COOKING LIGHT

the
fresh food
fast
cookbook

Cooking Light

the fresh food fast cookbook

Oxmoor House®

ISBN-13: 978-0-8487-3958-4
ISBN-10: 0-8487-3958-2
Library of Congress Control Number: 2013931807
Printed in the United States of America
First Printing 2013

Be sure to check with your health-care provider before making any changes in your diet.

Oxmoor House

Editorial Director: Leah McLaughlin
Creative Director: Felicity Keane
Brand Manager: Michelle Turner Aycock
Senior Editor: Andrea C. Kirkland, M.S., R.D.
Managing Editor: Rebecca Benton

Cooking Light® The Fresh Food Fast Cookbook

Editor: Meredith L. Butcher
Art Director: Claire Cormany
Assistant Designer: Allison Sperando Potter
Director, Test Kitchen: Elizabeth Tyler Austin
Assistant Directors, Test Kitchen: Julie Christopher, Julie Gunter
Recipe Developers and Testers: Wendy Ball, R.D., Victoria E. Cox, Tamara Goldis, Stefanie Maloney, Callie Nash, Karen Rankin, Leah Van Deren
Recipe Editor: Alyson Moreland Haynes
Food Stylists: Margaret Monroe Dickey, Catherine Crowell Steele
Photography Director: Jim Bathie
Senior Photographer: Helene Dujardin
Senior Photo Stylist: Kay E. Clarke
Photo Stylist: Mindi Shapiro Levine
Assistant Photo Stylist: Mary Louise Menendez
Senior Production Manager: Greg A. Amason
Production Manager: Tamara Nall Wilder

Contributors

Project Editor: Jena Hippensteel
Recipe Developer and Tester: Kathleen Royal Phillips
Copy Editor: Jacqueline Giovanelli
Proofreader: Julie Bosche
Indexer: Mary Ann Laurens
Interns: Megan Branagh, Frances Gunnells, Susan Kemp, Sara Lyon, Staley McIlwain, Jeffrey Preis, Maria Sanders, Julia Sayers
Food Stylist: Kellie Gerber Kelley
Photographer: Iain Bagwell
Photo Stylist: Mary Clayton Carl

Time Home Entertainment Inc.

Publisher: Jim Childs
VP, Strategy & Business Development: Steven Sandonato
Executive Director, Marketing Services: Carol Pittard
Executive Director, Retail & Special Sales: Tom Mifsud
Director, Bookazine Development & Marketing: Laura Adam
Executive Publishing Director: Joy Butts
Associate Publishing Director: Megan Pearlman
Finance Director: Glenn Buonocore
Associate General Counsel: Helen Wan

Cooking Light®

Editor: Scott Mowbray
Creative Director: Carla Frank
Executive Managing Editor: Phillip Rhodes
Executive Editor, Food: Ann Taylor Pittman
Special Publications Editor: Mary Simpson Creel, MS, RD
Senior Food Editors: Timothy Q. Cebula, Julianna Grimes
Senior Editor: Cindy Hatcher
Assistant Editor, Nutrition: Sidney Fry, MS, RD
Assistant Editors: Kimberly Holland, Phoebe Wu
Test Kitchen Director: Vanessa T. Pruett
Assistant Test Kitchen Director: Tiffany Vickers Davis
Recipe Testers and Developers: Robin Bashinsky, Adam Hickman, Deb Wise
Art Directors: Fernande Bondarenko, Shawna Kalish
Senior Deputy Art Director: Rachel Cardina Lasserre
Senior Designer: Anna Bird
Designer: Hagen Stegall
Assistant Designer: Nicole Gerrity
Photo Director: Kristen Schaefer
Assistant Photo Editor: Amy Delaune
Senior Photographer: Randy Mayor
Senior Prop Stylist: Cindy Barr
Chief Food Stylist: Kellie Gerber Kelley
Food Styling Assistant: Blakeslee Wright
Production Director: Liz Rhoades
Production Editor: Hazel R. Eddins
Assistant Production Editor: Josh Rutledge
Copy Chief: Maria Parker Hopkins
Assistant Copy Chief: Susan Roberts
Research Editor: Michelle Gibson Daniels
Administrative Coordinator: Carol D. Johnson
Cookinglight.com Editor: Allison Long Lowery
Associate Editor/Producer: Mallory Daugherty Brasseale

To order additional publications,
call 1-800-765-6400 or 1-800-491-0551

To search, savor, and share thousands of recipes,
visit **myrecipes.com**

Cover: Pasta with Roasted Tomatoes and Garlic, page 273
Back cover: Cornmeal-Yogurt Waffles, page 36; Pan Roasted Salmon and Tomatoes, page 286; Chili Lime Flank Steak, page 422
Page 2: Kalamata-Balsamic Chicken with Feta, page 375

welcome

Hectic weekdays call for simple, quick, and delicious meals. And if you're like most busy cooks, you need new and reliable recipes to expand your cooking repertoire. *Cooking Light: The Fresh Food Fast Cookbook* gives you just that, with more than 750 5-ingredient, 15-minute recipes guaranteed to deliver tasty dishes, save time, and make your life much easier.

Within these pages, we'll give you rave-worthy dishes for every meal. Start your morning right with the Lemon-Artichoke Frittata and Blueberry Citrus Salad (page 257). Need something that's kid-pleasing for lunch? Our Pasta Bolognese (page 415) or Shredded Chicken Tacos (page 349) guarantee they'll be grinning ear to ear. Or are you craving a decadent, guilt-free dessert? Indulge in our Fudgy Bourbon-Pecan Brownies (page 488).

Every Test Kitchen–rated recipe meets at least one of two criteria: It uses just 5 ingredients (excluding water, flour, cooking spray, oil, salt and pepper, and optional ingredients), or it can be prepared in 15 minutes or less. Many fit the bill for both.

Making fresh, delicious food that fits into your busy lifestyle is simple with hundreds of mouthwatering recipes; you'll be inspired every time you turn the page!

-The Cooking Light Editors

contents

33

74

199

344

362

529

fish & shellfish, 278

Fast-cooking fish offers a lighter option, ideal for any night of the week.

poultry, 346

Whether you start with a cooked rotisserie chicken or fresh chicken breast, these pleasing dishes come together in a flash.

meats, 410

Escape the dinnertime rut with this selection of beef, pork, and lamb entrées.

desserts, 478

Indulge your sweet tooth with these quick ice creams, beautiful tarts, and chocolate treats.

breakfast & brunch

Cornmeal-Yogurt Waffles,
page 36

Citrus-Ginger Salad

Prep: 6 minutes

For a light, refreshing breakfast at work, pack this salad in its own container, along with a container of low-fat cottage cheese or yogurt to add protein.

2	medium navel oranges
1	medium red grapefruit
1	lime
2	tablespoons finely chopped crystallized ginger
1	tablespoon honey

1. Peel and section oranges and grapefruit over a medium bowl, reserving juice.
2. Grate 1 teaspoon rind and squeeze 1 tablespoon juice from lime. Add lime rind and lime juice to orange mixture. Add ginger and honey; toss gently. Chill until ready to serve. Yield: 3 servings (serving size: ½ cup).

CALORIES 135; FAT 0.1g (sat 0g, mono 0g, poly 0g); PROTEIN 1.6g; CARB 34.7g; FIBER 3.4g; CHOL 0mg; IRON 0.4mg; SODIUM 4mg; CALC 79mg

Banana-Blueberry Smoothies

Prep: 5 minutes

1	cup frozen blueberries
½	cup silken tofu
2	tablespoons water
1	teaspoon vanilla extract
1½	medium-sized ripe bananas, broken into pieces
1	(5.3-ounce) container plain fat-free Greek yogurt

1. Place all ingredients in a blender; process until smooth, scraping sides as necessary. Yield: 2 servings (serving size: 1½ cups).

CALORIES 198; FAT 1.7g (sat 0g, mono 0.4g, poly 0.8g); PROTEIN 11.4g; CARB 34.1g; FIBER 5g; CHOL 0mg; IRON 0.7mg; SODIUM 35mg; CALC 138mg

Go-Getter Green Smoothies

Prep: 5 minutes

Loaded with fruit and packed with an extra boost of iron from spinach, this smoothie is a nutritious and sweet start to a busy day. Be sure to try it in the summer when ripe, sweet honeydew melon is available.

1	cup (½-inch) cubes honeydew melon
1	cup bagged baby spinach
1	cup sliced ripe banana, frozen (about 1 large)
½	cup vanilla light soy milk
1	(5.3-ounce) container fat-free Greek yogurt with honey
1	cubed peeled kiwifruit

1. Place all ingredients in a blender. Process until smooth. Serve immediately. Yield: 2 servings (serving size: 1½ cups).

CALORIES 224; FAT 1.1g (sat 0.2g, mono 0.2g, poly 0.5g); PROTEIN 9.4g; CARB 47.9g; FIBER 4.3g; CHOL 0mg; IRON 1mg; SODIUM 91mg; CALC 180mg

ingredient spotlight

Packaged fresh baby spinach, found in your grocer's produce section, provides a power punch of vitamins A and C, calcium, iron, and potassium. There's no need to trim the stems from the tender leaves, and their small size eliminates the need to chop them before adding to the blender.

Vanilla-Berry Smoothie

Prep: 3 minutes

Use a 6-ounce container of vanilla low-fat yogurt if you want a sweeter smoothie.

1	(5.3-ounce) container vanilla fat-free Greek yogurt
1	cup frozen mixed berries
½	cup fat-free milk
2	teaspoons honey
3	ice cubes

1. Place first 4 ingredients in a blender; process until smooth. Remove center cap from blender lid; with blender on, add ice cubes, 1 at a time, processing until smooth. Yield: 1 serving.

CALORIES 250; FAT 0.6g (sat 0.1g, mono 0.1g, poly 0.4g); PROTEIN 19.4g; CARB 45.9g; FIBER 4g; CHOL 2mg; IRON 0.4mg; SODIUM 118mg; CALC 174mg

Pineapple Parfait

Prep: 4 minutes • Cook: 3 minutes

Let the pineapple cool slightly before layering this tropical-inspired parfait.

1	teaspoon butter
⅔	cup cubed fresh pineapple
1	tablespoon brown sugar
1	(5.3-ounce) container vanilla fat-free Greek yogurt
1	tablespoon chopped macadamia nuts, toasted
1	tablespoon flaked sweetened coconut, toasted

1. Melt butter in a small nonstick skillet over medium-high heat. Add pineapple and brown sugar; cook 2 minutes or until pineapple is golden brown.
2. Layer half of yogurt in a small glass. Top with half of pineapple mixture. Repeat layers once. Sprinkle with nuts and coconut. Yield: 1 serving.

CALORIES 346; FAT 11.8g (sat 4.8g, mono 6.1g, poly 0.3g); PROTEIN 17.5g; CARB 44.8g; FIBER 2.7g; CHOL 10mg; IRON 0.7mg; SODIUM 145mg; CALC 33mg

Mixed Berry, Flaxseed, and Yogurt Parfait

Prep: 5 minutes

Layer this parfait in an insulated coffee mug before you head to work, and it will stay cold until you arrive.

½	cup plain low-fat yogurt
2	tablespoons low-sugar strawberry preserves
¼	teaspoon grated lemon rind
¼	cup low-fat granola without raisins
1	tablespoon sliced almonds, toasted
1	tablespoon flaxseed meal
⅔	cup mixed fresh berries

1. Combine first 3 ingredients in a small bowl. Combine granola, almonds, and flaxseed meal in a separate small bowl. Spoon half of yogurt mixture into bottom of 1 (10-ounce) glass; top with half of granola mixture and ⅓ cup berries. Repeat layers with remaining yogurt mixture, granola mixture, and berries. Yield: 1 serving.

CALORIES 321; FAT 9.1g (sat 1.7g, mono 3.3g, poly 2.2g); PROTEIN 11.2g; CARB 52.1g; FIBER 9.6g; CHOL 13mg; IRON 2.8mg; SODIUM 123mg; CALC 256mg

Mixed Berry, Flaxseed,
and Yogurt Parfait

Almond-Apricot
Granola

Yogurt with Orange-Honey Figs

Prep: 5 minutes

When fresh figs aren't in season, stir ¼ cup chopped dried figs into the yogurt with the orange marmalade. If you prefer a tangy taste to sweetness, use plain 2% reduced-fat Greek yogurt instead of vanilla.

1   (6-ounce) container vanilla fat-free Greek yogurt
1   tablespoon orange marmalade
2   fresh figs, quartered
2   teaspoons chopped pistachios
2   teaspoons orange blossom honey

1. Combine yogurt and orange marmalade in a small bowl. Top with figs; sprinkle with pistachios, and drizzle with honey. Yield: 1 serving.

CALORIES 315; FAT 2.7g (sat 0.3g, mono 1.3g, poly 0.9g); PROTEIN 18g; CARB 58.2g; FIBER 3.6g; CHOL 0mg; IRON 0.7mg; SODIUM 88mg; CALC 49mg

Almond-Apricot Granola

Prep: 6 minutes • Cook: 36 minutes

Make this granola ahead, and store in an airtight container for a quick topping for oatmeal or yogurt, or for an on-the-go breakfast all by itself.

2   cups old-fashioned rolled oats
1   cup sliced almonds
¼   cup honey
2   tablespoons canola oil
¼   teaspoon ground cinnamon
⅛   teaspoon salt
Cooking spray
1   cup dried apricots, coarsely chopped

1. Preheat oven to 300°.
2. Combine oats and almonds in a large bowl. Combine honey and oil in a small saucepan. Bring to a boil, stirring occasionally. Stir in cinnamon and salt; pour honey mixture over oat mixture, tossing until oats are thoroughly coated.
3. Spread oat mixture evenly onto a 17 x 12 x 1–inch pan coated with cooking spray. Bake at 300° for 35 to 38 minutes, stirring every 10 minutes, until granola is golden brown. Let cool on baking sheet. Stir in apricots. Store in an airtight container. Yield: 8 servings (serving size: about ½ cup).

CALORIES 271; FAT 10.8g (sat 1.2g, mono 4.8g, poly 4.1g); PROTEIN 5.6g; CARB 39.8g; FIBER 4.7g; CHOL 0mg; IRON 2.5mg; SODIUM 40mg; CALC 44mg

Tropical Muesli

Prep: 8 minutes • Other: 8 hours

Make this muesli just before bedtime, and then top it with fruit on your way out the door the next morning.

⅔   cup light coconut milk
3   tablespoons honey
1¼   cups unsweetened muesli
1   (6-ounce) container plain fat-free yogurt
1   cup chopped fresh pineapple
1   cup chopped peeled kiwifruit
1   cup chopped banana

1. Combine first 4 ingredients in a medium bowl, stirring well with a spoon. Cover and chill up to 8 hours. Stir in fruit just before serving. Yield: 4 servings (serving size: 1 cup).

CALORIES 288; FAT 4.6g (sat 0.5g, mono 2.1g, poly 1.4g); PROTEIN 8.2g; CARB 62.7g; FIBER 7.8g; CHOL 1mg; IRON 1.7mg; SODIUM 29mg; CALC 103mg

Savory Loaded Oatmeal

Prep: 2 minutes • Cook: 5 minutes

½	cup old-fashioned rolled oats
½	cup water
½	cup fat-free milk
⅛	teaspoon salt
2	tablespoons reduced-fat shredded sharp cheddar cheese
1	teaspoon butter
1	center-cut bacon slice, cooked and crumbled
1	tablespoon chopped green onions (optional)

1. Combine first 4 ingredients in a medium microwave-safe bowl. Microwave at MEDIUM 5 to 6 minutes or until liquid is absorbed.
2. Add cheese, butter, and bacon, stirring until cheese and butter melt. Sprinkle with green onions, if desired. Yield: 1 serving.

CALORIES 291; FAT 11.3g (sat 5.5g, mono 3.5g, poly 1.4g); PROTEIN 14.7g; CARB 33.6g; FIBER 4g; CHOL 28mg; IRON 1.8mg; SODIUM 582mg; CALC 256mg

Morning Wheat Berry Salad

Prep: 4 minutes • Cook: 1 hour
Other: 8 hours

Eating fiber-rich whole foods is the best way to add essential components to your diet. Whole-grain wheat berries are chewy, mild, and packed with fiber.

1	cup uncooked wheat berries
1	cup plain low-fat yogurt
¼	cup maple syrup
1	cup blueberries
1	cup sliced strawberries
½	cup sliced almonds, toasted (optional)

1. Place wheat berries in a bowl; cover with water to 2 inches above berries. Cover and let stand 8 hours. Drain.
2. Place wheat berries in a medium saucepan; cover with water to 2 inches above berries. Bring to a boil; reduce heat, and cook, uncovered, 1 hour or until wheat berries are tender. Drain.
3. Combine yogurt and syrup in a large bowl, stirring with a whisk. Add wheat berries, blueberries, and strawberries; toss well. Sprinkle with almonds, if desired. Yield: 6 servings (serving size: ¾ cup).

CALORIES 188; FAT 1.2g (sat 0.5g, mono 0.1g, poly 0.3g); PROTEIN 6.2g; CARB 40.5g; FIBER 5.1g; CHOL 3mg; IRON 0.3mg; SODIUM 31mg; CALC 82mg

make ahead

Cook the wheat berries for this whole-grain breakfast salad over the weekend so you can enjoy this dish throughout the week without much prep work.

Morning Wheat Berry Salad

Peanutty Granola Bars

Peanutty Granola Bars

Prep: 8 minutes • Cook: 25 minutes
Other: 1 hour

Cooking spray
2   cups old-fashioned rolled oats
1   cup unsalted, dry-roasted peanuts
1   cup flaked sweetened coconut
⅔   cup honey
¼   cup creamy peanut butter
3   tablespoons canola oil

1. Preheat oven to 325°.
2. Coat an 11 x 7–inch baking dish with cooking spray.
3. Combine oats, peanuts, and coconut on a 17½ x 12½ x 1–inch pan. Bake at 325° for 15 minutes or until lightly toasted. Transfer oat mixture to a large bowl.

4. Combine honey, peanut butter, and oil in a small saucepan. Bring to a boil over medium heat, stirring occasionally; pour over oat mixture, stirring to coat. Pour mixture into prepared dish pressing into an even layer with plastic wrap. Remove wrap.
5. Bake at 325° for 10 minutes or until golden brown. Cool 1 hour or until completely cool; cut into 16 bars. (Mixture will become firm when completely cool.) Yield: 16 bars (serving size: 1 bar).

CALORIES 211; FAT 12g (sat 3.2g, mono 5g, poly 2.9g); PROTEIN 4.6g; CARB 23.6g; FIBER 2.2g; CHOL 0mg; IRON 0.9mg; SODIUM 35mg; CALC 6mg

Chewy Date-Apple Bars

Prep: 5 minutes • Cook: 15 minutes
Other: 1 hour

Try a combination of other fruits and nuts with the dates.

2½   cups whole pitted dates
1   cup dried apples
½   cup walnuts, toasted
½   cup old-fashioned rolled oats
¼   teaspoon ground cinnamon

1. Preheat oven to 350°.
2. Place first 3 ingredients in food processor; process until fruit and nuts are finely chopped. Add oats and cinnamon; pulse 8 to 10 times or until moist and oats are chopped. Spoon mixture into a lightly greased 9 x 5–inch loaf pan, pressing into an even layer with plastic wrap. Remove wrap.
3. Bake at 350° for 15 minutes or until golden brown. Cool 1 hour or until completely cool; cut into 12 bars. Yield: 12 servings (serving size: 1 bar).

CALORIES 194; FAT 3.6g (sat 0.4g, mono 0.6g, poly 2.5g); PROTEIN 2.5g; CARB 41.9g; FIBER 4.5g; CHOL 0mg; IRON 0.9mg; SODIUM 67mg; CALC 25mg

Cranberry-Almond Cereal Bars

Prep: 5 minutes • Cook: 14 minutes
Other: 1 hour and 15 minutes

A creamy, sweet mix of almond butter and honey holds these bars together. Be sure to stir the almond butter before measuring it to reincorporate any oil that has separated.

½   cup almond butter
⅔   cup honey
5   cups crispy wheat cereal squares
¾   cup sweetened dried cranberries
½   cup slivered almonds, toasted
Cooking spray

1. Place almond butter and honey in a large Dutch oven. Bring to a boil over medium heat. Stir in cereal, cranberries, and almonds, tossing to coat. Spoon mixture into an 11 x 7–inch baking dish coated with cooking spray, pressing into an even layer with plastic wrap. Let stand 1 hour or until set. Cut into 12 bars. Yield: 12 servings (serving size: 1 bar).

CALORIES 268; FAT 9.2g (sat 0.9g, mono 5.6g, poly 2.1g); PROTEIN 5.3g; CARB 45g; FIBER 4.1g; CHOL 0mg; IRON 8.2mg; SODIUM 268mg; CALC 94mg

ingredient spotlight

Almond butter is an alternative to peanut butter and contains significantly more fiber, iron, and potassium.

Banana Bread Muffins

Prep: 8 minutes • Cook: 25 minutes

Wrap these muffins in plastic wrap, and freeze them in an airtight container. Take out what you need the night before, and let them thaw overnight in the refrigerator. Toast before serving.

Cooking spray
9   ounces all-purpose flour (about 2 cups)
1   cup sugar
1   teaspoon baking soda
½   teaspoon salt
2   large eggs
1½   cups mashed ripe banana (3 large)
⅓   cup plain low-fat yogurt
¼   cup canola oil

1. Preheat oven to 375°.
2. Place 16 paper muffin cup liners in muffin cups; coat liners with cooking spray.
3. Weigh or lightly spoon flour into dry measuring cups; level with a knife. Combine flour, sugar, baking soda, and salt in a medium bowl; make a well in center of mixture. Place eggs in a medium bowl; beat with a whisk. Add banana, yogurt, and oil, stirring with a whisk. Add egg mixture to flour mixture, stirring just until moist. Spoon batter into liners, filling three-fourths full.
4. Bake at 375° for 25 minutes or until muffins spring back when touched lightly in center. Remove muffins from pan, and cool on a wire rack. Yield: 16 servings (serving size: 1 muffin).

CALORIES 168; FAT 4.4g (sat 0.6g, mono 2.5g, poly 1.2g); PROTEIN 2.9g; CARB 29.8g; FIBER 1g; CHOL 27mg; IRON 0.9mg; SODIUM 165mg; CALC 16mg

Banana Bread
Muffins

Cappuccino–Chocolate Chip Muffins

Prep: 8 minutes • Cook: 20 minutes

Cooking spray
1¾   cups low-fat baking mix
½   cup sugar
½   cup hot water
2   tablespoons instant espresso granules
¼   cup canola oil
1   large egg
½   cup semisweet chocolate minichips

1. Preheat oven to 400°.
2. Place 12 paper muffin cup liners in muffin cups; coat liners with cooking spray.
3. Lightly spoon baking mix into dry measuring cups; level with a knife. Combine baking mix and sugar in a medium bowl; stir with a whisk. Make a well in center of mixture. Combine ½ cup hot water and coffee granules, stirring until coffee dissolves. Combine oil and egg, stirring with a whisk; stir in coffee mixture. Add coffee mixture to baking mix mixture, stirring just until moist. Stir in chocolate minichips.
4. Spoon batter into prepared liners. Bake at 400° for 20 minutes or until muffins spring back when touched lightly in center. Remove muffins from pans immediately; place on a wire rack. Serve warm. Yield: 12 servings (serving size: 1 muffin).

CALORIES 196; FAT 8.8g (sat 2.1g, mono 4.7g, poly 1.7g); PROTEIN 2.6g; CARB 27.2g; FIBER 0.4g; CHOL 15.5mg; IRON 0.7mg; SODIUM 196mg; CALC 92mg

Raisin Bran Muffins

Prep: 7 minutes • Cook: 17 minutes
Other: 15 minutes

Prepare this batter ahead, and keep it in your refrigerator for up to three days. Add six minutes of baking time if you're putting cold batter in the oven.

4.5   ounces all-purpose flour (about 1 cup)
1½   teaspoons baking soda
¼   teaspoon salt
1¼   cups fat-free milk
½   cup honey
2   tablespoons canola oil
1   large egg
2   cups wheat bran flakes cereal with raisins, crushed
½   cup golden raisins (optional)
Cooking spray

1. Preheat oven to 400°.
2. Weigh or lightly spoon flour into a dry measuring cup; level with a knife. Combine flour, baking soda, and salt in a large bowl, stirring with a whisk. Combine milk and next 3 ingredients in a medium bowl, stirring with a whisk. Stir in cereal. Add cereal mixture to flour mixture; stir just until moist. Fold in raisins, if desired. Let batter stand 15 minutes.
3. Spoon batter into 16 muffin cups coated with cooking spray. Bake at 400° for 17 minutes or until a wooden pick inserted in center comes out clean. Cool slightly on a wire rack. Serve warm. Yield: 16 servings (serving size: 1 muffin).

CALORIES 111; FAT 2.4g (sat 0.4g, mono 1g, poly 0.9g); PROTEIN 2.6g; CARB 21.2g; FIBER 1.1g; CHOL 14mg; IRON 2.2mg; SODIUM 204mg; CALC 31mg

Fig-Maple Drop Biscuits

Prep: 6 minutes • Cook: 16 minutes

Maple sugar is made from the sap of maple trees—the sap is boiled until nearly all the liquid is evaporated. Using a very sharp knife or kitchen shears will make chopping the dried figs easier.

10.1	ounces all-purpose flour (about 2¼ cups)
¾	cup maple sugar, divided
1	tablespoon baking powder
½	teaspoon salt
6	tablespoons chilled unsalted butter, cut into small pieces and divided
¾	cup fat-free milk
½	cup chopped dried Calimyrna figs (about 4 figs)

1. Preheat oven to 400°.

2. Weigh or lightly spoon flour into dry measuring cups; level with a knife. Combine flour, ½ cup plus 1 tablespoon maple sugar, baking powder, and salt in a large bowl. Cut in 5 tablespoons butter with a pastry blender or 2 knives until mixture resembles coarse meal. Add milk and figs, stirring until a soft dough forms.

3. Drop dough by heaping spoonfuls into 12 mounds 2 inches apart on a parchment paper–lined baking sheet. Melt remaining 1 tablespoon butter; brush evenly over biscuits. Sprinkle biscuits evenly with remaining 3 tablespoons maple sugar.

4. Bake at 400° for 16 minutes or until biscuits are golden. Yield: 12 servings (serving size: 1 biscuit).

CALORIES 189; FAT 6.1g (sat 3.7g, mono 1.5g, poly 0.3g); PROTEIN 3.2g; CARB 30.8g; FIBER 1.2g; CHOL 16mg; IRON 1.4mg; SODIUM 206mg; CALC 103mg

Fig-Maple Drop Biscuits

Sausage Drop Scones

Prep: 10 minutes • Cook: 15 minutes

Precooked sausage is a time-saver in this recipe; simply chop the sausage, and add it to the dough along with the cheese. You can also use veggie sausage patties.

3	cups low-fat baking mix
1½	teaspoons freshly ground black pepper
2	tablespoons chilled butter, cut into small pieces
¾	cup low-fat evaporated milk
4	fully cooked turkey sausage patties, chopped
½	cup (2 ounces) reduced-fat cheddar cheese with jalapeño peppers, shredded

Cooking spray

1. Preheat oven to 425°.
2. Combine baking mix and pepper in a large bowl. Cut in butter with a pastry blender or 2 knives until mixture resembles coarse meal. Add milk, sausage, and cheese; stir until just moist. Drop dough by ¼ cupfuls onto a baking sheet lined with parchment paper. Coat dough with cooking spray.
3. Bake at 425° for 15 minutes or until scones are golden. Yield: 15 servings (serving size: 1 scone).

CALORIES 135; FAT 4.8g (sat 1.6g, mono 1.9g, poly 0.6g); PROTEIN 5.5g; CARB 18g; FIBER 0.7g; CHOL 15mg; IRON 1mg; SODIUM 376mg; CALC 186mg

Sausage Drop Scones

Cherry Scones

Prep: 10 minutes • Cook: 20 minutes

You can replace half the flour in this recipe with white whole-wheat pastry flour if you'd like the extra benefits of whole grains.

9	ounces all-purpose flour (about 2 cups)
¼	cup granulated sugar
1½	teaspoons baking powder
¼	teaspoon salt
¼	cup chilled unsalted butter, cut into pieces
¾	cup dried tart cherries, chopped
¾	cup low-fat buttermilk
¼	teaspoon almond extract (optional)

Cooking spray

1	tablespoon turbinado sugar (optional)

1. Preheat oven to 425°.
2. Weigh or lightly spoon flour into dry measuring cups; level with a knife. Combine flour, sugar, baking powder, and salt in a large bowl, stirring well with a whisk. Cut in butter using a pastry blender until mixture resembles coarse meal. Stir in cherries. Add buttermilk and almond extract, if desired, stirring just until moist.
3. Turn dough out onto a lightly floured surface; knead lightly 3 times with floured hands. Form dough into an 8-inch circle on a baking sheet coated with cooking spray. Cut dough into 10 wedges, cutting into but not through dough. Coat top of dough with cooking spray. Sprinkle with turbinado sugar, if desired.
4. Place baking sheet on rack in upper third of oven. Bake at 425° for 20 minutes or until scones are golden. Yield: 10 servings (serving size: 1 scone).

CALORIES 191; FAT 5.1g (sat 3.1g, mono 1.3g, poly 0.3g); PROTEIN 3.5g; CARB 32.5g; FIBER 3.2g; CHOL 13mg; IRON 1.4mg; SODIUM 139mg; CALC 67mg

Cinnamon-Raisin Waffle Sandwich

Cinnamon-Raisin Waffle Sandwich

Prep: 3 minutes • Cook: 10 minutes

The sweetened cream cheese spread is also delicious on other breakfast breads, such as bagels and toast.

1	(1.33-ounce) frozen multigrain waffle
2	tablespoons (1 ounce) ⅓-less-fat cream cheese, softened
2	teaspoons brown sugar
¼	teaspoon ground cinnamon
1	tablespoon raisins
1	tablespoon chopped walnuts, toasted

1. Toast waffle according to package directions.
2. Combine cream cheese, brown sugar, and cinnamon until well blended. Spread cream cheese mixture evenly over waffle. Sprinkle evenly with raisins and walnuts. Cut waffle in half. Sandwich waffle halves together with filling in center. Yield: 1 serving.

CALORIES 279; FAT 14.7g (sat 4.3g, mono 4.3g, poly 4.7g); PROTEIN 5.5g; CARB 34.8g; FIBER 4.3g; CHOL 21mg; IRON 1.4mg; SODIUM 260mg; CALC 70mg

Bagel Sandwich with Pears
and Goat Cheese Spread

Mediterranean Breakfast Sandwich

Prep: 6 minutes • Cook: 6 minutes

Cooking spray
¼ cup chopped red bell pepper
2 tablespoons chopped frozen artichoke hearts, thawed
1 large egg
1 large egg white
½ teaspoon chopped fresh oregano
2 tablespoons crumbled feta cheese
½ cup fresh baby spinach leaves
1 whole-wheat pita half

1. Heat a medium nonstick skillet over medium-high heat. Coat pan with cooking spray. Add bell pepper; sauté 3 minutes. Add artichokes; sauté 1 minute or until thoroughly heated. Remove pepper mixture from pan. Wipe pan with paper towels. Coat pan with cooking spray.
2. Combine egg, egg white, and oregano in a small bowl, stirring with a whisk. Add egg mixture to pan; cook over medium heat 1 minute. Do not stir until mixture begins to set on bottom. Add pepper mixture and cheese. Draw a heat-resistant spatula through egg mixture to form large curds. Do not stir constantly. Cook just until egg mixture is thickened, but still moist.
3. Stuff spinach into pita half; add egg mixture. Yield: 1 serving.

CALORIES 253; FAT 10.7g (sat 4.6g, mono 3.4g, poly 1.2g); PROTEIN 16.7g; CARB 24.1g; FIBER 3.6g; CHOL 228mg; IRON 2.4mg; SODIUM 784mg; CALC 138mg

Bagel Sandwich with Pears and Goat Cheese Spread

Prep: 6 minutes • Cook: 2 minutes

½ cup (4 ounces) goat cheese, crumbled
½ cup (4 ounces) ⅓-less-fat cream cheese, softened
2 tablespoons honey
⅓ cup chopped toasted walnuts
1 cinnamon-raisin swirl mini-bagel, halved and toasted
¼ red Anjou pear, unpeeled and thinly sliced

1. Combine first 3 ingredients in a small bowl. Stir in walnuts. Spread 1 tablespoon goat cheese spread evenly onto cut sides of bagel. Place pear slices on bottom half of bagel. Replace bagel top. Cover and chill remaining spread up to one week. Yield: 1 serving.

CALORIES 152; FAT 4.2g (sat 1.8g, mono 0.8g, poly 1.2g); PROTEIN 4.5g; CARB 25.5g; FIBER 2.5g; CHOL 7mg; IRON 1.3mg; SODIUM 128mg; CALC 24mg

quick flip

Swap the flavor of the Mediterranean for south-of-the-border. Substitute frozen corn for the artichokes and cilantro, queso fresco, and avocado slices for the oregano, feta cheese, and spinach leaves.

Breakfast Egg Salad Sandwiches

Prep: 12 minutes

To shave time, purchase preboiled eggs. You can make this egg salad in advance for the week ahead.

6	hard-cooked large eggs, chopped
6	hard-cooked large egg whites, chopped
¼	cup canola mayonnaise
½	cup (2 ounces) shredded reduced-fat extra-sharp cheddar cheese
6	center-cut bacon slices, cooked and crumbled
½	teaspoon salt
¼	teaspoon freshly ground black pepper
16	(0.7-ounce) slices whole-wheat bread

1. Combine all ingredients except bread. Spoon mixture evenly onto 8 bread slices. Top with remaining bread slices. Yield: 8 servings (serving size: 1 sandwich).

CALORIES 238; FAT 12.6g (sat 3.2g, mono 6g, poly 2.6g); PROTEIN 15.7g; CARB 21g; FIBER 6g; CHOL 152.7mg; IRON 5.2mg; SODIUM 609mg; CALC 154mg

Sausage Breakfast Braid

Prep: 6 minutes • Cook: 19 minutes
Other: 5 minutes

Peaches or cubed watermelon sub nicely for the nectarines in the side salad.

1	(13.8-ounce) can refrigerated pizza crust dough
	Cooking spray
4	ounces light smoked sausage, chopped
3	large eggs, lightly beaten
¼	teaspoon freshly ground black pepper
¾	cup (3 ounces) shredded reduced-fat extra-sharp cheddar cheese
1	large egg white, lightly beaten

1. Preheat oven to 425°.
2. Unroll dough onto a baking sheet coated with cooking spray; pat dough into a 15 x 10–inch rectangle.
3. Heat a large skillet over medium heat. Coat pan with cooking spray. Add sausage; cook 2 minutes or until lightly browned, stirring occasionally. Stir in eggs and pepper; cook 1 minute or until set, stirring occasionally. Remove from heat.
4. Sprinkle ½ cup cheese lengthwise down center of dough, leaving a 2-inch border on each side. Spoon egg mixture evenly over cheese, and sprinkle with ¼ cup cheese.
5. Make 2-inch-long diagonal cuts about 1 inch apart on both sides of dough to within ½ inch of filling using a sharp knife or kitchen shears. Arrange dough strips over filling, alternating strips diagonally over filling. Press ends under to seal. Brush with egg white. Bake at 425° for 15 minutes or until golden brown. Let stand 5 minutes. Cut crosswise into slices. Yield: 8 servings (serving size: 1 slice).

CALORIES 212; FAT 7.8g (sat 3.4g, mono 2.3g, poly 1g); PROTEIN 11.5g; CARB 24g; FIBER 0.8g; CHOL 95mg; IRON 1.9mg; SODIUM 602mg; CALC 87mg

serve with:
Heirloom Tomato and Nectarine Salad

Prep: 6 minutes

2	large heirloom tomatoes, each cut into 8 slices
2	tablespoons fresh lemon juice
4	teaspoons extra-virgin olive oil
2	teaspoons honey
2	ripe nectarines, coarsely chopped
¼	cup vertically sliced sweet onion
1	tablespoon chopped fresh mint

1. Arrange tomato slices on a serving platter. Combine lemon juice, oil, and honey in a medium bowl; add nectarines and onion, tossing well. Spoon nectarine mixture over tomatoes; drizzle with any remaining juices. Sprinkle with fresh mint. Yield: 8 servings (serving size: 2 tomato slices and ¼ cup nectarine mixture).

CALORIES 53; FAT 2.6g (sat 0.3g, mono 1.8g, poly 0.2g); PROTEIN 0.6g; CARB 7.6g; FIBER 0.8g; CHOL 0mg; IRON 0.2mg; SODIUM 2mg; CALC 8mg

Sausage Breakfast Braid

Cast-Iron Breakfast Pizza

1. Preheat oven to 450°.
2. Roll out dough to a 12-inch circle. Press dough into bottom and 1 inch up sides of a well-seasoned 10-inch cast-iron skillet. Fold edges under and crimp.
3. Spread ricotta cheese in bottom of crust; top with bacon, mozzarella cheese, and pepper. Place skillet over high heat; cook 3 minutes. Transfer skillet to oven.
4. Bake at 450° for 18 minutes or until crust is lightly browned and cheese melts.
5. While pizza cooks, heat a large skillet over medium-high heat. Coat pan with cooking spray. Add spinach. Cook 1 minute or until spinach wilts, turning often with tongs. Remove spinach from pan; drain and squeeze out excess liquid. Top pizza with wilted spinach. Cut pizza into 8 wedges. Yield: 8 servings (serving size: 1 wedge).

CALORIES 260; FAT 8.2g (sat 3.7g, mono 1.4g, poly 1.1g); PROTEIN 13.7g; CARB 34.1g; FIBER 2g; CHOL 22mg; IRON 2.6mg; SODIUM 562mg; CALC 210mg

Cast-Iron Breakfast Pizza

Prep: 12 minutes • Cook: 23 minutes

Use a well-seasoned cast-iron skillet—it eliminates the need for extra oil to grease the pan. For a crisp pizza crust, heat the skillet on the cooktop before transferring it to the oven.

1   (16-ounce) package commercial pizza dough
1   cup part-skim ricotta cheese
5   lower-sodium bacon slices, cooked and crumbled
1   cup (4 ounces) shredded part-skim mozzarella cheese
¼   teaspoon freshly ground black pepper
Cooking spray
1   (6-ounce) package fresh baby spinach

serve with:

Broiled Sweet Peaches

Prep: 3 minutes • Cook: 8 minutes

8   peaches, halved and pitted
2   tablespoons butter, melted
¼   cup turbinado sugar
⅓   cup plain fat-free Greek yogurt

1. Preheat broiler. Place a rack 6 inches from the heat.
2. Place peach halves on a baking sheet lined with foil; brush with butter, and sprinkle with turbinado sugar. Broil 8 minutes or until sugar melts and is lightly browned. Spoon 1 teaspoon yogurt over each peach half. Yield: 8 servings (serving size: 2 peach halves).

CALORIES 104; FAT 3.3g (sat 1.9g, mono 0.9g, poly 0.2g); PROTEIN 2.2g; CARB 19.2g; FIBER 2.2g; CHOL 7.6mg; IRON 0.4mg; SODIUM 24mg; CALC 16mg

Baked Eggs with Spinach and Goat Cheese

Prep: 20 minutes • Cook: 10 minutes

These light, airy eggs are ideal for brunch. Serve with sliced tomatoes or fruit salad and toast.

Cooking spray
4   large egg whites
¼   teaspoon salt
¼   teaspoon freshly ground black pepper
¼   cup (2 ounces) goat cheese, crumbled
1   cup chopped fresh spinach
4   large egg yolks
2   tablespoons crème fraîche
1   tablespoon chopped fresh chives

1. Preheat oven to 350°.
2. Coat 4 (6-ounce) custard cups with cooking spray. Place egg whites, salt, and pepper in a medium bowl; beat with a mixer at high speed 1 minute or until stiff peaks form. Gently fold in cheese and spinach. Divide mixture evenly among prepared custard cups.
3. Make an indentation in the center of egg white mixture in each custard cup. Place 1 egg yolk into each indentation. Spoon 1½ teaspoons crème fraîche on top of each egg yolk. Place custard cups on a baking sheet.
4. Bake at 350° for 10 to 12 minutes or until egg white mixture is puffed and pale. (Yolks will not be set in center.) Sprinkle with chives, and serve immediately. Yield: 4 servings.

CALORIES 140; FAT 10.8g (sat 5.2g, mono 2.6g, poly 0.8g); PROTEIN 9.3g; CARB 1.3g; FIBER 0.3g; CHOL 225mg; IRON 1.4mg; SODIUM 280mg; CALC 52mg

Garden Scrambled Eggs

Prep: 5 minutes • Cook: 5 minutes

Bring garden freshness to your table with these veggie-laden scrambled eggs. Red tomato, juicy onion, and green bell pepper perk up this traditional breakfast dish.

Butter-flavored cooking spray
¾   cup refrigerated prechopped tomato, onion, and bell pepper mix
4   large eggs
4   large egg whites
2   tablespoons chopped fresh parsley
6   tablespoons reduced-fat sour cream
1   tablespoon Dijon mustard
Dash of salt
Dash of freshly ground black pepper

1. Heat a large nonstick skillet over medium heat. Coat pan with cooking spray; add tomato mixture. Coat vegetables with cooking spray; cook 3 minutes or until vegetables are tender, stirring often.
2. While vegetables cook, combine eggs, egg whites, and remaining ingredients in a medium bowl, stirring with a whisk.
3. Add egg mixture to pan; cook over medium heat 2 minutes. Do not stir until mixture begins to set on bottom. Draw a heat-resistant spatula through egg mixture to form large curds. Do not stir constantly. Egg mixture is done when thickened, but still moist. Serve immediately. Yield: 4 servings.

CALORIES 133; FAT 8g (sat 3.3g, mono 2.7g, poly 0.8g); PROTEIN 11g; CARB 4.3g; FIBER 0.5g; CHOL 220mg; IRON 1.2mg; SODIUM 263mg; CALC 59mg

serve with:

Garlic-Roasted Potatoes

Prep: 5 minutes • Cook: 20 minutes

1	pound small red potatoes (about 8 potatoes)
1	teaspoon olive oil
¼	teaspoon salt
¼	teaspoon garlic powder
¼	teaspoon freshly ground black pepper

Butter-flavored cooking spray

1. Preheat oven to 450°.
2. Scrub potatoes; cut each into 8 wedges. Place wedges in a large bowl. Drizzle with oil; toss well. Sprinkle with salt, garlic powder, and pepper; toss until potatoes are evenly coated with spices. Arrange wedges in a single layer on a large rimmed baking sheet coated with cooking spray.
3. Bake at 450° for 20 minutes or until browned. Yield: 4 servings (serving size: ¾ cup).

CALORIES 92; FAT 2g (sat 0.2g, mono 0.8g, poly 0.2g); PROTEIN 2.2g; CARB 18.2g; FIBER 2g; CHOL 0mg; IRON 0.8mg; SODIUM152mg; CALC 12mg

Garden Scrambled Eggs

Black Bean Omelet

Black Bean Omelet

Prep: 7 minutes • Cook: 6 minutes

This omelet, stuffed with Monterey Jack cheese, jalapeño peppers, and black beans, gets a fresh touch on top from tomato-avacado salsa.

2	large eggs
4	large egg whites
⅛	teaspoon salt
¼	teaspoon freshly ground black pepper
	Cooking spray
½	cup no-salt-added black beans, rinsed and drained
¼	cup (1 ounce) preshredded Monterey Jack cheese with jalapeño peppers
2	tablespoons sliced green onions
	Tomato-Avocado Salsa

1. Combine first 4 ingredients in a medium bowl; stir with a whisk until blended.
2. Heat an 8-inch pan over medium heat. Coat pan with cooking spray. Add egg mixture, and cook 3 minutes or until set (do not stir). Sprinkle with beans, cheese, and green onions. Loosen omelet with a spatula; fold in half. Cook 1 to 2 minutes or until cheese melts. Slide omelet onto a plate. Cut in half. Top each half with Tomato-Avocado Salsa. Yield: 2 servings (serving size: ½ omelet and ¼ cup salsa).

CALORIES 252; FAT 12.9g (sat 4.6g, mono 5.3g, poly 1.2g); PROTEIN 20.7g; CARB 14.2g; FIBER 4.9g; CHOL 227mg; IRON 2.2mg; SODIUM 571mg; CALC 149mg

Tomato-Avocado Salsa

Prep: 3 minutes

¼	cup chopped tomato
¼	cup chopped peeled avocado
1	tablespoon fresh lemon juice
⅛	teaspoon salt
⅛	teaspoon ground cumin

1. Combine all ingredients in a small bowl. Yield: 2 servings (serving size: ¼ cup).

CALORIES 37; FAT 2.8g (sat 0.4g, mono 1.8g, poly 0.4g); PROTEIN 0.6g; CARB 3.2g; FIBER 1.6g; CHOL 0mg; IRON 0.2mg; SODIUM 150mg; CALC 6mg

Cheese and Tomato Omelet

Prep: 5 minutes • Cook: 7 minutes

This veggie-packed omelet is perfect for brunch or a simple supper. For a delicious side, serve a medley of fresh fruit, such as Mandarin Oranges with Kiwifruit and Grapes.

2   large eggs
2   large egg whites
2   tablespoons water
1   tablespoon finely chopped fresh cilantro
¼   teaspoon salt
⅛   teaspoon coarsely ground black pepper
Cooking spray
¼   cup (1 ounce) reduced-fat shredded cheddar
       cheese
½   cup diced seeded tomato (1 small)
Chopped fresh cilantro (optional)

1. Combine first 6 ingredients in a medium bowl, stirring with a whisk.
2. Heat an 8-inch nonstick skillet over medium-high heat; coat pan with cooking spray. Add egg mixture, and cook until edges begin to set. Gently lift edges of egg mixture with a wide spatula, tilting pan to allow uncooked egg mixture to come in contact with pan. Cook 2 minutes or until egg mixture is almost set; sprinkle with cheese. Spoon tomato over half of omelet; fold in half.
3. Cut omelet in half crosswise, and slide one half onto each of 2 plates. Garnish with cilantro, if desired, and serve immediately. Yield: 2 servings (serving size: ½ omelet).

CALORIES 147; FAT 7.7g (sat 3.4g, mono 3g, poly 0.9g); PROTEIN 13.9g; CARB 3.8g; FIBER 0.5g; CHOL 190mg; IRON 1.4mg; SODIUM 510mg; CALC 132mg

serve with:

Mandarin Oranges with Kiwifruit and Grapes

Prep: 4 minutes

2   tablespoons light syrup from mandarin
       oranges
¾   cup mandarin oranges in light syrup, drained
½   cup cubed kiwifruit (about 1 kiwifruit)
¼   cup seedless red grape halves
1   teaspoon fresh lemon juice

1. Combine 2 tablespoons light syrup, oranges, and remaining ingredients. Yield: 2 servings (serving size: ¾ cup).

CALORIES 95; FAT 0.4g (sat 0g, mono 0.1g, poly 0.1g); PROTEIN 0.8g; CARB 24.1g; FIBER 1.9g; CHOL 0mg; IRON 0.5mg; SODIUM 6mg; CALC 19mg

Cheese and Tomato Omelet

Frittata with Mascarpone and Prosciutto

Prep: 4 minutes • Cook: 10 minutes

While the onion sautés, prepare the frittata ingredients. You'll have time to toss the salad topping as the frittata cooks.

Cooking spray
½   cup chopped onion
8   large eggs
⅛   teaspoon salt
¼   teaspoon freshly ground black pepper
2   ounces thinly sliced prosciutto, chopped
8   teaspoons mascarpone cheese
Arugula-Tomato Topping

1. Preheat broiler.
2. Heat a 10-inch ovenproof skillet over medium heat. Coat pan with cooking spray. Add onion; sauté 3 minutes or until onion is tender.
3. Combine eggs, salt, and pepper in a medium bowl; stir with a whisk until foamy. Stir in prosciutto. Pour egg mixture over onion in pan. Dollop 1 teaspoon mascarpone over egg mixture at each of 8 equal intervals around edge of eggs. (Each of 8 wedges, when cut, will contain a small dollop.) Cook 3 minutes or until almost set, gently lifting edges of frittata with a spatula and tilting pan so uncooked portion flows underneath.

4. Broil frittata 2 minutes or until completely set in center.
5. While frittata cooks, prepare Arugula-Tomato Topping. Spoon topping over frittata, and cut into 8 wedges just before serving. Yield: 8 servings (serving size: 1 wedge frittata and about ⅓ cup topping).

CALORIES 147; FAT 11.3g (sat 4.3g, mono 2.3g, poly 1.1g); PROTEIN 9.4g; CARB 2.6g; FIBER 0.5g; CHOL 229mg; IRON 1.1mg; SODIUM 340mg; CALC 54mg

Arugula-Tomato Topping

Prep: 2 minutes

2   cups arugula
1   cup grape tomatoes, halved
2   teaspoons olive oil
⅛   teaspoon salt
¼   teaspoon freshly ground black pepper

1. Combine all ingredients in a medium bowl, tossing gently. Serve immediately. Yield: 8 servings (serving size: about ⅓ cup).

CALORIES 15; FAT 1.2g (sat 0.2g, mono 0.8g, poly 0.1g); PROTEIN 0.3g; CARB 1g; FIBER 0.4g; CHOL 0mg; IRON 0.1mg; SODIUM 39mg; CALC 11mg

Mediterranean-Style Frittata

Prep: 8 minutes • Cook: 6 minutes

The deep green of the spinach in the frittata and the bright red of the Herb-Crusted Broiled Tomatoes create a vibrant combination for a vitamin-packed brunch. To speed up prep time, prepare the tomatoes while the frittata broils.

2	teaspoons olive oil
¾	cup packed fresh baby spinach
2	green onions
4	large egg whites
6	large eggs
⅓	cup (1.3 ounces) crumbled feta cheese with basil and sun-dried tomatoes
2	teaspoons salt-free Greek seasoning
¼	teaspoon salt

1. Preheat broiler.
2. Heat a 10-inch ovenproof skillet over medium heat. Add oil; swirl to coat. While oil heats, coarsely chop spinach and finely chop onions. Combine egg whites, eggs, cheese, Greek seasoning, and salt in a large bowl; stir well with a whisk. Add spinach and onions, stirring well.
3. Add egg mixture to pan; cook until edges begin to set, about 2 minutes. Gently lift edge of egg mixture, tilting pan to allow uncooked egg mixture to come in contact with pan. Cook 2 minutes or until egg mixture is almost set.
4. Broil 2 to 3 minutes or until center is set. Transfer frittata to a serving platter immediately; cut into 4 wedges. Yield: 4 servings (serving size: 1 wedge).

CALORIES 178; FAT 12g (sat 4g, mono 4.5g, poly 1.4g); PROTEIN 15.7g; CARB 2.2g; FIBER 0.6g; CHOL 326mg; IRON 1.7mg; SODIUM 438mg; CALC 86mg

serve with:
Herb-Crusted Broiled Tomatoes

Prep: 4 minutes • Cook: 3 minutes

¼	cup whole-wheat panko (Japanese breadcrumbs)
2	tablespoons grated fresh Parmesan cheese
1	teaspoon dried Italian seasoning
½	teaspoon freshly ground black pepper
¼	teaspoon seasoned salt
1	teaspoon unsalted butter, melted
2	tomatoes, cut in half horizontally

Cooking spray

1. Preheat broiler.
2. Combine first 5 ingredients in a small bowl. Stir butter into breadcrumb mixture. Place tomato halves on a rimmed baking sheet coated with cooking spray. Sprinkle breadcrumb mixture evenly over tomato halves. Broil 3 to 4 minutes or until topping is golden. Serve immediately. Yield: 4 servings (serving size: 1 tomato half).

CALORIES 48; FAT 2g (sat 1.1g, mono 0.5g, poly 0.1g); PROTEIN 2.3g; CARB 6.2g; FIBER 1.3g; CHOL 5mg; IRON 0.4mg; SODIUM 135mg; CALC 35mg

ingredient spotlight

Panko (Japanese breadcrumbs) is every bit as convenient but tastes better than bland dry breadcrumbs. Panko also gives a supercrisp crust.

Cinnamon-Apple–Stuffed French Toast

Prep: 7 minutes • Cook: 8 minutes

The butter and brown sugar cook with the apples to create a delicious syrup for drizzling over the French toast.

Cinnamon-Apple Filling
4   (1-ounce) slices diagonally cut French bread (about 1 inch thick)
½   cup fat-free milk
1   teaspoon vanilla extract
1   large egg
Cooking spray
1   tablespoon powdered sugar (optional)

1. Prepare Cinnamon-Apple Filling.
2. Cut a horizontal slit through the side of each bread slice to form a pocket. Stuff 3 tablespoons Cinnamon-Apple Filling into each pocket.
3. Place milk, vanilla, and egg in a shallow dish; stir with a whisk until blended. Heat a large skillet over medium-high heat. Coat pan with cooking spray.
4. Dip each side of stuffed bread in egg mixture to coat. Add stuffed bread to pan; cook 2 minutes on each side or until golden brown. Sprinkle with powdered sugar, if desired; top evenly with remaining filling. Yield: 4 servings (serving size: 1 toast slice and 5 tablespoons apple filling).

CALORIES 230; FAT 7.9g (sat 4.2g, mono 2.2g, poly 0.7g); PROTEIN 6.2g; CARB 34.6g; FIBER 2.2g; CHOL 69mg; IRON 1.4mg; SODIUM 259mg; CALC 73mg

Cinnamon-Apple Filling

Prep: 2 minutes • Cook: 4 minutes

2   tablespoons butter
2   cups chopped unpeeled Gala apple (about 1 large)
¼   cup brown sugar
½   teaspoon ground cinnamon

1. Melt butter in a large nonstick skillet over medium-high heat. Add remaining ingredients; sauté 3 minutes or until apples are golden. Yield: 4 servings (serving size: 5 tablespoons).

CALORIES 115; FAT 5.9g (sat 3.7g, mono 1.5g, poly 0.2g); PROTEIN 0.2g; CARB 16.9g; FIBER 1.5g; CHOL 15mg; IRON 0.2mg; SODIUM 44mg; CALC 16mg

Cinnamon-Apple–Stuffed French Toast

Tropical Waffles

Tropical Waffles

Prep: 4 minutes • Cook: 6 minutes

Coconut milk and banana replace the milk and sugar normally found in waffle batter, giving these waffles the flavor of the tropics.

4.5	ounces self-rising flour (about 1 cup)
1	cup light coconut milk
⅓	cup mashed ripe banana
1	large egg

Pineapple-Orange Syrup

1. Weigh or lightly spoon flour into a dry measuring cup; level with a knife. Place flour in a large bowl.
2. Combine coconut milk, banana, and egg in a medium bowl, stirring with a whisk until blended. Add to flour, stirring until smooth.
3. Preheat a nonstick Belgian waffle iron.
4. Spoon about ½ cup batter per 4-inch waffle onto hot waffle iron, spreading batter to edges. Cook 5 to 6 minutes or until steaming stops. Spoon Pineapple-Orange Syrup over waffles. Yield: 4 servings (serving size: 1 waffle and about 3 tablespoons syrup).

CALORIES 252; FAT 6.2g (sat 2.3g, mono 3g, poly 0.4g); PROTEIN 5.5g; CARB 44.4g; FIBER 2g; CHOL 53mg; IRON 1.9mg; SODIUM 436mg; CALC 118mg

Pineapple-Orange Syrup

Prep: 2 minutes • Cook: 30 seconds

¼	cup pineapple preserves
¼	cup fresh orange juice
2	tablespoons chopped macadamia nuts
2	tablespoons flaked sweetened coconut

1. Combine preserves and juice in a 1-cup glass measure. Microwave at HIGH 30 seconds or until preserves melt. Stir in macadamia nuts and coconut. Yield: 4 servings (serving size: about 3 tablespoons).

CALORIES 99; FAT 4g (sat 1.2g, mono 2.5g, poly 0.1g); PROTEIN 0.5g; CARB 16.5g; FIBER 0.6g; CHOL 0mg; IRON 0.2mg; SODIUM 19mg; CALC 5mg

Mediterranean Hash Brown Cakes

Prep: 9 minutes • Cook: 5 minutes

1   large egg
1   large egg white
2   cups frozen hash browns, thawed
¼   cup chopped red bell pepper
1   tablespoon chopped fresh parsley
¼   teaspoon salt
¼   teaspoon freshly ground black pepper
Cooking spray
Olive-Tomato Topping

1. Place egg and egg white in a large bowl; beat with a whisk until foamy. Stir in hash browns and next 4 ingredients.

2. Heat a large skillet over medium-high heat. Coat pan with cooking spray. Pour ⅓ cup potato mixture per potato cake onto hot pan; cook 2 minutes on each side or until browned. Serve with Olive-Tomato Topping. Yield: 2 servings (serving size: 2 cakes and ¼ cup topping).

CALORIES 183; FAT 9.1g (sat 2.9g, mono 4.9g, poly 0.9g); PROTEIN 9.8g; CARB 17.8g; FIBER 2.8g; CHOL 109mg; IRON 2.5mg; SODIUM 543mg; CALC 54mg

Olive-Tomato Topping

Prep: 4 minutes

¼   cup chopped seeded tomato
2   tablespoons crumbled goat cheese
2   tablespoons commercial olive tapenade
1   tablespoon chopped fresh parsley

1. Combine all ingredients in a small bowl. Yield: 2 servings (serving size: ¼ cup).

CALORIES 69; FAT 6.2g (sat 2g, mono 3.7g, poly 0.5g); PROTEIN 2.6g; CARB 2.1g; FIBER 1.3g; CHOL 3mg; IRON 1mg; SODIUM 178mg; CALC 35mg

fix it faster

Speed up the thawing process by putting your hash browns in the fridge the night before.

Mediterranean Hash Brown Cakes

Cornmeal-Yogurt Waffles

Prep: 14 minutes • Cook: 21 minutes

Use your favorite waffle toppings; these are dressed up with blueberries, maple syrup, and powdered sugar.

4.5	ounces self-rising flour (about 1 cup)
¾	cup yellow cornmeal
4	large eggs
1	cup water
1	(5.3-ounce) container vanilla organic Greek yogurt
2	tablespoons unsalted butter, melted
¼	cup powdered sugar (optional)
6	tablespoons maple syrup (optional)
2	cups blueberries (optional)

1. Preheat a waffle iron.
2. Weigh or lightly spoon flour into a dry measuring cup; level with a knife. Combine flour and cornmeal in a large mixing bowl, stirring with a whisk.
3. Separate eggs. Place egg whites in a large bowl. Combine 1 egg yolk, 1 cup water, yogurt, and butter in a medium bowl, stirring well with a whisk. (Discard or reserve remaining egg yolks for another use.) Add yogurt mixture to flour mixture, stirring until smooth.
4. Beat egg whites with a mixer at high speed until stiff peaks form. Gently fold one-quarter of egg whites into cornmeal mixture; fold in remaining egg whites.
5. Spoon about ⅓ cup batter per 4-inch waffle onto hot waffle iron, spreading batter to edges. Cook 4 to 5 minutes or until steaming stops; repeat procedure with remaining batter. Sift 1 teaspoon powdered sugar over each waffle, if desired; top with 1 tablespoon maple syrup and about ⅓ cup blueberries, if desired. Serve immediately. Yield: 6 servings (serving size: 2 waffles).

CALORIES 346; FAT 7.4g (sat 3.5g, mono 2.3g, poly 0.9g); PROTEIN 10.4g; CARB 58.6g; FIBER 2.3g; CHOL 134.2mg; IRON 2.2mg; SODIUM 395mg; CALC 124mg

Breakfast Bakers

Prep: 5 minutes • Cook: 10 minutes

4	(8-ounce) ready-to-microwave baking potatoes
4	large eggs, lightly beaten
¼	teaspoon salt
¼	teaspoon freshly ground black pepper
2	teaspoons butter
4	tablespoons ⅓-less-fat tub-style chive and onion cream cheese
½	cup (2 ounces) preshredded reduced-fat sharp cheddar cheese
2	center-cut bacon slices, cooked and crumbled

1. Microwave potatoes according to label directions.
2. While potatoes cook, combine eggs, salt, and pepper in a medium bowl, stirring with a whisk. Melt butter in a large nonstick skillet over medium-high heat. Pour egg mixture into pan. Cook 4 minutes or until soft-scrambled, stirring frequently. Remove from heat.
3. Cut potatoes in half. Scoop out pulp, leaving a ⅛-inch shell. Place pulp in a bowl; add cream cheese, and mash with a potato masher until cream cheese melts. Spoon potato mixture evenly into potato shells. Top evenly with scrambled eggs; sprinkle evenly with cheddar cheese and bacon. Yield: 4 servings (serving size: 1 stuffed potato, 2 tablespoons cheddar cheese, and 2 teaspoons bacon).

CALORIES 337; FAT 13g (sat 6.6g, mono 4.2g, poly 1.1g); PROTEIN 15.8g; CARB 39.6g; FIBER 2.7g; CHOL 237mg; IRON 1.6mg; SODIUM 488mg; CALC 158mg

Breakfast Bakers

Sausage Hash Browns
with Eggs

Sausage Hash Browns with Eggs

Prep: 2 minutes • Cook: 12 minutes

Sure to become a family favorite, these hash browns are delicious with eggs, but you can also substitute cheddar cheese.

4	ounces reduced-fat pork sausage
2	teaspoons olive oil
1	(20-ounce) package refrigerated diced potatoes with onions
1	cup refrigerated prechopped tricolor bell pepper mix
2	teaspoons chopped fresh thyme
¼	teaspoon salt
¼	teaspoon freshly ground black pepper
4	large eggs

Freshly ground black pepper (optional)

1. Cook sausage in a small nonstick skillet over medium-high heat 4 to 5 minutes or until lightly browned, stirring to crumble. Remove sausage from pan.

2. While sausage cooks, heat a large non-stick skillet over medium heat. Add oil to pan; swirl to coat. Add potatoes and bell pepper mix, spreading into a single layer. Cook 7 minutes or until vegetables are lightly browned, stirring occasionally. Stir in sausage, thyme, salt, and pepper.

3. Crack eggs into potato mixture, spacing an even distance apart near edge of pan. Cover and cook over medium heat 3 minutes or until egg whites are firm and yolks barely move when pan is touched. Sprinkle with additional pepper, if desired. Yield: 4 servings (serving size: 1 egg and ¼ of potato mixture).

CALORIES 300; FAT 12.5g (sat 3.7g, mono 5.8g, poly 1.6g); PROTEIN 14.7g; CARB 32.4g; FIBER 3.9g; CHOL 231mg; IRON 2.2mg; SODIUM 673mg; CALC 32mg

serve with:

Lemon Balm–Citrus Salad

Prep: 15 minutes

2	navel oranges
1	red grapefruit
½	cup seedless red grapes, halved
2	tablespoons chopped fresh lemon balm or mint
2	tablespoons agave nectar

1. Peel and section oranges and grapefruit over a bowl; squeeze membranes to extract juice. Add grapes, lemon balm, and agave nectar; toss well. Chill until ready to serve. Yield: 4 servings (serving size: about ½ cup).

CALORIES 101; FAT 0.2g (sat 0g, mono 0g, poly 0.1g); PROTEIN 1.1g; CARB 26.3g; FIBER 2.6g; CHOL 0mg; IRON 0.3mg; SODIUM 2mg; CALC 41mg

ingredient spotlight

Agave nectar is a versatile, ready-made liquid sweetener with a nice, neutral flavor you don't find in honey. It can be found in most grocery stores.

Sausage and Sweet Potato Hash

Prep: 2 minutes • Cook: 13 minutes

Use the shredder blade on your food processor to quickly grate the sweet potatoes.

8	ounces reduced-fat pork sausage
1	pound sweet potatoes
2	teaspoons canola oil
¾	cup prechopped onion
1¼	cups sliced cremini mushrooms
1	teaspoon chopped fresh thyme
½	teaspoon freshly ground black pepper
½	cup water
½	cup (2 ounces) preshredded fresh

Parmesan cheese (optional)

1. Cook sausage in a small nonstick skillet over medium-high heat 5 minutes or until browned; stir to crumble. Remove from skillet and keep warm.
2. While sausage cooks, peel sweet potatoes. Place potatoes in a food processor; using coarse-shredding disc, shred to measure 4 cups.
3. Heat a large nonstick skillet over medium-high heat. Add oil; swirl to coat. Cook sweet potato, onion, and next 3 ingredients in hot oil 7 minutes, stirring frequently and adding ½ cup water, 1 tablespoon at a time, as necessary to prevent sticking. Add sausage; cook, stirring constantly, 1 minute. Remove from heat; sprinkle with cheese. Serve immediately. Yield: 6 servings (serving size: 1 cup).

CALORIES 234; FAT 11.3g (sat 4.6g, mono 3.1g, poly 1.4g); PROTEIN 12.1g; CARB 21.5g; FIBER 3.2g; CHOL 33mg; IRON 1.4mg; SODIUM 451mg; CALC 154mg

Zucchini-Potato Pancakes with Eggs

Prep: 4 minutes • Cook: 13 minutes

These crispy pan-fried cakes showcase zucchini and potatoes topped with fried eggs.

2	cups refrigerated shredded hash brown potatoes
1	cup shredded zucchini (about 1 small)
¼	cup Italian-seasoned panko (Japanese breadcrumbs)
4	large egg whites, lightly beaten
¼	cup (1 ounce) shredded fresh Parmesan cheese
¼	teaspoon freshly ground black pepper

Cooking spray

4	large eggs
⅛	teaspoon freshly ground black pepper

Fresh salsa (optional)
Light sour cream (optional)

1. Combine first 6 ingredients in a large bowl.
2. Heat a large nonstick skillet over medium heat; heavily coat pan with cooking spray. Spoon about ½ cup potato mixture into 2 (5-inch) circles in pan. Cook 5 minutes; turn and cook 4 minutes or until potato is tender. Remove pancakes from pan, and keep warm. Repeat procedure with remaining potato mixture.
3. Reheat pan over medium-high heat; heavily recoat pan with cooking spray. Crack 4 eggs into pan; sprinkle with ⅛ teaspoon black pepper, and coat tops of eggs with cooking spray. Cover and cook 3 minutes or until whites have just set and yolks begin to thicken but are not hard or until desired degree of doneness. Slide 1 egg onto each pancake. Serve with salsa and sour cream, if desired. Yield: 4 servings (serving size: 1 pancake and 1 egg).

CALORIES 222; FAT 6.5g (sat 2.5g, mono 1.9g, poly 0.8g); PROTEIN 15.6g; CARB 24g; FIBER 1.6g; CHOL 186mg; IRON 1.4mg; SODIUM 392mg; CALC 120mg

serve with:

Spinach Salad with Strawberries

Prep: 4 minutes

1	tablespoon olive oil
1	tablespoon fresh lemon juice
1	teaspoon honey
¼	teaspoon salt
⅛	teaspoon freshly ground black pepper
3	cups bagged baby spinach leaves
1	cup quartered strawberries
⅓	cup (1.3 ounces) crumbled feta cheese (optional)

1. Combine first 5 ingredients in a large bowl, stirring well with a whisk. Add spinach and strawberries; toss well. Sprinkle with feta cheese, if desired. Yield: 2 servings (serving size: 2 cups).

CALORIES 108; FAT 7g (sat 0.9g, mono 5g, poly 0.8g); PROTEIN 1.5g; CARB 11.3g; FIBER 2.6g; CHOL 0mg; IRON 2mg; SODIUM 320mg; CALC 49mg

appetizers, beverages & snacks

Crab Salad in Wonton Cups,
page 43

Crab Salad in Wonton Cups

Prep: 3 minutes • Cook: 12 minutes

Wonton wrappers become a crispy golden shell for fresh crab salad: Simply coat them with cooking spray, mold them into mini muffin cups, and bake.

Cooking spray
18   wonton wrappers
Chile-Lime Dressing
½   pound jumbo lump crabmeat, drained and shell pieces removed
½   cup finely chopped celery (2 stalks)
⅓   cup finely chopped red onion

1. Preheat oven to 375°.
2. Coat 18 miniature muffin cups with cooking spray. Coat wonton wrappers with cooking spray; press 1 wrapper into each muffin cup. Bake at 375° for 12 minutes or until browned and crisp. Remove wonton cups from muffin cups.
3. While wonton cups bake, prepare Chile-Lime Dressing in a medium bowl. Add crab, celery, and onion to dressing, tossing to coat. Fill wonton cups evenly with crab mixture. Serve immediately. Yield: 9 servings (serving size: 2 filled wonton cups).

CALORIES 104; FAT 3g (sat 0.4g, mono 1.7g, poly 0.4g); PROTEIN 7.7g; CARB 10.8g; FIBER 0.7g; CHOL 28mg; IRON 0.9mg; SODIUM 227mg; CALC 39mg

quick flip

Don't have crabmeat? Make an easy sub with shredded cooked chicken.

Chile-Lime Dressing

Prep: 4 minutes

1   teaspoon grated lime rind
2½   tablespoons fresh lime juice
2   tablespoons minced green onions
1½   tablespoons olive oil
½   teaspoon chopped dried Thai chiles (2 chiles)
¼   teaspoon freshly ground black pepper
⅛   teaspoon salt

1. Combine all ingredients in a medium bowl, stirring with a whisk. Cover and chill until ready to serve. Yield: 9 servings (serving size: 2 teaspoons).

CALORIES 23; FAT 2.3g (sat 0.3g, mono 1.7g, poly 0.3g); PROTEIN 0.1g; CARB 0.7g; FIBER 0.2g; CHOL 0mg; IRON 0.1mg; SODIUM 34mg; CALC 2mg

Apricot-Stilton Bites

Prep: 6 minutes

This simple appetizer is also delicious with white Stilton or a white Stilton blend with ginger. You can substitute honey for the agave syrup, if you like. A glass of Vouvray would complement these snacks.

¼   cup (1 ounce) crumbled blue Stilton cheese
12   dried apricot halves
2   tablespoons coarsely chopped pistachios
1   tablespoon agave syrup
½   teaspoon chopped fresh thyme

1. Place 1 teaspoon cheese on each apricot; top each with ½ teaspoon pistachios. Drizzle evenly with syrup. Sprinkle evenly with thyme. Yield: 4 servings (serving size: 3 topped apricots).

CALORIES 92; FAT 4.3g (sat 1.9g, mono 1.6g, poly 0.6g); PROTEIN 2.8g; CARB 11.8g; FIBER 1.2g; CHOL 6.3mg; IRON 0.4mg; SODIUM 144mg; CALC 51mg

Broccoli Pesto Bruschetta

Prep: 4 minutes • Cook: 6 minutes

Take inspiration from these bruschetta, and spread leftover broccoli pesto on a sandwich.

12	(½-ounce) slices diagonally cut French bread baguette

Cooking spray

2	cups broccoli florets
1	garlic clove
¼	cup (1 ounce) grated fresh Parmesan cheese
2	tablespoons pine nuts
2	tablespoons olive oil
1½	ounces shaved fresh pecorino Romano cheese
¼	teaspoon freshly ground black pepper

1. Preheat oven to 450°.
2. Lightly coat bread slices with cooking spray; place on a baking sheet. Bake at 450° for 5 minutes or until crisp.
3. While bread bakes, cook broccoli in boiling water 6 minutes or just until tender; drain.
4. Drop garlic through food chute with processor on; process until minced. Add broccoli, Parmesan cheese, pine nuts, and olive oil. Process until smooth.
5. Top toast slices evenly with broccoli mixture and pecorino Romano cheese. Sprinkle evenly with pepper. Serve immediately. Yield: 12 servings (serving size: 1 bruschetta).

CALORIES 79; FAT 4.4g (sat 1g, mono 1.9g, poly 0.8g); PROTEIN 3g; CARB 7.5g; FIBER 0.7g; CHOL 3mg; IRON 0.6mg; SODIUM 149mg; CALC 52mg

Caramelized Onion and Goat Cheese Tartlets

Prep: 10 minutes • Cook: 22 minutes

A classy twist on onion dip, these tarts pair the complex flavor of caramelized onion with goat cheese in a pretty shell.

1	(1.9-ounce) package mini phyllo shells

Cooking spray

1	cup diced onion
2	tablespoons reduced-fat sour cream
½	teaspoon freshly ground black pepper
1	(4-ounce) package herbed goat cheese

Thyme sprigs (optional)

1. Preheat oven to 400°.
2. Arrange phyllo shells on a baking sheet. Heat a medium skillet over medium-high heat. Coat pan with cooking spray. Add onion to pan; coat with cooking spray. Cook onion, stirring frequently, 10 minutes or until golden brown and tender.
3. Combine sour cream, pepper, and cheese. Place 1 tablespoon cheese mixture into each mini phyllo shell. Top each with 1 teaspoon onion.
4. Bake at 400° for 10 to 12 minutes or until golden. Let cool on a wire rack. Garnish with thyme sprigs, if desired. Yield: 15 servings (serving size: 1 tartlet).

CALORIES 42; FAT 2.8g (sat 1.2g, mono 1.1g, poly 0.3g); PROTEIN 1.3g; CARB 3.2g; FIBER 0.2g; CHOL 3.7mg; IRON 0.2mg; SODIUM 48mg; CALC 11mg

Caramelized Onion and
Goat Cheese Tartlets

Carrot Soup
Shots

Carrot Soup Shots

Prep: 3 minutes • Cook: 5 minutes

Ginger and carrots are a classic combo. Here, the ginger blends with crème fraîche, a thick, mild-flavored dairy product that is popular in France. If you can't find it, you can substitute sour cream.

2	cups frozen sliced carrots
2	tablespoons water
1½	teaspoons unsalted butter
2	tablespoons chopped shallot (1 medium shallot)
2	cups organic vegetable broth, divided

Ginger Crème Fraîche

1. Place carrots and 2 tablespoons water in a medium microwave-safe bowl. Cover tightly with heavy-duty plastic wrap. Microwave at HIGH 5 minutes or until carrots are tender.
2. While carrots cook, melt butter in a 2-quart saucepan over medium-high heat. Add shallot; cook, stirring often, 3 minutes or just until tender.
3. Place shallot, half of cooked carrots, and 1 cup broth in a blender. Remove center piece of blender lid (to allow steam to escape); secure blender lid on blender. Place a clean towel over opening in blender lid (to avoid splatters). Blend until smooth. Pour into a large bowl. Repeat procedure with remaining carrots and broth. Stir to blend.
4. Serve soup, warm or chilled, in shot glasses with a dollop of Ginger Crème Fraîche. Yield: 20 servings (serving size: 2 tablespoons soup and about ½ teaspoon crème fraîche).

CALORIES 15; FAT 0.9g (sat 0.5g, mono 0.3g, poly 0g); PROTEIN 0.1g; CARB 1.5g; FIBER 0.4g; CHOL 3mg; IRON 0.1mg; SODIUM 64mg; CALC 6mg

Ginger Crème Fraîche

Prep: 2 minutes

2	tablespoons crème fraîche
1	teaspoon chopped green onions
¾	teaspoon grated peeled fresh ginger
¼	teaspoon fresh lemon juice

1. Combine all ingredients in a small bowl. Chill until ready to serve. Yield: 20 servings (serving size: about ½ teaspoon).

CALORIES 6; FAT 0.6g (sat 0.4g, mono 0.2g, poly 0g); PROTEIN 0g; CARB 0g; FIBER 0g; CHOL 2mg; IRON 0mg; SODIUM 0.6mg; CALC 1mg

Creamy Avocado Dip with Sweet Potato Chips

Prep: 6 minutes

Sour cream makes this dip extra smooth. Experiment with different chips: You might try plantain chips or taro root chips in place of the store-bought sweet potato chips.

1	ripe peeled avocado, coarsely mashed
⅓	cup light sour cream
2	tablespoons fresh lemon juice
½	teaspoon ground cumin
¼	teaspoon salt
¼	teaspoon freshly ground black pepper
32	sweet potato chips

1. Combine first 6 ingredients in a medium bowl. Serve with chips. Yield: 8 servings (serving size: 2 tablespoons dip and 4 chips).

CALORIES 78; FAT 5.2g (sat 1.1g, mono 2.4g, poly 0.9g); PROTEIN 1.3g; CARB 7g; FIBER 1.5g; CHOL 3.3mg; IRON 0.3mg; SODIUM 85mg; CALC 29mg

Curried Hummus

Prep: 4 minutes

Hummus, a Mediterranean classic, gets an Indian twist with curry.

2	(15-ounce) cans no-salt-added chickpeas (garbanzo beans), drained
2	tablespoons water
2	tablespoons extra-virgin olive oil
1	tablespoon fresh lemon juice
2	teaspoons curry powder
½	teaspoon salt

1. Place all ingredients in a food processor; process until smooth. Yield: 8 servings (serving size: ⅓ cup).

CALORIES 94; FAT 4.7g (sat 0.5g, mono 3g, poly 0.9g); PROTEIN 3.3g; CARB 10.2g; FIBER 2.9g; CHOL 0mg; IRON 1.1mg; SODIUM 224mg; CALC 24mg

serve with:

Spicy Cilantro Naan Chips

Prep: 5 minutes • Cook: 7 minutes

1	(9-ounce) package whole-wheat naan (2 naan)
	Olive oil–flavored cooking spray
½	teaspoon smoked paprika
¼	teaspoon kosher salt
¼	teaspoon ground red pepper
2	tablespoons chopped fresh cilantro

1. Preheat oven to 425°.
2. Cut each naan into 8 wedges. Arrange wedges in a single layer on a baking sheet. Coat wedges with cooking spray.
3. Combine smoked paprika, salt, and ground red pepper in a small bowl; sprinkle evenly over wedges. Lightly coat wedges with cooking spray. Sprinkle with cilantro.
4. Bake at 425° for 7 minutes or until browned and crisp. Yield: 8 servings (serving size: 2 chips).

CALORIES 87; FAT 2.6g (sat 0.5g, mono 0.8g, poly 0.8g); PROTEIN 2.6g; CARB 10.8g; FIBER 2.1g; CHOL 2.5mg; IRON 0.9mg; SODIUM 263mg; CALC 21mg

ingredient spotlight

Naan is leavened, oven-baked thick flatbread popular in many parts of Asia. Baked in a tandoor oven at extremely high heat, naan is known for its big bubbles, airy texture, and smoky flavor.

Curried Hummus

Fig and Caramelized
Onion Flatbread

Fig and Caramelized Onion Flatbread

Prep: 10 minutes • Cook: 27 minutes
Other: 5 minutes

Straight from the oven, this sweet and savory flat-bread wins rave reviews. Balsamic glaze is a sweet, tangy syrup made from balsamic vinegar. Look for it in grocery stores. You can substitute feta cheese or a young sheep's milk cheese for the ricotta salata.

1	tablespoon olive oil
1	large onion, thinly sliced
⅛	teaspoon freshly ground black pepper
1	cup water
¾	cup dried Mission figs, stems removed
1	(11-ounce) can refrigerated thin pizza crust dough
Cooking spray	
⅔	cup ricotta salata
1	tablespoon balsamic glaze

1. Preheat oven to 425°.
2. Heat a medium nonstick skillet over medium heat. Add oil; swirl to coat. Add onion; cook 10 minutes or until very soft and golden, stirring frequently. Stir in pepper, and remove from heat.
3. While onion cooks, combine water and figs in a small microwave-safe bowl. Microwave at HIGH 1 minute. Let stand 5 minutes.
4. While figs stand, unroll dough. Shape dough into a 15 x 12–inch rectangle on a baking sheet coated with cooking spray. Bake at 425° for 5 minutes.
5. Drain figs, and coarsely chop. Top crust with onion and figs; sprinkle with ricotta salata.
6. Bake at 425° for 10 minutes or until golden. Drizzle with balsamic glaze. Cut into pieces. Serve immediately. Yield: 18 servings (serving size: 1 piece).

CALORIES 89; FAT 3.1g (sat 1g, mono 1g, poly 0.8g); PROTEIN 2.3g; CARB 13.4g; FIBER 1.1g; CHOL 0mg; IRON 0.6mg; SODIUM 174mg; CALC 18mg

Goat Cheese–Stuffed
Piquillo Peppers

Goat Cheese–Stuffed Piquillo Peppers

Prep: 10 minutes

Piquillos are small, red, spicy-sweet roasted Spanish peppers; substitute roasted bell peppers if you can't find them in a specialty grocery store.

4	teaspoons olive oil, divided
2	tablespoons chopped pitted kalamata olives
¼	teaspoon garlic pepper
1	(4-ounce) package goat cheese
1½	teaspoons sherry vinegar
1	(9.5-ounce) jar pimientos del piquillo peppers
2	teaspoons chopped fresh chives

1. Combine 1 teaspoon oil and next 3 ingredients in a small bowl.
2. Combine 3 teaspoons oil and vinegar in another small bowl, stirring with a whisk.
3. Drain peppers, and pat dry. Carefully make a vertical slit down 1 side of each pepper. Open peppers and fill evenly with cheese mixture. Close edges of pepper over filling to seal. Place stuffed peppers, seam sides down, on a serving platter. Drizzle evenly with vinaigrette, and sprinkle evenly with chives. Serve immediately. Yield: 12 servings (serving size: 1 pepper).

CALORIES 52; FAT 3.9g (sat 1.6g, mono 1.9g, poly 0.3g); PROTEIN 1.8g; CARB 2g; FIBER 0.9g; CHOL 4.4mg; IRON 0.2mg; SODIUM 128mg; CALC 14mg

make ahead

For an easy make-ahead option, chill the stuffed peppers, covered, on the serving platter. When ready to serve, let them stand at room temperature 30 minutes, and then drizzle with the vinaigrette and sprinkle with chives.

Grilled Asparagus Pizzas

Prep: 7 minutes • Cook: 4 minutes

Use green, white, and purple asparagus for a stunning pizza.

¼	pound asparagus spears, trimmed
1½	teaspoons olive oil
½	teaspoon freshly ground black pepper, divided
¼	teaspoon salt
1	lemon
½	cup part-skim ricotta cheese
¼	cup (2 ounces) herbed goat cheese
½	(12-ounce) package whole-wheat naan (2 naan)
Cooking spray	

1. Preheat grill to medium-high heat.
2. Place asparagus in a bowl. Add oil, ¼ teaspoon pepper, and salt; toss to coat.
3. Grate 1 teaspoon rind and squeeze 1 tablespoon juice from lemon. Combine remaining ¼ teaspoon pepper, lemon rind, lemon juice, ricotta cheese, and goat cheese in a small bowl. Spread each naan with half of cheese mixture.
4. Place pizzas and asparagus on grill rack coated with cooking spray. Grill 4 minutes or until pizzas are crisp and asparagus is crisp-tender. Chop asparagus, and sprinkle evenly over pizzas. Cut each pizza into 8 wedges. Yield: 8 servings (serving size: 2 wedges).

CALORIES 111; FAT 4.5g (sat 1.9g, mono 1.4g, poly 0.6g); PROTEIN 5.6g; CARB 12.9g; FIBER 2.4g; CHOL 7.3mg; IRON 1.1mg; SODIUM 204mg; CALC 53mg

Barbecue Turkey Burger Sliders

Prep: 15 minutes • Cook: 10 minutes

While great for serving at small parties, you can also make this recipe into full-sized burgers for dinner.

1 pound ground turkey breast
3 tablespoons chopped fresh cilantro
2 tablespoons barbecue sauce
Cooking spray
12 (1.2-ounce) whole-wheat slider buns
Mustard Coleslaw

1. Combine first 3 ingredients in a medium bowl. Divide meat mixture into 12 equal portions; shape portions into ¼-inch-thick patties.
2. Heat a large nonstick skillet over medium-high heat. Coat pan with cooking spray. Add half of patties to pan; cook 3 minutes. Turn patties over; cook 2 minutes or until done. Transfer patties to a plate; keep warm. Repeat procedure with remaining patties.
3. Place 1 patty on bottom half of each bun. Top each patty with about 3 tablespoons Mustard Coleslaw and 1 bun top. Yield: 12 servings (serving size: 1 slider).

CALORIES 149; FAT 2.5g (sat 0.1g, mono 0.2g, poly 1.1g); PROTEIN 14.5g; CARB 19g; FIBER 1.3g; CHOL 15mg; IRON 0.5mg; SODIUM 207mg; CALC 47mg

Mustard Coleslaw

Prep: 5 minutes

¼ cup creamy mustard blend (such as Dijonnaise)
2 tablespoons white wine vinegar
¾ teaspoon sugar
¼ teaspoon freshly ground black pepper
¼ cup chopped red onion
1 (5-ounce) package cabbage-and-carrot coleslaw

1. Combine first 4 ingredients in a medium bowl, stirring with a whisk.
2. Add onion and coleslaw; toss to coat. Yield: 12 servings (serving size: about 3 tablespoons).

CALORIES 8; FAT 0g (sat 0g, mono 0g, poly 0g); PROTEIN 0.2g; CARB 1.6g; FIBER 0.3g; CHOL 0mg; IRON 0mg; SODIUM 27mg; CALC 7mg

Barbecue Turkey Burger Sliders

Cucumber-Gin Sipper

Prep: 5 minutes

This refreshing gin cocktail gains its herbal notes from an infusion of cucumber and shiso, as well as a touch of Pimm's No. 1. Use a vegetable peeler to make the cucumber ribbon. The drink is best with a lighter-style gin, such as Beefeater or Hendrick's.

4   (¼-inch-thick) slices English cucumber
4   green shiso leaves, divided
2   teaspoons Pimm's No. 1
2   tablespoons gin
1   teaspoon fresh lime juice
Crushed ice
¼   cup club soda
1   (6 x 2–inch) English cucumber ribbon
     (⅛ inch thick)

1. Place cucumber slices, 3 shiso leaves, and Pimm's in a martini shaker; crush leaves with back of a long spoon. Add gin and lime juice. Fill shaker with crushed ice; shake. Fill an old-fashioned glass with crushed ice. Strain mixture over ice in glass. Stir in club soda. Garnish with remaining 1 shiso leaf and a cucumber ribbon. Yield: 1 serving.

CALORIES 89; FAT 0g (sat 0g, mono 0g, poly 0g); PROTEIN 0.2g; CARB 0.9g; FIBER 0.1g; CHOL 0mg; IRON 0.1mg; SODIUM 1mg; CALC 6mg

ingredient spotlight

Shiso, also known as perilla, is an herb widely used in Japanese cuisine. The anise-flavored herb comes in both a red and a green variety; you can find it at Asian markets.

Kentucky Mule

Prep: 3 minutes • Other: 10 minutes

A twist on the Moscow Mule, which is traditionally made with vodka and ginger ale, this cocktail steps up the game with bourbon and ginger beer.

½   cup bourbon
2   tablespoons Cointreau (orange-flavored liqueur)
3   cups ginger beer
Icy Ginger Oranges

1. Fill 6 (8-ounce) glasses one-third full with ice. Combine bourbon and Cointreau; pour 1⅔ tablespoons bourbon mixture in each glass. Add ½ cup ginger beer to each glass. Garnish with Icy Ginger Oranges. Yield: 6 servings (serving size: about ⅔ cup and 1 orange slice).

CALORIES 171; FAT 0g (sat 0g, mono 0g, poly 0g); PROTEIN 0.2g; CARB 23g; FIBER 0.5g; CHOL 0mg; IRON 0.3mg; SODIUM 2mg; CALC 18mg

Icy Ginger Oranges

Prep: 2 minutes • Other: 10 minutes

1   tablespoon chopped crystallized ginger
2   tablespoons sugar
6   (⅛-inch-thick) slices navel orange

1. Place ginger and sugar in small food processor or spice grinder; pulse until minced. Dredge orange slices in ginger mixture; place in a single layer on a parchment paper–lined baking sheet. Freeze 10 minutes or until ready to use. Yield: 6 servings (serving size: 1 orange slice).

CALORIES 48; FAT 0.3g (sat 0g, mono 0g, poly 0g); PROTEIN 0.2g; CARB 12.3g; FIBER 0.5g; CHOL 0mg; IRON 0.3mg; SODIUM 2mg; CALC 18mg

Mango Mo-ritas

Prep: 7 minutes

What do you get when you combine the best of two favorites: a mojito and a margarita? A festive mo-rita!

1	cup cubed peeled ripe mango
¼	cup fresh mint leaves
2	tablespoons superfine sugar
2	tablespoons fresh lime juice
½	cup tequila
1	tablespoon Triple Sec (orange-flavored liqueur)

Crushed ice
1	cup club soda

Mint sprigs (optional)

1. Place first 4 ingredients in a blender; process until smooth. Stir in tequila and Triple Sec.
2. Fill each of 4 glasses with ½ cup crushed ice. Pour mango mixture evenly over ice, and fill each glass with ¼ cup club soda. Garnish with mint sprigs, if desired. Yield: 4 servings (serving size: about ⅔ cup).

CALORIES 130; FAT 0.1g (sat 0g, mono 0g, poly 0g); PROTEIN 0.3g; CARB 15.7g; FIBER 0.9g; CHOL 0mg; IRON 0.2mg; SODIUM 14mg; CALC 12mg

Mint Vodka and Iced Green Tea

Prep: 5 minutes • Cook: 8 minutes
Other: 2 hours and 10 minutes

Use your favorite brand of green tea for this refreshing drink; they often vary in strength and flavor. Add a lemon wedge, if you like.

4	cups water
2	tablespoons agave syrup
6	mint green tea bags
4	(5-inch) mint sprigs
1	cup sweet tea vodka

1. Place first 4 ingredients in a large saucepan; bring to a boil. Boil 5 minutes, stirring occasionally. Remove pan from heat; cover and let stand 10 minutes. Remove and discard tea bags and mint, squeezing tea bags to remove liquid. Stir in vodka; let cool completely. Pour tea mixture into a pitcher; cover and refrigerate until thoroughly chilled.
2. Serve tea over ice. Yield: 5 servings (serving size: about 1 cup).

CALORIES 127; FAT 0g (sat 0g, mono 0g, poly 0g); PROTEIN 0g; CARB 6.4g; FIBER 0g; CHOL 0mg; IRON 0mg; SODIUM 1mg; CALC 0mg

Raspberry Lemon Drop

Prep: 5 minutes • Cook: 3 minutes

½	cup sugar
½	cup water
¼	cup fresh lemon juice
6	lemon thyme sprigs
1	cup fresh raspberries
6	ounces raspberry-flavored vodka
1	cup club soda
4	lemon slices

Additional fresh raspberries (optional)

1. Combine first 4 ingredients in a small heavy saucepan. Cook over medium heat, stirring gently until sugar dissolves. Remove pan from heat. Remove and discard thyme sprigs.
2. Place ¼ cup raspberries in a cocktail shaker; crush with back of a wooden spoon. Add 1½ ounces vodka and 1 tablespoon thyme syrup. Fill shaker with crushed ice; shake until outside of glass is frosted. Pour mixture through a fine-mesh sieve into a glass; gently stir in ¼ cup soda. Repeat procedure with remaining raspberries, vodka, syrup, ice, and club soda, reserving remaining syrup for another use. Serve each drink with a lemon slice and additional raspberries, if desired. Yield: 4 servings (serving size: ½ cup).

CALORIES 152; FAT 0.3g (sat 0g, mono 0g, poly 0.1g); PROTEIN 0.5g; CARB 13.5g; FIBER 2.5g; CHOL 0mg; IRON 1.2mg; SODIUM 1.4mg; CALC 24mg

Raspberry Lemon Drop

Sparkling Peach Lemonade

Prep: 5 minutes • Cook: 4 minutes

Muddle mint leaves in the bottom of each glass for more flavor, or add 1⅓ cups citrus vodka for a spiked cocktail.

¼   cup fresh lemon juice
3   tablespoons sugar
2   cups lemon-flavored sparkling water, chilled
2   cups ginger ale, chilled
1½   cups peach nectar, chilled
Mint sprigs (optional)

1. Combine lemon juice and sugar in a small saucepan. Cook over medium heat, stirring constantly, 4 minutes or just until sugar dissolves. Pour into a large pitcher. Cover and chill.
2. Stir in sparkling water, ginger ale, and peach nectar just before serving. Serve over ice, and garnish with mint sprigs, if desired. Yield: 6 servings (serving size: about 1 cup).

CALORIES 88; FAT 0g (sat 0g, mono 0g, poly 0g); PROTEIN 0.2g; CARB 23g; FIBER 0.4g; CHOL 0mg; IRON 0.3mg; SODIUM 13mg; CALC 19mg

make ahead

Make the lemon juice and sugar syrup the night before and chill. Just add the rest of the ingredients when ready to serve.

Spicy Carrot Bloody Mary

Prep: 3 minutes

1   cup carrot juice, chilled
½   cup vodka
¼   teaspoon ground cumin
1   (15-ounce) can diced tomatoes with celery, onion, and green pepper
1   jalapeño pepper, coarsely chopped
5   small serrano peppers (optional)
5   carrot ribbons (optional)

1. Place first 5 ingredients in a blender. Blend until smooth. Serve over ice. Garnish with serrano peppers and carrot ribbons, if desired. Yield: 5 servings (serving size: about ¾ cup).

CALORIES 103; FAT 0.1g (sat 0g, mono 0g, poly 0g); PROTEIN 1.2g; CARB 11.5g; FIBER 1.9g; CHOL 0mg; IRON 0.8mg; SODIUM 187mg; CALC 40mg

quick flip

This version of a Bloody Mary mixes the heat of jalapeño with sweet carrot juice. Make the cocktails even spicier by using jalapeño or black pepper vodka.

Spicy Carrot Bloody Mary

White Cranberry–Peach Spritzers

Prep: 7 minutes

These spritzers combine white cranberry and peach juice with seasonal fresh peaches and lime-flavored sparkling water to create a light, summery drink.

2   cups white cranberry–peach juice
1   cup Lillet Blanc (French aperitif wine)
1   peach, halved
1½   cups lime-flavored sparkling water
4   lime slices

1. Combine juice and wine in a pitcher. Peel half of peach, and cut into slices. Add peach slices to juice mixture; muddle with liquid. Divide peach mixture evenly among 4 ice-filled glasses. Add 6 tablespoons (⅜ cup) lime-flavored sparkling water to each glass. Cut remaining peach half into 4 slices. Garnish each drink with 1 peach slice and 1 lime slice. Yield: 4 servings (serving size: 1¼ cups).

CALORIES 120; FAT 0.1g (sat 0g, mono 0g, poly 0g); PROTEIN 0.3g; CARB 20g; FIBER 0.6g; CHOL 0mg; IRON 0.1mg; SODIUM 20mg; CALC 11mg

ingredient spotlight

If you can't find Lillet Blanc, a white apertif wine, substitute a sweet white dessert wine.

Melon Chillers

Prep: 6 minutes

2   cups cubed fresh cantaloupe, frozen
⅓   cup orange juice
2   tablespoons fresh lime juice
¼   cup sugar
1   (12-ounce) can ginger ale, divided

1. Place first 4 ingredients and ½ cup ginger ale in a blender; process until smooth. Add remaining ginger ale; process until smooth. Yield: 4 servings (serving size: about 1 cup).

CALORIES 116; FAT 1g (sat 0.1g, mono 0g, poly 0.1g); PROTEIN 0.9g; CARB 29.2g; FIBER 0.1g; CHOL 0mg; IRON 0.4mg; SODIUM 19mg; CALC 13mg

Melon Chillers

Cranberry-Açai Spritzer

Sugared Spicy Nuts

Prep: 2 minutes • Cook: 11 minutes

Store nuts in your freezer to keep them fresh longer. For this recipe, let them come to room temperature first, or toast them a minute longer.

1	cup whole natural almonds
½	cup walnut halves
½	cup cashews
2	tablespoons butter
½	cup packed light brown sugar
1	tablespoon water
¼	teaspoon ground red pepper
¼	teaspoon salt
2	teaspoons chopped fresh thyme

Cooking spray

1. Place nuts in a large skillet. Cook over medium heat 8 minutes or until toasted, stirring often. Transfer to a small bowl.
2. Add butter and next 4 ingredients to pan. Cook over medium heat 1 minute, stirring until sugar dissolves. Add nuts and thyme, stirring to coat. Cook an additional 2 minutes or until nuts are glazed and golden brown.
3. Spread mixture in a single layer on a foil-lined baking sheet coated with cooking spray. Cool completely. Yield: 26 servings (serving size: 2 tablespoons).

CALORIES 83; FAT 6.1g (sat 1.1g, mono 2.8g, poly 1.8g); PROTEIN 1.9g; CARB 6.5g; FIBER 0.9g; CHOL 2mg; IRON 0.5mg; SODIUM 32mg; CALC 22mg

Cranberry-Açai Spritzers

Prep: 4 minutes

2	cups cranberry juice
1	(10.5-ounce) bottle organic açai juice blend
1	tablespoon fresh lime juice
1	(12-ounce) can ginger ale
2	cups crushed ice (optional)

Lime slices (optional)

1. Combine first 3 ingredients in a 1½-quart pitcher. Slowly add ginger ale. Serve over ice, and garnish with lime slices, if desired. Yield: 4 servings (serving size: about 1 cup).

CALORIES 136; FAT 1.2g (sat 0.3g, mono 0g, poly 0g); PROTEIN 0.3g; CARB 31.5g; FIBER 0.3g; CHOL 0mg; IRON 0.4mg; SODIUM 17mg; CALC 30mg

Blueberry-Yogurt Parfaits

Prep: 5 minutes

Layer the berries and yogurt ahead, and store in the refrigerator. Top with cereal just before serving for a satisfying afternoon snack or light breakfast.

1   cup plain fat-free Greek yogurt
¼   teaspoon grated lemon rind
2   teaspoons honey
½   cup blueberries
2   tablespoons multigrain cluster cereal

1. Combine first 3 ingredients in a small bowl. Spoon 2 tablespoons yogurt mixture into each of 2 parfait glasses. Top with 2 tablespoons blueberries. Repeat layers. Top each serving with 1 tablespoon cereal. Serve immediately. Yield: 2 servings (serving size: 1 parfait).

CALORIES 115; FAT 0.3g (sat 0g, mono 0.1g, poly 0.1g); PROTEIN 10.9g; CARB 17.8g; FIBER 1.4g; CHOL 0mg; IRON 0.2mg; SODIUM 56mg; CALC 81mg

Blueberry-Yogurt Parfaits

Apple-Avocado Smoothies

Prep: 6 minutes

Avocado adds creaminess and a very mild flavor to this healthy, refreshing smoothie.

1   Hass avocado
2   cups crushed ice
1   cup almond milk
2   tablespoons honey
2   teaspoons fresh lime juice
1   (6-ounce) carton vanilla low-fat yogurt
1   (3.9-ounce) container Granny Smith applesauce (about ½ cup)
2½ teaspoons sliced almonds, toasted (optional)

1. Cut avocado in half lengthwise; discard pit. Scoop pulp from avocado halves, and place in a blender. Add ice and next 5 ingredients; process until smooth. Garnish with almonds, if desired. Serve immediately. Yield: 5 servings (serving size: about ¾ cup).

CALORIES 143; FAT 6.8g (sat 1.1g, mono 4.3g, poly 0.8g); PROTEIN 2.2g; CARB 19.5g; FIBER 3.1g; CHOL 2mg; IRON 0.3mg; SODIUM 53mg; CALC 83mg

ingredient spotlight

Made from ground almonds, almond milk is a vegan and vegetarian substitute for milk. Be sure to buy the plain flavor for this recipe.

Mini Pesto Pretzels

Prep: 30 minutes • Cook: 12 minutes

1   (11-ounce) can refrigerated breadstick dough
⅓   cup grated fresh Parmesan cheese
3   tablespoons commercial pesto
Cooking spray

1. Preheat oven to 425°.
2. Unroll dough; separate into 12 breadsticks. Cut each breadstick in half lengthwise. Roll each breadstick half into a 16-inch rope. Cross one end of rope over the other to form a circle. Twist rope once at base of the circle. Fold ends over circle and into traditional pretzel shape, pinching gently to seal.
3. Place cheese in a shallow dish. Brush top side of pretzels evenly with pesto. Press pesto side of pretzels into cheese. Place pretzels, cheese side up, on a baking sheet coated with cooking spray.
4. Bake at 425° for 12 minutes or until golden brown. Yield: 24 servings (serving size: 1 pretzel).

CALORIES 51; FAT 1.9g (sat 0.8g, mono 0.8g, poly 0.2g); PROTEIN 1.9g; CARB 6.4g; FIBER 0.3g; CHOL 2mg; IRON 0.4mg; SODIUM 137mg; CALC 27mg

Cheddar-Apple Cracker Bites

Prep: 5 minutes

Using different cheeses or mustards, or even pears instead of apples, gives you more options for snack time or a buffet table.

2	(0.7-ounce) slices reduced-fat cheddar cheese, cut into quarters
8	(0.1-ounce, 3 x 1½–inch) flatbread crackers
16	thin vertical Fuji apple slices (1 medium)
1	tablespoon honey
2	teaspoons stone-ground mustard

1. Place 1 cheese quarter on top of each cracker. Top each with 2 apple slices.
2. Combine honey and mustard in small bowl. Drizzle evenly over apples. Yield: 8 servings (serving size: 1 topped cracker).

CALORIES 45; FAT 1.2g (sat 0.6g, mono 0.3g, poly 0g); PROTEIN 1.7g; CARB 7.3g; FIBER 0.6g; CHOL 4mg; IRON 0.2mg; SODIUM 78mg; CALC 72mg

Chocolate-Hazelnut Popcorn

Prep: 6 minutes • Cook: 23 minutes

This popcorn is a healthier alternative to a candy bar.

	Cooking spray
8	cups popcorn (popped without salt and fat)
½	cup chopped toasted hazelnuts
6	tablespoons chocolate-hazelnut spread
⅓	cup honey

1. Preheat oven to 300°.
2. Coat a large jelly-roll pan with cooking spray.

3. Place popcorn and hazelnuts on prepared pan. Combine chocolate-hazelnut spread and honey in a medium saucepan. Cook, stirring constantly, over medium-low heat 3 minutes or until melted and smooth. Drizzle hazelnut mixture over popcorn mixture, tossing gently to coat.
4. Bake at 300° for 20 minutes, stirring twice. Transfer mixture to a sheet of parchment paper; cool completely.
Yield: 16 servings (serving size: ½ cup).

CALORIES 97; FAT 4.5g (sat 2.2g, mono 1.7g, poly 0.4g); PROTEIN 1.5g; CARB 13.7g; FIBER 1.3g; CHOL 0mg; IRON 0.6mg; SODIUM 3mg; CALC 12mg

Curried Chutney–Stuffed Celery

Prep: 10 minutes

Walnuts are a delicious substitute if you don't have honey-roasted peanuts on hand.

6	tablespoons (4 ounces) ⅓-less-fat cream cheese, softened
2	tablespoons mango chutney
1	teaspoon grated onion
½	teaspoon red curry powder
9	celery stalks, each cut into 3 pieces
2	tablespoons finely chopped honey-roasted peanuts

1. Combine first 4 ingredients in a small bowl; stir well. Spread about 1½ teaspoons cheese mixture into each celery piece. Sprinkle cheese mixture evenly with peanuts. Serve immediately, or cover and chill. Yield: 9 servings (serving size: 3 stuffed celery pieces).

CALORIES 66; FAT 3.8g (sat 1.8g, mono 1.2g, poly 0.4g); PROTEIN 2.2g; CARB 6.2g; FIBER 1.2g; CHOL 9mg; IRON 0.3mg; SODIUM 134mg; CALC 35mg

Curried Yogurt Dip

Prep: 5 minutes

Pair this spicy dip with an assortment of vegetables, such as carrots, bell peppers, green beans, celery, cucumbers, radishes, or whatever fresh seasonal vegetables you have on hand.

½	cup plain 2% reduced-fat Greek yogurt
½	cup canola mayonnaise
1½	tablespoons chopped fresh cilantro
1	tablespoon fresh lime juice
1½	teaspoons hot curry powder
1	garlic clove, minced

1. Combine all ingredients in a small bowl. Yield: 4 servings (serving size: ¼ cup).

CALORIES 113; FAT 9.7g (sat 0.4g, mono 5.2g, poly 3g); PROTEIN 2.5g; CARB 2.1g; FIBER 0.3g; CHOL 2mg; IRON 0.2mg; SODIUM 190mg; CALC 24mg

make ahead

If you can, make this dip the day before, and refrigerate it overnight to allow the yogurt to fully absorb the flavors from the cilantro, lime, and hot curry powder.

Curried Yogurt Dip

Feta-Mint Dip

Prep: 7 minutes

Serve with fresh seasonal vegetables or whole-grain flaxseed crackers.

1	cup plain 2% reduced-fat Greek yogurt
½	cup (2 ounces) crumbled feta cheese
½	cup finely chopped English cucumber
3	tablespoons chopped fresh mint
2	tablespoons sliced green onions
¼	teaspoon grated lemon rind
¼	teaspoon salt
⅛	teaspoon freshly ground black pepper

Freshly ground black pepper (optional)

1. Place yogurt and feta in a food processor; process until smooth. Transfer to a small bowl. Stir in cucumber and next 5 ingredients. Sprinkle with additional black pepper, if desired. Yield: 8 servings (serving size: about 3½ tablespoons).

CALORIES 40; FAT 2g (sat 1.2g, mono 0.6g, poly 0.1g); PROTEIN 4g; CARB 2g; FIBER 0.4g; CHOL 7mg; IRON 0.2mg; SODIUM 165mg; CALC 43mg

Feta-Mint Dip

Fresh Salsa

Prep: 13 minutes

Tomato seeds can be bitter, so remove them. Seeding a tomato is easy: Cut it in half horizontally, and use a spoon or your finger to quickly scrape out the seeds.

1⅔	cups chopped seeded tomato (1 large)
½	cup chopped onion
¼	cup chopped fresh cilantro
2	tablespoons fresh lime juice
¼	teaspoon salt
2	garlic cloves, minced
1	jalapeño pepper, seeded and minced

1. Combine all ingredients in a medium bowl. Yield: 14 servings (serving size: 2 tablespoons).

CALORIES 8; FAT 0.1g (sat 0g, mono 0g, poly 0g); PROTEIN 0.3g; CARB 1.8g; FIBER 0.4g; CHOL 0mg; IRON 0.1mg; SODIUM 44mg; CALC 5mg

Lemon-Basil Ice Pops

Prep: 6 minutes • Cook: 2 minutes
Other: 8 hours and 30 minutes

1	cup water
¾	cup sugar
3	tablespoons chopped fresh basil
1	tablespoon grated lemon rind
1	cup fresh lemon juice
6	basil leaves

1. Combine first 4 ingredients in a small saucepan. Bring to a boil; remove from heat, and let stand 30 minutes. Strain lemon mixture through a sieve into a bowl. Stir in lemon juice. Pour mixture evenly into 6 (3-ounce) ice pop molds. Place 1 basil leaf into each mold. Freeze 8 hours or until firm. Yield: 6 servings (serving size: 1 pop).

CALORIES 109; FAT 0g (sat 0g, mono 0g, poly 0g); PROTEIN 0.2g; CARB 28.9g; FIBER 0.3g; CHOL 0mg; IRON 0.1mg; SODIUM 1mg; CALC 8mg

Lemon-Basil
Ice Pops

Lemon, Mint, and White Bean Dip

Prep: 5 minutes

1   garlic clove
1   (15-ounce) can no-salt-added cannellini beans, rinsed and drained
2   tablespoons chopped fresh mint
1   teaspoon grated lemon rind
1½   tablespoons fresh lemon juice
1   tablespoon extra-virgin olive oil
¼   teaspoon salt
¼   teaspoon freshly ground black pepper

1. Drop garlic through food chute with processor on; process until minced. Add beans and remaining ingredients; process until smooth. Cover and chill until ready to serve. Yield: 10 servings (serving size: 2 tablespoons).

CALORIES 35; FAT 1.6g (sat 0.2g, mono 1g, poly 0.2g); PROTEIN 1.4g; CARB 4.1g; FIBER 1.2g; CHOL 0mg; IRON 0.4mg; SODIUM 67mg; CALC 10mg

---

make ahead

Make this dip in advance, and store it in an airtight container in the refrigerator up to one week.

Peanut Butter–Banana Dip

Prep: 4 minutes

Try this great snack with apple wedges or celery sticks.

½   cup chunky peanut butter
⅓   cup mashed ripe banana
1   tablespoon honey
¼   teaspoon ground cinnamon
1   (6-ounce) carton vanilla fat-free organic yogurt

1. Combine all ingredients in a medium bowl. Yield: 8 servings (serving size: 3 tablespoons).

CALORIES 127; FAT 8g (sat 1.3g, mono 3.9g, poly 2.4g); PROTEIN 4.8g; CARB 10.9g; FIBER 1.7g; CHOL 1mg; IRON 0.3mg; SODIUM 91mg; CALC 37mg

Pimiento Cheese Poppers

Prep: 9 minutes

Pimiento cheese is a great snack with any fresh veggie. Try it with celery sticks or bell pepper wedges.

3   ounces ⅓-less-fat cream cheese, softened
3   ounces fat-free cream cheese, softened
8   ounces reduced-fat extra-sharp cheddar cheese, shredded
¼   cup canola mayonnaise
1   (4-ounce) jar diced pimientos, drained
2   tablespoons finely diced onion
Ground red pepper (optional)
24   tricolor sweet mini peppers, cut in half

1. Combine first 6 ingredients and ground red pepper, if desired, in a medium bowl. Stuff each pepper half with 2 teaspoons cheese mixture. Refrigerate until ready to serve. Yield: 24 servings (serving size: 2 stuffed pepper halves).

CALORIES 72; FAT 5.3g (sat 2g, mono 2.4g, poly 0.9g); PROTEIN 3.5g; CARB 2.1g; FIBER 0.4g; CHOL 11mg; IRON 0.1mg; SODIUM 142mg; CALC 84mg

Pecan Biscotti

Prep: 15 minutes • Cook: 50 minutes
Other: 10 minutes

These nutty biscotti are a delicious accompaniment to a cup of coffee or tea. Store them for up to two weeks in an airtight container.

1½   cups coarsely chopped pecans, toasted and divided
¾   cup sugar
9   ounces self-rising flour (about 2 cups)
1   teaspoon vanilla extract
3   large eggs

1. Preheat oven to 350°.
2. Line a large baking sheet with parchment paper.
3. Place ½ cup pecans and sugar in a food processor; process until finely ground. Transfer pecan mixture to a large bowl. Weigh or lightly spoon flour into dry measuring cups, and level with a knife. Add flour, vanilla, and eggs to bowl. Beat with a heavy-duty mixer at medium speed just until a soft dough forms. Stir in 1 cup pecans.
4. Using floured hands, divide dough in half. Form each half into a 10 x 2–inch log. Place logs 3 inches apart on prepared baking sheet.
5. Bake at 350° for 30 minutes or until lightly browned. Cool logs on pan 10 minutes.
6. Cut logs diagonally into ¼-inch-thick slices with a serrated knife. Arrange slices on baking sheet. Bake at 350° for 10 minutes. Turn slices over; bake an additional 10 minutes or until golden and crisp. Remove slices from pan. Cool completely on a wire rack. Yield: 32 servings (serving size: 1 biscotto).

CALORIES 88; FAT 4.2g (sat 0.5g, mono 2.3g, poly 1.2g); PROTEIN 1.8g; CARB 11.3g; FIBER 0.7g; CHOL 20mg; IRON 0.6mg; SODIUM 106mg; CALC 33mg

Pecan Biscotti

Roasted Edamame

Prep: 4 minutes • Cook: 15 minutes

Don't be tempted to stir the edamame too frequently—it's more flavorful when it's lightly charred.

1	(16-ounce) package frozen unshelled edamame (green soybeans), thawed
4	teaspoons olive oil
¼	teaspoon ground red pepper
2	garlic cloves, minced
½	teaspoon coarse sea salt

1. Preheat oven to 500°.
2. Pat edamame dry with paper towels. Place edamame, oil, red pepper, and garlic on a rimmed baking sheet, tossing to coat.
3. Bake at 500° for 15 minutes or until browned, stirring once. Sprinkle with salt. Yield: 8 servings (serving size: ½ cup).

CALORIES 101; FAT 5.6g (sat 0.7g, mono 2.8g, poly 1.6g); PROTEIN 6.7g; CARB 6.3g; FIBER 2g; CHOL 0mg; IRON 1.2mg; SODIUM 149mg; CALC 68mg

Strawberry-Ginger Yogurt Pops

Prep: 5 minutes • Cook: 5 minutes
Other: 8 hours

Spicy ginger is the perfect pairing with strawberries in these refreshing yogurt pops.

2	cups quartered strawberries
¼	cup sugar
2	tablespoons water
½	teaspoon grated peeled fresh ginger
1	cup plain low-fat Greek yogurt
1	teaspoon fresh lime juice

1. Combine first 4 ingredients in a medium saucepan. Bring to a boil; reduce heat, and simmer, uncovered, 5 minutes or until berries are softened, stirring occasionally. Place strawberry mixture in a blender; process until smooth. Add yogurt and lime juice. Process just until blended.
2. Fill 8 (3-ounce) ice pop molds with strawberry mixture, according to manufacturer's instructions. Freeze 8 hours or until firm. Yield: 8 servings (serving size: 1 pop).

CALORIES 91; FAT 1.1g (sat 0.6g, mono 0.3g, poly 0.1g); PROTEIN 4.3g; CARB 17.1g; FIBER 1.3g; CHOL 3mg; IRON 0.3mg; SODIUM 16mg; CALC 41mg

Sweet and Spicy Kettle Corn

Prep: 2 minutes • Cook: 5 minutes

Popped corn keeps fresh for a day or two if stored in a paper bag with the top folded down. Use other spices you like, such as coriander, cumin, or paprika.

½	teaspoon ground red pepper
1¼	teaspoons fine sea salt
¼	teaspoon ground chipotle chile pepper
3	tablespoons canola oil
½	cup popcorn, unpopped
¼	cup sugar

1. Combine first 3 ingredients in a small bowl.
2. Heat oil in a large Dutch oven over medium heat. Add oil; swirl to coat. Add popcorn; cover and cook 30 seconds. Sprinkle popcorn with sugar; cover. As soon as kernels begin to pop, begin shaking pan. Cook, shaking pan constantly, 4 minutes or until popping slows to 2 to 3 seconds between pops. Transfer popped corn to a large bowl. Sprinkle with red pepper mixture; toss well. Yield: 16 servings (serving size: 1 cup).

CALORIES 57; FAT 2.9g (sat 0.2g, mono 1.7g, poly 0.9g); PROTEIN 0.6g; CARB 7.4g; FIBER 0.9g; CHOL 0mg; IRON 0.2mg; SODIUM 175mg; CALC 0mg

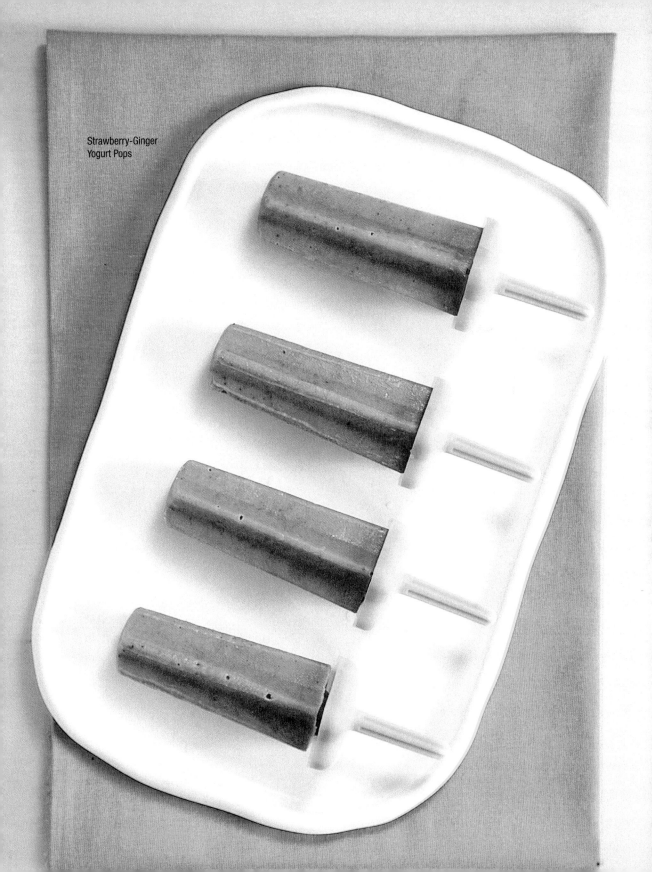

Strawberry-Ginger
Yogurt Pops

Toasted Cashew
Hummus

Toasted Cashew Hummus

Prep: 6 minutes • Cook: 7 minutes

Toasting the already roasted cashews deepens their flavor. Serve with pita chips or raw veggies.

1	cup jumbo cashews, roasted in sea salt
2	garlic cloves
¾	cup water
¼	cup tahini (roasted sesame seed paste)
2	tablespoons fresh lime juice
1	tablespoon olive oil
1	teaspoon ground cumin
¼	teaspoon salt
1	(15.5-ounce) can chickpeas (garbanzo beans), rinsed and drained
2	teaspoons chopped fresh cilantro (optional)

1. Preheat oven to 350°.
2. Spread cashews in a shallow pan. Bake at 350° for 7 minutes, stirring occasionally.
3. Drop garlic through food chute with processor on; process until minced. Add cashews, water, and next 6 ingredients; process until smooth. Garnish with cilantro, if desired. Yield: 10 servings (serving size: ¼ cup).

CALORIES 162; FAT 11.3g (sat 1.9g, mono 6g, poly 2.8g); PROTEIN 4.6g; CARB 12.7g; FIBER 2g; CHOL 0mg; IRON 1.6mg; SODIUM 234mg; CALC 27mg

Tomato-Avocado Dip

Prep: 5 minutes

1	cup chopped tomato
1½	teaspoons chopped fresh cilantro
1	tablespoon fresh lime juice
¼	teaspoon salt
¼	teaspoon ground cumin
1	ripe peeled avocado, coarsely mashed
1	garlic clove, minced
36	baked tortilla chips

1. Combine first 7 ingredients in a medium bowl. Serve immediately with chips. Yield: 6 servings (serving size: ¼ cup dip and 6 tortilla chips).

CALORIES 103; FAT 5.4g (sat 0.7g, mono 3.3g, poly 0.6g); PROTEIN 2.1g; CARB 13.6g; FIBER 3.4g; CHOL 0mg; IRON 0.4mg; SODIUM 177mg; CALC 24mg

Trail Mix Poppers

Prep: 11 minutes

Toss a few of these nutrient-packed poppers in a zip-top plastic bag, and you're ready to roll with snack in hand. Pair them with yogurt for a quick breakfast, too. Create a more complex flavor by adding three slices of crystallized ginger when mincing the fruit bits.

⅔	cup sliced almonds
¼	cup flaked sweetened coconut
1	(7-ounce) bag dried fruit bits
1½	tablespoons honey

1. Place almonds in a food processor; pulse 10 times or until minced. Transfer half of almonds to a medium bowl. Add coconut and fruit bits to remaining almonds in processor; process 30 seconds or until minced. Add honey. Pulse 10 times or just until blended.
2. Using a 1-inch scoop, shape mixture into 18 (1-inch) balls. Roll balls in reserved almonds. Store in an airtight container. Yield: 9 servings (serving size: 2 poppers).

CALORIES 119; FAT 3.4g (sat 0.8g, mono 1.7g, poly 0.7g); PROTEIN 1.8g; CARB 21.3g; FIBER 2.6g; CHOL 0mg; IRON 0.7mg; SODIUM 18mg; CALC 26mg

soups

Leek and Potato Soup,
page 78

Greek Lentil Soup with
Mint-Yogurt Sauce

Greek Lentil Soup with Mint-Yogurt Sauce

Prep: 9 minutes • Cook: 19 minutes

A great soup starter, canned lentils readily absorb the rich flavors of this hearty soup.

2	teaspoons olive oil
1	cup refrigerated prechopped onion
½	cup chopped carrot
2	cups organic vegetable broth
¼	teaspoon freshly ground pepper
⅛	teaspoon salt
2	(15-ounce) cans organic lentils

Mint-Yogurt Sauce
Fresh mint or cilantro sprigs (optional)

1. Heat a Dutch oven over medium-high heat. Add oil; swirl to coat. Add onion and carrot. Cook 4 minutes or until vegetables are lightly browned, stirring occasionally. Stir in broth and next 3 ingredients. Bring to a boil; reduce heat, and simmer, uncovered, 10 minutes or until carrot is tender. While soup simmers, prepare Mint-Yogurt Sauce. Ladle soup into bowls. Top with Mint-Yogurt Sauce and, if desired, fresh mint or cilantro. Yield: 4 servings (serving size: 1½ cups soup and 2 tablespoons sauce).

CALORIES 234; FAT 2.5g (sat 0.3g, mono 1.8g, poly 0.3g); PROTEIN 16.4g; CARB 36.6g; FIBER 16.2g; CHOL 0mg; IRON 0.4mg; SODIUM 628mg; CALC 43mg

Mint-Yogurt Sauce

Prep: 6 minutes

A minty yogurt sauce energizes this bold lentil soup and adds traditional Mediterranean flavor.

½	cup plain fat-free Greek yogurt
1	tablespoon chopped fresh mint
1	tablespoon chopped fresh cilantro
1	teaspoon ground cumin
1	teaspoon grated lemon rind
2	garlic cloves, minced

1. Combine all ingredients in a small bowl. Yield: 4 servings (serving size: 2 tablespoons).

CALORIES 20; FAT 0.1g (sat 0g, mono 0.1g, poly 0g); PROTEIN 2.7g; CARB 2g; FIBER 0.3g; CHOL 0mg; IRON 0.2mg; SODIUM 12mg; CALC 28mg

quick flip

Turn the Mint-Yogurt Sauce into Dill-Yogurt Sauce by substituting dill, parsley, and green onions for the mint, cilantro, and cumin. Fresh, wispy dill adds a sweet, citrusy hint to this Mediterranean-inspired sauce.

Minestrone

Prep: 3 minutes • Cook: 15 minutes

Healthy greens and sautéed pancetta add a contemporary flavor to this Italian mainstay. The Basil-Asiago Grissini, an update on crisp breadsticks, help kick off the fun. Cook the pasta separately to make the soup even faster.

¼   cup uncooked ditalini (very short tube-shaped macaroni)
2   ounces pancetta, chopped
1   cup refrigerated prechopped celery, onion, and bell pepper mix
½   cup chopped carrot
2   cups chopped Swiss chard
1   cup water
1   (15-ounce) can no-salt-added cannellini beans, rinsed and drained
1   (14.5-ounce) can no-salt-added diced tomatoes, undrained
1   (14-ounce) can fat-free, lower-sodium chicken broth

1. Cook pasta according to package directions, omitting salt and fat. Drain.
2. While pasta cooks, cook pancetta in a Dutch oven over medium-high heat 3 minutes or until browned, stirring frequently. Add celery mix and carrot; cook 3 minutes or until vegetables are tender and browned. Stir in chard and remaining ingredients. Bring mixture to a boil; cover, reduce heat, and simmer 6 minutes. Stir in pasta. Yield: 4 servings (serving size: 1½ cups soup).

CALORIES 176; FAT 5.5g (sat 2.1g, mono 2.4g, poly 1g); PROTEIN 8.1g; CARB 24.1g; FIBER 5.6g; CHOL 10mg; IRON 1.9mg; SODIUM 619mg; CALC 62mg

serve with:
Basil-Asiago Grissini

Prep: 3 minutes • Cook: 12 minutes

½   sheet frozen puff pastry dough, thawed
Cooking spray
1   large egg white, lightly beaten
⅓   cup (1.3 ounces) shredded Asiago cheese
½   teaspoon dried basil
¼   teaspoon garlic powder
¼   teaspoon freshly ground black pepper

1. Preheat oven to 400°.
2. Place pastry dough on a baking sheet coated with cooking spray. Press pastry into a 9½ x 5–inch rectangle. Brush egg white over pastry. Sprinkle evenly with cheese and remaining ingredients. Cut pastry into 8 thin strips. Carefully twist each strip into a curly breadstick about 10 inches long.
3. Bake at 400° for 12 to 13 minutes or until browned. Yield: 4 servings (serving size: 2 grissini).

CALORIES 62; FAT 3.9g (sat 2g, mono 0.9g, poly 0.9g); PROTEIN 4g; CARB 2.5g; FIBER 0.2g; CHOL 9mg; IRON 0.3mg; SODIUM 63mg; CALC 94mg

fix it faster

You can save a step by substituting refrigerated tortelloni stuffed with chicken and prosciutto for the ditalini and pancetta. The choice ingredients for the soup will still deliver the Italian flavor you desire.

Leek and Potato Soup

Prep: 6 minutes • Cook: 26 minutes

For the best results, use just the white portion of leeks; it has the mildest flavor. Avoid slicing too far into the green part, which can make the soup bitter.

2	leeks
1	(24-ounce) package refrigerated country-style mashed potatoes
2	center-cut bacon slices
1	cup fat-free, lower-sodium chicken broth, divided
¼	teaspoon salt
2	cups 2% low-fat milk
¼	teaspoon freshly ground black pepper

1. Remove roots, outer leaves, and tops from leeks, leaving only white part of leeks. Cut white part of leeks in half lengthwise. Cut crosswise into ½-inch-thick slices to measure 1 cup. Rinse with cold water; drain.
2. Microwave potatoes according to package directions.
3. While potatoes heat, cook bacon in a large saucepan over medium heat until crisp. Remove bacon from pan; crumble. Add leek to drippings in pan; sauté 3 minutes, adding 2 tablespoons broth to prevent sticking. Sauté 4 minutes or until tender.
4. Stir in remaining broth, scraping pan to loosen browned bits. Stir in potatoes and salt. Gradually add milk, stirring until smooth. Cook, uncovered, over medium heat 10 minutes or until thoroughly heated, stirring occasionally. Stir in pepper. Ladle soup into bowls; sprinkle with crumbled bacon. Yield: 4 servings (serving size: 1½ cups soup and 1 tablespoon bacon).

CALORIES 242; FAT 6.3g (sat 3.4g, mono 1.7g, poly 0.4g); PROTEIN 9.2g; CARB 37.2g; FIBER 3.6g; CHOL 20.4mg; IRON 1.5mg; SODIUM 554mg; CALC 173mg

serve with:
Mixed Greens with Hazelnut-Herb Vinaigrette

Prep: 9 minutes

1	(5-ounce) package mixed salad greens
¾	cup grape tomatoes, halved
½	cup drained canned quartered artichoke hearts
¼	cup torn fresh mint leaves (optional)
2	tablespoons white balsamic vinegar
1	tablespoon toasted hazelnut oil
1	teaspoon Dijon mustard
1	teaspoon honey
⅛	teaspoon salt
⅛	teaspoon freshly ground black pepper
2	tablespoons chopped hazelnuts, toasted

1. Combine first 3 ingredients and mint, if desired, in a large bowl. Combine balsamic vinegar and next 5 ingredients in a small bowl, stirring with a whisk.
2. Drizzle greens mixture with dressing, and sprinkle with toasted nuts. Yield: 4 servings (serving size: 1½ cups).

CALORIES 87; FAT 5.7g (sat 0.4g, mono 4.4g, poly 0.8g); PROTEIN 1.9g; CARB 8g; FIBER 1.5g; CHOL 0mg; IRON 0.9mg; SODIUM 182mg; CALC 9mg

Sweet Potato, Leek, and Ham Soup

Prep: 6 minutes • Cook: 28 minutes

Prechopped sweet potato is now available in most grocery stores. If you're unable to find it, peel and cube two small sweet potatoes to measure about 3 cups.

Olive oil–flavored cooking spray
1	cup diced cooked ham
1½	cups sliced leek (about 1 large)
2	tablespoons water (optional)
3	cups refrigerated cubed peeled sweet potato
1	cup fat-free, less-sodium chicken broth
2	cups water
1	(5-ounce) can evaporated fat-free milk
¼	teaspoon freshly ground black pepper

Thinly sliced leek (optional)
Thinly sliced green onions (optional)

1. Heat a large Dutch oven over medium heat. Coat pan with cooking spray. Add ham; cook 3 to 4 minutes or until browned, stirring frequently. Remove ham from pan; set aside.

2. Add leek to pan; coat with cooking spray. Cook leek, covered, 5 minutes or until very tender, stirring occasionally. Add 2 tablespoons water to pan, if needed, to prevent burning.

3. Add sweet potato and next 4 ingredients, scraping pan to loosen browned bits; bring mixture to a boil. Cover, reduce heat, and simmer 15 minutes or until sweet potato is very tender. Place half of potato mixture in a blender or food processor. Remove center piece of blender lid (to allow steam to escape); secure blender lid on blender.

Sweet Potato, Leek, and Ham Soup

4. Place a clean towel over opening in blender lid (to avoid splatters). Process until smooth. Pour puree into a large bowl. Repeat procedure with remaining mixture. Return pureed mixture to pan. Stir in ¾ cup reserved ham. Ladle soup into bowls; top servings evenly with ¼ cup reserved ham. Garnish with sliced leek and onions, if desired. Yield: 4 servings (serving size: about 1¼ cups soup).

CALORIES 193; FAT 1g (sat 0.2g, mono 0g, poly 0.1g); PROTEIN 15.5g; CARB 29.2g; FIBER 3.6g; CHOL 26mg; IRON 2mg; SODIUM 625mg; CALC 153mg

Sweet Potato Soup with Pancetta-Rosemary Croutons

Prep: 12 minutes • Cook: 28 minutes

To save time, use cubed peeled sweet potato from the produce department of your supermarket.

¼ cup finely chopped pancetta (about 1½ ounce)
2 cups chopped sweet onion
4 cups cubed peeled sweet potato (2 medium)
1 (12-ounce) can low-fat evaporated milk
2 cups water
¼ teaspoon salt
½ teaspoon freshly ground black pepper
Pancetta-Rosemary Croutons

1. Cook pancetta in a large Dutch oven over medium-low heat 4 minutes until golden brown and crisp. Add onion; cook 5 minutes, stirring occasionally. Add sweet potato and next 4 ingredients. Cover and bring to a boil. Cover, reduce heat, and simmer 15 minutes.
2. Place 3 cups soup in a blender. Remove center piece of blender lid (to allow steam to escape); secure blender lid on blender. Place a clean towel over opening in blender lid (to avoid splatters). Blend until smooth. Pour blended soup into a large bowl. Repeat procedure with remaining soup. Stir soup to blend. Ladle soup evenly into 6 bowls; sprinkle with Pancetta-Rosemary Croutons. Yield: 6 servings (serving size: 1 cup soup and about ⅓ cup croutons).

CALORIES 251; FAT 7.5g (sat 3.6g, mono 1.5g, poly 1.2g); PROTEIN 9.8g; CARB 36.2g; FIBER 3.7g; CHOL 22mg; IRON 1.5mg; SODIUM 630mg; CALC 198mg

Pancetta-Rosemary Croutons

Prep: 3 minutes • Cook: 13 minutes

⅓ cup finely chopped pancetta (about 2 ounces)
2 cups (1-inch) cubed sourdough bread
1 teaspoon chopped fresh rosemary

1. Cook pancetta in a nonstick skillet over medium-low heat 4 minutes or until golden brown and crisp. Remove pancetta from skillet; drain. Cook bread cubes in drippings in pan, stirring frequently, 7 minutes or until golden and crisp. Stir in rosemary; cook 1 minute. Stir pancetta into bread cubes. Yield: 6 servings (serving size: about ⅓ cup).

CALORIES 80; FAT 3.5g (sat 1.4g, mono 1g, poly 1g); PROTEIN 3.1g; CARB 9.3g; FIBER 0.6g; CHOL 7mg; IRON 0.8mg; SODIUM 263mg; CALC 18mg

ingredient spotlight

Pancetta is unsmoked pork belly that is cured in salt and spices. It adds a distinctive pork flavor to dishes without the smokiness of American bacon.

Corn and Bacon Chowder

Prep: 2 minutes • Cook: 14 minutes

To capture the freshness of yellow jewel-like corn without the fuss of shucking ears or cutting kernels off the cob, use packages of frozen baby gold and white corn. This chowder is so wonderfully sweet with the frozen corn that our taste testers gave it our highest rating.

2	bacon slices
½	cup refrigerated prechopped celery, onion, and bell pepper mix
2	(16-ounce) packages frozen baby gold and white corn, thawed and divided
2	cups 1% low-fat milk, divided
½	teaspoon salt
¼	teaspoon freshly ground black pepper
¾	cup (3 ounces) reduced-fat shredded extra-sharp cheddar cheese

Freshly ground black pepper (optional)

1. Cook bacon in a Dutch oven over medium heat until crisp. Remove bacon from pan; crumble and set aside. Add celery mixture and 1 package corn to drippings in pan; sauté 5 minutes or until vegetables are tender.

2. Place remaining 1 package corn and 1 cup milk in a blender, and process until smooth. Add pureed mixture to vegetables in pan; stir in remaining 1 cup milk, salt, black pepper, and cheese. Cook over medium heat (do not boil), stirring constantly, until cheese melts. Ladle chowder into bowls. Top each serving evenly with reserved crumbled bacon. Sprinkle with additional black pepper, if desired. Yield: 6 servings (serving size: 1 cup chowder).

CALORIES 215; FAT 6g (sat 3.1g, mono 1g, poly 0.6g); PROTEIN 10.8g; CARB 33.6g; FIBER 3.8g; CHOL 15mg; IRON 0.8mg; SODIUM 402mg; CALC 208mg

serve with:

Tomato, Avocado, and Onion Salad

Prep: 7 minutes

3	small heirloom tomatoes, sliced
½	Vidalia or other sweet onion, vertically thinly sliced
½	cup coarsely chopped ripe peeled avocado (about ½ avocado)
1½	tablespoons thinly sliced fresh basil
2	tablespoons light Northern Italian salad dressing with basil and Romano

1. Combine first 4 ingredients in a large bowl, tossing gently. Drizzle dressing evenly over salad; toss gently to coat. Yield: 6 servings (serving size: about ¾ cup).

CALORIES 46; FAT 3g (sat 0.3g, mono 1.2g, poly 0.3g); PROTEIN 0.9g; CARB 5g; FIBER 1.5g; CHOL 0mg; IRON 0.3mg; SODIUM 61mg; CALC 16mg

Corn and Bacon Chowder

Spicy Poblano and Corn Soup

Prep: 3 minutes • Cook: 10 minutes

The peak season for poblano chiles is summer and early fall. Ripe poblanos are reddish brown and sweeter than the green ones. Be sure to remove the seeds and membranes before cooking; that's where most of the heat-inducing capsaicin is found.

1   (16-ounce) package frozen baby gold and white corn, thawed and divided
2   cups fat-free milk, divided
4   poblano chiles, seeded and chopped (about 1 pound)
1   cup refrigerated prechopped onion
1   tablespoon water
¾   teaspoon salt
½   cup (2 ounces) reduced-fat shredded sharp cheddar cheese

1. Place 1 cup corn and 1½ cups milk in a Dutch oven. Bring mixture to a boil over medium heat.
2. Combine chopped chiles, onion, and 1 tablespoon water in a microwave-safe bowl. Cover and microwave at HIGH 4 minutes.
3. Meanwhile, place 2 cups corn and ½ cup milk in a blender; process until smooth. Add pureed mixture to corn mixture in pan. Stir in chile mixture and salt, and cook 6 minutes over medium heat. Ladle soup into bowls, and top each serving with cheddar cheese. Yield: 4 servings (serving size: about 1⅓ cups soup and 2 tablespoons cheese).

CALORIES 239; FAT 4g (sat 2.2g, mono 0.3g, poly 0.5g); PROTEIN 13.2g; CARB 42.3g; FIBER 4.9g; CHOL 13mg; IRON 1.5mg; SODIUM 633mg; CALC 275mg

Spicy Poblano and Corn Soup

make ahead

For even deeper flavor, make this yummy soup the night before. Reheat and top with cheddar cheese.

Gazpacho with Smoky Shrimp

Prep: 5 minutes • Cook: 4 minutes

Chilling this refreshing summer soup makes it a little more special and is worth the extra time if you have it. The fire-roasted tomatoes and paprika add a smoky zing.

1	(14.5-ounce) can fire-roasted diced tomatoes with garlic
1½	cups chopped cucumber
1	(8-ounce) container refrigerated prechopped tomato, onion, and bell pepper mix
1	cup water
2	tablespoons red wine vinegar
¼	teaspoon salt
¼	teaspoon freshly ground black pepper

Smoky Shrimp

Gazpacho with Smoky Shrimp

1. Place diced tomatoes in a food processor; process until smooth. Pour tomato puree into a bowl. Place cucumber and tomato, onion, and bell pepper mix in processor; pulse 5 times or just until chunky. Add cucumber mixture to tomato puree. Stir in 1 cup water and next 3 ingredients.
2. Prepare Smoky Shrimp.
3. Ladle soup into 4 bowls; top evenly with shrimp. Yield: 4 servings (serving size: about 1 cup soup and 7 to 8 shrimp).

CALORIES 171; FAT 2.2g (sat 0.5g, mono 0.5g, poly 1.1g); PROTEIN 24.8g; CARB 11.1g; FIBER 2.3g; CHOL 172mg; IRON 3.1mg; SODIUM 475mg; CALC 78mg

Smoky Shrimp

Prep: 2 minutes • Cook: 4 minutes

Take a tip from savvy shoppers to get dinner on the table fast: Buy shrimp already peeled and deveined. It's a clever shortcut and time-saver.

1	pound peeled and deveined large shrimp
1	large garlic clove, minced
1	teaspoon smoked paprika
¼	teaspoon salt
¼	teaspoon crushed red pepper

Cooking spray

1. Combine all ingredients except cooking spray in a bowl; toss well.
2. Heat a large nonstick skillet over medium-high heat. Coat pan with cooking spray. Add shrimp mixture; sauté 3 to 5 minutes or until shrimp reach desired degree of doneness. Yield: 4 servings (serving size: about 7 to 8 shrimp).

CALORIES 124; FAT 2g (sat 0.5g, mono 0.4g, poly 1g); PROTEIN 23.2g; CARB 1.6g; FIBER 0.2g; CHOL 172mg; IRON 2.8mg; SODIUM 314mg; CALC 62mg

Quick Shrimp Gumbo

Prep: 1 minute • Cook: 14 minutes

Gumbo in 15 minutes? You bet! The secret is to pre-pare the roux in the microwave. It can even be made ahead, cooled completely, covered, and chilled. Just reheat over low heat before using.

Cooking spray
4 ounces reduced-fat smoked turkey sausage, chopped
1 (16-ounce) package frozen gumbo vegetables
1 (14.5-ounce) can diced tomatoes with zesty mild green chiles, undrained
1½ cups water
2 teaspoons salt-free Cajun seasoning
¼ teaspoon freshly ground black pepper
1 bay leaf
2 tablespoons all-purpose flour
1 tablespoon canola oil
1 pound peeled and deveined medium shrimp
Hot sauce (optional)

1. Heat a Dutch oven over medium-high heat. Coat pan with cooking spray. Add sausage; cook 2 minutes or until browned, stirring occasionally. Add frozen vegetables; cook 2 minutes or until vegetables thaw, stirring occasionally. Stir in tomatoes and next 4 ingredients. Bring to a boil.
2. While soup comes to a boil, combine flour and oil in a small microwave-safe bowl, stirring until smooth. Microwave at HIGH 2 minutes to 2 minutes and 30 seconds, stirring after 30 seconds and then every 15 seconds. Stir flour mixture and shrimp into soup; cover, reduce heat, and simmer 4 minutes or until shrimp turn pink and soup is slightly thick. Remove bay leaf. Serve soup with hot sauce, if desired. Yield: 6 servings (serving size: 1½ cups gumbo).

CALORIES 191; FAT 5.4g (sat 1g, mono 2.4g, poly 1.9g); PROTEIN 19.8g; CARB 14.2g; FIBER 2.5g; CHOL 127mg; IRON 2.5mg; SODIUM 644mg; CALC 93mg

serve with:
Cajun Rice

Prep: 1 minute • Cook: 5 minutes

1 (8.8-ounce) package ready-to-serve whole-grain brown rice
Cooking spray
1 cup refrigerated prechopped celery, onion, and bell pepper mix
¼ cup fat-free, lower-sodium chicken broth
1 teaspoon salt-free Cajun seasoning
2 teaspoons chopped fresh oregano (optional)

1. Microwave rice according to package directions.
2. While rice cooks, heat a medium sauce-pan over medium-high heat. Coat pan with cooking spray. Add celery mix; cook 2 minutes or until tender, stirring occasionally. Stir in rice, chicken broth, Cajun seasoning, and, if desired, oregano. Cook 2 minutes or until liquid evaporates. Yield: 6 servings (serving size: about ⅓ cup).

CALORIES 73; FAT 1.3g (sat 0.2g, mono 0.5g, poly 0.5g); PROTEIN 1.8g; CARB 13.8g; FIBER 1g; CHOL 0mg; IRON 0.3mg; SODIUM 30mg; CALC 5mg

Quick Shrimp Gumbo

Provençal Fish Stew

Prep: 4 minutes • Cook: 11 minutes

1   teaspoon olive oil
1¼   cups chopped leek
½   cup chopped fennel bulb
1   garlic clove, minced
1   (14.5-ounce) can diced tomatoes
1¼   cups organic vegetable broth
¼   cup dry white wine
3   tablespoons chopped fresh parsley, divided
6   ounces grouper or other firm white fish, cut
        into 1½-inch pieces
¼   pound peeled and deveined medium shrimp
Parsley sprigs (optional)

1. Heat a large Dutch oven over medium-high heat. Add oil; swirl to coat. Add leek, fennel, and garlic to pan; sauté 4 minutes or until tender. Stir in tomatoes, broth, wine, and 1 tablespoon parsley; bring to a boil.
2. Add fish and shrimp; cook 3 minutes or until done. Sprinkle with remaining 2 tablespoons parsley, and garnish with parsley sprigs, if desired. Yield: 4 servings (serving size: 1¼ cups stew).

CALORIES 127; FAT 2g (sat 0.3g, mono 1.2g, poly 0.5g); PROTEIN 14.2g; CARB 10.5g; FIBER 2.5g; CHOL 58mg; IRON 2.1mg; SODIUM 391mg; CALC 60mg

---

ingredient spotlight

Fennel, an aromatic plant native to the Mediterranean region, has a licorice-like flavor and is delicious raw or cooked. Chopped and sautéed, the fennel bulb adds body and rich flavor to soups. Look for small, heavy, white bulbs that are firm and free of cracks, browning, or moist areas. Store fennel bulbs in a perforated plastic bag in the refrigerator for up to five days.

Coconut Shrimp Soup

Prep: 3 minutes • Cook: 6 minutes

Light coconut milk adds subtle flavor to this spicy soup for two.

1   cup light coconut milk
1   cup water
½   teaspoon red curry paste
¼   teaspoon salt
1   (2 x ½–inch) strip lime rind
¾   pound peeled and deveined large shrimp
¼   cup julienne-cut fresh basil

1. Combine first 5 ingredients in a large saucepan, stirring with a whisk. Bring to a boil over medium-high heat. Add shrimp; cover, reduce heat to medium, and cook 3 minutes or until shrimp turn pink. Remove and discard lime rind; stir in basil. Yield: 2 servings (serving size: 1⅔ cups soup).

CALORIES 199; FAT 7.5g (sat 6.1g, mono 0.7g, poly 0.7g); PROTEIN 28.7g; CARB 5.2g; FIBER 0.4g; CHOL 252mg; IRON 4.7mg; SODIUM 633mg; CALC 61mg

serve with:
Edamame Salad

Prep: 5 minutes

1   cup frozen shelled edamame
¾   cup frozen petite corn kernels
¼   cup chopped red onion
1   tablespoon chopped fresh parsley or cilantro
1½   tablespoons light olive oil vinaigrette

1. Place edamame and corn in a colander, and rinse under cool running water to thaw; drain well. Combine edamame, corn, red onion, parsley or cilantro, and vinaigrette in a medium bowl; toss well to coat. Serve immediately, or cover and chill until ready to serve. Yield: 2 servings (serving size: 1 cup).

CALORIES 152; FAT 5.6g (sat 0.2g, mono 1.5g, poly 3.9g); PROTEIN 8g; CARB 19.9g; FIBER 1.4g; CHOL 0mg; IRON 1.4mg; SODIUM 95mg; CALC 43mg

Coconut Shrimp Soup

Creamy Avocado Soup with Tomato–Lump Crab Relish

Prep: 9 minutes

2	ripe peeled avocados, coarsely chopped
2	cups fat-free, less-sodium chicken broth
1	(8-ounce) carton reduced-fat sour cream
2	tablespoons fresh lime juice
¼	teaspoon ground cumin
¼	teaspoon freshly ground black pepper
⅛	teaspoon salt
¼	pound fresh lump crabmeat, shell pieces removed
½	cup refrigerated prechopped tomato, onion, and bell pepper mix

Cilantro leaves (optional)

1. Place first 7 ingredients in a blender or food processor; process until smooth. Chill soup until ready to serve.
2. Ladle soup into bowls. Combine crabmeat and tomato mixture in a small bowl. Spoon crabmeat mixture evenly on top of soup in each bowl. Garnish with cilantro leaves, if desired. Yield: 4 servings (serving size: 1 cup soup).

CALORIES 295; FAT 23g (sat 6.8g, mono 9.7g, poly 2.1g); PROTEIN 12.6g; CARB 13.9g; FIBER 5.5g; CHOL 50mg; IRON 1.3mg; SODIUM 510mg; CALC 124mg

serve with:

Minted Mango and Jicama Salad

Prep: 12 minutes

1	tablespoon fresh lime juice
2	tablespoons reduced-sugar orange marmalade
1	teaspoon minced peeled fresh ginger
1	tablespoon chopped fresh mint
1	sliced peeled ripe mango
1	cup (3 x ¼–inch) strips peeled jicama

1. Combine first 4 ingredients in a small bowl; stir well with a whisk.
2. Combine mango and jicama in a medium bowl. Drizzle juice mixture over mango mixture; toss gently to coat. Yield: 4 servings (serving size: about ½ cup).

CALORIES 59; FAT 0.1g (sat 0g, mono 0.1g, poly 0g); PROTEIN 0.5g; CARB 14.9g; FIBER 2.5g; CHOL 0mg; IRON 0.3mg; SODIUM 3mg; CALC 10mg

ingredient spotlight

Nothing beats the aroma of a ripe, beautiful mango. Look for fruit with unblemished skin that is blushed with red. A mango is ready to eat when it becomes soft to the touch and very fragrant.

Asian Soup with Mushrooms, Bok Choy, and Shrimp

Prep: 3 minutes • Cook: 12 minutes

You can use most any greens in place of the baby bok choy, including spinach or napa (Chinese) cabbage.

2	teaspoons dark sesame oil

Cooking spray

2	(3½-ounce) packages shiitake mushrooms, trimmed and thinly sliced
3	tablespoons chopped peeled fresh ginger
3	cups fat-free, less-sodium chicken broth
3	cups water
1	tablespoon low-sodium soy sauce
3	cups coarsely chopped baby bok choy
2	tablespoons sliced green onions
2	tablespoons chopped fresh cilantro
1	pound peeled and deveined shrimp
¼	cup fresh lime juice (about 3 limes)

1. Heat a large Dutch oven over medium-high heat; coat pan with cooking spray. Add oil; swirl to coat. Sauté mushrooms and ginger 5 minutes or until liquid evaporates and mushrooms darken.
2. Add broth, 3 cups water, and soy sauce; bring mixture to a boil. Stir in bok choy and next 3 ingredients; cover, reduce heat, and simmer 3 minutes or until shrimp are done. Stir in lime juice just before serving. Yield: 6 servings (serving size: 1⅔ cups soup).

CALORIES 102; FAT 2g (sat 0.4g, mono 0.1g, poly 0.3g); PROTEIN 15.1g; CARB 4.9g; FIBER 0.9g; CHOL 112mg; IRON 2.7mg; SODIUM 534mg; CALC 63mg

serve with:
Sesame Wonton Crisps

Prep: 7 minutes • Cook: 5 minutes

2	teaspoons dark sesame oil
1	teaspoon water
18	wonton wrappers

Cooking spray

1	teaspoon sesame seeds
1	teaspoon black sesame seeds
¼	teaspoon salt
⅛	teaspoon five-spice powder

1. Preheat oven to 400°.
2. Combine sesame oil and 1 teaspoon water in a small bowl. Set aside.
3. Place wonton wrappers on a baking sheet coated with cooking spray. Brush evenly with oil mixture. Sprinkle evenly with sesame seeds, salt, and five-spice powder.
4. Bake at 400° for 5 minutes or until browned and crispy. Yield: 6 servings (serving size: 3 wonton crisps).

CALORIES 88; FAT 2g (sat 0.3g, mono 0.1g, poly 0.3g); PROTEIN 2.6g; CARB 14.2g; FIBER 0.5g; CHOL 2mg; IRON 0.9mg; SODIUM 234mg; CALC 17mg

Asian Soup with Mushrooms, Bok Choy, and Shrimp

Smoky Chicken Tortilla Soup

Prep: 3 minutes • Cook: 10 minutes

Chicken cooked at home is a healthier, lower-sodium option over rotisserie chicken. This soup puts leftover cooked chicken to good use.

1	teaspoon olive oil
½	cup chopped onion
1	garlic clove, minced
1	cup fat-free, lower-sodium chicken broth
1	cup water
2	cups shredded cooked chicken
2	tablespoons fresh lime juice
¼	teaspoon chipotle chile powder
1	(10-ounce) can diced tomatoes and green chiles, undrained
¼	cup tortilla strips

1. Heat a medium saucepan over medium-high heat. Add oil; swirl to coat. Add onion and garlic; sauté 3 minutes or until tender. Add broth and next 5 ingredients. Bring to a boil; reduce heat, and simmer, uncovered, 5 minutes. Ladle soup into 3 bowls, and sprinkle with tortilla strips. Yield: 3 servings (serving size: about 1⅓ cups soup and about 1 tablespoon tortilla strips).

CALORIES 280; FAT 8.4g (sat 1.4g, mono 3.6g, poly 2.3g); PROTEIN 31.4g; CARB 17.7g; FIBER 2.3g; CHOL 79.3mg; IRON 1.5mg; SODIUM 665mg; CALC 44mg

fix it faster

Pack the soup in an airtight container. Keep the tortilla strips in a separate container, and top your soup after it's heated.

Smoky Chicken
Tortilla Soup

Coconut Corn Chowder with Chicken

Prep: 2 minutes • Cook: 7 minutes

Using the microwave is the perfect way to jump-start this creamy creation.

3½	cups (½-inch) cubed medium-sized red potatoes (6 potatoes)
2	(14¾-ounce) cans no-salt-added cream-style corn
1	(13.5-ounce) can light coconut milk
3	cups pulled skinless, boneless rotisserie chicken
¼	teaspoon salt
¼	teaspoon freshly ground black pepper
¼	cup chopped green onions or chopped fresh cilantro (optional)

1. Place potato in a large microwave-safe bowl. Cover with plastic wrap; vent. Microwave at HIGH 3 minutes or until tender.
2. While potato cooks, combine corn and next 4 ingredients in a medium saucepan. Cook over medium heat 3 minutes or just until bubbly, stirring occasionally.
3. Stir potato into corn mixture. Bring to a boil; reduce heat, and simmer 2 minutes. Ladle soup into 6 bowls; sprinkle evenly with green onions or cilantro, if desired. Yield: 6 servings (serving size: 1⅓ cups chowder).

CALORIES 353; FAT 6.7g (sat 4.2g, mono 1.4g, poly 1.1g); PROTEIN 27.6g; CARB 50.2g; FIBER 4.2g; CHOL 60mg; IRON 2.7mg; SODIUM 335mg; CALC 28mg

serve with:
Mini Carrot Quiches

Prep: 4 minutes • Cook: 15 minutes
Other: 3 minutes

8	wonton wrappers
	Cooking spray
1	large egg
¼	teaspoon salt
¼	teaspoon ground ginger
½	cup shredded carrot
1	tablespoon evaporated fat-free milk

1. Preheat oven to 400°.
2. Press 1 wonton wrapper into each of 8 miniature muffin cups coated with cooking spray, forming small cups and allowing corners to extend over edges of cups. Coat wonton cups with cooking spray.
3. Bake at 400° on bottom oven rack for 5 minutes or just until slightly crisp.
4. While wonton cups bake, combine egg, salt, and ginger in a bowl, stirring with a whisk until foamy. Stir in carrot and milk. Spoon carrot mixture evenly into hot wonton cups. Bake on bottom rack an additional 10 minutes or until custard is set and edges of cups are golden. Let quiches cool in pan on a wire rack 3 minutes before serving. Yield: 8 servings (serving size: 1 quiche).

CALORIES 36; FAT 0.7g (sat 0.2g, mono 0.3g, poly 0.1g); PROTEIN 1.8g; CARB 5.4g; FIBER 0.3g; CHOL 27mg; IRON 0.4mg; SODIUM 130mg; CALC 13mg

Creamy Chicken Noodle Soup

Prep: 4 minutes • Cook: 24 minutes

A bit of flour mixed with broth replaces cream to give this comforting soup its luscious texture.

1	tablespoon olive oil
½	cup chopped carrot
1	(8-ounce) container refrigerated prechopped celery, onion, and bell pepper mix
2	tablespoons all-purpose flour
1	(32-ounce) carton fat-free, lower-sodium chicken broth, divided
1	cup water
2	cups pulled skinless, boneless rotisserie chicken breast
2	cups uncooked whole-grain extra-wide noodles
½	teaspoon freshly ground black pepper

Chopped fresh parsley (optional)

1. Heat a Dutch oven over medium-high heat. Add oil; swirl to coat. Add carrot and celery mix; cook 8 minutes, stirring frequently, until tender.

2. While vegetables cook, combine flour and 3 tablespoons broth in a small bowl, stirring with a whisk until smooth.

3. Add remaining broth, water, and chicken to vegetables. Bring to a boil; add noodles, and boil 7 minutes or until noodles are tender.

4. Stir flour mixture with a whisk until smooth; add to soup. Cook, stirring constantly, 3 minutes or until soup is slightly thickened. Stir in pepper. Garnish with chopped fresh parsley, if desired. Yield: 6 servings (serving size: 1 cup soup).

CALORIES 163; FAT 4.2g (sat 0.7g, mono 2.4g, poly 0.6g); PROTEIN 18.2g; CARB 14.5g; FIBER 2.3g; CHOL 42mg; IRON 0.9mg; SODIUM 619mg; CALC 25mg

Chicken Tortilla Soup

Prep: 4 minutes • Cook: 11 minutes

Start this spicy soup while the oven preheats for the tortilla strips. Then, while the soup comes to a boil, prepare and bake the tortilla strips to sprinkle on top.

1	(14-ounce) can fat-free, lower-sodium chicken broth
1	cup water
1	(10-ounce) can diced tomatoes with green chiles (such as Rotel), undrained
1½	cups frozen whole-kernel corn
2	cups shredded cooked chicken breast

Diced avocado (optional)
Lime wedges (optional)

1. Combine first 4 ingredients in a medium saucepan; bring to a boil. Stir in chicken; reduce heat, and simmer 2 minutes or until thoroughly heated. Top with avocado and lime wedges, if desired. Yield: 4 servings (serving size: 1½ cups soup).

CALORIES 180; FAT 3.1g (sat 0.9g, mono 1.1g, poly 0.9g); PROTEIN 24g; CARB 13.8g; FIBER 1.8g; CHOL 60mg; IRON 1mg; SODIUM 589mg; CALC 13mg

quick flip

Want to make this Mexican classic Italian? With just a few tweaks, it can be done. Simply omit the tomatoes with green chiles and frozen corn, and add 1 (14-ounce) can diced tomatoes with green peppers and onions, 1 (9-ounce) package refrigerated cheese-filled tortellini, chopped fresh parsley, and shredded fresh Parmesan cheese.

serve with:

Spicy Tortilla Strips

Prep: 3 minutes • Cook: 11 minutes

3	(6-inch) corn tortillas
2	teaspoons canola oil
Cooking spray	
½	teaspoon salt-free Southwest chipotle seasoning
¼	teaspoon ground cumin
⅛	teaspoon salt

1. Preheat oven to 350°.
2. Brush 1 side of tortillas evenly with oil. Place tortillas on a large rimmed baking sheet coated with cooking spray. Sprinkle evenly with chipotle seasoning, cumin, and salt. Cut tortillas into 2 x ¼–inch strips.
3. Bake at 350° for 11 minutes or until strips are crisp and golden. Yield: 4 servings (serving size: ¼ cup).

CALORIES 51; FAT 2.7g (sat 0.2g, mono 1.4g, poly 0.9g); PROTEIN 0.8g; CARB 6.8g; FIBER 0.8g; CHOL 0mg; IRON 0mg; SODIUM 77mg; CALC 9mg

Chicken Tortilla Soup

Southern Camp Stew

Southern Camp Stew

Prep: 2 minutes • Cook: 13 minutes

This hearty dish is reminiscent of Brunswick stew, a Southern comfort-food favorite made with pork, beef, and chicken. In this version, we opted to only use chicken to keep the ingredient list short and the preparation quick.

1½ cups frozen whole-kernel corn
1 cup chicken stock
2 tablespoons white vinegar
1 tablespoon light brown sugar
¼ cup no-salt-added tomato paste
1 (14.5-ounce) can no-salt-added diced tomatoes
1 (15.25) can medium-sized green lima beans, rinsed and drained
2 teaspoons hot sauce (optional)
1 small rotisserie chicken

1. Combine first 7 ingredients and hot sauce, if desired, in a large Dutch oven. Cover and bring to a boil; reduce heat, and simmer 6 minutes.
2. While soup simmers, skin and bone chicken. Shred chicken to measure 3½ cups; add chicken to soup. Cook 3 minutes. Yield: 6 servings (serving size: 1 cup stew).

CALORIES 225; FAT 2.9g (sat 0.8g, mono 1g, poly 0.7g); PROTEIN 27g; CARB 23.8g; FIBER 5g; CHOL 60mg; IRON 2.4mg; SODIUM 257mg; CALC 38mg

---

ingredient spotlight

Tomato paste is a richly flavored tomato concentrate made from ripened tomatoes that have been cooked for several hours, strained, and reduced. The final product is a thick red paste that's perfect for adding depth of flavor to soups and sauces.

Southwestern Chicken and White Bean Soup

Prep: 2 minutes • Cook: 13 minutes

We really like the extra zing of flavor from the fresh cilantro. It adds a nice burst of color to the dish as well. Simply toss some of the distinctive herb on top of the soup just before serving.

2 cups shredded cooked chicken breast
1 tablespoon 40%-less-sodium taco seasoning
Cooking spray
2 (14-ounce) cans fat-free, less-sodium chicken broth
1 (16-ounce) can cannellini beans or other white beans, rinsed and drained
½ cup green salsa
Light sour cream (optional)
Chopped fresh cilantro (optional)

1. Combine chicken and taco seasoning; toss well to coat. Heat a large saucepan over medium-high heat. Coat pan with cooking spray. Add chicken; sauté 2 minutes or until chicken is lightly browned. Add broth, scraping pan to loosen browned bits.
2. Place beans in a small bowl; mash until only a few whole beans remain. Add beans and salsa to pan, stirring well. Bring to a boil. Reduce heat; simmer 10 minutes or until slightly thick. Serve with sour cream and cilantro, if desired. Yield: 6 servings (serving size: 1 cup soup).

CALORIES 134; FAT 3g (sat 0.5g, mono 0.6g, poly 0.5g); PROTEIN 18g; CARB 8.5g; FIBER 1.8g; CHOL 40mg; IRON 1.1mg; SODIUM 623mg; CALC 22mg

Chicken-Escarole Soup

Prep: 1 minute • Cook: 14 minutes

To cut down on time and keep cleanup to a minimum, use kitchen shears to easily chop tomatoes while they're still in the can.

1	(14½-ounce) can Italian-style stewed tomatoes, undrained and chopped
1	(14-ounce) can fat-free, less-sodium chicken broth
1	cup chopped cooked chicken breast
2	cups coarsely chopped escarole (about 1 small head)
2	teaspoons extra-virgin olive oil

1. Combine tomatoes and broth in a large saucepan. Cover and bring to a boil over high heat. Reduce heat to low; simmer 5 minutes. Add chicken, escarole, and oil; cook 5 minutes. Yield: 4 servings (serving size: 1 cup soup).

CALORIES 118; FAT 4g (sat 0.7g, mono 2.1g, poly 0.6g); PROTEIN 13.5g; CARB 7.9g; FIBER 1.5g; CHOL 30mg; IRON 1.1mg; SODIUM 535mg; CALC 49mg

Chicken-Escarole Soup

Smoked Turkey–Lentil Soup

Prep: 5 minutes • Cook: 8 hours

Throw these ingredients into the slow cooker in the morning, and come home to a hearty and comforting meal without doing any further work. If you prefer to use dried oregano instead of the fresh, reduce the amount to ½ teaspoon. Dried herbs are very potent; a little goes a long way.

6	cups organic vegetable broth
1	(8-ounce) smoked turkey leg
½	pound dried lentils, rinsed and drained
1	(8-ounce) container refrigerated prechopped celery, onion, and bell pepper mix
2	teaspoons chopped fresh oregano
½	teaspoon freshly ground black pepper

Fat-free Greek yogurt (optional)
Oregano sprigs (optional)

1. Place first 6 ingredients in a 3- to 4-quart electric slow cooker. Cover and cook on LOW 8 to 10 hours or until lentils are tender and turkey falls off the bone.
2. Remove turkey leg from cooker. Remove and discard skin. Shred meat; return to cooker, discarding bone. Ladle soup into bowls; garnish with yogurt and oregano sprigs, if desired. Yield: 8 servings (serving size: 1 cup soup).

CALORIES 159; FAT 3g (sat 0.6g, mono 0.7g, poly 0.5g); PROTEIN 12.7g; CARB 21.3g; FIBER 5g; CHOL 17mg; IRON 2.2mg; SODIUM 648mg; CALC 26mg

Smoked Turkey–Lentil
Soup

serve with:
Fresh Lime and Oregano Spring Greens Salad

Prep: 7 minutes

1	garlic clove, minced
2	tablespoons water
1½	tablespoons extra-virgin olive oil
1	tablespoon fresh lime juice
1	teaspoon chopped fresh oregano
¼	teaspoon freshly ground black pepper
⅛	teaspoon salt
1	(5-ounce) package spring greens

1. Combine first 7 ingredients in a large bowl; stir well with a whisk. Add greens, and toss gently to coat. Yield: 4 servings (serving size: about 1 cup).

CALORIES 70; FAT 7g (sat 1.4g, mono 4g, poly 0.5g); PROTEIN 1.3g; CARB 2.1g; FIBER 0.6g; CHOL 3mg; IRON 0.2mg; SODIUM 171mg; CALC 38mg

Chicken-Vegetable-Barley Soup

Prep: 5 minutes • Cook: 21 minutes
Other: 5 minutes

5	cups fat-free, less-sodium chicken broth
2	cups shredded rotisserie chicken breast
½	teaspoon kosher salt
½	teaspoon freshly ground black pepper
1	(16-ounce) package frozen vegetable soup mix with tomatoes
¾	cup quick-cooking barley
2	cups chopped fresh baby spinach leaves

1. Combine first 5 ingredients in a large Dutch oven. Cover and bring to a boil. Stir in barley; cover, reduce heat, and simmer 10 minutes, stirring occasionally. Remove from heat; stir in spinach, and let stand 5 minutes. Yield: 8 servings (serving size: about 1 cup soup).

CALORIES 156; FAT 2.9g (sat 0.8g, mono 1.1g, poly 0.6g); PROTEIN 15.9g; CARB 17.6g; FIBER 3g; CHOL 29mg; IRON 0.8mg; SODIUM 494mg; CALC 11mg

Chicken-Vegetable-Barley Soup

Easy Vegetable-Beef Soup

Prep: 1 minute • Cook: 27 minutes

Italian-style stewed tomatoes and seasoning give this soup an Italian accent. Leftovers, if there are any, freeze beautifully.

Seasoning Blend
1	pound ground round
2½	cups water
1	(16-ounce) package frozen mixed vegetables
1	(14½-ounce) can Italian-style stewed tomatoes, undrained and chopped
1	(8-ounce) can tomato sauce

1. Prepare Seasoning Blend.
2. Cook beef and Seasoning Blend in a Dutch oven over medium-high heat until browned, stirring to crumble. Drain. Return meat mixture to pan. Stir in 2½ cups water and remaining ingredients. Bring to a boil over medium-high heat; reduce heat, cover, and simmer 20 minutes. Yield: 6 servings (serving size: 1½ cups soup).

CALORIES 241; FAT 8.1g (sat 3.6g, mono 3.7g, poly 0.7g); PROTEIN 18.4g; CARB 20.9g; FIBER 4.1g; CHOL 49mg; IRON 3.3mg; SODIUM 514mg; CALC 63mg

Easy Vegetable-Beef Soup

Seasoning Blend

Prep: 2 minutes

1	(8-ounce) container refrigerated prechopped onion
1½	tablespoons minced garlic
1	teaspoon dried Italian seasoning
½	teaspoon freshly ground black pepper
¼	teaspoon salt

1. Combine all ingredients in a small bowl. Yield: 1¾ cups (serving size: about ¼ cup).

CALORIES 23; FAT 0.4g (sat 0.1g, mono 0g, poly 0.3g); PROTEIN 0.4g; CARB 3.8g; FIBER 0.6g; CHOL 0mg; IRON 0.1mg; SODIUM 84mg; CALC 8mg

Beef and Barley Soup

Prep: 3 minutes • Cook: 28 minutes

This is not your mother's soup. But it's just as good. (Sorry, Mom!) To get that home-cooked taste, use a packaged pot roast as the base for rich flavor. It's ready to simmer in just 3 minutes.

1   (17-ounce) package refrigerated beef roast au jus
1   (32-ounce) carton fat-free, lower-sodium beef broth
¾   cup water
¾   cup uncooked quick-cooking barley
1   (16-ounce) package frozen vegetables for soup with tomatoes

1. Combine first 4 ingredients in a Dutch oven; cover and bring to a boil. Reduce heat, and simmer 10 minutes. Add frozen vegetables; return to a boil. Reduce heat and simmer, uncovered, 10 minutes or until vegetables are tender. Yield: 8 servings (serving size: 1 cup soup).

CALORIES 164; FAT 4g (sat 1.7g, mono 1.8g, poly 0.5g); PROTEIN 15.8g; CARB 17.9g; FIBER 2.8g; CHOL 32mg; IRON 1mg; SODIUM 441mg; CALC 0mg

ingredient spotlight

Barley adds bold and hearty taste to soups and dishes. Plus, it's full of fiber!

---

serve with:
Cornmeal-Herb Spirals

Prep: 6 minutes • Cook: 14 minutes

1   (11-ounce) can refrigerated breadstick dough
1   tablespoon olive oil
2   garlic cloves, pressed
2   tablespoons stone-ground yellow cornmeal
1   tablespoon minced fresh rosemary
Cooking spray

1. Preheat oven to 375°.
2. Unroll dough (do not separate dough into strips). Combine oil and garlic; brush evenly over dough. Combine cornmeal and rosemary; sprinkle over dough.
3. Separate and roll up each strip of dough in a spiral pattern with cornmeal mixture on the inside, pinching ends to seal. Place on a baking sheet coated with cooking spray; coat each roll with cooking spray.
4. Bake at 375° for 14 minutes or until lightly browned. Yield: 12 servings (serving size: 1 roll).

CALORIES 89; FAT 2.5g (sat 0.6g, mono 1.7g, poly 0.1g); PROTEIN 2.1g; CARB 13.8g; FIBER 0.6g; CHOL 0mg; IRON 0.8mg; SODIUM 194mg; CALC 2mg

quick flip

Any fresh herb can be swapped in for the fresh rosemary. Fresh basil is a Test Kitchen favorite substitute.

Mole Chili

Prep: 1 minute • Cook: 14 minutes

1	pound ground round
1	cup chopped onion (about 1 small onion)
1	garlic clove, minced
1	(14.5-ounce) can diced tomatoes, undrained
1	cup water
2	tablespoons chili powder
1	ounce semisweet chocolate, coarsely chopped
1	teaspoon ground cumin
1	teaspoon salt
½	teaspoon dried oregano

Reduced-fat sour cream (optional)
Chopped fresh cilantro (optional)

1. Cook beef in a large saucepan over medium-high heat until browned, stirring to crumble. Drain, if necessary, and return beef to pan. Add onion and garlic to pan; cook 4 minutes or until tender. Add tomatoes and remaining ingredients; cover and simmer 7 minutes. Serve immediately. Top with sour cream and cilantro, if desired. Yield: 6 servings (serving size: ¾ cup chili).

CALORIES 127; FAT 4.7g (sat 2.2g, mono 1.4g, poly 0.2g); PROTEIN 17.3g; CARB 8.2g; FIBER 1.8g; CHOL 40mg; IRON 1.9mg; SODIUM 597mg; CALC 25mg

ingredient spotlight

Chocolate is often added to savory Mexican dishes to cut the heat and enrich the flavor. In this recipe, chocolate adds richness and deepens the color of the chili without making it sweet.

serve with:
Jalapeño Corn Bread Mini Muffins

Prep: 9 minutes • Cook: 17 minutes

¾	cup self-rising white cornmeal mix
½	cup non-fat buttermilk
2	tablespoons minced seeded jalapeño pepper
1½	tablespoons canola oil
1	large egg

Cooking spray

1. Preheat oven to 425°. Lightly spoon self-rising white cornmeal mix into measuring cups; level with a knife, and place in a large bowl. Combine buttermilk, jalapeño pepper, oil, and egg in a small bowl. Pour buttermilk mixture into cornmeal mixture; stir just until combined. Coat 12 miniature muffin cups with cooking spray; spoon batter evenly into cups. Bake at 425° for 17 minutes or until lightly browned. Remove from pans immediately; serve warm. Yield: 6 servings (serving size: 2 mini muffins).

CALORIES 127; FAT 4.8g (sat 0.5g, mono 2.5g, poly 1.4g); PROTEIN 3.7g; CARB 17.4g; FIBER 1.3g; CHOL 30mg; IRON 1.2mg; SODIUM 312mg; CALC 93mg

Beer-Braised Beef Stew

Prep: 2 minutes • Cook: 13 minutes

This stew deserves to be on the menu as the perfect after-work Friday night dinner. The dark beer and tomato paste add a deep, rich flavor that belies the short cook time.

2	teaspoons olive oil
1	(1 pound) sirloin steak, trimmed and cut into ½-inch pieces
1	cup refrigerated prechopped onion
2	large carrots, cut into ½-inch chunks
1	(8-ounce) package sliced fresh mushrooms
2	tablespoons all-purpose flour
3	tablespoons water
1	tablespoon tomato paste
¾	cup dark beer
½	cup fat-free, lower-sodium beef broth
¼	teaspoon salt
¼	teaspoon freshly ground black pepper

1. Heat a Dutch oven over medium-high heat. Add oil; swirl to coat. Add steak. Cook 5 minutes or until browned, stirring once. Remove steak from pan; keep warm. Add onion, carrot, and mushrooms to drippings in pan. Cook, stirring frequently, 3 minutes or until browned.
2. While vegetables cook, combine flour and 3 tablespoons water in a medium bowl, stirring with a whisk until smooth. Add tomato paste, stirring until smooth. Stir in beer and broth.
3. Add steak, salt, and pepper to mushroom mixture; stir in beer mixture. Bring to a boil; cover, reduce heat, and simmer 2 minutes or until stew is thick.
4. Ladle stew into bowls. Sprinkle each serving with parsley, if desired. Yield: 4 servings (serving size: 1 cup stew).

CALORIES 247; FAT 7.2g (sat 2.3g, mono 3.9g, poly 0.9g); PROTEIN 27.8g; CARB 14.7g; FIBER 2.6g; CHOL 46mg; IRON 2.4mg; SODIUM 314mg; CALC 41mg

serve with:
Chive Cheese Biscuits

Prep: 5 minutes • Cook: 10 minutes

¾	cup low-fat baking mix
⅓	cup (1.3 ounces) reduced-fat shredded sharp cheddar cheese
1	tablespoon chopped fresh chives
¼	teaspoon freshly ground black pepper
¼	cup fat-free milk
2	tablespoons reduced-fat sour cream
Cooking spray	

1. Preheat oven to 425°.
2. Combine first 4 ingredients in a medium bowl. Add milk and sour cream, stirring just until moist.
3. Drop dough by heaping spoonfuls onto an ungreased baking sheet to form 8 mounds. Coat tops of mounds with cooking spray.
4. Bake at 425° for 10 minutes or until golden brown. Yield: 4 servings (serving size: 2 biscuits).

CALORIES 124; FAT 4.5g (sat 2g, mono 1.9g, poly 0.5g); PROTEIN 5g; CARB 17g; FIBER 0.3g; CHOL 10mg; IRON 0.9mg; SODIUM 256mg; CALC 181mg

Caldillo

Caldillo

Prep: 4 minutes • Cook: 45 minutes

Caldillo is a Mexican version of beef stew, full of tomatoes, green chiles, and potatoes.

1 pound boneless sirloin steak (about ½ inch thick), cut into bite-sized pieces
Cooking spray
1 (8-ounce) container refrigerated prechopped onion
3 cups water
2 (14½-ounce) cans diced tomatoes with zesty mild green chiles (such as Del Monte), undrained
1 teaspoon ground cumin
3 cups (½-inch) cubed unpeeled Yukon gold or red potato
¼ cup chopped fresh cilantro (optional)

1. Coat beef with cooking spray. Heat a large Dutch oven over high heat. Coat pan with cooking spray. Add beef to pan, cook 3 minutes. Stir in onion. Cook 5 minutes or until liquid evaporates and beef and onion are browned.
2. Stir in 3 cups water, tomatoes, and cumin; cover and bring to a boil. Reduce heat to medium; simmer 20 minutes.
3. Add potato; cover and simmer 10 minutes or until potato is tender. Remove from heat; stir in cilantro, if desired. Yield: 6 servings (serving size: 1⅓ cups stew).

CALORIES 165; FAT 3g (sat 1.2g, mono 1.6g, poly 0.2g); PROTEIN 18.3g; CARB 15.5g; FIBER 3.2g; CHOL 28mg; IRON 2mg; SODIUM 595mg; CALC 59mg

Brunswick Stew

Prep: 3 minutes • Cook: 12 minutes

During the summer months, use fresh lima beans and corn for a real treat. Add additional water or broth if the consistency becomes too thick.

1 cup pulled smoked pork
1 cup pulled skinless smoked chicken
1 cup fat-free, lower-sodium chicken broth
1 (14.5-ounce) can fire-roasted diced tomatoes, undrained
½ cup frozen baby lima beans
½ cup frozen whole-kernel corn
¼ cup Carolina sweet barbecue sauce
¼ teaspoon freshly ground black pepper

1. Combine all ingredients in a Dutch oven. Bring to boil. Cover, reduce heat, and simmer 12 minutes or until vegetables are tender. Yield: 4 servings (serving size: 1¼ cups stew).

CALORIES 293; FAT 11.4g (sat 4.1g, mono 4.6g, poly 1.7g); PROTEIN 28.1g; CARB 18.3g; FIBER 2.4g; CHOL 76mg; IRON 2.4mg; SODIUM 569mg; CALC 42mg

Brunswick Stew

Posole

Posole

Prep: 3 minutes • Cook: 30 minutes

The meat develops a rich, full-bodied flavor when it's cooked to a dark brown, so be sure not to stir the pork until it releases easily from the pan. Serve this fiery soup with warm flour tortillas.

Cooking spray
1   (1-pound) pork tenderloin, trimmed and cut into bite-sized pieces
2   teaspoons salt-free Southwest chipotle seasoning blend
1   (15.5-ounce) can white hominy, undrained
1   (14.5-ounce) can Mexican-style stewed tomatoes with jalapeño peppers and spices, undrained
1   cup water
¼   cup chopped fresh cilantro

1. Heat a large saucepan over medium-high heat. Coat pan with cooking spray. Sprinkle pork evenly with chipotle seasoning blend; coat evenly with cooking spray. Add pork to pan; cook 4 minutes or until browned. Stir in hominy, tomatoes, and 1 cup water. Bring to a boil; cover, reduce heat, and simmer 20 minutes or until pork is tender. Stir in cilantro. Yield: 4 servings (serving size: 1⅓ cups soup).

CALORIES 233; FAT 5g (sat 1.4g, mono 1.9g, poly 0.8g); PROTEIN 24.4g; CARB 23g; FIBER 4.4g; CHOL 68mg; IRON 2.3mg; SODIUM 610mg; CALC 33mg

ingredient spotlight

Some call it cilantro; others call it coriander or even Chinese parsley. This native of southern Europe and the Middle East has a pungent flavor, with a faint undertone of anise. The leaves are often mistaken for flat-leaf parsley. One of the most versatile herbs, cilantro adds a distinctive taste to salsas, soups, stews, curries, and salads, as well as vegetable, fish, and chicken dishes.

Jamaican Red Beans and Rice Soup

Prep: 3 minutes • Cook: 11 minutes

2   bacon slices, cut crosswise into thin strips
½   cup chopped onion (1 small)
2   (14-ounce) cans fat-free, less-sodium chicken broth
2   teaspoons Jamaican jerk seasoning
1   (16-ounce) can red beans, rinsed and drained
1   (8.8-ounce) package microwaveable precooked whole-grain brown rice
¼   cup chopped fresh cilantro

1. Cook bacon and onion in a large saucepan over medium heat 2 minutes.
2. While bacon mixture cooks, place broth in a large microwave-safe bowl. Cover with plastic wrap; vent. Microwave at HIGH 2 minutes.
3. Add hot broth and jerk seasoning to bacon mixture. Stir in beans, mashing slightly. Cover; bring to a boil over high heat. Uncover, reduce heat, and simmer 5 minutes. Stir in rice; cover and simmer 3 minutes. Ladle soup evenly into 4 bowls; sprinkle with cilantro. Yield: 4 servings (serving size: 1¼ cups soup).

CALORIES 199; FAT 2.4g (sat 0.6g, mono 0.6g, poly 0.4g); PROTEIN 10.3g; CARB 30.3g; FIBER 4.3g; CHOL 6mg; IRON 1.5mg; SODIUM 250mg; CALC 36mg

Sausage and Barley Soup

Prep: 5 minutes • Cook: 18 minutes

Fresh, delicate baby spinach doesn't hold up to hours of cooking, so it is added at the last minute. Pureeing the vegetables allows you to drastically cut cooking time while maintaining all the rich flavors of the vegetables.

Cooking spray
6   ounces turkey breakfast sausage
2½   cups frozen bell pepper stir-fry
2   cups water
1   (14½-ounce) can Italian-style stewed tomatoes, undrained and chopped
¼   cup uncooked quick-cooking barley
1   cup coarsely chopped fresh baby spinach

1. Heat a large saucepan over medium-high heat. Coat pan with cooking spray. Add sausage; cook 3 minutes or until browned. Remove from heat.
2. While sausage cooks, place stir-fry and 2 cups water in a blender; process until smooth. Add stir-fry puree, tomatoes, and barley to sausage in pan. Bring mixture to a boil over high heat; cover, reduce heat to low, and simmer 10 minutes. Stir in spinach; cook 1 minute or until spinach wilts. Yield: 4 servings (serving size: 1½ cups soup).

CALORIES 145; FAT 4g (sat 1.5g, mono 1.2g, poly 0.5g); PROTEIN 9.9g; CARB 17.9g; FIBER 2.6g; CHOL 33mg; IRON 1.6mg; SODIUM 493mg; CALC 53mg

serve with:
Asiago-Topped Garlic Bread

Prep: 6 minutes • Cook: 4 minutes

1   garlic clove, pressed
1   (6-ounce) whole-wheat French bread baguette, cut in half lengthwise
1½   tablespoons light olive oil vinaigrette
½   teaspoon chopped fresh rosemary
¼   cup (1 ounce) finely grated Asiago cheese

1. Preheat broiler.
2. Spread garlic on cut sides of bread; brush evenly with vinaigrette. Top evenly with rosemary and cheese.
3. Broil 4 minutes or until cheese melts and bread is lightly browned. Cut into 8 pieces. Yield: 4 servings (serving size: 2 pieces).

CALORIES 138; FAT 3g (sat 1.4g, mono 0.5g, poly 0.1g); PROTEIN 5.6g; CARB 20.2g; FIBER 0.7g; CHOL 7mg; IRON 1.1mg; SODIUM 283mg; CALC 70mg

Chorizo Rice and Bean Soup

Prep: 2 minutes • Cook: 23 minutes

Flavor-packed yellow rice and spicy chorizo make this soup a Spanish specialty. Accompany the soup with garlic and tomato–rubbed rustic toasts for a classic staple from the Catalan region of Spain.

8	ounces fresh chorizo
4	cups water
2	(15-ounce) cans reduced-sodium pinto beans, undrained
1	(5-ounce) package yellow rice mix
3	tablespoons chopped fresh cilantro

1. Remove casings from chorizo. Cook sausage in a Dutch oven over medium-high heat 5 minutes, stirring to crumble. Add 4 cups water, beans, and rice mix. Bring to a boil, stirring occasionally; reduce heat to low, cover, and simmer 15 minutes or until rice is tender.
2. Ladle soup into bowls; sprinkle evenly with cilantro. Serve immediately. Yield: 8 servings (serving size: 1 cup soup and about 1 teaspoon cilantro).

CALORIES 212; FAT 6.8g (sat 2.5g, mono 3.4g, poly 0.9g); PROTEIN 12.2g; CARB 28.9g; FIBER 5.9g; CHOL 0mg; IRON 2mg; SODIUM 411mg; CALC 40mg

serve with:
Rustic Tomato-Garlic Toasts

Prep: 4 minutes • Cook: 2 minutes

8 (½-inch) slices ciabatta
4 garlic cloves, halved
1 (12-ounce) ripe tomato, halved
4 teaspoons extra-virgin olive oil
¼ teaspoon salt

1. Heat a grill pan over medium-high heat. Add ciabatta slices to pan. Cook 1 minute on each side or until toasted.
2. Rub 1 side of each toast with a garlic half, cut side down, until toast is fragrant. Rub tomato halves over toasts to release juice onto toasts. Drizzle each toast with ½ teaspoon olive oil. Sprinkle toasts evenly with salt. Yield: 8 servings (serving size: 1 toast).

CALORIES 109; FAT 3.7g (sat 0.5g, mono 2.6g, poly 0.5g); PROTEIN 3g; CARB 17.6g; FIBER 1g; CHOL 0mg; IRON 1mg; SODIUM 269mg; CALC 7mg

Chorizo Rice and Bean Soup

White Bean and Lamb
Soup with Gremolata

White Bean and Lamb Soup with Gremolata

Prep: 1 minute • Cook: 20 minutes

Gremolata is a treat for the taste buds. This simple, zesty condiment of minced parsley, grated lemon rind, and garlic abounds with flavor. It's often served sprinkled over veal, but it adds a nice fresh flavor to any "meaty" dish.

2	teaspoons olive oil
1	pound lean boneless leg of lamb, cut into ½-inch pieces
½	cup refrigerated prechopped onion
4½	cups water
½	teaspoon freshly ground black pepper
1	(6-ounce) package dry Tuscan white bean soup mix
	Gremolata

1. Heat a Dutch oven over medium-high heat. Add oil to pan; swirl to coat. Add lamb and onion; sauté 5 minutes or until lamb is browned and onion is tender. Add 4½ cups water and pepper to lamb mixture. Bring to a boil; add soup mix, stirring 1 minute. Reduce heat, and simmer, uncovered, 12 minutes or until pasta is done.
2. While soup cooks, prepare Gremolata.
3. Ladle soup into 6 bowls. Top each serving with Gremolata. Yield: 6 servings (serving size: ¾ cup soup and 2 teaspoons Gremolata).

CALORIES 169; FAT 3.9g (sat 1.2g, mono 2.1g, poly 0.6g); PROTEIN 11.9g; CARB 20.3g; FIBER 5g; CHOL 23mg; IRON 1.8mg; SODIUM 459mg; CALC 40mg

Gremolata

Prep: 4 minutes

¼	cup minced fresh flat-leaf parsley
1½	teaspoons grated lemon rind
1	garlic clove, minced

1. Combine all ingredients in a small bowl. Yield: ¼ cup (serving size: 2 teaspoons).

CALORIES 1; FAT 0g (sat 0g, mono 0g, poly 0g); PROTEIN 0g; CARB 0.3g; FIBER 0.1g; CHOL 0mg; IRON 0mg; SODIUM 0.2mg; CALC 2mg

sandwiches

Margherita Piadine,
page 121

Pear-Walnut Sandwiches

Prep: 15 minutes

Crisp, ripe Bartlett pears and toasted walnuts from fall's harvest combine in these quick and tasty sandwiches. They pack nutrition and taste great for breakfast, lunch, or dinner.

½	cup (4 ounces) tub-style light cream cheese
8	(1.1-ounce) slices cinnamon-raisin bread, toasted
2	tablespoons finely chopped walnuts, toasted
2	Bartlett pears, cored and thinly sliced
1	cup alfalfa sprouts

1. Spread 1 tablespoon cream cheese evenly over each of 8 bread slices. Sprinkle ½ tablespoon walnuts evenly over each of 4 bread slices. Top each evenly with pear slices, sprouts, and 1 bread slice. Cut each sandwich in half diagonally. Yield: 4 servings (serving size: 1 sandwich).

CALORIES 335; FAT 11g (sat 3.7g, mono 0.4g, poly 1.8g); PROTEIN 8.7g; CARB 52.2g; FIBER 5.9g; CHOL 15mg; IRON 2mg; SODIUM 363mg; CALC 56mg

Blue Cheese and Pear Sandwiches

Prep: 4 minutes • Cook: 6 minutes

This "salad and sandwich in one" features a hearty slice of peasant bread topped with sweet pears, pungent blue cheese, and peppery watercress. Look for artisan peasant bread in the bakery at your supermarket.

4   (1½-ounce) slices peasant bread
Cooking spray
1⅓   cups coarsely chopped watercress
2   teaspoons olive oil
⅛   teaspoon salt
⅛   teaspoon freshly ground black pepper
2   medium pears, thinly sliced
½   cup (2 ounces) crumbled blue cheese

1. Preheat broiler.
2. Place bread slices on a baking sheet. Coat each slice with cooking spray; broil 2 minutes on each side or until lightly toasted.
3. While bread cooks, combine watercress, olive oil, salt, and pepper in a small bowl; toss gently.
4. Place pear slices evenly on bread slices; top evenly with blue cheese. Broil 2 to 3 minutes or until cheese melts. Remove from oven; top evenly with watercress mixture. Serve immediately. Yield: 4 servings (serving size: 1 sandwich).

CALORIES 211; FAT 6.9g (sat 3g, mono 2.8g, poly 0.4g); PROTEIN 7.5g; CARB 31.7g; FIBER 2.5g; CHOL 11mg; IRON 1.2mg; SODIUM 506mg; CALC 139mg

serve with:

White Balsamic–Dill Pasta Salad

Prep: 2 minutes • Cook: 14 minutes

2   cups uncooked farfalle (bow tie pasta)
2   tablespoons white balsamic vinegar
1   tablespoon olive oil
⅛   teaspoon salt
⅛   teaspoon freshly ground black pepper
½   cup prechopped tricolor bell pepper mix
1   tablespoon chopped fresh dill

1. Cook pasta according to package directions, omitting salt and fat. Rinse under cold water until cool; drain well.
2. While pasta cooks, combine vinegar and next 3 ingredients in a medium bowl, stirring with a whisk. Add pasta, bell pepper mix, and dill, and toss well. Yield: 4 servings (serving size: ¾ cup).

CALORIES 196; FAT 4.1g (sat 0.7g, mono 2.5g, poly 0.6g); PROTEIN 6g; CARB 34g; FIBER 1.7g; CHOL 0mg; IRON 1.5mg; SODIUM 77mg; CALC 12mg

ingredient spotlight

Similar to its darker cousin, white balsamic vinegar has a sweet and clean flavor. Since it is almost clear, it won't discolor lighter-colored foods, such as pasta salad.

Roasted Tomato and Goat Cheese Baguette with Parsley Aioli

Prep: 7 minutes • Cook: 12 minutes

Roasting the tomatoes and peppers intensifies their natural sweetness, which is the key to this simple sandwich's robust flavor. Round out your meal by adding crispy sweet potato chips.

8   (½-inch thick) slices large beefsteak tomatoes
1   large yellow bell pepper, quartered lengthwise
1   (10-ounce) whole-grain baguette, halved lengthwise
4   ounces goat cheese, crumbled
Parsley Aioli

1. Preheat broiler.
2. Place tomato slices and bell pepper on a baking sheet lined with foil. Broil 10 minutes or until bell pepper is charred. Cut bell pepper crosswise into thin strips.
3. Place baguette halves cut sides up on a baking sheet. Broil 2 minutes or until lightly toasted.
4. Arrange tomato slices in a single layer on top of cut side of bottom half of toasted baguette. Top tomato slices evenly with goat cheese and pepper strips.
5. Spread Parsley Aioli on cut side of top half of toasted baguette. Top pepper strips with top half of baguette. Cut crosswise into 4 equal portions. Yield: 4 servings (serving size: 1 sandwich).

CALORIES 294; FAT 10.8g (sat 6.1g, mono 3.2g, poly 0.9g); PROTEIN 12.3g; CARB 36.1g; FIBER 2.6g; CHOL 24mg; IRON 3.2mg; SODIUM 624mg; CALC 114mg

Parsley Aioli

Prep: 4 minutes

1   cup fresh parsley leaves
1   garlic clove, crushed
1   teaspoon extra-virgin olive oil
1   teaspoon Dijon mustard
¼   cup fat-free mayonnaise
⅛   teaspoon freshly ground black pepper

1. Place all ingredients in a food processor; process until blended. Yield: ⅓ cup (serving size: about 1 tablespoon).

CALORIES 32; FAT 1.7g (sat 0.3g, mono 1.2g, poly 0.1g); PROTEIN 0.4g; CARB 4.1g; FIBER 0.5g; CHOL 1mg; IRON 1mg; SODIUM 162mg; CALC 22mg

quick flip

Try swapping fresh basil leaves for the parsley leaves for a flavor twist.

Veggie Roll-Ups with Carrot–Red Onion Toss

Prep: 6 minutes • Cook: 1 minute

Bacon adds a little slice of heaven to these quick roll-ups. And let's face it, bacon makes just about any sandwich better.

½   cup refrigerated hummus (such as Athenos Original)
4   (8-inch) 96% fat-free whole-wheat flour tortillas (such as Mission)
4   precooked bacon slices
Carrot–Red Onion Toss
½   cup finely chopped cucumber

1. Spread hummus evenly over tortillas. Microwave bacon slices according to package directions; crumble bacon. Sprinkle bacon evenly over hummus. Top evenly with Carrot–Red Onion Toss and cucumber; roll up. Yield: 4 servings (serving size: 1 roll-up).

CALORIES 220; FAT 6.4g (sat 0.5g, mono 1.9g, poly 3.9g); PROTEIN 7.5g; CARB 34.4g; FIBER 4.8g; CHOL 5mg; IRON 0.6mg; SODIUM 688mg; CALC 11mg

Carrot–Red Onion Toss

Prep: 1 minute

1   cup matchstick-cut carrots
⅓   cup vertically sliced red onion
2   tablespoons light red wine vinaigrette
¼   teaspoon freshly ground black pepper

1. Combine all ingredients in a medium bowl; toss gently. Yield: 1¼ cups (serving size: about ⅓ cup).

CALORIES 18; FAT 0g (sat 0g, mono 0g, poly 0g); PROTEIN 0.4g; CARB 4.1g; FIBER 0.7g; CHOL 0mg; IRON 0.1mg; SODIUM 101mg; CALC 9mg

Veggie Roll-Ups with
Carrot–Red Onion Toss

Margherita Piadine

Prep: 5 minutes • Cook: 10 minutes

Cooking spray
1	(11-ounce) package refrigerated thin-crust pizza crust dough
2	teaspoons extra-virgin olive oil, divided
1	small garlic clove, minced
3	large basil leaves, cut into thin strips
¼	teaspoon freshly ground black pepper, divided
1	tablespoon balsamic vinegar
⅛	teaspoon salt
4	cups loosely packed arugula
1½	cups diced seeded plum tomato (about 2)
4	(0.67-ounce) slices reduced-fat provolone cheese

1. Preheat oven to 425°.
2. Coat a large baking sheet with cooking spray. Roll out dough onto prepared baking sheet; cut dough crosswise in half, creating 2 smaller rectangles. Brush surface of dough with 1 teaspoon oil; sprinkle with garlic, basil, and ⅛ teaspoon pepper. Bake at 425° for 8 minutes or until crust is golden but still pliable.
3. While crust bakes, combine remaining oil, remaining ⅛ teaspoon pepper, vinegar, and salt in a large bowl, stirring with a whisk. Add arugula and tomato; toss well.
4. Arrange cheese slices lengthwise down long side of crusts; top with arugula mixture. Fold dough over filling, creating 2 long rectangle sandwiches. Bake an additional 1 to 2 minutes or until cheese melts. Cut each rectangle crosswise in half. Serve immediately. Yield: 4 servings (serving size: 1 sandwich).

CALORIES 314; FAT 12.3g (sat 3.6g, mono 5g, poly 1.6g); PROTEIN 12.2g; CARB 39.8g; FIBER 2g; CHOL 10mg; IRON 2.2mg; SODIUM 730mg; CALC 188mg

serve with:
Lemony Chickpea Salad

Prep: 2 minutes • Cook: 2 minutes

1	tablespoon chopped fresh parsley
1	tablespoon fresh lemon juice
1	tablespoon extra-virgin olive oil
⅛	teaspoon crushed red pepper
1	small garlic clove, minced
1	(15-ounce) can chickpeas (garbanzo beans), rinsed and drained

1. Combine first 5 ingredients in a medium bowl. Stir in chickpeas. Serve at room temperature. Yield: 4 servings (serving size: about ½ cup).

CALORIES 117; FAT 4.2g (sat 0.6g, mono 2.7g, poly 0.7g); PROTEIN 3.6g; CARB 16.7g; FIBER 3.2g; CHOL 0mg; IRON 1.1mg; SODIUM 128mg; CALC 26mg

ingredient spotlight

A piadine is an Italian flatbread sandwich made by cooking dough over coals, and then folding the thin bread over dressed greens or vegetables. We bake our version in the oven and use refrigerated pizza crust for speed and ease.

Mediterranean Flatbread Sandwiches

Prep: 10 minutes

Soft, tender Mediterranean flatbread offers a delightful contrast to the crisp vegetables and crunchy pilaf in this hearty meatless recipe. Round out your meal with a sweet-tart Pomegranate Refresher.

1	(8.5-ounce) package 7-grain pilaf
1	cup diced English cucumber
1	cup chopped seeded tomato (1 medium)
½	cup (2 ounces) crumbled feta cheese
2	tablespoons fresh lemon juice
1	tablespoon olive oil
¼	teaspoon salt
¼	teaspoon freshly ground black pepper
1	(7-ounce) container hummus
3	(2.8-ounce) Mediterranean-style white flatbreads

1. Combine first 8 ingredients in a bowl. Spread hummus evenly over each flatbread. Spoon pilaf mixture evenly over half of each flatbread; fold flatbread over filling. Cut each sandwich in half, and serve immediately. Yield: 6 servings (serving size: ½ sandwich).

CALORIES 310; FAT 12.2g (sat 3.4g, mono 6.6g, poly 1.8g); PROTEIN 11.1g; CARB 39.2g; FIBER 6g; CHOL 11mg; IRON 1mg; SODIUM 549mg; CALC 80mg

serve with:
Pomegranate Refreshers

Prep: 4 minutes

2	cups pomegranate juice, chilled
¼	cup fresh lemon juice
3	tablespoons sugar
2	cups club soda, chilled
Ice cubes	
Lemon slices (optional)	

1. Combine first 3 ingredients in a small pitcher, stirring until sugar dissolves. Gently stir in club soda. Serve over ice, and garnish with lemon slices, if desired. Yield: 6 servings (serving size: about ¾ cup).

CALORIES 73; FAT 0g (sat 0g, mono 0g, poly 0g); PROTEIN 0.4g; CARB 18.8g; FIBER 0g; CHOL 0mg; IRON 0.1mg; SODIUM 27mg; CALC 18mg

Mediterranean Flatbread Sandwiches

Pesto Grilled Cheese Panini

Prep: 2 minutes • Cook: 11 minutes

Bursting with flavor, this grown-up grilled cheese makes a perfect warm lunch with simply dressed greens. Save leftover pesto to use as a sandwich spread, a pizza topping, or a sauce for pasta or fish.

1   red bell pepper, cut into 4 wedges
Olive oil–flavored cooking spray
¼   cup Basil-Walnut Pesto
8   (1-ounce) slices sourdough bread
4   (0.7-ounce) slices reduced-fat provolone cheese
½   cup (2 ounces) shredded part-skim mozzarella cheese
Cooking spray

1. Preheat panini grill.
2. Coat both sides of bell pepper wedges with cooking spray. Place on panini grill; cook 8 minutes or until tender and lightly charred.
3. While bell pepper cooks, prepare Basil-Walnut Pesto. Spread 1½ teaspoons pesto on each bread slice. Top each of 4 bread slices with 1 provolone slice, 2 tablespoons mozzarella, and 1 bell pepper wedge; top with remaining bread slices. Coat both sides of sandwiches with cooking spray.
4. Place sandwiches on panini grill. Grill 3 minutes or until bread is browned and cheese melts. Cut panini in half before serving, if desired. Yield: 4 servings (serving size: 1 panino).

CALORIES 293; FAT 15.2g (sat 6.1g, mono 5.2g, poly 2.8g); PROTEIN 12.2g; CARB 24.5g; FIBER 1.9g; CHOL 56mg; IRON 0.6mg; SODIUM 560mg; CALC 317mg

Pesto Grilled Cheese Panini

Basil-Walnut Pesto

Prep: 4 minutes

2   tablespoons coarsely chopped walnuts
1   garlic clove, peeled
2   cups basil leaves
¼   cup grated fresh pecorino Romano cheese
⅛   teaspoon salt
2   tablespoons extra-virgin olive oil

1. Drop nuts and garlic through food chute with food processor on; process until minced. Add basil, cheese, and salt; process until finely minced. With processor on, slowly pour oil through food chute; process until blended. Yield: 8 servings (serving size: 1 tablespoon).

CALORIES 59; FAT 5.6g (sat 1.3g, mono 3.1g, poly 1.2g); PROTEIN 1.5g; CARB 0.6g; FIBER 0.3g; CHOL 2mg; IRON 0.4mg; SODIUM 94mg; CALC 64mg

Fried Green Tomato
Sandwiches

Fried Green Tomato Sandwiches

Prep: 8 minutes • Cook: 7 minutes

To add a tangy bite to the sandwiches, use Dijonnaise rather than canola mayonnaise.

Fried Green Tomatoes
8   teaspoons canola mayonnaise
4   (1.5-ounce) whole-grain white sandwich thins
4   green leaf lettuce leaves
4   bacon slices, cooked and halved

1. Prepare Fried Green Tomatoes.
2. Spread 1 teaspoon mayonnaise on cut side of each sandwich thin half. Place 1 lettuce leaf and 2 Fried Green Tomato slices on bottom half of each sandwich thin; top each with 2 bacon slice halves. Cover with tops of sandwich thins. Yield: 4 servings (serving size: 1 sandwich).

CALORIES 292; FAT 11.2g (sat 1.4g, mono 5.7g, poly 2.8g); PROTEIN 10.5g; CARB 39.5g; FIBER 6.2g; CHOL 9mg; IRON 2.2mg; SODIUM 516mg; CALC 83mg

Fried Green Tomatoes

Prep: 5 minutes • Cook: 7 minutes

¼   cup nonfat buttermilk
1   large egg white
⅓   cup yellow cornmeal
2   tablespoons all-purpose flour
¼   teaspoon freshly ground black pepper
8   (¼-inch-thick) slices green tomato (about 2 medium tomatoes)
1   tablespoon canola oil
Cooking spray

1. Combine buttermilk and egg white in a shallow dish, stirring with a whisk. Combine cornmeal, flour, and pepper in another shallow dish.
2. Dip tomato slices in buttermilk mixture; dredge in cornmeal mixture.
3. Heat a large nonstick skillet over medium-high heat. Add oil; swirl to coat. Add tomato slices; cook 3 minutes. Coat slices with cooking spray. Turn slices over; cook 3 minutes or until golden. Yield: 4 servings (serving size: 2 tomato slices).

CALORIES 115; FAT 3.9g (sat 0.3g, mono 2.2g, poly 1g); PROTEIN 3.3g; CARB 16.7g; FIBER 0.9g; CHOL 0mg; IRON 0.8mg; SODIUM 34mg; CALC 26mg

Tofu Salad Sandwiches

Prep: 10 minutes

Toast the English muffins under a preheated broiler while preparing the filling. You can toast four muffins on a baking sheet in the same amount of time it takes to cook just one muffin in a toaster. Round out your meal with a handful of baked tortilla chips and a dill pickle spear.

4	green leaf lettuce leaves
4	honey wheat double-fiber English muffins, split and toasted
4	tomato slices

Tofu Salad
Freshly ground black pepper (optional)

1. Place 1 lettuce leaf on the bottom half of each English muffin; top each with 1 tomato slice. Spoon ⅓ cup Tofu Salad evenly over each tomato slice; sprinkle evenly with black pepper, if desired. Top sandwiches with remaining 4 muffin halves. Yield: 4 servings (serving size: 1 sandwich).

CALORIES 203; FAT 6g (sat 0.5g, mono 1.5g, poly 3.8g); PROTEIN 9.5g; CARB 30.9g; FIBER 6.1g; CHOL 4mg; IRON 2.7mg; SODIUM 510mg; CALC 195mg

Tofu Salad

Prep: 5 minutes

8	ounces extra-firm tofu
¼	cup reduced-calorie salad dressing (such as Miracle Whip Light)
1	tablespoon dill pickle relish
1	teaspoon prepared mustard
⅛	teaspoon salt
⅛	teaspoon dried dill
⅛	teaspoon freshly ground black pepper

1. Press tofu between paper towels to remove excess moisture; cut into ¼-inch cubes.
2. Combine salad dressing and next 5 ingredients in a medium bowl, stirring until blended. Add half of tofu, mashing with the back of a large spoon. Add remaining tofu, stirring gently. Yield: 1⅓ cups (serving size: ⅓ cup).

CALORIES 88; FAT 6g (sat 0.5g, mono 1.5g, poly 3.8g); PROTEIN 5.1g; CARB 3.8g; FIBER 0.8g; CHOL 4mg; IRON 1.1mg; SODIUM 287mg; CALC 109mg

Tofu Salad Sandwiches

Overstuffed Grilled Vegetable–Feta Sandwiches

Prep: 4 minutes • Cook: 11 minutes

Make sure your grill is nice and hot to create grill marks on the vegetables and bread.

1⅓	cups refrigerated presliced yellow squash and zucchini mix
4	(¼-inch-thick) slices red onion
Cooking spray	
¾	cup grape tomatoes, halved
3	tablespoons light Northern Italian salad dressing with basil and Romano
1	tablespoon chopped fresh basil
1	(8-ounce) loaf French bread, halved lengthwise
¾	cup (3 ounces) crumbled feta cheese

1. Preheat grill to medium-high heat.
2. Coat squash mix and onion evenly with cooking spray. Place vegetables on grill rack; grill 4 minutes on each side or until crisp-tender and beginning to brown.
3. Place tomato in a medium bowl; add dressing and basil, tossing gently to coat. Add cooked vegetables to tomato mixture; toss well.
4. Coat cut sides of bread with cooking spray. Grill bread 1 minute on each side or until lightly toasted. Spoon vegetable mixture over bottom half of bread; sprinkle evenly with cheese. Top with remaining bread half. Press down lightly; cut crosswise into 4 equal pieces. Yield: 4 servings (serving size: 1 piece).

CALORIES 283; FAT 8g (sat 3.5g, mono 1.2g, poly 0.7g); PROTEIN 11.6g; CARB 42.5g; FIBER 3.2g; CHOL 19mg; IRON 2.7mg; SODIUM 773mg; CALC 158mg

Overstuffed Grilled
Vegetable–Feta Sandwiches

Roasted Portobello Mushroom Sandwiches with Parmesan Mayonnaise

Prep: 7 minutes • Cook: 11 minutes

Begin assembling these sandwiches while the mushrooms broil, and add the hot-from-the-oven mushrooms at the end. Spread leftover Parmesan Mayonnaise on any of your favorite deli meat sandwiches—it adds a fantastic burst of flavor.

2	(6-ounce) packages presliced portobello mushrooms
12	sprays balsamic vinaigrette salad spritzer (such as Wish-Bone)
½	cup Parmesan Mayonnaise
8	(¾-ounce) slices crusty Chicago-style Italian bread (about ½ inch thick), toasted
1	(12-ounce) bottle roasted red bell peppers, drained
2	cups baby arugula

1. Preheat broiler.
2. Place mushrooms on a baking sheet; coat evenly with balsamic spritzer. Broil mushrooms 11 to 12 minutes or until browned and tender.
3. While mushrooms broil, spread 1 tablespoon Parmesan Mayonnaise over cut side of each bread slice; top each of 4 slices with about ⅔ cup bell pepper and ½ cup arugula. Arrange roasted mushrooms evenly over arugula. Top with remaining 4 bread slices. Yield: 4 servings (serving size: 1 sandwich).

CALORIES 276; FAT 13g (sat 2.3g, mono 3.0g, poly 7.4g); PROTEIN 7.4g; CARB 32.4g; FIBER 2.8g; CHOL 13mg; IRON 2mg; SODIUM 806mg; CALC 88mg

Roasted Portobello Mushroom Sandwiches with Parmesan Mayonnaise

Parmesan Mayonnaise

Prep: 3 minutes

½	cup light mayonnaise
1	garlic clove, pressed
2	tablespoons grated fresh Parmesan cheese
2	tablespoons minced red onion
¼	teaspoon freshly ground black pepper

1. Combine all ingredients in a small bowl, stirring until well blended. Yield: ⅔ cup (serving size: about 1 tablespoon).

CALORIES 46; FAT 4g (sat 0.8g, mono 0.9g, poly 2g); PROTEIN 0.5g; CARB 1.4g; FIBER 0.1g; CHOL 5mg; IRON 0.1mg; SODIUM 111mg; CALC 13mg

Portobello Melts with Smoky Red Pepper Mayo

Prep: 7 minutes • Cook: 10 minutes

Smoky Red Pepper Mayo and melted cheese transform this grilled mushroom sandwich into the perfect weeknight dinner.

4   large portobello mushroom caps
Olive oil–flavored cooking spray
4   (0.7-ounce) part-skim mozzarella slices
2   tablespoons shredded fresh Parmigiano-Reggiano cheese
Smoky Red Pepper Mayo
4   (1.5-ounce) whole-grain white sandwich thins

1. Preheat grill to medium-high heat.
2. Coat both sides of mushroom caps with cooking spray. Place mushroom caps, gill sides down, on grill rack coated with cooking spray. Grill 5 minutes; turn mushrooms over, and top evenly with cheeses. Grill 5 minutes or until cheeses melt.
3. Spread 2½ tablespoons Smoky Red Pepper Mayo evenly on cut sides of each sandwich thin. Place a mushroom cap, cheese side up, on bottom of each sandwich thin. Top with sandwich thin tops. Yield: 4 servings (serving size: 1 sandwich).

CALORIES 329; FAT 17.6g (sat 5.5g, mono 4.3g, poly 5.4g); PROTEIN 15.6g; CARB 29.6g; FIBER 7.4g; CHOL 28mg; IRON 1.8mg; SODIUM 680mg; CALC 288mg

Smoky Red Pepper Mayo

Prep: 4 minutes

½   cup light mayonnaise
2   tablespoons chopped bottled roasted red bell pepper
1   teaspoon fresh lemon juice
½   teaspoon smoked paprika
½   teaspoon minced garlic

1. Combine all ingredients in a small bowl. Yield: 10 tablespoons (serving size: 2½ tablespoons).

CALORIES 104; FAT 10g (sat 1.5g, mono 2.3g, poly 5.2g); PROTEIN 0.2g; CARB 3.1g; FIBER 0.1g; CHOL 11mg; IRON 0.1mg; SODIUM 253mg; CALC 2mg

ingredient spotlight

Make extra of this yummy red pepper mayo to spread on other sandwiches, such as roast turkey or beef. Store it in the refrigerator for up to one week.

Portobello Melts with
Smoky Red Pepper Mayo

Tuna Florentine Sandwiches with Lemon-Caper Vinaigrette

Prep: 4 minutes • Cook: 3 minutes

Fresh basil leaves and a homemade lemon-caper vinaigrette lend a vibrant Italian flair to this easy sandwich. For a simple, sweet-yet-healthful accompaniment, serve with juicy red grapes.

1	(12-ounce) can albacore tuna in water, drained and flaked
1½	cups bagged baby spinach leaves
1	cup basil leaves
Lemon-Caper Vinaigrette	
8	(1.5-ounce) multigrain bread slices, toasted

1. Combine first 4 ingredients; toss well. Spoon tuna mixture evenly over each of 4 toasted bread slices. Top with remaining bread slices. Yield: 4 servings (serving size: 1 sandwich).

CALORIES 326; FAT 7.2g (sat 0.5g, mono 2.9g, poly 2.9g); PROTEIN 25.3g; CARB 43.1g; FIBER 6g; CHOL 26mg; IRON 3.3mg; SODIUM 572mg; CALC 291mg

quick flip

Don't have canned tuna on hand? Cooked chicken is a yummy and healthy alternative.

Lemon-Caper Vinaigrette

Prep: 4 minutes

3	tablespoons fresh lemon juice
2½	tablespoons minced shallots (1 small)
1	tablespoon drained capers
1	tablespoon olive oil
½	teaspoon freshly ground black pepper
½	teaspoon Dijon mustard

1. Combine all ingredients in a small bowl, stirring with a whisk. Yield: ½ cup (serving size: 2 tablespoons).

CALORIES 39; FAT 3.5g (sat 0.5g, mono 2.5g, poly 0.5g); PROTEIN 0.4g; CARB 2.4g; FIBER 0.2g; CHOL 0mg; IRON 0.1mg; SODIUM 63mg; CALC 6mg

Tuna Florentine
Sandwiches with
Lemon-Caper Vinaigrette

Sardine, Caper, and
Radicchio Sandwiches

Sardine, Caper, and Radicchio Sandwiches

Prep: 5 minutes • Cook: 2 minutes

Sardine skeptics, take note: This tasty, highly nutritious open-faced sandwich is filled with omega-3 fatty acids and calcium. Mustardy sardines, capers, and citrus pair perfectly with slightly bitter Italian greens and toasted peasant bread for a mouthful of flavor.

4	(1½-ounce) slices peasant bread
1	tablespoon stone-ground mustard
2	teaspoons fresh lemon juice
2	teaspoons olive oil
¼	teaspoon freshly ground black pepper
4	cups torn romaine lettuce
2¼	cups radicchio, shredded
2	(4.375-ounce) cans low-sodium skinless, boneless sardines, drained
4	teaspoons drained capers

1. Preheat broiler.
2. Place bread slices on a baking sheet. Broil 1 minute on each side or until lightly toasted.
3. While bread cooks, combine mustard and next 3 ingredients in a medium bowl. Add lettuce and radicchio; toss gently.
4. Break sardines into chunks and place evenly on bread slices; sprinkle evenly with capers. Top evenly with lettuce mixture. Yield: 4 servings (serving size: 1 open-faced sandwich).

CALORIES 234; FAT 8.4g (sat 1.1g, mono 3.7g, poly 3g); PROTEIN 17.7g; CARB 22g; FIBER 1.3g; CHOL 75mg; IRON 3.3mg; SODIUM 626mg; CALC 221mg

Havarti-Dill Tuna Melts

Prep: 7 minutes • Cook: 2 minutes

Put a new spin on the patty melt using tuna. Top it with a pickle spear, if desired, and serve it while the cheese oozes. The prep time clocks in at under 10 minutes.

8	(1-ounce) slices 15-grain bread, toasted
	Cucumber Tuna Salad
4	(¾-ounce) slices Havarti cheese with dill
4	(¼-inch-thick) slices tomato

1. Preheat broiler.
2. Place 4 toast slices on a baking sheet; spread evenly with Cucumber Tuna Salad. Top evenly with cheese. Broil 2 minutes or until cheese melts.
3. Top with tomato and remaining toast slices. Yield: 4 servings (serving size: 1 sandwich).

CALORIES 342; FAT 16.7g (sat 6.2g, mono 4.6g, poly 5.8g); PROTEIN 24.1g; CARB 29.1g; FIBER 5.5g; CHOL 47mg; IRON 1.8mg; SODIUM 731mg; CALC 223mg

Cucumber Tuna Salad

Prep: 4 minutes

1	(6.4-ounce) pouch albacore tuna in water, flaked
⅓	cup finely chopped celery (1 stalk)
⅓	cup light mayonnaise
¼	cup finely chopped seeded cucumber
¼	teaspoon black pepper
⅛	teaspoon salt

1. Combine all ingredients in a medium bowl. Yield: 1½ cups (serving size: ⅓ cup).

CALORIES 124; FAT 7.2g (sat 1g, mono 1.8g, poly 4.4g); PROTEIN 12.2g; CARB 2.3g; FIBER 0.3g; CHOL 28mg; IRON 0.3mg; SODIUM 449mg; CALC 7mg

Open-Faced Avocado-Bacon Tuna Melts

Jazz up a traditional tuna melt with bacon and avocado.

Prep: 13 minutes • Cook: 2 minutes

1   (12-ounce) can albacore tuna in water, drained and flaked
3   tablespoons light mayonnaise
⅛   teaspoon freshly ground black pepper
4   (1-ounce) slices whole-wheat bread, toasted
4   center-cut bacon slices, cooked and halved
¼   avocado, thinly sliced
4   (0.74-ounce) slices reduced-fat Swiss cheese

1. Preheat oven to 425°.
2. Combine first 3 ingredients in a bowl. Spoon tuna mixture evenly over toasted bread slices. Top tuna mixture evenly with bacon, avocado, and cheese. Place sandwiches on a baking sheet.
3. Bake at 425° for 2 minutes or until cheese melts. Yield: 4 servings (serving size: 1 open-faced sandwich).

CALORIES 264; FAT 11.7g (sat 3.1g, mono 3.5g, poly 3.4g); PROTEIN 29.4g; CARB 11.1g; FIBER 3.6g; CHOL 47mg; IRON 1.2mg; SODIUM 514mg; CALC 269mg

serve with:

Spicy Sweet Potato Fries

Prep: 2 minutes • Cook: 16 minutes

2½   cups frozen sweet potato fries
Butter-flavored cooking spray
¼   kosher salt
⅛   teaspoon ground red pepper

1. Preheat oven to 425°.
2. Place potatoes in a single layer on a large baking sheet coated with cooking spray. Coat potatoes with cooking spray.
3. Bake at 425° for 16 minutes or until crisp and golden.
4. Combine salt and ground pepper in a small bowl. Remove fries from oven, and sprinkle with salt mixture. Yield: 4 servings (serving size: ½ cup).

CALORIES 202; FAT 8.2g (sat 1.7g, mono 3.7g, poly 2.3g); PROTEIN 2.7g; CARB 32.1g; FIBER 4.1g; CHOL 0mg; IRON 1mg; SODIUM 304mg; CALC 54mg

fix it faster

Shorten the prep time by baking the sweet potato fries while you make the sandwiches. Then add the assembled sandwiches to the baking sheet used for the potatoes during the last 2 minutes of cooking, so that everything is ready at the same time.

Open-Faced Salmon BLTs

Prep: 5 minutes • Cook: 10 minutes

Fresh salmon and a tangy dill spread dress up the conventional BLT. You'll need a knife and fork to handle this hearty sandwich. To save time, toast the bread slices while the fish cooks.

8	precooked hickory-smoked bacon, slices
2	(6-ounce) salmon fillets (about 1 inch thick)
¼	teaspoon freshly ground black pepper, divided

Cooking spray

¼	cup light mayonnaise
1½	tablespoons fresh lemon juice
1½	teaspoons minced fresh dill
4	(1-ounce) slices diagonally cut French bread, toasted
4	green leaf lettuce leaves
4	tomato slices, cut in half

1. Preheat broiler.
2. Microwave bacon slices according to package directions; set aside.
3. While bacon cooks, sprinkle fish with ⅛ teaspoon pepper. Place fish, skin sides down, on a broiler pan coated with cooking spray. Broil 10 to 13 minutes or until fish flakes easily when tested with a fork. Remove skin from fish, and cut fish into chunks.
4. While fish cooks, combine mayonnaise, lemon juice, dill, and remaining ⅛ teaspoon pepper. Spread 1 tablespoon dill mayonnaise on each French bread slice; top with 1 lettuce leaf, 2 tomato halves, 2 bacon slices, and one-fourth of salmon chunks. Drizzle remaining dill mayonnaise evenly over each sandwich. Yield: 4 servings (serving size: 1 open-faced sandwich).

CALORIES 331; FAT 15.6g (sat 3, mono 4.8g, poly 5.7g); PROTEIN 24.9g; CARB 21.4g; FIBER 1.3g; CHOL 55mg; IRON 1.7mg; SODIUM 505mg; CALC 31mg

Open-Faced Salmon BLTs

serve with:
Tomato and Cucumber Salad

Prep: 5 minutes

1	cup cherry tomatoes, halved
2	small salad cucumbers, sliced
½	cup coarsely chopped yellow or green bell pepper
½	cup light red wine vinaigrette
½	teaspoon freshly ground black pepper

1. Combine all ingredients in a medium bowl; toss well. Cover and chill until ready to serve. Yield: 4 servings (serving size: ¾ cup).

CALORIES 66; FAT 5.2g (sat 0.5g, mono 2g, poly 2g); PROTEIN 0.8g; CARB 5.6g; FIBER 1.1g; CHOL 0mg; IRON 0.3mg; SODIUM 283mg; CALC 12mg

Open-Faced Smoked
Salmon Sandwiches

Open-Faced Smoked Salmon Sandwiches

Prep: 9 minutes

Served with a mixed green salad, this light salmon sandwich is perfect for a warm summer's day.

Dill–Cream Cheese Spread
4   (1-ounce) slices pumpernickel bread, toasted
4   ounces thinly sliced smoked salmon
8   (¼-inch-thick) slices red onion
1   cup alfalfa sprouts

1. Spread 1 tablespoon Dill–Cream Cheese Spread over each of 4 bread slices. Top each with 1 ounce salmon, 2 onion slices, and ¼ cup sprouts. Yield: 4 servings (serving size: 1 open-faced sandwich).

CALORIES 176; FAT 5g (sat 1.9g, mono 0.9g, poly 0.7g); PROTEIN 10.7g; CARB 23.6g; FIBER 3.6g; CHOL 14mg; IRON 1.4mg; SODIUM 568mg; CALC 66mg

Dill–Cream Cheese Spread

Prep: 3 minutes

¼   cup (2 ounces) tub-style light chive-and-onion cream cheese
2   teaspoons chopped fresh dill
2   teaspoons capers, rinsed and drained

1. Combine all ingredients in a bowl, stirring until well blended. Yield: ¼ cup (serving size: 1 tablespoon).

CALORIES 30; FAT 2g (sat 1.5g, mono 0g, poly 0g); PROTEIN 1.5g; CARB 1.1g; FIBER 0.1g; CHOL 8mg; IRON 0mg; SODIUM 128mg; CALC 21mg

ingredient spotlight

Low in calories and rich in protein, alfalfa sprouts crown this sandwich with lots of vitamins and minerals—particularly vitamin C.

Smoked Paprika Salmon Sliders

Prep: 5 minutes • Cook: 10 minutes
Other: 5 minutes

These small sandwiches pack incredible flavor—and it's all about the rub.

Smoked Paprika Rub
3   (6-ounce) salmon fillets (1 inch thick)
Cooking spray
1   (10-ounce) package hearth-baked
      French rolls
2   tablespoons light mayonnaise
½   cup packed arugula or mixed baby
      salad greens

1. Preheat broiler.
2. Prepare Smoked Paprika Rub; rub over tops of fillets, reserving ½ teaspoon. Place salmon on a broiler pan coated with cooking spray. Broil 10 minutes or until desired degree of doneness. Let cool 5 minutes.
3. While salmon cools, reduce oven temperature to 425°. Heat rolls at 425° according to package directions. Combine mayonnaise and reserved ½ teaspoon rub; spread evenly onto cut sides of rolls.
4. Remove skin from salmon, and cut each fillet in half crosswise. Place salmon on roll bottoms. Top with arugula and roll tops. Yield: 6 servings (serving size: 1 slider).

CALORIES 238; FAT 4.9g (sat 0.6g, mono 2g, poly 2.1g); PROTEIN 21.2g; CARB 26.8g; FIBER 1.5g; CHOL 44mg; IRON 2.3mg; SODIUM 371mg; CALC 115mg

Smoked Paprika Salmon Sliders

Smoked Paprika Rub

Prep: 2 minutes

1   tablespoon smoked paprika
1   tablespoon brown sugar
1   teaspoon grated orange rind
¼   teaspoon salt
¼   teaspoon freshly ground black pepper

1. Combine all ingredients in a small bowl. Yield: 2½ tablespoons (serving size: 1¼ teaspoons).

CALORIES 13; FAT 0.1g (sat 0g, mono 0g, poly 0.1g); PROTEIN 0.2g; CARB 2.9g; FIBER 0.4g; CHOL 0mg; IRON 0.2mg; SODIUM 99mg; CALC 5mg

Tilapia Sandwiches with Greek Tapenade

Prep: 8 minutes • Cook: 6 minutes

Mâche, also known as lamb's lettuce or corn salad, is a tender green with a tangy, nutty flavor. Look for it in the premium salad greens section of the produce section–it is usually packaged in a plastic clamshell container.

Greek Tapenade
2	(6-ounce) tilapia fillets
1/8	teaspoon salt
1/8	teaspoon coarsely ground black pepper
Cooking spray	
4	(0.8-ounce) slices crusty Chicago-style Italian bread (about 1/2 inch thick), toasted
4	tomato slices
2/3	cup mâche

Tilapia Sandwiches with Greek Tapenade

1. Prepare Greek Tapenade; set aside.
2. Sprinkle fillets evenly with salt and pepper. Heat a large nonstick over medium-high heat; coat pan with cooking spray. Add fish; cook 2 to 3 minutes on each side or until fish flakes easily when tested with a fork.
3. Spread about 1 tablespoon Greek Tapenade on each bread slice. Top each of 2 slices with 1 fillet, 2 tomato slices, 1/3 cup mâche, and remaining bread slices. Yield: 2 servings (serving size: 1 sandwich).

CALORIES 347; FAT 8.9g (sat 3g, mono 3.4g, poly 1.7g); PROTEIN 39.9g; CARB 26g; FIBER 1.6g; CHOL 93mg; IRON .3mg; SODIUM 768mg; CALC 113mg

Greek Tapenade

Prep: 5 minutes

2	tablespoons chopped pitted kalamata olives
2	tablespoons crumbled feta cheese
1	tablespoon chopped bottled roasted red bell peppers
1/2	teaspoon grated lemon rind
1	teaspoon fresh lemon juice
1/2	teaspoon chopped fresh oregano

1. Place all ingredients in a mini food processor; pulse 2 or 3 times or until minced. Yield: 2 servings (serving size: 2 1/2 tablespoons).

CALORIES 52; FAT 4.3g (sat 1.7g, mono 2.2g, poly 0.3g); PROTEIN 1.5g; CARB 1.7g; FIBER 0.1g; CHOL 8mg; IRON 0mg; SODIUM 262mg; CALC 52mg

fix it faster

Use a minichopper—or take your time using a large chef's knife—to finely chop the olives, roasted peppers, and oregano for the Greek Tapenade before you spread the mixture over the toasted bread.

Grilled Grouper Sandwiches with Tartar Sauce

Prep: 6 minutes • Cook: 6 minutes

Grouper is a white-meat fish that is well suited for the grill. If you can't find grouper, use white sea bass or mahimahi. Look for fish that is free of blemishes, has a fresh smell, and has flesh that springs back when touched. Serve these fish sandwiches with fresh seasonal cherries and pineapple to add bright color and tart flavor to your meal.

4	(6-ounce) grouper fillets (about 1½ inches thick)
2	teaspoons olive oil
¼	teaspoon salt
¼	teaspoon freshly ground black pepper

Cooking spray
Tartar Sauce

4	(1.8-ounce) white-wheat hamburger buns
4	green leaf lettuce leaves

1. Preheat grill to medium-high heat.
2. Brush fillets evenly with olive oil; sprinkle evenly with salt and pepper. Place fillets on grill rack coated with cooking spray; grill 3 to 4 minutes on each side or until fish flakes easily when tested with a fork.
3. While fish cooks, prepare Tartar Sauce. Spread about 2½ tablespoons Tartar Sauce over cut sides of each bun; place 1 lettuce leaf on bottom half of each bun. Top lettuce with fish; top with remaining bun halves. Yield: 4 servings (serving size: 1 sandwich).

CALORIES 388; FAT 16g (sat 2.8g, mono 4.6g, poly 8.5g); PROTEIN 38.5g; CARB 26.3g; FIBER 5.5g; CHOL 73mg; IRON 4.6mg; SODIUM 783mg; CALC 311mg

Tartar Sauce

Prep: 4 minutes

½	cup light mayonnaise
2	tablespoons chopped green onions
1	tablespoon sweet pickle relish
1½	teaspoons capers, rinsed and drained
1½	teaspoons fresh lemon juice
½	teaspoon Worcestershire sauce

1. Combine all ingredients in a small bowl, stirring with a whisk until well blended. Yield: ⅔ cup (serving size: about 1 tablespoon).

CALORIES 43; FAT 4g (sat 0.6g, mono 0.8g, poly 2g); PROTEIN 0.1g; CARB 1.8g; FIBER 0.1g; CHOL 4mg; IRON 0.1mg; SODIUM 124mg; CALC 2mg

Grilled Grouper Sandwiches with Tartar Sauce

Shrimp Rolls

Prep: 10 minutes

We've chosen a traditional hot dog bun for this sandwich. However, for variety, you can also use a flour tortilla. Place a lettuce leaf on an 8-inch tortilla, spoon the shrimp mixture onto the lettuce, and then roll up the tortilla. Secure the roll with a round wooden pick, and cut it in half.

1	small lemon
¼	cup light mayonnaise
2	tablespoons chopped green onion tops
¾	pound chopped cooked shrimp
½	cup finely chopped celery
4	(1.5-ounce) white-wheat hot dog buns
4	Boston lettuce leaves

1. Grate ½ teaspoon lemon rind from lemon. Squeeze lemon to measure 1½ tablespoons juice. Combine lemon rind, juice, mayonnaise, and green onions in a large bowl. Add shrimp and celery; toss gently.
2. Top each bun with 1 lettuce leaf. Spoon shrimp mixture evenly onto lettuce leaves. Serve immediately. Yield: 4 servings (serving size: 1 roll).

CALORIES 220; FAT 7.4g (sat 1g, mono 1.2g, poly 3.4g); PROTEIN 23.1g; CARB 20.7; FIBER 4.5g; CHOL 171mg; IRON 5.5mg; SODIUM 514mg; CALC 296mg

---

quick flip

Feeling fancy? Cooked lobser is a rich substitution for the shrimp.

---

serve with:
Pear-Kiwi Salad

Prep: 6 minutes

2	tablespoons fresh lime juice
1	tablespoon finely chopped fresh mint
1	tablespoon honey
2	cups sliced pear (about 2 pears)
1¾	cups peeled, sliced kiwi

1. Combine lime juice, mint, and honey in a medium bowl, stirring with a whisk. Add pear and kiwi; toss gently. Yield: 4 servings (serving size: ¾ cup).

CALORIES 113; FAT 0.5g (sat 0g, mono 0.1g, poly 0.2g); PROTEIN 1.3g; CARB 29.2g; FIBER 5g; CHOL 0mg; IRON 0.4mg; SODIUM 4mg; CALC 36mg

Shrimp Rolls

Crushed Heirloom Tomato and Shrimp Bruschetta

Prep: 9 minutes • Cook: 4 minutes

These mile-high knife-and-fork sandwiches highlight heirloom tomatoes, summer's seasonal gems.

8	(0.7-ounce) diagonal slices French bread (½ inch thick)

Olive oil–flavored cooking spray

4	large garlic cloves, halved
½	cup (4 ounces) goat cheese, softened

Crushed Heirloom Tomato and Shrimp Topping

¼	teaspoon freshly ground black pepper
1	tablespoon extra-virgin olive oil
24	small basil leaves

1. Preheat grill to medium-high heat.
2. Coat bread with cooking spray. Grill 2 minutes on each side or until toasted. Rub cut sides of garlic on 1 side of each piece of toast. Spread goat cheese evenly over garlic on toast. Top each toast with ½ cup Crushed Heirloom Tomato and Shrimp Topping. Sprinkle with pepper, and drizzle with olive oil. Top each serving with basil leaves. Yield: 4 servings (serving size: 2 bruschetta).

CALORIES 355; FAT 13.3g (sat 6g, mono 5.1g, poly 2.1g); PROTEIN 32.3g; CARB 26.1g; FIBER 1.8g; CHOL 185mg; IRON 5.1mg; SODIUM 647mg; CALC 159mg

Crushed Heirloom Tomato and Shrimp Topping

Prep: 4 minutes • Cook: 4 minutes

1	pound peeled and deveined medium shrimp

Olive oil–flavored cooking spray

2	cups heirloom multicolored cherry tomatoes
1	teaspoon grated lemon rind
1	tablespoon fresh lemon juice
¼	teaspoon salt
¼	teaspoon crushed red pepper (optional)

1. Preheat grill to medium-high heat.
2. Coat shrimp with cooking spray; place shrimp in a grill basket. Grill 2 to 3 minutes on each side or until shrimp reach desired degree of doneness.
3. While shrimp cook, place tomatoes in a medium bowl. Press tomatoes with the back of a spoon or potato masher until lightly crushed. Add shrimp to tomatoes in bowl; stir in remaining ingredients. Yield: 4 servings (serving size: 1 cup).

CALORIES 139; FAT 2.4g (sat 0.5g, mono 0.7g, poly 1.1g); PROTEIN 23.7g; CARB 4.9g; FIBER 0.9g; CHOL 172mg; IRON 3.1mg; SODIUM 320mg; CALC 64mg

Crushed Heirloom Tomato and Shrimp Bruschetta

Blue Cheeseburgers

Prep: 6 minutes • Cook: 12 minutes

Blue cheese is the surprise ingredient in this burger. It boosts the flavor and keeps it juicy. Top the burger with your favorite condiments, and serve with steak fries to round out your meal.

1	pound 93% lean ground beef
¼	cup minced fresh onion
¼	cup (1 ounce) crumbled blue cheese
¼	teaspoon salt
⅛	teaspoon freshly ground black pepper
4	(1.8-ounce) white-wheat hamburger buns
4	(¼-inch-thick) slices tomato (optional)
4	green leaf lettuce leaves (optional)

1. Combine first 5 ingredients in a medium bowl; stir well. Divide beef mixture into 4 equal portions, shaping each into a ½-inch-thick patty.

2. Heat a nonstick grill pan over medium-high heat. Place hamburger patties in pan, and cook 6 minutes on each side or until desired degree of doneness.

3. Top bottom half of each bun with 1 patty, tomato, and lettuce, if desired, and remaining half of bun. Yield: 4 servings (serving size: 1 burger).

CALORIES 294; FAT 12.4g (sat 5.1g, mono 5g, poly 2.3g); PROTEIN 26.9g; CARB 22.2g; FIBER 5.2g; CHOL 61mg; IRON 5.5mg; SODIUM 556mg; CALC 297mg

Blue Cheeseburgers

Flank Steak Sandwiches with Carrot Slaw

Prep: 10 minutes • Cook: 13 minutes
Other: 5 minutes

Overlapping tasks keeps prep and cook time to a minimum for this recipe. Fire up the grill, and season the steak while the oven preheats and the rolls bake. Prepare the slaw while the steak is grilling. Assemble the sandwiches, and you're done.

4	(1.5-ounce) frozen ciabatta rolls
1	(1-pound) flank steak, trimmed
2	teaspoons olive oil
1	teaspoon five-spice powder
¼	teaspoon salt
¼	teaspoon freshly ground black pepper

Cooking spray
| 2 | cups bagged baby spinach leaves |

Carrot Slaw

1. Bake rolls according to package directions. Cut rolls horizontally in half.
2. Preheat grill to medium-high heat.
3. Rub steak with oil; sprinkle with five-spice powder, salt, and pepper. Place steak on grill rack coated with cooking spray. Grill 6 minutes on each side or until desired degree of doneness. Remove steak from grill, and let stand 5 minutes. Cut steak diagonally across grain into thin slices.
4. Place ½ cup spinach on roll bottoms. Top evenly with steak and Carrot Slaw. Place roll tops over slaw. Yield: 4 servings (serving size: 1 sandwich).

CALORIES 306; FAT 10g (sat 3.1g, mono 5.5g, poly 1.3g); PROTEIN 28.6g; CARB 23.6g; FIBER 1.8g; CHOL 39mg; IRON 4mg; SODIUM 583mg; CALC 56mg

Flank Steak Sandwiches
with Carrot Slaw

Carrot Slaw

Prep: 10 minutes

2	teaspoons rice vinegar
1	teaspoon grated peeled fresh ginger
1	teaspoon olive oil
¼	teaspoon salt
¼	teaspoon freshly ground black pepper
2	garlic cloves, minced
1	cup shredded carrot
¼	cup shredded radishes
1	tablespoon chopped fresh cilantro

1. Combine first 6 ingredients in a medium bowl. Add carrot, radishes, and cilantro; toss to coat. Cover and chill until ready to serve. Yield: 1 cup (serving size: ¼ cup).

CALORIES 26; FAT 1.2g (sat 0.2g, mono 0.8g, poly 0.2g); PROTEIN 0.4g; CARB 3.6g; FIBER 1g; CHOL 0mg; IRON 0.2mg; SODIUM 168mg; CALC 14mg

Black Pepper Sirloin Wraps with Kickin' Chipotle Spread

Prep: 6 minutes • Cook: 10 minutes
Other: 3 minutes

Mayonnaise, garlic, and adobo sauce create a spicy, smoky spread well suited for these satisfying steak wraps. To warm the tortillas, stack them together, and cover with a few layers of damp paper towels; then microwave at HIGH 1 minute or until the tortillas are soft and pliable.

1   (1-pound) lean boneless sirloin steak (¾ inch thick)
2   teaspoons coarsely ground black pepper
Cooking spray
6   (7-inch) flour tortillas
4   cups torn mixed salad greens
1   cup (3 x ¼-inch) julienne-cut red bell pepper (about 1 medium)
Kickin' Chipotle Spread

1. Preheat grill to medium-high heat.
2. Sprinkle both sides of steak with black pepper. Place steak on grill rack coated with cooking spray; grill 5 to 6 minutes on each side or until desired degree of doneness. Let stand 3 minutes before slicing.
3. While steak cooks, top tortillas evenly with salad greens and bell pepper. Top with steak slices; drizzle Kickin' Chipotle Spread evenly over steak. Roll up. Yield: 6 servings (serving size: 1 wrap).

CALORIES 235; FAT 9.8g (sat 2.4g, mono 3.8g, poly 1.7g); PROTEIN 18.9g; CARB 17.7g; FIBER 2.1g; CHOL 51mg; IRON 3.3mg; SODIUM 759mg; CALC 22mg

Kickin' Chipotle Spread

Prep: 2 minutes

⅓   cup light mayonnaise
2   teaspoons adobo sauce
1   garlic clove, minced
2   tablespoons water
¼   teaspoon salt

1. Combine all ingredients in a small bowl, stirring with a whisk. Yield: about ½ cup (serving size: about 1 tablespoon).

CALORIES 35; FAT 3.4g (sat 0.7g, mono 0.8g, poly 1.7g); PROTEIN 0g; CARB 0.9g; FIBER 0.1g; CHOL 3mg; IRON 0mg; SODIUM 166mg; CALC 1mg

Black Pepper Sirloin Wraps with Kickin' Chipotle Spread

Spicy Baja Beef Tortillas

Prep: 12 minutes

¼	cup light sour cream
1	tablespoon adobo sauce from canned chipotle chiles in adobo sauce (reserve chiles for another use)
4	(6-inch) low-fat whole-wheat tortillas
5	cups gourmet salad greens
6	ounces thinly sliced low-sodium deli roast beef
1	cup refrigerated prechopped tomato
⅓	cup mild pickled banana pepper rings
1	ripe peeled avocado, coarsely chopped

1. Combine ¼ cup sour cream and adobo sauce in a small bowl, stirring well. Place 1 tortilla on each of 4 plates. Spread 1 tablespoon sour cream mixture over each tortilla. Top each evenly with salad greens; arrange beef over greens.
2. Combine tomato, pepper rings, and avocado in a medium bowl; toss gently. Top beef evenly with tomato mixture. Yield: 4 servings (serving size: 1 tortilla).

CALORIES 284; FAT 13.1g (sat 3.5g, mono 4.8g, poly 1g); PROTEIN 16.9g; CARB 26.4g; FIBER 6.1g; CHOL 25mg; IRON 3.2mg; SODIUM 352mg; CALC 103mg

serve with:
Melon Kebabs with Lime and Chiles

Prep: 4 minutes

5	cups cubed cantaloupe, honeydew, and watermelon
1	teaspoon grated lime rind
¼	cup fresh lime juice
1	teaspoon agave syrup
1	teaspoon crushed chipotle chile flakes (such as Williams-Sonoma Crushed Chipotle Chili)
¼	teaspoon kosher salt

1. Thread 1 cup fruit onto each of 5 (8-inch) skewers, alternating cantaloupe, honeydew, and watermelon.
2. Combine lime rind, lime juice, and agave syrup in a small bowl, stirring with a small whisk. Brush syrup over fruit. Combine chile flakes and salt; sprinkle over skewers. Yield: 5 servings (serving size: 1 kebab).

CALORIES 175; FAT 0.3g (sat 0.1g, mono 0g, poly 0.1g); PROTEIN 1.2g; CARB 15.6g; FIBER 1.3g; CHOL 0mg; IRON 0.4mg; SODIUM 116mg; CALC 15mg

Spicy Baja Beef
Tortillas

Black and Blue Quesadillas

Black and Blue Quesadillas

Prep: 5 minutes • Cook: 11 minutes

A sweet and salty flavor combination is always a huge hit, and the blue cheese and balsamic glaze in these beefy quesadillas is no exception. Pair with Mixed Greens with Lime Vinaigrette for a sensational meal.

Cooking spray
⅓   cup thinly sliced red onion
4   (8-inch) fat-free flour tortillas
½   pound thinly sliced low-sodium deli roast beef
2   tablespoons crumbled blue cheese
4   teaspoons balsamic glaze

1. Heat a large nonstick skillet over medium heat. Coat pan with cooking spray. Add onion; sauté 3 to 4 minutes or until tender and lightly browned. Remove from heat.
2. Top half of each tortilla evenly with beef, onion, and cheese. Fold tortillas in half.

3. Return pan to heat. Coat pan and both sides of quesadillas evenly with cooking spray. Place 2 quesadillas in pan; cook 2 to 3 minutes on each side or until browned. Repeat procedure with remaining quesadillas. Cut each quesadilla into 4 wedges; drizzle with 1 teaspoon glaze. Yield: 4 servings (serving size: 1 quesadilla).

CALORIES 233; FAT 4g (sat 1.8g, mono 0.3g, poly 0g); PROTEIN 20.3g; CARB 27.9g; FIBER 2.3g; CHOL 33.5mg; IRON 1.5mg; SODIUM 484mg; CALC 26mg

serve with:
Mixed Greens with Lime Vinaigrette

Prep: 7 minutes

2   tablespoons white wine vinegar
1   tablespoon olive oil
½   teaspoon grated lime rind
¼   teaspoon freshly ground black pepper
⅛   teaspoon salt
6   cups mixed baby greens
1   peeled avocado, cut into 8 slices
1   cup cherry tomatoes, halved

1. Combine first 5 ingredients in a small bowl, stirring well with a whisk.
2. Arrange greens on plates. Top with avocado and tomato. Drizzle evenly with dressing. Yield: 4 servings (serving size: 1½ cups mixed greens, 2 slices avocado, and ¼ cup tomato).

CALORIES 177; FAT 15g (sat 3.7g, mono 7.3g, poly 1.5g); PROTEIN 4.9g; CARB 9.6g; FIBER 4.7g; CHOL 10mg; IRON 1.2mg; SODIUM 154mg; CALC 108mg

French Dip Sandwiches

Prep: 3 minutes • Cook: 12 minutes
Other: 5 minutes

Deglazing the pan with a couple of tablespoons of water while cooking the onions speeds up the browning process. The result is a "shortcut" caramelized onion that adds maximum flavor to this deli classic.

1   medium Vidalia or other sweet onion, peeled and thinly sliced
Cooking spray
2   teaspoons salt-free onion and herb seasoning blend, divided
½   cup plus 2 tablespoons water
1   cup fat-free, less-sodium beef broth
12   ounces very thinly sliced low-sodium deli roast beef
4   (2½-ounce) hoagie rolls, split lengthwise
4   (0.8-ounce) slices reduced-fat Swiss cheese, torn in half

1. Preheat oven to 500°.
2. Heat a large nonstick skillet over high heat; add onion. Coat onion with cooking spray; stir in ½ teaspoon seasoning blend. Sauté 11 to 12 minutes or until onion is tender and golden brown. While onion cooks, add 2 tablespoons water at a time; cook each time until liquid evaporates, scraping pan to loosen browned bits.
3. While onion cooks, combine broth and remaining 1½ teaspoons seasoning blend in a medium saucepan; cook over medium heat until hot. Remove pan from heat; add beef, pushing beef down into liquid until covered. Let stand 5 minutes.
4. While beef stands, place hoagie rolls, cut sides up, on a baking sheet. Bake at 500° for 4 minutes or until bread is lightly toasted.

5. Remove beef from broth, allowing excess broth to drip back into pan; reserve broth. Arrange beef evenly over bottom halves of rolls; top evenly with onion, cheese slices, and remaining bread halves. Serve with warm broth for dipping. Yield: 4 servings (serving size: 1 sandwich and 2 tablespoons broth).

CALORIES 395; FAT 10g (sat 4.5g, mono 2g, poly 1.7g); PROTEIN 37.4g; CARB 42.2g; FIBER 2.7g; CHOL 46mg; IRON 2.4mg; SODIUM 683mg; CALC 219mg

serve with:
Creamy Ranch-Style Coleslaw

Prep: 7 minutes

⅓   cup light mayonnaise
¼   cup nonfat buttermilk
1   teaspoon salt-free onion and herb seasoning blend
¼   teaspoon salt
⅛   teaspoon freshly ground black pepper
4   cups packaged coleslaw

1. Combine first 5 ingredients in a bowl, stirring well with a whisk. Pour dressing over slaw; toss well. Chill until ready to serve. Yield: 4 servings (serving size: 1 cup).

CALORIES 85; FAT 7g (sat 1.3g, mono 1.5g, poly 3.8g); PROTEIN 1.1g; CARB 4.8g; FIBER 1g; CHOL 6.8mg; IRON 0.2mg; SODIUM 328mg; CALC 39mg

Philly Cheese Steak Sandwiches

Prep: 6 minutes • Cook: 6 minutes

A number of different cheeses, from processed cheese sauce in a can to sharp provolone, typically crown this Philly favorite. We chose shredded reduced-fat extra-sharp cheddar to make it both tasty and fast to prepare.

Cheddar Cheese Sauce
¾   pound boneless sirloin steak
Cooking spray
2   cups refrigerated presliced green, yellow, and red bell pepper strips
½   cup refrigerated chopped onion
¼   teaspoon freshly ground black pepper
4   (2½-ounce) whole-wheat hoagie rolls

1. Prepare Cheddar Cheese Sauce.
2. While sauce cooks, cut steak diagonally across the grain into ⅛-inch-thick slices.
3. Heat a large cast-iron skillet 2 minutes over high heat. Coat pan with cooking spray. Add steak, bell pepper, and onion to pan. Sprinkle steak and vegetables with black pepper; sauté 6 minutes or until meat is browned and vegetables are tender. Drain.
4. Stand rolls on uncut edge; fill each roll with about ¾ cup steak mixture. Spoon about 3 tablespoons Cheddar Cheese Sauce over each sandwich. Serve immediately. Yield: 4 servings (serving size: 1 sandwich).

CALORIES 342; FAT 7.9g (sat 3.1g, mono 2.5g, poly 1.7g); PROTEIN 29g; CARB 40.9g; FIBER 5.3g; CHOL 52.3mg; IRON 2.9mg; SODIUM 442mg; CALC 189mg

Cheddar Cheese Sauce

Prep: 3 minutes • Cook: 4 minutes

1½   tablespoons all-purpose flour
¾   cup 1% low-fat milk
¼   cup (1 ounce) shredded reduced-fat extra-sharp Cheddar cheese
⅛   teaspoon salt
⅛   teaspoon ground red pepper
⅛   teaspoon onion powder

1. Place flour in a small saucepan. Gradually add milk, stirring with a whisk until smooth. Cook over medium-high heat until thick (about 3 minutes), stirring frequently. Remove from heat; add cheese, stirring until cheese melts. Stir in salt, pepper, and onion powder. Yield: 4 servings (serving size: about 3 tablespoons).

CALORIES 53; FAT 2g (sat 1.3g, mono 0.1g, poly 0g); PROTEIN 3.6g; CARB 4.9g; FIBER 0.1g; CHOL 7.3mg; IRON 0.2mg; SODIUM 155mg; CALC 109mg

Philly Cheese Steak Sandwiches

Mini Lamb Pitas with Minted Pea Hummus

Prep: 9 minutes • Cook: 12 minutes
Other: 5 minutes

Nothing says spring like these pita pockets loaded with delicate lamb and colorful Minted Pea Hummus. Green peas contribute bold color and are especially high in vitamin K, which helps protect against osteoporosis. Add fresh fruit as a side dish, and you've got a wonderfully healthy meal. Use leftover hummus as a refreshing and vibrant veggie dip.

1	pound lean ground lamb
¼	cup (1 ounce) crumbled reduced-fat feta cheese
¼	teaspoon ground cumin
¼	teaspoon freshly ground black pepper
	Cooking spray
8	(1-ounce) miniature whole-wheat pitas
½	cup Minted Pea Hummus
	Red onion slices (optional)
	Alfalfa sprouts (optional)
	Cucumber slices (optional)

1. Preheat grill to medium-high heat.
2. Combine first 4 ingredients. Divide mixture into 4 equal portions, shaping each into a ½-inch-thick patty.
3. Place patties on a grill rack coated with cooking spray; grill 6 minutes on each side or until a thermometer registers 165°. Remove from grill; let stand 5 minutes. Cut each patty in half. Split each pita in half horizontally, cutting to, but not through, opposite side. Spread 1 tablespoon Minted Pea Hummus on bottom half of each pita, and top with half of 1 patty. Add onion, sprouts, and cucumber, if desired. Yield: 4 servings (serving size: 2 stuffed pitas).

CALORIES 391; FAT 17g (sat 6.9g, mono 6.7g, poly 1.1g); PROTEIN 27.4g; CARB 33.9g; FIBER 4g; CHOL 77mg; IRON 3.7mg; SODIUM 354mg; CALC 84mg

Mini Lamb Pitas with Minted Pea Hummus

Minted Pea Hummus

Prep: 3 minutes

2	cups frozen petite green peas, thawed
2	garlic cloves
½	cup mint leaves
1½	teaspoons olive oil
1	teaspoon water
¼	teaspoon salt

1. Place all ingredients in a blender or food processor; process until smooth. Yield: 1¼ cups (serving size: 1 tablespoon).

CALORIES 15; FAT 0.5g (sat 0.1g, mono 0.3g, poly 0.1g); PROTEIN 0.7g; CARB 2.1g; FIBER 0.8g; CHOL 0mg; IRON 0.4mg; SODIUM 60mg; CALC 5mg

Lamb Wraps with Tzatziki

Prep: 16 minutes • Cook: 9 minutes

Soft, pillowy flatbreads hug a spicy lamb filling drizzled with refreshing cucumber-mint sauce in this take on a favorite Greek sandwich. Round out the meal with a healthy side of red grapes.

Cooking spray
¾   pound lean ground lamb
1   cup chopped onion
½   teaspoon black pepper
¼   teaspoon salt
2   cups shredded romaine lettuce
2   (3.8-ounce) Mediterranean-style white
     flatbreads
Tzatziki

1. Heat a large nonstick skillet over medium-high heat. Coat pan with cooking spray. Add lamb and onion; cook 8 minutes or until lamb is browned and onion is tender, stirring to crumble lamb. Drain. Stir in pepper and salt.
2. Divide lettuce evenly between flatbreads; spoon lamb mixture evenly over lettuce. Drizzle lamb mixture evenly with Tzatziki. Roll up flatbreads, and wrap in parchment paper or tie with string. Cut each wrap in half, and serve immediately. Yield: 4 servings (serving size: 1 wrap).

CALORIES 389; FAT 17.6g (sat 6.5g, mono 6.8g, poly 4.2g); PROTEIN 23.6g; CARB 33.1g; FIBER 3.5g; CHOL 58mg; IRON 1.5mg; SODIUM 532mg; CALC 67mg

Tzatziki

Prep: 5 minutes

½   cup plain 2% reduced-fat Greek yogurt
¼   cup shredded seeded peeled cucumber
1   tablespoon chopped fresh mint
1   tablespoon fresh lemon juice
⅛   teaspoon salt
2   garlic cloves, pressed

1. Combine all ingredients in a small bowl. Yield: about ⅔ cup (serving size: 2½ tablespoons).

CALORIES 26; FAT 0.7g (sat 0.5g, mono 0.2g, poly 0g); PROTEIN 3g; CARB 2.4g; FIBER 0.1g; CHOL 2mg; IRON 0.7mg; SODIUM 84mg; CALC 35mg

ingredient spotlight

A traditional Greek dip and gyro condiment, tzatziki makes a tasty topping for other sandwiches and even hamburgers.

Sweet-Spiked Pork Sandwiches

Prep: 2 minutes • Cook: 25 minutes
Other: 5 minutes

Although the slaw can be served as a side dish with this open-faced sandwich, we enjoyed piling it high on top of the sweet glazed pork as a condiment.

1   (1-pound) pork tenderloin, trimmed
¼   teaspoon salt
¾   teaspoon coarsely ground black pepper
Cooking spray
1   cup cola
¼   cup bourbon
2½   tablespoons country-style Dijon mustard
4   (0.8-ounce) Italian bread slices, crusty Chicago style, lightly toasted

1. Sprinkle pork evenly with salt and pepper; coat with cooking spray. Heat a large nonstick skillet over medium-high heat. Coat pan with cooking spray. Add pork; cook 3 minutes or until browned on 1 side.
2. Reduce heat to medium-low; turn pork over. Cover and cook 17 minutes or until a thermometer registers 160° (slightly pink). Remove pork from pan. Cover and let stand 5 minutes.
3. While pork is standing, increase heat to medium-high, and add cola and bourbon to pan. Bring to a boil; cook 7 minutes or until mixture is reduced to ¼ cup.
4. Spread mustard evenly on 1 side of bread slices. Cut pork into thin slices. Add pork slices to sauce, tossing to coat. Arrange pork slices over mustard. Spoon sauce evenly over pork. Yield: 4 servings (serving size: 1 open-faced sandwich).

CALORIES 275; FAT 4.7g (sat 1.5g, mono 1.9g, poly 0.7g); PROTEIN 25.9g; CARB 20.1g; FIBER 0.7g; CHOL 74mg; IRON 2.1mg; SODIUM 562mg; CALC 27mg

serve with:
Spicy Celery Seed Coleslaw

Prep: 5 minutes

3   tablespoons light mayonnaise
1   tablespoon sugar
1   tablespoon water
1   teaspoon cider vinegar
½   teaspoon celery seed
⅛   teaspoon crushed red pepper
⅛   teaspoon salt
¼   freshly ground black pepper
3   cups cabbage-and-carrot coleslaw

1. Combine all ingredients, except coleslaw, in a medium bowl; stir with a whisk. Add coleslaw; toss well. Yield: 4 servings (serving size: about ⅔ cup).

CALORIES 61; FAT 3.8g (sat 0.8g, mono 1g, poly 2g); PROTEIN 0.4g; CARB 6g; FIBER 0.8g; CHOL 4mg; IRON 0.3mg; SODIUM 169mg; CALC 20mg

Sweet-Spiked Pork Sandwiches

Grilled Pork Sliders with Honey BBQ Sauce

Prep: 5 minutes • Cook: 24 minutes
Other: 5 minutes

Crisp on the outside, soft on the inside, Herbed Sweet Potato Fries are the perfect side to pair with a barbecue pork sandwich. We guarantee you can't eat just one. And that's a good thing: Sweet potatoes are rich in beta carotene, vitamin C, and vitamin E.

½   cup bottled barbecue sauce
2   tablespoons dark rum
2   tablespoons honey
1   (1-pound) pork tenderloin, trimmed
Cooking spray
4   (1.8-ounce) white-wheat hamburger buns

1. Preheat grill to medium-high heat.
2. Combine barbecue sauce, rum, and honey in a medium saucepan; bring to a boil. Cook 2 minutes or until reduced to ½ cup. Reserve ¼ cup sauce for serving. Use remaining ¼ cup sauce for basting.
3. Place pork on grill rack coated with cooking spray; grill 8 minutes. Turn and baste pork with sauce; cook 8 minutes. Turn and baste with sauce. Cook 4 minutes or until a thermometer registers 160° (slightly pink). Let stand 5 minutes; cut into thin slices.
4. Place buns, cut sides down, on grill rack; toast 1 minute. Place 3 ounces pork on bottom half of each bun. Spoon 1 tablespoon sauce over each serving; top with remaining halves of buns. Yield: 4 servings (serving size: 1 slider).

CALORIES 319; FAT 6g (sat 1.8g, mono 1.5g, poly 1.4g); PROTEIN 27.6g; CARB 39.2g; FIBER 5.1g; CHOL 63mg; IRON 4mg; SODIUM 520mg; CALC 261mg

Grilled Pork Sliders with Honey BBQ Sauce

serve with:
Herbed Sweet Potato Fries

Prep: 3 minutes • Cook: 14 minutes

2   cups frozen sweet potato fries
Cooking spray
1   teaspoon chopped fresh thyme
1   teaspoon chopped fresh rosemary
¼   teaspoon salt
¼   teaspoon freshly ground black pepper

1. Preheat oven to 425°.
2. Arrange fries in a single layer on a rimmed baking sheet coated with cooking spray. Coat fries evenly with cooking spray; sprinkle remaining ingredients evenly over fries, tossing to coat.
3. Bake at 425° for 14 minutes or until golden. Yield: 4 servings (serving size: ½ cup).

CALORIES 86; FAT 3g (sat 1.3g, mono 0g, poly 0.1g); PROTEIN 1.2g; CARB 13.8g; FIBER 1.8g; CHOL 0mg; IRON 0.5mg; SODIUM 225mg; CALC 25mg

Avocado BLTs

Prep: 9 minutes • Cook: 5 minutes

A creamy, healthful avocado spread replaces the traditional mayonnaise in this sandwich loaded with bacon, gourmet greens, and juicy, ripe tomatoes.

½   cup Creamy Avocado Spread
8   (1-ounce) slices thin-sliced 15-grain bread, toasted
2   cups gourmet salad greens
4   (¼-inch-thick) slices tomato
8   center-cut bacon slices, cooked

1. Spread 2 tablespoons Creamy Avocado Spread over 4 bread slices. Top each of the 4 bread slices with ½ cup greens, 1 tomato slice, and 2 bacon slices. Top with remaining bread slices. Yield: 4 servings (serving size: 1 sandwich).

CALORIES 272; FAT 12.7g (sat 2.7g, mono 6.7g, poly 1.9g); PROTEIN 12.1g; CARB 31.5g; FIBER 8.5g; CHOL 15mg; IRON 1.7mg; SODIUM 680mg; CALC 45mg

Creamy Avocado Spread

Prep: 4 minutes

1   peeled ripe avocado, coarsely mashed
1   tablespoon fresh lemon juice
1   garlic clove, minced
¼   teaspoon salt
⅛   teaspoon ground red pepper

1. Combine all ingredients in a small bowl, stirring with a fork until blended. Yield: 4 servings (serving size: 2 tablespoons).

CALORIES 59; FAT 5.3g (sat 0.7g, mono 3.3g, poly 0.6g); PROTEIN 0.7g; CARB 3.5g; FIBER 2.4g; CHOL 0mg; IRON 0.2mg; SODIUM 150mg; CALC 6mg

Hawaiian Ham and Pineapple Panini

Prep: 6 minutes • Cook: 2 minutes

These grilled sandwiches balance sweet pineapple preserves against the subtle heat of Dijon mustard. Top with the lettuce after pressing them to keep the green leaves crisp.

¼   cup (2 ounces) ⅓-less-fat cream cheese, softened
1   tablespoon country-style Dijon mustard
4   (2.2-ounce) mini sub rolls
¼   cup pineapple preserves
8   ounces thinly sliced lower-sodium deli ham
4   green leaf lettuce leaves

1. Preheat panini grill.
2. Combine cream cheese and mustard. Spread cream cheese mixture evenly over bottom half of each roll. Spread preserves evenly over top halves of rolls. Top each portion of cheese mixture with 2 ounces ham. Replace roll tops. Grill panini 2 minutes or until toasted. Immediately lift top of each panino and insert 1 lettuce leaf. Serve immediately. Yield: 4 servings (serving size: 1 panino).

CALORIES 351; FAT 9.1g (sat 5g, mono 2.8g, poly 0.6g); PROTEIN 17.2g; CARB 50.9g; FIBER 1.1g; CHOL 70mg; IRON 1.9mg; SODIUM 793mg; CALC 52mg

quick flip

We prefer pineapple preserves, but any other mild fruit preserve will do, such as apricot or peach.

Hawaiian Ham and
Pineapple Panini

Mini Pork Buns

Prep: 8 minutes • Cook: 4 minutes

Find the pillowy-soft steamed Mandarin buns at an Asian grocery store. For the salad, blond sesame seeds will work if you don't have black.

1½   cups thin English cucumber slices
½   cup rice vinegar, divided
8   steamed Mandarin buns
1   cup pulled smoked pork
2   tablespoons hoisin sauce

1. Combine cucumber slices and ¼ cup vinegar in a medium bowl.
2. Microwave buns according to package directions. Split buns, and brush cut sides evenly with 3 tablespoons vinegar from cucumber mixture. Evenly divide and arrange cucumber slices on bottom halves of buns.
3. Combine pork, remaining ¼ cup vinegar, and hoisin sauce in a medium bowl. Spoon 2 tablespoons pork mixture over cucumber slices on each bun; top each with 4 additional cucumber slices. Cover with bun tops. Yield: 4 servings (serving size: 2 buns).

CALORIES 382; FAT 9.5g (sat 2.8g, mono 4.1g, poly 1.8g); PROTEIN 22.8g; CARB 50.7g; FIBER 0.8g; CHOL 34mg; IRON 2.7mg; SODIUM 750mg; CALC 32mg

serve with:
Asian Pear Salad

Prep: 4 minutes

2   cups sliced Asian pears
4   cups mixed baby greens
⅓   cup chopped green onions
⅓   cup light sesame-ginger dressing
1   tablespoon black sesame seeds

1. Combine all ingredients in a large bowl; toss well. Serve immediately, or cover and refrigerate until thoroughly chilled. Yield: 4 servings (serving size: 1 cup).

CALORIES 107; FAT 2.4g (sat 0.2g, mono 0.9g, poly 1g); PROTEIN 1.8g; CARB 21.8g; FIBER 6.9g; CHOL 0mg; IRON 1.2mg; SODIUM 244mg; CALC 34mg

Mini Pork Buns

Pork and Onion Jam Sandwiches

Prep: 5 minutes • Cook: 22 minutes
Other: 5 minutes

You can prepare these hearty and healthy sandwiches open-faced on peasant bread or other European-style bread.

1   (1-pound) pork tenderloin, trimmed
¼   teaspoon salt
½   teaspoon coarsely ground black pepper
Cooking spray
½   cup roasted garlic onion jam
1   tablespoon balsamic vinegar
1   (8.5-ounce) whole-grain baguette, halved
       lengthwise
2   cups baby watercress or baby arugula

1. Preheat broiler.
2. Sprinkle pork evenly with salt and pepper. Coat pork with cooking spray. Heat a large nonstick skillet over medium-high heat. Coat pan with cooking spray. Add pork; cook 3 minutes or until browned on 1 side.
3. Reduce heat to medium-low; turn pork over. Cover and cook 17 minutes or until a thermometer registers 145°, turning pork after 10 minutes. Remove pork from pan. Cover and let stand 5 minutes. Cut pork into ⅓-inch-thick slices.
4. While pork stands, combine onion jam and balsamic vinegar in a small bowl. Place baguette halves, cut sides up, on a baking sheet. Broil 2 minutes or until lightly toasted.
5. Spread onion jam mixture on cut sides of both baguette halves. Arrange pork slices evenly in a single layer on bottom half of baguette. Top pork with watercress. Cover watercress with top half of baguette. Cut sandwich crosswise into 4 equal portions. Yield: 4 servings (serving size: 1 sandwich).

CALORIES 371; FAT 3.2g (sat 0.8g, mono 0.9g, poly 0.4g); PROTEIN 29.2g; CARB 54.1g; FIBER 1.2g; CHOL 74mg; IRON 2.7mg; SODIUM 525mg; CALC 28mg

Pork and Onion Jam
Sandwiches

fix it faster

Cook the pork the night before and reheat right before you are ready to assemble the sandwiches.

Italian Grilled Cheese Sandwiches

Prep: 2 minutes • Cook: 7 minutes

This American classic borrows the flavors of Italy. Sun-dried tomatoes, fresh basil, and fontina cheese perk up this cheese sandwich that can be prepared in a panini grill or on a griddle like a traditional grilled cheese.

2   ounces thinly sliced pancetta
8   (0.8-ounce) slices Chicago Italian bread
¼   teaspoon freshly ground black pepper
4   (¾-ounce) slices fontina cheese
1¾   ounces large sun-dried tomatoes, packed without oil (about 12)
8   large basil leaves
Olive oil–flavored cooking spray

1. Preheat panini grill.
2. Cook pancetta in a large nonstick skillet over medium-high heat 5 minutes, turning often, until crisp. Remove pancetta from pan. Drain on paper towels.
3. Sprinkle 4 bread slices evenly with pepper; top evenly with pancetta, cheese slices, tomatoes, and basil leaves. Top sandwiches with remaining bread slices. Coat outsides of sandwiches with cooking spray.
4. Place sandwiches on panini grill; cook 2 minutes or until golden brown and cheese melts. Cut sandwiches in half, if desired. Yield: 4 servings (serving size: 1 sandwich).

CALORIES 274; FAT 13.1g (sat 6.5g, mono 4.6g, poly 2.1g); PROTEIN 12.4g; CARB 26.5g; FIBER 2g; CHOL 35mg; IRON 2mg; SODIUM 794mg; CALC 161mg

serve with:
Watermelon Salad

Prep: 5 minutes

1   tablespoon white balsamic vinegar
2   teaspoons extra-virgin olive oil
1   teaspoon honey
¼   teaspoon freshly ground black pepper
1   shallot, minced
4   cups baby arugula
2   cups cubed watermelon
¼   cup (1 ounce) crumbled reduced-fat feta cheese

1. Combine first 5 ingredients in a large bowl. Add arugula and watermelon; toss gently to coat. Divide watermelon mixture evenly among 4 plates. Sprinkle each serving with cheese. Yield: 4 servings (serving size: 1½ cups salad and 1 tablespoon cheese).

CALORIES 79; FAT 3.5g (sat 1g, mono 2g, poly 0.5g); PROTEIN 2.6g; CARB 10.7g; FIBER 0.8g; CHOL 2mg; IRON 0.6mg; SODIUM 105mg; CALC 57mg

ingredient spotlight

Fontina is one of the great cheeses of Italy. It has a mild, creamy flavor and melts well, making it super-versatile.

Buffalo Chicken Salad Sandwiches

Prep: 8 minutes

Rotisserie chicken is a cook's best friend. In this variation of chicken salad, we gave it the "wings" treatment complete with hot sauce, blue cheese, and celery. We used 1 tablespoon hot sauce for a medium kick—adjust up or down depending on your heat preference.

½	cup low-fat mayonnaise dressing
3	tablespoons crumbled blue cheese
1	tablespoon hot sauce
¼	teaspoon freshly ground black pepper
2	cups shredded skinless, boneless rotisserie chicken breast
¾	cup chopped celery
5	romaine lettuce leaves
5	(¼-inch-thick) slices tomato
5	(1.8-ounce) white-wheat hamburger buns

1. Combine first 4 ingredients in a medium bowl. Add chicken and celery, tossing to coat. Place 1 lettuce leaf, 1 tomato slice, and ½ cup chicken mixture on bottom half of each bun. Place remaining bun halves on top. Yield: 5 servings (serving size: 1 sandwich).

CALORIES 246; FAT 7.3g (sat 2.1g, mono 1.8g, poly 3.3g); PROTEIN 24g; CARB 26.6g; FIBER 5.8g; CHOL 51mg; IRON 0.8mg; SODIUM 693mg; CALC 354mg

serve with:

Two-Potato Peppered Fries

Prep: 3 minutes • Cook: 20 minutes

1¼	cups frozen Yukon Gold fries with sea salt
1¼	cups frozen sweet potato fries
	Olive oil–flavored cooking spray
1	tablespoon grated fresh Parmesan cheese
1	teaspoon freshly ground mixed peppercorns

1. Preheat oven to 450°.
2. Place fries on a large rimmed baking sheet; coat heavily with cooking spray. Combine cheese and pepper. Sprinkle cheese mixture over fries; toss well.
3. Bake at 450° for 15 minutes. Stir, and bake an additional 5 minutes or until fries are lightly browned. Yield: 5 servings (serving size: ½ cup).

CALORIES 110; FAT 4g (sat 0.4g, mono 2.6g, poly 0.8g); PROTEIN 2.1g; CARB 17g; FIBER 1.9g; CHOL 1mg; IRON 0.7mg; SODIUM 143mg; CALC 35mg

fix it faster

Using a precooked rotisserie chicken makes this sandwich extra easy and fast, although any leftover cooked chicken will work.

Greek Chicken Sandwich with Lemon-Feta Spread

Prep: 10 minutes

Oregano, lemon, and feta cheese brighten the flavor of deli-convenient chicken in this quick Greek-themed sandwich.

Lemon-Feta Spread
4   (1.5-ounce) whole-grain white sandwich thins
2   cups bagged baby spinach leaves
8   ounces thinly sliced lemon pepper roasted chicken breast (such as Boar's Head)
¼   cup thinly sliced red onion

1. Prepare Lemon-Feta Spread.
2. Spread 2 tablespoons Lemon-Feta Spread evenly on cut sides of sandwich thins. Layer spinach, chicken, and onion evenly on bottoms of sandwich thins. Top with sandwich thin tops. Yield: 4 servings (serving size: 1 sandwich).

CALORIES 227; FAT 7.4g (sat 1.1g, mono 3.6g, poly 2.6g); PROTEIN 18.9g; CARB 24.9g; FIBER 5.7g; CHOL 37mg; IRON 1.9mg; SODIUM 782mg; CALC 81mg

Lemon-Feta Spread

Prep: 5 minutes

¼   cup canola mayonnaise
3   tablespoons crumbled reduced-fat feta cheese
2   teaspoons grated lemon rind
1   teaspoon minced fresh oregano
½   teaspoon freshly ground black pepper

1. Combine all ingredients in a small bowl. Yield: ½ cup (serving size: 2 tablespoons).

CALORIES 60; FAT 5.4g (sat 0.8g, mono 2.9g, poly 1.6g); PROTEIN 1.4g; CARB 0.6g; FIBER 0.3g; CHOL 2mg; IRON 0mg; SODIUM 178mg; CALC 19mg

Lemongrass Chicken Lettuce Wraps

Prep: 9 minutes

What gives this wrap its charm is the fact that it's a sandwich and a salad rolled up into a convenient, hand-held package. If you want to make a lunch-box version, pack the lettuce, peanuts, and cilantro separate from the filling and assemble at lunchtime.

3   cups shredded cooked chicken breast
1   cup matchstick-cut carrots
Lemongrass Vinaigrette
12 Boston lettuce leaves
¼   cup chopped dry-roasted peanuts
Cilantro leaves (optional)

1. Combine first 3 ingredients in a medium bowl. Divide mixture evenly among lettuce leaves. Sprinkle with peanuts and, if desired, cilantro leaves. Yield: 4 servings (serving size: 3 wraps).

CALORIES 249; FAT 9.6g (sat 1.9g, mono 4.5g, poly 3g); PROTEIN 34.9g; CARB 5.2g; FIBER 1.2g; CHOL 89mg; IRON 1.6mg; SODIUM 403mg; CALC 34mg

Lemongrass Vinaigrette

Prep: 5 minutes

2   tablespoons fresh lime juice
1   tablespoon lemongrass paste
1   tablespoon chopped fresh cilantro
2   teaspoons canola oil
2   teaspoons fish sauce
1   teaspoon lower-sodium soy sauce
2   garlic cloves, minced

1. Combine all ingredients in a small bowl. Yield: ⅓ cup (serving size: about 1 tablespoon).

CALORIES 29; FAT 2.7g (sat 0.3g, mono 1.3g, poly 1g); PROTEIN 0.3g; CARB 1.8g; FIBER 0.1g; CHOL 0mg; IRON 0.1mg; SODIUM 272mg; CALC 3mg

Lemongrass Chicken
Lettuce Wraps

Mega Crostini Chicken Sandwiches with Pesto Mayo

Prep: 6 minutes • Cook: 1 minute

Cut the ciabatta on a sharp diagonal for these big, open-faced chicken sandwiches. A pesto-laced mayonnaise ramps up the flavor of this hearty sandwich.

4	(1-ounce) slices diagonally cut ciabatta, toasted
	Olive oil–flavored cooking spray
	Pesto Mayo
8	ounces thinly sliced lower-sodium deli chicken
2	(6-ounce) ripe tomatoes, cut into 4 slices each
½	cup alfalfa sprouts

1. Lightly coat ciabatta slices with cooking spray; spread Pesto Mayo evenly on 1 side of each slice. Place chicken evenly over pesto. Top evenly with tomato slices and sprouts. Yield: 4 servings (serving size: 1 sandwich).

CALORIES 208; FAT 8.1g (sat 1.6g, mono 3.3g, poly 3.2g); PROTEIN 16.9g; CARB 21.4g; FIBER 1.6g; CHOL 34mg; IRON 1.7mg; SODIUM 795mg; CALC 14mg

Pesto Mayo

Prep: 2 minutes

3	tablespoons light mayonnaise
1	tablespoon commercial pesto
¼	teaspoon ground red pepper

1. Combine all ingredients in a small bowl. Cover and chill. Yield: ¼ cup (serving size: 1 tablespoon).

CALORIES 60; FAT 6g (sat 1.3g, mono 1.9g, poly 2.7g); PROTEIN 0.3g; CARB 1.5g; FIBER 0g; CHOL 4mg; IRON 0.1mg; SODIUM 151mg; CALC 4mg

Chicken Marinara Panini

Prep: 9 minutes • Cook: 3 minutes

Serve this Italian-flavored sandwich with a bowl of fruit or a light side salad. Use home-cooked chicken breast if you're keeping an eye on sodium.

⅓	cup marinara sauce
8	(1-ounce) slices crusty Chicago-style Italian bread
16	basil leaves
2	cups shredded cooked chicken breast (about 8½ ounces)
½	cup (2 ounces) preshredded part-skim mozzarella cheese
½	cup (2 ounces) grated fresh Parmesan cheese
	Olive oil–flavored cooking spray

1. Preheat panini grill.
2. Spread marinara sauce evenly over 4 bread slices. Top evenly with basil leaves, shredded chicken, cheeses, and remaining bread slices. Coat outsides of sandwiches with cooking spray.
3. Place sandwiches on panini grill; cook 3 minutes or until golden and cheese melts. Cut panini in half before serving. Yield: 4 servings (serving size: 1 panino).

CALORIES 365; FAT 10.6g (sat 4.6g, mono 3.1g, poly 1.9g); PROTEIN 34.4g; CARB 30.9g; FIBER 2.1g; CHOL 77mg; IRON 2.7mg; SODIUM 715mg; CALC 287mg

Chicken Marinara
Panini

Shaved Chicken, Apple, and Cheddar
Sandwiches with Basil Mayo

Shaved Chicken, Apple, and Cheddar Sandwiches with Basil Mayo

Prep: 5 minutes • Cook: 8 minutes

Shards of crisp apples and sliced cheddar cheese balance sweetness with bite in this flavorful chicken sandwich. Have the deli shave the chicken into paper-thin slices.

4	(1.5-ounce) frozen focaccia rolls with Asiago and Parmesan cheese

Basil Mayo

6	ounces shaved deli maple-glazed roasted chicken breast
1	medium Granny Smith apple, thinly sliced
4	(0.7-ounce) slices reduced-fat sharp cheddar cheese

1. Bake focaccia according to package directions. Cut rolls horizontally in half.
2. Prepare Basil Mayo. Spread 1 tablespoon Basil Mayo evenly over cut sides of bread halves.
3. Layer roll bottoms evenly with chicken and apple; top with cheese and roll tops. Yield: 4 servings (serving size: 1 sandwich).

CALORIES 266; FAT 8.1g (sat 3.1g, mono 2.1g, poly 2.9g); PROTEIN 19.2g; CARB 31.1g; FIBER 1.7g; CHOL 40mg; IRON 0.9mg; SODIUM 788mg; CALC 175mg

Basil Mayo

Prep: 3 minutes

¼	cup low-fat mayonnaise dressing
1½	tablespoons chopped fresh basil
1	teaspoon Dijon mustard
½	teaspoon freshly ground black pepper

1. Combine all ingredients in a small bowl. Yield: ⅓ cup (serving size: 1 tablespoon).

CALORIES 17; FAT 1g (sat 0g, mono 0.2g, poly 0.8g); PROTEIN 0.1g; CARB 2.5g; FIBER 0.1g; CHOL 0mg; IRON 0.1mg; SODIUM 160mg; CALC 3mg

Open-Faced Chicken and Pear Sandwiches

Prep: 5 minutes • Cook: 2 minutes

2	tablespoons Dijon mustard
6	(1.2-ounce) slices rye pumpernickel bread
12	ounces shaved deli, lower-sodium chicken breast
1	ripe pear, sliced
6	(0.5-ounce) slices Swiss cheese

1. Preheat broiler.
2. Spread 1 teaspoon mustard on each bread slice. Top each with 2 ounces chicken. Top evenly with pear and cheese.
3. Broil 2 minutes or until cheese melts. Serve immediately. Yield: 6 servings (serving size: 1 sandwich).

CALORIES 192; FAT 5.3g (sat 2.6g, mono 1.3g, poly 0.5g); PROTEIN 19.4g; CARB 19.7g; FIBER 2.6g; CHOL 43mg; IRON 1.2mg; SODIUM 767mg; CALC 132mg

quick flip

Apple would be a good substitute for the pear, as would cheddar cheese instead of Swiss.

California Smoked Chicken Sandwiches

Prep: 5 minutes • Cook: 5 minutes

This California favorite begins with pulled chicken and ends with a smoky paprika aioli. In between are creamy avocado and tomato slices. If the chicken is already smoky, use regular paprika in the aioli.

12   (0.7-ounce) slices sourdough bread
Smoked Paprika Aioli
6   (¼-inch-thick) slices tomato
2   cups pulled skinless smoked chicken
1   medium avocado, cut into 12 slices

1. Toast bread. While bread toasts, prepare Smoked Paprika Aioli.
2. Spread aioli evenly on 6 bread slices. Layer tomato, chicken, and avocado over aioli. Top with remaining bread slices. Yield: 6 servings (serving size: 1 sandwich).

CALORIES 263; FAT 8.5g (sat 1.8g, mono 3.6g, poly 2.9g); PROTEIN 19.9g; CARB 25.8g; FIBER 2.5g; CHOL 42mg; IRON 2.3mg; SODIUM 356mg; CALC 32mg

Smoked Paprika Aioli

Prep: 5 minutes

3   tablespoons light mayonnaise
1   tablespoon finely chopped green onions
1   teaspoon smoked paprika
½   teaspoon grated lemon rind
1   garlic clove, minced

1. Combine all ingredients in a small bowl, stirring with a whisk. Cover and chill until ready to serve. Yield: ¼ cup (serving size: 2 teaspoons).

CALORIES 30; FAT 2.5g (sat 0.4g, mono 0.4g, poly 1.6g); PROTEIN 0.1g; CARB 0.9g; FIBER 0.1g; CHOL 3mg; IRON 0mg; SODIUM 60mg; CALC 2mg

ingredient spotlight

Smoked paprika is made from sweet bell peppers that are dried in the sun before smoked over wood fires and ground to a fine powder. Use this smoky seasoning in your favorite spice rubs.

California Smoked
Chicken Sandwiches

Grilled Chicken Sausages
with Caraway Slaw

4. Divide sausages evenly among buns. Top sausages evenly with slaw. Yield: 4 servings (serving size: 1 hot dog).

CALORIES 340; FAT 12.8g (sat 2.4g, mono 5.3g, poly 5g); PROTEIN 19.7g; CARB 36.8g; FIBER 1g; CHOL 88mg; IRON 2.3mg; SODIUM 740mg; CALC 16mg

Caraway Slaw

Prep: 6 minutes • Cook: 1 minute

1	teaspoon caraway seeds
1	tablespoon chopped fresh parsley
2	tablespoons light mayonnaise
2	teaspoons cider vinegar
½	teaspoon sugar
1	cup thinly sliced red cabbage
1	cup packaged angel hair slaw

1. Cook caraway seeds in a small skillet over medium-high heat, stirring constantly, 1 to 2 minutes or until fragrant. Combine seeds, parsley, and next 3 ingredients in a medium bowl. Add cabbage and slaw, tossing to coat. Cover and chill until ready to serve. Yield: 4 servings (serving size: ½ cup).

CALORIES 41; FAT 2.6g (sat 0.4g, mono 0.6g, poly 1.5g); PROTEIN 0.7g; CARB 4g; FIBER 1g; CHOL 3mg; IRON 0.3mg; SODIUM 70mg; CALC 16mg

fix it faster

Prepared produce, such as angel hair coleslaw, can shave minutes off your prep time. Look for bags of angel hair coleslaw near the bagged lettuce in the produce section of your supermarket. Always check the freshness date, and look closely at the cut edges for signs of deterioration.

Grilled Chicken Sausages with Caraway Slaw

Prep: 7 minutes • Cook: 6 minutes

Toasting the caraway seeds releases their aromatic oils and revs up the flavor of the colorful slaw in these updated hot dogs.

1	(12-ounce) package chicken apple sausage
	Cooking spray
4	(1.7-ounce) bakery-style hot dog buns
	Caraway Slaw

1. Preheat grill to medium-high heat.
2. Place sausages on grill rack coated with cooking spray. Grill 6 minutes or until sausages reach desired degree of doneness, turning once. During last minute of grilling, open buns and place, cut sides down, on grill rack. Toast 1 minute.
3. While sausages cook, prepare Caraway Slaw.

Pulled Chicken Sandwiches
with White Barbecue Sauce

Pulled Chicken Sandwiches with White Barbecue Sauce

Prep: 5 minutes

To make the sauce ahead, combine all the ingredients, store it in the refrigerator, and bring it to room temperature before serving.

2   cups packaged angel hair slaw
6   (1.8-ounce) white-wheat hamburger buns
3   cups shredded rotisserie chicken
¾   cup White Barbecue Sauce
12 hamburger dill pickle slices

1. Place ⅓ cup slaw on bottom half of each bun; top each with ½ cup chicken.
2. Top chicken with 2 tablespoons White Barbecue Sauce, 2 pickle slices, and a bun top. Yield: 6 servings (serving size: 1 sandwich).

CALORIES 379; FAT 8.6g (sat 2g, mono 1.9g, poly 2.8g); PROTEIN 52.3g; CARB 25.5g; FIBER 5.7g; CHOL 129mg; IRON 1.6mg; SODIUM 503mg; CALC 332mg

White Barbecue Sauce

Prep: 5 minutes

1   cup low-fat mayonnaise
¾   cup cider vinegar
2   tablespoons fresh lemon juice
1   tablespoon freshly ground black pepper
¼   teaspoon ground red pepper

1. Combine all ingredients in a small bowl, stirring with a whisk. Cover and store in refrigerator up to a week. Yield: 1¾ cups (serving size: 2 tablespoons).

CALORIES 22; FAT 1.2g (sat 0g, mono 0g, poly 0.6g); PROTEIN 0.1g; CARB 2.9g; FIBER 0.1g; CHOL 0mg; IRON 0.1mg; SODIUM 149mg; CALC 3mg

ingredient spotlight

White Barbecue Sauce, widely used in Alabama-style barbecue, is known for its vinegary taste and its use of mayonnaise as its base, rather than the usual tomato sauce.

Southwestern Chicken Lettuce Wraps with Spicy Chipotle Dipping Sauce

Prep: 7 minutes • Cook: 90 seconds

Crisp iceberg lettuce cradles a Southwest-inspired mix of rice, beans, chicken, and salsa. Find fresh salsa in the produce section of your supermarket. It generally has 50 percent less sodium than bottled salsa, and it tastes like it's homemade.

1	(8.8-ounce) package microwaveable precooked whole-grain brown rice
2	cups shredded rotisserie chicken
¾	cup fresh salsa
⅓	cup chopped green onion (about 3)
1	(15-ounce) can reduced-sodium black beans, rinsed and drained
12	iceberg lettuce leaves

Spicy Chipotle Dipping Sauce

1. Prepare rice according to package directions. Place rice in a large bowl. Stir in chicken and next 3 ingredients. Spoon chicken mixture evenly in center of lettuce leaves. Fold in edges of leaves; roll up, and secure with wooden picks. Serve with Spicy Chipotle Dipping Sauce. Yield: 6 servings (serving size: 2 wraps and 2 tablespoons sauce).

CALORIES 211; FAT 5.3g (sat 2.1g, mono 1.3g, poly 0.5g); PROTEIN 18.6g; CARB 21.4g; FIBER 3.3g; CHOL 48mg; IRON 1.6mg; SODIUM 183mg; CALC 52mg

Spicy Chipotle Dipping Sauce

Prep: 2 minutes

½	cup reduced-fat sour cream
1	tablespoon chopped fresh cilantro
1	tablespoon fresh lime juice
½	teaspoon ground cumin
¼	teaspoon chipotle chili powder

1. Combine all ingredients in a small bowl. Yield: ¾ cup (serving size: 2 tablespoons).

CALORIES 28; FAT 2.4g (sat 1.5g, mono 0.7g, poly 0.1g); PROTEIN 0.6g; CARB 1.1g; FIBER 0.1g; CHOL 8mg; IRON 0.1mg; SODIUM 12mg; CALC 23mg

Southwestern Chicken Lettuce Wraps with Spicy Chipotle Dipping Sauce

Greek Chicken Salad Pitas

Greek Chicken Salad Pitas

Prep: 11 minutes

You'll find prepared hummus in a variety of flavors. We used roasted red bell pepper hummus for this sandwich, but either spicy three-pepper or artichoke-and-garlic hummus would make a good choice, too. Round out your meal with a refreshing side of mixed melon.

2	cups sliced romaine lettuce
1	cup chopped roasted chicken breast
⅔	cup diced seeded cucumber
¼	cup thinly sliced red onion
¼	cup (1 ounce) crumbled feta cheese
2	tablespoons fresh lemon juice
2	tablespoons olive oil
¼	teaspoon salt
¼	teaspoon freshly ground black pepper
6	tablespoons roasted red bell pepper hummus
2	(6-inch) whole-wheat pitas, cut in half

1. Combine lettuce and next 4 ingredients in a large bowl. Add lemon juice, olive oil, salt, and pepper; toss gently.

2. Spread 1½ tablespoons hummus inside each pita half; spoon salad mixture evenly into halves. Serve immediately. Yield: 4 servings (serving size: 1 pita half).

CALORIES 278; FAT 13.5g (sat 2.9g, mono 7.3g, poly 1.8g); PROTEIN 16.7g; CARB 24.6g; FIBER 4.1g; CHOL 38mg; IRON 2mg; SODIUM 669mg; CALC 71mg

fix it faster

To make this meal even faster, forgo rinsing, slicing, and chopping the fresh vegetables and fruit yourself. Look in the produce section for packaged torn romaine lettuce and containers of presliced red onion, prechopped cucumber, and prechopped mixed melon. Sometimes these items may be more expensive, but the trade-off is time saved from prepping and cleaning.

Avocado Chicken Salad Sandwiches

Prep: 7 minutes • Cook: 4 minutes

Avocado gives this chicken salad a rich, creamy texture as well as a healthy dose of monounsaturated fat, which protects against heart disease.

3	cups (½-inch) cubed cooked chicken breast
¼	cup light mayonnaise
2	tablespoons chopped fresh cilantro
¼	teaspoon salt
⅛	teaspoon freshly ground black pepper
1	cup (½-inch) cubed avocado (about 1)
4	green leaf lettuce leaves
8	whole-wheat bread slices, toasted

1. Combine first 5 ingredients in a large bowl. Gently stir avocado into chicken mixture until combined.
2. Place 1 lettuce leaf onto each of 4 bread slices. Spoon chicken mixture evenly onto each lettuce leaf. Top with remaining bread slices. Yield: 4 servings (serving size: 1 sandwich).

CALORIES 364; FAT 16.4g (sat 2.7g, mono 7.9g, poly 3g); PROTEIN 41.4g; CARB 24.1g; FIBER 11.9g; CHOL 95mg; IRON 4.4mg; SODIUM 647mg; CALC 322mg

serve with:
Herbed Tomato-Cucumber Salad

Prep: 6 minutes

1	tablespoon olive oil
2	teaspoons champagne vinegar
¼	teaspoons salt
¼	teaspoon Italian seasoning
⅛	teaspoon freshly ground black pepper
½	teaspoon minced garlic
2	medium tomatoes, cut into wedges
1	cup cucumber slices
¼	cup diced sweet onion

1. Combine first 6 ingredients in a medium bowl, stirring with a whisk. Stir in remaining ingredients. Serve immediately. Yield: 4 servings (serving size: ¾ cup).

CALORIES 51; FAT 3.6g (sat 0.5g, mono 2.5g, poly 0.4g); PROTEIN 0.9g; CARB 4.6g; FIBER 1.1g; CHOL 0mg; IRON 0.3mg; SODIUM 150mg; CALC 14mg

Avocado Chicken Salad Sandwiches

Grilled Chicken and Tomato Pesto Baguettes

Prep: 7 minutes • Cook: 8 minutes

1	(8.5-ounce) thin whole-wheat baguette
2	(8-ounce) skinless, boneless chicken breast halves
¼	teaspoon salt
⅛	teaspoon freshly ground black pepper
1	red bell pepper, seeded and quartered

Cooking spray

¼	cup sun-dried tomato pesto
4	curly leaf lettuce leaves
4	(0.7-ounce) slices low-fat Swiss cheese, cut in half lengthwise

1. Preheat grill to medium-high heat.
2. Cut baguette in half lengthwise. Hollow out top half of baguette, leaving a ½-inch border; reserve torn bread for another use. Set aside.

3. Place chicken breast halves between 2 large sheets of heavy-duty plastic wrap; pound to ½-inch thickness using a meat mallet or small heavy skillet. Sprinkle chicken with salt and pepper.
4. Flatten bell pepper quarters with hands. Coat chicken breasts and bell pepper quarters with cooking spray; place on grill rack. Cover and grill 8 minutes or until chicken is done and bell peppers are tender, turning once. Place cut sides of baguette halves on grill during last 2 minutes of grilling to lightly toast. Cut each chicken breast in half crosswise.
5. Spread both cut halves of baguette evenly with pesto. Top bottom half with lettuce leaves, chicken breast halves, bell pepper quarters, and cheese slices. Place top half of baguette on top of cheese. Cut crosswise into 4 equal portions. Yield: 4 servings (serving size: ¼ of baguette).

CALORIES 345; FAT 7.2g (sat 3.2g, mono 1.8g, poly 1.9g); PROTEIN 39.3g; CARB 24.7g; FIBER 1.7g; CHOL 66mg; IRON 2.4mg; SODIUM 748mg; CALC 271mg

Grilled Chicken and
Tomato Pesto Baguettes

Grilled BBQ Chicken Sandwiches with Spicy Avocado Spread

Prep: 2 minutes • Cook: 6 minutes

The Spicy Avocado Spread is bursting with flavor, but if time is short, use prepared guacamole or a few slices of fresh avocado to still enjoy the benefits of the avocado's healthful plant fats. Serve with baked potato chips. If you prefer your bun toasted, place it on the grill during the last minute of cooking.

4	(3-ounce) skinless, boneless chicken breast cutlets
¼	cup barbecue sauce
Cooking spray	
4	(0.7-ounce) slices 2% reduced-fat sharp Cheddar cheese
Green leaf lettuce leaves (optional)	
Tomato slices (optional)	
4	(1.8-ounce) white-wheat hamburger buns
Spicy Avocado Spread	

1. Preheat grill to medium-high heat.
2. Brush both sides of chicken with barbecue sauce. Place chicken on grill rack coated with cooking spray. Grill 3 to 4 minutes on each side or until chicken is done, placing 1 cheese slice on each chicken breast during last minute of cooking.
3. Place lettuce and tomato, if desired, on bottom half of each bun; add 1 chicken breast. Top each with about 2½ tablespoons Spicy Avocado Spread. Place remaining bun halves on top. Yield: 4 servings (serving size: 1 sandwich and about 2½ tablespoons Spicy Avocado Spread).

CALORIES 368; FAT 16g (sat 5g, mono 5.1g, poly 2.3g); PROTEIN 31.9g; CARB 31.8g; FIBER 7.8g; CHOL 64mg; IRON 3.9mg; SODIUM 678mg; CALC 423mg

Grilled BBQ Chicken Sandwiches with Spicy Avocado Spread

Spicy Avocado Spread

Prep: 6 minutes

1	ripe peeled avocado, coarsely mashed
1	tablespoon minced jalapeño pepper
1	tablespoon minced red onion
1½	tablespoons fresh lime juice
1	garlic clove, pressed
2	teaspoons minced fresh cilantro
⅛	teaspoon salt

1. Combine all ingredients in a small bowl, stirring well. Yield: ½ cup plus 3 tablespoons (serving size: 1 tablespoon).

CALORIES 31; FAT 3g (sat 0.5g, mono 1.8g, poly 0.4g); PROTEIN 0.4g; CARB 1.8g; FIBER 1g; CHOL 0mg; IRON 0.2mg; SODIUM 28mg; CALC 3mg

Grilled Chicken and Pineapple Sandwiches

Prep: 6 minutes • Cook: 10 minutes

Tickle your palate with a taste of the tropics. Pineapple has a natural juiciness that gives this sandwich an irresistible taste. The fruit also offers a healthy reason for indulging: It's a good source of vitamin C.

4   (6-ounce) skinless, boneless chicken breast halves
½   teaspoon salt
¼   teaspoon freshly ground black pepper
Cooking spray
¼   cup fresh lime juice (about 2 limes)
4   (½-inch-thick) slices fresh pineapple
4   (1.5-ounce) whole-wheat hamburger buns, toasted
Light mayonnaise (optional)
4   large basil leaves

1. Preheat grill to medium-high heat.
2. Sprinkle chicken evenly with salt and pepper. Place chicken on grill rack coated with cooking spray; grill 5 to 6 minutes on each side or until done, brushing occasionally with lime juice. Grill pineapple 2 to 3 minutes on each side or until browned.
3. Spread mayonnaise on bottom halves of buns, if desired. Top each with 1 chicken breast half, 1 pineapple slice, 1 basil leaf, and 1 bun top. Serve immediately. Yield: 4 servings (serving size: 1 sandwich).

CALORIES 333; FAT 4g (sat 0.9g, mono 1g, poly 1.4g); PROTEIN 43.4g; CARB 30.5g; FIBER 4.1g; CHOL 99mg; IRON 2.5mg; SODIUM 608mg; CALC 75mg

serve with:
Guilt-Free Piña Coladas

Prep: 9 minutes

⅓   cup fat-free sweetened condensed milk
⅓   cup thawed orange-pineapple-apple juice concentrate, undiluted
1   (21-ounce) package frozen diced pineapple
½   cup white rum
¼   teaspoon coconut extract
Pineapple wedges (optional)

1. Place half of each ingredient except pineapple wedges in a blender; process until smooth. Pour into a pitcher. Repeat procedure. Pour into glasses, and garnish with pineapple wedges, if desired. Serve immediately. Yield: 4 servings (serving size: about ¾ cup).

CALORIES 263; FAT 0.1g (sat 0g, mono 0g, poly 0.1g); PROTEIN 2.8g; CARB 47.1g; FIBER 2.1g; CHOL 3mg; IRON 0.4mg; SODIUM 30mg; CALC 86mg

Grilled Chicken and Pineapple Sandwiches

Hot Turkey and Strawberry Sandwiches

1. Preheat broiler.
2. Place bread slices on a baking sheet; spread each slice with 1 tablespoon cream cheese. Place 2 ounces turkey over cream cheese on each of 4 slices. Broil 4 minutes or until cream cheese melts and turkey is thoroughly heated.
3. Slice and place 2 strawberries over turkey on each sandwich half. Top with remaining bread slices, cheese sides down.
4. Cut sandwiches in half, and serve immediately. Yield: 4 servings (serving size: 1 sandwich).

CALORIES 263; FAT 8.2g (sat 4.2g, mono 3g, poly 1g); PROTEIN 19.9g; CARB 23.2g; FIBER 3.7g; CHOL 41mg; IRON 2.2mg; SODIUM 628mg; CALC 62mg

Hot Turkey and Strawberry Sandwiches

Prep: 6 minutes • Cook: 4 minutes

Juicy strawberries dress up this cheesy hot turkey sandwich. And the flavor mix doesn't stop there. All that goodness is sandwiched between cinnamon-raisin bread for a perfect pairing with Mint Limeade.

8   (1-ounce) slices whole-wheat cinnamon-raisin bread
½   cup (4 ounces) tub-style ⅓-less-fat cream cheese
8   ounces thinly sliced 47% lower-sodium skinless turkey
8   large strawberries

serve with:
Mint Limeade

Prep: 4 minutes

4   cups water, divided
⅓   cup sugar
¼   cup mint leaves
1   lime, cut into quarters
Ice cubes
Mint leaves (optional)

1. Place 2 cups water and next 3 ingredients in a blender; process 1 minute or until mixture is pureed. Pour lime mixture through a sieve into a large pitcher. Stir in remaining 2 cups water. Pour limeade over ice cubes in glasses, and, if desired, garnish with mint leaves. Yield: 4 servings (serving size: about 1 cup).

CALORIES 71; FAT 0g (sat 0g, mono 0g, poly 0g); PROTEIN 0.1g; CARB 18.7g; FIBER 0.6g; CHOL 0mg; IRON 0.1mg; SODIUM 1mg; CALC 4mg

Turkey Cobb Salad Roll-Ups

Prep: 14 minutes

2	cups shredded romaine lettuce
1	cup chopped seeded tomato (1 medium)
¼	cup chopped green onions (2 medium)
3	tablespoons blue cheese–flavored yogurt dressing
½	teaspoon freshly ground black pepper
8	ounces thinly sliced roast turkey
1	avocado, diced
4	(1.9-ounce) multigrain flatbreads with flax

1. Combine first 7 ingredients in a medium bowl. Spoon turkey mixture evenly onto flatbreads; roll up. Yield: 4 servings (serving size: 1 roll-up).

CALORIES 301; FAT 13.3g (sat 2.3g, mono 6.4g, poly 3.4g); PROTEIN 28.8g; CARB 25.1g; FIBER 12g; CHOL 53mg; IRON 1.9mg; SODIUM 381mg; CALC 83mg

serve with:
Carrot Slaw

Prep: 5 minutes

2½	tablespoons fresh lemon juice
1	tablespoon olive oil
1	tablespoon honey
⅛	teaspoon salt
¼	teaspoon freshly ground black pepper
3½	cups grated carrot (about 1 pound)
1½	cups diced Granny Smith apple (1 small)

1. Combine first 5 ingredients in a medium bowl, stirring with a whisk. Add carrot and apple; toss well. Yield: 4 servings (serving size: about 1 cup).

CALORIES 115; FAT 3.6g (sat 0.5g, mono 2.5g, poly 0.5g); PROTEIN 1.1g; CARB 22g; FIBER 3.9g; CHOL 0mg; IRON 0.5mg; SODIUM 140mg; CALC 36mg

Turkey Cobb Sandwiches

Prep: 10 minutes

Bookend the traditional ingredients of a Cobb salad with two slices of fresh wheat bread, and you've got a flavorful Turkey Cobb Sandwich. As an added convenience, you can now purchase boiled eggs at your supermarket. If you can't find them in your local store, hard-cook your own a day ahead. It will make preparation for this recipe quick and easy. Serve the sandwich with waffle-cut carrot chips.

2	tablespoons reduced-fat mayonnaise
8	(1-ounce) slices double-fiber wheat bread, toasted
4	small green leaf lettuce leaves
4	tomato slices
6	ounces shaved deli turkey
1	peeled avocado, sliced
4	precooked bacon slices
2	hard-cooked large eggs, sliced

1. Spread ½ tablespoon mayonnaise evenly over each of 4 bread slices. Layer each evenly with lettuce and remaining ingredients. Top with remaining 4 bread slices. Cut each sandwich in half diagonally. Yield: 4 servings (serving size: 1 sandwich).

CALORIES 319; FAT 14.9g (sat 2.7g, mono 5.9g, poly 1.9g); PROTEIN 22.1g; CARB 32.1g; FIBER 12.9g; CHOL 126mg; IRON 3.5mg; SODIUM 712mg; CALC 25mg

Turkey Cobb Sandwiches

Turkey Burgers with Cranberry-Peach Chutney

Prep: 5 minutes • Cook: 6 minutes

1	pound ground turkey breast
1	large egg white
¼	teaspoon salt
¼	teaspoon freshly ground black pepper
Cooking spray	
4	lettuce leaves
4	(1½-ounce) whole-wheat hamburger buns
Cranberry-Peach Chutney	

1. Combine turkey and next 3 ingredients. Divide turkey mixture into 4 equal portions, shaping each into a ½-inch-thick patty.
2. Heat a large nonstick skillet over medium heat; coat pan with cooking spray. Add patties; cook 3 to 4 minutes on each side or until a thermometer registers 165°.
3. Place 1 lettuce leaf on bottom half of each bun; top each with 1 burger. Spread 2 tablespoons Cranberry-Peach Chutney on inside of each bun top; place each on top of 1 burger. Yield: 4 servings (serving size: 1 burger).

CALORIES 342; FAT 10g (sat 2.9g, mono 3.5g, poly 3.4g); PROTEIN 28.2g; CARB 35.8g; FIBER 3.6g; CHOL 71mg; IRON 2.8mg; SODIUM 447mg; CALC 92mg

Turkey Burgers with Cranberry-Peach Chutney

Cranberry-Peach Chutney

Prep: 4 minutes

⅓	cup prepared cranberry chutney
⅓	cup finely chopped peaches
1	tablespoon finely chopped green onions

1. Combine all ingredients in a small bowl, stirring well to blend. Yield: ½ cup (serving size: 1 tablespoon).

CALORIES 30; FAT 0g (sat 0g, mono 0g, poly 0g); PROTEIN 0.1g; CARB 6.7g; FIBER 0.1g; CHOL 0mg; IRON 0.3mg; SODIUM 1mg; CALC 1mg

Cranberry-Orange Turkey
Salad Sandwiches

Cranberry-Orange Turkey Salad Sandwiches

Prep: 7 minutes • Cook: 5 minutes

Leftover turkey gets a makeover with grated orange rind, cranberries, almonds, and ginger.

½   cup plain fat-free Greek yogurt
1   teaspoon grated orange rind
1   teaspoon grated peeled fresh ginger
½   teaspoon salt
2   cups chopped cooked turkey breast
⅓   cup dried cranberries
¼   cup sliced almonds, toasted
8   (1-ounce) slices 100% whole-wheat bread
4   romaine lettuce leaves

1. Combine first 4 ingredients in a medium bowl. Add turkey, cranberries, and almonds, tossing to coat.
2. Top each of 4 bread slices with 1 lettuce leaf and ½ cup turkey salad. Cover with remaining bread slices. Cut sandwiches in half diagonally. Yield: 4 servings (serving size: 1 sandwich).

CALORIES 320; FAT 5.4g (sat 0.8g, mono 2.8g, poly 1.2g); PROTEIN 32.8g; CARB 35.4g; FIBER 5.7g; CHOL 59mg; IRON 3mg; SODIUM 608mg; CALC 114mg

quick flip

Don't have dried cranberries on hand? Try other dried fruits like chopped apricots or raisins.

Turkey-Hummus Pitas

Prep: 12 minutes

Store the hummus in the refrigerator in an airtight container for up to a week.

½   cup Herbed Hummus
2   (6-inch) whole-wheat pitas, cut in half
8   ounces thinly sliced deli, lower-sodium turkey breast
4   (¼-inch-thick) slices tomato, halved
¼   cup crumbled feta cheese
1   cup bagged baby spinach leaves (optional)

1. Prepare Herbed Hummus.
2. Spread 2 tablespoons Herbed Hummus in each pita half. Fill each pita with 2 ounces turkey, 1 tomato slice, 1 tablespoon feta cheese, and ¼ cup spinach, if desired. Yield: 4 servings (serving size: 1 pita half).

CALORIES 220; FAT 6.8g (sat 2.1g, mono 3g, poly 1.1g); PROTEIN 17.7g; CARB 21.9g; FIBER 3.4g; CHOL 29mg; IRON 1.8mg; SODIUM 668mg; CALC 64mg

Herbed Hummus

Prep: 7 minutes

1   garlic clove, peeled
1   (16-ounce) can chickpeas (garbanzo beans), rinsed and drained
2   tablespoons olive oil
2   tablespoons fresh lemon juice
2   tablespoons water
2   tablespoons flat-leaf parsley leaves
2   teaspoons tahini (roasted sesame seed paste)
¼   teaspoon smoked paprika

1. Drop garlic through food chute with food processor on; process until minced. Add chickpeas and remaining ingredients; process until smooth, scraping sides of bowl once. Yield: 10 servings (serving size: 2 tablespoons).

CALORIES 65; FAT 3.6g (sat 0.5g, mono 2.3g, poly 0.7g); PROTEIN 1.6g; CARB 7.1g; FIBER 1.4g; CHOL 0mg; IRON 0.5mg; SODIUM 86mg; CALC 12mg

salads

Arugula Salad with Beets
and Pancetta Crisps,
page 222

Arugula-Orange Salad with Fig-Bacon Dressing

Prep: 13 minutes • Cook: 30 seconds

Fig-Bacon Dressing
1	(5-ounce) package prewashed arugula
1	(15-ounce) can cannellini beans, rinsed and drained
1	cup navel orange slices, peeled and quartered (2 oranges)
1/3	cup (1.3 ounces) crumbled goat cheese
1/2	teaspoon freshly ground black pepper

1. Prepare Fig-Bacon Dressing.
2. Place Fig-Bacon Dressing, arugula, beans, and orange in a large bowl; toss well.
3. Divide salad evenly among 4 salad plates. Sprinkle salads evenly with goat cheese and pepper. Yield: 4 servings (serving size: 2 cups salad, about 4 teaspoons cheese, and dash of pepper).

CALORIES 238; FAT 8.9g (sat 3.9g, mono 3.8g, poly 0.7g); PROTEIN 10.9g; CARB 29.8g; FIBER 5.5g; CHOL 12.3mg; IRON 2.1mg; SODIUM 318mg; CALC 152mg

Fig-Bacon Dressing

Prep: 3 minutes • Cook: 30 seconds

3	tablespoons fig preserves
1/4	cup cider vinegar
1	tablespoon olive oil
1/2	teaspoon grated orange rind
2	center-cut bacon slices, cooked and crumbled

1. Spoon fig preserves into a large microwave-safe bowl. Cover and microwave at HIGH 30 seconds or until preserves melt. Add vinegar, olive oil, rind, and bacon; stir with a whisk until blended. Yield: 4 servings (serving size: 2 tablespoons).

CALORIES 77; FAT 4g (sat 0.7g, mono 2.5g, poly 0.4g); PROTEIN 1g; CARB 8.5g; FIBER 0g; CHOL 2.5mg; IRON 0.1mg; SODIUM 44mg; CALC 2mg

Six Bean Salad

Prep: 7 minutes

Here's the perfect meatless main-dish salad; it's simple, quick, and nutritious, thanks to a vacuum-packed medley of beans. Add chopped cooked chicken for a heartier salad, if you like.

2	tablespoons extra-virgin olive oil
2	tablespoons fresh lemon juice
1/4	teaspoon salt
1/4	teaspoon freshly ground black pepper
1	(12.3-ounce) package six bean medley
1/2	cup refrigerated prechopped celery, onion, and bell pepper mix
2	tablespoons finely chopped fresh parsley
2	teaspoons finely chopped fresh rosemary
3	tablespoons crumbled goat cheese with herbs

1. Combine first 4 ingredients in a medium bowl, stirring with a whisk. Add bean medley and next 3 ingredients, tossing to coat. Top servings evenly with cheese. Yield: 3 servings (serving size: 3/4 cup salad and 1 tablespoon cheese).

CALORIES 275; FAT 14.3g (sat 4g, mono 8.1g, poly 1.3g); PROTEIN 10.5g; CARB 32.4g; FIBER 6.4g; CHOL 7mg; IRON 2.5mg; SODIUM 388mg; CALC 45mg

Six Bean Salad

Feta-Chickpea Salad

Prep: 7 minutes

Fresh herbs and lemon brighten canned chickpeas, a perfect protein-packed base for a meatless lunch.

½   cup chopped sun-dried tomatoes, packed without oil
1½   tablespoons chopped fresh basil
1½   tablespoons chopped fresh parsley
2   (16-ounce) cans chickpeas (garbanzo beans), rinsed and drained
2   ounces feta cheese, crumbled (½ cup)
1   small shallot, minced
2   tablespoons fresh lemon juice
1½   tablespoons extra-virgin olive oil
¼   teaspoon freshly ground black pepper

1. Combine first 6 ingredients in a medium bowl. Combine lemon juice, oil, and pepper in a small bowl; pour over chickpea mixture, tossing to coat. Serve immediately or refrigerate until ready to serve. Yield: 4 servings (serving size: 1 cup salad).

CALORIES 278; FAT 10g (sat 2.6g, mono 5g, poly 1.4g); PROTEIN 11.2g; CARB 38.6g; FIBER 7.5g; CHOL 10.4mg; IRON 3mg; SODIUM 559mg; CALC 99mg

make ahead

This salad is equally delicious chilled or at room temperature. Toss all ingredients together the night before to make your morning lunch preparation easy.

Grilled Peach and Granola Salad

Prep: 6 minutes   •   Cook: 6 minutes

If you prefer, remove the skins from the peaches after they're grilled.

4   large peaches, halved and pitted
      Cooking spray
8   cups mixed salad greens
⅓   cup light raspberry vinaigrette
1   cup fresh raspberries
1   cup fresh blueberries
½   cup sliced almonds, toasted
¾   cup low-fat granola
1   cup (4 ounces) crumbled goat cheese

1. Preheat grill to medium-high heat.
2. Coat peach halves with cooking spray. Place peaches, cut sides down, on grill rack coated with cooking spray. Grill 3 minutes on each side or until grill marks appear on peach halves. Cut each peach half into 4 wedges.
3. Place salad greens in a large bowl; drizzle with vinaigrette, tossing to coat. Add berries, almonds, and granola; toss gently. Place 2½ cups salad mixture on each of 4 salad plates. Sprinkle each serving with 2 tablespoons cheese; top each with 8 peach wedges. Yield: 4 servings (serving size: 1 salad).

CALORIES 356; FAT 13.5g (sat 4.6g, mono 5.2g, poly 2.2g); PROTEIN 13.4g; CARB 52.3g; FIBER 10.7g; CHOL 13mg; IRON 3.3mg; SODIUM 420mg; CALC 97mg

Grilled Peach and
Granola Salad

Pea, Carrot, and
Tofu Salad

Pea, Carrot, and Tofu Salad

Prep: 5 minutes • Cook: 10 minutes

To get a beautiful brown sear on the tofu, drain the tofu slices between several layers of paper towels to absorb the extra moisture before cooking. Sear the slices in a hot skillet, and while they cook, move them only to turn them over.

1	(14-ounce) package water-packed firm tofu, drained
2	tablespoons sesame oil
½	cup light sesame ginger dressing
1	(16-ounce) package frozen petite green peas, thawed
1	cup matchstick-cut carrots
1	(8-ounce) can water chestnuts, drained
½	cup thinly sliced red onion
¼	teaspoon freshly ground black pepper
1	medium head Bibb lettuce, torn
4	teaspoons roasted, unsalted sunflower seed kernels

1. Place tofu on several layers of heavy-duty paper towels. Cover tofu with additional paper towels; gently press out moisture. Cut tofu into 1-inch cubes.

2. Heat a large nonstick skillet over medium-high heat. Add oil; swirl to coat. Add tofu; cook 5 to 6 minutes on each side or until golden on all sides, stirring occasionally.

3. Combine tofu, dressing, and next 5 ingredients in a large bowl; toss gently to coat. Divide lettuce evenly among 4 plates. Top lettuce with 1¾ cups tofu mixture. Sprinkle evenly with sunflower seed kernels. Yield: 4 servings (serving size: about 1½ cups lettuce, 1¾ cups tofu mixture, and 1 teaspoon sunflower seed kernels).

CALORIES 312; FAT 14.6g (sat 2.1g, mono 4.5g, poly 7g); PROTEIN 15.9g; CARB 33.2g; FIBER 8.5g; CHOL 0mg; IRON 4.4mg; SODIUM 554mg; CALC 256mg

Heirloom Tomato and Goat Cheese Salad with Bacon Dressing

Prep: 7 minutes • Cook: 7 minutes

Three harmonious flavors converge in this simple salad: smoky bacon, earthy goat cheese, and acidic tomatoes. Serve with a warm baguette slice and a glass of dry white wine to complete the meal.

2   heirloom tomatoes, sliced
1   (4-ounce) package goat cheese, sliced
½   cup vertically sliced red onion
2   cups bagged baby spinach leaves
½   cup Bacon Dressing

1. Arrange layers of tomato slices and next 3 ingredients evenly on each of 4 serving plates. Drizzle salads evenly with Bacon Dressing. Yield: 4 servings (serving size: 1 salad and 2 tablespoons dressing).

CALORIES 173; FAT 8.5g (sat 4.9g, mono 2.4g, poly 1.2g); PROTEIN 10.2g; CARB 14.4g; FIBER 1.5g; CHOL 21mg; IRON 1.7mg; SODIUM 457mg; CALC 65mg

Heirloom Tomato and Goat Cheese Salad with Bacon Dressing

ingredient spotlight

We recommend using heirloom tomatoes, which are grown from the seeds of old-fashioned varieties, because of their full-bodied flavor and dazzling palette of colors. They vary from red to yellow and from green to purplish black. Look for them at farmers' markets during the summer months.

Bacon Dressing

Prep: 4 minutes • Cook: 7 minutes

6   center-cut 30%-less-fat bacon slices
¼   cup cider vinegar
2   tablespoons honey
¼   teaspoon kosher salt
½   teaspoon freshly ground black pepper
¼   cup minced green onions (1 large)

1. Cook bacon in a skillet over medium heat until crisp. Remove bacon from pan, reserving 1 tablespoon drippings in pan; drain bacon.
2. Add vinegar and remaining 4 ingredients to drippings in pan, stirring with a whisk. Remove pan from heat. Crumble bacon, and add to pan, stirring with a whisk. Yield: ⅔ cup (serving size: about 2½ tablespoons).

CALORIES 76; FAT 2.3g (sat 0.8g, mono 1g, poly 0.5g); PROTEIN 3.9g; CARB 9.5g; FIBER 0.3g; CHOL 8mg; IRON 0.5mg; SODIUM 337mg; CALC 7mg

Grilled Chicken Salad
with Dried Cherries and
Goat Cheese

Grilled Chicken Salad with Dried Cherries and Goat Cheese

Prep: 7 minutes • Cook: 6 minutes
Other: 2 minutes

Chicken cutlets or thinly sliced chicken breasts speed up the recipe; they take less time to grill.

1	pound thinly sliced skinless, boneless chicken breast halves
½	cup Herbed Balsamic Dressing, divided
¼	teaspoon salt
¼	teaspoon freshly ground black pepper
	Cooking spray
1	(5-ounce) package baby spring mix salad greens
½	cup dried cherries
½	cup (2 ounces) crumbled goat cheese

1. Preheat grill to medium-high heat.
2. Brush chicken with ¼ cup Herbed Balsamic Dressing; sprinkle with salt and pepper. Place chicken on grill rack coated with cooking spray; grill 3 to 4 minutes on each side or until chicken is done. Let chicken stand 2 minutes; cut crosswise into thin slices.
3. Combine salad greens, cherries, and remaining ¼ cup Herbed Balsamic Dressing, tossing gently to coat. Place 1¼ cups salad mixture on each of 4 salad plates. Arrange one-fourth of chicken over each salad. Sprinkle each serving with 2 tablespoons goat cheese. Yield: 4 servings (serving size: 1 salad).

CALORIES 334; FAT 11g (sat 3.4g, mono 5.2g, poly 1.1g); PROTEIN 28.3g; CARB 27.7g; FIBER 2.4g; CHOL 79.1mg; IRON 1.4mg; SODIUM 382mg; CALC 45mg

Herbed Balsamic Dressing

Prep: 5 minutes

⅓	cup balsamic vinegar
1½	tablespoons olive oil
2	tablespoons honey
1	teaspoon Dijon mustard
1	tablespoon minced shallots
2	tablespoons chopped fresh basil

1. Combine first 4 ingredients, stirring with a whisk. Stir in shallots and basil. Yield: 5 servings (serving size: about 2 tablespoons).

CALORIES 81; FAT 4.1g (sat 0.6g, mono 3g, poly 0.4g); PROTEIN 0.2g; CARB 10.2g; FIBER 0g; CHOL 0mg; IRON 0.2mg; SODIUM 28mg; CALC 7mg

Curried Chicken and Broccoli Salad

Prep: 8 minutes

It's all about the crunch from the crisp apples and crunchy broccoli coleslaw. Fresh ginger and curry deliver the flavor to this chicken salad. Serve over red leaf lettuce, if desired, with whole-wheat crackers to complete the meal.

Curry-Yogurt Dressing
3	cups pulled rotisserie chicken
2	cups chopped Fuji apple (2 apples)
½	cup raisins
1	(12-ounce) package broccoli coleslaw

1. Prepare Curry-Yogurt Dressing in a large bowl. Add chicken and remaining ingredients; toss well. Cover and chill until ready to serve. Yield: 6 servings (serving size: 1½ cups salad).

CALORIES 333; FAT 3.9g (sat 1.3g, mono 1.6g, poly 0.9g); PROTEIN 39.7g; CARB 34.5g; FIBER 6g; CHOL 89mg; IRON 2.6mg; SODIUM 505mg; CALC 90mg

Curried Chicken and Broccoli Salad

Curry-Yogurt Dressing

Prep: 4 minutes

¾	cup vanilla fat-free Greek yogurt
1	tablespoon chopped fresh cilantro
1	tablespoon grated peeled fresh ginger
1¼	teaspoons curry powder
¼	teaspoon salt

1. Combine all ingredients. Cover and refrigerate until ready to use. Yield: 6 servings (serving size: 2 tablespoons).

CALORIES 17; FAT 0.1g (sat 0g, mono 0.1g, poly 0g); PROTEIN 2.5g; CARB 1.6g; FIBER 0.2g; CHOL 0mg; IRON 0.1mg; SODIUM 108mg; CALC 21mg

Chicken-Edamame Salad with Wasabi Vinaigrette

Prep: 13 minutes

1½	cups frozen shelled edamame (green soybeans)
6	cups shredded napa (Chinese) cabbage
3	cups shredded cooked chicken breast
4	green onions, sliced
¾	cup Wasabi Vinaigrette

1. Place edamame in a wire mesh strainer; rinse with cold water until thawed. Drain well. Combine edamame and next 3 ingredients in a large bowl. Prepare Wasabi Vinaigrette. Add Wasabi Vinaigrette to edamame mixture; toss well. Yield: 4 servings (serving size: 2 cups salad).

CALORIES 404; FAT 13.8g (sat 2.1g, mono 6.4g, poly 5.2g); PROTEIN 42.9g; CARB 25.8g; FIBER 6.3g; CHOL 89mg; IRON 1.4mg; SODIUM 261mg; CALC 120mg

ingredient spotlight

Edamame are green soybeans. These folate-rich gems, packed with protein and fiber, can be simmered, steamed, microwaved, boiled, and sautéed. You can even puree edamame to make hummus.

Wasabi Vinaigrette

Prep: 3 minutes

Whip up this dressing the night before for a quick assembly the next day.

⅔	cup rice vinegar
2	tablespoons canola oil
3	tablespoons honey
2	teaspoons wasabi paste
¼	teaspoon salt
2	garlic cloves, pressed

1. Combine all ingredients, stirring well with a whisk. Yield: 1 cup (serving size: 3 tablespoons).

CALORIES 104; FAT 5.8g (sat 0.4g, mono 3.4g, poly 2g); PROTEIN 0.1g; CARB 12.1g; FIBER 0.1g; CHOL 0mg; IRON 0.1mg; SODIUM 159mg; CALC 3mg

Chicken-Edamame Salad with Wasabi Vinaigrette

Chicken, Spinach, and Blueberry Salad with Pomegranate Vinaigrette

Prep: 6 minutes • Cook: 7 minutes

Sweet blueberries pair well with distinctive blue cheese in this chicken salad, while a bold-flavored vinaigrette lightly coats the tender baby spinach leaves.

Cooking spray
8   chicken breast tenders (about ¾ pound)
1½   teaspoons coarsely ground black pepper
¼   teaspoon salt
8   cups bagged baby spinach leaves
Pomegranate Vinaigrette
½   cup thinly sliced red onion
1   cup fresh blueberries
¼   cup (1 ounce) crumbled blue cheese

1. Heat a grill pan or large nonstick skillet over medium-high heat. Coat pan with cooking spray. Sprinkle chicken with pepper and salt. Coat chicken with cooking spray, and add to pan. Cook 3 to 4 minutes on each side or until done.
2. Divide spinach evenly on each of 4 serving plates; drizzle evenly with Pomegranate Vinaigrette. Arrange chicken, onion, and blueberries evenly over spinach. Sprinkle evenly with cheese. Yield: 4 servings (serving size: 2 cups spinach, 2 chicken tenders, 3 tablespoons vinaigrette, 2 tablespoons onion, ¼ cup blueberries, and 1 tablespoon cheese).

CALORIES 203; FAT 4.4g (sat 1.7g, mono 1.6g, poly 0.7g); PROTEIN 23g; CARB 18.5g; FIBER 3.7g; CHOL 56mg; IRON 2.4mg; SODIUM 377mg; CALC 95mg

Chicken, Spinach, and Blueberry Salad with Pomegranate Vinaigrette

Pomegranate Vinaigrette

Prep: 2 minutes

½   cup pomegranate juice
3   tablespoons sugar
3   tablespoons balsamic vinegar
1   tablespoon canola oil
1   teaspoon grated orange rind

1. Combine all ingredients in a small bowl. Stir with a whisk until blended. Yield: ¾ cup (serving size: 3 tablespoons).

CALORIES 96; FAT 3.5g (sat 0.3g, mono 2.1g, poly 1g); PROTEIN 0.2g; CARB 15.9g; FIBER 0.1g; CHOL 0mg; IRON 0.1mg; SODIUM 7mg; CALC 9mg

quick flip

Can't find pomegranate juice? Try other antioxidant-rich fruit juices, like cranberry or raspberry.

Grilled Chicken and Peach Spinach Salad with Sherry Vinaigrette

Prep: 6 minutes • Cook: 8 minutes

Pairing peaches with chicken is the ultimate summer addition to a spinach salad. The Sherry Vinaigrette brings out the sweetness of the peaches, while grilling the fruit caramelizes the natural sugars.

Sherry Vinaigrette, divided
2   peaches, halved and pitted
4   (4-ounce) chicken breast cutlets
Cooking spray
4   cups bagged baby spinach leaves
⅓   cup pine nuts, toasted
1   (3-ounce) package goat cheese, crumbled

1. Preheat grill to medium-high heat.
2. Prepare Sherry Vinaigrette; set aside ¼ cup vinaigrette.
3. Coat peach halves and chicken with cooking spray; brush chicken with remaining 1½ tablespoons vinaigrette. Place peach halves and chicken on grill rack coated with cooking spray. Grill chicken 3 to 4 minutes on each side. Grill peach halves 1 to 2 minutes on each side; cut each half into 4 wedges.
4. Cut chicken crosswise into thin strips. Place peach wedges, chicken strips, spinach, and pine nuts in a large bowl; drizzle with reserved ¼ cup vinaigrette, and toss well. Place 2 cups salad mixture on each of 4 plates; sprinkle evenly with cheese. Yield: 4 servings (serving size: 2 cups salad and 1½ tablespoons cheese).

CALORIES 320; FAT 17.2g (sat 4.5g, mono 6g, poly 4.7g); PROTEIN 32.9g; CARB 8.6g; FIBER 1.9g; CHOL 76mg; IRON 2.9mg; SODIUM 327mg; CALC 74mg

Sherry Vinaigrette

Prep: 4 minutes

2½   tablespoons minced shallots (about 1 large)
1   tablespoon sherry vinegar
1   tablespoon olive oil
½   teaspoon ground mustard
½   teaspoon freshly ground black pepper
¼   teaspoon salt

1. Combine all ingredients, stirring with a whisk. Yield: 4 servings (serving size: about 1 tablespoon and 1 teaspoon).

CALORIES 38; FAT 3.4g (sat 0.5g, mono 2.5g, poly 0.4g); PROTEIN 0.2g; CARB 1.4g; FIBER 0.2g; CHOL 0mg; IRON 0.1mg; SODIUM 156mg; CALC 4mg

ingredient spotlight

If your peaches are firm, let them stand on the kitchen counter for a few days or until they're soft to the touch and display a deep, golden color.

Chicken Salad with Asparagus and Creamy Dill Dressing

Prep: 3 minutes • Cook: 5 minutes

This tasty salad is perfect for evenings when you're looking for a quick, no-fuss meal. We hand-pulled large pieces of chicken from a cooked chicken breast to achieve a chunky texture. Serve with crackers to complete the meal.

2½   cups (2-inch) diagonally cut asparagus
2   cups coarsely shredded cooked chicken
       breast (about 8 ounces)
½   cup thinly sliced radishes
Creamy Dill Dressing
8   tomato slices (about 1 large)
Freshly ground black pepper (optional)

1. Steam asparagus, covered, 3 minutes or until crisp-tender. Drain and plunge asparagus into ice water; drain.
2. Combine asparagus, chicken, radishes, and dressing in a large bowl; toss well. Arrange 2 tomato slices on each of 4 plates; top each serving with 1 cup chicken mixture. Sprinkle with pepper, if desired. Yield: 4 servings (serving size: 1 salad).

CALORIES 170; FAT 4.3g (sat 0.6g, mono 1.7g, poly 1.5g); PROTEIN 21.2g; CARB 12.2g; FIBER 2.8g; CHOL 49mg; IRON 2.6mg; SODIUM 467mg; CALC 79mg

Creamy Dill Dressing

Prep: 4 minutes

½   cup low-fat mayonnaise
½   cup nonfat buttermilk
1   tablespoon chopped fresh dill
1   tablespoon fresh lemon juice
¼   teaspoon kosher salt
¼   teaspoon freshly ground black pepper

1. Combine all ingredients in a medium bowl, stirring well with a whisk. Yield: 8 servings (serving size: 2 tablespoons).

CALORIES 21; FAT 1g (sat 0g, mono 0g, poly 0.5g); PROTEIN 0.6g; CARB 3.1g; FIBER 0g; CHOL 0.2mg; IRON 0mg; SODIUM 205mg; CALC 19mg

make ahead

This superfast homemade dressing can be made ahead; make extra to keep on hand to drizzle over side salads or to serve as vegetable dip.

Chicken Salad with Roasted Peppers

Prep: 10 minutes

2	cups chopped cooked chicken breast (about ¾ pound)
½	cup refrigerated prechopped green bell pepper
½	cup refrigerated prediced celery
½	cup dried cranberries
½	cup chopped bottled roasted red bell pepper
¼	cup refrigerated prechopped red onion
¼	cup chopped pecans, toasted
¼	cup light mayonnaise
2	teaspoons low-sodium soy sauce
¼	teaspoon crushed red pepper

1. Combine all ingredients in a medium bowl; toss well. Cover and chill until ready to serve. Yield: 4 servings (serving size: 1 cup salad).

CALORIES 280; FAT 13g (sat 2.2g, mono 4.1g, poly 2.4g); PROTEIN 23g; CARB 17.5g; FIBER 2.3g; CHOL 65mg; IRON 1.1mg; SODIUM 333mg; CALC 26mg

serve with:

Cantaloupe with Balsamic Berries and Cream

Prep: 8 minutes

12	(5-inch) slices cantaloupe
2	cups vanilla bean light ice cream
1	cup fresh raspberries
2	tablespoons balsamic glaze

1. Arrange cantaloupe slices on each of 4 dessert plates; top each with ice cream and raspberries. Drizzle balsamic glaze over each serving. Yield: 4 servings (serving size: 3 slices cantaloupe, ½ cup ice cream, ¼ cup raspberries, and 1½ teaspoons balsamic glaze).

CALORIES 174; FAT 4g (sat 2.1g, mono 0g, poly 0.2g); PROTEIN 4.4g; CARB 32.6g; FIBER 2g; CHOL 20mg; IRON 0.5mg; SODIUM 71mg; CALC 79mg

Chicken Salad with Roasted Peppers

Chicken BLT Salad with Creamy Avocado–Horned Melon Dressing

Prep: 7 minutes

The horned melon lends subtle cucumber flavor and creaminess to this crisp, colorful chicken BLT salad. You may store the remaining Creamy Avocado–Horned Melon Dressing in the refrigerator up to three days.

3	cups sliced cooked chicken breast (about 1 pound)
1	tomato, cut into wedges
1	(10-ounce) package romaine salad
¾	cup Creamy Avocado–Horned Melon Dressing
3	center-cut bacon slices, cooked and crumbled

Chicken BLT Salad with Creamy Avocado–Horned Melon Dressing

1. Combine first 3 ingredients in a large bowl; toss well. Drizzle Creamy Avocado–Horned Melon Dressing over salad; top with bacon. Yield: 6 servings (serving size: about 1¾ cups salad).

CALORIES 184; FAT 7g (sat 1.8g, mono 3.1g, poly 1.3g); PROTEIN 24.5g; CARB 5.8g; FIBER 2.9g; CHOL 63mg; IRON 1.5mg; SODIUM 186mg; CALC 42mg

Creamy Avocado–Horned Melon Dressing

Prep: 8 minutes

1	horned melon
1	small ripe peeled avocado
1	small garlic clove
¼	cup low-fat buttermilk
2	tablespoons fresh lemon juice
2	tablespoons water
¼	teaspoon salt
¼	teaspoon freshly ground black pepper

1. Cut horned melon in half lengthwise; scoop out pulp. Place pulp in a fine sieve over a bowl. Press pulp with the back of a spoon to extract juice; discard juice. Place pulp and remaining ingredients in a blender or food processor; process until smooth. Store in an airtight container in the refrigerator up to 3 days. Yield: 1¼ cups (serving size: 1 tablespoon).

CALORIES 21; FAT 2g (sat 0.3g, mono 0.9g, poly 0.3g); PROTEIN 0.5g; CARB 1.7g; FIBER 0.8g; CHOL 0mg; IRON 0.1mg; SODIUM 33mg; CALC 7mg

ingredient spotlight

Also known as kiwano melons, horned melons grow in New Zealand and are now commonly found in many grocery stores. They have a yellow-orange spiked exterior and a green jelly-like flesh similar in flavor to that of a cucumber.

Asian Chicken Salad with Sweet and Spicy Wasabi Dressing

Asian Chicken Salad with Sweet and Spicy Wasabi Dressing

Prep: 10 minutes

Don't be shy about using the wasabi powder—the dressing is full of flavor, not heat. Rotisserie chicken works well for this salad, although any shredded cooked chicken will do.

2	tablespoons rice vinegar
2	tablespoons maple syrup
2	tablespoons olive oil
¾	teaspoon wasabi powder (dried Japanese horseradish)
¼	teaspoon salt
⅛	teaspoon freshly ground black pepper
1	(11.4-ounce) package Asian supreme salad mix
1	(8¼-ounce) can mandarin oranges in light syrup, drained
2	cups shredded cooked chicken breast (about ¾ pound)
1	diagonally cut green onion

1. Combine first 6 ingredients in a large bowl; stir well with a whisk.
2. Add salad mix to vinegar mixture, reserving wonton strips for topping and sesame-orange dressing for another use. Add oranges and chicken; toss gently to coat. Top evenly with onion and reserved wonton strips. Yield: 4 servings (serving size: about 1½ cups salad and 3 wonton strips).

CALORIES 316; FAT 14g (sat 3.6g, mono 5.9g, poly 1.6g); PROTEIN 25.3g; CARB 23.5g; FIBER 2.5g; CHOL 67mg; IRON 1.5mg; SODIUM 279mg; CALC 100mg

Chicken Caesar Salad

Prep: 3 minutes • Cook: 4 minutes

For an easy addition to this salad, place baguette slices on the grill while you're cooking the chicken. Grill the bread slices for 2 minutes on each side; then rub the slices with the cut side of a halved garlic clove.

Caesar Dressing, divided
3   (4-ounce) chicken cutlets
Cooking spray
1   (10-ounce) package romaine salad
2   tomatoes, cut into wedges
¼   cup (1 ounce) grated fresh Parmesan cheese

1. Preheat grill to medium-high heat.
2. While grill heats, prepare Caesar Dressing. Reserve ⅓ cup dressing in a separate bowl; set aside.
3. Place chicken on grill rack coated with cooking spray. Grill 2 to 3 minutes on each side or until done, basting frequently with remaining dressing. Remove from grill. Cool slightly; slice.
4. Combine chicken, reserved ⅓ cup dressing, lettuce, and tomato in a large bowl; toss gently to coat. Divide salad evenly among each of 4 bowls. Sprinkle each serving with 1 tablespoon cheese. Yield: 4 servings (serving size: 2½ cups salad).

CALORIES 225; FAT 11g (sat 2.4g, mono 0.7g, poly 0.4g); PROTEIN 23.6g; CARB 9g; FIBER 2.6g; CHOL 68mg; IRON 1.8mg; SODIUM 446mg; CALC 114mg

> ## quick flip
> Try grilling shrimp instead of chicken for another variation on this classic salad.

Caesar Dressing

Prep: 5 minutes

6   tablespoons light mayonnaise
3   tablespoons fresh lemon juice
1½   tablespoons water
1½   teaspoons anchovy paste
3   large garlic cloves, minced
1   teaspoon dried oregano
½   teaspoon freshly ground black pepper

1. Combine all ingredients in a small bowl, stirring well with a whisk. Yield: about ⅔ cup (serving size: about 1 tablespoon).

CALORIES 33; FAT 3g (sat 0.5g, mono 0g, poly 0g); PROTEIN 0.2g; CARB 1.5g; FIBER 0.1g; CHOL 6mg; IRON 0.1mg; SODIUM 112mg; CALC 5mg

Chicken Caesar Salad

Chicken and Spring
Greens with Açai Dressing

Chicken and Spring Greens with Açai Dressing

Prep: 6 minutes

Serve this salad with multigrain crispbreads such as those made by Wasa.

8	cups mixed baby salad greens
2	cups chopped cooked chicken breast (about ¾ pound)
½	cup red onion slices
¼	cup chopped pecans, toasted
¾	cup Açai Dressing

1. Arrange 2 cups salad greens on each of 4 plates. Top each evenly with chicken, onion slices, and pecans. Drizzle 3 tablespoons dressing over each salad. Yield: 4 servings (serving size: 2 cups greens, ½ cup chicken, about 5 onion slices, 1 tablespoon pecans, and 3 tablespoons dressing).

CALORIES 293; FAT 14g (sat 1.7g, mono 7.2g, poly 3.9g); PROTEIN 24.5g; CARB 18.5g; FIBER 3.8g; CHOL 60mg; IRON 2.5mg; SODIUM 81mg; CALC 87mg

Açai Dressing

Prep: 4 minutes

½	cup açai juice blend
3	tablespoons sugar
1½	tablespoons grated orange rind
3	tablespoons rice vinegar
1½	tablespoons canola oil
¼	teaspoon crushed red pepper

1. Combine all ingredients in a small bowl, stirring well with a whisk. Yield: ¾ cup (serving size: 3 tablespoons).

CALORIES 100; FAT 6g (sat 0.5g, mono 3.1g, poly 1.6g); PROTEIN 0.1g; CARB 12.8g; FIBER 0.5g; CHOL 0mg; IRON 0.1mg; SODIUM 1mg; CALC 8mg

Chicken, Bean, and Blue Cheese Pasta Salad with Sun-Dried Tomato Vinaigrette

Prep: 6 minutes • Cook: 16 minutes

1½	cups uncooked rotini (corkscrew pasta)
1½	cups (2-inch) cut green beans (about 6 ounces)
2	cups diced cooked chicken breast (about ¾ pound)
¼	cup (1 ounce) crumbled blue cheese
¼	cup Sun-Dried Tomato Vinaigrette

1. Cook pasta according to package directions, omitting salt and fat. Add beans during last 5 minutes of cooking. Drain pasta and beans; rinse with cold water until cool.
2. Combine pasta mixture and remaining ingredients; toss gently to coat. Yield: 4 servings (serving size: 1 cup salad).

CALORIES 315; FAT 9g (sat 2.7g, mono 3.9g, poly 1.1g); PROTEIN 28.8g; CARB 30.1g; FIBER 2.8g; CHOL 65mg; IRON 2.5mg; SODIUM 192mg; CALC 75mg

Sun-Dried Tomato Vinaigrette

Prep: 4 minutes

2	tablespoons balsamic vinegar
1	tablespoon olive oil
1	tablespoon water
2	tablespoons chopped sun-dried tomatoes, packed without oil
1	tablespoon chopped fresh basil
1	tablespoon chopped red onion

1. Combine first 3 ingredients in a small bowl, stirring well with a whisk. Stir in tomatoes, basil, and onion. Yield: ¼ cup (serving size: 1 tablespoon).

CALORIES 43; FAT 4g (sat 0.5g, mono 2.5g, poly 0.5g); PROTEIN 0.3g; CARB 2.6g; FIBER 0.3g; CHOL 0mg; IRON 0.2mg; SODIUM 37mg; CALC 6mg

Chickpea, Fennel, and
Olive Chicken Salad

Chickpea, Fennel, and Olive Chicken Salad

Prep: 15 minutes

This Mediterranean-inspired salad showcases fresh fennel, olives, and protein-packed chickpeas tossed with a simple vinaigrette of lemon juice and olive oil.

1	tablespoon fresh lemon juice
1	tablespoon olive oil
½	teaspoon freshly ground black pepper
¼	teaspoon salt
2¼	cups finely chopped fennel bulb (1 medium)
1½	cups chopped rotisserie chicken breast
½	cup chopped radishes (6 radishes)
⅓	cup chopped pitted kalamata olives
¼	cup chopped fresh parsley
2	navel oranges, peeled and chopped
1	(16-ounce) can chickpeas (garbanzo beans), rinsed and drained

1. Combine first 4 ingredients in a medium bowl, stirring with a whisk. Add fennel and remaining ingredients; toss well. Yield: 5 servings (serving size: about 1⅓ cups salad).

CALORIES 194; FAT 7.6g (sat 1g, mono 4.6g, poly 0.8g); PROTEIN 15.2g; CARB 18g; FIBER 4.7g; CHOL 35mg; IRON 1.5mg; SODIUM 576mg; CALC 69mg

Mango Chicken Salad

Prep: 8 minutes

This tropical chicken salad derives its flavor from mango chutney, fresh cilantro, and lime juice.

½	cup plain 2% reduced-fat Greek yogurt
¼	cup chopped red onion
¼	cup mango chutney
3	tablespoons chopped fresh cilantro
1	tablespoon fresh lime juice
2	cups shredded rotisserie chicken breast
1	(6.5-ounce) package sweet butter-blend salad greens
¼	cup chopped dry-roasted cashews, salted

Mango Chicken Salad

1. Combine first 5 ingredients in a medium bowl. Add chicken, and toss well.
2. Place 1¼ cups salad greens on each of 4 salad plates. Top each serving with about ½ cup chicken mixture and 1 tablespoon chopped cashews. Yield: 4 servings (serving size: 1 salad).

CALORIES 244; FAT 7g (sat 1.8g, mono 3.3g, poly 1g); PROTEIN 25.1g; CARB 21.2g; FIBER 1.1g; CHOL 65mg; IRON 0.9mg; SODIUM 430mg; CALC 35mg

ingredient spotlight

Greek yogurt, which imparts a rich creaminess, replaces the usual mayonnaise and sour cream.

Lemon-Dill Chicken Salad

Prep: 15 minutes

Serve this salad as a sandwich or on top of mixed greens for a great lunch.

2	lemons
½	cup canola mayonnaise
1	tablespoon chopped fresh dill or fresh tarragon
¼	teaspoon salt
¼	teaspoon freshly ground black pepper
3	cups finely chopped cooked chicken breast
½	cup chopped celery
½	cup finely chopped onion
2	tablespoons slivered almonds, toasted

1. Grate 2 teaspoons rind and squeeze 3 tablespoons juice from lemons. Combine rind, juice, mayonnaise, and next 3 ingredients in a large bowl. Add chicken and remaining ingredients; toss gently. Cover and chill until ready to serve. Yield: 7 servings (serving size: ½ cup salad).

CALORIES 232; FAT 15.7g (sat 1.8g, mono 8.2g, poly 4.1g); PROTEIN 19.2g; CARB 2.4g; FIBER 0.6g; CHOL 57mg; IRON 0.8mg; SODIUM 249mg; CALC 21mg

Lemon-Dill Chicken Salad

Turkey, Apricot, and Pistachio Salad

Prep: 9 minutes

Smoked turkey, sweet dried apricots, and meaty pistachios provide the backbone to this light yet filling salad. Fresh thyme, citrus, and naturally sweet rice vinegar marry beautifully as a light vinaigrette to add subtle flavor without overpowering the star ingredients.

Lemon-Thyme Vinaigrette

1	(5-ounce) package gourmet salad greens (7 cups)
1½	cups coarsely chopped deli smoked turkey breast (8 ounces)
⅓	cup chopped dried apricots
¼	cup chopped pistachios

1. Prepare Lemon-Thyme Vinaigrette.
2. Place greens and remaining 3 ingredients in a large bowl; drizzle with vinaigrette, and toss well. Yield: 4 servings (serving size: 2 cups salad).

CALORIES 242; FAT 13.4g (sat 1.9g, mono 6.9g, poly 3.9g); PROTEIN 19.1g; CARB 12.7g; FIBER 2.5g; CHOL 43mg; IRON 2mg; SODIUM 595mg; CALC 30mg

Lemon-Thyme Vinaigrette

Prep: 4 minutes

3	tablespoons rice vinegar
2	tablespoons canola oil
1	tablespoon fresh lemon juice
1	teaspoon honey
½	teaspoon Dijon mustard
½	teaspoon chopped fresh thyme
¼	teaspoon freshly ground black pepper

1. Combine all ingredients, stirring with a whisk. Yield: 4 servings (serving size: 4 teaspoons).

CALORIES 70; FAT 7g (sat 0.5g, mono 4.4g, poly 2g); PROTEIN 0.1g; CARB 2.1g; FIBER 0.1g; CHOL 0mg; IRON 0.1mg; SODIUM 16mg; CALC 2mg

Turkey, Apricot, and
Pistachio Salad

Turkey–Blue Cheese Salad

Prep: 4 minutes

4   ounces thinly sliced deli smoked turkey breast
4   cups mixed salad greens
2   cups grape tomatoes
2   tablespoons crumbled blue cheese
¼   cup light balsamic vinaigrette

1. Stack turkey slices; roll up. Cut into 1-inch pieces.
2. Arrange greens on 4 plates. Top each with turkey, tomatoes, blue cheese, and vinaigrette. Yield: 4 servings (serving size: 1 cup greens, 1 ounce turkey, ½ cup tomatoes, ½ tablespoon blue cheese, and 1 tablespoon vinaigrette).

CALORIES 81; FAT 2.4g (sat 0.7g, mono 1.1g, poly 0.6g); PROTEIN 8.7g; CARB 7.2g; FIBER 2.2g; CHOL 18mg; IRON 0.9mg; SODIUM 509mg; CALC 26mg

quick flip

Here's the perfect lunch-break salad; it's simple, quick, and delicious. Substitute sliced deli chicken breast for the turkey, and feta cheese for blue cheese, if you like.

Turkey-Cranberry Salad

Prep: 6 minutes

No need to roast a turkey for this after-the-holiday favorite. Just visit your local deli and pick up the fixings.

1   (8-ounce) bag romaine, green leaf, and butter lettuce hearts mix
1   (8-ounce) slice deli turkey breast, cubed
1   (8¼-ounce) can mandarin oranges in light syrup, drained
1   cup seasoned croutons
½   cup dried cranberries
¼   teaspoon freshly ground black pepper
5   tablespoons chopped pecans (optional)
¼   cup fat-free raspberry vinaigrette

1. Divide lettuce evenly among 5 plates. Top evenly with turkey and next 4 ingredients. Sprinkle with pecans, if desired. Drizzle salads evenly with vinaigrette. Yield: 5 servings (serving size: about 2¼ cups salad).

CALORIES 159; FAT 2.2g (sat 0.5g, mono 1g, poly 0.5g); PROTEIN 12.4g; CARB 23.5g; FIBER 2.5g; CHOL 21mg; IRON 1.3mg; SODIUM 388mg; CALC 39mg

choice ingredient

Pecans add a toasty crunch and heart-healthy monounsaturated fat to salads. You can buy them in many forms–halves, pieces, and chopped–but whole pecans in the shell are best for freshness and flavor. A good rule of thumb is that 1 pound of unshelled pecans yields about half a pound, or about 2 cups, of nutmeat. Store any leftover unshelled pecans in a cool, dry place for up to six months.

Turkey-Cranberry Salad

Deviled Egg Salad with
Pickled Jalapeños

Deviled Egg Salad with Pickled Jalapeños

Prep: 8 minutes

If you'd like less heat, omit the Sriracha. You'll still get a bit of devilish kick from the mustard and jalapeño peppers.

¼	cup canola mayonnaise
2	tablespoons finely chopped pickled jalapeño pepper rings
1	tablespoon Creole mustard
1	teaspoon Sriracha (hot chile sauce)
¼	teaspoon freshly ground black pepper
4	hard-cooked large eggs, peeled
4	Boston lettuce leaves
2	tablespoons chopped green onion tops

1. Combine first 5 ingredients in a medium bowl.
2. Slice eggs in half lengthwise; remove yolks. Finely chop egg whites; press yolks through a sieve using the back of a spoon. Gently fold egg into mayonnaise mixture. Top each lettuce leaf with about ¼ cup egg salad and 1½ teaspoons green onion tops. Yield: 2 servings (serving size: 2 filled lettuce leaves).

CALORIES 259; FAT 19.7g (sat 3.3g, mono 9.1g, poly 4.4g); PROTEIN 12.9g; CARB 3.9g; FIBER 0.7g; CHOL 424mg; IRON 1.6mg; SODIUM 601mg; CALC 60mg

Asian Fresh Tuna Salad

Prep: 5 minutes • Cook: 6 minutes

Alongside this salad, fill your lunch box with rice crackers, fresh fruit, and sparkling water for a truly enjoyable meal. For the best flavor, pack the radishes separately, and serve them on the side.

1	(1-pound) tuna steak (1 inch thick)
	Cooking spray
¼	cup light sesame-ginger dressing
1	tablespoon fresh lime juice
2	teaspoons wasabi paste
¼	teaspoon freshly ground black pepper
⅛	teaspoon salt
¾	cup refrigerated shelled edamame (green soybeans)
⅓	cup finely chopped red onion
3	radishes, sliced
12	rice crackers
3	lime wedges

1. Heat a medium well-seasoned cast-iron skillet over medium-high heat until very hot. Coat tuna with cooking spray. Add tuna to pan. Cook 2 minutes on each side or to desired degree of doneness.
2. While tuna cooks, combine dressing, lime juice, and wasabi paste in a large bowl, stirring with a whisk. Break tuna into chunks in a bowl; sprinkle with pepper and salt.
3. Add tuna, edamame, and onion to dressing in bowl; toss gently to coat. Serve immediately, or cover and chill. Serve with radishes, rice crackers, and lime wedges. Yield: 3 servings (serving size: 1⅓ cups salad, 1 sliced radish, 4 rice crackers, and 1 lime wedge).

CALORIES 250; FAT 3.6g (sat 0.4g, mono 1g, poly 1.1g); PROTEIN 30.2g; CARB 20.7g; FIBER 3.4g; CHOL 51mg; IRON 1.5mg; SODIUM 394mg; CALC 43mg

Asian Fresh Tuna Salad

Tuna–Pita Chip Panzanella

Prep: 4 minutes

Panzanella is an Italian bread salad that's popular in the summer months. Traditionally, the recipe calls for soaking densely textured, day-old bread in water, and then squeezing it out, giving it the name of "leftover salad." Swap out the pita chips for 3 cups of cubed Italian loaf bread for a more authentic dish.

3	cups plain pita chips, coarsely broken
1½	cups chopped cucumber (about 1 large)
½	cup chopped red onion (about 1 small)
¼	cup pitted kalamata olives, coarsely chopped
1	(12-ounce) can albacore tuna in water, drained and flaked into large chunks
¼	cup light balsamic vinaigrette
¼	cup torn mint leaves
¼	teaspoon freshly ground black pepper

1. Combine first 5 ingredients in a bowl; toss gently. Drizzle with vinaigrette; toss. Sprinkle with mint leaves and pepper; toss well. Serve immediately. Yield: 6 servings (serving size: 1½ cups salad).

CALORIES 165; FAT 5.8g (sat 0.5g, mono 4g, poly 1.2g); PROTEIN 11.9g; CARB 16.8g; FIBER 1.9g; CHOL 16mg; IRON 0.4mg; SODIUM 475mg; CALC 14mg

Tuna–Pita Chip Panzanella

serve with:
Salt and Pepper Tomatoes

Prep: 3 minutes

2	medium-sized red tomatoes, each cut into 5 slices (about ¾ pound)
2	medium-sized yellow tomatoes, each cut into 4 slices (about 9 ounces)
¼	cup (1 ounce) crumbled reduced-fat feta cheese
¼	teaspoon freshly ground black pepper
⅛	teaspoon salt

1. Alternately overlap tomato slices on a platter; sprinkle with cheese, pepper, and salt. Cover and chill until ready to serve. Yield: 6 servings (serving size: 3 tomato slices and 2 teaspoons cheese).

CALORIES 30; FAT 0.9g (sat 0.5g, mono 0.2g, poly 0.1g); PROTEIN 2.1g; CARB 4.3g; FIBER 1.2g; CHOL 1mg; IRON 0.5mg; SODIUM 133mg; CALC 24mg

Smoked Trout Salad with Creamy Horseradish Dressing

Prep: 8 minutes • Cook: 5 minutes

1   pound fingerling or baby potatoes
        (about 22 potatoes)
Creamy Horseradish Dressing
6   cups gourmet salad greens
1   (8-ounce) package smoked trout, skinned
        and broken into pieces
1   tablespoon drained capers

Smoked Trout Salad with Creamy Horseradish Dressing

1. Scrub potatoes; pierce with a fork. Place potatoes in a single layer on a microwave-safe plate; cover with wax paper. Microwave at HIGH 5 minutes or until tender. Cut potatoes in half, if desired.
2. While potatoes cook, prepare Creamy Horseradish Dressing.
3. Place 1½ cups salad greens on each of 4 salad plates. Top greens evenly with smoked trout and potatoes. Drizzle 2½ tablespoons dressing evenly over salads; sprinkle each with ¾ teaspoon capers. Yield: 4 servings (serving size: 1 salad).

CALORIES 281; FAT 9.4g (sat 1.7g, mono 3.9g, poly 3g); PROTEIN 22.3g; CARB 27.1g; FIBER 3.8g; CHOL 47mg; IRON 2mg; SODIUM 242mg; CALC 49mg

Creamy Horseradish Dressing

Prep: 4 minutes

¼   cup plain 2% reduced-fat Greek yogurt
¼   cup canola mayonnaise
3   tablespoons water
2   teaspoons chopped fresh dill
1   tablespoon prepared horseradish
1   teaspoon grated lemon rind
1   tablespoon fresh lemon juice
1   teaspoon country-style Dijon mustard
⅛   teaspoon freshly ground black pepper

1. Combine all ingredients in a small bowl, stirring well. Yield: 4 servings (serving size: 2½ tablespoons).

CALORIES 71; FAT 5.2g (sat 0.5g, mono 2.5g, poly 1.5g); PROTEIN 2.9g; CARB 2.5g; FIBER 0.2g; CHOL 2mg; IRON 0mg; SODIUM 143mg; CALC 34mg

quick flip

Other fresh herbs, such as chives or tarragon, would work well in this creamy dressing.

Tuna, Artichoke, and Roasted Red Pepper Salad

Prep: 9 minutes

A medley of Mediterranean flavors perks up humble albacore tuna in this no-cook dish.

1	(12-ounce) jar marinated quartered artichoke hearts
¼	cup chopped fresh dill
1	tablespoon extra-virgin olive oil
1	tablespoon fresh lemon juice
½	teaspoon freshly ground black pepper
2	garlic cloves, minced
2	cups chopped bagged fresh baby spinach leaves
2	(5-ounce) cans albacore tuna in water, drained and flaked
1	(12-ounce) jar roasted red bell peppers, drained and chopped

1. Drain artichokes, reserving 2 tablespoons marinade. Coarsely chop artichokes. Combine artichokes, reserved marinade, dill, and next 4 ingredients in a large bowl. Add spinach, tuna, and roasted peppers, tossing well. Yield: 4 servings (serving size: 1¼ cups tuna salad).

CALORIES 153; FAT 6.8g (sat 0.5g, mono 3g, poly 2.7g); PROTEIN 15.1g; CARB 9.3g; FIBER 2.2g; CHOL 23mg; IRON 0.7mg; SODIUM 468mg; CALC 17mg

serve with:
Feta Pita Crisps

Prep: 4 minutes • Cook: 10 minutes

3	(6-inch) pitas
1	(3.5-ounce) package crumbled reduced-fat feta cheese, finely chopped

Olive oil–flavored cooking spray

1. Preheat oven to 425°.
2. Split pitas; cut each into 6 wedges. Arrange pita wedges in a single layer on a large baking sheet; sprinkle with cheese, and lightly coat with cooking spray.
3. Bake at 425° for 10 minutes or until crisp and golden. Yield: 4 servings (serving size: 9 pita crisps).

CALORIES 173; FAT 3.5g (sat 2.2g, mono 0.9g, poly 0.1g); PROTEIN 10.4g; CARB 25.5g; FIBER 1.1g; CHOL 7mg; IRON 2mg; SODIUM 463mg; CALC 103mg

make ahead

Make this hearty salad ahead for a lunch-to-go, or prepare it for dinner. Just add the spinach and toss before serving.

Tuna, Artichoke, and Roasted Red Pepper Salad

Mediterranean Tuna Salad

Prep: 11 minutes

This Mediterranean-style salad spotlights albacore tuna—a fish that is rich in omega-3 fatty acids. Serve the salad over sliced summer tomatoes with Greek-Style Pita Chips, or stuff the salad in a pita with shredded lettuce for lunch on the go.

1	(12-ounce) can albacore tuna in water, drained and flaked into large chunks
½	cup thinly sliced red onion
2	celery stalks, thinly sliced
2	tablespoons coarsely chopped pitted kalamata olives
2½	tablespoons fresh lemon juice
1	tablespoon olive oil
¼	teaspoon freshly ground black pepper
⅛	teaspoon kosher salt
2	large tomatoes, sliced

1. Combine first 4 ingredients in a medium bowl. Add lemon juice and next 3 ingredients; toss gently to combine. Serve salad over sliced tomatoes. Yield: 3 servings (serving size: 1 cup tuna salad and 2 tomato slices).

CALORIES 203; FAT 8g (sat 1g, mono 4.6g, poly 1g); PROTEIN 24.9g; CARB 9.1g; FIBER 2.3g; CHOL 39mg; IRON 0.5mg; SODIUM 593mg; CALC 31mg

serve with:

Greek-Style Pita Chips

Prep: 7 minutes • Cook: 7 minutes

2	(6-inch) pitas
	Olive oil–flavored cooking spray
½	teaspoon dried Greek seasoning

1. Preheat oven to 400°.
2. Cut each pita into 8 wedges. Separate each wedge into 2 triangles. Place triangles in a single layer on a large baking sheet. Coat top sides of triangles with cooking spray; sprinkle evenly with seasoning.
3. Bake at 400° for 7 to 8 minutes or until crisp and lightly browned; cool. Yield: 4 servings (serving size: 8 chips).

CALORIES 80; FAT 0g (sat 0g, mono 0g, poly 0g); PROTEIN 3.5g; CARB 16.5g; FIBER 0.5g; CHOL 0mg; IRON 1.4mg; SODIUM 201mg; CALC 20mg

Mediterranean Tuna Salad

Crab Salad with Buttermilk Dressing

Prep: 7 minutes

This seafood salad gets its creaminess from low-fat buttermilk and its zing from lemon zest.

Buttermilk Dressing
1	pound jumbo lump crabmeat, drained and shell pieces removed
4	large Bibb lettuce leaves
2	cups multicolored cherry tomatoes (about 12 ounces), quartered

1. Prepare Buttermilk Dressing.
2. Combine crabmeat and dressing; toss well. Place a lettuce leaf on each of 4 plates. Spoon about ⅔ cup crab salad on each lettuce leaf; sprinkle ½ cup tomatoes over each salad. Yield: 4 servings (serving size: 1 salad).

CALORIES 129; FAT 3.6g (sat 1.5g, mono 0.9g, poly 1.1g); PROTEIN 18.7g; CARB 7.3g; FIBER 1.1g; CHOL 108mg; IRON 1.4mg; SODIUM 498mg; CALC 90mg

Buttermilk Dressing

Prep: 4 minutes

½	cup low-fat buttermilk
¼	cup light sour cream
2	teaspoons grated lemon rind
1	teaspoon chopped fresh dill
¼	teaspoon freshly ground black pepper
⅛	teaspoon salt

1. Combine all ingredients in a small bowl, stirring with a whisk. Yield: 4 servings (serving size: 3 tablespoons).

CALORIES 31; FAT 1.3g (sat 0.9g, mono 0.2g, poly 0.1g); PROTEIN 1.6g; CARB 3.7g; FIBER 0.1g; CHOL 6mg; IRON 0mg; SODIUM 120mg; CALC 38mg

Crab Salad with Buttermilk Dressing

Salmon, Asparagus, and Orzo Salad with Lemon-Dill Vinaigrette

Prep: 3 minutes • Cook: 18 minutes

This savory salad epitomizes the concept of fresh food fast. It's quick and easy and loaded with flavorful ingredients such as crisp-tender asparagus, perfectly cooked pink salmon, red onion, and a refreshing lemon juice–based vinaigrette. It received our highest Test Kitchen rating.

6	cups water
1	pound asparagus, trimmed and cut into 3-inch pieces
1	cup uncooked orzo (rice-shaped pasta)
1	(1¼-pound) skinless salmon fillet
¼	teaspoon salt
¼	teaspoon freshly ground black pepper

Cooking spray

¼	cup thinly sliced red onion

Lemon-Dill Vinaigrette

1. Preheat broiler.
2. Bring 6 cups water to a boil in a large saucepan. Add asparagus; cook 3 minutes or until crisp-tender. Remove asparagus from water with tongs or a slotted spoon, reserving water in pan. Plunge asparagus into ice water; drain and set aside.
3. Return reserved water to a boil. Add orzo, and cook according to package directions, omitting salt and fat.

4. While orzo cooks, sprinkle fillet evenly with salt and pepper. Place fish on a foil-lined broiler pan coated with cooking spray. Broil 5 minutes or until fish flakes easily when tested with a fork or until desired degree of doneness. Using 2 forks, break fish into large chunks. Combine fish, orzo, asparagus, onion, and Lemon-Dill Vinaigrette in a large bowl; toss gently to coat. Yield: 6 servings (serving size: about 1¼ cups salad).

CALORIES 310; FAT 11g (sat 3.2g, mono 4.7g, poly 2g); PROTEIN 26g; CARB 24.6g; FIBER 2.2g; CHOL 56mg; IRON 1.4mg; SODIUM 333mg; CALC 67mg

Lemon-Dill Vinaigrette

Prep: 6 minutes

⅓	cup (1.3 ounces) crumbled feta cheese
1	tablespoon chopped fresh dill
3	tablespoons fresh lemon juice
2	teaspoons extra-virgin olive oil
¼	teaspoon salt
¼	teaspoon freshly ground black pepper

1. Combine all ingredients in a small bowl, stirring well with a whisk. Yield: ⅓ cup (serving size: about 1 tablespoon).

CALORIES 43; FAT 4g (sat 1.7g, mono 1.8g, poly 0.2g); PROTEIN 1.4g; CARB 1.2g; FIBER 0.1g; CHOL 8mg; IRON 0.1mg; SODIUM 214mg; CALC 48mg

make ahead

Blend the bright flavors of feta, lemon, and dill by making this dressing the night before.

Grilled Salmon and Grapefruit Salad with Blood Orange Vinaigrette

Prep: 11 minutes • Cook: 10 minutes

A generous portion of tender, flaky salmon tops this vitamin C–packed salad. To speed preparation, use a jar of fresh red grapefruit sections and bottled blood orange juice. Prepare the Blood Orange Vinaigrette while the salmon and onion are on the grill.

2	(6-ounce) salmon fillets (1 to 1¼ inches thick)
½	teaspoon salt
¼	teaspoon freshly ground black pepper
1	large Vidalia or other sweet onion, cut into ½-inch-thick slices
Cooking spray	
8	cups mixed baby salad greens
1	(24-ounce) jar red grapefruit sections, drained
Blood Orange Vinaigrette	

1. Preheat grill to medium-high heat.
2. Sprinkle fillets with salt and pepper. Coat fillets and onion slices with cooking spray. Place fish and onion on grill rack coated with cooking spray. Cover and grill 5 minutes on each side or until fish flakes easily when tested with a fork and onion is tender.
3. Cut onion into bite-sized chunks; break fish into chunks. Place 2 cups salad greens on each of 4 salad plates; arrange grapefruit sections, onion, and fish evenly over greens on each plate. Drizzle Blood Orange Vinaigrette evenly over salads. Yield: 4 servings (serving size: 2 cups greens, ½ cup grapefruit, about ⅓ cup onion, 2 ounces fish, and about 3 tablespoons Blood Orange Vinaigrette).

CALORIES 319; FAT 10g (sat 2.1g, mono 5.3g, poly 2.1g); PROTEIN 21.2g; CARB 35.8g; FIBER 2.5g; CHOL 43mg; IRON 2.5mg; SODIUM 493mg; CALC 69mg

Grilled Salmon and Grapefruit Salad with Blood Orange Vinaigrette

Blood Orange Vinaigrette

Prep: 4 minutes

⅓	cup blood orange juice
1	tablespoon minced shallots
2	tablespoons honey
1	tablespoon olive oil
1	teaspoon Dijon mustard
⅛	teaspoon salt
⅛	teaspoon freshly ground black pepper

1. Combine all ingredients in a small bowl, stirring well with a whisk. Yield: ⅔ cup plus 1 tablespoon (serving size: about 3 tablespoons).

CALORIES 75; FAT 4g (sat 0.5g, mono 2.5g, poly 0.5g); PROTEIN 0.2g; CARB 11.6g; FIBER 0.1g; CHOL 0mg; IRON 0.1mg; SODIUM 103mg; CALC 4mg

Shrimp and Noodle Salad with Asian Vinaigrette Dressing

Prep: 9 minutes • Cook: 5 minutes

Soy, ginger, and garlic give this nutty noodle salad an extra dimension of tantalizing flavor. Look for rice noodles in the ethnic-food section of your supermarket.

2   ounces dried rice noodles
Asian Vinaigrette Dressing
4   cups thinly sliced napa (Chinese) cabbage
¾   pound cooked peeled and deveined large shrimp
1   cup snow peas, trimmed and cut diagonally in half
3   cups fresh bean sprouts
3   tablespoons thinly sliced green onions (optional)
¼   cup chopped fresh cilantro (optional)

1. Cook noodles in boiling water 5 minutes, omitting salt and fat; drain and rinse with cold water. Drain.
2. While noodles cook, prepare Asian Vinaigrette Dressing; set aside.
3. Combine noodles, cabbage, and next 3 ingredients. Add dressing, and toss well. Sprinkle salad with green onions and cilantro, if desired. Yield: 4 servings (serving size: 2 cups salad).

CALORIES 243; FAT 6.2g (sat 0.9g, mono 2g, poly 2.9g); PROTEIN 26.9g; CARB 21.4g; FIBER 2g; CHOL 166mg; IRON 4.3mg; SODIUM 288mg; CALC 116mg

Asian Vinaigrette Dressing

Prep: 6 minutes

3   tablespoons fresh lime juice
1½   teaspoons fish sauce
1½   tablespoons creamy peanut butter
2   teaspoons sugar
2   teaspoons grated peeled fresh ginger
2   teaspoons reduced-sodium soy sauce
2   teaspoons dark sesame oil
2   garlic cloves, minced

1. Combine all ingredients, stirring with a whisk until smooth. Yield: 4 servings (serving size: about 2 tablespoons).

CALORIES 71; FAT 5.4g (sat 1g, mono 2.4g, poly 1.8g); PROTEIN 2g; CARB 5.1g; FIBER 0.5g; CHOL 0mg; IRON 0.2mg; SODIUM 272mg; CALC 6.8mg

Shrimp and Noodle Salad with Asian Vinaigrette Dressing

Sweet and Spicy Shrimp and Avocado Salad with Mango Vinaigrette

Prep: 8 minutes

Mango Vinaigrette
6	cups shredded romaine lettuce (2 hearts)
1	cup chopped red bell pepper (1 medium)
6	tablespoons thinly sliced green onions (optional)
1	pound peeled cooked shrimp
1	avocado, peeled and diced

Sweet and Spicy Shrimp and Avocado Salad with Mango Vinaigrette

1. Place Mango Vinaigrette in a large bowl. Add lettuce, bell pepper, and green onions, if desired; toss well. Add shrimp and avocado; toss gently. Yield: 4 servings (serving size: 2¾ cups salad).

CALORIES 249; FAT 10.3g (sat 1.7g, mono 6g, poly 1.8g); PROTEIN 26.1g; CARB 15.1g; FIBER 5g; CHOL 221mg; IRON 5mg; SODIUM 412mg; CALC 86mg

Mango Vinaigrette

Prep: 9 minutes

¼	cup fresh lime juice
2	tablespoons chopped fresh cilantro
1	tablespoon olive oil
½	teaspoon crushed red pepper
½	teaspoon sugar
¼	teaspoon salt
¼	teaspoon freshly ground black pepper
1	garlic clove, minced
¾	cup diced mango (about 1 medium)

1. Combine first 8 ingredients in a bowl, stirring with a whisk. Stir in mango. Yield: 4 servings (serving size: about ¼ cup).

CALORIES 58; FAT 3.5g (sat 0.5g, mono 2.5g, poly 0.4g); PROTEIN 0.3g; CARB 7.6g; FIBER 0.7g; CHOL 0mg; IRON 0.1mg; SODIUM 147mg; CALC 8mg

quick flip

Don't have mango on hand? Try diced pineapple instead. The sweetness complements the shrimp and avocado.

Grilled Southwestern Shrimp Salad with Lime-Cumin Dressing

Prep: 2 minutes • Cook: 12 minutes

We tested this recipe with peeled and deveined shrimp. Whether you have your fishmonger peel and devein them or if you do it yourself, you'll need to start with 1 pound of unpeeled shrimp.

¾   pound peeled and deveined large shrimp
1   teaspoon chili powder
2   ears corn
Cooking spray
6   cups chopped romaine lettuce
2   large tomatoes, cut into 8 wedges
Lime-Cumin Dressing
1   cup diced peeled avocado (1 small)

1. Preheat grill to medium-high heat.
2. Sprinkle shrimp evenly with chili powder. Remove husks from corn; scrub silks from corn. Place corn on grill rack coated with cooking spray. Grill 12 minutes, turning occasionally. Add shrimp to grill rack after 6 minutes; grill 3 minutes on each side. Cut kernels from ears of corn. Discard cobs.
3. Combine shrimp, corn, lettuce, and tomato in a large bowl; drizzle with Lime-Cumin Dressing, and toss well. Add avocado; toss gently. Serve immediately. Yield: 4 servings (serving size: 3¼ cups salad).

CALORIES 266; FAT 11.2g (sat 1.5g, mono 5.7g, poly 2.7g); PROTEIN 21.4g; CARB 24g; FIBER 5.9g; CHOL 129mg; IRON 3.8mg; SODIUM 404mg; CALC 90mg

Lime-Cumin Dressing

Prep: 4 minutes

¼   cup fresh lime juice
1   tablespoon canola oil
1   tablespoon honey
½   teaspoon kosher salt
½   teaspoon ground cumin
⅛   teaspoon coarsely ground black pepper

1. Combine all ingredients in a small bowl, stirring with a whisk. Yield: 4 servings (serving size: 1½ tablespoons).

CALORIES 52; FAT 3.6g (sat 0.3g, mono 2.1g, poly 1g); PROTEIN 0.1g; CARB 5.8g; FIBER 0.2g; CHOL 0mg; IRON 0.1mg; SODIUM 236mg; CALC 5mg

Grilled Southwestern Shrimp Salad with Lime-Cumin Dressing

Roast Beef, Beet, and Arugula Salad with Orange Vinaigrette

Prep: 8 minutes • Cook: 8 minutes

Sweet beets marry well with the peppery bite of arugula in this roast beef salad, while a citrusy vinaigrette provides a bright counterpoint to the richness of the meat, goat cheese, and pine nuts.

3	small beets, trimmed
8	cups loosely packed arugula

Orange Vinaigrette

1	(4-ounce) slice low-sodium deli roast beef (about ¼ inch thick), cut into strips
½	cup (2 ounces) crumbled goat cheese
2	tablespoons pine nuts, toasted

1. Place beets in a microwave-safe bowl; add enough water to come halfway up sides of bowl. Cover with plastic wrap; vent. Microwave at HIGH 8 minutes or until tender; drain and cool. Peel and slice into wedges.
2. While beets cook, combine arugula and Orange Vinaigrette, tossing gently to coat. Arrange arugula mixture evenly on each of 4 plates. Top evenly with beef, beets, cheese, and nuts. Yield: 4 servings (serving size: about 1½ cups arugula salad, 1 ounce beef, 3 beet wedges, 2 tablespoons cheese, and ½ tablespoon nuts).

CALORIES 226; FAT 16g (sat 4.6g, mono 6.7g, poly 2.4g); PROTEIN 13.4g; CARB 10.4g; FIBER 2.6g; CHOL 26mg; IRON 2.4mg; SODIUM 234mg; CALC 120mg

Orange Vinaigrette

Prep: 8 minutes

1	orange
2	tablespoons white wine vinegar
1	tablespoon minced shallots
2	teaspoons Dijon mustard
¼	teaspoon sugar
2	tablespoons olive oil

1. Grate 1 teaspoon orange rind; squeeze 2 tablespoons juice from orange over a bowl.
2. Combine orange rind and juice, white wine vinegar, and next 3 ingredients in a small bowl, stirring well with a whisk. Slowly add oil, stirring well with a whisk. Yield: ⅓ cup (serving size: about 1 tablespoon).

CALORIES 52; FAT 5g (sat 0.7g, mono 3.7g, poly 0.5g); PROTEIN 0.1g; CARB 1.6g; FIBER 0.1g; CHOL 0mg; IRON 0.1mg; SODIUM 46mg; CALC 2mg

ingredient spotlight

When selecting beets, buy small to medium globes with stems and leaves attached. You will usually find about three beets per bunch. The skins should be smooth, firm, and free of soft spots. Be sure to wear disposable latex gloves when handling the beets to protect your hands from staining.

Arugula Salad with Beets and Pancetta Crisps

Prep: 5 minutes • Cook: 5 minutes

The best time to make this salad is when there's a leftover end of French bread hanging around on the counter. Once the bread is dry and hard, it's the perfect addition to this salad.

8	very thin slices pancetta (1½ ounces)
4	cups arugula
1½	cups (1-inch) cubes day-old French bread, toasted
¼	cup chopped pitted dates
3	tablespoons prechopped green onions
3	tablespoons light balsamic vinaigrette
1	(8-ounce) package steamed peeled ready-to-eat baby red beets, quartered
1	cup (4 ounces) crumbled goat cheese

1. Cook pancetta in a large nonstick skillet over medium heat 5 minutes or until crisp, turning occasionally. Remove pancetta from skillet; drain on paper towels.
2. Combine arugula and next 3 ingredients in a large bowl. Drizzle with vinaigrette; toss gently to coat. Divide greens mixture evenly among 4 bowls. Top salads evenly with beets and pancetta; sprinkle evenly with cheese. Yield: 4 servings (serving size: 1¼ cups greens mixture, about 7 beet wedges, 2 pancetta slices, and about 1 ounce cheese).

CALORIES 220; FAT 10g (sat 5.4g, mono 2.8g, poly 0.8g); PROTEIN 10.8g; CARB 24.4g; FIBER 2.7g; CHOL 20.6mg; IRON 2.2mg; SODIUM 567mg; CALC 96mg

Prosciutto and Spicy Green Olive Pasta Salad

Prep: 11 minutes • Cook: 14 minutes

Serve this pasta salad with cantaloupe slices—a common partner for prosciutto—to cap off your meal.

1¾	cups uncooked multigrain penne
2	cups bagged baby spinach leaves
8	jalapeño-stuffed green olives, sliced
2	ounces thinly sliced prosciutto, chopped
2	tablespoons chopped fresh oregano
1	tablespoon extra-virgin olive oil
½	cup (2 ounces) crumbled reduced-fat feta cheese

1. Cook pasta according to package directions, omitting salt and fat. Drain and rinse with cold water.
2. While pasta cooks, combine spinach and next 4 ingredients in a large bowl. Add pasta and cheese; toss well. Yield: 4 servings (serving size: about 1½ cups pasta salad).

CALORIES 235; FAT 9g (sat 2.3g, mono 3.8g, poly 1.9g); PROTEIN 12g; CARB 32.6g; FIBER 5.2g; CHOL 13mg; IRON 2.1mg; SODIUM 585mg; CALC 83mg

ingredient spotlight

Prosciutto is an Italian ham that's air-cured with salt and seasonings pressed into the densely textured meat. The best prosciutto sold in the United States comes from the Parma area of Italy; it is made from larger pork legs than American prosciutto and is aged longer.

Prosciutto and Spicy
Green Olive Pasta Salad

Prosciutto-Fig Salad

Prep: 10 minutes

Substitute dried Calimyrna figs when fresh figs are no longer in season. You can toast the walnuts quickly in a dry skillet over medium-high heat. Sitr frequently, and remove them from the heat as soon as you begin to smell that wonderful nutty aroma.

¼   cup sherry vinegar
2   tablespoons olive oil
¼   teaspoon freshly ground black pepper
2   (6-ounce) packages fresh baby spinach
¼   cup chopped walnuts, toasted
8   fresh figs, quartered
3   ounces thinly sliced prosciutto, torn
¼   cup (1 ounce) crumbled Gorgonzola cheese

1. Combine first 3 ingredients in a large bowl, stirring with a whisk. Add spinach and next 3 ingredients; toss gently to coat. Divide spinach mixture evenly among 4 bowls. Sprinkle each serving with cheese. Yield: 4 servings (serving size: about 2½ cups spinach mixture and 1 tablespoon cheese).

CALORIES 292; FAT 16.1g (sat 3.7g, mono 7.2g, poly 4.6g); PROTEIN 11.5g; CARB 30.3g; FIBER 7.7g; CHOL 18mg; IRON 3.6mg; SODIUM 611mg; CALC 140mg

Prosciutto-Fig Salad

Black and Blue Salad

Prep: 3 minutes • Cook: 7 minutes
Other: 5 minutes

Serve this salad chilled or warm for a summer or
fall dinner.

2   (4-ounce) beef tenderloin steaks
Cooking spray
4   cups sliced romaine lettuce hearts
       (1½ romaine hearts)
½   cup vertically sliced red onion
2   plum tomatoes, quartered
Blue Cheese Dressing
½   to 1 teaspoon freshly ground black pepper

1. Heat a medium cast-iron or nonstick skillet over medium-high heat. Coat beef with
cooking spray. Add steaks to pan. Cook
steaks 2 to 3 minutes on each side or until
desired degree of doneness. Remove steaks
from pan; let stand 5 minutes. Cut each
steak into thin slices.
2. Place 2 cups lettuce on each of 2 large
plates. Sprinkle each salad with ¼ cup
onion slices. Arrange 4 tomato quarters
around edge of each salad. Place 1 sliced
steak in center of each salad; drizzle
Blue Cheese Dressing evenly over salads.
Sprinkle pepper evenly over salads. Yield:
2 servings (serving size: 1 salad and 3
tablespoons dressing).

CALORIES 295; FAT 16.5g (sat 3.8g, mono 8.2g, poly 3.2g); PROTEIN 26.1g;
CARB 10.5g; FIBER 3.3g; CHOL 69.9mg; IRON 2.6mg; SODIUM 233mg;
CALC 88mg

fix it faster

Look for packages of chopped romaine lettuce
hearts to make this delicious salad even faster.

Blue Cheese Dressing

Prep: 5 minutes

¼   cup nonfat buttermilk
1½   tablespoons canola mayonnaise
⅛   teaspoon hot sauce
1½   tablespoons crumbled blue cheese

1. Combine first 3 ingredients in a small
bowl, stirring with a whisk. Stir in cheese.
Yield: 2 servings (serving size: 3 tablespoons).

CALORIES 105; FAT 9.8g (sat 1.3g, mono 5.7g, poly 2.7g); PROTEIN 2.3g;
CARB 1.9g; FIBER 0g; CHOL 8.4mg; IRON 0mg; SODIUM 177mg; CALC 28mg

Black and Blue Salad

Taco Salad with Cilantro-Lime Vinaigrette

Prep: 5 minutes • Cook: 5 minutes

An ice-cold beer is all you need with this main-dish salad that's topped with a zesty cilantro-lime dressing. The mushrooms add meaty texture and flavor. Look for meatless crumbles in the produce section near the tofu and other soy products.

Cooking spray
1   (8-ounce) package presliced mushrooms
2   cups refrigerated meatless fat-free crumbles
2   teaspoons 40%-less-sodium taco seasoning
1   (8-ounce) package shredded iceberg lettuce
1   cup (⅛-inch-thick) slices red onion
Fresh salsa (optional)
Cilantro-Lime Vinaigrette
Preshredded reduced-fat Mexican blend cheese
        (optional)
16 light restaurant-style tortilla chips

quick flip

Try rolling up the salad mixture in iceberg lettuce leaves for a quick-and-easy variation.

1. Heat a large nonstick skillet over medium-high heat. Coat pan with cooking spray. Add mushrooms; sauté 3 minutes or until lightly browned. Add crumbles and taco seasoning. Cook 2 minutes or until thoroughly heated; set aside.
2. Layer lettuce, onion, and crumbles mixture evenly on each of 4 plates. Top with salsa, if desired; drizzle evenly with Cilantro-Lime Vinaigrette. Top with cheese, if desired. Serve each salad with tortilla chips. Yield: 4 servings (serving size: 1½ cups taco salad, about 1 tablespoon dressing, and 4 chips).

CALORIES 198; FAT 11g (sat 1.5g, mono 5.8g, poly 2.5g); PROTEIN 11.7g; CARB 16.7g; FIBER 4.3g; CHOL 0mg; IRON 2.3mg; SODIUM 328mg; CALC 35mg

Cilantro-Lime Vinaigrette

Prep: 6 minutes

2   tablespoons finely chopped fresh cilantro
3   tablespoons red wine vinegar
2   tablespoons olive oil
1   teaspoon grated lime rind
1   teaspoon minced garlic

1. Combine all ingredients, stirring well with a whisk. Yield: ⅓ cup (serving size: about 1 tablespoon).

CALORIES 69; FAT 8g (sat 1.1g, mono 5.5g, poly 0.8g); PROTEIN 0.1g; CARB 0.3g; FIBER 0.1g; CHOL 0mg; IRON 0.1mg; SODIUM 1mg; CALC 2mg

Spinach Salad with Grilled Pork Tenderloin and Nectarines

Prep: 6 minutes • Cook: 10 minutes
Other: 10 minutes

Grilling heightens the sweetness and flavor of the nectarines. Because they have such thin skins, nectarines don't require peeling for this dish. However, you may substitute fresh peeled peaches, if you prefer.

1	(1-pound) peppercorn-flavored pork tenderloin, trimmed
3	nectarines, halved
	Cooking spray
2	(6-ounce) packages fresh baby spinach
¼	cup light balsamic vinaigrette
¼	cup (1 ounce) crumbled feta cheese
	Freshly ground black pepper (optional)

1. Preheat grill to medium-high heat.
2. Cut pork horizontally through center of meat, cutting to, but not through, other side using a sharp knife; open flat as you would a book. Place pork and nectarine halves, cut sides down, on grill rack coated with cooking spray. Grill pork 5 minutes on each side or until a thermometer registers 160°. Grill nectarine halves 4 to 5 minutes on each side or until thoroughly heated. Remove pork and nectarine halves from grill. Let pork rest 10 minutes.
3. Cut nectarine halves into slices. Thinly slice pork. Combine spinach and vinaigrette in a large bowl; toss gently to coat.
4. Divide spinach mixture evenly on each of 6 plates. Top each serving evenly with nectarine slices and pork slices. Sprinkle with cheese. Sprinkle evenly with pepper, if desired. Yield: 6 servings (serving size: 1⅔ cups spinach salad, ½ nectarine, about 2 ounces pork, and 2 teaspoons cheese).

CALORIES 169; FAT 6g (sat 2g, mono 1.5g, poly 0.9g); PROTEIN 16g; CARB 15.8g; FIBER 3.9g; CHOL 41mg; IRON 2.9mg; SODIUM 766mg; CALC 86mg

Warm Pork Salad with Apples

Prep: 6 minutes • Cook: 7 minutes

Pork and apples are simply meant for each other. The pungent dressing marries well with tart Granny Smith apples.

6	teaspoons olive oil, divided
1	(1-pound) pork tenderloin, cut into 12 slices
1¼	teaspoons ground cumin, divided
½	teaspoon salt, divided
¼	teaspoon freshly ground black pepper, divided
2	tablespoons cider vinegar
2	teaspoons light brown sugar
1	(7-ounce) package torn radicchio and butter lettuce
1	large Granny Smith apple, cored and thinly sliced

1. Heat a large nonstick skillet over medium-high heat. Add 2 teaspoons oil; swirl to coat. Sprinkle pork evenly with 1 teaspoon cumin, ¼ teaspoon salt, and ⅛ teaspoon pepper. Add pork to pan; cook 3 minutes on each side or until done.
2. Combine vinegar, brown sugar, remaining 4 teaspoons oil, remaining ¼ teaspoon cumin, remaining ¼ teaspoon salt, and remaining ⅛ teaspoon pepper in a small bowl, stirring with a whisk.
3. Place lettuce, apple, and 2 tablespoons dressing in a large bowl; toss gently to coat. Divide salad evenly among 4 plates; top each with 3 slices of pork, and drizzle remaining dressing evenly over pork. Yield: 4 servings (serving size: 3 slices pork, 2 cups salad, and 1 teaspoon dressing).

CALORIES 237; FAT 11g (sat 2.3g, mono 4.1g, poly 4.3g); PROTEIN 23.4g; CARB 12g; FIBER 2.1g; CHOL 63mg; IRON 1.6mg; SODIUM 344mg; CALC 16mg

serve with:

Pomegranate-Orange Sparkler

Prep: 2 minutes

1   cup pomegranate juice, chilled
1   cup orange juice, chilled
¼   cup sugar
2   cups sparkling water, chilled
4   lemon wedges

1. Combine pomegranate juice, orange juice, and sugar in a large pitcher; stir until sugar dissolves. Stir in sparkling water, and serve immediately over ice with lemon wedges. Yield: 4 servings (serving size: 1 cup sparkler and 1 lemon wedge).

CALORIES 154; FAT 0.2g (sat 0g, mono 0g, poly 0g); PROTEIN 0.8g; CARB 38.7g; FIBER 0.1g; CHOL 0mg; IRON 0.2mg; SODIUM 13mg; CALC 18mg

Warm Pork Salad with Apples

Mediterranean Pasta Salad

Prep: 6 minutes • Cook: 10 minutes

8   ounces uncooked multigrain farfalle (bow tie pasta)
Olive-Parmesan Vinaigrette
1   cup chopped zucchini (about 1 medium)
½   cup julienne-cut sun-dried tomatoes, packed without oil
Basil leaves (optional)

1. Cook pasta according to package directions, omitting salt and fat. While pasta cooks, prepare Olive-Parmesan Vinaigrette. Add zucchini to pasta during the last 1 to 2 minutes of cook time. Drain. Rinse pasta mixture under cold water; drain and place in a large bowl. Add tomatoes; drizzle with Olive-Parmesan Vinaigrette, tossing to coat. Garnish with basil, if desired, and serve immediately. Yield: 6 servings (serving size: 1 cup pasta salad).

CALORIES 247; FAT 8.1g (sat 1.7g, mono 4.5g, poly 1.7g); PROTEIN 10.4g; CARB 33.1g; FIBER 5.1g; CHOL 3mg; IRON 2.7mg; SODIUM 245mg; CALC 100mg

Olive-Parmesan Vinaigrette

Prep: 4 minutes

¼   cup (1 ounce) grated fresh Parmesan cheese
¼   cup red wine vinegar
¼   cup olive tapenade
1   tablespoon extra-virgin olive oil
1   teaspoon Dijon mustard
¼   teaspoon freshly ground black pepper

1. Place all ingredients in a blender; process until smooth. Cover and refrigerate until ready to serve. Yield: 6 servings (serving size: 2 tablespoons).

CALORIES 73; FAT 6.7g (sat 1.7g, mono 4.1g, poly 0.8g); PROTEIN 2.7g; CARB 0.9g; FIBER 0.7g; CHOL 3mg; IRON 0.5mg; SODIUM 204mg; CALC 81mg

Asian Soba Noodle Salad

Prep: 10 minutes • Cook: 10 minutes

Soba noodles, made from buckwheat and wheat flour, are generally easy to find in the Asian food section. If unavailable, use whole-wheat spaghetti.

1	(8-ounce) package soba noodles
1½	cups frozen shelled edamame (green soybeans)
1½	cups matchstick-cut carrots
	Orange Vinaigrette
	Cooking spray
1	pound chicken breast tenders, cut into thin strips
¼	teaspoon salt
¼	teaspoon freshly ground black pepper

1. Cook noodles in boiling water 7 minutes or until almost al dente. Add edamame and carrots to pan; cook 1 minute or until tender. Drain; rinse under cold water. While noodle mixture cooks, prepare Orange Vinaigrette in a large bowl. Add noodle mixture to bowl; set aside.

2. While noodles cook, heat a large non-stick skillet over medium-high heat. Coat pan with cooking spray. Sprinkle chicken evenly with salt and pepper. Add chicken to pan. Cook 3 minutes on each side or until browned. Add chicken to noodle mixture; toss gently to coat. Cover and chill until ready to serve. Yield: 6 servings (serving size: about 1 cup salad).

CALORIES 322; FAT 7.6g (sat 1.2g, mono 2.9g, poly 3.4g); PROTEIN 25.6g; CARB 36.3g; FIBER 4g; CHOL 42mg; IRON 1.2mg; SODIUM 446mg; CALC 16mg

Asian Soba Noodle Salad

Orange Vinaigrette

Prep: 6 minutes

3	tablespoons fresh orange juice
1	tablespoon finely chopped green onions
1	tablespoon mirin (sweet rice wine)
1	tablespoon lower-sodium soy sauce
1	tablespoon dark sesame oil
2	teaspoons grated peeled fresh ginger
2	large garlic cloves, minced

1. Combine all ingredients in a bowl, stirring with a whisk. Yield: 6 servings (serving size: 1 tablespoon).

CALORIES 33; FAT 2.4g (sat 0.3g, mono 0.9g, poly 1.1g); PROTEIN 0.3g; CARB 2.4g; FIBER 0.1g; CHOL 0mg; IRON 0.1mg; SODIUM 101mg; CALC 4mg

Chickpea, Feta, and Orzo Salad

Prep: 7 minutes • Cook: 10 minutes

This Mediterranean-style salad combines the chewy texture of chickpeas with the tangy flavor of feta. Chopped tomato adds a pop of color.

1	cup uncooked orzo (rice-shaped pasta)
	Cucumber-Thyme Relish
1	cup refrigerated prechopped tomato
1	(16-ounce) can chickpeas (garbanzo beans), rinsed and drained
¼	teaspoon salt
⅓	cup (1.3 ounces) crumbled feta cheese with basil and sun-dried tomatoes

1. Cook pasta according to package directions; drain and rinse under cold water. Drain well. While pasta cooks, prepare Cucumber-Thyme Relish.
2. Combine tomato and chickpeas in a large bowl, tossing gently; stir in pasta, salt, and Cucumber-Thyme Relish. Add feta cheese; toss gently. Yield: 4 servings (serving size: 1½ cups salad).

CALORIES 294; FAT 7.7g (sat 1.6g, mono 4.2g, poly 1.9g); PROTEIN 10.6g; CARB 46.6g; FIBER 5.3g; CHOL 7mg; IRON 1.3mg; SODIUM 488mg; CALC 60mg

---

ingredient spotlight

Orzo is a tiny rice-shaped pasta. Perfect in soups and salads, it cooks in a flash. It's available in both short, plump "grains" and long, thin "grains."

Cucumber-Thyme Relish

Prep: 4 minutes

1½	tablespoons fresh lemon juice
1	tablespoon extra-virgin olive oil
½	cup chopped English cucumber
2	tablespoons finely chopped red onion
1	tablespoon thyme leaves
¼	teaspoon salt
¼	teaspoon freshly ground black pepper

1. Combine lemon juice and olive oil in a medium bowl, stirring with a whisk. Stir in cucumber and remaining ingredients. Yield: ⅔ cup (serving size: about 3 tablespoons).

CALORIES 37; FAT 3.5g (sat 0.5g, mono 2.5g, poly 0.5g); PROTEIN 0.2g; CARB 1.6g; FIBER 0.3g; CHOL 0mg; IRON 0.2mg; SODIUM 146mg; CALC 7mg

---

quick flip

Try fresh mint instead of thyme leaves for a cooler flavor.

Couscous, Sweet Potato, and Black Soybean Salad

Prep: 5 minutes • Cook: 5 minutes
Other: 5 minutes

Choose this lime-basil-infused salad—with chunks of beta-carotene-laced sweet potatoes and tender, high-fiber, protein-rich black soybeans—for a healthy meatless main dish you can have on the table in 15 minutes.

¾	cup water
⅔	cup wheat couscous
1	(16-ounce) package refrigerated cubed peeled sweet potato
¼	cup fat-free lime-basil vinaigrette
½	teaspoon freshly ground black pepper
¼	teaspoon salt
1	(15-ounce) can no-salt-added black soybeans, rinsed and drained
2	cups bagged baby spinach leaves
5	tablespoons crumbled reduced-fat feta cheese
3	green onions, chopped

1. Bring ¾ cup water to boil in a medium saucepan; gradually stir in couscous. Remove from heat; cover and let stand 5 minutes. Fluff with a fork.
2. While couscous stands, place sweet potato on a microwave-safe plate. Microwave at HIGH 5 minutes or until tender.
3. Combine vinaigrette, pepper, and salt in a large bowl; stir well with a whisk. Add couscous, sweet potato, soybeans, and spinach; toss gently to coat. Top each serving with cheese; sprinkle evenly with onions. Yield: 5 servings (serving size: about 1⅓ cups couscous salad and 1 tablespoon cheese).

CALORIES 228; FAT 4g (sat 1.1g, mono 0.7g, poly 1.7g); PROTEIN 10.5g; CARB 39.8g; FIBER 7.3g; CHOL 3mg; IRON 2.4mg; SODIUM 287mg; CALC 102mg

Couscous, Sweet Potato, and
Black Soybean Salad

Tarragon-Chicken Quinoa Salad

Prep: 4 minutes • Cook: 18 minutes

Packed with protein, this whole-grain salad combines tender rotisserie chicken and juicy grapes with an apple-yogurt dressing. Granny Smith apple slices make a great accompaniment.

1   cup uncooked quinoa
2   cups water
Creamy Apple Dressing
2   cups pulled rotisserie chicken
2   cups halved red seedless grapes
½   teaspoon salt

1. Place quinoa in a fine sieve. Rinse quinoa under cold water until water runs clear; drain well.
2. Combine quinoa and 2 cups water in a medium saucepan; bring to a boil. Cover, reduce heat, and simmer 15 minutes or until grains are translucent and the germ has spiraled out from each grain. While quinoa cooks, prepare Creamy Apple Dressing. Rinse quinoa under cold water until cool; drain well.
3. Place quinoa, chicken, and grapes in a large bowl. Combine Creamy Apple Dressing and salt, stirring with a whisk; add to quinoa mixture, tossing until coated. Serve immediately, or cover and refrigerate until thoroughly chilled. Yield: 6 servings (serving size: 1 cup quinoa salad).

CALORIES 273; FAT 6.1g (sat 1.4g, mono 3g, poly 1.6g); PROTEIN 20.6g; CARB 35.4g; FIBER 2.6g; CHOL 41mg; IRON 3.4mg; SODIUM 444mg; CALC 52mg

Creamy Apple Dressing

Prep: 5 minutes

½   cup plain low-fat Greek yogurt
1   Granny Smith apple, cored and quartered
1   tablespoon olive oil
1   teaspoon fresh tarragon
¼   teaspoon salt
¼   teaspoon white pepper

1. Place all ingredients a blender; process 1 minute or until apple is pureed. Cover and chill until ready to serve. Yield: 6 servings (serving size: about 3 tablespoons).

CALORIES 54; FAT 2.7g (sat 0.6g, mono 1.7g, poly 0.3g); PROTEIN 2g; CARB 6.2g; FIBER 0.4g; CHOL 1mg; IRON 0.1mg; SODIUM 105mg; CALC 23mg

Tarragon-Chicken
Quinoa Salad

Beet, Bulgur, and Orange Salad with Parsley Vinaigrette

Prep: 7 minutes • Cook: 10 minutes
Other: 10 minutes

To quickly remove the peel from an orange, cut a thin slice from the top and bottom of the orange so the fruit will stand upright. Stand the orange vertically on the cutting board. Using a sharp knife, remove the skin in ½-inch slices. Be sure to remove the white pith, which can be very bitter.

Beet, Bulgur, and Orange Salad
with Parsley Vinaigrette

1¾	cups water
1	cup uncooked bulgur
1	medium beet, peeled
2	navel oranges
	Parsley Vinaigrette
½	cup (4 ounces) crumbled goat cheese
	Parsley leaves (optional)

1. Bring water to a boil in a medium saucepan; stir in bulgur. Cover, remove from heat; let stand 10 minutes. Rinse with cold water; drain.
2. While water for bulgur comes to a boil, place beet on a plate; cover with 3 layers of damp paper towels. Microwave at HIGH 6 minutes or until tender.
3. While beet cooks, peel oranges; cut crosswise into thin wagon wheel–shaped slices.
4. Cut beet in half lengthwise. Turn beet halves, cut sides down, and cut into thin half moon–shaped slices; place in a bowl. Add 3 tablespoons Parsley Vinaigrette; toss until coated.
5. Stir remaining vinaigrette into bulgur. Spoon bulgur evenly onto each of 4 serving plates. Top evenly with beets and orange slices; sprinkle with cheese and parsley, if desired. Yield: 4 servings (serving size: 1 salad).

CALORIES 301; FAT 13.6g (sat 5.2g, mono 6.5g, poly 1.4g); PROTEIN 10.6g; CARB 37.8g; FIBER 8.6g; CHOL 13mg; IRON 1.8mg; SODIUM 274mg; CALC 89mg

Parsley Vinaigrette

Prep: 3 minutes

2	tablespoons coarsely chopped fresh parsley
2	tablespoons red wine vinegar
2	tablespoons olive oil
¼	teaspoon salt
¼	teaspoon freshly ground black pepper

1. Combine all ingredients in a small bowl, stirring with a whisk. Yield: 4 servings (serving size: about 4 teaspoons).

CALORIES 63; FAT 7g (sat 1g, mono 5g, poly 1g); PROTEIN 0.1g; CARB 0.2g; FIBER 0.1g; CHOL 0mg; IRON 0.2mg; SODIUM 147mg; CALC 4mg

fix it faster

We shaved minutes off the cook time of this meatless main-dish salad by microwaving the beet. Traditional cooking methods, such as baking, boiling, steaming, and roasting, can require 45 minutes or longer.

Couscous Salad with Roasted Chicken

Prep: 8 minutes • Cook: 2 minutes
Other: 5 minutes

The flavors of this salad meld as it chills. Be sure to prepare enough to have leftovers—it makes a great portable lunch.

⅓   cup uncooked couscous
1½   cups chopped roasted chicken breast
1   cup chopped English cucumber
1   cup halved grape tomatoes
¼   cup crumbled feta
1   cup chopped fresh parsley
¼   cup chopped fresh mint
4   green onions, chopped
1   garlic clove, minced
¼   cup fresh lemon juice
2   tablespoons olive oil
¼   teaspoon salt

1. Prepare couscous according to package directions, omitting salt and fat. Fluff couscous with a fork.
2. Combine couscous, chicken, and next 7 ingredients in a large bowl. Set aside.
3. Combine lemon juice, olive oil, and salt in a small bowl; stir well with a whisk. Pour dressing over couscous mixture; toss gently. Yield: 4 servings (serving size: about 1 cup salad).

CALORIES 230; FAT 9.3g (sat 1.6g, mono 5.7g, poly 1.5g); PROTEIN 19.7g; CARB 17.7g; FIBER 2.8g; CHOL 45mg; IRON 2.7mg; SODIUM 356mg; CALC 66mg

serve with:
Greek Pita Chips

Prep: 6 minutes • Cook: 15 minutes

2   (6-inch) pitas
Olive oil–flavored cooking spray
¼   teaspoon salt-free Greek seasoning
¼   teaspoon salt

1. Preheat oven to 350°.
2. Split pitas; cut into 8 wedges. Arrange pita wedges in a single layer on a large baking sheet; coat lightly with cooking spray. Sprinkle evenly with Greek seasoning and salt. Bake at 350° for 15 minutes or until crisp. Yield: 4 servings (serving size: 8 chips).

CALORIES 82; FAT 0.2g (sat 0g, mono 0g, poly 0g); PROTEIN 3.5g; CARB 16.5g; FIBER 0.5g; CHOL 0mg; IRON 1.4mg; SODIUM 225mg; CALC 20mg

Couscous Salad with Roasted Chicken

Chicken and Wild Rice Salad with Orange-Mango Vinaigrette

Prep: 5 minutes • Cook: 15 minutes
Other: 30 minutes

Slivered almonds add just the right amount of crunch to this nourishing salad, which you can make up to a day ahead.

1	(2.75-ounce) package quick-cooking wild rice
1	(3½-ounce) bag boil-in-bag brown rice
2	cups chopped cooked chicken breast (8 ounces)

Orange-Mango Vinaigrette
¼   cup slivered almonds, toasted

1. Cook wild rice and brown rice according to package directions, omitting salt and fat. Combine wild rice and brown rice; spread rice mixture in a thin layer in a baking pan. Refrigerate 30 minutes or until cool, stirring occasionally. Combine chilled rice mixture, chicken, and Orange-Mango Vinaigrette in a large bowl; toss well. Spoon rice mixture evenly onto each of 4 serving plates; sprinkle evenly with almonds. Yield: 4 servings (serving size: 1½ cups rice mixture and 1 tablespoon almonds).

CALORIES 421; FAT 10.1g (sat 1.5g, mono 5.9g, poly 1.9g); PROTEIN 30.1g; CARB 45.6g; FIBER 4.2g; CHOL 60mg; IRON 2.7mg; SODIUM 352mg; CALC 80mg

Orange-Mango Vinaigrette

Prep: 7 minutes

½	cup refrigerated orange-mango juice
1	cup chopped green onions
¼	cup chopped fresh flat-leaf parsley
2	tablespoons white balsamic vinegar
2	tablespoons minced shallots
1	tablespoon chopped fresh thyme
1	tablespoon extra-virgin olive oil
½	teaspoon salt
½	teaspoon freshly ground black pepper

1. Combine all ingredients in a small bowl, stirring with a whisk. Yield: 8 servings (serving size: 2 tablespoons).

CALORIES 35; FAT 1.8g (sat 0.3g, mono 1.3g, poly 0.2g); PROTEIN 0.4g; CARB 4.5g; FIBER 0.5g; CHOL 0mg; IRON 0.4mg; SODIUM 149mg; CALC 14mg

make ahead

To get a jump-start on this dish, cook and chill the rice up to two days before making the salad.

Curried Chicken-Rice Salad

Prep: 8 minutes • Cook: 3½ minutes
Other: 8 minutes

Crisp Gala apple and crunchy celery give this nutrient-rich salad an extra dimension of tantalizing texture and color. An excellent source of vitamin C, celery helps strengthen the immune system.

1	(10-ounce) package frozen microwaveable brown rice
1	cup vanilla fat-free yogurt
1	teaspoon curry powder
¼	teaspoon salt
3	cups chopped cooked chicken breast (about 1 pound)
1½	cups chopped Gala apple (about 1 medium)
½	cup chopped celery
¼	cup cherry-flavored sweetened dried cranberries

Green leaf lettuce leaves (optional)

1. Prepare rice according to package directions. Spread rice in a shallow pan; place in freezer 8 to 10 minutes.
2. While rice chills, combine yogurt, curry powder, and salt in a large bowl. Add chicken and next 3 ingredients to yogurt mixture, stirring until coated.
3. Stir chilled rice into chicken mixture. Spoon chicken salad onto lettuce leaves, if desired. Yield: 6 servings (serving size: 1 cup salad).

CALORIES 238; FAT 3g (sat 0.8g, mono 1g, poly 0.7g); PROTEIN 25.3g; CARB 26.5g; FIBER 1.9g; CHOL 60mg; IRON 1mg; SODIUM 187mg; CALC 97mg

Feta-Chicken Couscous Salad with Basil

Prep: 9 minutes • Cook: 2 minutes
Other: 5 minutes

Serve this salad with crispbreads and red pepper hummus for a light summer meal.

1¼	cups water
⅔	cup uncooked whole-wheat couscous
1	cup diced cooked chicken breast
¼	cup chopped fresh basil
3	tablespoons capers, rinsed and drained
1	tablespoon extra-virgin olive oil
1	teaspoon grated lemon rind
1	tablespoon fresh lemon juice
2	cups mixed baby salad greens
¼	cup (1 ounce) crumbled reduced-fat feta cheese

1. Bring 1¼ cups water to a boil in a medium saucepan. Add couscous; cover and let stand 5 minutes.
2. While couscous stands, combine chicken and next 5 ingredients in a large bowl, tossing gently to coat.
3. Fluff couscous with a fork. Add couscous, salad greens, and cheese to chicken mixture; toss gently to coat. Yield: 4 servings (serving size: 1 cup couscous salad).

CALORIES 208; FAT 7g (sat 1.8g, mono 2.9g, poly 0.8g); PROTEIN 17.2g; CARB 20.7g; FIBER 2.7g; CHOL 33mg; IRON 1.1mg; SODIUM 366mg; CALC 56mg

ingredient spotlight

Whether it's juice, lemon zest (rind), or slices, the acidity of lemon adds to the final balance of flavor in all types of food, from savory to sweet. Look for lemons with smooth, brightly colored skin that are heavy for their size.

Feta-Chicken Couscous Salad
with Basil

Chicken, Edamame, and Rice Salad

Prep: 11 minutes • Cook: 5 minutes
Other: 2 minutes

The distinct and powerful taste combination of fresh ginger and mint lends a burst of flavor to this main-dish salad.

1	(8.8-ounce) pouch microwaveable cooked long-grain rice
1¼	cups frozen shelled edamame (green soybeans)
3	tablespoons water
1	cup diced cooked chicken breast
2	tablespoons chopped fresh mint
1	tablespoon grated peeled fresh ginger
2	tablespoons rice vinegar
1	tablespoon canola oil
¼	teaspoon salt
4	radicchio leaves

1. Microwave rice according to package directions. Set aside; keep warm.
2. Combine edamame and 3 tablespoons water in a small bowl. Cover with plastic wrap. Microwave at HIGH 3 minutes. Let stand 2 minutes; drain.
3. Combine rice, edamame, chicken, and next 5 ingredients in a large bowl; toss to coat. Serve over radicchio. Yield: 4 servings (serving size: about ¾ cup salad and 1 radicchio leaf).

CALORIES 235; FAT 8g (sat 0.6g, mono 2.5g, poly 1.3g); PROTEIN 16.6g; CARB 23.5g; FIBER 2.4g; CHOL 30mg; IRON 1.6mg; SODIUM 399mg; CALC 49mg

serve with:

Green Tea–Kiwi and Mango Smoothies

Prep: 15 minutes

2½	cups frozen diced mango
¾	cup vanilla fat-free yogurt, divided
¼	cup honey, divided
2	tablespoons water
½	teaspoon grated lime rind
3	ripe kiwifruit, peeled and quartered
2	cups ice cubes
½	cup packed bagged baby spinach leaves
2	tablespoons bottled green tea
Kiwifruit slices (optional)	

1. Place mango, ½ cup yogurt, 2 tablespoons honey, 2 tablespoons water, and lime rind in a blender; process until smooth, stirring occasionally. Divide mango mixture into each of 4 serving glasses; place glasses in freezer.
2. Rinse blender container. Place remaining ¼ cup yogurt, remaining 2 tablespoons honey, kiwifruit, and next 3 ingredients in blender; process until smooth, stirring occasionally. Gently spoon green tea–kiwi mixture onto mango mixture in reserved glasses, working carefully around inside of each glass to create a clean horizontal line. Garnish with kiwifruit slices, and stir to combine flavors, if desired. Serve immediately. Yield: 4 servings (serving size: 1 cup).

CALORIES 234; FAT 0.4g (sat 0.1g, mono 0.1g, poly 0.2g); PROTEIN 3.2g; CARB 59.3g; FIBER 2.8g; CHOL 1mg; IRON 0.5mg; SODIUM 58mg; CALC 107mg

Chicken Bulgur Salad

Chicken Bulgur Salad

Prep: 3 minutes • Cook: 11 minutes

Reminiscent of tabbouleh, this Lebanese-inspired dish is a smart choice if you want to incorporate more fiber into your diet. Serve this salad with warmed whole-wheat pita bread.

1	cup water
½	cup uncooked quick-cooking bulgur
1½	cups cubed cooked chicken breast (about ½ pound)
1	cup finely chopped fresh parsley
1	(14-ounce) can quartered artichoke hearts, drained and coarsely chopped
1	cup grape tomatoes, halved
⅓	cup light Northern Italian salad dressing with basil and Romano (such as Ken's Steak House Lite)
2	tablespoons fresh lemon juice

1. Bring 1 cup water to a boil in a medium saucepan; stir in bulgur. Return to a boil; reduce heat, cover, and simmer 8 minutes or until liquid is absorbed. Drain bulgur, and rinse with cold water; drain well.
2. Combine chicken and remaining ingredients in a large bowl, tossing to coat. Add bulgur; toss gently to coat. Yield: 4 servings (serving size: 1¼ cups salad).

CALORIES 228 (23% from fat); FAT 6g (sat 1g, mono 1g, poly 0.5g); PROTEIN 21.2g; CARB 22.8g; FIBER 4.5g; CHOL 45mg; IRON 3mg; SODIUM 435mg; CALC 56mg

ingredient spotlight

Bulgur—wheat berries that have been steamed, dried, and ground—is the basis of many salads in the Middle East.

Multigrain Tuna Tabbouleh with Creamy Black Olive Vinaigrette

Prep: 9 minutes

Tabbouleh is a Mediterranean grain salad that traditionally includes chopped cucumber. Instead of tossing the cucumber into the salad, we cut an English cucumber into thin planks and spooned the pilaf mixture over the planks for a crunchier variation. Toss the extra vinaigrette with salad greens or steamed vegetables.

1	(8.5-ounce) package 7 whole-grain pilaf (such as Kashi)
1	(6-ounce) can albacore tuna in water, drained and flaked
1	cup chopped tomato
½	cup finely chopped fresh parsley
⅓	cup finely chopped red onion
⅓	cup Creamy Black Olive Vinaigrette
½	teaspoon coarsely ground black pepper
¼	teaspoon salt

1. Combine all ingredients in a large bowl; toss well. Serve immediately, or cover and chill until ready to serve. Yield: 4 servings (serving size: 1 cup salad).

CALORIES 275; FAT 15.9g (sat 2.2g, mono 10.8g, poly 2.6g); PROTEIN 12.3g; CARB 25.6g; FIBER 5.1g; CHOL 14mg; IRON 1.8mg; SODIUM 578mg; CALC 46mg

Creamy Black Olive Vinaigrette

Prep: 4 minutes

¾	cup drained large ripe olives
¼	cup fat-free, lower-sodium chicken broth
2	tablespoons red wine vinegar
2	teaspoons Dijon mustard
½	teaspoon black pepper
3	tablespoons extra-virgin olive oil

1. Place olives in a food processor; pulse 3 times until chopped. Add broth and next 3 ingredients; pulse 3 to 4 times or until blended. With processor on, slowly add oil though food chute. Yield: 8 servings (serving size: 2 tablespoons).

CALORIES 64; FAT 6.8g (sat 1g, mono 4.9g, poly 0.9g); PROTEIN 0.2g; CARB 1.3g; FIBER 0.5g; CHOL 0mg; IRON 0.5mg; SODIUM 122mg; CALC 13mg

Multigrain Tuna Tabbouleh with Creamy Black Olive Vinaigrette

meatless main dishes

Mushroom Macaroni and
Cheese, page 269

Black Bean and Corn–Topped Potatoes

Prep: 4 minutes • Cook: 10 minutes

Also enjoy this bountiful Southwestern-style topping with baked tortilla chips. When corn is in season, feel free to substitute fresh sweet corn kernels for frozen.

4	(6-ounce) baking potatoes
Cooking spray	
½	cup chopped onion
2	garlic cloves, minced
1	teaspoon ground cumin
½	teaspoon chili powder
1	(15-ounce) can no-salt-added black beans, rinsed and drained
1½	cups frozen whole-kernel corn
1½	cups fresh salsa
¼	cup (1 ounce) reduced-fat shredded Cheddar-Jack cheese
¼	cup chopped fresh cilantro

1. Pierce potatoes with a fork; arrange in a circle on paper towels in microwave oven. Microwave at HIGH 10 minutes, turning and rearranging potatoes after 5 minutes.
2. While potatoes cook, heat a large non-stick skillet over medium-high heat. Coat pan with cooking spray. Add onion and next 3 ingredients; sauté 3 minutes. Reduce heat to low. Add beans, corn, and salsa; cook 4 minutes or until thoroughly heated.
3. Split potatoes lengthwise, cutting to, but not through, other side. Fluff with a fork. Spoon about 1 cup bean mixture over each potato. Top each serving evenly with cheese and cilantro. Yield: 4 servings (serving size: 1 potato, about 1 cup bean mixture, 1 table-spoon cheese, and 1 tablespoon cilantro).

CALORIES 332; FAT 3g (sat 1.7g, mono 0.1g, poly 0.3g); PROTEIN 11g; CARB 64.1g; FIBER 9g; CHOL 7mg; IRON 3.5mg; SODIUM 308mg; CALC 106mg

Curried Paneer and Spinach–Stuffed Potatoes

Prep: 2 minutes • Cook: 12 minutes

Queso blanco, a Mexican cheese made almost exactly the same way as paneer, has a very similar flavor. It is available in most large supermarkets.

2	microwave-ready baking potatoes
Cooking spray	
1	teaspoon olive oil
½	cup prechopped onion
1	cup chopped tomato
1	teaspoon red curry powder
1	teaspoon ground fresh ginger paste
¼	teaspoon salt
1	cup chopped bagged baby spinach leaves
1	cup (4 ounces) diced paneer or queso blanco
¼	teaspoon garam masala
1	tablespoon chopped fresh cilantro (optional)

1. Microwave potatoes according to package directions for cooking 2 potatoes at one time.
2. While potatoes cook, heat a large nonstick skillet over medium-high heat. Coat pan with cooking spray. Add oil to pan; swirl to coat. Add onion; sauté onion in hot oil 2 minutes. Add tomato, red curry powder, ginger, and salt; cook 2 minutes, stirring occasionally. Remove from heat. Add spinach; stirring until spinach wilts. Stir in cheese and garam masala.
3. Unwrap potatoes. Cut a slit down top of each potato; push ends toward center to open potatoes. Spoon about ¾ cup tomato mixture into center of each potato. Garnish with cilantro, if desired. Yield: 2 servings (serving size: 1 stuffed potato).

CALORIES 293; FAT 7.9g (sat 3.4g, mono 3.4g, poly 0.6g); PROTEIN 11.5g; CARB 46.1g; FIBER 5g; CHOL 18mg; IRON 1.8mg; SODIUM 399mg; CALC 202mg

Tofu-Chickpea Patties

Prep: 10 minutes • Cook: 16 minutes

Serve these hearty meatless patties with Cucumber-Tomato Relish or Greek yogurt spiked with fresh cilantro and cumin.

1	(16-ounce) package cilantro-flavored firm tofu, drained
3	garlic cloves
1	(15-ounce) can lower-sodium chickpeas (garbanzo beans), rinsed and drained
4	teaspoons olive oil, divided
1	large egg
½	cup dry breadcrumbs
½	teaspoon freshly ground black pepper
¼	teaspoon salt

1. Place tofu between paper towels until barely moist. Cut tofu into 1-inch cubes.
2. With food processor running, drop garlic through food chute; process until minced. Add tofu and chickpeas. Pulse twice; scrape sides. Add 1 teaspoon oil, egg, and next 3 ingredients; pulse 4 times or just until beans are finely chopped (do not overprocess). Shape mixture into 8 (4-inch-round, ½-inch-thick) patties.
3. Heat in a large nonstick skillet over medium heat. Add 1½ teaspoons oil; swirl to coat. Add half of patties to pan; cook 4 minutes. Carefully turn patties over; cook 4 minutes or until browned. Repeat procedure with remaining oil and patties. Serve immediately. Yield: 4 servings (serving size: 2 patties).

CALORIES 312; FAT 15.5g (sat 2.4g, mono 6.3g, poly 6.5g); PROTEIN 19.4g; CARB 23.1g; FIBER 4.5g; CHOL 46.5mg; IRON 2mg; SODIUM 327mg; CALC 54mg

serve with:

Cucumber-Tomato Relish

Prep: 9 minutes

2	cups chopped English cucumber
½	cup chopped red onion
2	tablespoons chopped fresh mint
3	tablespoons fresh lemon juice
1½	tablespoons olive oil
½	teaspoon ground cumin
⅛	teaspoon salt
⅛	teaspoon freshly ground black pepper
1	(8-ounce) tomato, chopped

1. Place all ingredients except tomato in a food processor; pulse twice. Transfer mixture to a medium bowl, and stir in tomato. Yield: 4 servings (serving size: ¾ cup).

CALORIES 75; FAT 5.3g (sat 0.7g, mono 3.7g, poly 0.6g); PROTEIN 1.6g; CARB 6.6g; FIBER 2g; CHOL 0mg; IRON 0.4mg; SODIUM 78mg; CALC 15mg

ingredient spotlight

Put late-summer tomatoes to good use in this bright relish. For even more color, leave the cucumber unpeeled–English cucumber skin is thin enough to be palatable.

Chili-Cheese Sweet
Potato Fries

Chili-Cheese Sweet Potato Fries

Prep: 1 minute • Cook: 18 minutes

1   (20-ounce) package frozen julienne-cut
sweet potato fries
Butter-flavored cooking spray
1   (15-ounce) can vegetarian chili with beans
1   cup (4 ounces) reduced-fat shredded sharp
cheddar cheese
¼   cup sliced green onions

1. Preheat oven to 450°.
2. Arrange fries on a large rimmed baking
sheet. Coat fries with cooking spray. Bake at
450° for 18 to 22 minutes or until crisp.
3. While fries bake, cook chili in a small
saucepan over medium heat 3 minutes or
until thoroughly heated.
4. Transfer fries to a serving platter. Spoon
chili over fries; sprinkle with cheese and
green onions. Serve hot. Yield: 6 servings
(serving size: ⅙ chili-cheese fries).

CALORIES 282; FAT 11.5g (sat 3.5g, mono 3.5g, poly 4.4g); PROTEIN 10.5g;
CARB 37.8g; FIBER 6.4g; CHOL 15mg; IRON 0.9mg; SODIUM 381mg;
CALC 193mg

fix it faster

Don't have fresh strawberries on hand? Frozen
strawberries work in a pinch, but it will take a
little longer to blend.

serve with:
Mini Strawberry Milkshakes

Prep: 5 minutes

2½   cups vanilla low-fat ice cream
2   cups sliced strawberries
½   cup 1% low-fat milk
½   teaspoon vanilla extract

1. Place all ingredients in a blender; process
just until smooth. Yield: 6 servings (serving
size: about ⅔ cup).

CALORIES 111; FAT 3.3g (sat 1.8g, mono 1.1g, poly 0.3g); PROTEIN 3.5g;
CARB 17.8g; FIBER 1.1g; CHOL 18mg; IRON 0.2mg; SODIUM 48mg;
CALC 84mg

Tropical Black Beans

Prep: 7 minutes • Cook: 8 minutes

Light coconut milk, not to be confused with coconut cream, adds a creamy finish and exotic flavor boost to the nutty-flavored brown rice side dish that partners with the hearty black bean main dish.

2	teaspoons olive oil
1½	cups refrigerated prechopped tricolor bell pepper mix
¾	cup chopped red onion
2	garlic cloves, minced
1	cup (½-inch) chunks mango (1 mango)
⅓	cup fresh orange juice
½	teaspoon ground allspice
½	teaspoon freshly ground black pepper
2	(15-ounce) cans reduced-sodium black beans, rinsed and drained
½	cup (4 ounces) crumbled queso fresco

Tropical Black Beans

1. Heat a large nonstick skillet over medium-high heat. Add oil; swirl to coat. Add bell pepper mix, onion, and garlic; sauté 4 minutes or until tender. Stir in mango and next 4 ingredients. Cook 3 to 4 minutes or until thoroughly heated. Sprinkle with cheese. Yield: 4 servings (serving size: 1¼ cups bean mixture and 2 tablespoons cheese).

CALORIES 237; FAT 5.4g (sat 1.8g, mono 2.6g, poly 0.8g); PROTEIN 12.2g; CARB 40.8g; FIBER 8.4g; CHOL 9mg; IRON 3.4mg; SODIUM 198mg; CALC 177mg

quick flip

Consider subbing coconut curry broth for the light coconut milk. Lighter than light coconut milk, this broth nicely mingles flavors of coconut and curry. The hint of curry adds an ever-so-mild touch of heat.

serve with:
Coconut Rice

Prep: 2 minutes • Cook: 13 minutes
Other: 5 minutes

1	cup light coconut milk
¼	teaspoon salt
1	cup instant brown rice
¼	cup chopped green onions
1½	teaspoons Pickapeppa sauce
2	tablespoons flaked sweetened coconut, toasted

1. Combine coconut milk and salt in a 2-quart saucepan. Bring to a boil; gradually stir in rice. Cover, reduce heat, and simmer 10 minutes or until liquid is absorbed. Remove from heat; let stand, covered, 5 minutes. Fluff with a fork. Stir in remaining ingredients. Yield: 4 servings (serving size: ½ cup).

CALORIES 122; FAT 4.4g (sat 3.5g, mono 0.4g, poly 0.4g); PROTEIN 2.3g; CARB 21g; FIBER 1.5g; CHOL 0mg; IRON 0.6mg; SODIUM 175mg; CALC 5mg

Falafel Patties with Tzatziki

Prep: 6 minutes • Cook: 8 minutes

Falafel, a popular Middle Eastern food, consists of seasoned pureed chickpeas that are shaped into balls or patties and then deep fried and served stuffed inside pita bread. In our version, we've opted to lightly pan-fry the patties and serve them nestled in Boston lettuce leaves with a side of fresh, soft pita triangles.

2	garlic cloves
1	(15-ounce) can chickpeas (garbanzo beans), rinsed and drained
¼	cup all-purpose flour
¼	cup flat-leaf parsley leaves
2	tablespoons tahini (roasted sesame seed paste)
1	teaspoon baking powder
1	teaspoon ground cumin
1	teaspoon grated lemon rind
½	teaspoon salt
½	teaspoon freshly ground black pepper
2	tablespoons olive oil

Tzatziki

1. With food processor on, drop garlic through food chute; process until minced. Add chickpeas and next 8 ingredients to garlic in food processor; process until chickpeas are finely ground. Shape mixture into 4 (3-inch) patties.
2. Heat a large nonstick skillet over medium-high heat. Add oil to pan; swirl to coat. Add patties to pan; cook 4 minutes on each side or until browned. Serve patties with Tzatziki. Yield: 4 servings (serving size: 1 patty and about ⅓ cup Tzatziki).

CALORIES 286; FAT 12.8g (sat 2.1g, mono 6.9g, poly 3.2g); PROTEIN 10.6g; CARB 33.8g; FIBER 7.1g; CHOL 5mg; IRON 18.7mg; SODIUM 573mg; CALC 291mg

Tzatziki

Prep: 3 minutes

You'll need only one lemon for this meal, so be sure to grate the lemon rind for the falafel before squeezing the juice for the Tzatziki.

1½	cups coarsely chopped English cucumber (½ medium)
¾	cup plain low-fat yogurt
½	cup chopped fresh mint
1	tablespoon fresh lemon juice

1. Combine all ingredients in a bowl. Yield: 4 servings (serving size: about ⅓ cup).

CALORIES 62; FAT 1.1g (sat 0.5g, mono 0.3g, poly 0.3g); PROTEIN 4.6g; CARB 9g; FIBER 3g; CHOL 5mg; IRON 16.6mg; SODIUM 54mg; CALC 223mg

Sautéed Vegetables
and Spicy Tofu

Sautéed Vegetables and Spicy Tofu

Prep: 5 minutes • Cook: 9 minutes

Thanks to a seasoned packaged of tofu, this easy stir-fry comes together in a snap. This dish is delicious served alone, but for heartier fare serve it on top of rice noodles.

1	(16-ounce) package spicy tofu, drained
2	tablespoons olive oil, divided
2	tablespoons fresh lemon juice
½	teaspoon salt
¼	teaspoon crushed red pepper
2	large garlic cloves, pressed
1	large zucchini, halved lengthwise and cut crosswise into thin slices
1	cup thinly sliced red bell pepper

Lemon wedges (optional)

1. Place tofu on several layers of heavy-duty paper towels. Cover tofu with additional paper towels; gently press out moisture. Cut tofu into ½-inch cubes.
2. Combine 1 tablespoon oil and next 4 ingredients in a medium bowl. Set aside.
3. Heat remaining 1 tablespoon oil in a large nonstick skillet over medium-high heat. Add remaining 1 tablespoon oil; swirl to coat. Add tofu, zucchini, and bell pepper; stir-fry 8 to 10 minutes or until tofu is browned and vegetables are crisp-tender. Add oil mixture; cook 1 minute, stirring gently. Serve with lemon wedges, if desired. Yield: 4 servings (serving size: 1 cup).

CALORIES 196; FAT 13.7g (sat 2.3g, mono 5g, poly 5g); PROTEIN 15g; CARB 7.9g; FIBER 3.2g; CHOL 0mg; IRON 3mg; SODIUM 302mg; CALC 154mg

Asparagus and Basil Omelet

Prep: 4 minutes • Cook: 7 minutes

Simple to prepare, this garden-fresh omelet is a quick-fix brunch, lunch, or dinner. Serve it with whole-wheat toast and orange juice.

Cooking spray

12	asparagus spears, diagonally cut into 1-inch pieces (about 1 cup)
2	large eggs
½	cup egg substitute
¼	cup water
¼	teaspoon salt
¼	teaspoon coarsely ground black pepper
½	cup (2 ounces) reduced-fat shredded Swiss cheese
2	tablespoons basil leaves

1. Heat an 8-inch nonstick skillet over medium-high heat; coat pan with cooking spray. Add asparagus, and sauté 3 minutes; set aside.
2. Combine eggs and next 4 ingredients in a medium bowl; stir with a whisk until blended.
3. Wipe pan with paper towels. Heat pan over medium heat; recoat pan with cooking spray. Add egg mixture, and cook 3 minutes or until set (do not stir). Sprinkle with asparagus, cheese, and basil. Loosen omelet with a spatula; fold in half. Cook 1 to 2 minutes or until cheese melts. Slide omelet onto a plate. Cut in half. Yield: 2 servings (serving size: ½ omelet).

CALORIES 203; FAT 7.7g (sat 2.7g, mono 3g, poly 1.9g); PROTEIN 24.1g; CARB 7g; FIBER 2.1g; CHOL 191mg; IRON 4.5mg; SODIUM 548mg; CALC 360mg

Spanakopita

Prep: 11 minutes • Cook: 37 minutes

This Greek spinach pie with a fancy name requires some special tips. When working with phyllo, always keep the remaining portion covered with a damp cloth towel to prevent it from drying out. And be sure to drain the spinach well before combining with cheeses to keep the crust from becoming soggy.

Spinach Filling
12   (12 x 9–inch) sheets frozen phyllo dough, thawed
Olive oil–flavored cooking spray
2   tablespoons grated fresh Parmesan cheese

1. Preheat oven to 375°.
2. Prepare Spinach Filling.
3. Place 1 phyllo sheet on a large cutting board or work surface (cover remaining dough to prevent drying); coat with cooking spray. Top with 1 dough sheet; coat with cooking spray. Repeat procedure with 4 additional dough sheets and cooking spray.
4. Fit dough stack in an 11 x 7–inch baking dish coated with cooking spray, allowing phyllo to extend up sides of pan. Spread Spinach Filling over phyllo. Fold edges over filling even with edges of dish. Sprinkle with Parmesan cheese.
5. Place 1 phyllo sheet on work surface (cover remaining phyllo to prevent drying); coat with cooking spray. Top with 1 dough sheet; coat with cooking spray. Repeat procedure with 4 remaining sheets and cooking spray.

6. Place dough stack over spinach mixture. Fold edges over dough even with edges of dish. Coat dough with cooking spray.
7. Bake at 375° for 30 minutes or until golden. Cut into rectangles. Yield: 8 servings (serving size: 1 rectangle).

CALORIES 191; FAT 7g (sat 2.6g, mono 3.4g, poly 0.8g); PROTEIN 10.1g; CARB 21g; FIBER 2.3g; CHOL 56mg; IRON 2.6mg; SODIUM 481mg; CALC 155mg

Spinach Filling

Prep: 1 minute • Cook: 7 minutes

2   teaspoons olive oil
1   (8-ounce) container refrigerated prechopped onion
2   (6-ounce) packages fresh baby spinach
¾   cup part-skim ricotta cheese
1   (3.5-ounce) package crumbled reduced-fat feta cheese with basil and sun-dried tomatoes
¼   teaspoon salt
2   large eggs, lightly beaten

1. Heat a large nonstick skillet over medium heat. Add oil; swirl to coat. Add onion; sauté 5 minutes or until tender. Gradually add 1 package spinach. Cook, stirring constantly, 1 minute or just until spinach wilts slightly. Gradually add remaining package spinach; cook, stirring constantly, just until spinach wilts. Remove from heat. Drain spinach mixture through a fine sieve, pressing with the back of a spoon; place in a bowl. Stir in cheeses, salt, and eggs. Yield: 3½ cups.

CALORIES 98; FAT 4.7g (sat 1.9g, mono 2.2g, poly 0.5g); PROTEIN 7.3g; CARB 6g; FIBER 1.8g; CHOL 54mg; IRON 1.7mg; SODIUM 312mg; CALC 127mg

Lemon-Artichoke Frittata

Prep: 1 minute • Cook: 17 minutes

This lemony frittata with a sunny flavor is similar to an omelet but easier. Packed with artichoke hearts, it makes a great light main course for the time-starved cook.

1	tablespoon olive oil
1	lemon
6	large eggs
4	large egg whites
⅓	cup light garlic-and-herbs spreadable cheese
1	(14-ounce) can quartered artichoke hearts, drained

1. Preheat oven to 450°.
2. Heat a 10-inch ovenproof skillet over medium heat. Add oil; swirl to coat.
3. While oil heats, grate rind and squeeze juice from lemon to measure 2 teaspoons rind and 2 teaspoons juice. Combine lemon rind, lemon juice, eggs, egg whites, and cheese, stirring with a whisk. Stir in artichoke hearts.
4. Add egg mixture to pan; reduce heat to medium-low, and cook until edges begin to set, about 2 minutes. Gently lift edge of egg mixture, tilting pan to allow uncooked egg mixture to come in contact with pan. Cook 2 minutes or until egg mixture is almost set.
5. Bake at 450° for 11 minutes or until center is set. Transfer frittata to a serving platter immediately; cut into 8 wedges. Yield: 4 servings (serving size: 2 wedges).

CALORIES 182; FAT 11.9g (sat 4.2g, mono 5.8g, poly 1.8g); PROTEIN 15.8g; CARB 7g; FIBER 0.1g; CHOL 282mg; IRON 2.3mg; SODIUM 325mg; CALC 44mg

serve with:

Blueberry Citrus Salad

Prep: 5 minutes • Other: 30 minutes

3	navel oranges
2	tablespoons chopped fresh mint
2	tablespoons honey
2	cups fresh blueberries

1. Peel and section oranges over a bowl; squeeze membranes to extract juice. Stir in mint and honey. Add blueberries, and toss gently. Cover and chill 30 minutes. Yield: 4 servings (serving size: about ⅔ cup).

CALORIES 126; FAT 0.4g (sat 0g, mono 0.1g, poly 0.2g); PROTEIN 1.6g; CARB 32.7g; FIBER 4.2g; CHOL 0mg; IRON 0.4mg; SODIUM 3mg; CALC 52mg

Lemon-Artichoke Frittata

Southwest Rice Frittata

Prep: 5 minutes • Cook: 35 minutes
Other: 10 minutes

Spicy rice and sweet bell peppers make this open-faced frittata a standout. Bake it until it's golden brown and crispy on top.

1   (8.5-ounce) package Santa Fe–flavored microwavable precooked whole-grain rice medley
Cooking spray
1   (16-ounce) package frozen bell pepper stir-fry
3   large eggs
3   large egg whites
½   cup all-natural salsa

1. Preheat oven to 400°.
2. Microwave rice according to package directions. Heat a large skillet over medium-high heat. Coat pan with cooking spray. Add bell pepper stir-fry to pan; cook 3 minutes or until thawed and thoroughly heated, stirring frequently. Drain.
3. While bell pepper stir-fry cooks, combine eggs and egg whites in a large bowl, stirring with a whisk. Stir rice, bell pepper stir-fry, and salsa into egg mixture.
4. Spoon rice mixture into an 8-inch springform pan coated with cooking spray, pressing down firmly with the back of a spoon.
5. Bake at 400° for 35 minutes or until set and golden. Let cool 10 minutes on a wire rack. Cut frittata into 4 wedges. Yield: 4 servings (serving size: 1 wedge).

CALORIES 198; FAT 4.2g (sat 0.9g, mono 2g, poly 1.2g); PROTEIN 11.5g; CARB 26.3g; FIBER 4.1g; CHOL 135mg; IRON 1.3mg; SODIUM 446mg; CALC 40mg

Southwest Rice Frittata

serve with:

Jalapeño Black Beans and Corn

Prep: 2 minutes • Cook: 8 minutes

1   (15-ounce) can no-salt-added black beans, drained
1   (11-ounce) can whole-kernel corn, drained
¼   cup sliced drained pickled jalapeños
2   tablespoons fresh lime juice
2   tablespoons chopped fresh cilantro

1. Combine first 4 ingredients in a medium saucepan. Cook over medium-high heat 8 minutes or until bubbly and thoroughly heated, stirring occasionally. Stir in cilantro. Yield: 4 servings (serving size: ¾ cup).

CALORIES 151; FAT 1.5g (sat 0g, mono 0.4g, poly 1g); PROTEIN 7.1g; CARB 25.6g; FIBER 7.1g; CHOL 0mg; IRON 1.8mg; SODIUM 266mg; CALC 61mg

Meatless Hash and Eggs

Prep: 3 minutes • Cook: 16 minutes

This meat-free dish, adapted from a traditional recipe for corned beef and hash, earned our Test Kitchen's highest rating.

2½ cups frozen shredded hash brown potatoes
1½ cups frozen meatless crumbles
1½ cups prechopped tomato, green bell pepper, and onion mix
½ teaspoon salt
¼ teaspoon freshly ground black pepper
Cooking spray
1 tablespoon olive oil
4 large eggs

1. Combine first 5 ingredients in a medium bowl.
2. Heat a large nonstick skillet over medium heat. Coat pan with cooking spray. Add oil to pan; swirl to coat. Add potato mixture, and cook 5 to 7 minutes or until potato mixture is thoroughly heated, stirring occasionally. Form 4 (3-inch) indentations in potato mixture using the back of a spoon.

Break 1 egg into each indentation. Cover and cook 10 minutes or until eggs are done. Yield: 4 servings (serving size: 1 egg and 1 cup potato mixture).

CALORIES 271; FAT 10.8g (sat 2.3g, mono 4.7g, poly 3g); PROTEIN 15.2g; CARB 30.3g; FIBER 3.9g; CHOL 212mg; IRON 3.4mg; SODIUM 527mg; CALC 59mg

serve with:
Citrus-Jicama Salad

Prep: 9 minutes

1 (24-ounce) jar red grapefruit sections
2 tablespoons fresh mint, chopped
⅛ teaspoon ground cinnamon
⅔ cup jicama, peeled and matchstick-cut

1. Drain red grapefruit sections, reserving ¼ cup juice. Combine juice, mint, and cinnamon in a medium bowl; stir with a whisk. Add grapefruit sections and jicama; toss gently. Yield: 4 servings (serving size: about ½ cup).

CALORIES 91; FAT 0g (sat 0g, mono 0g, poly 0g); PROTEIN 1.6g; CARB 21.1g; FIBER 2g; CHOL 0mg; IRON 1mg; SODIUM 22mg; CALC 9mg

Meatless Hash and Eggs

Goat Cheese–Mushroom Naan Pizzas

Prep: 9 minutes • Cook: 18 minutes

Rustic naan, an East Indian yeast flatbread tradition-ally baked in a tandoor oven, makes a flavorful, sturdy base for this meatless pizza. Look for it with pita breads, wraps, and other flatbreads in your grocery store.

2	teaspoons olive oil
2	(4-ounce) packages presliced exotic mushroom blend (such as shiitake, cremini, and oyster)
2	(3-ounce) whole-wheat naan
Cooking spray	
¼	cup sun-dried tomato pesto
¾	cup (3 ounces) crumbled goat cheese with herbs

1. Preheat oven to 450°.
2. Heat a large nonstick skillet over medium-high heat. Add oil; swirl to coat. Add mushrooms; cook 7 minutes or until lightly browned, stirring once.
3. While mushrooms cook, place naan on a large baking sheet coated with cooking spray. Spread 2 tablespoons pesto over each naan, spreading to within ½ inch of edges. Sprinkle mushrooms evenly over each; top with goat cheese.
4. Bake at 450° for 10 minutes or until cheese softens. Cut each pizza in half. Yield: 4 servings (serving size: ½ pizza).

CALORIES 235; FAT 9.7g (sat 3.6g, mono 3.6g, poly 2.4g); PROTEIN 10.3g; CARB 27.8g; FIBER 5g; CHOL 8mg; IRON 2.3mg; SODIUM 420mg; CALC 34mg

serve with:

Butter Lettuce–Orange Salad with Sweet and Sour Dressing

Prep: 5 minutes

1	large navel orange
3	tablespoons white wine vinegar
1	tablespoon olive oil
1	tablespoon honey
¼	teaspoon salt
⅛	teaspoon freshly ground black pepper
1	(6.5-ounce) package sweet butter lettuce blend salad greens
¼	cup mint leaves, torn

1. Peel and section orange over a large bowl, squeezing membranes to extract juice and placing sections in a separate bowl. Add vinegar and next 4 ingredients to orange juice, stirring with a whisk. Add orange sections, lettuce, and mint; toss gently. Serve immediately. Yield: 4 servings (serving size: 1¼ cups).

CALORIES 70; FAT 3.4g (sat 0.5g, mono 2.5g, poly 0.4g); PROTEIN 0.9g; CARB 10.1g; FIBER 1.5g; CHOL 0mg; IRON 0.8mg; SODIUM 147mg; CALC 33mg

Goat Cheese–Mushroom Naan Pizzas

Fig and Arugula Pizzas
with Goat Cheese

1. Preheat oven to 450°.

2. Prepare Fig-Arugula Pesto. Place naan on a baking sheet coated with cooking spray. Spread half of Fig-Arugula Pesto on each naan, spreading to within 1 inch of edges. Arrange goat cheese slices evenly over pizzas.

3. Bake at 450° for 15 minutes or until naan is crisp and goat cheese is golden and bubbly. Top evenly with pear and walnuts. Cut each pizza into 4 slices. Yield: 4 servings (serving size: 2 slices).

CALORIES 412; FAT 19.1g (sat 5.8g, mono 5.7g, poly 7.4g); PROTEIN 12.1g; CARB 50.4g; FIBER 4.6g; CHOL 13mg; IRON 2.3mg; SODIUM 595mg; CALC 118mg

Fig-Arugula Pesto

Prep: 10 minutes

½	cup fig preserves
¼	cup chopped toasted walnuts
1	tablespoon extra-virgin olive oil
½	teaspoon salt
¼	teaspoon freshly ground black pepper
1	(5-ounce) package arugula

1. Place first 5 ingredients in a food processor; pulse 5 times or until blended. Add arugula; pulse 10 times or until arugula is finely chopped. Yield: 1⅓ cups (serving size: about 10 tablespoons).

CALORIES 177; FAT 8.5g (sat 1g, mono 3.2g, poly 4.1g); PROTEIN 2g; CARB 24.4g; FIBER 1.1g; CHOL 0mg; IRON 0.7mg; SODIUM 300mg; CALC 65mg

Fig and Arugula Pizzas with Goat Cheese

Prep: 15 minutes • Cook: 15 minutes

We subbed naan, a ready-made flatbread, for crust in this cheesy, fruity pizza variation. Flatbreads, such as naan, make quick and easy pizza crusts.

	Fig-Arugula Pesto
2	(4.4-ounce) naan
	Cooking spray
4	ounces goat cheese, sliced
1	cup thinly sliced red Bartlett pear (1 pear)
2	tablespoons walnuts, toasted and coarsely chopped

Mini White Pizzas with Vegetables

Prep: 5 minutes • Cook: 9 minutes

We used whole-wheat pita rounds to help with portion control and to speed up the cook time. For a Greek-inspired flavor variation, substitute hummus for the spreadable cheese.

4	(6-inch) whole-wheat pitas

Olive oil–flavored cooking spray

1	medium zucchini, thinly sliced
¼	cup thinly sliced red onion, separated into rings
¼	teaspoon freshly ground black pepper
⅛	teaspoon salt
½	cup light garlic-and-herbs spreadable cheese
6	tablespoons shredded Asiago cheese

1. Preheat broiler.
2. Place pitas on a baking sheet; broil 3 minutes.
3. Heat a nonstick skillet over medium-high heat; coat pan with cooking spray. Add zucchini, onion, pepper, and salt; sauté 3 minutes or until vegetables are crisp-tender.
4. Remove pitas from oven, and spread 2 tablespoons garlic-and-herbs spreadable cheese over each pita. Top evenly with vegetables and Asiago cheese. Broil 3 minutes or until edges are lightly browned and cheese melts. Yield: 4 servings (serving size: 1 pizza).

CALORIES 272; FAT 8.7g (sat 4.6g, mono 1, poly 1g); PROTEIN 11.9g; CARB 40.2g; FIBER 5.5g; CHOL 24mg; IRON 2.2mg; SODIUM 505mg; CALC 137mg

Mini White Pizzas with Vegetables

Roasted Mushroom and Shallot Pizza

1. Preheat oven to 450°.
2. Spread cream cheese over pizza crust. Top with Roasted Mushrooms and Shallots and cheese slices.
3. Bake pizza directly on oven rack at 450° for 8 minutes or until crust is golden and cheese melts. Sprinkle with oregano, and serve immediately. Yield: 6 servings (serving size: 1 slice).

CALORIES 280; FAT 11.3g (sat 5.4g, mono 2.8g, poly 3g); PROTEIN 12.9g; CARB 32g; FIBER 2.5g; CHOL 19mg; IRON 2.7mg; SODIUM 520mg; CALC 302mg

Roasted Mushrooms and Shallots

Prep: 15 minutes • Cook: 15 minutes

1	tablespoon extra-virgin olive oil
¼	teaspoon salt
¾	teaspoon freshly ground black pepper
4	garlic cloves, minced
1	(8-ounce) package baby portobello mushrooms, quartered
1	(3.5-ounce) package shiitake mushrooms, stems removed and quartered
2	(3-ounce) packages small shallots, peeled and quartered lengthwise

Cooking spray

1. Preheat oven to 450°.
2. Combine first 4 ingredients in a large bowl. Add mushrooms and shallots; toss to coat. Spread mushroom mixture in a single layer in a jelly-roll pan coated with cooking spray.
3. Bake at 450° for 15 minutes (do not stir). Yield: 2 cups (serving size: ⅓ cup).

CALORIES 55; FAT 2.5g (sat 0.3g, mono 1.8g, poly 0.3g); PROTEIN 2g; CARB 6.4g; FIBER 1.2g; CHOL 0mg; IRON 0.7mg; SODIUM 105mg; CALC 15mg

Roasted Mushroom and Shallot Pizza

Prep: 5 minutes • Cook: 8 minutes

Lorraine cheese, which comes in long slices, is similar in flavor to Swiss cheese. If you don't have fresh oregano, you can substitute ½ teaspoon dried oregano.

½	(8-ounce) tub light chive-and-onion cream cheese
1	(10-ounce) cheese-flavored thin pizza crust
2	cups Roasted Mushrooms and Shallots
3	(1-ounce) slices reduced-fat Lorraine cheese
2	tablespoons oregano leaves

Whole-Wheat Pita Pizzas with Spinach, Fontina, and Onions

Whole-Wheat Pita Pizzas with Spinach, Fontina, and Onions

Prep: 4 minutes • Cook: 11 minutes

3   teaspoons olive oil, divided
3   garlic cloves, minced
2   cups vertically sliced red onion
2   cups bagged baby spinach leaves
4   (7-inch) whole-wheat pitas
¼   cup (2 ounces) shredded Fontina cheese

1. Preheat oven to 450°.
2. Heat a medium nonstick skillet over medium-high heat. Add 1 teaspoon oil; swirl to coat. Add garlic and onion; sauté 5 minutes or until tender.
3. Add spinach and sauté 2 minutes or just until spinach begins to wilt. Remove from heat.
4. Place pitas on a large baking sheet; brush with remaining 2 teaspoons olive oil. Top pitas evenly with garlic-spinach mixture and cheese. Bake at 450° for 4 minutes or until cheese melts and pitas are brown. Yield: 4 servings (serving size: 1 pizza).

CALORIES 287; FAT 9.5g (sat 3.5g, mono 3.9g, poly 1.3g); PROTEIN 11g; CARB 42.6g; FIBER 6.2g; CHOL 16mg; IRON 2.6mg; SODIUM 466mg; CALC 118mg

serve with:
Arugula Salad

Prep: 2 minutes

1   tablespoon balsamic vinegar
2   teaspoons olive oil
½   teaspoon freshly ground black pepper
¼   teaspoon salt
4   cups arugula leaves
1   cup cherry tomatoes, halved

1. Combine first 4 ingredients in a large bowl, stirring with a whisk. Add arugula and tomato halves; toss well. Yield: 4 servings (serving size: about 1 cup).

CALORIES 37; FAT 2.5g (sat 0.4g, mono 1.7g, poly 0.4g); PROTEIN 0.9g; CARB 3.3g; FIBER 0.8g; CHOL 0mg; IRON 0.5mg; SODIUM 155mg; CALC 36mg

Grape, Blue Cheese, and Walnut Pizza

Prep: 4 minutes • Cook: 10 minutes

We made our own balsamic syrup for this unique thin-crust pizza, but you can substitute bottled balsamic glaze found in the vinegar section of your supermarket. This recipe can easily be doubled to serve two.

1   (2.8-ounce) whole-wheat flatbread
¾   cup seedless red grapes, halved
2   tablespoons crumbled blue cheese
2   tablespoons chopped walnuts, toasted
2   tablespoons balsamic vinegar
1   cup arugula leaves

1. Preheat oven to 375°.
2. Place flatbread on rack in oven; bake at 375° for 3 minutes or until lightly browned. Remove flatbread from oven; top with grapes, cheese, and walnuts. Place flatbread back on rack in oven; bake 5 minutes or until cheese melts and crust is browned.
3. While pizza bakes, bring vinegar to a boil in a small saucepan. Boil 1 minute or until vinegar thickens and reduces to about ½ tablespoon. Top pizza with arugula; drizzle with balsamic syrup. Serve immediately. Yield: 1 serving (serving size: 1 pizza).

CALORIES 479; FAT 17g (sat 3.2g, mono 2g, poly 6g); PROTEIN 18.3g; CARB 66g; FIBER 6.2g; CHOL 13mg; IRON 3.2mg; SODIUM 682mg; CALC 157mg

Grilled Heirloom Tomato and Goat Cheese Pizza

Prep: 11 minutes • Cook: 4 minutes

1   (13.8-ounce) can refrigerated pizza crust
     dough
Cooking spray
1   garlic clove, halved
1   large heirloom tomato, seeded and chopped
     (about 10 ounces)
½   cup (2 ounces) shredded part-skim
     mozzarella cheese
¾   cup (3 ounces) crumbled herbed goat cheese

1. Preheat grill to medium heat.
2. Unroll dough onto a large baking sheet coated with cooking spray; pat dough into a 12 x 9–inch rectangle. Lightly coat dough with cooking spray.

3. Place dough on grill rack coated with cooking spray; grill 1 minute or until lightly browned. Turn crust over. Rub with garlic; sprinkle with tomato and cheeses. Close grill lid; grill 3 minutes. Serve immediately. Yield: 6 servings (serving size: 1 slice).

CALORIES 242; FAT 8g (sat 4.4g, mono 1.4g, poly 0.2g); PROTEIN 10.7g; CARB 33.1g; FIBER 0.4g; CHOL 17mg; IRON 2.2mg; SODIUM 590mg; CALC 107mg

serve with:
Peanut Butter–Chocolate Banana Splits

Prep: 7 minutes • Cook: 1 minute

¼   cup plus 2 tablespoons chocolate syrup
1½   tablespoons reduced-fat peanut butter
3   bananas, cut in half lengthwise
3   cups vanilla bean light ice cream
3   tablespoons chopped unsalted peanuts

1. Combine chocolate syrup and peanut butter in a 1-cup glass measure. Microwave at HIGH 40 seconds or until peanut butter melts. Stir until smooth.
2. Cut each banana half crosswise into 2 pieces. Arrange 2 banana pieces in each of 6 dessert dishes; top banana with ice cream and hot chocolate sauce. Sprinkle with peanuts. Serve immediately. Yield: 6 servings (serving size: 2 pieces banana, ½ cup ice cream, about 1½ tablespoons chocolate sauce, and 1½ teaspoons peanuts).

CALORIES 255; FAT 7g (sat 2.6g, mono 1.1g, poly 0.7g); PROTEIN 6g; CARB 44.9g; FIBER 2.1g; CHOL 20mg; IRON 0.6mg; SODIUM 82mg; CALC 62mg

Grilled Heirloom Tomato and Goat Cheese Pizza

Roasted Vegetable Pizza

Prep: 3 minutes • Cook: 12 minutes

Roast the grape tomatoes and zucchini ahead, and refrigerate. Use the mixture as a topping for this hearty pizza or as a side dish for grilled chicken or fish.

1   (10-ounce) Italian cheese-flavored thin pizza crust
⅓   cup commercial pesto
3   cups Roasted Zucchini and Tomatoes
1   cup (4 ounces) preshredded part-skim mozzarella cheese
2   tablespoons grated fresh Parmesan cheese

1. Preheat oven to 500°. Place pizza crust on rack in oven while preheating, and heat 5 minutes.
2. Remove crust from oven; place on an ungreased baking sheet. Spread pesto evenly over crust. Top with Roasted Zucchini and Tomatoes; sprinkle evenly with cheeses. Bake at 500° for 7 minutes or until cheeses melt. Yield: 6 servings (serving size: 1 slice).

CALORIES 309; FAT 15g (sat 4.9g, mono 6.1g, poly 3.4g); PROTEIN 13.6g; CARB 31.8g; FIBER 3g; CHOL 17mg; IRON 2.3mg; SODIUM 629mg; CALC 277mg

Roasted Vegetable Pizza

Roasted Zucchini and Tomatoes

Prep: 4 minutes • Cook: 18 minutes

1   (8-ounce) container refrigerated prechopped red onion
2   medium zucchini, coarsely chopped
1   cup grape tomatoes
2   teaspoons olive oil
¼   teaspoon salt
¼   teaspoon freshly ground black pepper
1   tablespoon chopped fresh basil

1. Preheat oven to 500°.
2. Combine first 6 ingredients; toss well. Place on a large rimmed baking sheet. Bake at 500° for 18 minutes or until vegetables are tender and lightly browned, stirring after 12 minutes. Add basil to roasted vegetables; toss gently. Yield: 3 cups (serving size: ½ cup).

CALORIES 44; FAT 2g (sat 0.3g, mono 1.1g, poly 0.3g); PROTEIN 1.5g; CARB 6.8g; FIBER 1.7g; CHOL 0mg; IRON 0.4mg; SODIUM 106mg; CALC 22mg

Mushroom Macaroni and Cheese

Prep: 1 minute • Cook: 33 minutes

Fontina dresses up this hearty macaroni and cheese. Its creamy texture and nutty flavor are a delicious counterpoint to the earthiness of roasted mushrooms.

Sherry-Roasted Wild Mushrooms
8   ounces uncooked multigrain elbow macaroni
1.1   ounces all-purpose flour (about ¼ cup)
2½   cups evaporated fat-free milk
1   cup (4 ounces) shredded fontina cheese
¼   teaspoon salt
¼   teaspoon freshly ground black pepper
Cooking spray
Oregano leaves (optional)

1. Prepare Sherry-Roasted Wild Mushrooms. While mushrooms roast, cook pasta according to package directions, omitting salt and fat. Drain well.
2. While mushrooms roast and pasta cooks, weigh or lightly spoon flour into a dry measuring cup; level with a knife. Place flour in a large saucepan; gradually add milk, stirring with a whisk until blended. Cook over medium heat 6 minutes or until thick and bubbly; stir constantly with a whisk. Add cheese, salt, and pepper, stirring until cheese melts. Remove from heat. Stir in Sherry-Roasted Wild Mushrooms and pasta. Spoon into a 2-quart baking dish coated with cooking spray.
3. Lower oven temperature to 400°. Bake pasta mixture at 400° for 25 minutes or until bubbly. Sprinkle with oregano leaves, if desired, and serve immediately. Yield: 6 servings (serving size: about 1 cup).

CALORIES 349; FAT 9.1g (sat 4g, mono 3.7g, poly 1.3g); PROTEIN 20.7g; CARB 45.7g; FIBER 3.5g; CHOL 22mg; IRON 1.9mg; SODIUM 499mg; CALC 392mg

Sherry-Roasted Wild Mushrooms

Prep: 3 minutes • Cook: 15 minutes

3   (4-ounce) packages fresh gourmet-blend mushrooms
1   tablespoon olive oil
¼   teaspoon salt
¼   teaspoon freshly ground black pepper
2   garlic cloves, thinly sliced
Cooking spray
2   tablespoons dry sherry
2   teaspoons chopped fresh oregano

1. Preheat oven to 450°.
2. Combine first 5 ingredients on a large rimmed baking sheet coated with cooking spray. Bake at 450° for 15 to 20 minutes or until browned. Stir in sherry and oregano. Yield: 6 servings (serving size: about ½ cup).

CALORIES 38; FAT 2.5g (sat 0.3g, mono 1.7g, poly 0.4g); PROTEIN 1.9g; CARB 2.4g; FIBER 0.6g; CHOL 0mg; IRON 0.3mg; SODIUM 100mg; CALC 6mg

make ahead

Roast the wild mushrooms ahead of time. Just be sure to reheat before adding them to the cheese sauce.

Spaghetti with Zucchini and White Beans

Prep: 5 minutes • Cook: 10 minutes

Tender spaghetti noodles capture the fresh taste of the chunky bean and vegetable sauce, while a sprinkling of feta cheese adds a finishing touch.

6   ounces uncooked spaghetti
Olive oil–flavored cooking spray
3   cups (¼-inch) diced zucchini (2 medium)
⅓   cup water
1   tablespoon tomato paste
¼   teaspoon kosher salt
⅛   teaspoon coarsely ground black pepper
1   (15.8-ounce) can Great Northern beans, rinsed and drained
1   (14.5-ounce) can diced tomatoes with basil, garlic, and oregano, undrained
½   cup (2 ounces) crumbled feta cheese

1. Cook spaghetti according to package directions, omitting salt and fat.
2. While pasta cooks, heat a large nonstick skillet over medium-high heat; coat pan with cooking spray. Add zucchini to pan; cook 5 minutes or until lightly browned, stirring occasionally. Stir in water and next 5 ingredients; cover and simmer 4 minutes.
3. Place pasta evenly on each of 4 plates. Top pasta evenly with zucchini mixture and cheese. Yield: 4 servings (serving size: about ⅔ cup pasta, 1 cup zucchini mixture, and 2 tablespoons cheese).

CALORIES 311; FAT 4.1g (sat 2.4g, mono 0.8g, poly 0.5g); PROTEIN 14.7g; CARB 55.3g; FIBER 7.5g; CHOL 13mg; IRON 3.3mg; SODIUM 452mg; CALC 147mg

serve with:

Mixed Greens with Honey-Dijon Vinaigrette

Prep: 7 minutes

2   tablespoons balsamic vinegar
1   tablespoon extra-virgin olive oil
1   teaspoon honey
¼   teaspoon Dijon mustard
⅛   teaspoon coarsely ground black pepper
4   cups torn mixed salad greens
½   cup red seedless grape halves

1. Combine first 5 ingredients in a large bowl, stirring with a whisk. Add greens; toss gently. Divide greens mixture among 4 plates; top evenly with grape halves. Yield: 4 servings (serving size: about 1 cup salad and 2 tablespoons grapes).

CALORIES 66; FAT 3.7g (sat 0.5g, mono 2.5g, poly 0.6g); PROTEIN 1.1g; CARB 8.2g; FIBER 1.4g; CHOL 0mg; IRON 0.9mg; SODIUM 24mg; CALC 35mg

quick flip

For a slight twist in flavor, swap out grape halves for fresh blueberries.

Roasted Vegetable Pasta

Prep: 9 minutes • Cook: 15 minutes

This aromatic, colorful, and delicious pasta will please your senses of smell, sight, and taste.

3   cups (8 ounces) uncooked farfalle
    (bow tie pasta)
2   cups Roasted Vegetables
1   cup frozen petite green peas, thawed
¼   cup chopped fresh parsley
¼   cup (1½ ounces) thinly shaved fresh
    Parmesan cheese

1. Cook pasta according to package directions, omitting salt and fat. Drain; keep warm.
2. Combine pasta, Roasted Vegetables, and peas in a large bowl. Top with parsley and cheese. Yield: 4 servings (serving size: 1½ cups pasta, 1 tablespoon parsley, and 1 tablespoon cheese).

CALORIES 338; FAT 6g (sat 1.8g, mono 2.5g, poly 0.7g); PROTEIN 14.3g; CARB 54.9g; FIBER 5.5g; CHOL 5mg; IRON 3mg; SODIUM 485mg; CALC 106mg

Roasted Vegetables

Prep: 5 minutes • Cook: 22 minutes

1   (8-ounce) package baby portobello
    mushrooms, halved
2   cups grape or cherry tomatoes
1   red onion, sliced
1   tablespoon olive oil
½   teaspoon salt
¼   teaspoon freshly ground black pepper
¼   cup dry white wine

1. Preheat oven to 475°.
2. Combine first 6 ingredients in a bowl; toss well to coat. Arrange mushroom mixture in a single layer on a jelly-roll pan.
3. Bake at 475° for 15 minutes; turn vegetables over. Drizzle wine evenly over vegetables; bake an additional 7 minutes or until vegetables are tender and lightly browned. Yield: 2 cups (serving size: ½ cup).

CALORIES 84; FAT 3.9g (sat 0.6g, mono 2.5g, poly 0.7g); PROTEIN 2.4g; CARB 9.3g; FIBER 2.2g; CHOL 0mg; IRON 0.8mg; SODIUM 302mg; CALC 15mg

Roasted Vegetable Pasta

Pasta with Roasted
Tomatoes and Garlic

Pasta with Roasted Tomatoes and Garlic

Prep: 4 minutes • Cook: 14 minutes

Height-of-summer tomatoes burst with flavor and need little embellishment to create a spectacular dish. Churning the oil into boiling liquid emulsifies the mixture, yielding a creamy sauce that coats.

1	tablespoon kosher salt
8	ounces uncooked spaghetti
¼	cup extra-virgin olive oil, divided
2	pints multicolored cherry tomatoes
4	garlic cloves, thinly sliced
½	teaspoon kosher salt
¼	teaspoon freshly ground black pepper
2	ounces Parmigiano-Reggiano cheese, shaved
¼	cup small basil leaves

1. Preheat oven to 450°.
2. Bring a large pot of water to a boil; add 1 tablespoon salt. Add pasta; cook 10 minutes or until al dente. Drain pasta in a colander over a bowl, reserving 6 tablespoons cooking liquid. Return pasta to pan. Combine reserved liquid and 2 tablespoons oil in a small saucepan; bring to a boil. Boil 4 minutes or until mixture measures ⅓ cup. Add oil mixture to pan with pasta; toss to coat.
3. While pasta cooks, combine remaining 2 tablespoons oil, tomatoes, and garlic on a jelly-roll pan, tossing to combine. Bake at 450° for 11 minutes or until tomatoes are lightly browned and begin to burst. Add tomato mixture, ½ teaspoon salt, and pepper to pasta; toss to coat. Top with cheese and basil. Yield: 4 servings (serving size: about 1 cup).

CALORIES 417 (XX% from fat); FAT 18.4g (sat 4.4g, mono 11.1g, poly 2g); PROTEIN 14.1g; CARB 49.8g; FIBER 3.7g; CHOL 10mg; IRON 2.6mg; SODIUM 599mg; CALC 205mg

Vietnamese Noodle-
Vegetable Toss

Vietnamese Noodle-Vegetable Toss

Prep: 7 minutes • Cook: 5 minutes
Other: 3 minutes

Vietnamese cuisine is truly light Asian food. Rice noodles make this a hearty dish without leaving you feeling overly full.

6	cups water
6	ounces uncooked linguine-style rice noodles
1	tablespoon sugar
2	tablespoons water
1	tablespoon fish sauce
1	tablespoon fresh lime juice
2	cups packaged tricolor slaw mix
1	cup grated English cucumber
1	cup fresh bean sprouts
1	cup cilantro leaves
½	cup chopped unsalted, dry-roasted peanuts

1. Bring 6 cups water to a boil in a large saucepan. Remove from heat; add rice noodles. Let soak 3 minutes or until tender. Drain.
2. While noodles soak, combine sugar and next 3 ingredients in a small bowl, stirring well with a whisk.
3. Combine noodles, slaw mix, and next 3 ingredients in a large bowl. Toss with sugar mixture. Sprinkle with peanuts. Serve immediately. Yield: 3 servings (serving size: 1⅓ cups).

CALORIES 388; FAT 12g (sat 1.7g, mono 6g, poly 3.9g); PROTEIN 10.7g; CARB 61g; FIBER 3.8g; CHOL 0mg; IRON 2mg; SODIUM 397mg; CALC 49mg

ingredient spotlight

English, or seedless, cucumbers are usually twice the size of regular cucumbers and contain fewer seeds and less water. They're also typically milder in flavor than regular cucumbers.

Arugula, White Bean, and Sun-Dried Tomato Cream Quesadillas

Prep: 6 minutes • Cook: 4 minutes

A combo of tangy goat cheese and reduced-fat cream cheese adds a creamy texture to these lightened vegetarian quesadillas. They also get a considerable amount of flavor from the sun-dried tomatoes and peppery arugula.

2	ounces ⅓-less-fat cream cheese, softened
¼	cup chopped drained oil-packed sun-dried tomato halves
2	(8-inch) whole-wheat tortillas
½	cup rinsed and drained cannellini beans
¼	cup crumbled goat cheese
2	cups baby arugula
Cooking spray	

1. Combine cream cheese and sun-dried tomato in a small bowl; spread evenly over tortillas. Mash beans with a fork. Spread beans evenly over cream cheese mixture. Top evenly with goat cheese and arugula. Fold tortillas in half.
2. Heat a large skillet over medium heat. Coat pan with cooking spray. Place quesadillas in pan; cook 2 to 3 minutes on each side or until golden and cheese melts. Cut each quesadilla into 3 wedges. Serve immediately. Yield: 2 servings (serving size: 3 wedges).

CALORIES 299; FAT 12.4g (sat 6.5g, mono 4.1g, poly 0.9g); PROTEIN 13.1g; CARB 34.5g; FIBER 4.9g; CHOL 27mg; IRON 2.4mg; SODIUM 536mg; CALC 157mg

Spicy Vegetable Fried Rice

Prep: 2 minutes • Cook: 9 minutes

The crushed red pepper adds a hint of heat to this Asian favorite. If you're sensitive to spices, simply omit it.

1½ cups frozen broccoli stir-fry
1   cup frozen shelled edamame
Cooking spray
½   cup egg substitute
2   teaspoons dark sesame oil
2   teaspoons minced garlic
¼   teaspoon crushed red pepper
2   (8.8-ounce) pouches microwavable cooked brown rice
2½ tablespoons lower-sodium soy sauce
Toasted sesame seeds (optional)
Sliced green onions (optional)

1. Combine broccoli stir-fry and edamame in a microwave-safe bowl. Microwave at HIGH 2 minutes or until thawed; set aside.
2. While vegetables thaw, heat a large non-stick skillet over medium-high heat; coat pan with cooking spray. Add egg substitute; cook 2 minutes, stirring frequently, until scrambled. Remove from pan. Wipe pan with paper towels.
3. Heat pan over medium-high heat. Add oil to pan; swirl to coat. Add garlic and crushed red pepper. Cook 1 minute or until fragrant. Stir in vegetables and rice; cook 2 minutes or until thoroughly heated. Stir in soy sauce and reserved egg. Garnish with sesame seeds and onions, if desired. Yield: 4 servings (serving size: about 1⅓ cups).

CALORIES 289; FAT 8g (sat 0.8g, mono 3.6g, poly 2.9g); PROTEIN 11.5g; CARB 42.6g; FIBER 4g; CHOL 0mg; IRON 2mg; SODIUM 447mg; CALC 35mg

serve with:
Broiled Pineapple

Prep: 6 minutes • Cook: 6 minutes

1   cored fresh pineapple, cut into 8 slices
2   tablespoons butter, melted
½   cup packed brown sugar
⅓   cup flaked sweetened coconut

1. Preheat broiler.
2. Place pineapple slices on a jelly-roll pan. Drizzle with butter; sprinkle with sugar. Broil 4 minutes or until sugar melts. Sprinkle coconut over pineapple; broil 2 minutes or until coconut is toasted. Yield: 4 servings (serving size: 2 slices).

CALORIES 239; FAT 8g (sat 5.2g, mono 1.6g, poly 0.3g); PROTEIN 0.9g; CARB 45g; FIBER 2.3g; CHOL 15mg; IRON 1mg; SODIUM 70mg; CALC 41mg

quick flip

Turn this yummy side dish into an even better dessert by topping the slices of pineapple with a small scoop of light vanilla ice cream.

fish & shellfish

Shrimp and Summer Vegetable
Sauté, page 287

Grilled Citrus Halibut

Prep: 5 minutes • Cook: 8 minutes

Toss halibut fillets and orange slices in a quick vinaigrette of lemon juice, honey, mint, and ginger, and then grill. Place orange halves on the grill alongside the fish, and squeeze their sweet juice over the fish right before serving.

2	large navel oranges, divided
2	tablespoons fresh lemon juice
1	tablespoon chopped fresh mint
1	tablespoon olive oil
2	teaspoons grated peeled fresh ginger
1	teaspoon honey
¼	teaspoon salt
¼	teaspoon freshly ground black pepper
4	skinless halibut fillets (about 1¼ pounds)

Cooking spray
Mint sprigs (optional)

1. Preheat grill to medium-high heat.
2. Cut 1 orange in half. Cut remaining orange into 8 slices. Combine lemon juice and next 6 ingredients in a large bowl. Add fish and orange slices; toss gently to coat.
3. Place fish and orange slices on grill rack coated with cooking spray, discarding lemon mixture. Place orange halves, cut sides down, on grill rack. Grill 8 minutes or until fish flakes easily when tested with a fork, turning fish and orange slices after 4 minutes. Place 1 fillet on each of 4 plates. Top each with 2 orange slices. Squeeze orange halves evenly over fish and orange slices. Garnish with mint sprigs, if desired. Yield: 4 servings (serving size: 1 fillet, 2 orange slices, and about 1 tablespoon orange juice).

CALORIES 231; FAT 7g (sat 1g, mono 3.7g, poly 1.4g); PROTEIN 30.2g; CARB 11.2g; FIBER 1.7g; CHOL 45mg; IRON 1.4mg; SODIUM 223mg; CALC 99mg

Meyer Lemon and Dill Fish Parcels

Prep: 4 minutes • Cook: 15 minutes

Orange-yellow Meyer lemons are a hybrid of the mandarin orange and lemon, which gives them a sweeter flavor than their run-of-the-mill counterparts. If you have difficulty finding them, you can use regular lemons, such as Eurekas, instead.

4	(6-ounce) halibut fillets (¾ inch thick)
½	teaspoon salt
½	teaspoon freshly ground black pepper
8	(¼-inch-thick) slices Meyer lemon (2 lemons)
1	tablespoon butter, quartered
4	teaspoons chopped fresh dill

1. Preheat oven to 375°.
2. Cut 4 (15-inch) squares of parchment paper. Fold each square in half. Open folded parchment paper; place 1 fillet near fold on each square. Sprinkle fillets evenly with salt and pepper. Top evenly with lemon slices, butter quarters, and dill. Fold paper; seal edges with narrow folds. Place packets on a large baking sheet.
3. Bake at 375° for 15 minutes or until paper is puffy and lightly browned. Place 1 packet on each of 4 serving plates, and cut open. Serve immediately. Yield: 4 servings (serving size: 1 packet).

CALORIES 221; FAT 6.7g (sat 2.4g, mono 2g, poly 1.4g); PROTEIN 35.5g; CARB 2.7g; FIBER 1.1g; CHOL 62mg; IRON 1.5mg; SODIUM 403mg; CALC 92mg

serve with:

Sweet Potato Salad

Prep: 7 minutes • Cook: 6 minutes
Other: 30 minutes

3	medium-sized sweet potatoes (1½ pounds)
2	tablespoons chopped green onions
2	tablespoons fresh lime juice
1	tablespoon olive oil
¼	teaspoon salt
¼	teaspoon freshly ground black pepper

1. Scrub potatoes; place in a single layer in a microwave-safe casserole dish (do not pierce potatoes with a fork). Cover bowl with plastic wrap (do not allow plastic wrap to touch food); vent. Microwave at HIGH 6 minutes or until tender. Let stand 30 minutes or until cool to the touch.
2. Peel potatoes, and cut into 1-inch cubes. Place in a medium bowl. Sprinkle with onions and remaining ingredients; toss gently. Yield: 4 servings (serving size: ¾ cup).

CALORIES 164; FAT 3.4g (sat 0.5g, mono 2.5g, poly 0.4g); PROTEIN 2.7g; CARB 31.1g; FIBER 5.4g; CHOL 0mg; IRON 1.1mg; SODIUM 238mg; CALC 30mg

quick flip

Try swapping the lime juice for orange juice, which also complements the sweet potatoes.

Confetti Flounder Packets with Orange-Tarragon Butter

Prep: 6 minutes • Cook: 12 minutes
Other: 5 minutes

8	fresh snow peas, trimmed
1	cup matchstick-cut carrots
½	cup diced yellow bell pepper
2	tablespoons water
4	(6-ounce) flounder fillets (¼ inch thick)
¼	teaspoon salt
¼	teaspoon black pepper

Orange-Tarragon Butter
Orange wedges (optional)

1. Preheat oven to 400°.
2. Cut snow peas lengthwise into strips and in half crosswise. Place snow pea strips, carrots, bell pepper, and water in a microwave-safe bowl. Cover with plastic wrap; vent. Microwave at HIGH 2 minutes.
3. Sprinkle fillets with salt and pepper. Cut 4 (15 x 12–inch) squares of parchment paper. Fold each square in half. Open folded parchment paper; place 1 fillet near fold on each square. Top each fillet with one-fourth of carrot mixture; crumble or spread 1 tablespoon Orange-Tarragon Butter over carrot mixture. Fold paper; seal edges with narrow folds. Place packets on a large baking sheet.
4. Bake at 400° for 10 minutes. Let stand 5 minutes. Place 1 packet on each of 4 plates; cut open, and serve immediately. Garnish with orange wedges, if desired. Yield: 4 servings (serving size: 1 packet).

CALORIES 291; FAT 13.5g (sat 7.7g, mono 3.4g, poly 2g); PROTEIN 33.7g; CARB 5.8g; FIBER 1.8g; CHOL 112mg; IRON 1.5mg; SODIUM 442mg; CALC 72mg

Orange-Tarragon Butter

Prep: 3 minutes

¼	cup butter, softened
1	tablespoon finely chopped fresh tarragon
1½	teaspoons grated orange rind
⅛	teaspoon salt
⅛	teaspoon ground red pepper

1. Combine all ingredients in a bowl. Stir with a spoon until blended. Cover and chill until ready to serve. Yield: 4 servings (serving size: 1 tablespoon).

CALORIES 105; FAT 11.5g (sat 7.2g, mono 3g, poly 0.5g); PROTEIN 0.4g; CARB 0.9g; FIBER 0.2g; CHOL 30mg; IRON 0.4mg; SODIUM 154mg; CALC 18mg

quick flip

For another bright flavored butter, try finely chopped fresh parsley and grated lemon rind instead.

Grilled Halibut with Onion, Spicy Tomatoes, and Avocado

Grilled Halibut with Onion, Spicy Tomatoes, and Avocado

Prep: 7 minutes • Cook: 8 minutes

The pungent green onions mellow as they grill. Be sure to place the onions crosswise on the grill rack. Use kitchen shears to easily cut the cooked onions into 1-inch pieces. For a quick accompaniment, grill slices of bread alongside the fish and onions.

4	(6-ounce) halibut fillets
1	bunch green onions (about 10 onions), trimmed

Cooking spray

¼	teaspoon freshly ground black pepper
⅛	teaspoon salt
1	(10-ounce) can mild diced tomatoes and green chiles, undrained
1	avocado, peeled and diced
4	lime wedges

1. Preheat grill to medium-high heat.
2. Coat fillets and onions with cooking spray. Sprinkle fish evenly with pepper and salt. Place fish and onions on grill rack coated with cooking spray; cover and grill fish 4 minutes on each side or until fish flakes easily when tested with a fork or until desired degree of doneness. Grill onions 3 minutes on each side or until charred and tender.
3. While fish and onions grill, combine tomatoes and avocado in a small bowl.
4. Cut grilled onions into 1-inch pieces. Place 1 fillet on each of 4 plates. Top with tomato mixture; sprinkle with grilled onions. Squeeze 1 lime wedge over each serving. Yield: 4 servings (serving size: 1 fillet, ½ cup tomato topping, and about ¼ cup onions).

CALORIES 292; FAT 12g (sat 1.8g, mono 6.1g, poly 2.3g); PROTEIN 37.6g; CARB 9.5g; FIBER 4.3g; CHOL 54mg; IRON 2.7mg; SODIUM 460mg; CALC 128mg

Halibut with Quick Lemon Pesto

Prep: 3 minutes • Cook: 8 minutes

Grated lemon rind and juice lend tartness to the pesto that enhances the natural flavors of this simple grilled fish.

4	(6-ounce) halibut or other firm white fish fillets

Cooking spray

¼	teaspoon salt, divided
⅛	teaspoon freshly ground black pepper
⅔	cup firmly packed basil leaves
¼	cup (1 ounce) grated fresh Parmesan cheese
2	tablespoons extra-virgin olive oil
2	garlic cloves, peeled
1	tablespoon grated lemon rind
1	tablespoon fresh lemon juice

1. Preheat grill to medium-high heat.
2. Place fillets on grill rack coated with cooking spray. Sprinkle fish evenly with ⅛ teaspoon salt and pepper. Cover and grill 4 minutes on each side or until fish flakes easily when tested with a fork or until desired degree of doneness.
3. While fish grills, place remaining ⅛ teaspoon salt, basil, and remaining 5 ingredients in a blender or food processor. Process until finely minced. Serve grilled fish over pesto. Yield: 4 servings (serving size: 1 fillet and about 1 tablespoon pesto).

CALORIES 283; FAT 13g (sat 2.6g, mono 6.3g, poly 2.3g); PROTEIN 38.7g; CARB 1.4g; FIBER 0.5g; CHOL 59mg; IRON 1.7mg; SODIUM 363mg; CALC 195mg

serve with:
Grilled Zucchini and Red Bell Pepper with Corn

Prep: 5 minutes • Cook: 10 minutes

1	medium zucchini, halved lengthwise
1	red bell pepper, halved lengthwise and seeded

Cooking spray

1	cup frozen whole-kernel corn, thawed and drained
1½	tablespoons Parmesan and roasted garlic salad dressing
¼	teaspoon salt
⅛	teaspoon crushed red pepper

1. Preheat grill to medium-high heat.
2. Coat zucchini and bell pepper halves with cooking spray; place on grill rack. Cover and grill 5 minutes on each side or until bell pepper is charred and zucchini is tender.
3. Remove vegetables from grill; cut into 1-inch pieces. Place in a medium bowl. Stir in corn and remaining 3 ingredients, tossing gently to combine. Yield: 4 servings (serving size: about ½ cup).

CALORIES 74; FAT 3g (sat 0.5g, mono 0.1g, poly 0.2g); PROTEIN 2.3g; CARB 12.9g; FIBER 2.3g; CHOL 0mg; IRON 0.6mg; SODIUM 217mg; CALC 11mg

Pan-Roasted Salmon and Tomatoes

Prep: 3 minutes • Cook: 11 minutes

As the tomatoes, wine, and capers cook, the tomatoes begin to burst and release their juices, enhancing the pan sauce.

4	(6-ounce) salmon fillets
¼	teaspoon salt
¼	teaspoon freshly ground black pepper
Cooking spray	
2	cups grape tomatoes, halved
¼	cup dry white wine
1	tablespoon drained capers
¼	cup chopped fresh basil

1. Sprinkle salmon with salt and pepper. Heat a large nonstick skillet over medium-high heat. Coat pan with cooking spray. Add fillets, skin side up, to pan. Cook 3 minutes or until browned. Carefully turn fillets over. Add tomatoes, wine, and capers. Cover and cook 7 minutes or until salmon flakes when tested with a fork or until desired degree of doneness. Sprinkle with basil. Yield: 4 servings (serving size: 1 fillet and ¼ cup tomato mixture).

CALORIES 226; FAT 6.1g (sat 1g, mono 1.7g, poly 2.3g); PROTEIN 34.6; CARB 3.6g; FIBER 1.2g; CHOL 89mg; IRON 1.5mg; SODIUM 327mg; CALC 40mg

Pan-Roasted Salmon and Tomatoes

serve with:

Asparagus with Lemon-Basil Yogurt Sauce

Prep: 4 minutes • Cook: 2 minutes

1	pound asparagus spears
½	cup low-fat Greek yogurt
2	tablespoons chopped fresh basil
½	teaspoon grated lemon rind
2	tablespoons fresh lemon juice
¼	teaspoon salt
¼	teaspoon freshly ground black pepper

1. Snap off tough ends of asparagus. Cook asparagus in boiling water to cover 2 minutes or until crisp-tender; drain. Plunge asparagus into ice water; drain.
2. Combine yogurt and remaining ingredients in a small bowl. Serve over asparagus. Yield: 4 servings (serving size: ¼ of asparagus and 2 tablespoons sauce).

CALORIES 46; FAT 0.6g (sat 0.4g, mono 0.2g, poly 0g); PROTEIN 4.9g; CARB 6.8g; FIBER 2.6g; CHOL 1.9mg; IRON 0.5mg; SODIUM 155mg; CALC 47mg

Sautéed Tilapia Tacos with Grilled Peppers and Onion

Prep: 7 minutes • Cook: 18 minutes
Other: 5 minutes

2	(½-inch-thick) slices white onion
1	(8-ounce) package mini sweet bell peppers
	Cooking spray
¾	teaspoon salt, divided
½	teaspoon freshly ground black pepper, divided
4	(5-ounce) tilapia fillets
8	(6-inch) corn tortillas
1	small jalapeño pepper, thinly sliced
8	lime wedges (optional)

1. Preheat grill to medium-high heat.
2. Arrange onion slices and bell peppers on grill rack coated with cooking spray. Grill onions 12 minutes, turning after 6 minutes. Grill bell peppers 12 minutes, turning occasionally. Remove onions and bell peppers from grill, and let stand 5 minutes. Slice onion rings in half. Thinly slice bell peppers; discard stems and seeds. Combine onion, bell peppers, ¼ teaspoon salt, and ⅛ teaspoon black pepper in a small bowl.
3. Sprinkle fish evenly with remaining ½ teaspoon salt and remaining ⅜ teaspoon black pepper. Heat a large nonstick skillet over medium-high heat. Coat pan with cooking spray. Add fish to pan, and cook 3 minutes on each side or until fish flakes easily when tested with a fork or until desired degree of doneness.
4. Warm tortillas according to package directions. Divide fish, onion mixture, and jalapeño slices evenly among tortillas. Serve with lime wedges, if desired. Yield: 4 servings (serving size: 2 tacos).

CALORIES 292; FAT 4.4g (sat 1.2g, mono 1.2g, poly 1.3g); PROTEIN 32.6g; CARB 32g; FIBER 4.8g; CHOL 71mg; IRON 1.9mg; SODIUM 526mg; CALC 120mg

Shrimp and Summer Vegetable Sauté

Prep: 1 minute • Cook: 14 minutes

Pick juicy tomatoes at their peak in the summer, or visit a local farmers' market for vegetables until early fall. Small pods of okra are more tender.

4	bacon slices
2	cups fresh corn kernels
1½	cups chopped tomato (1 large)
1	cup sliced fresh okra
½	cup chopped onion
1¼	pounds peeled and deveined large shrimp
¼	teaspoon salt
¼	teaspoon freshly ground black pepper
	Cooking spray
2	tablespoons torn fresh basil
2	teaspoons fresh lemon juice
	Lemon wedges (optional)

1. Cook bacon in a large nonstick skillet over medium heat until crisp. Remove bacon from pan; crumble. Increase to medium-high heat. Add corn and next 3 ingredients to drippings in pan; sauté 3 minutes or until browned. Remove corn mixture from pan. Keep warm. Wipe pan with a paper towel.
2. Sprinkle shrimp with salt and pepper. Heat pan over medium-high heat. Coat pan with cooking spray. Add shrimp; sauté 2 minutes or until shrimp are done.
3. Add corn mixture to shrimp. Stir in crumbled bacon, basil, and lemon juice. Serve with lemon wedges, if desired. Yield: 4 servings (serving size: about 1½ cups).

CALORIES 267; FAT 5.6g (sat 1.8g, mono 1.5g, poly 1.5g); PROTEIN 34.5g; CARB 21.4g; FIBER 3.5g; CHOL 223mg; IRON 4.3mg; SODIUM 509mg; CALC 110mg

Tandoori Salmon

Prep: 3 minutes • Cook: 9 minutes

The spices on this broiled salmon give it the same flavors as many tandoori-cooked dishes.

1	teaspoon ground ginger
1	teaspoon ground turmeric
½	teaspoon ground cumin
¼	teaspoon salt
¼	teaspoon freshly ground black pepper
4	(6-ounce) salmon fillets

Cooking spray
Cilantro-Yogurt Sauce

1. Preheat broiler.
2. Combine first 5 ingredients in a small bowl; rub over fillets. Place fillets on a broiler pan coated with cooking spray; broil 9 minutes or until fish flakes easily when tested with a fork or until desired degree of doneness. Serve with Cilantro-Yogurt Sauce. Yield: 4 servings (serving size: 1 fillet and ¼ cup sauce).

CALORIES 246; FAT 7.2g (sat 1.6g, mono 2g, poly 2.4g); PROTEIN 37.4g; CARB 5.8g; FIBER 0.3g; CHOL 92mg; IRON 1.8mg; SODIUM 303mg; CALC 141mg

Cilantro-Yogurt Sauce

Prep: 5 minutes

1	cup plain low-fat yogurt
1	tablespoon chopped fresh cilantro
1	teaspoon grated lime rind
1	teaspoon fresh lime juice
2	garlic cloves, minced

1. Combine all ingredients in a small bowl. Cover and chill until ready to serve. Yield: 4 servings (serving size: ¼ cup).

CALORIES 41; FAT 1g (sat 0.6g, mono 0.3g, poly 0g); PROTEIN 3.3g; CARB 4.9g; FIBER 0g; CHOL 4mg; IRON 0.1mg; SODIUM 43mg; CALC 115mg

serve with:
Sautéed Okra

Prep: 2 minutes • Cook: 5 minutes

1	teaspoon canola oil
1	pound okra pods, cut in half lengthwise
¼	teaspoon salt
¼	teaspoon freshly ground black pepper

1. Heat a large nonstick skillet over medium-high heat. Add oil; swirl to coat. Add okra, and sauté 5 minutes or until lightly browned. Sprinkle with salt and freshly ground black pepper. Yield: 4 servings (serving size: ¼ cup of okra).

CALORIES 46; FAT 1.3g (sat 0.1g, mono 0.8g, poly 0.4g); PROTEIN 2.3g; CARB 8.1g; FIBER 3.7g; CHOL 0mg; IRON 0.9mg; SODIUM 157mg; CALC 93mg

quick flip

Spice up the flavors of this okra dish by sautéing garlic and crushed red pepper before adding okra.

Green Curry Snapper

Prep: 4 minutes • Cook: 10 minutes

Flavorful green curry, a variety of spices and herbs, and coconut milk provide a fragrant sauce for fresh snapper fillets. Coconut milk adds a rich, velvety texture to the savory dish. If snapper is unavailable, substitute another firm white fish.

½   cup coconut milk
1   tablespoon fresh lime juice
2   teaspoons green curry paste
2   teaspoons lemongrass paste
1   teaspoon ginger paste
4   (6-ounce) snapper fillets
⅛   teaspoon salt
2   teaspoons olive oil
2   garlic cloves, minced
¼   cup chopped fresh cilantro

1. Combine first 5 ingredients in a small bowl. Sprinkle fillets evenly with salt.
2. Heat a large nonstick skillet over medium-high heat. Add oil; swirl to coat. Add garlic; sauté 30 seconds. Add fillets. Cook 2 to 3 minutes on each side. Pour coconut milk mixture over fillets. Cover; bring to a simmer. Simmer 2 minutes or until fish flakes easily when tested with a fork or until desired degree of doneness. Carefully place 1 fillet on each of 4 plates. Spoon curry sauce evenly over fillets; sprinkle evenly with cilantro. Yield: 4 servings (serving size: 1 fillet, 1 tablespoon sauce, and 1 tablespoon cilantro).

CALORIES 260; FAT 11.2g (sat 6.2g, mono 2.5g, poly 1.3g); PROTEIN 35.6g; CARB 3.1g; FIBER 0g; CHOL 63mg; IRON 1.4mg; SODIUM 337mg; CALC 66mg

serve with:
Tropical Jasmine Rice

Prep: 2 minutes • Cook: 12 minutes
Other: 5 minutes

¾   cup water
½   cup jasmine rice
2   teaspoons butter
¼   teaspoon salt
⅓   cup finely chopped fresh pineapple
2   tablespoons diagonally cut green onions
2   tablespoons flaked sweetened coconut, toasted

1. Combine first 4 ingredients in a small saucepan. Bring to a boil; reduce heat, cover, and simmer 10 minutes. Remove pan from heat; let stand, covered, 5 minutes. Add pineapple, green onions, and coconut; fluff gently with a fork. Yield: 4 servings (serving size: ½ cup).

CALORIES 117; FAT 2.7g (sat 1.9g, mono 0.5g, poly 0.1g); PROTEIN 1.7g; CARB 21.4g; FIBER 1.1g; CHOL 5mg; IRON 0.3mg; SODIUM 173mg; CALC 15mg

Green Curry Snapper

Grilled Halibut with Hoisin Glaze

3. Place fillets on grill rack coated with cooking spray. Brush fillets with hoisin mixture. Grill 3 minutes on each side or until fish flakes easily when tested with a fork or until desired degree of doneness, basting occasionally with hoisin mixture. Garnish with orange rind, if desired. Yield: 4 servings (serving size: 1 fillet).

CALORIES 179; FAT 2.6g (sat 0.5g, mono 0.9g, poly 0.6g); PROTEIN 31.9g; CARB 4.9g; FIBER 0.3g; CHOL 84mg; IRON 0.4mg; SODIUM 443mg; CALC 16mg

serve with:

Grilled Baby Bok Choy

Prep: 5 minutes • Cook: 11 minutes

4	baby bok choy, halved lengthwise (about 1 pound)
2	tablespoons water
1	tablespoon dark sesame oil
¼	teaspoon salt
¼	teaspoon freshly ground black pepper

Cooking spray

| 2 | teaspoons toasted sesame seeds |

1. Preheat grill to medium-high heat.
2. Place bok choy halves and 2 tablespoons water in a microwave-safe dish. Cover dish with heavy-duty plastic wrap; vent. Microwave at HIGH 5 minutes or until tender. Drain.
3. Drizzle bok choy with sesame oil, and sprinkle with salt and pepper. Place on grill rack coated with cooking spray. Grill 3 minutes on each side or until bok choy begins to char. Sprinkle with toasted sesame seeds. Yield: 4 servings (serving size: 2 bok choy halves).

CALORIES 54; FAT 4.5g (sat 0.6g, mono 1.8g, poly 1.9g); PROTEIN 2.1g; CARB 2.3g; FIBER 1.3g; CHOL 0mg; IRON 1.3mg; SODIUM 187mg; CALC 107mg

Grilled Halibut with Hoisin Glaze

Prep: 4 minutes • Cook: 6 minutes

Sriracha, orange juice, and hoisin sauce give halibut a slightly sweet, Asian flavor. Use another firm white fish in place of the halibut, if you can't find it.

2	tablespoons fresh orange juice, divided
4	(6-ounce) halibut fillets
¼	teaspoon salt
¼	teaspoon freshly ground black pepper
2	tablespoons hoisin sauce
2	teaspoons Sriracha (hot chile sauce)

Cooking spray
Grated orange rind (optional)

1. Preheat grill to medium-high heat.
2. Brush 1 tablespoon orange juice evenly over fillets; sprinkle evenly with salt and pepper. Combine hoisin sauce, Sriracha, and remaining 1 tablespoon orange juice in a small bowl.

Pan-Seared Flounder with Fried Rosemary and Garlic

Prep: 2 minutes • Cook: 9 minutes

Cooking garlic and rosemary in the oil infuses it with flavor. This double dose of tastiness is imparted to the fish as it cooks.

1½	tablespoons olive oil
3	large garlic cloves, thinly sliced
4	rosemary sprigs
4	(6-ounce) flounder fillets
¼	teaspoon salt
¼	teaspoon freshly ground black pepper
¼	teaspoon paprika

Lemon wedges (optional)

1. Heat a large nonstick skillet over medium heat. Add oil; swirl to coat. Add garlic and rosemary. Cook 3 minutes or until garlic is browned and rosemary is crisp. Using a slotted spoon, transfer garlic and rosemary to paper towels, reserving oil in pan.
2. Return oil to medium-high heat. Sprinkle fish evenly with salt, pepper, and paprika. Cook fish in hot oil 3 minutes on each side or until desired degree of doneness. Divide fish evenly among 4 plates. Top with reserved garlic and rosemary. Serve with lemon wedges, if desired. Yield: 4 servings (serving size: 1 fillet).

CALORIES 204; FAT 7.1g (sat 1.4g, mono 4.3g, poly 1.3g); PROTEIN 32.2g; CARB 1g; FIBER 0.2g; CHOL 82mg; IRON 0.7mg; SODIUM 284mg; CALC 37mg

serve with:

Lemony Mashed Potatoes

Prep: 5 minutes • Cook: 8 minutes

1½	pounds Yukon Gold potatoes, peeled and cut into 1-inch pieces
1	tablespoon water
⅓	cup 1% low-fat milk
¼	cup reduced-fat sour cream
1½	teaspoons grated lemon rind
½	teaspoon garlic powder
¼	teaspoon salt
¼	teaspoon freshly ground black pepper

1. Place potato in a single layer in a microwave-safe bowl; add 1 tablespoon water. Cover bowl with plastic wrap (do not allow plastic wrap to touch food); vent. Microwave at HIGH 8 minutes or until tender.
2. Add remaining ingredients to potato in bowl; mash with a potato masher to desired consistency. Yield: 4 servings (serving size: about ⅔ cup).

CALORIES 171; FAT 2g (sat 1.3g, mono 0.6g, poly 0.1g); PROTEIN 5.2g; CARB 32.1g; FIBER 2.2g; CHOL 7mg; IRON 1.5mg; SODIUM 172mg; CALC 43mg

fix it faster

Put down the potato peeler, open up a package of refrigerated mashed potatoes, and turn up the flavor with a dash of garlic powder, a pinch of pepper, and a sprinkle of lemon zest. In just a few minutes, your side dish is ready to serve.

Halibut with Bacon and Balsamic Tomatoes

Prep: 1 minute • Cook: 18 minutes

Sweet tomatoes and smoky bacon enhance the mild flavor of halibut. A flat fish with a medium-firm white flesh, halibut hails from the cold waters of the northern Pacific and Atlantic oceans.

4   center-cut bacon slices
4   (6-ounce) skinless halibut fillets (about ½ to ¾ inch thick)
¼   teaspoon salt
¼   teaspoon freshly ground black pepper
2   cups grape tomatoes
2   tablespoons balsamic vinegar
Chopped fresh parsley (optional)

1. Cook bacon in a large nonstick skillet over medium-high heat 4 minutes or until crisp. Remove bacon from pan, reserving drippings in pan; crumble bacon.
2. Sprinkle fish evenly with salt and pepper. Add fillets to hot drippings in pan; cook 4 to 5 minutes on each side or until desired degree of doneness. Remove from pan, and keep warm.
3. Add tomatoes to pan. Sauté 4 minutes or until tomatoes begin to burst. Add vinegar; cook 1 minute or until sauce thickens, pressing tomatoes with the back of a spoon to release juice.
4. Spoon tomato mixture evenly over each fillet. Sprinkle with crumbled bacon and, if desired, parsley. Yield: 4 servings (serving size: 1 fillet, 6 tablespoons tomato mixture, and 1 tablespoon bacon).

CALORIES 228; FAT 5.2g (sat 1.3g, mono 2g, poly 1.8g); PROTEIN 38g; CARB 4.5g; FIBER 1g; CHOL 59mg; IRON 1.5mg; SODIUM 329mg; CALC 95mg

serve with:

Grilled Asparagus with Shallot-Dijon Vinaigrette

Prep: 4 minutes • Cook: 5 minutes

1   pound fresh asparagus, trimmed
Cooking spray
1   shallot, minced
1   tablespoon chopped fresh parsley
1   tablespoon sherry vinegar
1   tablespoon extra-virgin olive oil
1   teaspoon Dijon mustard
¼   teaspoon salt
¼   teaspoon freshly ground black pepper

1. Preheat grill to medium-high heat.
2. Place asparagus on grill rack coated with cooking spray. Cook 4 to 5 minutes or until tender, turning occasionally.
3. While asparagus cooks, combine shallots and next 6 ingredients in a large bowl, stirring well with a whisk.
4. Place asparagus on a serving plate; drizzle with vinaigrette. Serve immediately. Yield: 4 servings (serving size: ¼ of asparagus).

CALORIES 67; FAT 3.7g (sat 0.6g, mono 2.5g, poly 0.6g); PROTEIN 2.7g; CARB 6g; FIBER 2.5g; CHOL 0mg; IRON 2.6mg; SODIUM 179mg; CALC 32mg

ingredient spotlight

When selecting asparagus, reach for green instead of white. The green variety is higher in vitamins A and C and in folate. Choose asparagus spears with tight, compact tips and a similar diameter so they'll all cook at the same rate.

Sweet and Smoky Glazed Salmon

Prep: 3 minutes • Cook: 10 minutes
Other: 10 minutes

Crisp and glazed on the outside, this salmon cooks up tender and moist inside. The citrusy-sweet glaze with a smoky note adds a flavorful finish.

2	tablespoons frozen lemonade concentrate, thawed
1	tablespoon water
1	tablespoon honey
1	teaspoon smoked paprika
4	(6-ounce) salmon fillets
2	teaspoons canola oil
¼	teaspoon salt
¼	teaspoon freshly ground black pepper

1. Preheat broiler.
2. Combine first 4 ingredients in a large heavy-duty zip-top plastic bag. Add fish to bag; seal. Refrigerate 10 minutes, turning bag once.
3. Remove fish from bag, reserving marinade. Place marinade in a microwave-safe bowl; microwave at HIGH 40 seconds or until bubbly.
4. Heat a cast-iron skillet over medium-high heat. Add oil; swirl to coat. Sprinkle fish with salt and pepper. Add fish to pan; cook 3 minutes. Turn fish over; brush marinade evenly over fish. Broil 5 minutes or until desired degree of doneness. Yield: 4 servings (serving size: 1 fillet).

CALORIES 253; FAT 8.3g (sat 1.4g, mono 3.4g, poly 3.4g); PROTEIN 34.1g; CARB 9g; FIBER 0.2g; CHOL 89mg; IRON 1.5mg; SODIUM 260mg; CALC 25mg

Sweet and Smoky Glazed Salmon

Horseradish-Dill Salmon

Prep: 1 minute • Cook: 7 minutes

The essence of horseradish in this creamy sauce wakes up the flavor of the fish, which has a medium-firm flesh. Prepared horseradish is grated fresh horseradish root preserved in vinegar. It can be kept refrigerated for several months or until it begins to darken or hits a sour note.

4	(6-ounce) skinless salmon fillets (1 inch thick)
¼	teaspoon salt
¼	teaspoon freshly ground black pepper
Olive oil–flavored cooking spray	
2	tablespoons fat-free sour cream
2	tablespoons light mayonnaise
1	tablespoon prepared horseradish
1	tablespoon chopped fresh dill
1	tablespoon chopped drained capers
1	teaspoon grated lemon rind
2	teaspoons fresh lemon juice

1. Sprinkle fillets evenly with salt and pepper.
2. Heat a large nonstick skillet over medium-high heat; coat pan with cooking spray. Add fillets to pan; cook 3 to 4 minutes on each side or until desired degree of doneness.
3. While fillets cook, combine sour cream and next 6 ingredients in a small bowl. Spoon sauce over each fillet. Yield: 4 servings (serving size: 1 fillet and 2 tablespoons sauce).

CALORIES 235; FAT 8.6g (sat 1.6g, mono 2.8g, poly 4.1g); PROTEIN 34.6g; CARB 2.8g; FIBER 0.3g; CHOL 92mg; IRON 1.4mg; SODIUM 376mg; CALC 42mg

serve with:

Roasted Broccoli with Garlic and Pine Nuts

Prep: 3 minutes • Cook: 17 minutes

1	(12-ounce) package fresh broccoli florets
4	garlic cloves, crushed
2	teaspoons olive oil
¼	teaspoon salt
¼	teaspoon crushed red pepper (optional)
Cooking spray	
2	tablespoons pine nuts
2	teaspoons fresh lemon juice

1. Preheat oven to 450°.
2. Combine first 4 ingredients and, if desired, red pepper on a rimmed baking sheet coated with cooking spray.
3. Bake at 450° for 15 minutes or until browned and almost tender. Add pine nuts. Bake an additional 2 minutes or until nuts are toasted. Drizzle broccoli with lemon juice just before serving. Yield: 4 servings (serving size: ¼ cup).

CALORIES 77; FAT 5.5g (sat 0.7g, mono 2.8g, poly 1.9g); PROTEIN 3.3g; CARB 6.2g; FIBER 2.7g; CHOL 0mg; IRON 1.1mg; SODIUM 169mg; CALC 47mg

Horseradish-Dill Salmon

Parmesan-Broiled Tilapia

Prep: 4 minutes • Cook: 11 minutes

Sustainable tilapia and a rich-tasting cheesy coating combine the best of good eats. Grouper and orange roughy fillets work equally well in this simple-to-fix entrée.

6   (6-ounce) tilapia fillets
Cooking spray
¼   cup (1 ounce) grated fresh Parmesan cheese
3   tablespoons chopped green onions
3   tablespoons light mayonnaise
1   tablespoon yogurt-based spread
¼   teaspoon salt
¼   teaspoon freshly ground black pepper
1   garlic clove, pressed

1. Preheat broiler.
2. Pat fish dry with a paper towel. Arrange fish on rack of a broiler pan coated with cooking spray.
3. Combine cheese and next 6 ingredients in a small bowl. Spread mixture evenly over fish.
4. Broil 11 minutes or until desired degree of doneness. Yield: 6 servings (serving size: 1 fillet).

CALORIES 217; FAT 7.5g (sat 2.2g, mono 2.3g, poly 2.8g); PROTEIN 36.3g; CARB 1g; FIBER 0.2g; CHOL 88mg; IRON 1mg; SODIUM 339mg; CALC 88mg

quick flip

Try dried rosemary or a mix of other dried herbs with the potatoes.

serve with:

Lavender Potatoes

Prep: 3 minutes • Cook: 20 minutes

1½   pounds baby Yukon gold potatoes (about 24 potatoes)
1   tablespoon olive oil
1½   teaspoons dried lavender
¼   teaspoon salt
¼   teaspoon freshly ground black pepper

1. Preheat oven to 450°.
2. Cut potatoes in half crosswise. Place potato, oil, and remaining ingredients in a bowl, tossing to coat. Spread potato mixture in a single layer on a large rimmed baking sheet. Bake at 450° for 20 minutes. Yield: 6 servings (serving size: ½ cup).

CALORIES 114; FAT 2.3g (sat 0.3g, mono 1.6g, poly 0.2g); PROTEIN 2.7g; CARB 20.2g; FIBER 1.4g; CHOL 0mg; IRON 1mg; SODIUM 104mg; CALC 0mg

Parmesan-Broiled Tilapia

Trout with Onion Jam and Bacon

Prep: 4 minutes • Cook: 8 minutes

We turned up the flavor of trout fillets and cilantro slaw using sweet-savory garlic and onion jam with both. If you can't get trout fillets in your area, substitute farm-raised tilapia or other thin white fish fillets.

4	(6-ounce) trout fillets
¼	teaspoon salt
¼	teaspoon freshly ground black pepper
¼	cup roasted garlic onion jam
Cooking spray	
4	precooked bacon slices

1. Preheat broiler.
2. Sprinkle trout with salt and pepper. Stir jam well; brush tops of fillets evenly with jam. Place fillets on the rack of a broiler pan coated with cooking spray. Broil 8 to 10 minutes or until desired degree of doneness.
3. Heat bacon according to package directions. Coarsely crumble 1 bacon slice over each fillet before serving. Yield: 4 servings (serving size: 1 fillet and 1 bacon slice).

CALORIES 247; FAT 7.5g (sat 2.4g, mono 3.1g, poly 1.9g); PROTEIN 30.5g; CARB 13.1g; FIBER 0g; CHOL 146mg; IRON 0.5mg; SODIUM 331mg; CALC 30mg

serve with:
Cilantro Slaw

Prep: 1 minute • Cook: 1 minute

¼	cup roasted garlic onion jam
1	tablespoon brown sugar
1	tablespoon white vinegar
2	cups packaged 3-color coleslaw
¼	cup chopped fresh cilantro

1. Combine first 3 ingredients in a microwave-safe bowl. Microwave at HIGH 45 seconds or until jam melts. Cool slightly. Stir in coleslaw and cilantro. Yield: 2 cups (serving size: ½ cup).

CALORIES 72; FAT 0g (sat 0g, mono 0g, poly 0g); PROTEIN 0.4g; CARB 18.1g; FIBER 0.7g; CHOL 0mg; IRON 0.1mg; SODIUM 9mg; CALC 4mg

make ahead

If you have time to chill the Cilantro Slaw, all the better to boost the flavor.

Trout with Onion Jam and Bacon

Cornmeal-Crusted Trout with Bourbon-Pecan Butter Sauce

Prep: 4 minutes • Cook: 13 minutes

Trout fillets can vary in size. Generally, one 6-ounce uncooked fillet is the standard serving size. If trout isn't available, try grouper, the "other flaky white fish." Serve with sautéed spinach.

¼   cup stone-ground yellow cornmeal
3   tablespoons panko (Japanese breadcrumbs)
4   (6-ounce) rainbow trout fillets
¼   teaspoon salt
¼   teaspoon freshly ground black pepper
2   teaspoons olive oil
Bourbon-Pecan Butter Sauce

1. Combine cornmeal and panko in a shallow dish; sprinkle fish with salt and pepper. Heat a large nonstick skillet over medium-high heat. Add oil; swirl to coat. Dredge tops of fish in cornmeal mixture.
2. Place fish, breading sides down, in pan; cook 4 minutes or until browned. Turn fish over; cook 3 to 4 minutes or until desired degree of doneness. Remove fish from pan; cover and keep warm.
3. Prepare Bourbon-Pecan Butter Sauce; spoon sauce evenly over fish. Yield: 4 servings (serving size: 1 fillet and about 1 tablespoon Bourbon-Pecan Butter Sauce).

CALORIES 376; FAT 15.9g (sat 3.5g, mono 7.7g, poly 4.7g); PROTEIN 36.6g; CARB 12.2g; FIBER 2.1g; CHOL 104mg; IRON 1.8mg; SODIUM 242mg; CALC 127mg

Cornmeal-Crusted Trout with Bourbon-Pecan Butter Sauce

Bourbon-Pecan Butter Sauce

Prep: 1 minute • Cook: 5 minutes

Butter-flavored cooking spray
¼   cup pecan pieces
¼   cup bourbon
1   tablespoon light brown sugar
2   tablespoons fat-free, lower-sodium chicken broth
1   tablespoon light butter
Dash of ground red pepper

1. Heat a medium nonstick skillet over medium-high heat. Coat pan with cooking spray. Add pecans; sauté 2 minutes or until toasted. Remove from pan. Add bourbon, brown sugar, and broth to pan; bring to a boil. Boil 1 minute or until reduced by half. Remove from heat; add butter and pepper, stirring until butter melts. Yield: 4 servings (serving size: about 1 tablespoon).

CALORIES 115; FAT 7.4g (sat 1.7g, mono 3.7g, poly 1.8g); PROTEIN 0.8g; CARB 4.4g; FIBER 0.7g; CHOL 4mg; IRON 0.3mg; SODIUM 33mg; CALC 10mg

Grilled Amberjack with Country-Style Dijon Cream Sauce

Prep: 2 minutes • Cook: 7 minutes

Prepare the cream sauce ahead, if you like—just be sure to reserve the lemon juice for the fish. Pick up a whole-wheat baguette from the bakery at your supermarket, and steam fresh asparagus to make this meal quick and easy.

2	teaspoons salt-free steak grilling blend
1½	teaspoons chopped fresh tarragon
	Cooking spray
4	(6-ounce) amberjack fillets (about ¾ inch thick)
1	lemon
	Country-Style Dijon Cream Sauce

1. Combine steak seasoning and tarragon in a small bowl; set aside.
2. Heat a grill pan over medium-high heat. Coat pan with cooking spray. Coat fillets with cooking spray, and rub with seasoning mixture. Add fish to pan. Cook 3 to 4 minutes on each side until fillets flake easily when tested with a fork or until desired degree of doneness.
3. While fish cooks, grate 1 teaspoon rind from lemon; squeeze juice to measure 1 tablespoon. Reserve lemon rind for Country-Style Dijon Cream Sauce.
4. Place 1 fillet on each of 4 serving plates. Drizzle fillets evenly with lemon juice, and top with a dollop of cream sauce. Yield: 4 servings (serving size: 1 fillet, about ¾ teaspoon lemon juice, and 3 tablespoons cream sauce).

CALORIES 256; FAT 8g (sat 0.8g, mono 4g, poly 3g); PROTEIN 37.2g; CARB 6.3g; FIBER 0.6g; CHOL 83mg; IRON 0.1mg; SODIUM 473mg; CALC 39mg

Country-Style Dijon Cream Sauce

Prep: 4 minutes

¼	cup light mayonnaise
¼	cup fat-free sour cream
3	tablespoons water
1½	tablespoons country-style Dijon mustard
1½	teaspoons chopped fresh tarragon
1	teaspoon grated lemon rind
¼	teaspoon salt

1. Combine all ingredients in a small bowl. Yield: 4 servings (serving size: 3 tablespoons).

CALORIES 71; FAT 4.9g (sat 0.8g, mono 1g, poly 2.5g); PROTEIN 1.1g; CARB 5g; FIBER 0.1g; CHOL 8mg; IRON 0.1mg; SODIUM 413mg; CALC 33mg

Grilled Amberjack with
Country-Style Dijon
Cream Sauce

Blackened Catfish

Blackened Catfish

Prep: 3 minutes • Cook: 6 minutes

A combination of a few pantry spices lends authentic Cajun flavor to catfish. The Sautéed Corn and Cherry Tomatoes are delicious served alone as a side dish or as a relish spooned over the catfish.

1	tablespoon thyme leaves, minced
1	teaspoon onion powder
1	teaspoon garlic powder
1	teaspoon paprika
1	teaspoon freshly ground black pepper
½	teaspoon ground red pepper
¼	teaspoon salt
3	teaspoons olive oil, divided
4	(6-ounce) catfish fillets

1. Combine first 7 ingredients in a small bowl.
2. Heat a large nonstick skillet over medium-high heat. Add 2 teaspoons oil to pan; swirl to coat. Brush fillets with remaining 1 teaspoon olive oil. Rub fillets with spice mixture, and add to pan; cook 3 minutes on each side or until fillets flake easily when tested with a fork. Yield: 4 servings (serving size: 1 fillet).

CALORIES 200; FAT 8.3g (sat 1.7g, mono 3.9g, poly 1.9g); PROTEIN 28.2g; CARB 1.9g; FIBER 0.5g; CHOL 99mg; IRON 0.9mg; SODIUM 220mg; CALC 37mg

serve with:

Sautéed Corn and Cherry Tomatoes

Prep: 4 minutes • Cook: 6 minutes

2	teaspoons olive oil
1	garlic clove, minced
2	cups fresh corn kernels (about 3 ears)
1	cup cherry tomatoes, quartered (about 10)
3	tablespoons chopped green onions (about 2 large)
1	tablespoon sherry vinegar
2	teaspoons minced fresh thyme
½	teaspoon freshly ground black pepper
¼	teaspoon salt

1. Heat a large nonstick skillet over medium heat. Add oil; swirl to coat. Add garlic to pan; sauté 1 minute. Add corn and tomatoes; cook 3 minutes or until vegetables are tender, stirring often. Remove from heat; stir in onions and remaining ingredients. Yield: 4 servings (serving size: about ½ cup).

CALORIES 89; FAT 3.2g (sat 0.5g, mono 1.9g, poly 0.7g); PROTEIN 2.6g; CARB 15g; FIBER 2.4g; CHOL 0mg; IRON 0.7mg; SODIUM 158mg; CALC 12mg

Baked Bayou Catfish with Spicy Sour Cream Sauce

Prep: 5 minutes • Cook: 14 minutes

For a crisp texture similar to fried fish, coat the fillets with cornmeal and bake them at a high temperature. Try squeezing a lemon wedge over the fillets to enhance the flavor.

Cooking spray
2½   tablespoons hot sauce, divided
4   (6-ounce) catfish fillets
1   teaspoon Cajun seasoning
½   cup yellow cornmeal
½   cup light sour cream
⅛   teaspoon salt
1   lemon, cut into wedges (optional)
Chopped fresh parsley (optional)

1. Preheat oven to 400°.
2. Line a large baking sheet with foil; coat foil with cooking spray.
3. Brush 1½ tablespoons hot sauce evenly on both sides of fillets; sprinkle with Cajun seasoning, and dredge in cornmeal, pressing gently. Place fillets on prepared pan. Coat fillets with cooking spray. Bake at 400° for 14 minutes or until fillets flake easily when tested with a fork.
4. While fillets bake, combine remaining 1 tablespoon hot sauce, sour cream, and salt in a small bowl, stirring with a whisk. Serve fillets with sauce and lemon wedges, if desired. Sprinkle with parsley, if desired. Yield: 4 servings (serving size: 1 fillet and 2 tablespoons sauce).

CALORIES 322; FAT 15.7g (sat 4.6g, mono 6.2g, poly 4.9g); PROTEIN 28.7g; CARB 15.7g; FIBER 1.3g; CHOL 90mg; IRON 2.1mg; SODIUM 524mg; CALC 77mg

Baked Bayou Catfish with Spicy Sour Cream Sauce

serve with:
Sweet-and-Sour Broccoli Slaw

Prep: 4 minutes

1   tablespoon sugar
2   tablespoons cider vinegar
1   tablespoon canola oil
¼   teaspoon poppy seeds
⅛   teaspoon salt
⅛   teaspoon freshly ground black pepper
Dash of ground red pepper
2½   cups packaged broccoli coleslaw

1. Combine first 7 ingredients in a medium bowl, stirring with a whisk. Add coleslaw; toss well. Serve immediately. Yield: 4 servings (serving size: about ⅔ cup).

CALORIES 62; FAT 3.6g (sat 0.3g, mono 2.1g, poly 1.1g); PROTEIN 1.3g; CARB 5.7g; FIBER 1.3g; CHOL 0mg; IRON 0.4mg; SODIUM 88mg; CALC 13.5mg

Pan-Seared Grouper with Sweet Ginger Relish

Prep: 2 minutes • Cook: 13 minutes

Make a quick side by heating precooked jasmine rice in the microwave and tossing it with fresh chopped mint.

1	tablespoon reduced-sodium soy sauce
1	tablespoon chili oil
¼	teaspoon freshly ground black pepper
2	garlic cloves, pressed
4	(6-ounce) grouper fillets (about 1 inch thick)

Cooking spray
Sweet Ginger Relish

1. Combine first 4 ingredients; brush mixture over fillets.
2. Heat a large nonstick skillet over medium-high heat. Coat pan with cooking spray. Add fillets; cook 6 to 7 minutes on each side or until fillets flake easily when tested with a fork. Serve with Sweet Ginger Relish. Yield: 4 servings (serving size: 1 fillet and ¼ cup Sweet Ginger Relish).

CALORIES 211; FAT 5.4g (sat 0.9g, mono 1.1g, poly 2.9g); PROTEIN 33.8g; CARB 5.5g; FIBER 0.8g; CHOL 63mg; IRON 2mg; SODIUM 225mg; CALC 60mg

Sweet Ginger Relish

Prep: 10 minutes

½	cup finely chopped red bell pepper
¼	cup chopped fresh mint
¼	cup finely chopped red onion
1	tablespoon grated peeled fresh ginger
1	tablespoon fresh lime juice
1	teaspoon sugar

1. Combine all ingredients in a small bowl. Toss gently. Yield: 4 servings (serving size: ¼ cup).

CALORIES 19; FAT 0.2g (sat 0g, mono 0g, poly 0.1g); PROTEIN 0.5g; CARB 4.5g; FIBER 0.7g; CHOL 0mg; IRON 0.4mg; SODIUM 2mg; CALC 11mg

Pan-Seared Grouper with Sweet Ginger Relish

Pistou Halibut

Prep: 4 minutes • Cook: 6 minutes

Like Italian pesto, French pistou (pee-STOO) is made of basil, garlic, and olive oil. Here we use pistou to season fish, but it is also delicious when tossed with potatoes and pasta, so make an extra batch or two to freeze or keep on hand to use later in the week.

⅓ cup minced fresh basil
1 tablespoon olive oil
½ teaspoon salt
¼ teaspoon freshly ground black pepper
2 garlic cloves, minced
4 (6-ounce) skinless halibut fillets
   (1 inch thick)
Cooking spray
4 lemon wedges

1. Combine first 5 ingredients in a small bowl; rub over both sides of fillets.
2. Heat a large nonstick skillet over medium heat. Coat pan with cooking spray. Add fillets; cook 2 to 3 minutes on each side or until fillets flake easily when tested with a fork. Serve with lemon wedges. Yield: 4 servings (serving size: 1 fillet and 1 lemon wedge).

CALORIES 223; FAT 7.3g (sat 1g, mono 3.7g, poly 1.6g); PROTEIN 35.7g; CARB 1.4g; FIBER 0.4g; CHOL 54mg; IRON 1.6mg; SODIUM 383mg; CALC 91mg

serve with:
Sautéed Garlicky Spinach

Prep: 2 minutes • Cook: 3 minutes

1 tablespoon olive oil
3 garlic cloves, thinly sliced
2 (6-ounce) packages baby spinach
¼ teaspoon salt
¼ teaspoon freshly ground black pepper

1. Heat a large deep skillet or Dutch oven over medium heat. Add oil; swirl to coat. Add garlic; cook 1 minute or until golden. Add half of spinach; cook, 1 minute, turning with tongs. Add remaining half of spinach, cook 1 minute, turning with tongs, until spinach wilts. Stir in salt and pepper. Yield: 4 servings (serving size: ½ cup).

CALORIES 54; FAT 3.4g (sat 0.5g, mono 2.5g, poly 0.4g); PROTEIN 2.2g; CARB 3.8g; FIBER 2.1g; CHOL 0mg; IRON 2.8mg; SODIUM 211mg; CALC 85mg

Pistou Halibut

Teriyaki Salmon with Mushrooms

Prep: 3 minutes • Cook: 15 minutes

Get a healthy dose of omega-3 fatty acids, the fatty acids that lower the risk of heart disease, from this pan-seared salmon served with a rich mushroom sauce.

¼   cup dry sherry
¼   cup low-sodium teriyaki sauce
2   tablespoons light brown sugar
1   teaspoon canola oil
1   (8-ounce) package presliced baby portobello mushrooms
4   (6-ounce) skinless salmon fillets (about 1 to 1½ inches thick)

1. Combine first 3 ingredients in a small bowl; stir to dissolve sugar.
2. Heat a large nonstick skillet over medium-high heat. Add oil; swirl to coat. Add mushrooms, and sauté 4 minutes or until tender. Add ⅓ cup sherry mixture to mushrooms. Reduce heat, and simmer 1 to 2 minutes or until liquid almost evaporates. Spoon mushroom mixture into a bowl; set aside.
3. Heat pan over medium-high heat; add fillets. Cook 3 to 4 minutes on each side or until browned on all sides. Add mushrooms and remaining sherry mixture to pan; cook 2 minutes. Transfer fillets to a serving platter, and top with sauce and mushrooms. Yield: 4 servings (serving size: 1 fillet and 2 tablespoons mushroom mixture).

CALORIES 335; FAT 14.3g (sat 3.2g; mono 5g; poly 5g); PROTEIN 37.6g; CARB 9.5g; FIBER 0.9g; CHOL 87mg; IRON 1.2mg; SODIUM 346mg; CALC 32mg

serve with:

Orange-Ginger Sugar Snaps

Prep: 4 minutes • Cook: 5 minutes

1   teaspoon dark sesame oil
2   green onions, sliced
½   teaspoon grated peeled fresh ginger
1   (8-ounce) package sugar snap peas
1   teaspoon grated orange rind
¼   teaspoon salt

1. Heat a nonstick skillet over medium heat; Add oil; swirl to coat. Add onions and ginger. Sauté 2 minutes; add sugar snap peas, and sauté 2 minutes or just until crisp-tender. Remove from heat; stir in orange rind and salt. Yield: 4 servings (serving size: ½ cup).

CALORIES 40; FAT 1.2g (sat 0.2g; mono 0.5; poly 0.5); PROTEIN 1.5g; CARB 5.4g; FIBER 1.6g; CHOL 0mg; IRON 0.8mg; SODIUM 153mg; CALC 46mg

quick flip

Want another flavor idea? Swap out ginger and orange rind for garlic and lemon rind.

Roasted Salmon with Tomatillo–Red Onion Salsa

Prep: 3 minutes • Cook: 20 minutes

Cooking spray
4   (6-ounce) salmon fillets (1 inch thick)
2   teaspoons ground cumin
1½   teaspoons smoked paprika
1½   teaspoons coarsely ground black pepper
¼   teaspoon salt
Tomatillo–Red Onion Salsa
1   lemon, cut into 4 wedges

1. Preheat oven to 350°.
2. Line a baking sheet with foil; coat foil with cooking spray. Arrange fillets on prepared pan.
3. Combine cumin and next 3 ingredients. Rub spice mixture over tops of fillets. Coat fillets with cooking spray.
4. Bake at 350° for 20 minutes or until desired degree of doneness. Place 1 fillet on each of 4 individual plates. Spoon Tomatillo–Red Onion Salsa evenly over fillets. Serve with lemon wedges. Yield: 4 servings (serving size: 1 fillet, ¼ cup salsa, and 1 lemon wedge).

CALORIES 257; FAT 10g (sat 1.5g, mono 4.3g, poly 1.8g); PROTEIN 34.7g; CARB 6g; FIBER 2.1g; CHOL 88mg; IRON 2.1mg; SODIUM 408mg; CALC 46mg

ingredient spotlight

Although they look like small green tomatoes, tomatillos, also known as husk tomatoes, are actually related to gooseberries. In this recipe, their tart-yet-subtle apple and lemon-like flavors cut the richness of the salmon. Remove the papery skin from the tomatillos, wash them well, and pat them dry before chopping them.

Tomatillo–Red Onion Salsa

Prep: 6 minutes

This Latin-inspired salsa, which is primarily made of chopped red onion, chopped tomatillos, lemon juice, and extra-virgin olive oil, takes little time and effort to prepare. It's tasty and versatile enough to serve over grilled chicken and steak or with tacos and fajitas. For a tropical variation, try substituting chopped pineapple for the tomatillo.

⅔   cup chopped tomatillos (3 medium)
⅓   cup finely chopped red onion
2   teaspoons grated lemon rind
2   tablespoons fresh lemon juice
1   tablespoon extra-virgin olive oil
¼   teaspoon salt

1. Combine all ingredients in a small bowl. Yield: 4 servings (serving size: ¼ cup).

CALORIES 46; FAT 3.7g (sat 0.5g, mono 2.7g, poly 0.4g); PROTEIN 0.4g; CARB 3.4g; FIBER 0.8g; CHOL 0mg; IRON 0.2mg; SODIUM 146mg; CALC 7mg

Snapper Piccata

Prep: 5 minutes • Cook: 9 minutes

The wine and lemon juice combine to deglaze the skillet, capturing the flavorful browned bits that remain after the fish cooks. You can substitute fat-free, lower-sodium chicken broth for the wine, if desired. Cook the pasta while you prepare the fish so that both dishes will be ready at the same time.

1   tablespoon olive oil
4   (6-ounce) snapper fillets (about ¾ inch thick)
¼   teaspoon salt
¼   teaspoon freshly ground black pepper
½   cup dry white wine
2   tablespoons fresh lemon juice
2   tablespoons capers
2   tablespoons chopped fresh parsley

1. Heat a large nonstick skillet over medium-high heat. Add oil; swirl to coat. Sprinkle fillets evenly with salt and pepper. Add fillets to pan, and cook 3 to 4 minutes on each side or until fillets flake easily when tested with a fork. Remove fillets from pan; keep warm.
2. Add wine and juice to pan; bring to a boil. Reduce heat, and simmer 2 minutes or until slightly thick, scraping pan to loosen browned bits. Stir in capers and parsley. Spoon sauce evenly over fillets. Yield: 4 servings (serving size: 1 fillet and about 1½ tablespoons sauce).

CALORIES 205; FAT 5.8g (sat 1g; mono 3.6; poly 1); PROTEIN 35.4g; CARB 1.4g; FIBER 0.1g; CHOL 63mg; IRON 0.6mg; SODIUM 416mg; CALC 63mg

serve with:
Parsley-Buttered Pasta

Prep: 3 minutes • Cook: 10 minutes

4   ounces angel hair pasta
1   (8-ounce) slice light whole-wheat bread
1   tablespoon light butter
2   teaspoons chopped fresh parsley
¼   teaspoon salt
⅛   teaspoon freshly ground black pepper

1. Cook pasta according to package directions, omitting salt and fat.
2. While pasta cooks, place bread in a food processor; pulse 10 times or until coarse crumbs measure ½ cup. Combine cooked pasta, breadcrumbs, butter, parsley, salt, and pepper; toss gently. Serve immediately. Yield: 4 servings (serving size: ½ cup).

CALORIES 125; FAT 2.3g (sat 1g; mono 0.8; poly 0.5); PROTEIN 4.4g; CARB 23.3g; FIBER 1.6g; CHOL 4mg; IRON 1.2mg; SODIUM 196mg; CALC 17mg

Snapper Piccata

Snapper with Warm Italian-Style Salsa

Prep: 2 minutes • Cook: 11 minutes

Three words describe this dependable weeknight dish: quick, easy, and delicious. If red snapper is unavailable, use halibut or sea bass. Serve the fish over a bed of rice tossed with garlic, green onions, and, if desired, fresh herbs.

Warm Italian-Style Salsa
1½ teaspoons extra-virgin olive oil
4 (6-ounce) snapper fillets
¼ teaspoon freshly ground black pepper
Cooking spray
2 tablespoons crumbled reduced-fat
 feta cheese

1. Prepare Warm Italian-Style Salsa. Cover and keep warm.
2. Heat a large nonstick skillet over medium-high heat. Add oil; swirl to coat. Sprinkle fillets with pepper; coat with cooking spray. Add fillets to pan. Cook 5 minutes on each side or until fillets flake easily when tested with a fork.
3. Place 1 fillet on each of 4 serving plates; top evenly with Warm Italian-Style Salsa.

Sprinkle evenly with cheese. Yield: 4 servings (serving size: 1 fillet, ¼ cup salsa, and 1½ teaspoons cheese).

CALORIES 240; FAT 8.2g (sat 1.6g, mono 4.4g, poly 1.4g); PROTEIN 36.4g; CARB 3.2g; FIBER 1g; CHOL 64mg; IRON 0.4mg; SODIUM 392mg; CALC 86mg

Warm Italian-Style Salsa

Prep: 5 minutes • Cook: 3 minutes

1 tablespoon extra-virgin olive oil
1½ cups grape tomatoes, halved
2 tablespoons oregano leaves
2 tablespoons drained capers
1 medium garlic clove, minced
¼ teaspoon crushed red pepper (optional)
2 tablespoons water
¼ teaspoon salt

1. Heat a large nonstick skillet over medium-high heat. Add oil; swirl to coat. Add tomatoes, next 3 ingredients, and red pepper, if desired. Sauté 1 to 2 minutes or until tomato begins to soften. Stir in water and salt. Yield: 4 servings (serving size: ¼ cup).

CALORIES 46; FAT 3.6g (sat 0.5g, mono 2.7g, poly 0.3g); PROTEIN 0.6g; CARB 3g; FIBER 0.9g; CHOL 0mg; IRON 0.1mg; SODIUM 225mg; CALC 22mg

Snapper with Warm Italian-Style Salsa

Panko Pan-Fried Fish Strips

Prep: 8 minutes • Cook: 12 minutes

The delightful crunchy crust in this family-friendly dish comes from panko, Japanese breadcrumbs. Reminiscent of fried fish fingers, this recipe will please even the pickiest of eaters.

½	teaspoon garlic powder
½	teaspoon salt
¼	teaspoon freshly ground black pepper
4	(6-ounce) tilapia fillets, cut in half lengthwise
¾	cup low-fat buttermilk
1½	cups panko (Japanese breadcrumbs)
1½	tablespoons olive oil, divided

1. Combine first 3 ingredients; sprinkle evenly over fish.
2. Place buttermilk in a shallow dish. Place panko in another shallow dish. Working with 1 piece of fish at a time, dip fish into buttermilk, and dredge in panko.
3. Heat a large nonstick skillet over medium-high heat. Add half of oil to pan; swirl to coat. Add half of fish. Reduce heat to medium; cook 4 minutes on each side or until fish flakes easily when tested with a fork. Repeat procedure with remaining oil and fish. Yield: 4 servings (serving size: 2 fish strips).

CALORIES 311; FAT 9.1g (sat 1.9g, mono 4.6g, poly 2.2g); PROTEIN 38.8g; CARB 17.5g; FIBER 0.8g; CHOL 87mg; IRON 1mg; SODIUM 491mg; CALC 71mg

Panko Pan-Fried Fish Strips

serve with:

Dijon Green Beans

Prep: 2 minutes • Cook: 5 minutes

1	(12-ounce) package trimmed fresh green beans
1	tablespoon light butter, melted
2	teaspoons Dijon mustard
1	tablespoon finely chopped fresh parsley
½	teaspoon grated lemon rind
¼	teaspoon salt

1. Microwave beans according to package directions.
2. While beans cook, combine butter and remaining ingredients in a small bowl. Place beans in a serving bowl. Add butter mixture; toss well. Serve immediately. Yield: 4 servings (serving size: ¾ cup).

CALORIES 36; FAT 1.5g (sat 0.9g, mono 0g, poly 0g); PROTEIN 1.1g; CARB 6g; FIBER 3.1g; CHOL 4mg; IRON 0.4mg; SODIUM 230mg; CALC 43mg

Grilled Thai-Spiced
Tuna Steaks

Grilled Thai-Spiced Tuna Steaks

Prep: 3 minutes • Cook: 4 minutes

Red curry paste gives this tuna dish spiciness and depth of flavor. The sweetness from the vibrantly colored accompanying salad balances the heat and adds a burst of fresh flavor to the meal. Use less curry paste, if you prefer.

4   (6-ounce) sushi-grade tuna steaks
      (1 inch thick)
½   teaspoon salt
1   tablespoon olive oil
1   tablespoon red curry paste
Cooking spray
4   lime wedges

1. Preheat grill to medium-high heat.
2. Sprinkle fish with salt. Combine olive oil and curry paste; brush over fish.
3. Place fish on grill rack coated with cooking spray. Grill 2 minutes on each side or until desired degree of doneness. Serve with lime wedges. Yield: 4 servings (serving size: 1 tuna steak and 1 lime wedge).

CALORIES 224; FAT 3.4g (sat 0.5g, mono 2.5g, poly 0.4g); PROTEIN 42.1g; CARB 2.3g; FIBER 0.5g; CHOL 78mg; IRON 1.1mg; SODIUM 436mg; CALC 361mg

serve with:

Edamame and Roasted Red Pepper Salad

Prep: 8 minutes

1   cup chopped bottled roasted red bell
      peppers
¼   cup chopped fresh cilantro
2   tablespoons sesame ginger dressing
1   tablespoon minced peeled fresh ginger
1   (10-ounce) package refrigerated
      ready-to-eat shelled edamame

1. Combine all ingredients in a medium bowl, toss to coat. Yield: 4 servings (serving size: about ⅔ cup).

CALORIES 123; FAT 3.7g (sat 0.1g, mono 2.4g, poly 1.2g) ; PROTEIN 8.4g; CARB 13.1g; FIBER 4.2g; CHOL 0mg; IRON 2mg; SODIUM 333mg; CALC 54mg

Baked Flounder with Dill and Caper Cream

Prep: 8 minutes • Cook: 12 minutes

Fresh dill contributes sharp flavor and feathery elegance to this simple flounder recipe. Since heat diminishes the potency of fresh dill, it's best to add it to the dish near the end of the suggested cooking time.

¼	teaspoon freshly ground black pepper
⅛	teaspoon salt
4	(6-ounce) flounder fillets

Cooking spray

1	tablespoon chopped fresh dill
½	cup reduced-fat sour cream
2	tablespoons capers, drained
4	lemon wedges

1. Preheat oven to 425°.
2. Sprinkle pepper and salt evenly over fillets. Place fish on a foil-lined baking sheet coated with cooking spray. Bake at 425° for 10 minutes; sprinkle evenly with dill. Bake an additional 2 minutes or until fish flakes easily when tested with a fork or until desired degree of doneness.
3. While fish bakes, combine sour cream and capers in a small bowl. Place fish on a serving plate. Squeeze 1 lemon wedge over each serving. Serve with caper cream. Yield: 4 servings (serving size: 1 fillet and about 2 tablespoons cream).

CALORIES 205; FAT 6g (sat 2.9g, mono 0.4g, poly 0.6g); PROTEIN 33.6g; CARB 2.8g; FIBER 0.2g; CHOL 97mg; IRON 0.7mg; SODIUM 356mg; CALC 83mg

Baked Flounder with Dill and Caper Cream

Pistachio-Crusted
Grouper with Lavender
Honey Sauce

Pistachio-Crusted Grouper with Lavender Honey Sauce

Prep: 12 minutes • Cook: 12 minutes

The delicate, subtle flavors of roasted pistachios and lavender honey transform this baked grouper into an easy, yet refined meal that family and friends will remember. Serve with sautéed spinach.

5	tablespoons dry breadcrumbs
5	tablespoons finely chopped unsalted shelled dry-roasted pistachios
4	(6-ounce) grouper fillets
¼	teaspoon salt
¼	teaspoon freshly ground black pepper
2	large egg whites, lightly beaten

Lavender Honey Sauce
Lemon wedges (optional)
Lavender sprigs (optional)

1. Preheat oven to 450°.
2. Combine breadcrumbs and pistachios in a shallow dish. Sprinkle fillets evenly with salt and pepper. Dip fillets in egg whites; dredge in breadcrumb mixture.

3. Place fish on a jelly-roll pan lined with parchment paper; bake at 450° for 12 minutes or until fish flakes easily when tested with a fork or until desired degree of doneness. Drizzle fillets evenly with Lavender Honey Sauce. Garnish with lemon wedges and lavender sprigs, if desired. Yield: 4 servings (serving size: 1 fillet and about 1 tablespoon sauce).

CALORIES 337; FAT 12g (sat 4.7g, mono 4.3g, poly 2.3g); PROTEIN 37.7g; CARB 18.1g; FIBER 1.5g; CHOL 78mg; IRON 2.4mg; SODIUM 360mg; CALC 76mg

Lavender Honey Sauce

Prep: 2 minutes • Cook: 2 minutes

2	tablespoons butter
2	tablespoons lavender honey
1	tablespoon fresh lemon juice

1. Melt butter in a small saucepan over medium heat. Add honey and lemon juice, stirring to combine. Yield: about ¼ cup (serving size: about 1 tablespoon).

CALORIES 83; FAT 6g (sat 3.6g, mono 1.5g, poly 0.2g); PROTEIN 0.1g; CARB 9.1g; FIBER 0g; CHOL 15mg; IRON 0.1mg; SODIUM 41mg; CALC 3mg

Sunflower Seed–Crusted
Orange Roughy

Sunflower Seed–Crusted Orange Roughy

Prep: 8 minutes • Cook: 10 minutes
Other: 10 minutes

When breading the fish, use one hand for the dry mixture and the other hand for the wet, so you don't lose any panko crumbs. Serve with steamed asparagus tossed with grated lemon rind.

2	large egg whites
½	teaspoon freshly ground black pepper
½	teaspoon grated lemon rind
½	cup Italian-seasoned panko (Japanese breadcrumbs)
3	tablespoons unsalted sunflower seed kernels
4	(6-ounce) orange roughy fillets (about ½ inch thick)

Cooking spray
Lemon slices (optional)

1. Preheat oven to 475°. Place a jelly-roll pan in oven while preheating.
2. Combine first 3 ingredients in a medium bowl; stir with a whisk until foamy. Combine panko and sunflower seed kernels in a shallow dish. Dip fillets in egg white mixture; dredge in panko mixture. Place fish on a wire rack; let stand 10 minutes.
3. Remove jelly-roll pan from oven; coat pan with cooking spray. Coat fish with cooking spray; place on pan. Bake at 475° for 10 minutes or until fish flakes easily when tested with a fork or until desired degree of doneness. Serve with lemon slices, if desired. Yield: 4 servings (serving size: 1 fillet).

CALORIES 206; FAT 4g (sat 0.3g, mono 1g, poly 2.2g); PROTEIN 31.5g; CARB 9.1g; FIBER 1.7g; CHOL 102mg; IRON 2.4mg; SODIUM 212mg; CALC 21mg

Seared Salmon Fillets with Edamame Succotash

Prep: 1 minute • Cook: 14 minutes

Applewood-smoked bacon imbues this upscale version of succotash with its sweet, smoky essence. Green soybeans replace the traditional limas.

3	applewood-smoked bacon slices
4	(6-ounce) salmon fillets (about 1 inch thick)
¼	teaspoon salt
¼	teaspoon freshly ground black pepper
¼	cup water
1	(8-ounce) container refrigerated prechopped tomato, onion, and bell pepper mix
1	cup frozen yellow and white whole-kernel corn
1	cup frozen shelled edamame (green soybeans)
½	teaspoon dried thyme
⅛	teaspoon salt

1. Cook bacon in a large nonstick skillet over medium heat 7 minutes or until crisp.
2. While bacon cooks, sprinkle fillets evenly with ¼ teaspoon salt and black pepper. When bacon is done, transfer it to paper towels to drain; crumble bacon.
3. Add fillets, skin sides up, to drippings in pan. Cook 4 minutes over medium-high heat or until browned. Turn fish over; add crumbled bacon, ¼ cup water, and remaining ingredients to pan. Cover and steam 3 minutes or until fish flakes easily when tested with a fork or until desired degree of doneness. Serve fillets over succotash. Yield: 4 servings (serving size: 1 fillet and about ¾ cup succotash).

CALORIES 397; FAT 19g (sat 4.7g, mono 6g, poly 3.4g); PROTEIN 43.3g; CARB 13.7g; FIBER 3.2g; CHOL 95mg; IRON 1.6mg; SODIUM 468mg; CALC 49mg

Chili-Garlic Glazed Salmon

Prep: 4 minutes • Cook: 7 minutes

The sweet, salty, and spicy flavors of this colorful glaze permeate the salmon as it cooks, creating a succulent dish that tantalizes the taste buds.

3   tablespoons chili sauce with garlic
3   tablespoons minced green onions (about 3 green onions)
1½ tablespoons low-sugar orange marmalade
¾   teaspoon lower-sodium soy sauce
4   (6-ounce) salmon fillets
Cooking spray

1. Preheat broiler.
2. Combine first 4 ingredients in a small bowl; brush half of chili sauce mixture over fillets. Place fillets, skin sides down, on a baking sheet coated with cooking spray. Broil fish 5 minutes; brush with remaining chili sauce mixture. Broil 2 more minutes or until fish flakes easily when tested with a fork or until desired degree of doneness. Yield: 4 servings (serving size: 1 fillet).

CALORIES 298; FAT 13g (sat 3.1g, mono 5.7g, poly 3.2g); PROTEIN 36.3g; CARB 5.6g; FIBER 0.5g; CHOL 87mg; IRON 0.6mg; SODIUM 171mg; CALC 23mg

serve with:

Minted Sugar Snap Peas

Prep: 2 minutes • Cook: 3 minutes

1   teaspoon canola oil
1   (8-ounce) package fresh sugar snap peas
1   tablespoon chopped fresh mint
1   teaspoon grated orange rind
¼   teaspoon salt

1. Heat a large nonstick skillet over medium-high heat. Add oil; swirl to coat. Add peas. Sauté 2 minutes or just until peas are crisp-tender. Stir in mint, orange rind, and salt. Yield: 4 servings (serving size: ½ cup).

CALORIES 38; FAT 1g (sat 0.1g, mono 0.7g, poly 0.4g); PROTEIN 1.4g; CARB 4.9g; FIBER 1.4g; CHOL 0mg; IRON 0.8mg; SODIUM 152mg; CALC 42mg

Chili-Garlic Glazed Salmon

Peach-Glazed Salmon
with Raspberries

3. Sprinkle fish evenly with salt. Place fish, skin sides up, on grill rack coated with cooking spray; grill 4 minutes. Turn fish over; grill 4 minutes or until fish flakes easily when tested with a fork, basting with reserved 2 tablespoons sauce. Spoon raspberry sauce evenly over fillets. Yield: 4 servings (serving size: 1 fillet and ¼ cup sauce).

CALORIES 391; FAT 13g (sat 3.1g, mono 5.7g, poly 3.2g); PROTEIN 36.5g; CARB 30.7g; FIBER 0g; CHOL 87mg; IRON 0.8mg; SODIUM 229mg; CALC 32mg

serve with:

Balsamic Grilled Peaches

Prep: 2 minutes • Cook: 6 minutes

2	large firm ripe peaches, halved and pitted

Cooking spray

3	tablespoons balsamic glaze, divided
4	tablespoons crumbled blue cheese
¼	teaspoon freshly ground black pepper

1. Preheat grill to medium-high heat.
2. Place peaches, cut sides down, on grill rack coated with cooking spray, and grill 3 minutes. Turn peaches; brush tops and sides with 2 tablespoons glaze. Grill 3 minutes or until tender. Sprinkle with cheese and pepper; drizzle with remaining 1 tablespoon glaze. Yield: 4 servings (serving size: 1 peach half and 1 tablespoon cheese).

CALORIES 86; FAT 3g (sat 1.8g, mono 0.1g, poly 0.1g); PROTEIN 2.8g; CARB 13.4g; FIBER 1.5g; CHOL 9mg; IRON 0.2mg; SODIUM 134mg; CALC 49mg

Peach-Glazed Salmon with Raspberries

Prep: 5 minutes • Cook: 11 minutes

The addition of Balsamic Grilled Peaches makes this menu exceptional. Simply grill the peach halves alongside the fish to quickly caramelize their natural sugars. The mahogany-hued balsamic glaze pools in the center of the peaches, and a sprinkle of blue cheese provides a sharp flavor contrast.

½	cup peach spread
1½	tablespoons dark brown sugar
2	tablespoons balsamic vinegar
⅛	teaspoon crushed red pepper
1	cup fresh raspberries
4	(6-ounce) salmon fillets
¼	teaspoon salt

Cooking spray

1. Preheat grill to medium-high heat.
2. Combine peach spread and next 3 ingredients in a medium saucepan over medium-high heat; cook 2 minutes, stirring frequently. Reserve 2 tablespoons sauce. Add raspberries to pan; cook over medium heat 1 minute, stirring gently.

Pan-Seared Snapper with
Fennel-Olive Topping

Pan-Seared Snapper with Fennel-Olive Topping

Prep: 6 minutes • Cook: 13 minutes

Fennel bulb, when eaten raw in salads, has a subtle licorice flavor and crisp texture. When cooked, it mellows and softens. In this recipe the sautéed fennel combines with the piquant tapenade to create a saucy and savory vegetable topping for the fish. Serve over rice.

4	(6-ounce) red snapper or other firm white fish fillets
½	teaspoon salt
¼	teaspoon freshly ground black pepper
	Cooking spray
1	fennel bulb, thinly sliced (about 3½ cups)
½	cup thinly sliced onion
1	large tomato, chopped
3	tablespoons refrigerated olive tapenade
2	tablespoons fresh lemon juice

1. Sprinkle fillets evenly with salt and pepper. Heat a large nonstick skillet over medium-high heat; coat pan and fillets with cooking spray. Add fish to pan, skin sides up. Cook 3 minutes or until lightly browned. Remove from pan.
2. Coat pan with cooking spray. Add fennel and onion; sauté 3 minutes. Add tomato, tapenade, and lemon juice; stir well. Return fillets to pan, nestling them into fennel mixture. Cover and cook 7 minutes or until fish flakes easily when tested with a fork or until desired degree of doneness. Spoon fennel mixture over fillets to serve. Yield: 4 servings (serving size: 1 fillet and ¾ cup fennel topping).

CALORIES 238; FAT 6g (sat 1.3g, mono 0.4g, poly 0.8g); PROTEIN 37g;
CARB 8.9g; FIBER 3.4g; CHOL 63mg; IRON 1.4mg; SODIUM 545mg;
CALC 107mg

Lemon Red Snapper with Herbed Butter

Prep: 9 minutes • Cook: 13 minutes

A fragrant herbed butter and roasted lemon slices complement the sweet, nutty flavor of red snapper for a super-fresh dish. Complete the meal with colorful Sautéed Zucchini and Bell Peppers.

2	lemons
	Cooking spray
4	(6-ounce) red snapper or other firm white fish fillets
¼	teaspoon salt
¼	teaspoon paprika
¼	teaspoon freshly ground black pepper
2	tablespoons butter, softened
1½	teaspoons chopped fresh herbs (such as rosemary, thyme, basil, or parsley)
	Herb sprigs (optional)

1. Preheat oven to 425°.
2. Cut 1 lemon into 8 slices. Place slices, in pairs, on a rimmed baking sheet coated with cooking spray. Grate remaining lemon to get 1 teaspoon lemon rind; set aside. Reserve lemon for another use.
3. Place 1 fillet on top of each pair of lemon slices. Combine salt, paprika, and pepper; sprinkle evenly over fish. Bake at 425° for 13 minutes or until fish flakes easily when tested with a fork or until desired degree of doneness.
4. While fish bakes, combine reserved lemon rind, butter, and herbs in a small bowl.
5. Place fish and lemon slices on individual serving plates; top each fillet with herbed butter, spreading to melt, if desired. Garnish with herb sprigs, if desired. Yield: 4 servings (serving size: 1 fillet and about 1½ teaspoons herbed butter).

CALORIES 223); FAT 8g (sat 4.1g, mono 1.9g, poly 1g); PROTEIN 34g; CARB 2.9g; FIBER 0.9g; CHOL 75mg; IRON 0.5mg; SODIUM 259mg; CALC 62mg

serve with:

Sautéed Zucchini and Bell Peppers

Prep: 3 minutes • Cook: 7 minutes

1	teaspoon olive oil
1	medium zucchini, quartered lengthwise and cut into 2-inch pieces
1	cup refrigerated prechopped tricolor bell pepper
1	garlic clove, minced
¼	teaspoon salt

1. Heat a large nonstick skillet over medium-high heat. Add oil; swirl to coat. Add zucchini and remaining ingredients; sauté 7 minutes. Yield: 4 servings (serving size: ½ cup).

CALORIES 28; FAT 1g (sat 0.2g, mono 0.8g, poly 0.2g); PROTEIN 1.1g; CARB 3.9g; FIBER 0.8g; CHOL 0mg; IRON 0.4mg; SODIUM 148mg; CALC 14mg

Lemon Red Snapper with Herbed Butter

Spicy Louisiana Tilapia Fillets with Sautéed Vegetable Relish

Prep: 5 minutes • Cook: 10 minutes

Louisiana hot sauce is not as spicy as other hot sauces. Use a hotter sauce if you prefer more heat.

Cooking spray
1   (8-ounce) container refrigerated prechopped tomato, onion, and bell pepper mix
4   (6-ounce) tilapia fillets
2   tablespoons water
2   teaspoons Louisiana hot sauce
1½   teaspoons chopped fresh thyme
½   teaspoon salt
1   tablespoon butter

1. Heat a large nonstick skillet over medium-high heat; coat pan with cooking spray. Add tomato mixture; sauté 2 minutes. Remove from pan.
2. Coat pan and fillets with cooking spray; add fish to pan. Cook 2 minutes or until lightly browned. Turn fillets over; add tomato mixture to pan, spooning mixture over and around fillets. Cover and cook 5 minutes or until fish flakes easily when tested with a fork or until desired degree of doneness.
3. While fish cooks, combine 2 tablespoons water, hot sauce, thyme, and salt in a small bowl.
4. Carefully remove fish and tomato mixture from pan; place on a serving platter. Reduce heat to medium; add hot sauce mixture and butter to pan. Cook until butter melts. Spoon butter mixture evenly over fish and tomato mixture. Yield: 4 servings (serving size: 1 fillet and about ¼ cup tomato mixture).

CALORIES 210; FAT 6g (sat 2.8g, mono 1.6g, poly 0.8g); PROTEIN 35g; CARB 4.8g; FIBER 1.4g; CHOL 93mg; IRON 1.4mg; SODIUM 465mg; CALC 34mg

serve with:
Hoppin' John–Style Rice

Prep: 4 minutes • Cook: 4 minutes

2   teaspoons olive oil
¼   cup finely chopped green onions
1   garlic clove, minced
1   (15.8-ounce) can black-eyed peas, rinsed and drained
1   (8.8-ounce) pouch microwavable cooked brown rice

1. Heat a large nonstick skillet over medium-high heat. Add oil; swirl to coat. Add onions and garlic. Sauté 30 seconds or until lightly browned. Add peas; cook 2 minutes or until thoroughly heated.
2. While peas cook, microwave rice according to package directions.
3. Add rice to pea mixture; toss well. Yield: 4 servings (serving size: ¾ cup).

CALORIES 176; FAT 5g (sat 0.7g, mono 1.7g, poly 0.5g); PROTEIN 5.8g; CARB 28.6g; FIBER 3.4g; CHOL 0mg; IRON 1.1mg; SODIUM 131mg; CALC 20mg

fix it faster

Whip up this Southern dish in no time with the help of canned black-eyed peas and cooked brown rice.

Almond-Crusted Tilapia

Prep: 5 minutes • Cook: 6 minutes

Reminiscent of a restaurant-style fish amandine, this recipe easily doubles to serve a small dinner party. Almonds add such a rich, nutty flavor to the tilapia that even the pickiest eater will think it is delicious. Serve with green beans and Mashed Red Potatoes with Chives.

¼   cup whole natural almonds
2   tablespoons dry breadcrumbs
1   teaspoon salt-free garlic and herb seasoning blend
⅛   teaspoon freshly ground black pepper
1   tablespoon canola oil
1   tablespoon Dijon mustard
2   (6-ounce) tilapia fillets
Chopped fresh parsley (optional)

1. Place first 4 ingredients in a blender or food processor; process 45 seconds or until finely ground. Transfer crumb mixture to a shallow dish.
2. Heat a large nonstick skillet over medium heat. Add oil; swirl to coat. Brush mustard over both sides of fillets; dredge in crumb mixture. Add fish to pan; cook 3 minutes on each side or until fish flakes easily when tested with a fork or until desired degree of doneness. Sprinkle with parsley, if desired. Yield: 2 servings (serving size: 1 fillet).

CALORIES 367; FAT 19g (sat 2.1g, mono 10.6g, poly 4.8g); PROTEIN 38.9g; CARB 9.9g; FIBER 2.5g; CHOL 85mg; IRON 1.3mg; SODIUM 321mg; CALC 28mg

serve with:
Mashed Red Potatoes with Chives

Prep: 1 minute • Cook: 8 minutes

1   red potato (about ½ pound)
1   garlic clove, minced
2   tablespoons reduced-fat sour cream
1½   tablespoons fat-free milk
1   tablespoon yogurt-based spread
⅛   teaspoon salt
⅛   teaspoon freshly ground black pepper
½   tablespoon minced fresh chives

1. Scrub potato; place in a medium-sized microwave-safe bowl (do not pierce potato with a fork). Cover bowl with plastic wrap (do not allow plastic wrap to touch food); vent. Microwave at HIGH 8 minutes or until tender.
2. Add garlic and next 5 ingredients to potatoes. Mash to desired consistency. Stir in chives. Yield: 2 servings (serving size: about ½ cup).

CALORIES 120; FAT 4g (sat 1.1g, mono 0g, poly 0.1g); PROTEIN 3.0g; CARB 20g; FIBER 2g; CHOL 4mg; IRON 1mg; SODIUM 208mg; CALC 41mg

Almond-Crusted Tilapia

Tilapia with Warm Olive Salsa

Prep: 3 minutes • Cook: 9 minutes

Squeeze a lemon wedge over the fish before drizzling with olive oil to tie together the components of this dish. Any thin white fillets, such as sole or flounder, can be substituted for tilapia.

Cooking spray
1	cup chopped plum tomato (about ⅓ pound)
12	small pimiento-stuffed olives, chopped
2	tablespoons chopped fresh parsley
1½	teaspoons chopped fresh oregano, divided
4	(6-ounce) tilapia fillets, rinsed and patted dry
¼	teaspoon salt
¼	teaspoon freshly ground black pepper
4	lemon wedges
1	tablespoon extra-virgin olive oil

Tilapia with Warm Olive Salsa

1. Heat a large nonstick skillet over medium-high heat. Coat pan with cooking spray. Add tomato; cook 1 minute or until thoroughly heated. Combine cooked tomato, olives, parsley, and ¾ teaspoon oregano in a small bowl; keep warm.
2. Wipe pan dry with a paper towel; return pan to medium-high heat. Recoat pan with cooking spray. Sprinkle fillets evenly with remaining ¾ teaspoon oregano, salt, and pepper. Add fillets to pan; cook 3 minutes on each side or until fish flakes easily when tested with a fork or until desired degree of doneness. Squeeze 1 lemon wedge over each fillet; drizzle each evenly with oil. Top evenly with olive salsa. Yield: 4 servings (serving size: 1 fillet and ¼ cup olive salsa).

CALORIES 218; FAT 8g (sat 1.7g, mono 4.5g, poly 1.1g); PROTEIN 34.8g; CARB 3.1g; FIBER 1g; CHOL 85mg; IRON 1.4mg; SODIUM 485mg; CALC 36mg

serve with:
Lemon Couscous with Toasted Pine Nuts

Prep: 3 minutes • Cook: 5 minutes
Other: 5 minutes

1	cup water
⅔	cup uncooked whole-wheat couscous
1	teaspoon grated lemon rind
¼	cup pine nuts, toasted
2	teaspoons extra-virgin olive oil
¼	teaspoon salt

1. Bring 1 cup water to a boil in a small saucepan. Stir in couscous and lemon rind. Remove from heat; cover and let stand 5 minutes. Add pine nuts and remaining ingredients; fluff with a fork. Yield: 4 servings (serving size: about ½ cup).

CALORIES 148; FAT 8g (sat 0.7g, mono 3.4g, poly 3.1g); PROTEIN 3.8g; CARB 16.2g; FIBER 2.7g; CHOL 0mg; IRON 1.1mg; SODIUM 146mg; CALC 9mg

Pan-Seared Tarragon Trout

Prep: 7 minutes • Cook: 8 minutes

Steelhead, also known as ocean trout, is a fine choice for its bright pink color and rich flavor, but you can use any trout.

1   lemon
2   tablespoons all-purpose flour
2   (6-ounce) trout fillets
¼   teaspoon salt
¼   teaspoon freshly ground black pepper
1   tablespoon butter
1   garlic clove, minced
¼   cup dry white wine
1   teaspoon dried tarragon

1. Zest and juice lemon, reserving ¼ teaspoon zest and 1 teaspoon juice.
2. Place flour in a shallow dish. Sprinkle fish evenly with salt and pepper; dredge fish in flour.
3. Melt butter in a large nonstick skillet over medium-high heat. Add fish; cook 2 to 3 minutes on each side or until fish flakes easily when tested with a fork or until desired degree of doneness. Remove fish from pan; keep warm.
4. Add garlic to pan; sauté 1 minute or until browned. Add wine; cook until liquid almost evaporates, scraping pan to loosen browned bits. Stir in tarragon and reserved lemon zest and juice. Pour garlic sauce over fish. Yield: 2 servings (serving size: 1 fillet and about 1 tablespoon sauce).

CALORIES 293; FAT 12g (sat 4.8g, mono 3.4g, poly 2.4g); PROTEIN 36g; CARB 6.2g; FIBER 0.4g; CHOL 115mg; IRON 1.8mg; SODIUM 385mg; CALC 133mg

serve with:
Fig, Carrot, and Ginger Rice Pilaf

Prep: 4 minutes • Cook: 5 minutes

1   (8.8-ounce) pouch microwavable cooked brown rice
1   tablespoon olive oil
1   cup matchstick-cut carrots
1   tablespoon minced peeled fresh ginger
2   garlic cloves, minced
½   cup small dried figs, quartered

1. Heat rice according to package directions; keep warm.
2. While rice cooks, heat oil in a large nonstick skillet over medium-high heat. Add oil; swirl to coat. Add carrots, ginger, and garlic. Sauté 3 minutes or until browned. Add figs; sauté 2 minutes or until hot. Remove from heat; stir in rice. Serve immediately. Yield: 4 servings (serving size: about ½ cup).

CALORIES 217; FAT 6g (sat 0.8g, mono 2.6g, poly 0.6g); PROTEIN 3.7g; CARB 39.8g; FIBER 4.3g; CHOL 0mg; IRON 1mg; SODIUM 24mg; CALC 52mg

Pan-Seared Tarragon Trout

Seared Sesame Tuna with Orange-Ginger Sauce

Prep: 7 minutes • Cook: 7 minutes

The sesame seeds tend to pop out of the skillet as the tuna cooks, so use caution and wear an oven mitt when you turn the fish over.

1	garlic clove, minced
3	tablespoons orange-ginger sauce and glaze
1	tablespoon seasoned rice vinegar
1	teaspoon lower-sodium soy sauce
½	teaspoon dark sesame oil
2	teaspoons canola oil
4	(6-ounce) tuna steaks (about 1 inch thick)
⅛	teaspoon salt
3	tablespoons sesame seeds
3	tablespoons black sesame seeds
	Cooking spray
¼	cup sliced green onions

1. Combine first 5 ingredients, stirring well with a whisk; set aside.
2. Heat a large nonstick skillet over medium-high heat. Add canola oil; swirl to coat. Sprinkle steaks evenly with salt. Combine sesame seeds and black sesame seeds in a shallow dish. Dredge steaks in sesame seeds. Lightly coat both sides of fish with cooking spray. Add fish to pan; cook 3 minutes on each side or until desired degree of doneness. Sprinkle evenly with onions; serve with orange-ginger sauce. Yield: 4 servings (serving size: 1 steak and 1½ tablespoons sauce).

CALORIES 317; FAT 11g (sat 1.6g, mono 4.2g, poly 4.1g); PROTEIN 42.3g; CARB 10.4g; FIBER 1.9g; CHOL 77mg; IRON 3.3mg; SODIUM 302mg; CALC 165mg

serve with:

Edamame and Corn Salad

Prep: 7 minutes

¼	cup seasoned rice vinegar
2	tablespoons water
1	tablespoon olive oil
1	teaspoon brown sugar
1	teaspoon minced peeled fresh ginger
⅛	teaspoon salt
1	(10-ounce) package refrigerated shelled edamame (green soybeans)
1	cup frozen whole-kernel corn, thawed and drained
1	tablespoon chopped fresh cilantro

1. Combine first 6 ingredients in a medium bowl, stirring well with a whisk. Add edamame, corn, and cilantro; toss gently to coat. Yield: 4 servings (serving size: ⅔ cup).

CALORIES 156; FAT 7g (sat 0.5g, mono 2.6g, poly 0.6g); PROTEIN 8.4g; CARB 17.7g; FIBER 4.3g; CHOL 0mg; IRON 1.7mg; SODIUM 376mg; CALC 45mg

ingredient spotlight

Fresh soybeans (edamame) are packed with potential health benefits. Each ½-cup serving contains 4 grams of fiber and only 3 grams of fat, all of which are the heart-healthy mono- and polyunsaturated kind. The beans are also high in soy protein, which may help reduce cholesterol when part of a low-fat diet.

Grilled Tuna Steaks with Cucumber–Pickled Ginger Relish

Grilled Tuna Steaks with Cucumber–Pickled Ginger Relish

Prep: 9 minutes • Cook: 6 minutes

The pickled ginger adds a sweet, spicy bite to the cucumber relish. Prepare the relish while the tuna grills. Make a quick side by steaming snow peas in the microwave.

4	(6-ounce) tuna steaks (about 1 inch thick)
1	tablespoon canola oil
½	teaspoon freshly ground black pepper
¼	teaspoon salt
Cooking spray	
1	cup diced seeded peeled cucumber
6	tablespoons finely chopped red onion
6	tablespoons pickled ginger, coarsely chopped
3	tablespoons chopped fresh cilantro
1½	tablespoons fresh lime juice

1. Preheat grill to medium-high heat.
2. Brush steaks with oil; sprinkle evenly with pepper and salt. Place fish on grill rack coated with cooking spray; grill 3 minutes on each side or until medium-rare or until desired degree of doneness.
3. While fish cooks, combine cucumber and remaining 4 ingredients in a medium bowl, tossing well. Serve relish over fish. Yield: 4 servings (serving size: 1 tuna steak and about ⅓ cup relish).

CALORIES 257; FAT 5g (sat 0.7g, mono 2.3g, poly 1.5g); PROTEIN 40.2g; CARB 8.8g; FIBER 1g; CHOL 77mg; IRON 1.6mg; SODIUM 360mg; CALC 49mg

Spicy Thai Tuna Cakes with Cucumber Aioli

Prep: 10 minutes • Cook: 2 minutes

Cool cucumber aioli puts out the fire of the Thai spices in these tuna cakes. Although the cakes are portioned as a main dish, you can also form eight smaller appetizer cakes when entertaining guests.

3	(5-ounce) cans Thai chili-flavored tuna, drained
1	large egg white, lightly beaten
½	cup panko (Japanese breadcrumbs)
2	tablespoons chopped fresh cilantro
Cooking spray	
½	cup shredded cucumber
¼	cup light mayonnaise

1. Combine first 4 ingredients in a medium bowl. Divide tuna mixture into 4 equal portions, shaping each into a ¾-inch-thick patty.
2. Heat a large nonstick skillet over medium heat. Coat pan and patties with cooking spray. Add patties; cook 1 to 2 minutes on each side or until lightly browned.
3. While patties cook, combine cucumber and mayonnaise in a small bowl. Serve with tuna cakes. Yield: 4 servings (serving size: 1 cake and 2 tablespoons aioli).

CALORIES 173; FAT 9g (sat 1.2g, mono 3.8g, poly 3.6g); PROTEIN 10.1g; CARB 11.9g; FIBER 0.9g; CHOL 26mg; IRON 0.8mg; SODIUM 413mg; CALC 4mg

Spicy Thai Tuna Cakes with Cucumber Aioli

serve with:

Orange and Radish Cabbage Slaw

Prep: 6 minutes

4	cups shredded napa (Chinese) cabbage
½	cup sliced radishes (about 3 radishes)
⅓	cup orange sections (about 1 small orange)
2	tablespoons rice vinegar
1	tablespoon canola oil
2	teaspoons sugar
1	teaspoon dark sesame oil

1. Combine first 3 ingredients in a large bowl.
2. Combine vinegar and remaining 3 ingredients in a small bowl, stirring well with a whisk. Pour vinegar mixture over cabbage mixture; toss gently to coat. Yield: 4 servings (serving size: 1¼ cups).

CALORIES 76; FAT 5g (sat 0.4g, mono 2.1g, poly 1g); PROTEIN 1.2g; CARB 8g; FIBER 1.6g; CHOL 0mg; IRON 0mg; SODIUM 11mg; CALC 70mg

Catfish with Cilantro-Chipotle Rice

Catfish with Cilantro-Chipotle Rice

Prep: 5 minutes • Cook: 14 minutes

| 4 | (6-ounce) farm-raised catfish fillets |
Cooking spray
¼	teaspoon salt
¼	teaspoon freshly ground black pepper
¼	cup bottled chipotle salsa, divided
Lime wedges
Cilantro-Chipotle Rice

1. Heat a large nonstick skillet over medium-high heat. Coat pan and fillets with cooking spray. Sprinkle fillets evenly with salt and pepper. Add 2 fillets to pan, flat sides up; cook 4 minutes on 1 side or until browned. Turn fillets over; spoon 1 tablespoon salsa over each fillet. Cook 3 minutes or until fish flakes easily when tested with a fork or until desired degree of doneness. Repeat procedure with remaining 2 fillets. Serve with lime wedges and Cilantro-Chipotle Rice. Yield: 4 servings (serving size: 1 fillet and ½ cup rice).

CALORIES 322; FAT 13g (sat 3.1g, mono 6.3g, poly 2.8g); PROTEIN 28.6g; CARB 19.1g; FIBER 2.1g; CHOL 80mg; IRON 0.9mg; SODIUM 507mg; CALC 28mg

Cilantro-Chipotle Rice

Prep: 2 minutes • Cook: 4 minutes

1	(10-ounce) package frozen brown rice
⅓	cup bottled chipotle salsa
¼	cup chopped fresh cilantro

1. Heat rice according to package directions. Transfer rice to a medium bowl. Stir in salsa and cilantro. Serve immediately. Yield: 4 servings (serving size: ½ cup).

CALORIES 85; FAT 1g (sat 0.1g, mono 0.2g, poly 0.2g); PROTEIN 2.1g; CARB 17.5g; FIBER 1.6g; CHOL 0mg; IRON 0mg; SODIUM 156mg; CALC 11mg

Shrimp with Capers, Garlic, and Rice

Prep: 7 minutes • Cook: 5 minutes

The clean tastes of fresh lemon juice and thyme complement the saltiness of the capers in this shrimp and rice dish. Starting with peeled and deveined shrimp from the fish counter and a package of precooked rice makes this a fast and satisfying meal after a busy day.

2	teaspoons olive oil
2	tablespoons chopped fresh thyme
2	tablespoons drained capers
3	garlic cloves, minced
1½	pounds large shrimp, peeled and deveined
1	tablespoon fresh lemon juice
1	(8.8-ounce) package precooked long-grain rice

1. Heat a large nonstick skillet over medium-high heat. Add oil; swirl to coat. Add thyme, capers, and garlic; sauté 1 minute. Add shrimp and lemon juice; sauté 4 minutes or until shrimp are done. **2.** Microwave rice according to package directions. Serve shrimp mixture over rice. Yield: 4 servings (serving size: ¾ cup shrimp mixture and about ⅓ cup rice).

CALORIES 296; FAT 6.4g (sat 0.9g, mono 2.1g, poly 1.4g); PROTEIN 36.7g; CARB 20.9g; FIBER 0.8g; CHOL 259mg; IRON 5.2mg; SODIUM 333mg; CALC 126mg

ingredient spotlight

The most pungent of all alliums, garlic becomes stronger in taste the more it is chopped or minced. Be careful when you sauté garlic. If burned, garlic will add an acrid, bitter flavor to the finished dish.

serve with:

Greek-Style Green Beans

Prep: 5 minutes • Cook: 4 minutes

1	(12-ounce) package trimmed fresh green beans
¼	cup (⅛-inch) sliced shallots (about 2)
¼	cup crumbled feta cheese
2	tablespoons fresh lemon juice
1	tablespoon olive oil
2	tablespoons fresh lemon juice
⅛	teaspoon freshly ground black pepper

1. Microwave green beans according to package directions. Plunge beans into ice water; drain. Place in a large bowl. Add shallots and remaining ingredients; toss well. Yield: 4 servings (serving size: ¾ cup).

CALORIES 93; FAT 5.6g (sat 1.9g, mono 2.9g, poly 0.5g); PROTEIN 3.2g; CARB 9.3g; FIBER 2.8g; CHOL 8mg; IRON 0.8mg; SODIUM 107mg; CALC 87mg

Shrimp with Capers, Garlic, and Rice

Pan-Fried Shrimp

Prep: 4 minutes • Cook: 4 minutes

Processing the panko and cilantro creates fine crumbs that adhere well to the shrimp. To save time, buy a peeled, cored fresh pineapple and presliced mango for the slaw. Enjoy the rest of it later in the week as part of a fresh fruit salad.

1	cup panko (Japanese breadcrumbs)
2	tablespoons chopped fresh cilantro
1	pound extra-large shrimp, peeled and deveined (about 15)
¼	teaspoon salt
¼	teaspoon freshly ground black pepper
1	large egg, beaten
2	teaspoons water
2	tablespoons canola oil

Pan-Fried Shrimp

1. Place panko and cilantro in a food processor; pulse 2 to 3 times or until cilantro is finely minced. Transfer to a shallow dish.
2. Sprinkle shrimp with salt and pepper. Combine egg and water in a shallow dish. Dip half of shrimp in egg mixture; dredge in crumb mixture, and place in a single layer on a plate. Repeat procedure with remaining shrimp, egg mixture, and crumb mixture.
3. Heat a large nonstick skillet over medium-high heat. Add oil; swirl to coat. Add shrimp, and cook 2 minutes on each side or until done. Drain shrimp on paper towels. Yield: 3 servings (serving size: about 5 shrimp).

CALORIES 295; FAT 12.6g (sat 1.4g, mono 6.4g, poly 3.5g); PROTEIN 28.8g; CARB 13.9g; FIBER 0.7g; CHOL 284mg; IRON 3.9mg; SODIUM 532mg; CALC 55mg

serve with:
Tropical Slaw

Prep: 5 minutes • Other: 15 minutes

3¼	cups packaged coleslaw
¾	cup chopped fresh mango
½	cup chopped fresh pineapple
2	tablespoons light mayonnaise
¼	teaspoon salt
¼	teaspoon freshly ground black pepper
1	tablespoon finely chopped fresh cilantro

1. Combine first 6 ingredients in a large bowl; toss well. Cover and chill 15 minutes. Stir in cilantro. Yield: 3 servings (serving size: 1 cup).

CALORIES 87; FAT 3.5g (sat 0.1g, mono 1.7g, poly 1g); PROTEIN 0.9g; CARB 14.4g; FIBER 2.2g; CHOL 3mg; IRON 0.4mg; SODIUM 287mg; CALC 30mg

Smoky BBQ Shrimp

Prep: 8 minutes • Cook: 6 minutes

Like your 'cue cooked low and slow? The enticing aroma of this speedy grilled shrimp just might change your mind. We liked the smoky flavor that bacon and barbecue sauce add to the shrimp.

32	peeled and deveined large shrimp (about 1½ pounds)
⅓	cup spicy barbecue sauce
2	applewood-smoked bacon slices, cooked and finely crumbled
1½	tablespoons low-sugar orange marmalade
Cooking spray	

1. Preheat grill to medium-high heat.
2. Thread shrimp onto 4 (12-inch) metal skewers.
3. Combine barbecue sauce, bacon, and marmalade; brush evenly over shrimp, using all sauce. Place skewers on grill rack coated with cooking spray; grill 3 to 4 minutes on each side or until shrimp reach desired degree of doneness. Yield: 4 servings (serving size: about 8 shrimp).

CALORIES 227; FAT 5.2g (sat 1.6g, mono 1.6g, poly 1.9g); PROTEIN 37g; CARB 7.4g; FIBER 0g; CHOL 264mg; IRON 4.1mg; SODIUM 502mg; CALC 89mg

Smoky BBQ Shrimp

Grilled Shrimp Salad with
Honey-Lime Dressing

Grilled Shrimp Salad with Honey-Lime Dressing

Prep: 5 minutes • Cook: 8 minutes

The slightly sweet dressing would also be excellent drizzled over fresh fruit.

1   pound peeled and deveined shrimp (about 20 shrimp)
1   tablespoon olive oil
1   tablespoon fiery 5-pepper seasoning, divided
1   (1¼-pound) cored fresh pineapple, cut into ½-inch-thick slices
Cooking spray
Honey-Lime Dressing
2   (4-ounce) packages lettuce and herb blend salad greens
¼   cup chopped fresh cilantro (optional)
4   lime wedges (optional)

1. Preheat grill to medium-high heat.
2. Thread shrimp onto 3 (12-inch) metal skewers. Brush shrimp with oil; sprinkle with 1½ teaspoons seasoning. Sprinkle pineapple slices with remaining 1½ teaspoons seasoning.
3. Place skewers and pineapple slices on grill rack coated with cooking spray. Grill 8 minutes or until lightly browned, turning once. Cut each pineapple slice into 4 pieces.
4. While shrimp and pineapple cook, prepare Honey-Lime Dressing.
5. Divide greens evenly among 4 plates, and top evenly with grilled shrimp and pineapple. Drizzle salads with Honey-Lime Dressing. Sprinkle each serving with 1 tablespoon chopped fresh cilantro, and serve with 1 lime wedge, if desired. Yield: 4 servings (serving size: 5 shrimp, 2¼ cups greens, ⅔ cup pineapple, and 2 tablespoons dressing).

CALORIES 366; FAT 16.7g (sat 1.9g, mono 8.9g, poly 4.2g); PROTEIN 25.2g; CARB 30g; FIBER 2.7g; CHOL 177mg; IRON 3.2mg; SODIUM 360mg; CALC 105mg

Honey-Lime Dressing

Prep: 3 minutes

¼   cup organic canola mayonnaise
2   tablespoons honey
1½   tablespoons fresh lime juice
1   tablespoon chopped fresh cilantro
Dash of ground red pepper

1. Combine all ingredients in a small bowl. Yield: 4 servings (serving size: 2 tablespoons).

CALORIES 133; FAT 11g (sat 1g, mono 6g, poly 3g); PROTEIN 0.1g; CARB 9g; FIBER 0g; CHOL 5mg; IRON 0mg; SODIUM 100mg; CALC 1mg

Shrimp Scampi

Prep: 3 minutes • Cook: 7 minutes

This intensely flavored, garlic-infused scampi served over angel hair pasta won us over for its flavor and quick prep time. You're in and out of the kitchen superfast.

1½   tablespoons olive oil
1½   tablespoons minced garlic
1½   pounds peeled and deveined jumbo shrimp
¼   cup finely chopped fresh flat-leaf parsley
1½   tablespoons fresh lemon juice
½   teaspoon salt
⅛   teaspoon ground red pepper

1. Heat a large nonstick skillet over medium-low heat. Add oil; swirl to coat. Add garlic, and cook 1 minute. Add shrimp, and cook 5 minutes or until shrimp reach desired degree of doneness, stirring occasionally; remove pan from heat. Stir in parsley and remaining ingredients. Yield: 4 servings (serving size: about 5 shrimp).

CALORIES 233; FAT 8.1g (sat 1.3g, mono 4.1g, poly 1.7g); PROTEIN 34.9g; CARB 3.4g; FIBER 0.2g; CHOL 259mg; IRON 4.4mg; SODIUM 549mg; CALC 100mg

Shrimp with Creamy Orange-Chipotle Sauce

Prep: 3 minutes • Cook: 6 minutes

The half-and-half and grated orange rind create a citrusy cream sauce that tames the spiciness of the chipotle chile.

⅔   cup half-and-half
1   large chipotle chile, canned in adobo sauce
1   teaspoon grated orange rind
Cooking spray
1½   pounds peeled and deveined large shrimp
¾   teaspoon ground cumin
¼   teaspoon salt
2   tablespoons chopped fresh cilantro
Hot cooked linguine (optional)

1. Place first 3 ingredients in a blender; process until smooth.
2. Heat a large nonstick skillet over medium-high heat. Coat pan with cooking spray; add shrimp. Coat shrimp with cooking spray; sprinkle with cumin and salt. Sauté 4 minutes or until shrimp are done, stirring frequently. Transfer shrimp to a serving platter. Reduce heat to medium, add half-and-half mixture to pan, and cook 1 minute, stirring constantly. Pour sauce over shrimp; sprinkle with cilantro. Serve over linguine, if desired. Yield: 4 servings (serving size: ½ cup shrimp and 2 tablespoons sauce).

CALORIES 186; FAT 6g (sat 3.3g, mono 0.3g, poly 0.6g); PROTEIN 28.3g; CARB 2.6g; FIBER 0.5g; CHOL 267mg; IRON 4.3mg; SODIUM 494mg; CALC 97mg

Spicy Green Curry–Cilantro Shrimp

Prep: 2 minutes • Cook: 12 minutes

Serve this fiery, Thai-inspired dish over boil-in-bag jasmine rice and with Honey-Spiced Pineapple.

Cooking spray
1½   pounds peeled and deveined medium shrimp
1   cup light coconut milk
2   tablespoons sugar
2   tablespoons fresh lime juice (about 1 lime)
1   tablespoon green curry paste
1   teaspoon cornstarch
¼   teaspoon salt
⅓   cup chopped fresh cilantro
4 lime wedges

1. Heat a large nonstick skillet over medium-high heat. Coat pan with cooking spray. Add shrimp; cook 3 minutes, stirring occasionally.
2. While shrimp cook, combine coconut milk and next 5 ingredients, stirring with a whisk until smooth. Add to shrimp in pan; bring to a boil. Reduce heat; simmer 5 minutes or until slightly thickened. Sprinkle with cilantro; serve with lime wedges. Yield: 4 servings (serving size: 1 cup).

CALORIES 189; FAT 4g (sat 2.9g, mono 0.3g, poly 0.6g); PROTEIN 27.8g; CARB 10.1g; FIBER 0.1g; CHOL 252mg; IRON 4.3mg; SODIUM 517mg; CALC 53mg

serve with:

Honey-Spiced Pineapple

Prep: 2 minutes • Cook: 6 minutes

1	tablespoon butter
3	cups fresh pineapple chunks
1	tablespoon honey
½	teaspoon curry powder

1. Melt butter in a large nonstick skillet over medium-high heat. Add pineapple, honey, and curry powder; cook 3 minutes or until thoroughly heated, stirring frequently. Yield: 4 servings (serving size: ¾ cup).

CALORIES 120; FAT 3g (sat 1.8g, mono 0.8g, poly 0.2g); PROTEIN 1g; CARB 25.1g; FIBER 2.4g; CHOL 8mg; IRON 0.6mg; SODIUM 22mg; CALC 24mg

Spicy Green Curry–Cilantro Shrimp

Pesto Shrimp Pasta

Prep: 8 minutes • Cook: 15 minutes

This delectable pasta dish features swirls of tender angel hair, plump shrimp, and grape tomatoes tossed with pesto. Garnish with sprigs of basil just before serving for extra color and a burst of freshness.

4	ounces uncooked angel hair pasta
6	cups water
1¼	pounds peeled and deveined large shrimp
¼	cup commercial pesto, divided
1	cup halved grape tomatoes
¼	cup (1 ounce) shaved fresh Parmesan cheese

Basil sprigs (optional)

1. Cook pasta according to package directions, omitting salt and fat; drain.

2. While pasta cooks, bring 6 cups water to a boil in a large saucepan. Add shrimp; cook 2 to 3 minutes or until done. Drain shrimp; toss with 2 tablespoons pesto and tomatoes. Stir in pasta and remaining 2 tablespoons pesto. Top with cheese. Garnish with basil, if desired. Yield: 4 servings (serving size: 1 cup shrimp pasta and 1 tablespoon cheese).

CALORIES 320; FAT 11g (sat 2.7g, mono 6.3g, poly 1.7g); PROTEIN 31.4g; CARB 23.6g; FIBER 1.9g; CHOL 220mg; IRON 4.7mg; SODIUM 505mg; CALC 189mg

ingredient spotlight

Basil is one of the most important culinary herbs. Sweet basil, the most common type, is redolent of licorice and cloves. In the south of France, basil stars in pistou, the Italian cousin of pesto. Used in sauces, sandwiches, soups, and salads, basil is in top form when married with tomatoes.

Pesto Shrimp Pasta

Creamy Garlic Shrimp
and Pasta

Creamy Garlic Shrimp and Pasta

Prep: 2 minutes • Cook: 9 minutes

To save prep time, have your fishmonger peel and devein the shrimp. Or if you'd like to do it yourself, be sure to start with 1¼ pounds of unpeeled shrimp.

3	quarts water
1	(9-ounce) package fresh linguine
1	pound peeled and deveined large shrimp
¼	cup dry white wine
⅓	cup plus 1½ tablespoons (3 ounces) light garlic-and-herbs spreadable cheese
½	cup fat-free milk
3	garlic cloves, pressed
½	teaspoon salt
1½	tablespoons chopped fresh oregano

Oregano sprigs (optional)

1. Bring 3 quarts water to a boil in a large Dutch oven; add pasta and shrimp. Cook 3 to 4 minutes or until pasta is tender and shrimp are done. Drain, and keep warm.
2. While pasta and shrimp cook, combine wine and next 4 ingredients in a large non-stick skillet over medium-high heat. Bring to a boil. Reduce heat; simmer 2 minutes or until slightly thickened, stirring constantly.
3. Add pasta and shrimp to sauce in pan, tossing to coat. Stir in chopped oregano just before serving. Garnish with oregano sprigs, if desired. Yield: 4 servings (serving size: 1¼ cups).

CALORIES 337; FAT 7g (sat 3.3g, mono 0.2g, poly 0.4g); PROTEIN 28.7g; CARB 38.4g; FIBER 1.6g; CHOL 220mg; IRON 4.1mg; SODIUM 571mg; CALC 116mg

Spicy Grilled Shrimp Kebabs with Avocado and Papaya Salad

Prep: 5 minutes • Cook: 4 minutes

We loved the way the spicy kick from the shrimp mellowed with each bite of sweet papaya and cool, creamy avocado—so much, in fact, that we gave this dish our highest rating.

24	jumbo shrimp, peeled and deveined with tails intact (about 1½ pounds)
1	tablespoon olive oil
¼	teaspoon salt
¼	teaspoon crushed red pepper

Cooking spray
Avocado and Papaya Salad
Lime wedges (optional)

1. Preheat grill or grill pan to medium-high heat.
2. Thread 3 shrimp onto each of 8 skewers. Brush with olive oil; sprinkle evenly with salt and red pepper. Place kebabs on grill rack or grill pan coated with cooking spray; grill over medium-high heat 2 minutes on each side or until shrimp are done. Keep warm.
3. Serve kebabs with Avocado and Papaya Salad. Garnish with lime wedges, if desired. Yield: 4 servings (serving size: 2 kebabs and about ⅔ cup salad).

CALORIES 353; FAT 20g (sat 3.3g, mono 12.4g, poly 3.1g); PROTEIN 29.3g; CARB 16.3g; FIBER 5.7g; CHOL 252mg; IRON 5.1mg; SODIUM 592mg; CALC 72mg

Spicy Grilled Shrimp Kebabs with Avocado and Papaya Salad

fix it faster

To cut down on prep time, we recommend using metal skewers. If you prefer to use wooden ones, be sure to soak them in water 30 minutes before grilling.

Avocado and Papaya Salad

Prep: 5 minutes

3	tablespoons fresh lime juice (about 2 limes)
1	tablespoon honey
¼	teaspoon salt
1	cup diced peeled papaya (about 1 medium)
2	avocados, peeled and diced

1. Combine first 3 ingredients in a bowl, stirring well with a whisk. Add papaya and avocado; toss gently to coat. Yield: 2⅔ cups (serving size: about ⅔ cup).

CALORIES 194; FAT 15g (sat 2.5g, mono 9.7g, poly 2g); PROTEIN 2.3g; CARB 16.2g; FIBER 5.7g; CHOL 0mg; IRON 1.2mg; SODIUM 157mg; CALC 21mg

Scallops in Buttery Wine Sauce

Prep: 1 minute • Cook: 7 minutes

Pat the scallops dry with a paper towel to remove any excess moisture before searing. This step ensures a nicely browned exterior.

1½   pounds large sea scallops
1   tablespoon olive oil
½   cup dry white wine
1½   teaspoons chopped fresh tarragon
¼   teaspoon salt
1   tablespoon butter
Freshly ground black pepper (optional)

1. Pat scallops dry with paper towels. Heat a large nonstick skillet over medium-high heat. Add oil; swirl to coat. Add scallops. Cook 3 minutes on each side or until done. Transfer scallops to a serving platter; keep warm.
2. Add white wine, tarragon, and salt to pan, scraping pan to loosen browned bits. Boil 1 minute. Remove from heat; add butter, stirring until butter melts. Pour sauce over scallops. Sprinkle with pepper, if desired; serve immediately. Yield: 4 servings (serving size: about 3 scallops and about 1 tablespoon sauce).

CALORIES 225; FAT 8g (sat 2.4g, mono 3.3g, poly 1.1g); PROTEIN 28.6g; CARB 4.7g; FIBER 0g; CHOL 64mg; IRON 0.6mg; SODIUM 441mg; CALC 45mg

Scallops in Buttery Wine Sauce

serve with:
Asparagus with Feta and Oregano

Prep: 2 minutes • Cook: 4 minutes

1   cup water
1   pound asparagus spears, trimmed
1   teaspoon extra-virgin olive oil
1½   teaspoons chopped fresh oregano
¼   teaspoon salt
3   tablespoons crumbled feta cheese

1. Bring 1 cup water to a boil in a large nonstick skillet; add asparagus. Cover, reduce heat, and simmer 4 to 5 minutes or until asparagus is crisp-tender. Drain well; place on a serving platter. Drizzle oil over asparagus. Sprinkle with oregano and salt; toss well. Sprinkle with cheese. Yield: 4 servings (serving size: ¼ of asparagus spears).

CALORIES 40; FAT 2g (sat 0.7g, mono 0.8g, poly 0.2g); PROTEIN 2.7g; CARB 3.1g; FIBER 1.6g; CHOL 2mg; IRON 1.5mg; SODIUM 222mg; CALC 35mg

Crispy Curry Scallops

Prep: 5 minutes • Cook: 5 minutes

Panko—or Japanese breadcrumbs—is swoon material! It gives these succulent scallops a light, crispy crust and a delightful crunch. Look for panko on the baking aisle along with other varieties of breadcrumbs or on the ethnic foods aisle of your supermarket.

1½	pounds large sea scallops (about 12)
½	cup panko (Japanese breadcrumbs)
2	teaspoons lower-sodium soy sauce
1	teaspoon curry powder
2	teaspoons canola oil

Lime wedges

1. Pat scallops dry with paper towels. Place panko in a shallow dish.
2. Toss scallops with soy sauce in a medium bowl; sprinkle evenly with curry powder. Dredge in panko.
3. Heat a large nonstick skillet over medium-high heat. Add oil; swirl to coat. Add scallops to pan; cook 2 to 3 minutes on each side or until browned. Serve with lime wedges. Yield: 4 servings (serving size: about 3 scallops).

CALORIES 207; FAT 3.9g (sat 0.3g, mono 1.6g, poly 1.1g); PROTEIN 29.4g; CARB 11.1g; FIBER 1.3g; CHOL 56mg; IRON 0.6mg; SODIUM 388mg; CALC 43mg

serve with:

Chile-Ginger Sugar Snaps

Prep: 2 minutes • Cook: 4 minutes

3	tablespoons water
½	teaspoon grated peeled fresh ginger
½	teaspoon sambal oelek (ground fresh chile paste)
⅛	teaspoon salt

Cooking spray
1	(8-ounce) package fresh sugar snap peas

1. Combine 3 tablespoons water and next 3 ingredients in a small bowl; stir with a whisk.
2. Heat a large nonstick skillet over medium-high heat. Coat pan with cooking spray. Add sugar snap peas, and sauté 1 minute. Add water mixture to pan, tossing to coat peas. Cook 2 minutes or until sugar snap peas are crisp-tender. Yield: 4 servings (serving size: ½ cup).

CALORIES 31; FAT 0.2g (sat 0g, mono 0.2g, poly 0g); PROTEIN 1.4g; CARB 6.5g; FIBER 1.4g; CHOL 0mg; IRON 0.5mg; SODIUM 87mg; CALC 29mg

Green Curry Scallops with Shiitakes

Prep: 2 minutes • Cook: 11 minutes

1½	pounds sea scallops (about 16 scallops)
¼	teaspoon salt
¼	teaspoon freshly ground black pepper

Olive oil–flavored cooking spray

1	pound shiitake mushrooms, stems removed
1	cup light coconut milk
2	tablespoons green curry paste
2	cups cooked basmati rice (optional)
2	tablespoons chopped fresh basil (optional)

1. Rinse scallops. Drain well, and pat dry with paper towels. Sprinkle scallops with salt and pepper. Heat a large nonstick skillet over medium-high heat. Coat pan with cooking spray. Add scallops to pan; cook 3 minutes on each side or until done. Remove scallops from pan; keep warm.
2. Recoat pan with cooking spray; add mushrooms to pan. Sauté 3 minutes or until tender. Add coconut milk and curry paste. Bring to a simmer, stirring often. Pour sauce over scallops. Serve over basmati rice, and sprinkle with basil, if desired. Yield: 4 servings (serving size: about 4 scallops and about ⅔ cup sauce).

CALORIES 253; FAT 4.8g (sat 3.2g, mono 0.8g, poly 0.7g); PROTEIN 31.1g; CARB 23.6g; FIBER 2.4g; CHOL 56mg; IRON 1.3mg; SODIUM 574mg; CALC 45mg

serve with:
Mango Lassi

Prep: 4 minutes

2	cups vanilla fat-free yogurt
½	cup fat-free milk
1/16	teaspoon salt
2	peeled ripe mangoes, sliced

1. Place all ingredients in a blender; process until smooth. Cover and refrigerate until ready to serve. Yield: 6 servings (serving size: ¾ cup).

CALORIES 140; FAT 0.3g (sat 0.1g, mono 0.1g, poly 0.1g); PROTEIN 5.2g; CARB 29.8g; FIBER 1.6g; CHOL 2mg; IRON 0.1mg; SODIUM 97mg; CALC 180mg

ingredient spotlight

Green curry paste is typically made with fresh ingredients and all things Asian such as lemongrass, galangal (a cousin of ginger), garlic, onions, green or red chiles, and cilantro. The paste also comes in red and yellow, depending on the ingredients used. The heat index for green curry paste can soar!

Sesame-Crusted Scallops with Teriyaki Glaze

Prep: 3 minutes • Cook: 14 minutes

To get the desirable finish on scallops, be sure to pat them dry with a paper towel before cooking. Any moisture on scallops, and they'll steam instead of sear. Try them with the easy two-ingredient sauce. Use it as a dipping sauce for spring rolls or lettuce wraps, or in other Asian-inspired dishes.

1½ pounds large sea scallops (about 12)
¼ teaspoon salt
¼ teaspoon freshly ground black pepper
3½ tablespoons sesame seeds
1 tablespoon olive oil, divided
5 tablespoons salt-free spicy teriyaki marinade
1½ tablespoons mirin (sweet rice wine)
1½ tablespoons water
Sliced green onions (optional)

1. Pat scallops dry with paper towels. Sprinkle scallops with salt and pepper; dredge in sesame seeds.
2. Heat a large nonstick skillet over medium-high heat. Add 1½ teaspoons oil; swirl to coat. Add half of scallops; cook 3 minutes on each side. Remove scallops from pan; keep warm. Repeat procedure with remaining oil and scallops.
3. Combine teriyaki marinade, mirin, and 1½ tablespoons water, stirring with a whisk. Add to pan; cook 1 minute. Spoon sauce over scallops. Garnish with onions, if desired. Yield: 4 servings (serving size: about 3 scallops and 2 tablespoons sauce).

CALORIES 269; FAT 9.2g (sat 1.4g, mono 4.6g, poly 3g); PROTEIN 30g; CARB 12.7g; FIBER 1g; CHOL 56mg; IRON 1.7mg; SODIUM 420mg; CALC 119mg

serve with:

Green Onion Soba Noodles

Prep: 3 minutes • Cook: 7 minutes

3 ounces uncooked soba noodles
1 teaspoon dark sesame oil
½ cup sliced green onions
2 garlic cloves, minced
1 tablespoon lower-sodium soy sauce

1. Prepare noodles according to package directions, omitting salt and fat. Drain.
2. While noodles cook, heat a nonstick skillet over medium-high heat. Add oil; swirl to coat. Add onions; sauté 2 minutes. Add garlic; cook 30 seconds. Add drained noodles and soy sauce to pan; toss well. Yield: 4 servings (serving size: ½ cup).

CALORIES 96; FAT 1.5g (sat 0.2g, mono 0.6g, poly 0.6g); PROTEIN 2.6g; CARB 17.1g; FIBER 1g; CHOL 0mg; IRON 0.6mg; SODIUM 273mg; CALC 14mg

Sesame-Crusted Scallops with Teriyaki Glaze

Scallops with Lemon-Basil Sauce

Prep: 3 minutes • Cook: 12 minutes

Look for dry-packed sea scallops at your local seafood market. They haven't been soaked in a liquid solution, which increases their weight and sodium content.

1	large lemon
1½	pounds large sea scallops
¼	teaspoon salt, divided
¼	teaspoon freshly ground black pepper, divided
1	tablespoon butter, divided
¾	cup dry white wine
1	tablespoon water
½	teaspoon cornstarch
1	tablespoon finely chopped fresh basil

1. Finely grate lemon rind, reserving ¼ teaspoon. Squeeze lemon, reserving 2 tablespoons juice. Pat scallops dry with paper towels.
2. Sprinkle scallops with ⅛ teaspoon each salt and pepper. Melt 2 teaspoons butter in a large nonstick skillet over medium heat. Add scallops; cook 3 to 4 minutes on each side or until done. Remove scallops from pan; keep warm.
3. Add wine and reserved lemon juice to pan, and bring to a boil. Reduce heat, and simmer 2 minutes, stirring to loosen browned bits from bottom of pan. Combine water and cornstarch; add to pan. Cook, stirring constantly, 2 minutes or until sauce begins to thicken. Add reserved lemon rind, remaining 1 teaspoon butter, remaining ⅛ teaspoon each salt and pepper, and basil. Remove from heat. Serve over scallops. Yield: 4 servings (serving size: 5 ounces scallops and about 1 tablespoon sauce).

CALORIES 185; FAT 4.1g (sat 1.9g; mono 1; poly 0.9g); PROTEIN 28.9g; CARB 7g; FIBER 0.7g; CHOL 64mg; IRON 0.8mg; SODIUM 447mg; CALC 51mg

Scallops with Lemon-Basil Sauce

serve with:
Buttery Angel Hair Pasta with Parmesan Cheese

Prep: 3 minutes • Cook: 5 minutes

4	ounces uncooked angel hair pasta
¼	cup grated fresh Parmesan cheese
1	tablespoon butter

1. Cook pasta according to package directions, omitting salt and fat. Drain. Combine cooked pasta, cheese, and butter; toss well. Yield: 4 servings (serving size: about ½ cup).

CALORIES 161; FAT 5.5g (sat 3g; mono 0.8g; poly 0.2g); PROTEIN 6.6g; CARB 21.8g; FIBER 0.5g; CHOL 13mg; IRON 1mg; SODIUM 145mg; CALC 101m

Seared Scallops with Warm Fruit Salsa

Prep: 2 minutes • Cook: 8 minutes

A hot skillet is key to a deep golden sear on the scallops. Prepare the Warm Fruit Salsa in the same skillet as the scallops for an easy one-pan cleanup. Jasmine rice rounds out the meal.

1¼   pounds large sea scallops (about 12)
Cooking spray
¼   teaspoon freshly ground black pepper
⅛   teaspoon salt
Warm Fruit Salsa
4   teaspoons sliced green onions

1. Pat scallops dry with paper towels. Heat a large nonstick skillet over medium-high heat. Coat pan with cooking spray. Sprinkle scallops evenly with pepper and salt. Add scallops to pan; cook 3 minutes on each side or until done. Remove scallops from pan; keep warm.
2. Prepare Warm Fruit Salsa.
3. Discard any accumulated juices from scallops; top evenly with Warm Fruit Salsa and onions. Serve immediately. Yield: 4 servings (serving size: about 3 scallops and about ⅔ cup salsa).

CALORIES 202; FAT 4g (sat 0.5g, mono 1.7g, poly 0.8g); PROTEIN 24.9g; CARB 17.7g; FIBER 2.2g; CHOL 47mg; IRON 1mg; SODIUM 394mg; CALC 52mg

Warm Fruit Salsa

Prep: 8 minutes • Cook: 4 minutes

2   teaspoons olive oil
1   garlic clove, minced
2   cups diced pineapple
1¼   cups chopped red bell pepper
¼   cup green tea with mango (such as Snapple)
2   teaspoons low-sodium soy sauce
1   tablespoon chopped fresh mint

1. Heat a large nonstick skillet over medium-high heat. Add oil; swirl to coat. Add garlic; sauté 1 minute. Stir in pineapple and next 3 ingredients, scraping pan to loosen browned bits; cook 3 minutes. Stir in mint. Yield: 2¾ cups (serving size: about ⅔ cup).

CALORIES 77; FAT 3g (sat 0.4g, mono 1.7g, poly 0.4g); PROTEIN 1.1g; CARB 14.3g; FIBER 2.2g; CHOL 0mg; IRON 1mg; SODIUM 166mg; CALC 18mg

Seared Scallops with Warm Fruit Salsa

Fresh Garlic Linguine
with Clams

Fresh Garlic Linguine with Clams

Prep: 3 minutes • Cook: 8 minutes

Pay close attention to the clams when scrubbing them. If some are opened slightly, give them a gentle tap. If they close, they're fine; if they don't, discard them. If any clams remain closed after they have cooked, discard them as well.

1	(9-ounce) package refrigerated linguine or angel hair pasta
2	teaspoons olive oil
4	garlic cloves, minced
½	cup chopped bottled roasted red bell pepper
24	littleneck clams, scrubbed
¼	cup dry white wine
⅓	cup finely chopped fresh parsley, divided
¾	cup (3 ounces) grated Asiago cheese, divided

1. Cook pasta according to package directions, omitting salt and fat. Drain, reserving ¼ cup pasta water.
2. While pasta cooks, heat a large nonstick skillet over medium-high heat. Add oil; swirl to coat. Add garlic and bell peppers. Cook 1 minute, stirring constantly. Add clams and wine. Cover and cook 3 to 4 minutes or until shells open. Discard any unopened shells.
3. Add pasta and half of parsley to clams in pan, tossing well to blend. Add reserved ¼ cup pasta water and half of cheese, tossing well to blend. Sprinkle remaining parsley and cheese evenly over each serving. Yield: 4 servings (serving size: about 6 clams and 1 cup pasta).

CALORIES 339; FAT 11g (sat 4.9g, mono 3.3g, poly 0.7g); PROTEIN 20.8g; CARB 38.1g; FIBER 1.7g; CHOL 75mg; IRON 9.3mg; SODIUM 155mg; CALC 258mg

poultry

Moroccan Chicken Kebabs,
page 352

Orecchiette with Chicken, Bacon, and Tomato Ragù

Prep: 2 minutes • Cook: 12 minutes

1½ cups (5 ounces) uncooked orecchiette ("little ears" pasta)
2   center-cut bacon slices
1   cup refrigerated prechopped onion
1   (28-ounce) can no-salt-added whole tomatoes in puree
2   cups shredded cooked chicken
¼   cup basil leaves
½   teaspoon salt
¼   teaspoon freshly ground black pepper
¼   cup (1 ounce) shaved fresh Pecorino-Romano cheese

1. Cook pasta according to package directions, omitting salt and fat; drain.
2. While pasta cooks, cook bacon in a large nonstick skillet over medium heat 5 minutes or until crisp. Remove bacon from pan; crumble. Add onion to drippings in pan; sauté over medium-high heat 3 minutes or until tender.
3. Snip tomatoes in can with kitchen shears until chopped. Add tomatoes to onion. Cook 2 minutes or until sauce thickens, stirring occasionally. Stir in bacon, chicken, and next 3 ingredients. Cook 2 minutes or until thoroughly heated. Stir in pasta. Divide mixture evenly among 4 shallow bowls. Top evenly with cheese. Yield: 4 servings (serving size: 1½ cups pasta mixture and 1 tablespoon cheese).

CALORIES 336; FAT 5.4g (sat 2g, mono 2g, poly 1.3g); PROTEIN 30.2g; CARB 40.9g; FIBER 5.3g; CHOL 67mg; IRON 3.8mg; SODIUM 510mg; CALC 151mg

serve with:
Broccolini with Spicy Walnut "Butter"

Prep: 1 minute • Cook: 11 minutes

2   bunches Broccolini, trimmed (12 ounces)
2   tablespoons yogurt-based spread
2   tablespoons chopped walnuts, toasted
1   teaspoon grated lemon rind
¼   teaspoon crushed red pepper
Cooking spray

1. Pour water into a large nonstick skillet to a depth of 1 inch. Bring to a boil. Add Broccolini; cover and cook 4 minutes or until almost tender, turning after 2 minutes. Drain.
2. While Broccolini cooks, combine yogurt-based spread and next 3 ingredients in a small bowl.
3. Wipe pan dry, and return to medium-high heat; coat pan with cooking spray. Add Broccolini and "butter" to pan. Cook 2 minutes or until Broccolini is crisp-tender. Yield: 4 servings (serving size: ¼ of Broccolini).

CALORIES 82; FAT 4.9g (sat 0.7g, mono 1g, poly 3.2g); PROTEIN 3.6g; CARB 6.6g; FIBER 1.3g; CHOL 0mg; IRON 0.8mg; SODIUM 70mg; CALC 64mg

Barbecue-Stuffed Potatoes

Barbecue-Stuffed Potatoes

Prep: 5 minutes • Cook: 12 minutes

4   (6-ounce) baking potatoes
½   cup reduced-fat sour cream
2   green onions, finely chopped and divided
1⅓   cups shredded barbecue chicken
½   cup (2 ounces) reduced-fat shredded extra-sharp cheddar cheese

1. Pierce potatoes with a fork; arrange in a circle on paper towels in microwave oven. Microwave at HIGH 10 minutes or until done, rearranging potatoes after 5 minutes.
2. While potatoes cook, combine sour cream and 2 tablespoons onions; set aside.
3. Place chicken in a microwave-safe bowl; cover with plastic wrap (do not allow plastic wrap to touch food). Remove potatoes from microwave; place chicken in microwave. Microwave at HIGH 2 minutes or until thoroughly heated.
4. Slice potatoes lengthwise, cutting to, but not through, other side; fluff with fork. Top each potato evenly with chicken, sour cream mixture, cheese, and remaining onions. Yield: 4 servings (serving size: 1 potato, about ⅓ cup chicken, about 2 tablespoons sour cream mixture, and 2 tablespoons cheese).

CALORIES 367; FAT 9g (sat 5.3g, mono 2.4g, poly 1.2g); PROTEIN 16.5g; CARB 57.6g; FIBER 4.2g; CHOL 43mg; IRON 3.2mg; SODIUM 619mg; CALC 117mg

Shredded Chicken Tacos

Prep: 17 minutes • Cook: 18 minutes

Charring the corn brings out its natural sweetness.

2   ears shucked corn
1   (12-ounce) package baby heirloom tomatoes
½   teaspoon freshly ground black pepper
¼   teaspoon salt
8   (6-inch) corn tortillas
2   cups shredded skinless, boneless rotisserie chicken breast
1   peeled avocado, cut into 16 slices
8   lime wedges (optional)

1. Preheat broiler.
2. Place corn on a jelly-roll pan; broil 18 minutes or until charred on all sides, rotating every 6 minutes. Cut kernels from corn; place kernels in a medium bowl. Cut tomatoes into quarters. Add tomatoes to corn, and sprinkle corn mixture with black pepper and salt.
3. Heat tortillas according to package directions. Divide chicken evenly among tortillas; top each taco with ¼ cup corn mixture and 2 avocado slices. Serve with lime wedges, if desired. Yield: 4 servings (serving size: 2 tacos).

CALORIES 420; FAT 13.5g (sat 2.3g, mono 7.1g, poly 2.4g); PROTEIN 39.2g; CARB 40.6g; FIBER 8.4g; CHOL 101mg; IRON 2mg; SODIUM 554mg; CALC 123mg

Roasted Chicken and White
Beans with Greek Dressing

Roasted Chicken and White Beans with Greek Dressing

Prep: 8 minutes

For variation and added crunch, toast the pita wedges while you're preparing the chicken and bean mixture. For crispy wedges, split the pita rounds in half, coat the cut sides with butter-flavored cooking spray, and stack the split rounds. Cut the rounds into wedges, and place the wedges on a large baking sheet. Bake the pita wedges at 350° for 10 minutes or until golden and crisp.

2½   cups shredded skinless, boneless rotisserie
      chicken
1   (15.5-ounce) can cannellini beans, rinsed
      and drained
1   cup chopped red onion
Greek Dressing
2   (7-inch) whole-wheat pitas, each cut into
      8 wedges

1. Combine first 3 ingredients in a large bowl. Drizzle Greek Dressing over chicken mixture, and toss well. Serve with pita wedges. Yield: 4 servings (serving size: 1¼ cups chicken mixture and 4 pita wedges).

CALORIES 400; FAT 14g (sat 5g, mono 5.9g, poly 2.5g); PROTEIN 36.3g; CARB 31.5g; FIBER 5.6g; CHOL 93mg; IRON 3.1mg; SODIUM 550mg; CALC 159mg

Greek Dressing

Prep: 3 minutes

1½   tablespoons red wine vinegar
1½   tablespoons olive oil
½   teaspoon dry mustard
2   tablespoons minced fresh rosemary
¾   cup (3 ounces) crumbled feta cheese
½   teaspoon freshly ground black pepper
2   garlic cloves, minced

1. Combine all ingredients in a small bowl. Yield: 4 servings (serving size: 2 tablespoons).

CALORIES 108; FAT 9.8g (sat 3.9g, mono 4.7g, poly 0.7g); PROTEIN 3.3g; CARB 1.8g; FIBER 0.3g; CHOL 19mg; IRON 0.3mg; SODIUM 238mg; CALC 113mg

Thai Green Curry Chicken

Prep: 5 minutes • Cook: 10 minutes

Thanks to a deli rotisserie chicken, this dish lets you enjoy Thai cuisine with minimal effort. We packed this classic curry dish with colorful peppers and used light coconut milk to cut some of the fat. Serve it over fragrant jasmine rice to soak up the sauce.

Cooking spray
1   medium onion, halved and vertically sliced
1   small zucchini, halved lengthwise and sliced
1   small red bell pepper, cut into thin strips
2   teaspoons green curry paste
2   cups thinly sliced roasted chicken breast
1   cup fat-free, lower-sodium chicken broth
⅔   cup light coconut milk
3   tablespoons cilantro leaves
Lime wedges (optional)
Cilantro sprigs (optional)

1. Heat a large nonstick skillet over medium-high heat. Coat pan with cooking spray. Add onion, and sauté 5 minutes. Add zucchini and bell pepper, and sauté 3 minutes; stir in curry paste. Add chicken, broth, and coconut milk to pan; bring to a boil. Reduce heat, and simmer 3 minutes. Spoon evenly into 4 bowls; sprinkle evenly with cilantro. Serve with lime wedges, and garnish with cilantro sprigs, if desired. Yield: 4 servings (serving size: 1 cup chicken mixture).

CALORIES 159; FAT 4.7g (sat 2.6g; mono 0.9g; poly 0.6g); PROTEIN 23.9g; CARB 4.9g; FIBER 0.8g; CHOL 63mg; IRON 1.1mg; SODIUM 224mg; CALC 22mg

serve with:
Cucumber, Pineapple, and Mint Salad

Prep: 5 minutes

1   medium cucumber, coarsely chopped
1   cup coarsely chopped pineapple
2   green onions, thinly sliced
3   tablespoons chopped fresh mint
1   tablespoon seasoned rice vinegar
1   tablespoon fish sauce

1. Combine all ingredients in a medium bowl; toss well. Chill until ready to serve. Yield: 4 servings (serving size: ¾ cup).

CALORIES 37; FAT 0.1g (sat 0g; mono 0g; poly 0g); PROTEIN 1.4g; CARB 8.5g; FIBER 1.1g; CHOL 0mg; IRON 0.6mg; SODIUM 424mg; CALC 30mg

Thai Green Curry Chicken

Moroccan Chicken Kebabs

Prep: 5 minutes • Cook: 10 minutes

Moroccan cooking often combines meat with dried fruits and spices.

½	cup apricot preserves
1	teaspoon ground cumin
1	teaspoon ground cinnamon
½	teaspoon ground coriander
½	teaspoon salt
4	(6-ounce) skinless, boneless chicken breast halves, cut into 1½-inch pieces
4	metal skewers

Cooking spray

1. Preheat grill to medium-high heat.
2. Combine first 5 ingredients in a large bowl. Place chicken pieces in bowl, turning to coat. Thread chicken onto skewers.
3. Coat chicken with cooking spray; place on grill rack coated with cooking spray. Grill 5 minutes on each side or until done. Yield: 4 servings (serving size: 1 kebab).

CALORIES 283; FAT 4.2g (sat 1.3g, mono 1.6g, poly 1.1g); PROTEIN 34.7g; CARB 26.4g; FIBER 0.6g; CHOL 94mg; IRON 1.7mg; SODIUM 390mg; CALC 36mg

serve with:

Whole-Wheat Couscous with Ginger and Currants

Prep: 6 minutes • Cook: 4 minutes
Other: 5 minutes

¾	cup water
1	tablespoon extra-virgin olive oil
¼	teaspoon salt
⅔	cup uncooked whole-wheat couscous
½	cup currants
2	teaspoons grated peeled fresh ginger
1	tablespoon chopped fresh mint

1. Bring first 3 ingredients to a boil in a medium saucepan. Stir in couscous, currants, and ginger. Remove from heat; cover and let stand 5 minutes. Add mint, and fluff with a fork. Yield: 4 servings (serving size: about ½ cup).

CALORIES 151; FAT 3.8g (sat 0.5g, mono 2.6g, poly 0.7g); PROTEIN 3.2g; CARB 28.7g; FIBER 3.4g; CHOL 0mg; IRON 1.2mg; SODIUM 146mg; CALC 28mg

quick flip

Swap the exotic locale of Morocco for the flavor of the Mediterranean. Substitute mango chutney for the apricot preserves and 1 tablespoon of an all-in-one Mediterranean-spiced sea salt for the cumin, cinnamon, coriander, and salt.

Stir-Fried Lemon Chicken

Prep: 2 minutes • Cook: 10 minutes

This fresh and simple chicken stir-fry is best served right from the skillet. Make sure all the ingredients are prepped ahead and ready to go. Stir-frying is a brisk cooking method. It's easy eating and even easier cleanup.

1	pound skinless, boneless chicken breast, cut into bite-sized pieces
½	teaspoon freshly ground black pepper
¼	teaspoon salt
Cooking spray	
4	garlic cloves, minced
¾	cup matchstick-cut carrots
2	tablespoons water
1	(8.8-ounce) package microwavable precooked jasmine rice
1	tablespoon grated lemon rind

1. Sprinkle chicken with pepper and salt. Heat a large nonstick skillet over medium-high heat. Coat pan with cooking spray. Add chicken; stir-fry 5 minutes or until done. Add garlic; stir-fry 1 minute. Transfer chicken to a serving plate; cover and keep warm.
2. Recoat pan with cooking spray. Add carrots to pan; stir-fry 2 minutes or just until tender, adding 2 tablespoons water to prevent sticking. Add rice and lemon rind; stir-fry 1 minute. Add chicken; stir-fry 1 minute. Serve immediately. Yield: 4 servings (serving size: about ¾ cup).

CALORIES 263; FAT 4g (sat 0.9g, mono 1.8g, poly 1.3g); PROTEIN 25.9g; CARB 29.6g; FIBER 1.1g; CHOL 63mg; IRON 1.8mg; SODIUM 206mg; CALC 35mg

Stir-Fried Lemon Chicken

serve with:
Sugared Asparagus

Prep: 1 minute • Cook: 3 minutes

1	pound asparagus spears, trimmed
Cooking spray	
1	tablespoon sugar
¼	teaspoon freshly ground black pepper

1. Preheat grill to medium-high heat.
2. Place asparagus on a jelly-roll pan. Coat asparagus with cooking spray; sprinkle with sugar and pepper. Toss gently to coat.
3. Place asparagus on grill rack coated with cooking spray. Grill 3 minutes or until crisp-tender, turning occasionally. Yield: 4 servings (serving size: ¼ of asparagus).

CALORIES 41; FAT 0.1g (sat 0g, mono 0g, poly 0.1g); PROTEIN 2.5g; CARB 7.6g; FIBER 2.4g; CHOL 0mg; IRON 2.4mg; SODIUM 2mg; CALC 28mg

Rotini with Chicken, Asparagus, and Tomatoes

Prep: 7 minutes • Cook: 8 minutes

Reminiscent of pasta salad, this recipe calls for mixing rotini with tender, garden-fresh vegetables and a basil-flecked balsamic vinaigrette. This dish is delicious served warm or chilled, which makes it a great lunch-box option. Serve with a side of fresh bread from the bakery.

8   ounces uncooked rotini (corkscrew pasta)
Cooking spray
1   pound skinless, boneless chicken breast, cut into ¼-inch strips
½   teaspoon kosher salt
½   teaspoon freshly ground black pepper
1   cup (1-inch) slices asparagus
2   cups cherry tomatoes, halved
2   garlic cloves, minced
2   tablespoons chopped fresh basil
2   tablespoons balsamic vinegar
1   tablespoon extra-virgin olive oil
¼   cup (1 ounce) crumbled goat cheese

1. Cook pasta according to package directions, omitting salt and fat.
2. While pasta cooks, heat a large nonstick skillet over medium-high heat; coat with cooking spray. Sprinkle chicken with salt and pepper. Add chicken and asparagus to pan; sauté 5 minutes. Add tomatoes and garlic to pan; sauté 1 minute. Remove from heat. Stir pasta, basil, vinegar, and oil into chicken mixture in pan. Top with cheese. Yield: 4 servings (serving size: 2 cups).

CALORIES 419; FAT 9.5g (sat 3.2g, mono 4.1g, poly 1.6g); PROTEIN 33.9g; CARB 48.5g; FIBER 3.4g; CHOL 70mg; IRON 3.2mg; SODIUM 324mg; CALC 105mg

serve with:
Spinach Salad with Balsamic Vinaigrette

Prep: 3 minutes

2   tablespoons minced shallots
1   tablespoon olive oil
1   tablespoon balsamic vinegar
⅛   teaspoon salt
Dash of freshly ground black pepper
6   cups bagged baby spinach leaves

1. Combine first 5 ingredients in a large bowl, stirring with a whisk. Add spinach; toss well. Yield: 4 servings (serving size: about 1½ cups).

CALORIES 52; FAT 3.5g (sat 0.5g, mono 2.5g, poly 0.5g); PROTEIN 1g; CARB 5.4g; FIBER 1.8g; CHOL 0mg; IRON 1.3mg; SODIUM 132mg; CALC 29mg

Rotini with Chicken, Asparagus, and Tomatoes

Chicken and Olives

Prep: 1 minute • Cook: 11 minutes

Moroccan dishes often combine sweet and savory. Enjoy savory, paprika-spiced chicken with squash that has a sweet and spicy twist from orange, ginger, and cumin.

4	(4-ounce) chicken cutlets
½	teaspoon paprika
¼	teaspoon salt

Cooking spray

1¾	cups thin vertical onion slices
½	cup mixed pitted olives, halved
½	cup dry white wine

1. Sprinkle chicken evenly with paprika and salt. Heat a large skillet over medium-high heat. Coat pan with cooking spray. Add chicken to pan. Cook 2 minutes on each side or until done. Transfer chicken to a serving dish, and keep warm.
2. Coat pan with cooking spray; add onion slices. Sauté 4 minutes or until tender. Return chicken to pan; add olives and white wine. Cook 3 minutes or until liquid is reduced by half. Serve warm. Yield: 4 servings (serving size: 1 chicken cutlet and ½ cup onion mixture).

CALORIES 187; FAT 5g (sat 0.7g, mono 0.9g, poly 0.5g); PROTEIN 24.7g; CARB 6.2g; FIBER 0.9g; CHOL 72.6mg; IRON 0.6mg; SODIUM 415mg; CALC 19mg

serve with:
Moroccan Squash

Prep: 1 minute • Cook: 4 minutes

1	(12-ounce) package refrigerated steam-in-bag cubed butternut squash
2	tablespoons orange marmalade
1	teaspoon grated peeled fresh ginger
¼	teaspoon ground cumin
1	tablespoon chopped fresh cilantro

1. Microwave squash according to package directions. Place squash in a bowl. Add marmalade, ginger, and cumin; toss gently. Sprinkle with cilantro. Serve immediately. Yield: 4 servings (serving size: about ½ cup).

CALORIES 55; FAT 0.1g (sat 0g, mono 0g, poly 0g); PROTEIN 0.7g; CARB 14.4g; FIBER 2.4g; CHOL 0mg; IRON 0.5mg; SODIUM 9mg; CALC 35mg

Chicken and Olives

Grilled Rosemary Chicken with Chunky Tomato-Avocado Salsa

Prep: 3 minutes • Cook: 6 minutes
Other: 30 minutes

Assertive feta cheese pairs well with acidic tomatoes and rich avocados in this 5-minute salsa. Make this salsa right before serving, and avoid refrigerating it—the texture of the tomato will soften. Serve this dish with a side of grilled vegetables.

2   tablespoons olive oil
2   tablespoons red wine vinegar
1   tablespoon chopped fresh rosemary
1   tablespoon minced garlic
4   (4-ounce) chicken cutlets
¼   teaspoon salt
¼   teaspoon freshly ground black pepper
Cooking spray
Chunky Tomato-Avocado Salsa

1. Combine first 4 ingredients in a large heavy-duty zip-top plastic bag. Place chicken between 2 sheets of plastic wrap; pound to ¼-inch thickness using a meat mallet or small heavy skillet. Sprinkle chicken with salt and pepper, and add to bag; seal. Marinate in refrigerator 30 minutes.
2. Preheat grill to medium-high heat.
3. Remove chicken from marinade, discarding marinade. Place chicken on grill rack coated with cooking spray. Grill 3 minutes on each side or until done. Serve with Chunky Tomato-Avocado Salsa. Yield: 4 servings (serving size: 1 chicken cutlet and ¾ cup salsa).

CALORIES 393; FAT 21.8g (sat 4.5g, mono 12.3g, poly 3.9g); PROTEIN 39.4g; CARB 7.3g; FIBER 3.1g; CHOL 101mg; IRON 1.7mg; SODIUM 430mg; CALC 84mg

Chunky Tomato-Avocado Salsa

Prep: 5 minutes

1   tablespoon chopped fresh oregano
1   tablespoon extra-virgin olive oil
2   tablespoons red wine vinegar
1   garlic clove, minced
2   cups grape tomatoes, halved
½   cup (2 ounces) crumbled reduced-fat feta cheese with basil and sun-dried tomatoes
1   ripe peeled avocado, chopped

1. Combine first 4 ingredients in a large bowl, stirring with a whisk. Add tomato halves, cheese, and avocado; toss gently. Yield: 4 servings (serving size: ¾ cup).

CALORIES 132; FAT 10.6g (sat 2.4g, mono 5.9g, poly 1.9g); PROTEIN 4.2g; CARB 6.3g; FIBER 3g; CHOL 4mg; IRON 0.4mg; SODIUM 199mg; CALC 64mg

quick flip

Leave the Mediterranean for Mexico by swapping the rosemary and oregano for cilantro and the red wine vinegar and feta for lime juice and queso.

Schnitzel Chicken

Prep: 5 minutes • Cook: 12 minutes

1.1	ounces all-purpose flour (about ¼ cup)
1	large egg, beaten
1	cup whole-wheat panko (Japanese breadcrumbs)
4	(¼-inch-thick) chicken breast cutlets
⅜	teaspoon salt
¼	teaspoon freshly ground black pepper
2	teaspoons olive oil, divided

Cooking spray

4	lemon wedges

1. Place flour, egg, and panko each in a shallow dish. Sprinkle chicken cutlets evenly with salt and pepper. Dredge each chicken cutlet in flour. Dip in egg; dredge in panko.

2. Heat a large nonstick skillet over medium-high heat. Add 1 teaspoon oil; swirl to coat. Add half of chicken to pan. Cook 3 minutes or until golden; coat chicken with cooking spray. Turn chicken over. Cook an additional 3 minutes or until chicken is done. Transfer to a plate; cover and keep warm. Repeat procedure with remaining 1 teaspoon oil, chicken, and cooking spray. Serve with lemon wedges. Yield: 4 servings (serving size: 1 chicken cutlet and 1 lemon wedge).

CALORIES 268; FAT 7g (sat 1.4g, mono 3.1g, poly 1.2g); PROTEIN 29.5g; CARB 20.8g; FIBER 2.4g; CHOL 119mg; IRON 1.8mg; SODIUM 394mg; CALC 16mg

serve with:
Pan-Fried Slaw

Prep: 1 minute • Cook: 5 minutes

Cooking spray

2	(10-ounce) packages angel hair slaw
⅓	cup rice vinegar
½	teaspoon caraway seeds
¼	teaspoon freshly ground black pepper
⅛	teaspoon salt

1. Heat a large nonstick skillet over medium-high heat. Coat pan with cooking spray. Add slaw. Coat slaw with cooking spray. Sauté 3 minutes or until wilted and beginning to brown. Add vinegar and remaining ingredients; sauté 1 minute. Yield: 4 servings (about 1 cup).

CALORIES 37; FAT 0.2g (sat 0.1g, mono 0g, poly 0g); PROTEIN 1.9g; CARB 8.4g; FIBER 3.7g; CHOL 0mg; IRON 0.7mg; SODIUM 100mg; CALC 59mg

Schnitzel Chicken

Grilled Sun-Dried Tomato Chicken Breast

Prep: 7 minutes • Cook: 6 minutes

Chicken cutlets are a great convenience because they adapt to a variety of quick-cooking techniques, such as grilling, searing, and baking. Dress them up with jarred sun-dried tomato pesto embellished with fresh herbs and garlic.

2   tablespoons sun-dried tomato pesto
2   tablespoons chopped fresh basil
1   tablespoon chopped fresh oregano
2   garlic cloves, minced
4   (4-ounce) chicken breast cutlets
¼   teaspoon salt
¼   teaspoon freshly ground black pepper
Cooking spray

1. Preheat grill to medium-high heat.
2. Combine first 4 ingredients. Sprinkle chicken with salt and pepper; coat with cooking spray.
3. Place chicken on grill rack coated with cooking spray. Grill 3 minutes on each side or until done. Spoon pesto mixture evenly over chicken. Yield: 4 servings (serving size: 1 chicken cutlet and about 1 tablespoon pesto mixture).

CALORIES 137; FAT 3.3g (sat 0.9g, mono 0.9g, poly 0.8g); PROTEIN 23.4g; CARB 1.8g; FIBER 0.2g; CHOL 63mg; IRON 1mg; SODIUM 279mg; CALC 21mg

serve with:

Warm Cannellini Bean Salad

Prep: 3 minutes • Cook: 10 minutes

1   tablespoon olive oil
1   red onion, vertically cut into thin slices
3   garlic cloves, minced
1   (19-ounce) can cannellini beans, rinsed
      and drained
1   (12-ounce) jar roasted red bell peppers
4   cups baby arugula
4   teaspoons balsamic glaze

1. Heat a large nonstick skillet over medium heat. Add oil; swirl to coat. Add onion; cook 6 minutes or until lightly browned and tender, stirring occasionally.
2. Add garlic; sauté 1 minute. Add beans, peppers, and arugula; cook 1 to 2 minutes or just until arugula begins to wilt. Spoon salad evenly onto 4 serving plates. Drizzle with balsamic glaze. Yield: 4 servings (serving size: about 1 cup salad and 1 teaspoon glaze).

CALORIES 134; FAT 3.9g (sat 0.5g, mono 2.5g, poly 0.7g); PROTEIN 4g; CARB 20.3g; FIBER 3.9g; CHOL 0mg; IRON 1.5mg; SODIUM 347mg; CALC 67mg

Chicken Saltimbocca

Chicken Saltimbocca

Prep: 8 minutes • Cook: 19 minutes

"Saltimbocca" means "jump in the mouth" in Italian, and with the bold flavors of prosciutto, sage, and Marsala, this chicken entrée certainly lives up to its name. Serve with thin spaghetti or mashed potatoes on the side.

4	(6-ounce) skinless, boneless chicken breast halves
¼	teaspoon freshly ground black pepper
18	large sage leaves, divided
4	(½-ounce) thin slices prosciutto
1.1	ounces all-purpose flour (about ¼ cup)
Cooking spray	
1	cup dry Marsala wine

1. Preheat oven to 350°.
2. Sprinkle chicken evenly with pepper. Place 4 sage leaves on top of each chicken breast. Top each with 1 slice prosciutto, pressing lightly to adhere. Place flour in a shallow dish. Carefully dredge each chicken breast in flour, patting to adhere flour to chicken and shaking off any excess.
3. Heat a large nonstick skillet over medium-high heat. Coat pan with cooking spray. Add chicken; cook 3 to 4 minutes on each side or until golden. Place on a rack coated with cooking spray set in a rimmed baking sheet.
4. Bake at 350° for 8 minutes or until done.
5. Add wine to drippings in skillet, scraping pan to loosen browned bits. Add remaining 2 sage leaves. Bring to a boil over medium-high heat. Reduce heat; simmer, uncovered, 5 minutes or until reduced to 2 tablespoons. Remove sage from sauce. Serve sauce over chicken. Yield: 4 servings (serving size: 1 chicken breast and 1½ teaspoons sauce).

CALORIES 293; FAT 6.1g (sat 1.5g, mono 2.1g, poly 0.8g); PROTEIN 41.1g; CARB 10.1g; FIBER 0.2g; CHOL 120mg; IRON 1.2mg; SODIUM 579mg; CALC 24mg

Pan-Seared Chicken Cutlets with Tarragon-Mustard Cream Sauce

Prep: 3 minutes • Cook: 14 minutes

Tarragon is a flavorful herb popular in French cooking. It shows up in eggs, sauces, vegetables, fish, and chicken dishes. It's mostly known as the herb that flavors béarnaise sauce, a silky butter sauce.

3	tablespoons all-purpose flour
¼	teaspoon salt
¼	teaspoon freshly ground black pepper
4	(4-ounce) chicken breast cutlets (1 pound)
2	teaspoons olive oil

Cooking spray

¾	cup fat-free, lower-sodium chicken broth
¼	cup half-and-half
2	teaspoons stone-ground mustard
1	tablespoon chopped fresh tarragon

1. Combine first 3 ingredients in a heavy-duty zip-top plastic bag; add chicken. Seal bag; shake to coat chicken.
2. Heat a large nonstick skillet over medium-high heat. Add oil; swirl to coat. Coat chicken with cooking spray. Add chicken to pan; cook 3 minutes on each side or until browned.
3. Combine broth and next 3 ingredients, stirring with a whisk. Add to pan; bring to a boil. Reduce heat, and simmer 6 minutes or until chicken is done and sauce is slightly thick. Yield: 4 servings (serving size: 1 chicken cutlet and 2 tablespoons sauce).

CALORIES 186; FAT 6.8g (sat 2.2g, mono 3.4g, poly 1.1g); PROTEIN 24.2g; CARB 5.5g; FIBER 0.2g; CHOL 68mg; IRON 1.1mg; SODIUM 342mg; CALC 31mg

serve with:
Orange Roasted Carrots

Prep: 3 minutes • Cook: 18 minutes

| 1 | (12-ounce) package carrot sticks (about 3 cups) |

Cooking spray

¼	teaspoon salt
¼	teaspoon freshly ground black pepper
1	tablespoon olive oil
1	tablespoon honey
2	teaspoons grated orange rind

1. Preheat oven to 500°.
2. Cut larger carrot sticks in half lengthwise. Arrange carrots on a jelly-roll pan coated with cooking spray. Coat carrots with cooking spray, and sprinkle with salt and pepper. Toss well.
3. Bake at 500° for 10 minutes.
4. Combine oil, honey, and orange rind; add to carrots, and toss well. Bake an additional 8 minutes or until carrots are browned and tender. Yield: 4 servings (serving size: ½ cup).

CALORIES 82; FAT 3.4g (sat 0.5g, mono 2.5g, poly 0.4g); PROTEIN 1.1g; CARB 12.7g; FIBER 2.2g; CHOL 0mg; IRON 0.4mg; SODIUM 146mg; CALC 23mg

Pistachio-Crusted Chicken

Prep: 3 minutes • Cook: 22 minutes

Buy shelled pistachios to save time. You can also use other nuts in this recipe: Try almonds, pine nuts, cashews, or peanuts.

¾	cup pistachios
2	large egg whites, lightly beaten
4	(6-ounce) skinless, boneless chicken breast halves
¼	teaspoon salt
¼	teaspoon freshly ground black pepper
Cooking spray	

1. Preheat oven to 400°.
2. Place pistachios in a food processor. Process until finely chopped; transfer to a shallow bowl. Place egg whites in a shallow bowl. Sprinkle chicken with salt and pepper. Dip chicken into egg whites; dredge in pistachios, pressing lightly to adhere.
3. Heat a large nonstick ovenproof skillet over medium-high heat. Coat pan with cooking spray. Add chicken to pan; cook 4 minutes. Coat chicken with cooking spray. Turn chicken over; cook 4 minutes. Place pan in oven.
4. Bake, uncovered, at 400° for 14 minutes or until done. Cut chicken crosswise into slices. Yield: 4 servings (serving size: 3 ounces chicken).

CALORIES 329; FAT 13g (sat 1.9g, mono 6.2g, poly 3.7g); PROTEIN 46g; CARB 6.6g; FIBER 2.4g; CHOL 99mg; IRON 2.3mg; SODIUM 286mg; CALC 46mg

serve with:
Strawberry Salad

Prep: 5 minutes

1	(6-ounce) package fresh baby spinach
1½	cups quartered strawberries
¼	cup thinly sliced red onion
¼	teaspoon freshly ground black pepper
3	tablespoons blush wine vinaigrette
1	tablespoon chopped fresh mint (optional)
2	ounces goat cheese, crumbled

1. Combine first 5 ingredients and mint, if desired, in a large bowl; toss. Sprinkle with cheese. Yield: 4 servings (serving size: about 1⅔ cups salad).

CALORIES 124; FAT 5.8g (sat 2.3g, mono 1.7g, poly 0.6g); PROTEIN 4.1g; CARB 15.4g; FIBER 3.4g; CHOL 7mg; IRON 1.9mg; SODIUM 278mg; CALC 62mg

Chicken with Creamy Tomato Topping

Prep: 2 minutes • Cook: 16 minutes

4	(6-ounce) skinless, boneless chicken breast halves
½	teaspoon freshly ground black pepper
¼	teaspoon salt
	Cooking spray
2	cups grape tomatoes, halved
¼	cup refrigerated reduced-fat pesto
2	tablespoons fat-free cream cheese, softened

1. Sprinkle chicken with pepper and salt. Heat a large nonstick skillet over medium-high heat. Coat pan with cooking spray. Add chicken, and cook 5 minutes on each side or until done. Transfer to a serving dish, and keep warm.

2. Add tomatoes to hot pan; sauté 4 minutes or until tomatoes soften and begin to release their juices. Add pesto and cream cheese, stirring until smooth.
3. Cut chicken crosswise into ½-inch-thick medallions; place medallions from 1 chicken breast half on each of 4 plates. Spoon sauce evenly over medallions. Serve immediately. Yield: 4 servings (serving size: 1 chicken breast half and ¼ cup tomato topping).

CALORIES 264; FAT 8.8g (sat 2.4g, mono 4.6g, poly 1.8g); PROTEIN 37.6g; CARB 5.8g; FIBER 1.6g; CHOL 98mg; IRON 1.2mg; SODIUM 405mg; CALC 93mg

serve with:
Lemon-Parmesan Barley

Prep: 1 minute • Cook: 15 minutes
Other: 5 minutes

1½	cups water
1	tablespoon extra-virgin olive oil
¼	teaspoon freshly ground black pepper
¾	cup uncooked quick-cooking barley
¼	cup (1 ounce) shaved fresh Parmesan cheese
1	tablespoon grated lemon rind
1	tablespoon chopped fresh parsley

1. Combine first 3 ingredients in a medium saucepan; bring to a boil. Stir in barley; cover, reduce heat, and simmer 13 minutes or until tender and liquid evaporates.
2. Remove pan from heat; stir in cheese, lemon rind, and parsley. Cover and let stand 5 minutes. Fluff with a fork before serving. Yield: 4 servings (serving size: about ½ cup).

CALORIES 152; FAT 5.8g (sat 1.7g, mono 3.1g, poly 0.9g); PROTEIN 5.6g; CARB 21.5g; FIBER 3g; CHOL 6mg; IRON 0.6mg; SODIUM 109mg; CALC 82mg

Tomatillo Chicken

Prep: 3 minutes • Cook: 15 minutes

Tomatillos or green tomatoes cook up quickly for a fresh take on tomato sauce. This small round fruit imparts a lemony, apple, herb flavor. Be sure to remove the papery husks from the tomatillos, and wash them well to remove the sticky residue.

2	teaspoons ground cumin
½	teaspoon salt
½	teaspoon freshly ground black pepper
4	(6-ounce) skinless, boneless chicken breast halves

Cooking spray

1	tablespoon olive oil
1½	cups chopped tomatillos (about 4 tomatillos)
2	tablespoons minced seeded jalapeño pepper (1 pepper)

Lime wedges (optional)

1. Combine first 3 ingredients in a small bowl; rub mixture over chicken.
2. Place a large nonstick skillet over medium-high heat. Coat pan with cooking spray. Add chicken; cook 6 minutes on each side or until done. Remove chicken from pan, and keep warm.
3. Add oil to pan; swirl to coat. Stir in tomatillos and jalapeño pepper. Cook, stirring constantly, 3 minutes or until tender and saucy. Place chicken breast half on each of 4 plates. Spoon sauce evenly over chicken. Garnish with lime wedges, if desired. Yield: 4 servings (serving size: 1 chicken breast half and ¼ cup sauce).

CALORIES 235; FAT 8.1g (sat 1.9g, mono 4.4g, poly 1.7g); PROTEIN 35g; CARB 3.7g; FIBER 1.5g; CHOL 94mg; IRON 1.9mg; SODIUM 375mg; CALC 30mg

fix it faster

To beat the clock with this recipe, use ready-to-serve tomatillo salsa or salsa verde instead of chopping tomatillos and mincing and seeding jalapeño pepper. Look for these prepared sauces on the ethnic foods aisle of your supermarket.

Tomatillo Chicken

Chicken Milanese

Prep: 9 minutes • Cook: 19 minutes

A simple, chunky, fresh tomato sauce adds the magical finish to this chicken cooked Milanese-style. That means the food is breaded and fried. Incredibly light, crispy Italian-seasoned panko breadcrumbs add the crunchy layer of flavor to this chicken. Be sure the oil is hot before pan-frying for best results.

Fresh Milanese Sauce
1½   tablespoons olive oil
½   cup Italian-seasoned panko (Japanese
       breadcrumbs)
¼   cup (1 ounce) grated fresh Parmesan cheese
4   (6-ounce) skinless, boneless chicken breast
       halves
Olive oil–flavored cooking spray

1. Prepare Fresh Milanese Sauce; keep warm.
2. Heat a large nonstick skillet over medium heat until hot. Add olive oil; swirl to coat.
3. While pan heats, combine panko and cheese in a shallow dish; coat both sides of chicken with cooking spray, and dredge in panko mixture.
4. Cook chicken in hot oil over medium heat 7 minutes on each side or until done. Place 1 chicken breast half on each of 4 plates. Spoon Fresh Milanese Sauce evenly over chicken. Yield: 4 servings (serving size: 1 chicken breast half and 6 tablespoons tomato sauce).

CALORIES 347; FAT 13.8g (sat 3.3g, mono 8.1g, poly 2.2g); PROTEIN 39.2g; CARB 12.4g; FIBER 2.3g; CHOL 99mg; IRON 1.2mg; SODIUM 427mg; CALC 141mg

Chicken Milanese

Fresh Milanese Sauce

Prep: 5 minutes • Cook: 5 minutes

2   teaspoons olive oil
2   cups grape tomatoes, halved lengthwise
1   large shallot, chopped
¼   teaspoon salt
¼   teaspoon freshly ground black pepper
½   cup basil leaves
¼   cup dry red wine

1. Heat a large nonstick skillet over medium-high heat until hot. Add oil; swirl to coat. Stir in tomatoes and next 3 ingredients. Cook 4 minutes or until shallots are tender, stirring often.
2. While tomato mixture cooks, coarsely chop basil.
3. Stir wine into tomato mixture. Cook 30 seconds. Remove pan from heat, and stir in basil. Yield: 4 servings (serving size: 6 tablespoons).

CALORIES 53; FAT 2.3g (sat 0.3g, mono 1.7g, poly 0.3g); PROTEIN 0.8g; CARB 4.9g; FIBER 1.3g; CHOL 0mg; IRON 0.3mg; SODIUM 150mg; CALC 23mg

Skillet Barbecue Chicken

Prep: 6 minutes • Cook: 9 minutes

With this dish, you'll get the flavor of barbecue without having to fire up the grill. Two of the best features of this easy chicken dish are that it dresses up a store-bought barbecue sauce and everything is cooked in the same skillet. Use presliced onion and bell pepper to make preparing the slaw even faster.

4	(6-ounce) chicken breast halves
3	garlic cloves, minced
1	tablespoon salt-free Southwest chipotle seasoning blend
¼	teaspoon kosher salt
1	tablespoon olive oil
½	cup honey-roasted garlic barbecue sauce
¼	cup water

1. Place chicken between 2 sheets of plastic wrap; pound to ½-inch thickness using a meat mallet or small heavy skillet. Rub garlic over chicken, and sprinkle evenly with seasoning blend and salt.
2. Heat a large nonstick skillet over medium-high heat. Add oil; swirl to coat. Add chicken; cook 3 to 4 minutes on each side. Add barbecue sauce and water, scraping pan to loosen browned bits; cook 1 to 2 minutes or until chicken is done. Yield: 4 servings (serving size: 1 chicken breast half and ¼ cup sauce).

CALORIES 266; FAT 7.3g (sat 1.6g, mono 3.8g, poly 1.5g); PROTEIN 34.4g; CARB 11.7g; FIBER 0.1g; CHOL 94mg; IRON 1.2mg; SODIUM 580mg; CALC 21mg

serve with:
Sweet-and-Sour Slaw

Prep: 5 minutes • Other: 10 minutes

¼	cup cider vinegar
1	tablespoon olive oil
2	tablespoons honey
½	teaspoon salt
½	teaspoon freshly ground black pepper
4	cups packaged coleslaw
1	cup thinly sliced red bell pepper
⅓	cup thinly vertically sliced red onion

1. Combine first 5 ingredients in a large bowl, stirring with a whisk. Add coleslaw, bell pepper, and onion, tossing to coat. Cover and chill 10 minutes. Toss well before serving. Yield: 4 servings (serving size: 1 cup slaw).

CALORIES 93; FAT 3.5g (sat 0.5g, mono 2.5g, poly 0.4g); PROTEIN 1.1g; CARB 14.9g; FIBER 2g; CHOL 0mg; IRON 0.5mg; SODIUM 301mg; CALC 28mg

make ahead

Go ahead and make the slaw early–the flavors get better the longer it sits.

Herb-Crusted Chicken with Feta Sauce

Prep: 2 minutes • Cook: 11 minutes

A tangy Greek sauce made of mint, lemon, and feta cheese is a welcome addition to succulent breaded chicken breast. Serve it over a bed of orzo combined with chopped fresh basil. Use leftover sauce as a dressing spooned over romaine lettuce or tossed with fresh veggies such as tomatoes and cucumbers.

⅔ cup whole-wheat panko (Japanese breadcrumbs)
2 tablespoons Italian seasoning
4 (6-ounce) skinless, boneless chicken breast halves
½ teaspoon salt
¼ teaspoon freshly ground black pepper
4 teaspoons olive oil
6 tablespoons Feta Sauce

1. Combine panko and Italian seasoning in a shallow bowl. Sprinkle chicken with salt and pepper; dredge in panko mixture.
2. Heat a large nonstick skillet over medium-high heat. Add oil; swirl to coat. Add chicken; cook 5 minutes or until browned. Turn chicken over; reduce heat to medium, and cook 5 minutes or until done. Place 1 chicken breast half on each of 4 plates, and spoon about 1½ tablespoons Feta Sauce over each serving. Yield: 4 servings (serving size: 1 chicken breast and about 1½ tablespoons sauce).

CALORIES 323; FAT 13.3g (sat 3.4g, mono 6.7g, poly 2.8g); PROTEIN 39.3g; CARB 10.3g; FIBER 1.6g; CHOL 98mg; IRON 1.8mg; SODIUM 584mg; CALC 51mg

Feta Sauce

Prep: 4 minutes

1 lemon
1 tablespoon chopped fresh mint
4 teaspoons extra-virgin olive oil
Dash of freshly ground black pepper
(3.5-ounce) package reduced-fat feta cheese

1. Grate rind and squeeze juice from lemon to measure ½ teaspoon and 2 tablespoons, respectively. Combine rind, juice, mint, oil, and pepper in a small bowl, stirring with a whisk. Add cheese, stirring with a whisk. Yield: 7 servings (serving size: about 1½ tablespoons).

CALORIES 55; FAT 4.5g (sat 1.6g, mono 2.1g, poly 0.5g); PROTEIN 2.9g; CARB 0.8g; FIBER 0.3g; CHOL 4mg; IRON 0mg; SODIUM 196mg; CALC 34mg

Herb-Crusted Chicken with Feta Sauce

Green Salsa Chicken

Prep: 5 minutes • Cook: 18 minutes

You'll only need to purchase one package of pre-chopped green, yellow, and red bell pepper to use in the salsa and the corn.

1	lime
4	tomatillos, husks and stems removed
¼	cup refrigerated prechopped tricolor bell pepper mix
2	tablespoons chopped fresh cilantro
2	(6-ounce) skinless, boneless chicken breast halves

Cooking spray

1. Preheat grill to medium-high heat.
2. Grate rind from lime and squeeze juice to measure ⅛ teaspoon and 1 tablespoon, respectively. Place rind and juice in a medium bowl. Cut tomatillos in half.
3. Heat a medium nonstick skillet over medium-high heat. Add tomatillo halves, skin sides down; cook 4 minutes or until lightly charred on edges. Turn tomatillos over, and move to one side of pan; add bell pepper on the other side. Cook 2 minutes or until bell pepper is lightly charred, stirring occasionally (do not stir tomatillos). Remove pan from heat; remove tomatillos from pan, and coarsely chop. Add tomatillo, bell pepper, and cilantro to lime juice mixture; toss well.
4. Place chicken on grill rack coated with cooking spray. Grill 6 minutes on each side or until done. Spoon tomatillo salsa over chicken. Yield: 2 servings (serving size: 1 chicken breast half and about ⅓ cup salsa).

CALORIES 309; FAT 4.7g (sat 1.2g, mono 1.5g, poly 1.6g); PROTEIN 35g; CARB 31.1g; FIBER 2.3g; CHOL 94mg; IRON 1.6mg; SODIUM 437mg; CALC 22mg

serve with:
Cumin Corn

Prep: 5 minutes • Cook: 10 minutes

2	ears corn
2	teaspoons butter
¼	cup finely chopped onion
¼	cup refrigerated prechopped tricolor bell pepper mix
¼	teaspoon ground cumin
⅛	teaspoon salt
⅛	teaspoon freshly ground black pepper

1. Remove husks from corn; scrub silks from corn. Cut kernels from ears of corn; set corn aside. Discard cobs.
2. Melt butter in a nonstick skillet over medium heat. Add onion and bell pepper mix; cook, stirring constantly, 3 to 4 minutes until crisp-tender. Stir in cumin, salt, and pepper; cook 1 minute. Stir in corn; cook 5 minutes or until corn is crisp-tender, stirring frequently. Yield: 2 servings (serving size: ½ cup).

CALORIES 122; FAT 5g (sat 2.6g, mono 1.3g, poly 0.7g); PROTEIN 3.3g; CARB 19.6g; FIBER 3.1g; CHOL 10mg; IRON 0.7mg; SODIUM 187mg; CALC 10mg

Chicken Scaloppini

Prep: 10 minutes • Cook: 15 minutes

Scaloppini are cuts of meat that are pounded thin, and then cooked to perfection in about six minutes. For a beautifully browned crust, make sure the pan and oil are hot—the chicken should hiss as it hits the pan.

4   (6-ounce) skinless, boneless chicken breast halves
1   large egg white
2   teaspoons water
½   cup Italian-seasoned breadcrumbs
2   teaspoons olive oil, divided
½   cup fat-free, lower-sodium chicken broth
1   tablespoon fresh lemon juice

1. Place chicken between 2 sheets of plastic wrap. Pound to ¼-inch thickness using a meat mallet or small heavy skillet.
2. Combine egg white and water in a shallow dish, stirring with a whisk. Place breadcrumbs in another shallow dish. Dip each chicken breast half in egg mixture; dredge in breadcrumbs.
3. Heat a large nonstick skillet over medium-high heat. Add 1 teaspoon oil; swirl to coat. Add half of chicken to pan. Cook 3 minutes on each side or until golden. Transfer to a plate; cover and keep warm. Repeat procedure with remaining oil and chicken.
4. Add broth and lemon juice to pan, stirring to loosen browned bits. Cook, uncovered, over high heat 2 to 3 minutes or until reduced to ⅓ cup. Drizzle sauce over chicken. Yield: 4 servings (serving size: 1 chicken breast half and about 1 tablespoon sauce).

CALORIES 265; FAT 7g (sat 1.4g, mono 3g, poly 2.1g); PROTEIN 37.4g; CARB 10.5g; FIBER 0.5g; CHOL 94mg; IRON 1.9mg; SODIUM 380mg; CALC 38mg

serve with:

Pan-Roasted Asparagus and Tomatoes

Prep: 5 minutes • Cook: 6 minutes

1   pound asparagus spears, trimmed
1   tablespoon olive oil
2   cups grape tomatoes
¼   teaspoon salt
¼   teaspoon freshly ground black pepper

1. Rinse asparagus (do not dry). Heat a large nonstick skillet over medium-high heat. Add oil; swirl to coat. Add asparagus; cook 3 minutes. Add tomatoes; cook 2 minutes or until asparagus is crisp-tender and tomatoes just begin to burst, turning asparagus occasionally with tongs. Sprinkle with salt and pepper. Yield: 4 servings (serving size: ¼ of asparagus-tomato mixture).

CALORIES 72; FAT 3.5g (sat 0.5g, mono 2.5g, poly 0.4g); PROTEIN 3g; CARB 7.5g; FIBER 3.4g; CHOL 0mg; IRON 2.5mg; SODIUM 151mg; CALC 40mg

Apricot-Lemon Chicken

Prep: 4 minutes • Cook: 14 minutes

Start with an apricot fruit spread to create a sauce that transforms simply prepared chicken breasts into this elegant dish.

1	teaspoon curry powder
½	teaspoon salt
¼	teaspoon freshly ground black pepper
4	(6-ounce) skinless, boneless chicken breast halves
Cooking spray	
⅓	cup apricot spread
2	tablespoons fresh lemon juice
2	tablespoons water
2	teaspoons grated lemon rind

1. Combine first 3 ingredients in a small bowl; rub mixture over chicken.
2. Place a large nonstick skillet over medium-high heat. Coat pan with cooking spray. Cook chicken 6 minutes on each side or until done. Remove chicken from pan, and keep warm.
3. Add apricot spread, lemon juice, and 2 tablespoons water to pan, stirring until smooth. Cook over medium heat 1 minute. Spoon sauce over chicken; sprinkle with lemon rind. Yield: 4 servings (serving size: 1 chicken breast half and about 1½ tablespoons apricot-lemon sauce).

CALORIES 245; FAT 2g (sat 0.6g, mono 0.5g, poly 0.5g); PROTEIN 39.4g; CARB 14.5g; FIBER 0.3g; CHOL 99mg; IRON 1.4mg; SODIUM 402mg; CALC 24mg

serve with:

Sweet Lemon-Mint Pear Salad

Prep: 9 minutes

1	tablespoon sugar
3	tablespoons fresh lemon juice
2	teaspoons canola oil
4	cups packed baby spinach and spring greens mix
1	firm pear, thinly sliced
½	cup sliced red onion
¼	cup torn mint leaves

1. Combine first 3 ingredients in a large bowl, stirring with a whisk. Add greens mix and remaining ingredients; toss well. Serve immediately. Yield: 4 servings (serving size: 1½ cups salad).

CALORIES 72; FAT 2g (sat 0.2g, mono 1.4g, poly 0.7g); PROTEIN 1g; CARB 13g; FIBER 2.3g; CHOL 0mg; IRON 1mg; SODIUM 20mg; CALC 35mg

ingredient spotlight

Perfectly ripe pears are sweet with a subtle, intoxicating perfume. To ripen, place pears on the kitchen counter in a brown paper bag, and check them daily. It may take three to five days for them to fully ripen. If the neck area yields to gentle thumb pressure, the pear is ready to eat or cook.

Tarragon Chicken

Prep: 4 minutes • Cook: 7 minutes

Add the remaining olive oil–tarragon mixture at the final stage of the cooking process to preserve its full-bodied taste and citrus essence. This fast and easy entrée is ideal for weeknight guests.

4	(6-ounce) skinless, boneless chicken breast halves
¼	teaspoon salt
2	tablespoons extra-virgin olive oil
1	teaspoon grated lemon rind
2	tablespoons fresh lemon juice
1	garlic clove, minced
2	teaspoons minced fresh tarragon
⅛	teaspoon salt

1. Place each chicken breast half between 2 sheets of heavy-duty plastic wrap; pound to ¼-inch thickness using a meat mallet or small heavy skillet. Sprinkle chicken evenly with ¼ teaspoon salt.
2. Combine olive oil and remaining 5 ingredients in a small bowl, stirring well with a whisk. Heat a large nonstick skillet over medium-high heat. Add 2 teaspoons oil mixture to pan, spreading evenly over bottom of pan with a wide spatula. Add chicken; cook 2 minutes. Drizzle chicken with 2 teaspoons oil mixture. Turn chicken over; cook 2 minutes. Drizzle remaining oil mixture over chicken; reduce heat to low. Cover and cook 2 minutes or until done. Transfer chicken to a serving platter. Pour pan drippings over chicken; serve immediately. Yield: 4 servings (serving size: 1 chicken breast half).

CALORIES 251; FAT 9g (sat 1.6g, mono 5.5g, poly 1.5g); PROTEIN 39.4g; CARB 1.1g; FIBER 0.1g; CHOL 99mg; IRON 1.3mg; SODIUM 329mg; CALC 23mg

serve with:
Kalamata Barley

Prep: 1 minute • Cook: 13 minutes
Other: 5 minutes

1⅓	cups water
⅔	cup uncooked quick-cooking barley
½	cup refrigerated prechopped tricolor bell pepper mix
10	pitted kalamata olives, chopped
2	tablespoons chopped fresh parsley
1	teaspoon extra-virgin olive oil
⅛	teaspoon salt

1. Bring 1⅓ cups water to a boil in a medium saucepan; add barley. Cover and cook 12 minutes. Remove pan from heat; stir in bell pepper and remaining ingredients. Let stand 5 minutes; fluff with a fork before serving. Yield: 4 servings (serving size: about ½ cup).

CALORIES 122; FAT 4g (sat 0.5g, mono 2.8g, poly 0.4g); PROTEIN 2.9g; CARB 20.5g; FIBER 3g; CHOL 0mg; IRON 0.6mg; SODIUM 227mg; CALC 8mg

Tarragon Chicken

Kalamata-Balsamic Chicken with Feta

Prep: 4 minutes • Cook: 14 minutes

To keep the total time to 15 minutes, start cooking the chicken first. It will be done by the time the other ingredients are ready.

4   (6-ounce) skinless, boneless chicken
        breast halves
½   teaspoon freshly ground black pepper
Cooking spray
1   cup grape tomatoes, halved
16   pitted kalamata olives, halved
3   tablespoons light balsamic vinaigrette
3   tablespoons crumbled feta cheese
2   tablespoons small basil leaves

1. Sprinkle chicken evenly with pepper.
2. Heat a large nonstick skillet over medium-high heat. Coat pan with cooking spray. Cook chicken 6 to 7 minutes on each side or until done. Transfer chicken to a serving platter; keep warm.
3. While chicken cooks, combine tomatoes, olives, and vinaigrette in a medium bowl.
4. Add tomato mixture to pan; cook 1 to 2 minutes or until tomatoes soften. Spoon over chicken. Top evenly with cheese and basil. Yield: 4 servings (serving size: 1 chicken breast half, ¼ cup tomato mixture, and ¾ tablespoon cheese).

CALORIES 273; FAT 9g (sat 2.3g, mono 3.9g, poly 1g); PROTEIN 40.9g; CARB 4.1g; FIBER 0.7g; CHOL 105mg; IRON 1.5mg; SODIUM 612mg; CALC 65mg

serve with:
Orzo with Spring Greens and Rosemary

Prep: 1 minute • Cook: 10 minutes

¾   cup uncooked orzo (rice-shaped pasta)
1   cup spring greens mix, coarsely chopped
4   teaspoons pine nuts, toasted
1   tablespoon extra-virgin olive oil
½   teaspoon minced fresh rosemary
¼   teaspoon salt

1. Cook orzo according to package directions, omitting salt and fat. Drain pasta; place in a medium bowl.
2. Add greens mix and remaining ingredients, tossing well. Yield: 4 servings (serving size: about ⅔ cup).

CALORIES 171; FAT 6g (sat 0.6g, mono 3g, poly 1.5g); PROTEIN 4.6g; CARB 24.7g; FIBER 1.5g; CHOL 0mg; IRON 0.4mg; SODIUM 149mg; CALC 9mg

Balsamic Chicken with Roasted Tomatoes

Prep: 5 minutes • Cook: 12 minutes

The juices escaping from the roasting tomatoes combine with the honey and olive oil to make a syrupy glaze to coat the tomatoes and the chicken.

1	pint grape tomatoes
1	tablespoon honey
1½	teaspoons olive oil
½	teaspoon salt, divided
4	(6-ounce) skinless, boneless chicken breast halves
½	teaspoon freshly ground black pepper

Cooking spray
Balsamic vinaigrette salad spritzer

1. Preheat oven to 450°.
2. Combine first 3 ingredients in a small bowl; place tomato mixture on a foil-lined jelly-roll pan. Bake at 450° for 12 minutes or until tomato skins burst and begin to wrinkle, stirring once. Transfer tomatoes to a bowl, scraping juices into bowl. Stir ¼ teaspoon salt into tomato mixture.
3. Place each chicken breast half between 2 sheets of heavy-duty plastic wrap; pound to ¼-inch thickness using a meat mallet or small heavy skillet. Sprinkle chicken evenly with remaining ¼ teaspoon salt and pepper.
4. Heat a large nonstick skillet over medium-high heat. Coat pan with cooking spray. Add chicken; cook 3 to 4 minutes on each side. Place chicken on individual plates; coat each breast half with 2 to 3 sprays of balsamic spritzer. Spoon tomatoes evenly over chicken. Yield: 4 servings (serving size: 1 chicken breast half and about ¼ cup tomatoes).

CALORIES 238; FAT 4g (sat 0.8g, mono 1.8g, poly 0.8g); PROTEIN 40g; CARB 7.7g; FIBER 1g; CHOL 99mg; IRON 1.5mg; SODIUM 431mg; CALC 28mg

serve with:

Mushroom and Zucchini Orzo

Prep: 6 minutes • Cook: 12 minutes

1	cup uncooked orzo (rice-shaped pasta)

Cooking spray

1	cup sliced mushrooms
1	cup diced zucchini
1	tablespoon butter
½	teaspoon dried oregano
¼	teaspoon salt
¼	teaspoon freshly ground black pepper

1. Cook orzo according to package directions, omitting salt and fat. Drain and keep warm.
2. While orzo cooks, heat a large nonstick skillet over medium-high heat. Coat pan with cooking spray. Add mushrooms and zucchini; sauté 6 minutes or until tender and browned.
3. Combine orzo, mushroom mixture, and remaining ingredients in a large bowl, tossing gently. Yield: 4 servings (serving size: ¾ cup).

CALORIES 197; FAT 4g (sat 1.8g, mono 0.7g, poly 0.1g); PROTEIN 6.3g; CARB 34.2g; FIBER 2.1g; CHOL 8mg; IRON 0.3mg; SODIUM 171mg; CALC 11mg

choice ingredient

Zucchini has thin, edible skin and soft seeds. In peak form from June through late August, zucchini can be used in almost anything from salads and breads to gratins. It will keep in the refrigerator for about five days.

Mushroom-Herb Chicken

Prep: 5 minutes • Cook: 14 minutes

Marjoram is oregano's mild cousin. Crush the dried leaves to release their delicate flavor. For this recipe, use the largest shallots you can find; three large shallots should yield 1 cup of slices. Refrigerated mashed potatoes and broccoli complete the meal.

4	(6-ounce) skinless, boneless chicken breast halves
¼	teaspoon salt
¼	teaspoon freshly ground black pepper
Cooking spray	
3	large shallots, peeled
1	(8-ounce) package presliced mushrooms
⅓	cup dry sherry
1	teaspoon dried marjoram, crushed
Freshly ground black pepper (optional)	

1. Place each chicken breast half between 2 sheets of heavy-duty plastic wrap; pound to ⅓-inch thickness using a meat mallet or small heavy skillet. Sprinkle chicken evenly with salt and ¼ teaspoon pepper; coat with cooking spray. Heat a large non-stick skillet over medium-high heat. Add chicken to pan; cook 5 to 6 minutes on each side or until browned.

2. While chicken cooks, cut shallots vertically into thin slices. Remove chicken from pan. Coat pan with cooking spray. Add mushrooms and shallots to pan; coat vegetables with cooking spray. Cook 1 minute, stirring constantly. Stir in sherry and marjoram. Return chicken to pan; cover and cook 3 to 4 minutes or until mushrooms are tender and chicken is done. Transfer chicken to a platter. Pour mushroom mixture over chicken; sprinkle with freshly ground pepper, if desired. Serve immediately. Yield: 4 servings (serving size: 1 chicken breast half and ⅓ cup mushroom sauce).

CALORIES 226; FAT 3g (sat 0.6g, mono 0.5g, poly 0.6g); PROTEIN 41.6g; CARB 5g; FIBER 1g; CHOL 99mg; IRON 1.9mg; SODIUM 262mg; CALC 33mg

Mushroom-Herb Chicken

Chicken and Shiitake Marsala

Prep: 1 minute • Cook: 14 minutes

Marsala, a fortified Italian wine recognized for its golden brown color and sweet, nutty flavor, works well in both sweet and savory dishes. Along with the smoky mushrooms in this recipe, the wine creates a rich, aromatic sauce. Dry sherry is a good substitute for Marsala.

4	(6-ounce) skinless, boneless chicken breast halves
Cooking spray	
¼	teaspoon salt
¼	teaspoon black pepper
2	(3½-ounce) packages shiitake mushrooms, sliced
½	cup Marsala wine
2	green onions, finely chopped (about ⅓ cup) and divided
2	tablespoons butter

1. Place each chicken breast half between 2 sheets of heavy-duty plastic wrap; pound to ½-inch thickness using a meat mallet or small heavy skillet.

2. Heat a large nonstick skillet over medium-high heat. Coat pan with cooking spray. Sprinkle chicken evenly with salt and pepper. Add chicken to pan. Cook 5 to 6 minutes on each side or until done. Remove chicken and drippings from pan; set aside, and keep warm.

3. Heat pan over medium-high heat; coat pan with cooking spray. Add mushrooms. Coat mushrooms with cooking spray; cook 2 minutes or until tender, stirring frequently. Add wine and 3 tablespoons onions. Cook 30 seconds over high heat. Reduce heat; add butter, stirring until butter melts.

4. Add chicken and drippings to pan, stirring gently. Place chicken on a platter. Spoon mushroom sauce over chicken; sprinkle with remaining onions. Yield: 4 servings (serving size: 1 chicken breast half and about ¼ cup mushroom sauce).

CALORIES 291; FAT 8g (sat 4.2g, mono 2g, poly 0.7g); PROTEIN 40.9g; CARB 6.2g; FIBER 0.6g; CHOL 114mg; IRON 1.6mg; SODIUM 303mg; CALC 40mg

Chicken and Shiitake Marsala

Grilled Chicken and Veggies with Chimichurri Sauce

Prep: 8 minutes • Cook: 12 minutes

Chimichurri is a very flavorful and vinegary condiment made from parsley, garlic, and olive oil that is served in Argentina with grilled meats.

4	(6-ounce) skinless, boneless chicken breast halves
2	yellow squash, cut into ¼-inch slices
1	red bell pepper, cut into 2-inch squares
1	red onion, cut into ¼-inch slices

Cooking spray
½   teaspoon salt
½   teaspoon freshly ground black pepper
Chimichurri Sauce

1. Preheat grill to medium-high heat.
2. Coat chicken and vegetables with cooking spray; sprinkle with salt and pepper.
3. Place chicken and vegetables on grill rack coated with cooking spray. Grill chicken 6 minutes on each side or until done; grill vegetables 3 minutes on each side. Serve chicken with Chimichurri Sauce. Yield: 4 servings (serving size: 3 ounces chicken, about 1 cup vegetables, and ⅓ cup sauce).

CALORIES 351; FAT 14.9g (sat 2.6g, mono 8.9g, poly 2.5g); PROTEIN 37.8g; CARB 17g; FIBER 3.7g; CHOL 94mg; IRON 3.5mg; SODIUM 542mg; CALC 140mg

make ahead
Make the sauce up to a day ahead and store it in the refrigerator.

Chimichurri Sauce

Prep: 13 minutes

10	garlic cloves
2	cups flat-leaf parsley leaves
1	cup chopped onion
½	cup chopped fresh oregano
½	cup white wine vinegar
3	tablespoons olive oil
2	tablespoons fresh lemon juice
1	teaspoon grated lemon rind
½	teaspoon freshly ground black pepper
¼	teaspoon salt

1. With food processor on, drop garlic through food chute; process until minced. Add parsley and remaining ingredients; process 1 minute or until finely minced. Yield: 4 servings (serving size: about ⅓ cup sauce).

CALORIES 138; FAT 10.7g (sat 1.5g, mono 7.5g, poly 1.1g); PROTEIN 2.1g; CARB 10.2g; FIBER 2g; CHOL 0mg; IRON 2.2mg; SODIUM 166mg; CALC 104mg

Grilled Chicken and Veggies with Chimichurri Sauce

Rosemary-Fig Chicken with Port

Prep: 4 minutes • Cook: 15 minutes

This company-worthy dish received top reviews in our Test Kitchens because it's quick, easy, and simply unbeatable in terms of taste. Use garlic powder instead of fresh garlic; it won't burn when you sear the chicken.

½	teaspoon salt
½	teaspoon garlic powder
½	teaspoon freshly ground black pepper
4	(6-ounce) skinless, boneless chicken breast halves

Butter-flavored cooking spray

⅔	cup fig preserves
1	tablespoon minced fresh rosemary
6	tablespoons port or other sweet red wine

1. Sprinkle first 3 ingredients evenly over chicken. Coat chicken with cooking spray.
2. Heat a large nonstick skillet over medium-high heat. Add chicken; cook 3 minutes on each side or until browned. Combine fig preserves, rosemary, and wine in a bowl; add to chicken, stirring gently. Cover, reduce heat to medium, and cook 6 minutes or until chicken is done. Uncover and cook 1 minute over medium-high heat or until sauce is slightly thick. Serve sauce over chicken. Yield: 4 servings (serving size: 1 chicken breast half and about 3 tablespoons sauce).

CALORIES 329; FAT 2g (sat 0.6g, mono 0.5g, poly 0.5g); PROTEIN 39.4g; CARB 31.4g; FIBER 0.2g; CHOL 99mg; IRON 1.3mg; SODIUM 403mg; CALC 23mg

serve with:

Lemon-Scented Broccoli Rabe

Prep: 1 minute • Cook: 14 minutes

4	quarts hot water
1½	pounds broccoli rabe (rapini)
½	teaspoon garlic powder
¼	teaspoon salt
¼	teaspoon crushed red pepper
1	tablespoon olive oil
2	teaspoons grated lemon rind

1. Bring 4 quarts hot water to a boil in a large, covered Dutch oven. Trim coarse ends from broccoli rabe. Combine garlic powder, salt, and red pepper; set aside.
2. Place broccoli rabe in boiling water; cook, uncovered, 5 to 6 minutes or until crisp-tender. Drain and plunge broccoli rabe into ice water; drain.
3. Heat a large nonstick skillet over medium-high heat. Add oil; swirl to coat. Stir in garlic powder mixture. Add broccoli rabe, tossing to coat. Cook, turning every 1 to 2 minutes, until thoroughly heated. Sprinkle with lemon rind; toss well. Serve immediately. Yield: 4 servings (serving size: 1 cup).

CALORIES 69; FAT 4g (sat 0.5g, mono 2.5g, poly 0.5g); PROTEIN 4.6g; CARB 6.5g; FIBER 0.2g; CHOL 0mg; IRON 1.1mg; SODIUM 183mg; CALC 62mg

South-of-the-Border Grilled Chicken and Green Tomatoes

Prep: 6 minutes • Cook: 12 minutes
Other: 30 minutes

The shortcut marinade begins with the flavorful drained liquid from the salsa. Choose a fresh juicy salsa with chunks of tomatoes and onions, which you can find in the deli or produce section of your supermarket, rather than a thick, tomato sauce–based product. Serve with tortillas.

1	(16-ounce) container fresh salsa
1	tablespoon olive oil
¼	teaspoon salt
¼	teaspoon freshly ground black pepper
4	(6-ounce) skinless, boneless chicken breast halves
2	green tomatoes, each cut into 4 (½-inch-thick) slices
	Cooking spray
½	cup (2 ounces) crumbled queso fresco

1. Drain salsa in a colander over a bowl, reserving liquid. Set salsa aside.
2. Combine reserved liquid, oil, salt, and pepper in a large zip-top plastic bag. Add chicken and tomato to bag; seal and shake gently to coat. Chill 30 minutes.
3. Preheat grill to medium-high heat.
4. Remove chicken and tomato from bag, reserving marinade. Place chicken on grill rack coated with cooking spray. Place tomato slices on grill rack. Grill chicken 6 minutes on each side or until done. Grill tomatoes 5 minutes on each side or until lightly browned. Serve chicken with tomatoes; top with reserved salsa and queso fresco. Yield: 4 servings (serving size: 2 tomato slices, 1 chicken breast half, about ½ cup salsa, and 2 tablespoons queso fresco).

CALORIES 314; FAT 8g (sat 2.7g, mono 3.8g, poly 1.1g); PROTEIN 43.7g; CARB 8.7g; FIBER 0.7g; CHOL 109mg; IRON 1.7mg; SODIUM 588mg; CALC 115mg

South-of-the-Border Grilled
Chicken and Green Tomatoes

ingredient spotlight

There are two types of green tomatoes. The most common type is an immature tomato that's picked before it ripens. These green tomatoes have a sharp, tart taste and firm flesh. You wouldn't want to eat them raw, but cooking green tomatoes softens the flesh and balances the acidity. Green zebra tomatoes are yellowish green with dark green striations and remain green at full maturity. The flavor is mildly spicy and slightly tart.

Grilled Chicken with Rustic Mustard Cream

Prep: 6 minutes • Cook: 12 minutes

The pronounced lemon-pine character of rosemary goes well with olive oil and Dijon mustard, giving this grilled chicken a rustic Mediterranean flair.

1	tablespoon plus 1 teaspoon whole-grain Dijon mustard, divided
1	tablespoon olive oil
1	teaspoon chopped fresh rosemary
¼	teaspoon salt
¼	teaspoon freshly ground black pepper
4	(6-ounce) skinless, boneless chicken breast halves

Cooking spray
3	tablespoons light mayonnaise
1	tablespoon water

Rosemary sprigs (optional)

1. Preheat grill to medium-high heat.
2. Combine 1 teaspoon mustard, oil, and next 3 ingredients in a small bowl; brush evenly over chicken. Place chicken on grill rack coated with cooking spray; grill 6 minutes on each side or until done.
3. While chicken grills, combine 1 tablespoon mustard, mayonnaise, and 1 tablespoon water in a bowl. Serve mustard cream with grilled chicken. Garnish with rosemary sprigs, if desired. Yield: 4 servings (serving size: 1 chicken breast half and 1 tablespoon mustard cream).

CALORIES 262; FAT 10g (sat 1.8g, mono 4g, poly 3g); PROTEIN 39.6g; CARB 1.7g; FIBER 0.2g; CHOL 102mg; IRON 1.4mg; SODIUM 448mg; CALC 25mg

Grilled Chicken with Rustic Mustard Cream

serve with:

Pan-Roasted Tomatoes with Herbs

Prep: 2 minutes • Cook: 4 minutes
Other: 5 minutes

2	teaspoons olive oil, divided
1	pint multicolored grape tomatoes
1	teaspoon chopped fresh oregano
½	teaspoon chopped fresh rosemary
¼	teaspoon salt
¼	teaspoon crushed red pepper

1. Heat a medium nonstick skillet over medium-high heat. Add 1 teaspoon oil; swirl to coat. Add tomatoes; cook 3 to 4 minutes or until tomatoes begin to blister. Remove from heat; stir in remaining 1 teaspoon oil and remaining ingredients, tossing gently to combine. Let stand 5 minutes. Yield: 4 servings (serving size: ½ cup).

CALORIES 34; FAT 3g (sat 0.4g, mono 1.7g, poly 0.4g); PROTEIN 0.7g; CARB 3.1g; FIBER 0.9g; CHOL 0mg; IRON 0.2mg; SODIUM 149mg; CALC 10mg

Cumin-Seared Chicken with Pineapple-Mint Salsa

Prep: 1 minute • Cook: 14 minutes

Buying refrigerated precubed pineapple makes it a breeze to put together this colorful salsa.

1	teaspoon ground cumin
½	teaspoon salt
⅛	teaspoon ground red pepper
4	(6-ounce) skinless, boneless chicken breast halves
Cooking spray	
1½	cups cubed pineapple, finely chopped
½	cup chopped fresh mint
¼	cup finely chopped red onion
2	tablespoons rice vinegar
2	teaspoons grated peeled fresh ginger

1. Combine cumin, salt, and red pepper; sprinkle evenly over chicken.
2. Heat a large nonstick skillet over medium-high heat. Coat pan with cooking spray. Add chicken; cook 7 to 8 minutes on each side or until done.
3. While chicken cooks, combine pineapple and remaining ingredients; toss gently to blend. Serve with chicken. Yield: 4 servings (serving size: 1 chicken breast half and ½ cup salsa).

CALORIES 224; FAT 2g (sat 0.6g, mono 0.5g, poly 0.5g); PROTEIN 39.9g; CARB 9.2g; FIBER 1.5g; CHOL 99mg; IRON 1.8mg; SODIUM 405mg; CALC 41mg

Cumin-Seared Chicken with Pineapple-Mint Salsa

serve with:
Almond-Coconut Rice

Prep: 2 minutes • Cook: 6 minutes

1	(10-ounce) package frozen whole-grain brown rice
⅓	cup slivered almonds
3	tablespoons flaked sweetened coconut
½	teaspoon ground cumin
⅛	teaspoon salt

1. Microwave rice according to package directions.
2. While rice cooks, heat a medium non-stick skillet over medium-high heat. Add almonds and coconut; cook 2 minutes or until lightly browned, stirring constantly. Remove from heat; add rice, cumin, and salt, stirring to blend. Yield: 4 servings (serving size: ¾ cup).

CALORIES 147; FAT 6g (sat 1.4g, mono 3.1g, poly 1.3g); PROTEIN 4.2g; CARB 19.8g; FIBER 2.5g; CHOL 0mg; IRON 0.5mg; SODIUM 86mg; CALC 35mg

Chicken with Pomegranate-Sake Poached Raisins

Prep: 4 minutes • Cook: 17 minutes

Most of the sake's alcohol content will evaporate during cooking, but stirring an extra tablespoon of sake into the finished sauce enhances the dish without overpowering it.

4	(6-ounce) skinless, boneless chicken breast halves
¼	teaspoon salt
¼	teaspoon ground red pepper
Cooking spray	
½	cup plus 1 tablespoon sake (rice wine), divided
½	cup pomegranate-cherry juice
½	cup raisins or dried sweet cherries

1. Sprinkle both sides of chicken with salt and red pepper, rubbing to evenly distribute spices. Coat chicken with cooking spray.
2. Heat a large nonstick skillet over medium-high heat. Coat pan with cooking spray; add chicken. Cook 4 minutes on each side or until browned; add ½ cup sake, juice, and raisins. Cover and cook 6 minutes or until chicken is done. Uncover and transfer chicken to individual plates. Cook raisin mixture, stirring constantly, 2 to 3 minutes or until liquid almost evaporates.
3. Remove pan from heat; stir in remaining 1 tablespoon sake. Spoon raisin sauce evenly over chicken. Yield: 4 servings (serving size: 1 chicken breast half and 2 tablespoons raisin sauce).

CALORIES 280; FAT 2g (sat 0.6g, mono 0.5g, poly 0.5g); PROTEIN 39.9g; CARB 19.2g; FIBER 0.7g; CHOL 99mg; IRON 1.6mg; SODIUM 265mg; CALC 28mg

serve with:

Roasted Green Beans with Onions

Prep: 3 minutes • Cook: 13 minutes

1	(12-ounce) package trimmed green beans
1	cup sliced onion (about ½ medium onion)
1	teaspoon dark sesame oil
¼	teaspoon salt
Sesame seeds, toasted (optional)	

1. Preheat oven to 500°.
2. Combine first 4 ingredients in a large bowl; toss to coat. Arrange bean mixture in a single layer on a jelly-roll pan. Bake at 500° for 10 minutes; stir beans. Bake an additional 3 minutes or until beans are tender. Sprinkle with sesame seeds, if desired. Yield: 4 servings (serving size: ¾ cup).

CALORIES 39; FAT 1g (sat 0.2g, mono 0g, poly 0.1g); PROTEIN 1.5g; CARB 6.6g; FIBER 2.8g; CHOL 0mg; IRON 0.8mg; SODIUM 150mg; CALC 31mg

ingredient spotlight

Dark sesame oil is made from extracting the oil from toasted sesame seeds. Look for it on the ethnic foods aisle of your local grocery store.

Roasted Chicken Breasts and Butternut Squash with Herbed Wine Sauce

Roasted Chicken Breasts and Butternut Squash with Herbed Wine Sauce

Prep: 9 minutes • Cook: 38 minutes

Butternut squash's natural sugars caramelize during roasting. When paired with fine herbs and wine, they create a flavor explosion that rivals any bistro specialty.

4	bone-in chicken breast halves (about 2 pounds), skinned

Cooking spray

1	tablespoon olive oil, divided
½	teaspoon salt, divided
½	teaspoon freshly ground black pepper, divided
5	cups (½-inch) cubed peeled butternut squash (2¼ pounds)
1	teaspoon fine herbs
3	tablespoons dry white wine

1. Preheat oven to 450°.
2. Place chicken in a large roasting pan coated with cooking spray. Brush chicken with 1½ teaspoons olive oil; sprinkle with ¼ teaspoon salt and ¼ teaspoon pepper.
3. Place squash in a large bowl. Drizzle with remaining olive oil, and sprinkle with fine herbs, remaining salt, and remaining pepper; toss well. Add squash to pan. Bake at 450° for 38 minutes or until chicken is done. Transfer chicken and squash to a serving platter; keep warm.
4. Add wine to pan drippings; bring to a boil over high heat, scraping pan to loosen browned bits. Reduce heat; cook 2 minutes or until reduced to ¼ cup. Place 1 chicken breast half on each of 4 plates. Spoon 1 tablespoon sauce over each chicken breast. Serve with squash. Yield: 4 servings (serving size: 1 chicken breast half, 1 cup squash, and 1 tablespoon sauce).

CALORIES 370; FAT 7.9g (sat 1.7g, mono 4g, poly 1.4g); PROTEIN 40.1g; CARB 36.5g; FIBER 6.1g; CHOL 102mg; IRON 3mg; SODIUM 539mg; CALC 164mg

make it faster

Peeling and cubing a butternut squash isn't difficult, but it will require a few extra minutes of your time. To prepare this recipe even quicker, look for precubed butternut squash in the produce section of your supermarket. It may cost a little extra, but the trade-off is time saved in prepping this meal.

Roasted Chicken with Shallots, Grapes, and Thyme

Prep: 4 minutes • Cook: 33 minutes

Savor this beautiful browned chicken dish that boasts sweet red grapes roasted to coax out their sweetness.

2   teaspoons olive oil, divided
4   (8-ounce) skinless, bone-in chicken leg quarters
½   teaspoon freshly ground black pepper
¼   teaspoon salt
2   cups seedless red grapes
1   tablespoon thyme leaves
4   large shallots, peeled and quartered
Thyme sprigs (optional)

1. Preheat oven to 425°.
2. Heat a 12-inch cast-iron skillet or other ovenproof skillet over medium-high heat. Add 1 teaspoon oil; swirl to coat. Sprinkle chicken with pepper and salt. Add chicken to pan; cook 4 minutes on each side or until browned. Remove pan from heat.
3. While chicken cooks, combine remaining 1 teaspoon oil, grapes, thyme, and shallots. Spoon grape mixture around chicken in pan. Bake, uncovered, at 425° for 22 to 25 minutes or until chicken is done.
4. Place 1 chicken quarter on each of 4 plates. Spoon shallot mixture evenly over chicken. Garnish with thyme sprigs, if desired. Yield: 4 servings (serving size: 1 chicken quarter and about ½ cup shallot mixture).

CALORIES 293; FAT 8.7g (sat 2.3g, mono 4.1g, poly 2.2g); PROTEIN 35.4g; CARB 17.5g; FIBER 1.2g; CHOL 136mg; IRON 2.4mg; SODIUM 297mg; CALC 37mg

serve with:
Mushroom–Whole-Grain Rice Pilaf

Prep: 2 minutes • Cook: 5 minutes

1   (8.5-ounce) package microwavable seven-whole-grain rice mixture
1   teaspoon olive oil
1   cup sliced mushrooms
2   garlic cloves, minced
2   tablespoons coarsely chopped pecans, toasted

1. Microwave rice according to package directions.
2. While rice cooks, heat a large nonstick skillet over medium-high heat. Add oil; swirl to coat. Add mushrooms and garlic; sauté 4 minutes or until mushrooms are browned and tender, stirring in pecans during the last minute. Stir in hot rice. Yield: 4 servings (serving size: ½ cup).

CALORIES 139; FAT 5.6g (sat 0.6g, mono 3.2g, poly 1.7g); PROTEIN 4.2g; CARB 21.6g; FIBER 3.9g; CHOL 0mg; IRON 0.2mg; SODIUM 1mg; CALC 6mg

Roasted Chicken with Shallots, Grapes, and Thyme

Chicken Pasta Primavera

Prep: 1 minute • Cook: 9 minutes

Zesty Italian seasoning, brightly colored vegetables, and nutty-flavored Parmigiano-Reggiano cheese perfume this Italian classic.

6	ounces uncooked whole-wheat fusilli (short twisted spaghetti)
¾	pound frozen chicken thigh strips, thawed
1	teaspoon salt-free Italian medley seasoning blend
1	tablespoon olive oil, divided
1	cup refrigerated tricolor bell pepper strips
1	(12-ounce) package fresh-cut vegetable stir-fry with broccoli, carrot, red cabbage, and snow peas
¼	cup dry white wine
⅓	cup (1.3 ounces) grated fresh Parmigiano-Reggiano cheese
½	teaspoon freshly ground black pepper
¼	teaspoon salt
3	tablespoons chopped fresh basil

1. Cook pasta according to package directions, omitting salt and fat; drain.
2. While pasta cooks, sprinkle chicken with Italian seasoning blend. Heat a large non-stick skillet over medium-high heat until hot. Add 2 teaspoons oil; swirl to coat. Add chicken to pan; sauté 4 minutes or until chicken is done and is lightly browned.

3. Remove chicken from pan. Add remaining 1 teaspoon oil to pan. Add bell pepper and vegetable stir-fry. Stir-fry over medium-high heat 3 minutes or just until vegetables are almost tender. Stir in wine. Stir in hot pasta. Add cheese, black pepper, salt, and chicken; toss well. Divide pasta mixture evenly among 4 plates, and sprinkle evenly with basil. Yield: 4 servings (serving size: 1¾ cups pasta mixture and about 1½ teaspoons basil).

CALORIES 385; FAT 14.1g (sat 3.6g, mono 6.8g, poly 3.6g); PROTEIN 23.1g; CARB 40.2g; FIBER 6.3g; CHOL 56mg; IRON 3.4mg; SODIUM 325mg; CALC 98

serve with:
Mâche Salad with Dijon Dressing

Prep: 4 minutes • Cook: 4 minutes

3	tablespoons rice vinegar
1	tablespoon honey
2	teaspoons extra-virgin olive oil
2	teaspoons Dijon mustard
1	(3.5-ounce) package mâche (about 6 cups)
2	tablespoons coarsely chopped walnuts, toasted

1. Combine first 4 ingredients in a large bowl; add mâche, and toss gently to coat. Divide salad evenly among 4 plates; sprinkle evenly with walnuts. Yield: 4 servings (serving size: 1½ cups salad and 1½ teaspoons walnuts).

CALORIES 68; FAT 4.7g (sat 0.6g, mono 2g, poly 2.1g); PROTEIN 1.1g; CARB 6.4g; FIBER 0.8g; CHOL 0mg; IRON 0.6mg; SODIUM 61mg; CALC 28mg

Apricot-Glazed Grilled Chicken Thighs

Prep: 3 minutes • Cook: 16 minutes

Two types of pepper—black and red—ignite these grilled chicken thighs. The apricot glaze is a saucy surprise flavor. Accompany the chicken with grilled summer squash and coleslaw.

3	tablespoons apricot preserves
2	tablespoons red wine vinegar
1½	tablespoons olive oil
1	garlic clove, minced
½	teaspoon salt, divided
8	skinless, boneless chicken thighs (about 1½ pounds)
¼	teaspoon freshly ground black pepper
⅛	teaspoon ground red pepper

Cooking spray

1. Preheat grill to medium-high heat.
2. Combine first 4 ingredients and ¼ teaspoon salt in a small bowl, stirring well.
3. Sprinkle chicken with remaining ¼ teaspoon salt and peppers; coat with cooking spray. Place chicken on grill rack coated with cooking spray. Grill 6 minutes on each side. Brush with half of apricot mixture; grill 2 minutes. Turn chicken over; brush with remaining apricot mixture. Grill 2 minutes or until chicken is done. Yield: 4 servings (serving size: 2 chicken thighs).

CALORIES 289; FAT 12g (sat 2.4g, mono 5.8g, poly 2.2g); PROTEIN 33.6g; CARB 10.1g; FIBER 0.1g; CHOL 141mg; IRON 1.9mg; SODIUM 444mg; CALC 23mg

quick flip

Don't have apricot preserves and red wine vinegar on hand? Try honey and cider vinegar for another delicious flavor.

Braised Chicken with Saffron and Olives

Prep: 1 minute • Cook: 11 minutes

Meaty chicken thighs nestle in flavor and brightness thanks to a colorful medley of bell peppers and deep-red saffron. The chicken simmers in a broth-based stew. And it all comes together quickly—in under 15 minutes.

Braised Chicken with Saffron and Olives

8	thighs skinless, boneless chicken thighs (about 1½ pounds)
Cooking spray	
¾	teaspoon paprika
½	teaspoon freshly ground black pepper
¼	teaspoon salt
2	teaspoons olive oil
2	cups refrigerated prechopped tricolor bell pepper mix
¾	cup fat-free, lower-sodium chicken broth
1	tablespoon thyme leaves
¾	teaspoon saffron threads
3	garlic cloves, minced
⅓	cup halved small green olives
Thyme sprigs or leaves (optional)	

1. Coat chicken with cooking spray. Combine paprika, black pepper, and salt; sprinkle evenly over chicken.
2. Heat a large nonstick skillet over medium-high heat. Add oil; swirl to coat. Add chicken; cook 3 minutes on each side or until lightly browned. Remove from pan; keep warm.
3. Add bell pepper to pan. Stir in broth and next 3 ingredients, scraping pan to loosen browned bits. Return chicken to pan. Cover, reduce heat to medium, and cook 3 minutes or just until chicken is done and sauce is slightly thick. Stir in olives; cook 1 minute. Garnish with thyme sprigs, if desired. Yield: 4 servings (serving size: 2 chicken thighs and ⅓ cup vegetable mixture).

CALORIES 309; FAT 16.5g (sat 4.2g, mono 8.2g, poly 4g); PROTEIN 32.6g; CARB 5g; FIBER 1g; CHOL 113mg; IRON 2.3mg; SODIUM 543mg; CALC 22mg

serve with:
Sugared Almond Basmati Rice

Prep: 1 minute • Cook: 6 minutes

1	tablespoon light butter
2	tablespoons brown sugar
2	tablespoons sliced almonds
1	(8.8-ounce) package microwavable precooked basmati rice
⅛	teaspoon salt
1	teaspoon grated lemon rind

1. Melt butter in a medium nonstick skillet over medium heat. Add brown sugar and almonds; cook 3 minutes or until almonds are lightly browned, stirring often.
2. While almonds cook, microwave rice according to package directions.
3. Stir salt into almond mixture. Stir in rice and lemon rind. Cook 1 minute or until thoroughly heated. Yield: 4 servings (serving size: about ½ cup).

CALORIES 163; FAT 4.7g (sat 1.2g, mono 2.2g, poly 1.1g); PROTEIN 3.6g; CARB 28g; FIBER 0.9g; CHOL 4mg; IRON 1.1mg; SODIUM 97mg; CALC 27mg

Chicken Thighs with Chipotle-Peach Sauce

Prep: 3 minutes • Cook: 12 minutes

While the chicken and vegetables grill, prepare the chipotle-peach sauce.

8   thighs skinless, boneless chicken thighs (about 1½ pounds)
½   teaspoon salt, divided
½   teaspoon freshly ground black pepper
Olive oil–flavored cooking spray
2   medium peaches, peeled, pitted, and quartered
2   tablespoons honey
1   chipotle chile in adobo sauce

1. Preheat grill to medium-high heat.
2. Sprinkle chicken with ¼ teaspoon salt and ½ teaspoon pepper; coat with cooking spray. Place chicken on grill rack coated with cooking spray. Grill 12 minutes or until done, turning chicken once.
3. While chicken cooks, puree peaches, honey, chile, and remaining ¼ teaspoon salt in a food processor. Reserve ¾ cup chipotle-peach sauce to serve with chicken; brush remaining ½ cup sauce over chicken during last 2 minutes of cooking. Yield: 4 servings (serving size: about 2 thighs and 3 tablespoons sauce).

CALORIES 307; FAT 13.2g (sat 3.6g; mono 4.9g; poly 4.3g); PROTEIN 31.1g; CARB 15.1g; FIBER 1.2g; CHOL 112mg; IRON 1.8mg; SODIUM 423mg; CALC 20mg

serve with:
Grilled Corn and Red Pepper Salad

Prep: 7 minutes • Cook: 12 minutes

2   ears corn, shucked
2   red bell peppers, seeded and halved
Olive oil–flavored cooking spray
2   green onions, chopped
2   tablespoons fresh lime juice
¼   teaspoon salt
¼   teaspoon freshly ground black pepper

1. Preheat grill to medium-high heat.
2. Coat corn and bell peppers with cooking spray. Place on grill rack coated with cooking spray. Grill 6 minutes on each side or until slightly charred.
3. Cut corn from cob; cut bell pepper into strips. Place in a bowl with green onions and remaining ingredients. Toss well. Yield: 4 servings (serving size: about ⅔ cup).

CALORIES 57; FAT 0.9g (sat 0.1g; mono 0.1g; poly 0.3g); PROTEIN 2.1g; CARB 12.7g; FIBER 2.8g; CHOL 0mg; IRON 0.6mg; SODIUM 155mg; CALC 13mg

Chicken Thighs with Chipotle-Peach Sauce

Moroccan-Spiced Chicken Thighs

Prep: 8 minutes • Cook: 15 minutes

Chicken thighs cooked in a smoky, acidic tomato sauce combine seamlessly with a sweet, nutty couscous to create a hearty North African–inspired meal. While the chicken simmers, prepare the couscous so both dishes will be ready at the same time.

¼ teaspoon salt
½ teaspoon smoked paprika
½ teaspoon ground cumin
½ teaspoon dried thyme
8 skinless, boneless chicken thighs (about 1½ pounds)
Cooking spray
1 (14.5-ounce) can fire-roasted diced tomatoes with garlic, undrained
Chopped fresh cilantro (optional)

1. Combine first 4 ingredients. Rub chicken thighs with spice mixture.
2. Heat a large nonstick skillet over medium-high heat. Coat pan with cooking spray. Add chicken; cook 2 minutes. Turn chicken over; stir in tomatoes. Bring to a boil; cover, reduce heat, and simmer 10 minutes. Uncover and cook 1 minute or until liquid is reduced by half. Sprinkle with cilantro, if desired. Yield: 4 servings (serving size: 2 chicken thighs and ¼ cup tomato sauce).

CALORIES 273; FAT 12.9g (sat 3.6g, mono 4.9g, poly 3.6g); PROTEIN 31.4g; CARB 5.4g; FIBER 1.2g; CHOL 112mg; IRON 3mg; SODIUM 479mg; CALC 42mg

Moroccan-Spiced Chicken Thighs

serve with:
Whole-Wheat Couscous and Apricots

Prep: 5 minutes • Cook: 5 minutes
Other: 5 minutes

2 teaspoons olive oil
¾ cup whole-wheat couscous
1 cup fat-free, lower-sodium chicken broth
⅓ cup diced dried apricots
⅓ cup slivered almonds, toasted

1. Heat a medium saucepan over medium heat. Add oil; swirl to coat. Add couscous; sauté 1 minute. Stir in broth and apricots. Bring to a boil; remove from heat. Let stand 5 minutes or until liquid is absorbed. Add almonds; fluff with a fork. Yield: 4 servings (serving size: about ⅔ cup).

CALORIES 196; FAT 7.6g (sat 0.8g, mono 4.7g, poly 1.4g); PROTEIN 6.6g; CARB 27.7g; FIBER 4.4g; CHOL 0mg; IRON 1.7mg; SODIUM 19mg; CALC 39mg

Chicken Thighs with Orange-Ginger Glaze

Prep: 1 minute • Cook: 14 minutes

Honey—combined with fresh ginger, orange rind, and orange juice—is all that's needed to create this spicy-sweet glaze. Round out your meal with white rice.

8	skinless, boneless chicken thighs (about 1½ pounds)
½	teaspoon salt
¼	teaspoon freshly ground black pepper
⅛	teaspoon garlic powder
1½	teaspoons olive oil
1	navel orange
3	tablespoons honey
1	teaspoon grated peeled fresh ginger

Chopped green onions (optional)

1. Sprinkle chicken with salt, pepper, and garlic powder. Heat a large nonstick skillet over medium-high heat. Add oil; swirl to coat. Add chicken; cook 3 to 4 minutes on each side or until browned.
2. While chicken cooks, grate rind and squeeze juice from orange to measure 1 teaspoon and ¼ cup, respectively. Add orange rind, juice, honey, and ginger to chicken, scraping to loosen browned bits. Bring to a boil; reduce heat, and simmer, uncovered, 7 minutes or until chicken is done and orange mixture is syrupy. Sprinkle with green onions, if desired. Yield: 4 servings (serving size: 2 chicken thighs and about 1½ tablespoons sauce).

CALORIES 327; FAT 14.5g (sat 3.8g, mono 6.4g, poly 3.6g); PROTEIN 30.9g; CARB 17.7g; FIBER 0.9g; CHOL 112mg; IRON 1.7mg; SODIUM 395mg; CALC 31mg

serve with:
Roasted Broccoli with Almonds

Prep: 6 minutes • Cook: 14 minutes

1¼	pounds fresh broccoli crowns (about 3)

Cooking spray
1	tablespoon olive oil
1	garlic clove, pressed
¼	teaspoon salt
¼	teaspoon freshly ground black pepper
3	tablespoons sliced almonds

1. Preheat oven to 475°.
2. Cut broccoli into 3-inch-long spears; cut thick stems in half lengthwise. Place broccoli in a single layer on a jelly-roll pan coated with cooking spray.
3. Combine olive oil and garlic; drizzle broccoli with oil mixture, and toss well. Sprinkle with salt and pepper. Bake at 475° for 14 minutes (do not stir).
4. While broccoli roasts, cook almonds, stirring constantly, in a small skillet over medium heat 2 minutes or until toasted. Sprinkle roasted broccoli with toasted almonds. Yield: 4 servings (serving size: about 1 cup).

CALORIES 97; FAT 6.1g (sat 0.7g, mono 3.9g, poly 1.1g); PROTEIN 5.2g; CARB 8.6g; FIBER 4.8g; CHOL 0mg; IRON 1.5mg; SODIUM 184mg; CALC 81mg

Five-Spice Grilled Chicken Thighs with Blackberry Glaze

Prep: 7 minutes • Cook: 12 minutes

Rev up simple grilled chicken thighs with aromatic Chinese five-spice powder—a blend of cinnamon, cloves, fennel seed, star anise, and Szechuan peppercorns. The glaze thickens as it cools; simply reheat it in the microwave for 10 seconds for the right consistency.

1	tablespoon five-spice powder
½	teaspoon salt
¼	teaspoon freshly ground black pepper
8	skinless, boneless chicken thighs (about 1½ pounds)

Cooking spray

¾	cup sugar-free seedless blackberry jam
3	tablespoons cider vinegar
1	tablespoon water
¾	teaspoon grated peeled fresh ginger

Fresh blackberries (optional)

1. Preheat grill to medium-high heat.
2. Combine first 3 ingredients in a small bowl. Sprinkle spice mixture evenly over chicken. Place chicken on grill rack coated with cooking spray; cook chicken 6 minutes on each side or until done.
3. While chicken grills, combine jam and next 3 ingredients in a nonstick skillet. Simmer over medium-low heat 8 minutes or until glaze is reduced to ½ cup. Drizzle glaze evenly over chicken; garnish with blackberries, if desired. Serve immediately. Yield: 4 servings (serving size: 2 chicken thighs and 2 tablespoons glaze).

CALORIES 285; FAT 13g (sat 3.6g, mono 4.9g, poly 2.9g); PROTEIN 30.6g; CARB 17.3g; FIBER 0g; CHOL 112mg; IRON 2.7mg; SODIUM 395mg; CALC 32mg

Five-Spice Grilled Chicken Thighs with Blackberry Glaze

serve with:
Yellow Rice with Spring Peas

Prep: 3 minutes • Cook: 18 minutes

Cooking spray

½	cup chopped onion
1	(3½-ounce) bag boil-in-bag long-grain rice
½	teaspoon ground turmeric
¾	cup fat-free, lower-sodium chicken broth
½	cup water
⅛	teaspoon salt
½	cup frozen petite green peas

1. Heat a large nonstick skillet over medium-high heat. Coat pan with cooking spray. Add onion to pan; sauté 4 minutes or until tender. Cut open rice bag; pour rice into pan. Add turmeric; sauté 2 minutes. Add broth, ½ cup water, and salt; bring to a boil. Cover, reduce heat, and simmer 12 minutes or until rice is tender and liquid is absorbed. Stir in peas. Yield: 4 servings (serving size: ½ cup).

CALORIES 54 (1% from fat); FAT 0g (sat 0g, mono 0g, poly 0g); PROTEIN 2.2g; CARB 10.9g; FIBER 1.3g; CHOL 0mg; IRON 0.6mg; SODIUM 219mg; CALC 5mg

Smothered Green Chile Pepper Chicken

Prep: 4 minutes • Cook: 35 minutes

Whole green chiles hug the chicken thighs and impart a mild, roasted flavor to both the meat and broth. The chiles used in this recipe come three per 4-ounce can.

8	skinless, boneless chicken thighs (about 1½ pounds)
1	tablespoon fresh lime juice (about ½ lime)
3	tablespoons reduced-sodium taco seasoning
8	canned whole green chiles, drained
½	cup (2 ounces) shredded part-skim mozzarella cheese

1. Preheat oven to 400°.
2. Arrange chicken in an 8-inch square baking dish; pour lime juice evenly over chicken. Sprinkle evenly with taco seasoning.
3. Slice chiles lengthwise, cutting to, but not through, other side; open flat. Place 1 chile over each chicken thigh. Cover dish with foil; bake at 400° for 30 minutes. Sprinkle cheese evenly over chiles and chicken; bake, uncovered, an additional 5 minutes or until cheese melts. Yield: 4 servings (serving size: 2 chicken thighs and 3 tablespoons broth).

CALORIES 301; FAT 15g (sat 5g, mono 5.5g, poly 3g); PROTEIN 34.1g; CARB 4.7g; FIBER 0.5g; CHOL 120mg; IRON 2mg; SODIUM 574mg; CALC 116mg

serve with:
Corn-Filled Mini-Muffins

Prep: 7 minutes • Cook: 13 minutes
Other: 2 minutes

1	(6.5-ounce) package corn muffin mix
⅓	cup fat-free milk
2	tablespoons canola oil
2	egg whites
1	cup frozen shoepeg white corn
Butter-flavored cooking spray	

1. Preheat oven to 400°.
2. Combine all ingredients except cooking spray in a medium bowl; stir just until combined. Spoon batter evenly into 24 miniature muffin cups coated with cooking spray. Bake at 400° for 11 minutes. Spray tops of muffins with cooking spray; bake an additional 2 minutes. Remove from oven; let stand in pan 2 minutes. Yield: 12 servings (serving size: 2 muffins).

CALORIES 102; FAT 4g (sat 0.6g, mono 2g, poly 0.8g); PROTEIN 2.2g; CARB 13.8g; FIBER 0.6g; CHOL 4mg; IRON 0.4mg; SODIUM 147mg; CALC 29mg

Smothered Green Chile Pepper Chicken

Sweet Mustard Chicken Thighs

Prep: 3 minutes • Cook: 6 minutes

These Carolina-style barbecue chicken thighs are smothered with a tangy-sweet sauce that will please the whole family.

½   cup prepared mustard
⅓   cup packed dark brown sugar
1   teaspoon ground allspice
¼   teaspoon crushed red pepper
8   skinless, boneless chicken thighs (about 1½ pounds)
Cooking spray

1. Preheat grill to medium-high heat.
2. Combine first 4 ingredients in a small bowl, stirring well. Reserve and set aside ¼ cup sauce mixture.
3. Place chicken on grill rack coated with cooking spray. Brush half of remaining ½ cup sauce mixture over one side of chicken. Grill chicken 3 to 4 minutes. Turn chicken over; brush with remaining half of sauce mixture. Cook 3 to 4 minutes or until done. Place chicken on a serving platter; drizzle with reserved ¼ cup sauce mixture. Yield: 4 servings (serving size: 2 chicken thighs and 1 tablespoon sauce).

CALORIES 317; FAT 13g (sat 3.6g, mono 4.9g, poly 2.9g); PROTEIN 30.5g; CARB 18.3g; FIBER 0.3g; CHOL 112mg; IRON 1.9mg; SODIUM 471mg; CALC 34mg

serve with:

Warm Balsamic Potato Salad

Prep: 5 minutes • Cook: 7 minutes

1   pound mixed baby potatoes (such as fingerling, purple, and red), cut into wedges
1   tablespoon water
¼   cup light balsamic vinaigrette
½   cup chopped bottled roasted red bell pepper
2   tablespoons chopped fresh basil
¼   cup (1 ounce) crumbled goat cheese

1. Place potato wedges in a large microwave-safe bowl; add 1 tablespoon water. Cover with plastic wrap; vent (do not allow plastic wrap to touch food). Microwave at HIGH 7 minutes or until tender; drain.
2. Stir in vinaigrette, bell pepper, and basil. Top each serving with cheese. Yield: 4 servings (serving size: about ¾ cup potatoes and 1 tablespoon cheese).

CALORIES 131; FAT 4g (sat 1.8g, mono 0.5g, poly 0.1g); PROTEIN 3.7g; CARB 19.9g; FIBER 2g; CHOL 6mg; IRON 1mg; SODIUM 329mg; CALC 35mg

Chicken Under a Brick

Prep: 5 minutes • Cook: 40 minutes
Other: 8 hours

The weight of the bricks helps the chicken cook evenly, leaving the breast moist and juicy, while the legs cook fully. Marinating the chicken tenderizes the meat and also adds a pleasant tangy flavor.

1   (3¼-pound) whole chicken
½   cup light mayonnaise
⅓   cup cider vinegar
¼   cup water
2   tablespoons sugar
1   tablespoon chopped fresh rosemary
Cooking spray

1. Remove backbone from chicken using kitchen shears. Combine mayonnaise and next 4 ingredients in a large heavy-duty zip-top plastic bag; add chicken. Seal and turn to coat. Marinate in refrigerator 8 hours, turning bag occasionally.
2. Remove chicken from marinade, and discard marinade. Heat a large cast-iron skillet over medium-high heat. Coat pan with cooking spray. Add chicken to pan. Place 2 bricks wrapped in heavy-duty foil over chicken, pressing down to flatten. Cook 20 minutes; turn chicken over. Reposition bricks. Cook an additional 20 minutes or until chicken is done. Remove skin from chicken, and cut into quarters. Carve chicken. Yield: 4 servings (serving size: about 4 ounces).

CALORIES 290; FAT 10.5g (sat 2.1g, mono 4.7g, poly 3.5g); PROTEIN 75g; CARB 4.7g; FIBER 0g; CHOL 253mg; IRON 4mg; SODIUM 397mg; CALC 44mg

serve with:
Summer Succotash

Prep: 5 minutes • Cook: 10 minutes

2   center-cut bacon slices
1   cup frozen baby lima beans
2   ears corn
1   large garlic clove, minced
1   cup grape tomatoes, halved
¼   teaspoon salt
¼   teaspoon freshly ground black pepper
1   tablespoon chopped fresh basil

1. Cook bacon in a large nonstick skillet over medium-high heat until crisp. Remove bacon from pan, reserving drippings in pan; crumble bacon, and set aside.
2. While bacon cooks, thaw lima beans in a colander under warm water.
3. Cut kernels from ears of corn. Add corn and garlic to drippings. Sauté 4 minutes or until corn is golden. Stir in lima beans, tomato halves, salt, and pepper. Sauté 3 minutes or until thoroughly heated. Stir in bacon and basil just before serving. Yield: 4 servings (serving size: about ⅔ cup).

CALORIES 104; FAT 1.3g (sat 0.4g, mono 0.4g, poly 0.3g); PROTEIN 5.8g; CARB 19.2g; FIBER 4.5g; CHOL 3mg; IRON 1.2mg; SODIUM 210mg; CALC 23mg

fix it faster

Thawed frozen corn can work in a pinch if fresh corn isn't in season.

Spinach-Chicken Burgers

Prep: 5 minutes • Cook: 6 minutes

Sun-dried tomatoes pack flavor into this aioli-topped chicken burger. Just a couple tablespoons of oats in the patty keep the burger juicy.

1	pound ground chicken breast
⅓	cup frozen chopped spinach, thawed, drained, and squeezed dry
2	tablespoons old-fashioned rolled oats
¼	teaspoon salt
¼	teaspoon freshly ground black pepper

Cooking spray

4	Bibb lettuce leaves (optional)
4	(1.5-ounce) 100% whole-wheat hamburger buns

Sun-Dried Tomato Aioli

1. Combine first 5 ingredients. Divide chicken mixture into 4 equal portions, shaping each into a ½-inch-thick patty.
2. Heat a large nonstick skillet over medium-high heat; coat pan with cooking spray. Add patties; cook 3 minutes on each side or until thermometer registers 165°.

3. Place 1 lettuce leaf on bottom half of each bun, if using. Place 1 burger on bottom half of each bun. Spread 2½ tablespoons Sun-Dried Tomato Aioli on inside of each bun top; place tops on burgers. Yield: 4 servings (serving size: 1 burger).

CALORIES 374; FAT 18.2g (sat 1.8g, mono 9g, poly 5.1g); PROTEIN 29.1g; CARB 25.8g; FIBER 4.2g; CHOL 72mg; IRON 1.6mg; SODIUM 654mg; CALC 67mg

Sun-Dried Tomato Aioli

Prep: 3 minutes

1	garlic clove
⅓	cup canola mayonnaise
3	tablespoons drained oil-packed sun-dried tomatoes
1	tablespoon fresh lemon juice
⅛	teaspoon salt

1. Drop garlic through food chute with food processor on; process until minced. Add remaining ingredients; process until smooth. Yield: 4 servings (serving size: 2½ tablespoons).

CALORIES 146; FAT 15.4g (sat 1.4g, mono 8.5g, poly 4.1g); PROTEIN 0.3g; CARB 1.8g; FIBER 0.3g; CHOL 7mg; IRON 0.2mg; SODIUM 220mg; CALC 4mg

Spinach-Chicken Burgers

Pomegranate-Glazed Duck Breast

Prep: 2 minutes • Cook: 11 minutes

Duck, with its dark, succulent flesh, calls for a bold-flavored sauce, and this pomegranate molasses fills the bill. It's a thick syrup made by reducing pomegranate juice and imparts a rich depth of flavor to meats. Look for it on the ethnic foods aisle of your supermarket or in specialty markets.

4   (6-ounce) boneless duck breast halves, skinned
¼   teaspoon salt
2   tablespoons sliced almonds
Cooking spray
¼   cup water
2   tablespoons pomegranate molasses
1   tablespoon honey
½   teaspoon ground cinnamon
Pomegranate seeds (optional)

1. Sprinkle duck evenly with salt. Heat a large nonstick skillet over medium-high heat. Add almonds; cook, stirring constantly, 2 minutes or until toasted. Remove almonds from pan. Coat pan with cooking spray. Add duck; cook 4 minutes on each side or until desired degree of doneness. Remove from pan, and keep warm.
2. Stir in ¼ cup water and next 3 ingredients, scraping pan to loosen browned bits. Cook, stirring constantly, 1 minute or until slightly thick. Remove pan from heat.
3. Add duck and almonds to sauce, turning to coat. Cut duck across grain into thin slices. Drizzle with sauce; sprinkle with pomegranate seeds, if desired. Yield: 4 servings (serving size: 1 duck breast and about 1 tablespoon sauce).

CALORIES 312; FAT 9.5g (sat 3.2g, mono 4.4g, poly 1.8g); PROTEIN 34.7g; CARB 19g; FIBER 0.7g; CHOL 131mg; IRON 9.1mg; SODIUM 243mg; CALC 50mg

serve with:

Red Onion and Orange Salad

Prep: 4 minutes

1   tablespoon chopped fresh mint
1   tablespoon extra-virgin olive oil
¼   teaspoon salt
1   cup vertically sliced red onion
2   navel oranges, cut crosswise into thin slices
½   cup (2 ounces) crumbled goat cheese

1. Combine first 3 ingredients in a medium bowl. Add onion and orange slices, turning orange slices in dressing to coat. Divide salad among 4 plates; sprinkle evenly with cheese. Yield: 4 servings (serving size: ¾ cup salad and 2 tablespoons cheese).

CALORIES 109; FAT 6.6g (sat 2.6g, mono 3.2g, poly 0.6g); PROTEIN 3.5g; CARB 10.4g; FIBER 1.8g; CHOL 7mg; IRON 0.4mg; SODIUM 200mg; CALC 53mg

quick flip

For a little more tang in the salad, try substituting feta for the goat cheese. This white crumbly Greek cheese adds plenty of zip to appetizers, salads, and sides.

Seared Turkey Cutlets with Cranberry–Caramelized Onion Salsa

Prep: 2 minutes • Cook: 12 minutes

Don't reserve turkey and cranberries just for the holidays. This meal uses dried cranberries, which you can find year-round. Serve with a buttered baked sweet potato.

2	teaspoons olive oil
8	ounces turkey cutlets (about 4 cutlets)
3/8	teaspoon salt, divided
1/4	teaspoon freshly ground black pepper, divided
1	cup prechopped onion
1/4	cup water
3	tablespoons sweetened dried cranberries, chopped
2	tablespoons white balsamic vinegar

Chopped fresh parsley (optional)

1. Heat a large nonstick skillet over medium-high heat. Add oil; swirl to coat. Sprinkle turkey with 1/8 teaspoon salt and 1/8 teaspoon pepper. Add turkey to pan; cook 2 minutes on each side or until done. Divide turkey between 2 plates; keep warm.
2. Add onion to pan. Cook 3 minutes, stirring frequently; add remaining 1/4 teaspoon salt and remaining 1/8 teaspoon pepper. Cook 5 minutes or until onion is tender and golden, stirring frequently. Stir in water, cranberries, and vinegar; cook 2 minutes or until cranberries are tender. Remove from heat; stir in parsley, if desired. Yield: 2 servings (serving size: 2 turkey cutlets and about 1/2 cup salsa).

CALORIES 249; FAT 7.4g (sat 1.4g, mono 4.2g, poly 1.6g); PROTEIN 23.8g; CARB 22g; FIBER 2.1g; CHOL 63mg; IRON 1mg; SODIUM 494mg; CALC 32mg

serve with:
Roasted Brussels Sprouts à l'Orange

Prep: 3 minutes • Cook: 14 minutes

2½	cups trimmed Brussels sprouts (about 8 ounces), halved lengthwise
2	teaspoons olive oil
1/4	teaspoon salt
1/8	teaspoon freshly ground black pepper
1/2	teaspoon grated orange rind
2	tablespoons fresh orange juice

1. Preheat oven to 425°.
2. Place Brussels sprouts in a large bowl. Add oil, salt, and pepper; toss to coat. Place Brussels sprouts in a single layer on a foil-lined baking sheet. Roast at 425° for 7 minutes. Turn Brussels sprouts over, using a wide spatula. Bake an additional 7 minutes or until tender and browned.
3. Place Brussels sprouts in a bowl. Combine orange rind and juice in a small bowl. Drizzle juice mixture over Brussels sprouts; toss well. Yield: 2 servings (serving size: 1⅓ cups).

CALORIES 96; FAT 4.9g (sat 0.7g, mono 3.3g, poly 0.7g); PROTEIN 4g; CARB 12g; FIBER 4.4g; CHOL 0mg; IRON 1.7mg; SODIUM 319mg; CALC 51mg

Orange-Glazed Turkey with Cranberry Rice

Prep: 8 minutes • Cook: 7 minutes

Orange-scented dried cranberries stud quick-cooking rice that accompanies pan-fried turkey cutlets and broccoli.

1	(8.8-ounce) package microwavable precooked brown rice
½	cup orange-flavored dried sweetened cranberries
2	tablespoons chopped pecans, toasted
⅛	teaspoon salt
1½	pounds turkey cutlets (about 12 cutlets)
¼	teaspoon salt, divided
	Butter-flavored cooking spray
⅓	cup low-sugar orange marmalade

1. Prepare rice in microwave according to package directions. Place cranberries in a medium bowl. Pour hot rice over cranberries; let stand 1 minute. Stir pecans and ⅛ teaspoon salt into rice mixture; cover and keep warm.

2. Sprinkle turkey cutlets evenly with ⅛ teaspoon salt. Heat a large nonstick skillet over medium-high heat. Coat pan with cooking spray.

3. Add cutlets to pan, salted sides down. Cook 1 minute; coat cutlets with cooking spray, and sprinkle with remaining ⅛ teaspoon salt. Turn cutlets; cook 1 minute. Transfer turkey to a platter. Turn off heat; add marmalade to hot pan, and stir 30 seconds. Return turkey and accumulated juices to pan, turning to coat cutlets.

4. Spoon rice mixture onto 4 plates. Top rice mixture with turkey cutlets; spoon sauce over cutlets. Yield: 4 servings (serving size: about ½ cup rice, about 3 cutlets, and ½ tablespoon sauce).

CALORIES 357; FAT 3.9g (sat 0.5g, mono 1.9g, poly 1.1g); PROTEIN 44.2g; CARB 35.2g; FIBER 2.0g; CHOL 68mg; IRON 2.3mg; SODIUM 370mg; CALC 12mg

Orange-Glazed Turkey with Cranberry Rice

quick flip

Skinless, boneless turkey cutlets, also known as turkey scaloppini, are ideal for this recipe. However, chicken cutlets or veal cutlets make a great substitution, too. Any of these three ingredients are perfect for sautéed dishes. Flip it for your convenience or personal taste.

Sage Turkey Meat Loaves with Onion and Cider Gravy

Prep: 10 minutes • Cook: 25 minutes

Cooking meat loaf in single-serving portions cuts the cooking time in half and keeps the ground turkey moist. Be sure to gently shape the turkey mixture into loaves—overworking the mixture will make them tough. For a hearty meal, serve with green beans and mashed potatoes.

1½	pounds ground turkey
1	cup shredded peeled apple (about 1 medium)
½	cup dry breadcrumbs
2	tablespoons minced fresh sage
½	teaspoon salt
½	teaspoon freshly ground black pepper
Cooking spray	
Onion and Cider Gravy	

1. Preheat oven to 425°.
2. Combine first 6 ingredients in a large bowl. Divide turkey mixture into 6 equal portions, shaping each into an oval-shaped loaf. Place loaves on a broiler pan coated with cooking spray. Bake at 425° for 25 minutes or until a thermometer inserted in center registers 165°.
3. While meat loaves bake, prepare Onion and Cider Gravy. Serve meat loaves with gravy. Yield: 6 servings (serving size: 1 meat loaf and about ¼ cup gravy).

CALORIES 283; FAT 11.9g (sat 3.9g, mono 4g, poly 3.4g); PROTEIN 22.5g; CARB 21g; FIBER 1.2g; CHOL 95mg; IRON 1.6mg; SODIUM 567mg; CALC 33mg

Onion and Cider Gravy

Prep: 3 minutes • Cook: 34 minutes

1	tablespoon butter
1	large Vidalia or other sweet onion, vertically sliced
1	cup apple cider
1	cup fat-free, lower-sodium chicken broth
1	tablespoon cornstarch
1	tablespoon water
¼	teaspoon salt

1. Melt butter in a large nonstick skillet over medium-high heat; add onion. Cook 10 minutes or until golden brown, stirring frequently.
2. While onion cooks, bring cider and broth to a boil in a medium saucepan; boil 23 minutes or until reduced to 1 cup. Combine cornstarch, water, and salt; add to reduced cider mixture, stirring constantly with a whisk. Cook over medium heat 1 minute or until slightly thickened. Stir in onion. Yield: 4 servings (serving size: about ¼ cup).

CALORIES 64; FAT 1.9g (sat 1.2g, mono 0.5g, poly 0.1g); PROTEIN 0.8g; CARB 11.2g; FIBER 0.5g; CHOL 5mg; IRON 0.2mg; SODIUM 190mg; CALC 12mg

Sage Turkey Meat Loaves with Onion and Cider Gravy

Turkey-Basil Rolls

Prep: 10 minutes • Cook: 5 minutes

Thai seasoning blend is packed with flavor, but isn't spicy. Look for it in the Asian section of your supermarket. Prepare the filling ahead, if desired, but assemble the rolls just before serving.

Cooking spray
¾   pound ground turkey
½   teaspoon salt-free Thai seasoning blend
¼   teaspoon freshly ground black pepper
⅛   teaspoon salt
¾   cup cabbage-and-carrot coleslaw
6   (8-inch) round sheets rice paper
12   basil leaves
6   tablespoons light sesame-ginger dressing

1. Heat a large nonstick skillet over medium-high heat. Coat with cooking spray. Add turkey and next 3 ingredients; cook 5 minutes or until done. Combine turkey mixture and coleslaw in a medium bowl.
2. Add hot water to a large, shallow dish to a depth of 1 inch. Place 1 rice paper sheet in dish; let stand 30 seconds or just until soft. Place sheet on a flat surface. Arrange 2 basil leaves on top third of sheet. Arrange ⅓ cup turkey mixture on bottom third of sheet. Folding sides of sheet over filling and starting with filled side, roll up jelly-roll fashion. Gently press seam to seal. Place roll, seam side down, on a serving platter (cover to keep from drying).
3. Repeat procedure with remaining sheets, basil, and turkey mixture. Slice each roll in half diagonally. Serve rolls with dressing as a dipping sauce. Yield: 3 servings (serving size: 2 rolls and 2 tablespoons dipping sauce).

CALORIES 263; FAT 9g (sat 2g, mono 4.5g, poly 2.3g); PROTEIN 24.5g; CARB 20.8g; FIBER 0.4g; CHOL 65mg; IRON 2.3mg; SODIUM 589mg; CALC 9mg

serve with:
Mandarin Oranges with Grand Marnier and Mascarpone

Prep: 8 minutes

¼   cup reduced-fat sour cream
2   tablespoons mascarpone cheese
4   teaspoons sugar
1   (15-ounce) can mandarin oranges in light syrup, drained
1½   tablespoons Grand Marnier (orange-flavored liqueur)
Mint leaves (optional)

1. Combine first 3 ingredients in a small bowl, stirring with a whisk until sugar dissolves.
2. Combine oranges and liqueur; spoon evenly into 3 wineglasses or dessert dishes. Spoon sour cream mixture over oranges; garnish with mint leaves, if desired. Yield: 3 servings (serving size: about 2½ tablespoons oranges and 1 tablespoon sour cream topping).

CALORIES 200; FAT 11g (sat 6.2g, mono 0g, poly 0g); PROTEIN 3g; CARB 19.9g; FIBER 0.8g; CHOL 34mg; IRON 0.3mg; SODIUM 28mg; CALC 72mg

Smoked Sausage and Corn Frittata

Prep: 3 minutes • Cook: 16 minutes
Other: 2 minutes

Browning intensifies the smokiness of the sausage, allowing you to use less sausage while achieving maximum results in this simple-to-prepare frittata.

Cooking spray
4	ounces smoked turkey sausage, quartered lengthwise and diced
1½	cups frozen shoepeg white corn, thawed
¼	teaspoon ground red pepper (optional)
1	large egg
4	large egg whites
½	cup (2 ounces) reduced-fat shredded sharp cheddar cheese
3	tablespoons chopped fresh cilantro, divided

1. Heat a medium nonstick skillet over medium-high heat. Coat pan with cooking spray. Add sausage; sauté 4 minutes or until browned. Stir in corn and, if desired, red pepper; reduce heat to medium-low.
2. Combine egg and egg whites in a small bowl; stir with a whisk. Drizzle evenly over sausage mixture. Cover and cook 8 minutes or until almost set. Remove pan from heat; sprinkle evenly with cheese and 1½ tablespoons cilantro. Cover and let stand 2 minutes. Sprinkle with remaining 1½ tablespoons cilantro. Cut into 4 wedges. Yield: 4 servings (serving size: 1 wedge).

CALORIES 174; FAT 6g (sat 2.9g, mono 0.5g, poly 0.2g); PROTEIN 13.8g; CARB 14.5g; FIBER 1.6g; CHOL 76mg; IRON 0.6mg; SODIUM 472mg; CALC 121mg

Smoked Sausage and Corn Frittata

serve with:
Sweet Lemon-Splashed Melon

Prep: 3 minutes

1	tablespoon sugar
½	teaspoon grated lemon rind
1	tablespoon fresh lemon juice
3	cups cubed peeled cantaloupe

1. Combine all ingredients in a medium bowl; toss gently to coat. Yield: 4 servings (serving size: ¾ cup).

CALORIES 54; FAT 0g (sat 0.1g, mono 0g, poly 0.1g); PROTEIN 1g; CARB 13.3g; FIBER 0g; CHOL 0mg; IRON 0.3mg; SODIUM 19mg; CALC 11mg

Smoked Sausage-and-Vegetable Pile-Up

Prep: 4 minutes • Cook: 11 minutes

Popular fast-food "all-in-one" bowls are loaded with fat and sodium. Our quick alternative is much healthier.

Cooking spray
7   ounces smoked turkey sausage, diagonally sliced
1   cup refrigerated prechopped onion
1   cup refrigerated prechopped tricolor bell pepper mix
1   cup refrigerated presliced zucchini
1   (20-ounce) package refrigerated garlic mashed potatoes
2   cups frozen whole-kernel corn

1. Heat a large nonstick skillet over medium-high heat. Coat pan with cooking spray. Add sausage; sauté 2 minutes or until browned. Remove from skillet; keep warm.
2. Return pan to heat; coat with cooking spray. Add onion, bell pepper, and zucchini. Coat vegetables with cooking spray; sauté 5 minutes or until tender and beginning to brown.
3. While vegetables cook, heat potatoes according to package directions.
4. Add corn and cooked sausage to onion mixture. Sauté 4 minutes or until thoroughly heated. Serve sausage mixture over mashed potatoes. Yield: 4 servings (serving size: 1 cup sausage and vegetables and ½ cup mashed potatoes).

CALORIES 306; FAT 9g (sat 4.6g, mono 1.1g, poly 3.3g); PROTEIN 12.9g; CARB 46.2g; FIBER 6g; CHOL 37mg; IRON 1.8mg; SODIUM 434mg; CALC 77mg

meats

Slow-Cooker Beef
Pot Roast, page 442

Pub Burgers

Prep: 5 minutes • Cook: 10 minutes

A slathering of blue cheese spread dotted with bits of crisp bacon sends this burger right over the top.

1   pound ground sirloin
¼   teaspoon salt
¼   teaspoon freshly ground black pepper
Cooking spray
4   (¼-inch-thick) slices red onion
Blue Cheese–Bacon Spread
4   (1.8-ounce) white-wheat hamburger buns
4   green leaf lettuce leaves (optional)

1. Preheat grill to high heat.
2. Combine first 3 ingredients in a medium bowl. Divide mixture into 4 equal portions, shaping each into a ½-inch-thick patty. Place burgers on grill rack coated with cooking spray. Grill 5 minutes. Turn patties over. Coat onion slices with cooking spray; place on grill rack. Grill patties and onion 5 minutes or until patties are done, turning onion halfway through cooking time.
3. While patties and onion slices cook, prepare Blue Cheese–Bacon Spread.
4. Spread Blue Cheese–Bacon Spread on cut sides of each bun; top each bun bottom with 1 lettuce leaf, if desired, 1 patty, and 1 onion slice. Cover with bun tops. Yield: 4 servings (serving size: 1 burger).

CALORIES 230; FAT 13.8g (sat 5.7g, mono 4.3g, poly 1.3g); PROTEIN 28.4g; CARB 27.2g; FIBER 4.8g; CHOL 71mg; IRON 4.7mg; SODIUM 570mg; CALC 300mg

Blue Cheese–Bacon Spread

Prep: 4 minutes

¼   cup (2 ounces) tub-style ⅓-less-fat cream cheese
2   tablespoons nonfat buttermilk
2   tablespoons crumbled blue cheese
1   bacon slice, cooked and crumbled
¼   teaspoon freshly ground black pepper

1. Combine first 3 ingredients in a small bowl, stirring until smooth. Stir in bacon and pepper. Yield: 4 servings (serving size: 1½ tablespoons).

CALORIES 58; FAT 4.7g (sat 2.7g, mono 1.3g, poly 0.2g); PROTEIN 2.8g; CARB 1.2g; FIBER 0g; CHOL 16mg; IRON 0mg; SODIUM 136mg; CALC 36mg

Pub Burgers

Dolmathes

Prep: 18 minutes • Cook: 31 minutes

Dolmathes is a traditional Greek dish of meat and rice stuffed in grape leaves and topped with a delicate lemon avgolemono sauce.

Dolmathes

18   bottled large grape leaves
1   pound ground round
1   cup butter-and-garlic–flavored microwavable
      cooked rice
½   teaspoon freshly ground black pepper
¼   teaspoon salt
Cooking spray
1   cup fat-free, lower-sodium chicken broth
2   teaspoons olive oil
Avgolemono Sauce
Chopped fresh mint or parsley (optional)

1. Rinse grape leaves under cold water; drain and pat dry with paper towels. Remove stems, and discard.
2. Combine beef and next 3 ingredients in a medium bowl. Spoon 2 tablespoons beef mixture onto center of each grape leaf. Bring 2 opposite points of leaf to center, and fold over filling. Beginning at 1 short side, roll up leaf tightly, jelly-roll fashion. Repeat procedure with remaining grape leaves.
3. Place stuffed grape leaves close together, seam sides down, in a Dutch oven coated with cooking spray. Add broth and oil; bring to a boil. Cover, reduce heat, and simmer 30 minutes. Using a slotted spoon, transfer to a serving platter, and keep warm until ready to serve.
4. Prepare Avgolemono Sauce. Serve Dolmathes with Avgolemono Sauce, and garnish with chopped mint or parsley, if desired. Yield: 6 servings (serving size: 3 Dolmathes and about 1½ tablespoons sauce).

CALORIES 209; FAT 10.7g (sat 3.9g, mono 5.4g, poly 1.2g); PROTEIN 17.6g; CARB 9.3g; FIBER 1.4g; CHOL 79mg; IRON 2.5mg; SODIUM 407mg; CALC 61mg

Avgolemono Sauce

Prep: 2 minutes • Cook: 4 minutes

1   large egg
1   tablespoon fresh lemon juice
⅓   cup fat-free, lower-sodium chicken broth
1   tablespoon chopped fresh parsley
1   tablespoon chopped fresh mint

1. Place egg and lemon juice in a blender; process until egg is well beaten.
2. Place chicken broth in a 1-cup glass measure; microwave at HIGH 30 seconds or until hot. Remove center piece of blender lid; with blender on, gradually add hot broth to egg mixture. Process until blended.
3. Pour mixture into a small saucepan. Cook over medium-high heat, stirring constantly with a whisk, 2 minutes or until slightly thick (do not boil). Stir in parsley and mint. Yield: 6 servings (serving size: about 1½ tablespoons).

CALORIES 14; FAT 0.7g (sat 0.2g, mono 0.3g, poly 0.1g); PROTEIN 1.1g; CARB 0.6g; FIBER 0.1g; CHOL 30mg; IRON 0.2mg; SODIUM 43mg; CALC 6mg

Shepherd's Pie

Prep: 2 minutes • Cook: 13 minutes

An English meat pie originally devised as a way to use leftover lamb, shepherd's pie just might be the first-ever casserole. This all-in-one meal features beef joined by a medley of veggies and topped with a pillow-soft mountain of mashed potatoes.

¾   pound 93% lean ground beef
1½   cups frozen baby vegetable mix
1   (14.5-ounce) can diced tomatoes with basil, garlic, and oregano, undrained
1   (8-ounce) can no-salt-added tomato sauce
2   cups country-style refrigerated mashed potatoes
Cooking spray
⅛   teaspoon freshly ground black pepper

1. Preheat broiler.
2. Cook beef in a large nonstick skillet over medium-high heat until browned, stirring to crumble. Add vegetable mix, tomatoes, and tomato sauce. Cook 5 minutes or until mixture is slightly thick and thoroughly heated, stirring occasionally.
3. While beef mixture cooks, place potatoes in a microwave-safe bowl. Cover with plastic wrap; vent. Microwave at HIGH 2 minutes or until thoroughly heated.
4. Spoon beef mixture evenly into each of 4 (8-ounce) broiler-safe ramekins coated with cooking spray. Top evenly with potatoes; sprinkle with pepper. Place ramekins on a baking sheet. Broil 2 to 3 minutes or until potatoes are golden. Yield: 4 servings (serving size: 1 pie).

CALORIES 305; FAT 10.7g (sat 5.6g, mono 3.8g, poly 0.4g); PROTEIN 20.6g; CARB 32.4g; FIBER 4.8g; CHOL 56mg; IRON 3.7mg; SODIUM 490mg; CALC 59mg

Shepherd's Pie

Pasta Bolognese

Prep: 3 minutes • Cook: 12 minutes

This tastes-like-you-cooked-it-all-day sauce is perfect tossed with linguine.

1   (13.25-ounce) package whole-grain linguine
2   (4-ounce) links hot turkey Italian sausage
Olive oil–flavored cooking spray
1   pound 93% lean ground beef
1   cup chopped onion
1   (8-ounce) package button mushrooms, chopped
1   tablespoon finely chopped fresh rosemary
1   (28-ounce) can petite diced tomatoes, undrained
½   cup fat-free evaporated milk
¼   teaspoon freshly ground black pepper
⅛   teaspoon salt
Shaved fresh Parmesan cheese (optional)

1. Cook pasta in a large Dutch oven according to package directions, omitting salt and fat; drain, return to pan, and keep warm.
2. While pasta cooks, remove casings from sausage. Heat a large nonstick skillet over medium-high heat. Coat pan with cooking spray. Add sausage, beef, and onion; cook 2 minutes, stirring to crumble; drain, if necessary. Add mushrooms and rosemary. Cook 5 minutes or until browned.
3. Stir in tomatoes; reduce heat, and simmer, uncovered, 3 minutes. Stir in milk, pepper, and salt; cook 2 minutes. Add sauce to pasta, tossing well. Sprinkle with cheese, if desired. Yield: 8 servings (serving size: 1½ cups).

CALORIES 324; FAT 9.4g (sat 2g, mono 4g, poly 3.1g); PROTEIN 23.9g; CARB 43.6g; FIBER 7.2g; CHOL 47.3mg; IRON 3.7mg; SODIUM 444mg; CALC 81mg

serve with:

Shaved Fennel Salad

Prep: 8 minutes

3   tablespoons olive oil
3   tablespoons fresh lemon juice
¼   teaspoon salt
¼   teaspoon freshly ground black pepper
8   cups shaved fennel bulb (about 2 bulbs)
1   (10-ounce) package Italian-blend salad greens (about 8 cups)
⅓   cup loosely packed celery leaves, coarsely chopped
½   cup shaved fresh Parmesan cheese

1. Combine first 4 ingredients in a large bowl, stirring with a whisk. Add fennel, greens, and celery leaves; toss well. Add cheese, and toss gently. Yield: 8 servings (serving size: 1½ cups).

CALORIES 110; FAT 7.3g (sat 1.7g, mono 4.1g, poly 1.2g); PROTEIN 4.6g; CARB 8.3g; FIBER 3.2g; CHOL 5mg; IRON 1mg; SODIUM 251mg; CALC 154mg

make ahead

This hearty sauce freezes well and can be ready in minutes with a quick thaw in the microwave.

Stuffed Peppers

Prep: 4 minutes • Cook: 10 minutes

Beef and rice seasoned with herbs and a robust pasta sauce fill these tender, flavorful peppers. If you don't have dried Italian seasoning, use ½ teaspoon dried basil and ½ teaspoon dried oregano. Make sure the bell peppers are 10 ounces or larger so the beef stuffing will fit.

2	large green bell peppers (about 10 ounces each)
¾	pound ground sirloin
¼	cup chopped onion
1	teaspoon dried Italian seasoning
¼	teaspoon salt
¼	teaspoon freshly ground black pepper
1	(8.8-ounce) package precooked whole-grain brown rice
1	cup tomato-basil pasta sauce
1	cup shredded part-skim mozzarella cheese

1. Cut bell peppers in half lengthwise; discard seeds and membranes. Place bell pepper halves, cut sides up, in an 11 x 7–inch baking dish. Microwave at HIGH 6 to 7 minutes or until tender.
2. While bell peppers cook, heat a large nonstick skillet over medium-high heat. Cook beef and onion until browned, stirring to crumble beef. Drain, if necessary; return to pan. Stir in dried Italian seasoning, salt, black pepper, brown rice, and pasta sauce. Cook 1 to 2 minutes or until warm, stirring occasionally.
3. Fill bell pepper halves with beef mixture; sprinkle evenly with cheese. Microwave at HIGH 2 to 3 minutes or until cheese melts. Yield: 4 servings (serving size: ½ pepper).

CALORIES 312; FAT 9.8g (sat 4.6g, mono 3.3g; poly 1.5g); PROTEIN 27.4g; CARB 29.9g; FIBER 4.1g; CHOL 61mg; IRON 2.4mg; SODIUM 543mg; CALC 242mg

ingredient spotlight

Microwavable precooked rice, such as whole-grain brown, long-grain white, jasmine, or basmati, is a great shortcut instead of cooking rice from scratch. Precooked rice can be used as a stuffing, stirred into soups, or served as a healthy 90-second side. It comes in an assortment of flavors, but be sure to look at each one's nutrition label—some seasoned varieties can be high in sodium.

Stuffed Peppers

Individual Salsa Meat Loaves

Prep: 10 minutes • Cook: 30 minutes

Making meat loaf in single-serving portions reduces the cooking time by half and keeps the meat juicy.

2	large egg whites
⅓	cup quick-cooking oats
½	cup plus 2 tablespoons chipotle salsa, divided
¼	cup ketchup, divided
1	pound ground beef, extra lean

Cooking spray

1. Preheat oven to 350°.
2. Combine egg whites in a large bowl, stirring well with a whisk. Stir in oats, ½ cup salsa, and 2 tablespoons ketchup. Add beef; mix well. Divide beef mixture into 4 equal portions, shaping each into an oval-shaped loaf. Coat a foil-lined rimmed baking sheet with cooking spray. Place loaves on prepared pan.
3. Bake at 350° for 30 minutes or until done.
4. Combine remaining 2 tablespoons salsa and remaining 2 tablespoons ketchup in a small bowl; spread mixture evenly over loaves. Yield: 4 servings (serving size: 1 meat loaf).

CALORIES 190; FAT 6g (sat 2.1g, mono 2.1g, poly 0.7g); PROTEIN 25g; CARB 10.9g; FIBER 1.7g; CHOL 60mg; IRON 2.2mg; SODIUM 548mg; CALC 7mg

serve with:
Green Beans with Country Mustard and Herbs

Prep: 2 minutes • Cook: 5 minutes

1	(12-ounce) package trimmed green beans
1	tablespoon butter
2	tablespoons chopped fresh parsley
1½	teaspoons minced fresh oregano
2	teaspoons whole-grain Dijon mustard
¼	teaspoon salt

1. Microwave green beans according to package directions.
2. While beans cook, place butter and remaining ingredients in a serving bowl. Add beans; toss gently until butter melts. Yield: 4 servings (serving size: ½ cup).

CALORIES 55; FAT 3g (sat 1.8g, mono 0.8g, poly 0.2g); PROTEIN 1.7g; CARB 6.8g; FIBER 3g; CHOL 8mg; IRON 1mg; SODIUM 232mg; CALC 37mg

Individual Salsa Meat Loaves

Ginger-Lime Beef Stir-Fry

Prep: 4 minutes • Cook: 5 minutes

Peppery ginger adds a lively herbal note to this stir-fry. Serve over cellophane noodles.

1	tablespoon sugar
1	tablespoon grated peeled fresh ginger
2	tablespoons fresh lime juice (about 1 lime)
1½	teaspoons lower-sodium soy sauce
¼	teaspoon crushed red pepper
1	tablespoon canola oil
12	ounces boneless sirloin steak, trimmed and cut into thin strips
½	cup diagonally cut green onions (optional)
4	lime wedges (optional)

1. Combine first 5 ingredients in a small bowl; stir well with a whisk.

2. Heat a large nonstick skillet over medium-high heat. Add oil; swirl to coat. Add steak; cook 4 minutes or until browned, stirring frequently. Remove from heat; drizzle evenly with ginger-lime mixture. Garnish with onions and lime wedges, if desired. Yield: 3 servings (serving size: ⅔ cup).

CALORIES 197; FAT 9g (sat 2g, mono 4.5g, poly 2g); PROTEIN 22.4g; CARB 5.5g; FIBER 0.1g; CHOL 42mg; IRON 2.8mg; SODIUM 197mg; CALC 16mg

ingredient spotlight

Look for fresh ginger in the produce section of your supermarket. Choose the freshest, youngest-looking roots you can find because they are more flavorful and tender and less fibrous than old rhizomes.

Ginger-Lime Beef
Stir-Fry

Orange Beef and Broccoli

Prep: 7 minutes • Cook: 7 minutes

For convenience, ask the butcher to cut the steak into thin slices. Round out this restaurant-inspired meal with a side of hot cooked rice and, for dessert, Wasabi Ice Cream with Honey.

1	(12-ounce) package refrigerated broccoli florets
⅓	cup fat-free, lower-sodium beef broth
⅓	cup low-sugar orange marmalade
2	tablespoons lower-sodium soy sauce
¼	teaspoon salt
2	tablespoons cornstarch
1	(1-pound) flank steak, trimmed and cut into thin slices

Cooking spray

1. Microwave broccoli according to package directions.
2. While broccoli cooks, combine broth and next 3 ingredients in a small bowl, stirring with a whisk; set aside.
3. Place cornstarch in a shallow dish. Dredge steak in cornstarch.
4. Heat a large nonstick skillet over medium-high heat. Coat pan with cooking spray. Add steak; sauté 5 minutes or until browned on all sides. Add broth mixture; cook 1 minute or until thick. Stir in broccoli. Serve immediately. Yield: 4 servings (serving size: 1 cup).

CALORIES 238; FAT 7g (sat 2.4g, mono 2.2g, poly 0.4g); PROTEIN 27.7g; CARB 16.6g; FIBER 2.5g; CHOL 37mg; IRON 2.6mg; SODIUM 570mg; CALC 68mg

serve with:

Wasabi Ice Cream with Honey

Prep: 4 minutes • Cook: 4 minutes
Other: 2 hours and 46 minutes

1½	cups water
¾	cup sugar
1	tablespoon wasabi paste
4	teaspoons fresh lemon juice
1¼	cups whole milk
3	tablespoons honey

1. Combine 1½ cups water and sugar in a saucepan; bring to a boil, stirring until sugar dissolves. Remove pan from heat; add wasabi paste and lemon juice, stirring with a whisk. Cover and chill completely.
2. Stir in milk. Pour mixture into the freezer can of an ice-cream freezer; freeze according to manufacturer's instructions. Spoon ice cream into a freezer-safe container; cover and freeze 1 hour or until firm. Drizzle each serving with honey. Yield: 6 servings (serving size: about ½ cup ice cream and 1½ teaspoons honey).

CALORIES 178; FAT 2g (sat 1g, mono 0.4g, poly 0.1g); PROTEIN 1.7g; CARB 37.7g; FIBER 0g; CHOL 5mg; IRON 0.1mg; SODIUM 71mg; CALC 59mg

Mongolian Beef

Mongolian Beef

Prep: 4 minutes • Cook: 6 minutes

This spicy Asian favorite gets its flavor from hoisin sauce and dark sesame oil. Hoisin sauce is a versatile, sweet-and-spicy condiment that is used in Chinese cooking and dining much the same way Westerners use ketchup. The dark sesame oil imparts a distinctive nutty taste and aroma to the dish. Serve with boil-in-bag jasmine rice and steamed snow peas.

1	(1-pound) flank steak, trimmed and cut into thin slices
	Butter-flavored cooking spray
⅓	cup hoisin sauce
2	tablespoons water
2	teaspoons minced peeled fresh ginger
1	teaspoon bottled minced roasted garlic
2	teaspoons dark sesame oil
½	teaspoon crushed red pepper
4	green onions

1. Heat a large nonstick skillet over medium-high heat. Coat steak with cooking spray. Cook steak in pan over medium-high heat 3 minutes or until browned and liquid has almost evaporated, stirring occasionally.
2. While steak cooks, combine hoisin sauce and next 5 ingredients in a small bowl. Cut onions crosswise into 1-inch pieces. Add sauce mixture and onions to meat in pan; cook 1 to 2 minutes or until sauce is slightly reduced (do not overcook meat). Serve immediately. Yield: 4 servings (serving size: about ½ cup).

CALORIES 240; FAT 10g (sat 2.8g, mono 3.4g, poly 2.6g); PROTEIN 25.5g; CARB 11.1g; FIBER 1.1g; CHOL 38mg; IRON 2.2mg; SODIUM 410mg; CALC 45mg

Horseradish-Garlic Flank Steak

Prep: 3 minutes • Cook: 8 minutes
Other: 5 minutes

Horseradish gives grilled flank steak a tangy kick of spiciness.

2   tablespoons prepared horseradish
1   tablespoon olive oil
½   teaspoon salt
4   garlic cloves, minced
1   (1-pound) flank steak, trimmed
Cooking spray

1. Preheat grill to medium-high heat.
2. Combine first 4 ingredients in a bowl, stirring with a whisk. Spread mixture onto both sides of steak.
3. Place steak on grill rack coated with cooking spray. Grill 4 to 5 minutes on each side or until desired degree of doneness. Remove from grill; let stand 5 minutes. Cut steak diagonally across grain into thin slices. Yield: 4 servings (serving size: 3 ounces).

CALORIES 198; FAT 9.6g (sat 2.8g, mono 4.7g, poly 0.6g); PROTEIN 24.7g; CARB 1.8g; FIBER 0.3g; CHOL 37mg; IRON 1.9mg; SODIUM 377mg; CALC 37mg

> ## quick flip
> Can't find flank steak? Spread the horseradish mixture on your favorite cut of meat.

serve with:
Lemony Arugula Salad

Prep: 4 minutes

2   tablespoons extra-virgin olive oil
1   tablespoon fresh lemon juice
1   tablespoon water
½   teaspoon Dijon mustard
⅛   teaspoon salt
¼   teaspoon freshly ground black pepper
1   (5-ounce) bag arugula
¼   cup (1 ounce) shaved fresh Parmesan cheese

1. Combine first 6 ingredients in a large bowl, stirring with a whisk. Add arugula; toss to coat. Divide arugula mixture evenly among 4 plates; top evenly with cheese. Yield: 4 servings (serving size: 1 cup salad and 1 tablespoon cheese).

CALORIES 102; FAT 9.1g (sat 2.2g, mono 5.9g, poly 0.8g); PROTEIN 3.5g; CARB 2.1g; FIBER 0.6g; CHOL 4.8mg; IRON 0.6mg; SODIUM 211mg; CALC 142mg

Horseradish-Garlic
Flank Steak

Steak with Creamy Mushroom Gravy

Prep: 3 minutes • Cook: 16 minutes
Other: 5 minutes

Cheesy polenta is a no-fuss alternative to mashed potatoes as a side for this dinnertime classic.

1	(1-pound) flat-iron steak, trimmed
½	teaspoon salt, divided
½	teaspoon freshly ground black pepper, divided
1	tablespoon canola oil
1	(4-ounce) package gourmet mushroom blend
½	cup fat-free, lower-sodium beef broth
2	teaspoons chopped fresh rosemary
¼	cup reduced-fat sour cream

1. Sprinkle steak evenly with ¼ teaspoon salt and ¼ teaspoon pepper.
2. Heat a large nonstick skillet over medium-high heat. Add 1 tablespoon oil; swirl to coat. Add steak. Cook 5 minutes on each side or until desired degree of doneness. Remove steak from pan. Let stand 5 minutes.
3. Add mushrooms to pan; sauté 3 minutes or until tender. Stir in broth, rosemary, remaining ¼ teaspoon salt, and remaining ¼ teaspoon pepper. Bring to a boil; cover, reduce heat, and simmer 3 minutes.
4. Place sour cream in a medium bowl. Gradually add mushroom mixture, stirring constantly with a whisk.
5. Cut steak diagonally across grain into thin slices. Serve with gravy. Yield: 4 servings (serving size: 3 ounces steak and 3 tablespoons gravy).

CALORIES 221; FAT 12.7g (sat 4.6g, mono 6.5g, poly 1.5g); PROTEIN 24.8g; CARB 2.6g; FIBER 0.3g; CHOL 86.6mg; IRON 3mg; SODIUM 455mg; CALC 46mg

Chili-Lime Flank Steak

Prep: 5 minutes • Cook: 14 minutes
Other: 5 minutes

This boneless steak from a well-exercised part of the cow requires some TLC—and that's where the smoky-citrusy rub comes in. It brings out the flavor, while the zesty lime juice tenderizes it. A trio of colorful roasted bell peppers brightens this Southwestern-style favorite.

1	tablespoon chili powder
2	teaspoons grated lime rind
½	teaspoon salt
½	teaspoon freshly ground black pepper
1	(1½-pound) flank steak, trimmed
2	tablespoons fresh lime juice
Cooking spray	
3	tablespoons chopped fresh cilantro or cilantro leaves

1. Preheat grill to medium-high heat.
2. Combine first 4 ingredients in a small bowl. Sprinkle steak with lime juice. Rub steak with spice mixture.
3. Place steak on grill rack coated with cooking spray. Grill 7 to 8 minutes on each side or until desired degree of doneness. Let stand 5 minutes. Cut steak diagonally across grain into thin slices. Sprinkle each serving with cilantro. Yield: 6 servings (serving size: 3 ounces).

CALORIES 158; FAT 5.7g (sat 2.6g, mono 2.5g, poly 0.5g); PROTEIN 24.4g; CARB 0.7g; FIBER 0.2g; CHOL 39mg; IRON 1.8mg; SODIUM 294mg; CALC 27mg

serve with:

Roasted Bell Peppers, Potatoes, and Onion

Prep: 5 minutes • Cook: 25 minutes
Other: 5 minutes

3	medium bell peppers (1 each, green, red, and yellow)
9	small red potatoes (about 1 pound), cut into wedges
1	medium-sized sweet onion, cut into wedges
1	tablespoon olive oil
1	teaspoon garlic powder
½	teaspoon paprika
¼	teaspoon salt
¼	teaspoon freshly ground black pepper

Cooking spray

1. Preheat oven to 450°.
2. Cut bell peppers in half, discarding seeds and membranes. Combine bell pepper, potato, and next 6 ingredients on a large rimmed baking sheet coated with cooking spray. Bake at 450° for 25 minutes or until vegetables are browned and tender. Place peppers in a zip-top plastic bag; seal. Let stand 5 minutes.
3. While peppers stand, place potato mixture in a bowl. Peel and cut bell pepper into bite-sized pieces; add to potato mixture, and toss well. Yield: 6 servings (serving size: about 1 cup).

CALORIES 117; FAT 2.5g (sat 0.4g, mono 1.7g, poly 0.3g); PROTEIN 2.9g; CARB 21.3g; FIBER 2.7g; CHOL 0mg; IRON 1.1mg; SODIUM 109mg; CALC 17mg

Chili-Lime
Flank Steak

Steak Soft Tacos with Grilled Onion

Steak Soft Tacos with Grilled Onion

Prep: 15 minutes • **Cook:** 14 minutes
Other: 5 minutes

Prepared Southwest chipotle seasoning is a merry mix of red pepper, lime juice, onion, garlic, and salt, blended with smoky chipotle chiles.

1	(¾-pound) flank steak, trimmed
1	tablespoon olive oil, divided
1	tablespoon salt-free Southwest chipotle seasoning, divided
½	teaspoon salt, divided
½	teaspoon freshly ground black pepper, divided
1	large sweet onion, cut into ½-inch-thick slices

Cooking spray
Cilantro Cream

4	(8-inch) flour tortillas with chipotle chili and peppers

1. Preheat grill to medium-high heat.
2. Rub flank steak with 1 teaspoon oil; sprinkle with 1 teaspoon chipotle seasoning, ¼ teaspoon salt, and ¼ teaspoon black pepper.
3. Coat both sides of onion slices with cooking spray. Combine remaining 2 teaspoons oil, 2 teaspoons chipotle seasoning, ¼ teaspoon salt, and ¼ teaspoon pepper in a small bowl; brush on both sides of onion slices.
4. Place steak and onion slices on grill rack coated with cooking spray. Grill 7 minutes on each side or until steak reaches desired degree of doneness and onion is slightly charred and almost tender. Remove steak and onion from grill; cover steak, and let stand 5 minutes. Cut steak diagonally across grain into thin slices.
5. While steak stands, prepare Cilantro Cream. Stack onion slices, and cut crosswise into quarters. Microwave tortillas according to package directions until warm. Place 1 tortilla on each of 4 plates. Spread tortillas evenly with Cilantro Cream; top evenly with steak and onion. Fold sides of tortillas over, and serve immediately. Yield: 4 servings (serving size: 1 taco).

CALORIES 317; FAT 12g (sat 4.1g, mono 6.2g, poly 1.5g); PROTEIN 23.5g; CARB 30.6g; FIBER 1.9g; CHOL 35mg; IRON 3.4mg; SODIUM 459mg; CALC 175mg

Cilantro Cream

Prep: 4 minutes

¼	cup reduced-fat sour cream
2	tablespoons chopped fresh cilantro
⅛	teaspoon ground cumin
2	large garlic cloves, minced

1. Combine all ingredients in a small bowl, stirring with a whisk. Yield: 4 servings (serving size: 1 tablespoon).

CALORIES 23; FAT 1.8g (sat 1.1g, mono 0.5g, poly 0.1g); PROTEIN 0.6g; CARB 1.1g; FIBER 0.1g; CHOL 6mg; IRON 0.1mg; SODIUM 7mg; CALC 19mg

Jamaican-Spiced Hanger Steak with Banana-Mango Chutney

Prep: 7 minutes • Cook: 23 minutes
Other: 1 hour and 5 minutes

Hanger steak shares texture and flavor with flank steak. Here, the spicy Jamaican wet rub makes it tender, juicy, and flavorful.

Jamaican Rub
1   (1-pound) hanger steak, trimmed
Cooking spray
½   cup chopped banana
½   cup mango chutney

1. Prepare Jamaican Rub.
2. Reserve 2 tablespoons Jamaican Rub. Pat remaining rub onto steak. Place steak in a large heavy-duty zip-top plastic bag; seal bag, and marinate in refrigerator at least 1 hour.
3. Preheat oven to 450°.
4. Heat a large cast-iron or ovenproof skillet over medium-high heat. Coat pan with cooking spray. Add steak; cook 3 minutes on each side or until browned. Bake at 450° for 15 minutes or to desired degree of doneness. Transfer steak to a serving platter; cover and let steak rest 5 minutes.
5. Place reserved rub in a small saucepan. Add banana and chutney; cook, stirring constantly, over medium-high heat 1 minute or until thoroughly heated.
6. Thinly cut steak across grain into thin slices. Spoon chutney over steak. Yield: 4 servings (serving size: 3 ounces steak and ½ cup chutney).

CALORIES 305; FAT 8.2g (sat 3.6g, mono 3.6g, poly 0.9g); PROTEIN 24.4g; CARB 30.8g; FIBER 1.3g; CHOL 39mg; IRON 0.4mg; SODIUM 615mg; CALC 23mg

Jamaican Rub

Prep: 4 minutes

2   tablespoons dark brown sugar
1   tablespoon thyme leaves
2   tablespoons white vinegar
2   tablespoons grated peeled fresh ginger
2   teaspoons ground allspice
1   teaspoon crushed red pepper
½   teaspoon salt
4   garlic cloves, minced

1. Place all ingredients in a small bowl; mash to a paste with a fork. Yield: 4 servings (serving size: 2 tablespoons).

CALORIES 39; FAT 0.2g (sat 0g, mono 0g, poly 0.1g); PROTEIN 0.4g; CARB 9.4g; FIBER 0.9g; CHOL 0mg; IRON 0.4mg; SODIUM 295mg; CALC 23mg

Jamaican-Spiced
Hanger Steak with
Banana-Mango Chutney

Mustard-Molasses Flank Steak

Prep: 4 minutes • Cook: 10 minutes
Other: 30 minutes

⅓ cup balsamic vinegar
¼ cup fat-free, lower-sodium beef broth
2 tablespoons molasses
2 tablespoons whole-grain Dijon mustard
¼ teaspoon salt
¼ teaspoon freshly ground black pepper
1 (1-pound) flank steak, trimmed
Cooking spray
Chopped green onions (optional)

1. Combine first 7 ingredients in a large zip-top plastic bag; seal. Marinate in refrigerator 30 minutes.

2. Preheat broiler.
3. Remove steak from bag, reserving marinade. Place steak on a broiler pan coated with cooking spray; broil 5 minutes on each side or until desired degree of doneness. Remove steak from oven; loosely cover with foil.
4. While steak broils, place reserved marinade in a small nonstick skillet. Bring to a boil; cook until reduced to ⅓ cup (about 6 minutes), stirring occasionally.
5. Cut steak diagonally across the grain into ¼-inch-thick slices. Drizzle mustard-molasses sauce over steak. Top with onions, if desired. Yield: 4 servings (serving size: 3 ounces steak and about 1½ tablespoons sauce).

CALORIES 219; FAT 7g (sat 2.3g, mono 2.2g, poly 0.2g); PROTEIN 25.2g; CARB 12.4g; FIBER 0.3g; CHOL 37mg; IRON 2.6mg; SODIUM 397mg; CALC 60mg

Mustard-Molasses Flank Steak

Cowboy Flank Steak

Prep: 3 minutes • Cook: 12 minutes
Other: 5 minutes

Instant coffee granules may seem like an odd ingredient to use in a meat rub, but we found that it actually deepens the flavor. The coffee also helps caramelize the steak's surface, sealing in its natural juices and creating a tastier, more tender bite.

2   teaspoons chili powder
1   teaspoon instant coffee granules
½   teaspoon ground cumin
½   teaspoon brown sugar
1   (1-pound) flank steak, trimmed
½   teaspoon salt
¼   teaspoon freshly ground black pepper
Cooking spray

1. Preheat broiler.
2. Combine first 4 ingredients in a bowl, stirring with a small whisk until blended. Sprinkle steak with salt and pepper; rub steak with spice mixture. Place steak on a broiler pan coated with cooking spray.
3. Broil steak 4 inches from heat 12 minutes or until desired degree of doneness (do not turn steak). Remove steak from oven; loosely cover with foil, and let stand 5 minutes.
4. Cut steak diagonally across the grain into thin slices. Yield: 4 servings (serving size: 3 ounces steak).

CALORIES 181; FAT 8.2g (sat 3.4g, mono 3.3g, poly 1.3g); PROTEIN 24.2g; CARB 0.9g; FIBER 0.1g; CHOL 40mg; IRON 1.9mg; SODIUM 393mg; CALC 32mg

serve with:
Mini Cheddar Potato Skins

Prep: 5 minutes • Cook: 7 minutes
Other: 5 minutes

1   pound red fingerling potatoes (about 20)
1   tablespoon butter, melted
¼   teaspoon salt
¼   teaspoon freshly ground black pepper
3   tablespoons reduced-fat shredded extra-sharp cheddar cheese
2   tablespoons thinly sliced green onion tops

1. Preheat broiler.
2. Scrub potatoes; place in a single layer in a microwave-safe bowl (do not pierce potatoes with a fork). Cover bowl with plastic wrap (do not allow plastic wrap to touch food); vent. Microwave at HIGH 5 to 6 minutes or until tender. Let stand 5 minutes or until cool enough to touch. Cut potatoes in half; drizzle evenly with butter, and sprinkle evenly with salt and pepper. Top evenly with cheese. Broil 2 minutes or until cheese melts, and sprinkle evenly with green onions. Yield: 4 servings (serving size: about 5 potato halves).

CALORIES 149; FAT 4.2g (sat 2.6g, mono 1g, poly 0.2g); PROTEIN 3.9g; CARB 24.4g; FIBER 2.5g; CHOL 12mg; IRON 0.8mg; SODIUM 174mg; CALC 55mg

Grilled Flank Steak with Balsamic Glaze and Orange Gremolata

Prep: 2 minutes • Cook: 12 minutes
Other: 5 minutes

Gremolata, a zesty Italian garnish traditionally made of minced parsley, lemon rind, and garlic, is simple to prepare and great for adding a burst of fresh flavor to a variety of dishes. Here, orange rind stands in for the lemon rind. Serve with mashed sweet potatoes.

1	(1-pound) flank steak, trimmed
½	teaspoon salt
¼	teaspoon freshly ground black pepper
1	medium-size red onion, cut into 8 wedges
	Cooking spray
½	cup balsamic vinegar
¼	cup finely chopped shallots
	Orange Gremolata

1. Preheat grill to medium-high heat.
2. Sprinkle steak with salt and pepper. Place steak and onion wedges on grill rack coated with cooking spray. Grill 5 minutes on each side or until desired degree of doneness. Let stand 5 minutes. Cut steak diagonally across grain into thin slices.
3. While steak grills, combine balsamic vinegar and shallots in a small saucepan. Bring to a boil; reduce heat, and simmer 7 minutes or until reduced to ¼ cup. Drizzle balsamic mixture over steak slices, and sprinkle with Orange Gremolata. Yield: 4 servings (serving size: 3 ounces steak, 1 tablespoon glaze, 2 onion wedges, and 1 tablespoon Orange Gremolata).

CALORIES 236; FAT 8.3g (sat 3.4g, mono 3.6g, poly 0.8g); PROTEIN 25.6g; CARB 12.2g; FIBER 1.6g; CHOL 40mg; IRON 3.4mg; SODIUM 378mg; CALC 86mg

Orange Gremolata

Prep: 5 minutes

¼	cup minced fresh parsley
1	tablespoon grated orange rind
2	garlic cloves, minced

1. Combine all ingredients in a small bowl. Yield: 4 servings (serving size: 1 tablespoon).

CALORIES 5; FAT 0.1g (sat 0g, mono 0g, poly 0g); PROTEIN 0.2g; CARB 1.1g; FIBER 0.3g; CHOL 0mg; IRON 0.3mg; SODIUM 2mg; CALC 10mg

make ahead

Prepare this flavorful gremolata ahead of time and store covered in the refrigerator for up to 3 days. Make a double batch and use it to top other dishes.

Skirt Steak with Green Olive Tapenade

Prep: 3 minutes • Cook: 6 minutes
Other: 8 hours and 5 minutes

This topping capitalizes on bold-tasting olives and capers to deliver a huge amount of flavor. To make this meal even quicker, use a store-bought tapenade instead of making your own. If you can't find skirt steak, you can use flank steak. Serve with an arugula and tomato salad.

1½	pounds skirt steak, trimmed and cut in half crosswise
¼	teaspoon freshly ground black pepper
⅛	teaspoon salt
¼	cup balsamic vinegar
2	tablespoons olive oil
1	garlic clove, minced
	Cooking spray
	Green Olive Tapenade

1. Sprinkle steak on both sides with pepper and salt. Combine vinegar, olive oil, and garlic in a large heavy-duty zip-top plastic bag. Add steak to bag; seal. Marinate in refrigerator 8 hours, turning occasionally.
2. Preheat grill to medium-high heat.
3. Remove steak from bag, discarding marinade. Place steak on grill rack coated with cooking spray. Grill 6 to 8 minutes or until desired degree of doneness. Remove steak from grill; cover and let stand 5 minutes. Cut diagonally across the grain into thin slices. Serve with Green Olive Tapenade. Yield: 6 servings (serving size: 3 ounces steak and 2 tablespoons Green Olive Tapenade).

CALORIES 287; FAT 19.3g (sat 4.9g, mono 12g, poly 1.9g); PROTEIN 21.6g; CARB 3g; FIBER 0.3g; CHOL 60mg; IRON 2.9mg; SODIUM 335mg; CALC 22mg

Green Olive Tapenade

Prep: 3 minutes

1	lemon
12	large garlic-stuffed green olives
1	tablespoon drained capers
1	tablespoon chopped fresh flat-leaf parsley
2	tablespoons olive oil

1. Grate rind and squeeze juice from lemon to equal 1 tablespoon and 2½ tablespoons, respectively. Process lemon rind, juice, olives, and remaining ingredients in a food processor until coarsely chopped. Yield: 6 servings (serving size: 2 tablespoons).

CALORIES 51; FAT 5.4g (sat 0.7g, mono 3.9g, poly 0.6g); PROTEIN 0.2g; CARB 1g; FIBER 0.3g; CHOL 0mg; IRON 0.2mg; SODIUM 208mg; CALC 8mg

Skirt Steak with Green Olive Tapenade

Beef Tenderloin with Peppery Fig-Port Sauce

Prep: 5 minutes • Cook: 15 minutes
Other: 5 minutes

Grilled beef tenderloin steaks become decadent when drizzled with fig-studded port sauce, which is also delicious served with lamb and game.

4	(4-ounce) beef tenderloin steaks, trimmed (about ¾ inch thick)
½	teaspoon salt
½	teaspoon freshly ground black pepper, divided
	Cooking spray
1	cup tawny port or other sweet red wine
1½	tablespoons finely chopped shallots
8	small dried Mission figs, quartered
1	rosemary sprig

1. Preheat grill to medium-high heat.
2. Sprinkle steaks with salt and ¼ teaspoon pepper. Place steaks on grill rack coated with cooking spray. Grill 3 minutes on each side or until desired degree of doneness. Let stand 5 minutes.
3. While steaks cook, combine remaining ¼ teaspoon black pepper, port, and remaining 3 ingredients in a small saucepan. Bring to a boil; boil 15 minutes or until reduced to ½ cup. Remove rosemary sprig. Spoon port sauce over steaks. Yield: 4 servings (serving size: 1 steak and 2 tablespoons sauce).

CALORIES 302; FAT 7.5g (sat 2.8g, mono 3g, poly 0.4g); PROTEIN 25.7g; CARB 16.8g; FIBER 1.3g; CHOL 76mg; IRON 2.3mg; SODIUM 361mg; CALC 55mg

Beef Tenderloin with Peppery Fig-Port Sauce

serve with:
Grilled Fennel and Red Onion

Prep: 5 minutes • Cook: 12 minutes

¼	cup balsamic vinegar
1	tablespoon olive oil
¼	teaspoon salt
¼	teaspoon freshly ground black pepper
1	large red onion, cut into 4 (½-inch-thick) slices
2	medium fennel bulbs with stalks (about 2 pounds), trimmed and cut into ¼-inch-thick slices
	Cooking spray

1. Preheat grill to medium-high heat.
2. Combine first 4 ingredients in a large bowl. Add onion and fennel, tossing to coat.
3. Place onion and fennel on grill rack coated with cooking spray. Grill 12 minutes or until tender, turning once. Yield: 4 servings (serving size: ¾ cup).

CALORIES 127; FAT 4.1g (sat 0.5g, mono 2.6g, poly 0.4g); PROTEIN 3.3g; CARB 22.4g; FIBER 7.7g; CHOL 0mg; IRON 1.9mg; SODIUM 269mg; CALC 125mg

Apricot-Glazed Beef Tenderloin

Prep: 1 minute • Cook: 8 minutes

Spicy and creamy meet savory and sweet in this comforting meal with a little kick. The tangy-sweet apricot glaze on the beef balances the lively jalapeño grits sidekick.

1	tablespoon butter
4	(4-ounce) beef tenderloin steaks, trimmed (about 1 inch thick)
½	teaspoon ground cumin
½	teaspoon freshly ground black pepper
¼	teaspoon salt
½	cup apricot preserves
2	tablespoons water

1. Melt butter in a large nonstick skillet over medium-high heat.
2. While butter melts, sprinkle steaks evenly with cumin, pepper, and salt. Cook steaks in melted butter 3 minutes on each side or until desired degree of doneness. Transfer steaks to a serving platter; keep warm. Reduce heat to medium.
3. Stir preserves and 2 tablespoons water into drippings, scraping pan to loosen browned bits. Cook, stirring constantly, over medium heat 1 minute or until bubbly.
4. Place 1 steak on each of 4 plates. Spoon sauce evenly over steaks. Yield: 4 servings (serving size: 1 steak and 2 tablespoons sauce).

CALORIES 300; FAT 10.3g (sat 5.1g, mono 4.2g, poly 0.9g); PROTEIN 25.2g; CARB 26.3g; FIBER 0.2g; CHOL 84mg; IRON 1.9mg; SODIUM 230mg; CALC 31mg

serve with:
Jalapeño Grits

Prep: 2 minutes • Cook: 7 minutes

1½	cups water
¼	teaspoon salt
½	cup uncooked quick-cooking grits
1½	tablespoons minced seeded jalapeño pepper (1 pepper)
½	cup fat-free milk
2	(0.5-ounce) slices reduced-fat Monterey Jack cheese with jalapeño peppers, chopped

Freshly ground black pepper (optional)

1. Bring 1½ cups water and salt to a boil in a medium saucepan. Gradually stir in grits. Add jalapeño pepper; cover, reduce heat, and simmer 5 minutes or until thick. Stir in milk. Remove from heat; add cheese, stirring until cheese melts. Garnish with freshly ground black pepper, if desired. Yield: 4 servings (serving size: ½ cup).

CALORIES 105; FAT 1.8g (sat 0.9g, mono 0.6g, poly 0.2g); PROTEIN 4.7g; CARB 17.6g; FIBER 0.4g; CHOL 5mg; IRON 0.8mg; SODIUM 223mg; CALC 83mg

fix it faster

These grits are a cinch to make using Monterey Jack cheese studded with jalapeño pepper. The all-in-one cheese eliminates seeding and mincing the chile pepper and gives the grits the desired creamy texture with a hit of hot.

Beef Tenderloin with Mushroom Gravy

Prep: 3 minutes • Cook: 12 minutes

Tenderloin, prized for its rich flavor and tenderness, can be a bit pricey, but the melt-in-your-mouth results are worth the splurge. It's the most tender cut of beef you can buy. Beef tenderloin steaks are often labeled "filet mignon." Round out your meal with Garlicky Smashed Potatoes and a side of steamed haricots verts.

4	(4-ounce) beef tenderloin steaks, trimmed
½	teaspoon freshly ground black pepper
¼	teaspoon salt

Cooking spray

½	cup minced shallots
1	(8-ounce) package presliced baby portobello mushrooms
1	(1.25-ounce) package mushroom-and-herb gravy mix
1	cup water

1. Sprinkle steaks with pepper and salt. Heat a large nonstick skillet over medium-high heat. Add steaks to pan, and cook 3 to 4 minutes on each side or until desired degree of doneness. Remove steaks from pan; keep warm.
2. Coat pan with cooking spray. Add shallots and mushrooms; cook 5 minutes. Empty gravy mix into a small bowl. Gradually add 1 cup water, stirring with a whisk until blended. Add gravy to pan, scraping pan to loosen browned bits. Cook 1 minute. Spoon gravy over steaks. Yield: 4 servings (serving size: 1 steak and ¼ cup gravy).

CALORIES 242; FAT 8.7g (sat 2.8g, mono 3.3g, poly 0.4g); PROTEIN 28g; CARB 10.8g; FIBER 1.1g; CHOL 81mg; IRON 2.3mg; SODIUM 216mg; CALC 48mg

serve with:
Garlicky Smashed Potatoes

Prep: 2 minutes • Cook: 4 minutes

1	(24-ounce) package country-style mashed potatoes
¼	cup light garlic-and-herbs spreadable cheese
¼	teaspoon freshly ground black pepper

1. Heat potatoes according to package directions. Stir in cheese and pepper. Yield: 6 servings (serving size: ½ cup).

CALORIES 108; FAT 4.5g (sat 3.3g, mono 0.9g, poly 0.1g); PROTEIN 2.5g; CARB 15g; FIBER 1.9g; CHOL 16mg; IRON 0.7mg; SODIUM 214mg; CALC 29mg

Beef Tenderloin with Mushroom Gravy

Grecian Steaks

Prep: 2 minutes • Cook: 5 minutes

Tangy feta cheese and briny kalamata olives add Mediterranean flair to these steaks. Flatten the filets with your palm to speed cooking time. Our taste panel rated this bistro-style meal a hall-of-famer!

4   (4-ounce) beef tenderloin steaks, trimmed (about 1 inch thick)
½   teaspoon freshly ground black pepper
Olive oil–flavored cooking spray
2   tablespoons fresh lemon juice
¼   cup (1 ounce) crumbled feta cheese
2   tablespoons coarsely chopped pitted kalamata olives
Oregano leaves (optional)

1. Press steaks with palm of hand to flatten, if desired. Sprinkle steaks with pepper; coat with cooking spray. Heat a large cast-iron skillet over medium-high heat. Coat pan with cooking spray. Add steaks to pan; cook 2 to 3 minutes on each side or until desired degree of doneness. Remove pan from heat. Drizzle steaks with lemon juice, and sprinkle with cheese and olives. Garnish with oregano, if desired. Yield: 4 servings (serving size: 1 steak, about 1½ teaspoons pan juices, and 1 tablespoon cheese).

CALORIES 185; FAT 11g (sat 4.9g, mono 5.2g, poly 0.9g); PROTEIN 19.1g; CARB 1.5g; FIBER 0.1g; CHOL 60mg; IRON 2.5mg; SODIUM 199mg; CALC 3mg

serve with:
Lemon-Pepper Fries

Prep: 1 minute • Cook: 17 minutes

3   cups frozen extra-crispy crinkle-cut fries
Cooking spray
2   teaspoons salt-free lemon pepper seasoning
2   teaspoons grated lemon rind

1. Preheat oven to 450°.
2. Place fries on a large baking sheet coated with cooking spray. Coat fries with cooking spray, and sprinkle with seasoning; toss well. Arrange fries in a single layer.
3. Bake at 450° for 17 minutes or until browned, stirring once. Stir in lemon rind. Yield: 4 servings (serving size: about ¾ cup).

CALORIES 151; FAT 4.1g (sat 2.3g, mono 1.3g, poly 0.5g); PROTEIN 2.3g; CARB 24.5g; FIBER 2.4g; CHOL 0mg; IRON 0mg; SODIUM 360mg; CALC 1mg

quick flip

Substitute ¼ cup (1 ounce) crumbled blue cheese for the feta and kalamata olives. Assertive blue cheese is a small but bold modification for these succulent steaks. Just a sprinkling adds more wow!

Mojito Strip Steaks with Pico de Gallo

Prep: 3 minutes • Cook: 4 minutes
Other: 33 minutes

Strip steaks are tender and full of flavor, so they're a great choice for broiling or grilling. One steak will generally weigh about 8 ounces when purchased raw because it's a long, thick cut of meat. For portion control, we've called for 2 (8-ounce) steaks cut in half. Serve with grilled corn on the cob.

1	lime
¼	cup chopped fresh mint
2	tablespoons light rum
2	(½-inch-thick) beef strip steaks, trimmed and cut in half crosswise (about 1 pound)
	Pico de Gallo
½	teaspoon salt
½	teaspoon freshly ground black pepper
	Cooking spray

1. Grate rind and squeeze juice from lime to measure 1 teaspoon and 1 tablespoon, respectively. Combine rind, juice, mint, and rum in a large zip-top plastic bag. Add steak to bag, and seal bag. Marinate in refrigerator 30 minutes, turning occasionally.
2. While steak marinates, prepare Pico de Gallo.
3. Preheat grill to medium-high heat.
4. Remove steaks from marinade, discarding marinade. Sprinkle steaks with salt and pepper. Place steaks on grill rack coated with cooking spray. Grill 2 minutes on each side or until desired degree of doneness. Let stand 3 minutes. Cut steak into slices. Serve with Pico de Gallo. Yield: 4 servings (serving size: 4 ounces steak and ½ cup Pico de Gallo).

CALORIES 217; FAT 7.6g (sat 2.8g, mono 3.2g, poly 1.4g); PROTEIN 22.4g; CARB 7.2g; FIBER 1.7g; CHOL 76mg; IRON 2.4mg; SODIUM 506mg; CALC 24mg

Pico de Gallo

Prep: 8 minutes

2	cups chopped seeded tomato (2 medium)
⅓	cup chopped red onion
⅓	cup chopped fresh cilantro
2	tablespoons fresh lime juice (2 limes)
1½	tablespoons chopped seeded jalapeño (about 1)
¼	teaspoon salt
¼	teaspoon freshly ground black pepper

1. Combine all ingredients in a medium bowl; toss well. Yield: 4 servings (serving size: ½ cup).

CALORIES 28; FAT 0.4g (sat 0.1g, mono 0.1g, poly 0.1g); PROTEIN 1g; CARB 6.4g; FIBER 1.4g; CHOL 0mg; IRON 0.5mg; SODIUM 155mg; CALC 11mg

Mojito Strip Steaks with Pico de Gallo

Coffee-Marinated Beef Tenderloin Steaks

Prep: 5 minutes • Cook: 4 minutes
Other: 8 hours

If you look in your pantry, you'll probably find the staple items needed to make this marinade. Make an extra cup of joe the morning you plan to prepare the marinade. Store the marinade in the refrigerator until you're ready to use it.

1   cup strong brewed coffee
1½   tablespoons dark brown sugar
½   teaspoon salt
½   teaspoon freshly ground black pepper
¼   teaspoon ground red pepper
2   garlic cloves, minced
4   (4-ounce) beef tenderloin steaks, trimmed
        (½-inch-thick)
Cooking spray

1. Combine first 6 ingredients in a large zip-top plastic bag. Add steaks; seal bag. Marinate in refrigerator 8 hours, turning occasionally.
2. Preheat grill to medium-high heat.
3. Remove steaks from marinade, discarding marinade. Place steaks on grill rack coated with cooking spray. Grill 2 minutes on each side or until desired degree of doneness. Yield: 4 servings (serving size: 1 steak).

CALORIES 174; FAT 6.3g (sat 2.4g, mono 2.5g, poly 1.2g); PROTEIN 22g;
CARB 5.8g; FIBER 0.1g; CHOL 59mg; IRON 1.5mg; SODIUM 339mg;
CALC 24mg

serve with:
Grilled Asparagus and Tomatoes

Prep: 2 minutes • Cook: 6 minutes

1   pound fresh asparagus, trimmed
4   plum tomatoes, halved
1   tablespoon olive oil
Cooking spray
¼   teaspoon salt
⅛   teaspoon freshly ground black pepper
½   teaspoon grated lemon rind

1. Preheat grill to medium-high heat.
2. Place asparagus and tomato halves in an 11 x 7–inch baking dish. Drizzle vegetables with oil; toss gently to coat. Place vegetables on a grill rack coated with cooking spray. Grill asparagus 3 minutes on each side; grill tomato 1 minute on each side. Return asparagus and tomato to dish. Sprinkle vegetables with salt, pepper, and lemon rind. Yield: 4 servings (serving size: ¼ of asparagus and 2 tomato halves).

CALORIES 62; FAT 3.7g (sat 0.5g, mono 2.5g, poly 0.4g); PROTEIN 3.8g;
CARB 5.7g; FIBER 1.3g; CHOL 0mg; IRON 0.9mg; SODIUM 151mg;
CALC 27mg

Grilled Beef Tenderloin with
Horseradish-Walnut Sauce

Grilled Beef Tenderloin with Horseradish-Walnut Sauce

Prep: 6 minutes • Cook: 6 minutes

1	tablespoon chopped fresh thyme
2	teaspoons olive oil
½	teaspoon salt
¼	teaspoon freshly ground black pepper
4	garlic cloves, minced
4	(4-ounce) beef tenderloin steaks (about ¾ inch thick)

Cooking spray
Horseradish-Walnut Sauce

1. Preheat grill to medium-high heat.
2. Combine first 5 ingredients in a small bowl; rub herb mixture over steaks. Place steaks on grill rack coated with cooking spray. Grill 3 minutes on each side or until desired degree of doneness. Serve with Horseradish-Walnut Sauce. Yield: 4 servings (serving size: 1 steak and 1½ tablespoons sauce).

CALORIES 246; FAT 14.9g (sat 4.2g, mono 4.5g, poly 5.8g); PROTEIN 23.3g; CARB 3.5g; FIBER 0.4g; CHOL 62mg; IRON 1.9mg; SODIUM 419mg; CALC 34mg

Horseradish-Walnut Sauce

Prep: 4 minutes

2½	tablespoons light sour cream
2½	tablespoons light mayonnaise
2	tablespoons finely chopped walnuts, toasted
1	tablespoon finely chopped green onions
2	teaspoons prepared horseradish
¼	teaspoon freshly ground black pepper

1. Combine all ingredients in a small bowl. Yield: 4 servings (serving size: 1½ tablespoons).

CALORIES 70; FAT 6.3g (sat 1.5g, mono 1.3g, poly 3.3g); PROTEIN 1.3g; CARB 2.2g; FIBER 0.3g; CHOL 3mg; IRON 0.2mg; SODIUM 83mg; CALC 7mg

Beer-Braised Beef

Prep: 4 minutes • Cook: 8 hours and
7 minutes • Other: 10 minutes

An oval 3- to 3½-quart slow cooker works best for
this recipe because of the shape of the meat. If you
don't own an oval slow cooker, cut the meat in half
to fit the one you have. Spoon this fork-tender, saucy
beef over mashed potatoes.

1	cup refrigerated prechopped onion
Cooking spray	
1	(1-pound) boneless top round steak, trimmed
1	(14.5-ounce) can diced tomatoes with basil, garlic, and oregano, undrained
½	cup light beer
2	tablespoons molasses
¼	teaspoon salt

1. Place onion in a 3- to 3½-quart electric
slow cooker coated with cooking spray.
2. Heat a large nonstick skillet over medium-
high heat; coat pan with cooking spray. Add
steak; cook 3 minutes on each side or until
browned. Place steak over onion in cooker;
pour tomatoes and beer over steak. Cover
and cook on LOW for 8 hours or until steak
is very tender.
3. Shred steak with 2 forks in slow cooker;
stir in molasses and salt. Let steak stand
10 minutes before serving. Yield: 4 servings
(serving size: 1 cup).

CALORIES 265; FAT 8g (sat 3.1g, mono 3.4g, poly 0.3g); PROTEIN 25.5g;
CARB 20.4g; FIBER 1.5g; CHOL 64mg; IRON 3.7mg; SODIUM 514mg;
CALC 64mg

Beer-Braised Beef

Seared Beef Tenderloin Steaks with Dark Beer Reduction and Blue Cheese

Prep: 2 minutes • Cook: 13 minutes

2   teaspoons steak rub
4   (4-ounce) beef tenderloin steaks, trimmed (about 1 inch thick)
1   teaspoon olive oil
1   (12-ounce) bottle dark lager
2   tablespoons light brown sugar
2   tablespoons crumbled blue cheese

1. Preheat oven to 450°.
2. Rub steak seasoning over both sides of steaks.
3. Heat a large nonstick skillet over medium-high heat. Add oil; swirl to coat. Add steaks; cook 2 minutes on each side or until browned. Remove steaks from pan; place on a baking sheet. Bake at 450° for 4 to 5 minutes or until desired degree of doneness.
4. While steaks bake, combine beer and brown sugar in a medium bowl; add to skillet, scraping pan to loosen browned bits. Cook 6 minutes or until mixture is slightly syrupy and reduced to about ¼ cup. Serve steaks with reduced sauce; sprinkle evenly with cheese. Yield: 4 servings (serving size: 1 steak, about 1½ tablespoons sauce, and 1½ teaspoons cheese).

CALORIES 209; FAT 8g (sat 3.2g, mono 3.4g, poly 0.4g); PROTEIN 22.7g; CARB 6.2g; FIBER 0g; CHOL 62mg; IRON 1.5mg; SODIUM 362mg; CALC 37mg

Beef Tenderloin Steaks with Red Wine–Mushroom Sauce

Prep: 1 minute • Cook: 10 minutes

Stirring the mushrooms constantly helps release their juices, allowing them to caramelize quickly. Complete the meal with Wedge Salad with Sour Cream–Mustard Seed Dressing.

4	(4-ounce) beef tenderloin steaks, trimmed (about ½ inch thick)
¼	teaspoon salt
¼	teaspoon freshly ground black pepper

Butter-flavored cooking spray

1	(8-ounce) package presliced baby portobello mushrooms
1	cup dry red wine
2	tablespoons butter
1	teaspoon minced fresh rosemary

1. Heat a large nonstick skillet over medium-high heat. Sprinkle steaks with salt and pepper; coat with cooking spray. Add steaks to pan; cook 3 minutes on each side or until desired degree of doneness. Transfer steaks to a serving platter; keep warm.
2. Add mushrooms to pan. Coat mushrooms with cooking spray; sauté 3 minutes or until browned. Stir in wine, scraping pan to loosen browned bits. Cook until liquid almost evaporates. Remove pan from heat; add butter and rosemary, stirring until butter melts. Pour sauce over steaks. Yield: 4 servings (serving size: 1 steak and ¼ cup sauce).

CALORIES 244; FAT 13g (sat 6g, mono 4g, poly 0.9g); PROTEIN 23.3g; CARB 3.8g; FIBER 0.9g; CHOL 74mg; IRON 1.9mg; SODIUM 235mg; CALC 24mg

serve with:

Wedge Salad with Sour Cream–Mustard Seed Dressing

Prep: 6 minutes

⅓	cup reduced-fat sour cream
3	tablespoons water
2	tablespoons light mayonnaise
2	teaspoons whole-grain Dijon mustard
1	garlic clove, minced
⅛	teaspoon salt
½	head iceberg lettuce, cut into 4 wedges
½	cup diced plum tomato (about 1 tomato)

Freshly ground black pepper

1. Combine first 6 ingredients in a medium bowl, stirring well with a whisk.
2. Place 1 lettuce wedge on each of 4 plates. Drizzle with dressing. Top with tomato and pepper. Yield: 4 servings (serving size: 1 lettuce wedge, about 3 tablespoons dressing, and 2 tablespoons tomato).

CALORIES 73; FAT 5g (sat 2g, mono 0.7g, poly 2.4g); PROTEIN 1.8g; CARB 5.5g; FIBER 1g; CHOL 13mg; IRON 0.4mg; SODIUM 212mg; CALC 49mg

Slow-Cooker Beef Pot Roast

Prep: 4 minutes • Cook: 7 hours and 7 minutes

Pair this home-style favorite with mashed potatoes to soak up the sauce. Leftover meat makes great hot roast beef sandwiches the next day.

1	(8-ounce) package presliced mushrooms
1	(8-ounce) container refrigerated prechopped green bell pepper

Cooking spray

¼	cup plus 2 tablespoons ketchup
¼	cup water
1	tablespoon Worcestershire sauce
½	teaspoon freshly ground black pepper
¼	teaspoon salt
1	(2-pound) boneless shoulder pot roast

1. Place mushrooms and bell pepper in a 3½- to 4-quart electric slow cooker coated with cooking spray.
2. Combine ketchup and next 4 ingredients in a small bowl, stirring until blended.
3. Heat a large nonstick skillet over medium-high heat. Coat pan and roast with cooking spray. Cook roast 3 minutes on each side or until browned. Place roast over vegetables in cooker; pour ketchup mixture over roast. Cover and cook on HIGH for 1 hour. Reduce heat to LOW; cook 6 to 7 hours or until roast is very tender. Serve vegetables and sauce over roast. Yield: 6 servings (serving size: 3 ounces beef and ½ cup vegetables and sauce).

CALORIES 228; FAT 8g (sat 2g, mono 3.1g, poly 0.1g); PROTEIN 31.3g; CARB 7.4g; FIBER 1.1g; CHOL 89mg; IRON 4.2mg; SODIUM 397mg; CALC 21mg

Feta-Lamb Patties with Cucumber Sauce

Prep: 5 minutes • Cook: 9 minutes

Substitute Greek yogurt for the sour cream and omit the vinegar for a tangier cucumber sauce. Complete this meal with tomatoes, thinly sliced onion, and pita bread, if you wish.

1	pound lean ground lamb
¼	cup crumbled feta cheese
2	teaspoons chopped fresh oregano
2	garlic cloves, pressed
¼	teaspoon salt, divided
½	teaspoon freshly ground black pepper, divided
¼	cup shredded English cucumber
¾	cup fat-free sour cream
1	teaspoon chopped fresh dill
½	teaspoon red wine vinegar

1. Combine first 4 ingredients, ⅛ teaspoon salt, and ¼ teaspoon pepper in a bowl. Divide lamb mixture into 4 equal portions, shaping each into a ½-inch-thick patty.
2. Heat a large nonstick skillet over medium-high heat. Add patties; cook 4 minutes. Turn patties over; cook 4 minutes or until done.
3. While patties cook, combine remaining ⅛ teaspoon salt, remaining ¼ teaspoon pepper, cucumber, and next 3 ingredients in a small bowl. Serve with patties. Yield: 4 servings (serving size: 1 patty and 3½ table-spoons cucumber sauce).

CALORIES 225; FAT 8.6g (sat 3.9g, mono 2.8g, poly 0.6g); PROTEIN 26.8g; CARB 8.6g; FIBER 0.1g; CHOL 86mg; IRON 2.2mg; SODIUM 362mg; CALC 133mg

Feta-Lamb Patties with
Cucumber Sauce

Spiced Lamb

Prep: 7 minutes • Cook: 9 minutes

Greek yogurt lends moisture to these lamb patties, keeping them tender and juicy as they cook. If you can't find ground lamb, substitute ground beef.

1   pound ground lamb
¼   cup chopped onion
½   teaspoon garam masala
¼   teaspoon salt
½   cup plain fat-free Greek yogurt, divided
Cooking spray
1   tablespoon chopped fresh cilantro

1. Combine first 4 ingredients and 1 tablespoon yogurt; shape into 12 (½-inch-thick) oblong patties.
2. Heat a large nonstick skillet over medium-high heat. Coat pan with cooking spray. Add patties to pan. Cook 4 to 5 minutes on each side or until done.
3. While patties cook, combine remaining yogurt and cilantro in a small bowl. Serve yogurt mixture with patties. Yield: 4 servings (serving size: 3 lamb patties and about 2 tablespoons yogurt mixture).

CALORIES 179; FAT 6.3g (sat 2.2g, mono 2.5g, poly 0.6g); PROTEIN 25.8g; CARB 3.3g; FIBER 0.5g; CHOL 74mg; IRON 2.2mg; SODIUM 232mg; CALC 38mg

serve with:
Fruited Couscous

Prep: 5 minutes • Cook: 2 minutes
Other: 5 minutes

1   cup water
1   cup uncooked couscous
3   tablespoons coarsely chopped dried apricots
3   tablespoons golden raisins
2   tablespoons slivered almonds, toasted
1   tablespoon chopped fresh mint
1   tablespoon fresh lemon juice
1   tablespoon olive oil
½   teaspoon salt

1. Bring 1 cup water to a boil in a medium saucepan; gradually stir in couscous. Remove from heat; cover and let stand 5 minutes. Add apricots and remaining ingredients. Fluff with a fork. Yield: 4 servings (serving size: ¾ cup).

CALORIES 253; FAT 5.3g (sat 0.6g, mono 3.5g, poly 0.9g); PROTEIN 6.6g; CARB 44.5g; FIBER 3.4g; CHOL 0mg; IRON 1mg; SODIUM 306mg; CALC 30mg

ingredient spotlight

Garam masala is a North Indian spice mixture and can be stored in an airtight continer for up to six months. Spicy heat from black pepper, cinnamon, and chile is underscored by smoky cumin, fragrant cardamom, warm cloves, and nutmeg.

Lamb Chops with Minted Yogurt Sauce

Prep: 4 minutes • Cook: 6 minutes

Tender lamb loin chops dressed up with a tangy, yogurt dipping sauce and served with Couscous Salad offer a mouthwatering meal with minimal effort.

½   cup plain fat-free yogurt
1   tablespoon chopped fresh mint
1   teaspoon fresh lemon juice
1   small garlic clove, minced
½   teaspoon salt, divided
½   teaspoon freshly ground black pepper, divided
8   (4-ounce) lamb loin chops, trimmed
Cooking spray

1. Preheat grill to medium-high heat.
2. Combine yogurt and next 3 ingredients. Stir in ⅛ teaspoon salt and ⅛ teaspoon pepper. Chill.
3. Sprinkle lamb evenly with remaining ⅜ teaspoon each salt and pepper. Place lamb on grill rack coated with cooking spray; grill 3 minutes on each side or until desired degree of doneness. Serve with yogurt sauce. Yield: 4 servings (serving size: 2 chops and 2 tablespoons sauce).

CALORIES 221; FAT 9.3g (sat 3.3g; mono 4.4g; poly 1.6g); PROTEIN 29.9g; CARB 3g; FIBER 0.1g; CHOL 91mg; IRON 2mg; SODIUM 388mg; CALC 59mg

Lamb Chops with Minted Yogurt Sauce

serve with:
Couscous Salad

Prep: 6 minutes • Cook: 3 minutes
Other: 5 minutes

½   cup water
½   cup uncooked wheat couscous
¾   cup chopped seeded plum tomato
⅓   cup minced fresh parsley
⅓   cup minced fresh mint
2   tablespoons fresh lemon juice
1   tablespoon olive oil
⅛   teaspoon salt

1. Bring water to a boil in a small saucepan. Stir in couscous. Cover, remove from heat, and let stand 5 minutes.
2. While couscous stands, combine tomato, parsley, mint, lemon juice, oil, and salt in a small bowl. Add couscous, and stir to combine. Serve at room temperature or chilled. Yield: 4 servings (serving size: ½ cup).

CALORIES 110; FAT 4.2g (sat 0.5g; mono 3.2g; poly 0.5g); PROTEIN 3.2g; CARB 16.6g; FIBER 1.9g; CHOL 0mg; IRON 0.7mg; SODIUM 78mg; CALC 16mg

Grilled Lamb Chops with Cherry Port Sauce

Prep: 3 minutes • Cook: 16 minutes

Port, a sweet fortified wine, creates a vibrant sauce for the lamb. The unique flavor of port is hard to match, but if you need a substitute, use a fruity red wine or ⅔ cup pomegranate-cherry juice and ½ teaspoon sugar.

8   (4-ounce) lamb loin chops, trimmed
½   teaspoon salt, divided
½   teaspoon freshly ground black pepper
⅔   cup tawny port
1   teaspoon cornstarch
1   teaspoon water
¾   cup frozen pitted dark sweet cherries
1   teaspoon minced fresh thyme
Cooking spray

1. Preheat grill to medium-high heat.
2. Sprinkle lamb evenly with ¼ teaspoon salt and pepper; set aside.
3. Bring port to a boil in a medium skillet over high heat. Boil, uncovered, 2 to 3 minutes or until reduced to ⅓ cup. Reduce heat to medium. Combine cornstarch and water in a separate bowl, stirring until smooth. Add cornstarch mixture and cherries to pan. Simmer 1 minute or until sauce is slightly thick. Remove from heat; stir in thyme and remaining ¼ teaspoon salt.
4. Coat lamb with cooking spray; place on grill rack. Grill 5 minutes on each side or until desired degree of doneness. Serve cherry sauce over lamb. Yield: 4 servings (serving size: 2 chops and about 2½ tablespoons sauce).

CALORIES 295; FAT 9.3g (sat 3.3g; mono 4.3g; poly 1.6g); PROTEIN 28.9g; CARB 11.2g; FIBER 0.9g; CHOL 91mg; IRON 2.1mg; SODIUM 374mg; CALC 28mg

serve with:

Grilled Red Onion and Zucchini

Prep: 2 minutes • Cook: 10 minutes

3   tablespoons balsamic vinegar
2   teaspoons olive oil
¾   teaspoon Greek seasoning
1   large red onion, cut into 4 (½-inch-thick) slices
2   large zucchini, halved lengthwise
Cooking spray

1. Preheat grill to medium-high heat.
2. Combine first 3 ingredients in a large bowl. Add onion and zucchini; toss to coat.
3. Place vegetables on grill rack coated with cooking spray; cover and grill 10 to 12 minutes or until vegetables are tender. Yield: 4 servings (serving size: 1 zucchini half and 1 onion slice).

CALORIES 68; FAT 2.7g (sat 0.4g; mono 1.8g; poly 0.5g); PROTEIN 2.4g; CARB 10.4g; FIBER 2.4g; CHOL 0mg; IRON 0.6mg; SODIUM 202mg; CALC 33mg

Grilled Lamb Chops with Cherry Port Sauce

Sweet-Spiced Grilled Lamb Chops

Prep: 2 minutes • Cook: 8 minutes

On cold days when you don't want to brave the outdoor grill, broil these lamb chops in the oven instead.

¾   teaspoon ground cinnamon
½   teaspoon freshly ground black pepper
¼   teaspoon ground allspice
¼   teaspoon ground cumin
⅛   teaspoon salt
⅛   teaspoon ground red pepper
8   (4-ounce) lamb loin chops, trimmed (about 1 inch thick)
Cooking spray
Lime wedges (optional)

1. Preheat grill to medium-high heat.
2. Combine first 6 ingredients in a small bowl. Rub mixture evenly over lamb. Place lamb on grill rack coated with cooking spray. Grill 4 to 5 minutes on each side or until desired degree of doneness. Serve with lime wedges, if desired. Yield: 4 servings (serving size: 2 lamb chops).

CALORIES 209; FAT 9g (sat 3.3g, mono 4.1g, poly 0.6g); PROTEIN 28.7g; CARB 0.7g; FIBER 0.4g; CHOL 90mg; IRON 2.1mg; SODIUM 153mg; CALC 26mg

serve with:

Bulgur–Golden Raisin Pilaf

Prep: 3 minutes • Cook: 11 minutes
Other: 2 minutes

1   cup water
½   cup bulgur wheat with soy grits hot cereal
½   cup golden raisins
¼   teaspoon crushed red pepper
¼   cup slivered almonds, toasted
2   teaspoons butter
¼   teaspoon salt

1. Combine first 4 ingredients in a medium saucepan; bring to a boil. Cover, reduce heat, and simmer 8 minutes or until water is almost absorbed.
2. Remove from heat; stir in remaining ingredients. Let stand, uncovered, 2 minutes. Yield: 4 servings (serving size: ½ cup).

CALORIES 176; FAT 6g (sat 1.5g, mono 2.7g, poly 0.9g); PROTEIN 7.2g; CARB 28.8g; FIBER 3.2g; CHOL 5mg; IRON 1.6mg; SODIUM 161mg; CALC 49mg

Sweet-Spiced Grilled Lamb Chops

Broiled Lamb Chops with Lemon-Arugula Pesto

Prep: 3 minutes • Cook: 10 minutes

Broiled Lamb Chops with Lemon-Arugula Pesto

Arugula subs for the traditional basil to give this bright green sauce a hint of peppery flavor. The chops and carrots can broil at the same time, allowing you to get dinner on the table even faster.

8	(4-ounce) lamb loin chops, trimmed
½	teaspoon salt, divided
½	teaspoon freshly ground black pepper, divided

Cooking spray

1	lemon
1	tablespoon pine nuts, toasted
2	garlic cloves
4	cups baby arugula leaves
2	teaspoons olive oil
2	tablespoons water

1. Preheat broiler.
2. Sprinkle lamb evenly with ¼ teaspoon salt and ¼ teaspoon pepper. Arrange lamb in a single layer on a broiler pan coated with cooking spray; broil 5 to 6 minutes on each side or until desired degree of doneness.
3. While lamb broils, grate 1 teaspoon lemon rind; squeeze juice from lemon to measure 2 teaspoons.
4. Place pine nuts and garlic in a blender or food processor; process until minced. Add lemon rind, lemon juice, arugula, oil, 2 tablespoons water, remaining ¼ teaspoon salt, and remaining ¼ teaspoon pepper; process until smooth. Serve with lamb. Yield: 4 servings (serving size: 2 lamb chops and 2 tablespoons pesto).

CALORIES 249; FAT 13g (sat 3.8g, mono 6.1g, poly 1.7g); PROTEIN 29.5g; CARB 2g; FIBER 0.6g; CHOL 90mg; IRON 2.4mg; SODIUM 376mg; CALC 55mg

serve with:

Honey-Roasted Carrots

Prep: 3 minutes • Cook: 16 minutes

1	(12-ounce) package carrot sticks (about 3 cups)

Cooking spray

¼	teaspoon salt
¼	teaspoon freshly ground black pepper
1	tablespoon butter, melted
1	tablespoon brown sugar
1	tablespoon honey
2	teaspoons chopped fresh parsley

1. Preheat broiler.
2. Arrange carrot sticks on a jelly-roll pan coated with cooking spray. Coat carrots with cooking spray. Sprinkle evenly with salt and pepper, tossing to coat.
3. Broil 14 minutes or until carrots begin to brown, stirring once.
4. While carrots broil, combine butter, brown sugar, and honey in a small bowl. Pour butter mixture over carrots, tossing to coat. Broil 2 minutes or until carrots are browned and tender. Sprinkle with parsley. Yield: 4 servings (serving size: ¾ cup).

CALORIES 85; FAT 3g (sat 1.8g, mono 0.8g, poly 0.2g); PROTEIN 0.9g; CARB 14.9g; FIBER 2.5g; CHOL 8mg; IRON 0.4mg; SODIUM 226mg; CALC 33mg

Veal Piccata

Veal Piccata

Prep: 18 minutes • Cook: 8 minutes

Round out this delicious meal by serving the veal over cooked angel hair pasta. The lemon-caper pan sauce can do double duty in moistening both the veal and the pasta. Just place the veal cutlet on top of the pasta before pouring the pan sauce over it.

4	(4-ounce) veal cutlets (about ¼ inch thick)
¼	teaspoon salt
¼	teaspoon freshly ground black pepper
2	tablespoons all-purpose flour
Olive oil–flavored cooking spray	
1	garlic clove, minced
½	cup dry white wine
¼	cup fat-free, lower-sodium chicken broth
2	tablespoons fresh lemon juice
2	tablespoons drained capers
1	tablespoon butter

1. Sprinkle veal with salt and pepper. Combine veal and flour in a large zip-top plastic bag; seal bag, and shake to coat with flour.
2. Heat a large nonstick skillet over medium-high heat. Coat pan with cooking spray. Add veal; cook 2 minutes on each side or until browned. Remove veal from pan; keep warm.
3. Recoat pan with cooking spray. Add garlic; sauté 30 seconds. Add wine and next 3 ingredients. Bring to a boil; reduce heat, and simmer, uncovered, 3 minutes or until reduced by half, stirring occasionally. Stir in butter; pour sauce over veal. Yield: 4 servings (serving size: 1 veal cutlet and ¼ cup sauce).

CALORIES 248; FAT 13.9g (sat 6g, mono 5.1g, poly 0.9g); PROTEIN 19.7g; CARB 4.9g; FIBER 0.3g; CHOL 81mg; IRON 1mg; SODIUM 379mg; CALC 23mg

Thai Pork Roll-Ups

Prep: 10 minutes • Cook: 4 minutes

Look for rice paper at Asian markets or in the Asian ingredients section of the supermarket. If you can't find it, substitute two whole-grain tortillas.

Cooking spray	
1	(4-ounce) boneless center-cut loin pork chop, cut into 8 thin strips
½	cup shredded napa (Chinese) cabbage
½	cup matchstick-cut carrots
2	tablespoons spicy peanut sauce
4	(8-inch) round sheets rice paper
2	tablespoons cilantro leaves
2	tablespoons lightly salted peanuts

1. Heat a small nonstick skillet over medium-high heat. Coat pan with cooking spray. Add pork; sauté 3 minutes or until lightly browned. Remove from pan.
2. Combine cabbage, carrots, and peanut sauce in a medium bowl.
3. Pour hot water to a depth of 1 inch into a large shallow dish. Place 1 rice paper sheet in hot water; let stand 30 seconds or until softened. Remove rice paper from water; place on work surface. Arrange 2 pieces pork on one-half of rice paper sheet; top with one-fourth of cabbage mixture, 1½ teaspoons cilantro, and 1½ teaspoons peanuts. Fold sides over filling, and roll up. Place roll in an airtight container. Repeat procedure with remaining rice paper sheets, pork, cabbage mixture, cilantro, and peanuts, placing rolls in a single layer in container. Cover and store in refrigerator until ready to serve. Yield: 2 servings (serving size: 2 roll-ups).

CALORIES 241; FAT 9.4g (sat 1.9g, mono 4g, poly 2.2g); PROTEIN 16.5g; CARB 22.3g; FIBER 1.7g; CHOL 33mg; IRON 0.7mg; SODIUM 339mg; CALC 30mg

Hoisin Pork and Boston
Lettuce Wraps

Hoisin Pork and Boston Lettuce Wraps

Prep: 11 minutes • Cook: 4 minutes

Tender strips of pork, coated with a lime-infused hoisin sauce, nestle in the delicate folds of soft, buttery Boston lettuce leaves. A crunchy coleslaw tops them. Three wraps are perfect for a light summer meal; individual wraps make excellent appetizers.

⅓   cup hoisin sauce
1   tablespoon plus 1 teaspoon fresh lime juice
1   tablespoon plus 1 teaspoon water
3   cups packaged cabbage-and-carrot coleslaw
½   cup chopped fresh cilantro
⅓   cup unsalted peanuts
Cooking spray
3   (4-ounce) boneless center-cut loin pork chops, cut into 24 thin strips
12   Boston lettuce leaves

1. Combine first 3 ingredients in a small bowl; set aside.
2. Combine coleslaw, cilantro, and peanuts; set aside.
3. Heat a large nonstick skillet over medium-high heat. Coat pan with cooking spray. Add pork; sauté 4 minutes or until lightly browned. Remove from pan.
4. Arrange 3 lettuce leaves on each of 4 plates. Top each lettuce leaf with 2 slices pork, hoisin-lime sauce, and coleslaw. Yield: 4 servings (serving size: 3 lettuce leaves, 6 slices pork, about 2 tablespoons hoisin-lime sauce, and about ¾ cup coleslaw).

CALORIES 252; FAT 12g (sat 2.7g, mono 5.4g, poly 2.6g); PROTEIN 22.2g; CARB 14.9g; FIBER 2.6g; CHOL 49mg; IRON 1.4mg; SODIUM 389mg; CALC 57mg

Curried Pork and Chai Rice

Prep: 3 minutes • Cook: 12 minutes
Other: 5 minutes

Delight your palate by cooking with chai tea. Chai is a fragrantly spiced, sweetened black tea served in India. It typically includes a combination of cinnamon, cloves, cardamom, and black peppercorns.

1   large navel orange
¾   cup plus 2 tablespoons water
2   spiced chai tea bags
1   cup uncooked instant brown rice
½   teaspoon salt, divided
4   (4-ounce) boneless center-cut loin pork chops (about ½ inch thick)
1   teaspoon curry powder
¼   teaspoon ground cumin (optional)
Cooking spray

1. Grate rind from orange to measure 1 teaspoon. Squeeze juice from orange to measure 6 tablespoons. Combine 2 tablespoons orange juice, ¾ cup plus 2 tablespoons water, and tea bags in a medium saucepan; bring to a boil. Add rice; cover, reduce heat, and simmer 5 minutes. Remove from heat; let stand, covered, 5 minutes. Remove tea bags; stir in orange rind and ¼ teaspoon salt.
2. While rice cooks, sprinkle pork evenly with remaining ¼ teaspoon salt, curry powder, and cumin, if desired. Heat a large nonstick skillet over medium-high heat. Coat pan with cooking spray. Add pork; cook 4 minutes on each side or until done. Transfer to a serving platter, and keep warm. Add remaining 4 tablespoons orange juice to pan; cook 1 minute, scraping pan to loosen browned bits or until reduced to 2 tablespoons. Drizzle sauce over pork; serve with rice. Yield: 4 servings (serving size: 1 pork chop and ½ cup rice).

CALORIES 254; FAT 7g (sat 2.4g, mono 2.9g, poly 0.5g); PROTEIN 25.8g; CARB 22.2g; FIBER 2g; CHOL 65mg; IRON 1.1mg; SODIUM 344mg; CALC 43mg

Apple-Mustard–Glazed Pork Chops

Prep: 5 minutes • Cook: 10 minutes
Other: 3 minutes

Fruity apple juice and tangy mustard are a perfect flavor combo for these grilled pork chops.

1	tablespoon canola oil
4	(4-ounce) boneless center-cut loin pork chops (about ½ inch thick)
½	teaspoon salt
¼	teaspoon ground red pepper, divided
¼	cup thawed apple juice concentrate, undiluted
1	tablespoon cider vinegar
1	tablespoon water
2	teaspoons stone-ground mustard

Cooking spray

1. Preheat grill to medium-high heat.
2. Rub oil over both sides of pork; sprinkle with salt and ⅛ teaspoon red pepper.

3. Combine remaining ⅛ teaspoon red pepper, apple juice concentrate, and next 3 ingredients. Place pork on grill rack coated with cooking spray; grill 5 minutes on each side or until a meat thermometer inserted into thickest portion registers 145°, basting frequently with apple juice mixture. Let chops stand 3 minutes before serving. Yield: 4 servings (serving size: 1 pork chop).

CALORIES 208; FAT 7.9g (sat 1.5g, mono 3.9g, poly 1.5g); PROTEIN 25g; CARB 7.4g; FIBER 0g; CHOL 78mg; IRON 0.8mg; SODIUM 389mg; CALC 21mg

serve with:
Broccolini with Bacon

Prep: 2 minutes • Cook: 10 minutes

3	quarts water
1	pound Broccolini
2	center-cut bacon slices
½	cup coarsely chopped sweet onion
¼	cup fat-free, lower-sodium chicken broth
⅛	teaspoon salt
⅛	teaspoon freshly ground black pepper

1. Bring 3 quarts water to a boil. Add Broccolini to boiling water; cook 4 minutes or until crisp-tender. Drain.
2. Cook bacon in a large nonstick skillet over medium heat until crisp. Remove bacon from pan; crumble. Add onion to drippings in pan; sauté 4 minutes or until tender. Stir in broth, salt, and pepper, scraping pan to loosen browned bits. Add Broccolini; toss well. Sprinkle with bacon. Yield: 4 servings.

CALORIES 66; FAT 0.8g (sat 0.3g, mono 0.3g, poly 0.1g); PROTEIN 5.3g; CARB 10g; FIBER 1.7g; CHOL 3mg; IRON 1.1mg; SODIUM 187mg; CALC 85mg

Apple-Mustard–Glazed
Pork Chops

Pork Chops with Mustard Cream Sauce

Prep: 3 minutes • Cook: 14 minutes

Using fat-free half-and-half gives this dish a creamy, rich flavor that fat-free milk can't. Sprinkle the finished dish with chopped fresh parsley, if desired.

4	(4-ounce) boneless center-cut loin pork chops (about ½ inch thick)
½	teaspoon salt
¼	teaspoon freshly ground black pepper
Cooking spray	
½	cup fat-free, lower-sodium chicken broth
⅔	cup fat-free half-and-half
1	tablespoon Dijon mustard
2	teaspoons fresh lemon juice
Chopped fresh parsley (optional)	

1. Sprinkle both sides of pork with salt and pepper.
2. Heat a large nonstick skillet over medium-high heat. Coat pan with cooking spray. Add pork, and cook 4 to 5 minutes on each side or until lightly browned and done. Transfer pork to a serving plate, and keep warm.
3. Add broth to pan, scraping pan to loosen browned bits. Stir in half-and-half, mustard, and lemon juice. Reduce heat, and simmer, uncovered, 6 minutes or until sauce is slightly thick. Spoon sauce over pork; sprinkle with parsley, if desired. Yield: 4 servings (serving size: 1 pork chop and 2 tablespoons sauce).

CALORIES 193; FAT 6.4g (sat 2.3g; mono 2.7g; poly 1.2g); PROTEIN 24.3g; CARB 5.2g; FIBER 0g; CHOL 65mg; IRON 0.7mg; SODIUM 539mg; CALC 52mg

Pork Chops with Mustard Cream Sauce

serve with:
Roasted Potato Wedges

Prep: 3 minutes • Cook: 20 minutes

1	pound small red potatoes, quartered
2	teaspoons olive oil
¼	cup panko (Japanese breadcrumbs) with Italian seasoning
2	tablespoons grated Parmesan-Romano cheese blend
Cooking spray	

1. Preheat oven to 475°.
2. Combine potatoes and oil in a medium bowl, tossing to coat. Combine panko and cheese in a large zip-top plastic bag; add potatoes, tossing to coat. Place potatoes on a jelly-roll pan coated with cooking spray; discard remaining breadcrumb mixture. Bake at 475° for 20 minutes or until browned and crispy. Yield: 4 servings (serving size: about ¾ cup).

CALORIES 123; FAT 3.7g (sat 1.1g; mono 2g; poly 0.6g); PROTEIN 3.9g; CARB 19.9g; FIBER 2.2g; CHOL 4mg; IRON 0.9mg; SODIUM 88mg; CALC 56mg

Seared Pork Chops with Spicy Roasted Pepper Sauce

Prep: 2 minutes • Cook: 10 minutes

Rather than searing the chops in oil, extra-virgin olive oil is drizzled over the cooked chops just before serving for a boost of flavor. Though not ideal as a cooking fat due to its low smoke point, extra-virgin olive oil has a richer, more complex character than refined varieties. Serve this dish with steamed green beans.

4   (4-ounce) boneless center-cut loin pork chops (about ½ inch thick)
2   teaspoons 25%-less-sodium Montreal steak seasoning
Olive oil–flavored cooking spray
1   cup bottled roasted red bell pepper, drained
1   chipotle chile, canned in adobo sauce
2   tablespoons water
½   teaspoon ground cumin
2   teaspoons extra-virgin olive oil

1. Sprinkle pork evenly with steak seasoning. Heat a large nonstick skillet over medium-high heat. Coat pork with cooking spray. Add pork to pan; cook 4 minutes. Turn pork over; cook 3 minutes.

2. While pork cooks, place bell pepper and next 3 ingredients in a blender; process until smooth. When pork is done, remove pan from heat. Remove pork from pan; cover and keep warm.

3. Add bell pepper mixture to pan; return pan to medium heat. Cook 1 to 2 minutes, stirring often. Spoon 2 tablespoons sauce onto each of 4 serving plates. Top each with a pork chop; drizzle with ½ teaspoon oil. Yield: 4 servings (serving size: 1 pork chop and 2 tablespoons sauce).

CALORIES 194; FAT 9g (sat 2.7g, mono 4.7g, poly 0.7g); PROTEIN 23.9g; CARB 1.7g; FIBER 0.3g; CHOL 65mg; IRON 0.8mg; SODIUM 443mg; CALC 27mg

Seared Pork Chops with Spicy Roasted Pepper Sauce

Spiced Pork Chops with Butternut Squash

Prep: 4 minutes • Cook: 21 minutes

Don't reserve pumpkin pie spice for desserts alone; sprinkle this blend of cinnamon, ginger, nutmeg, and allspice on pork chops for a fragrant, home-style dish.

Cooking spray
4   (4-ounce) boneless center-cut loin pork chops (about ¾ inch thick)
1   teaspoon pumpkin pie spice
½   teaspoon freshly ground black pepper
¼   teaspoon salt, divided
1   butternut squash (about 1¼ pounds)
1   cup refrigerated prechopped onion
¼   cup water
1   tablespoon chopped fresh mint

1. Heat a large nonstick skillet over medium-high heat. Coat pan with cooking spray. Sprinkle pork evenly with spice, pepper, and ⅛ teaspoon salt. Add pork to pan; sauté 3 to 4 minutes on each side or until done. Remove pork from pan; keep warm.
2. While pork cooks, pierce squash several times with a fork; place on paper towels in microwave oven. Microwave at HIGH 1 minute. Peel squash; cut in half lengthwise. Discard seeds and membrane. Coarsely chop squash.
3. Coat pan with cooking spray. Add squash; cover and cook 7 minutes, stirring occasionally. Add onion; cook, uncovered, 5 minutes, stirring frequently. Add ¼ cup water; cook until liquid evaporates, scraping pan to loosen browned bits. Remove from heat; stir in remaining ⅛ teaspoon salt and mint. Spoon squash mixture evenly over pork. Yield: 4 servings (serving size: 1 pork chop and ¾ cup squash).

CALORIES 232; FAT 7g (sat 2.4g, mono 2.9g, poly 0.5g); PROTEIN 25.6g; CARB 18.2g; FIBER 3.2g; CHOL 65mg; IRON 1.7mg; SODIUM 200mg; CALC 96mg

serve with:

Ginger Couscous with Jalapeños and Cilantro

Prep: 2 minutes • Cook: 2 minutes
Other: 5 minutes

⅔   cup uncooked whole-wheat couscous
1   jalapeño pepper, seeded and minced
2   tablespoons chopped fresh cilantro
1½   teaspoons grated peeled fresh ginger
2   teaspoons canola oil
¼   teaspoon salt

1. Prepare couscous according to package directions for 2 servings, omitting salt and fat. Fluff with a fork; stir in jalapeño pepper and remaining ingredients. Yield: 4 servings (serving size: about ½ cup).

CALORIES 92; FAT 3g (sat 0.2g, mono 1.4g, poly 0.7g); PROTEIN 2.7g; CARB 15.4g; FIBER 2.5g; CHOL 0mg; IRON 0.6mg; SODIUM 146mg; CALC 8mg

quick flip

Want a sweeter side dish? Swap out jalapeño and cilantro for apricots and mint.

Lemon-Herb Skillet
Pork Chops

1. Sprinkle both sides of pork evenly with salt and pepper. Combine flour and next 3 ingredients in a shallow dish. Dredge pork in flour mixture.
2. Heat a large nonstick skillet over medium-high heat. Add oil to pan; swirl to coat. Add pork; cook 4 minutes on each side or until pork is done. Serve with lemon wedges. Yield: 4 servings (serving size: 1 pork chop and 1 lemon wedge).

CALORIES 218; FAT 10g (sat 2.9g, mono 5.4g, poly 1g); PROTEIN 24.7g; CARB 5.9g; FIBER 0.7g; CHOL 65mg; IRON 1.1mg; SODIUM 340mg; CALC 41mg

serve with:

Sweet Pea and Bell Pepper Toss

Prep: 1 minute • Cook: 7 minutes

Cooking spray
1   cup refrigerated prechopped onion
1   cup refrigerated prechopped tricolor bell pepper mix
1   cup frozen petite green peas
¼   teaspoon salt

1. Heat a large nonstick skillet over medium-high heat. Coat pan with cooking spray. Add onion to pan; coat with cooking spray. Cook 2 minutes. Add bell pepper; coat with cooking spray. Cook 3 minutes or until vegetables are tender and lightly browned, stirring frequently.
2. Stir in peas and salt; cook 1 to 2 minutes or until thoroughly heated, stirring frequently. Yield: 4 servings (serving size: ½ cup).

CALORIES 34; FAT 0g (sat 0g, mono 0g, poly 0.1g); PROTEIN 1.4g; CARB 7.5g; FIBER 1.7g; CHOL 0mg; IRON 0.4mg; SODIUM 160mg; CALC 15mg

Lemon-Herb Skillet Pork Chops

Prep: 2 minutes • Cook: 11 minutes

A squeeze of fresh lemon completes the dish and provides a hint of tartness that enhances the natural mild sweetness of the chops.

4   (4-ounce) boneless center-cut loin pork chops (about ½ inch thick)
½   teaspoon salt
½   teaspoon freshly ground black pepper
3   tablespoons all-purpose flour
¾   teaspoon dried thyme
¾   teaspoon paprika
¼   teaspoon dried rubbed sage
1   tablespoon olive oil
4   lemon wedges

Asiago-Crusted Pork Chops

Prep: 5 minutes • Cook: 9 minutes

Asiago cheese—a popular Italian cow's milk cheese—and crunchy breadcrumbs form a delicate crust on these fork-tender pork chops. Accompany with Broccoli with Sour Cream Sauce for a hearty meal that can be on the table in less than 15 minutes.

4	(4-ounce) boneless center-cut loin pork chops
1	large egg white, lightly beaten
½	cup panko (Japanese breadcrumbs)
¼	cup (1 ounce) grated Asiago cheese
¼	teaspoon salt
¼	teaspoon freshly ground black pepper
1	tablespoon extra-virgin olive oil
4	lemon wedges
2	teaspoons chopped fresh thyme

1. Place pork between 2 sheets of plastic wrap; pound to an even thickness (about ¼-inch) using a meat mallet or a small heavy skillet.
2. Place egg white in a shallow dish. Combine panko, cheese, salt, and pepper in a shallow dish. Dip pork in egg white; dredge in panko mixture, pressing gently with fingers to coat.
3. Heat oil in a large nonstick skillet over medium heat. Add pork; cook 3 to 4 minutes on each side or until lightly browned. Squeeze 1 lemon wedge over each pork chop; sprinkle each evenly with thyme. Yield: 4 servings (serving size: 1 pork chop).

CALORIES 253; FAT 12g (sat 4.1g, mono 5.4g, poly 1g); PROTEIN 27.4g; CARB 6.2g; FIBER 0.6g; CHOL 71mg; IRON 0.7mg; SODIUM 297mg; CALC 83mg

Asiago-Crusted Pork Chops

serve with:
Broccoli with Sour Cream Sauce

Prep: 2 minutes • Cook: 6 minutes

1	(12-ounce) package refrigerated broccoli florets
⅓	cup reduced-fat sour cream
2	tablespoons 1% low-fat milk
1	teaspoon Dijon mustard
¼	teaspoon salt

1. Microwave broccoli according to package directions.
2. While broccoli cooks, combine sour cream and remaining ingredients in a small saucepan. Cook over medium heat until thoroughly heated, stirring frequently (do not boil).
3. Arrange broccoli on a serving plate; drizzle with sauce. Yield: 4 servings (serving size: about 1 cup broccoli and about 1½ tablespoons sauce).

CALORIES 60; FAT 3g (sat 1.7g, mono 0g, poly 0.2g); PROTEIN 3.7g; CARB 6.4g; FIBER 2.5g; CHOL 11mg; IRON 0.8mg; SODIUM 214mg; CALC 84mg

Orange-Ginger Pork Chops

Orange-Ginger Pork Chops

Prep: 5 minutes • Cook: 12 minutes

1   navel orange
2   tablespoons lower-sodium soy sauce
2   teaspoons grated peeled fresh ginger
½   teaspoon freshly ground black pepper
4   (4-ounce) boneless center-cut loin pork
       chops (about ½ inch thick)
Cooking spray

1. Grate 2 teaspoons rind and squeeze ¼ cup juice from orange. Combine orange rind, orange juice, soy sauce, ginger, and pepper in a shallow dish. Add pork, turning to coat.
2. Heat a medium nonstick skillet over medium heat. Coat pan with cooking spray. Remove pork from marinade, reserving marinade. Add pork to pan; cook 5 minutes on each side or until done. Remove from pan, and keep warm. Add marinade to pan. Bring to a boil; boil 1 minute. Spoon sauce evenly over pork. Yield: 4 servings (serving size: 1 pork chop and 1½ teaspoons sauce).

CALORIES 157; FAT 5.8g (sat 1.7g, mono 2.1g, poly 0.7g); PROTEIN 21.8g; CARB 2.7g; FIBER 0.2g; CHOL 66mg; IRON 0.7mg; SODIUM 347mg; CALC 23mg

Pork Schnitzel

Prep: 8 minutes • Cook: 9 minutes

Schnitzel is German for cutlet. Thinly pounded, breaded, and fried, this dish of thin pork chops is traditionally served with spaetzle, tiny noodlelike dumplings. Panko keeps the pork light and crispy with a satisfying crunch.

4   (4-ounce) boneless loin pork chops
½   teaspoon salt
½   teaspoon freshly ground black pepper
1.1   ounces all-purpose flour (about ¼ cup)
1   large egg, lightly beaten
1   cup panko (Japanese breadcrumbs)
Cooking spray
3   teaspoons canola oil, divided
4   lemon wedges
Chopped fresh parsley (optional)

1. Place pork between 2 sheets of heavy-duty plastic wrap; pound to ⅛-inch thickness using a meat mallet or small heavy skillet. Cut each piece in half.
2. Sprinkle pork evenly with salt and pepper. Place flour, egg, and panko each in a shallow dish. Dredge pork in flour; dip in egg. Dredge in panko.
3. Heat a large nonstick skillet over medium-high heat. Coat pan with cooking spray. Add 1½ teaspoons oil to pan; swirl to coat. Add half of pork. Cook 2 minutes on each side or until desired degree of doneness. Repeat procedure with remaining 1½ teaspoons oil and remaining pork. Serve with lemon wedges, and, if desired, sprinkle with parsley. Yield: 4 servings (serving size: 2 pieces of pork).

CALORIES 348; FAT 17.9g (sat 5.8g, mono 9.1g, poly 2.9g); PROTEIN 27.2g; CARB 17.1g; FIBER 1g; CHOL 107mg; IRON 1.4mg; SODIUM 385mg; CALC 32mg

serve with:

Sautéed Brussels Sprouts and Red Cabbage with Bacon

Prep: 1 minute • Cook: 12 minutes

2   center-cut bacon slices
2   cups shredded Brussels sprouts
2   cups thinly sliced red cabbage
1   cup refrigerated prechopped onion
1   tablespoon brown sugar
2   tablespoons cider vinegar
¼   teaspoon salt
¼   teaspoon freshly ground black pepper

1. Cook bacon in a large nonstick skillet over medium heat until crisp. Remove bacon from pan; crumble. Add Brussels sprouts, cabbage, and onion to drippings in pan; sauté 4 minutes or until tender.
2. Stir in brown sugar and next 3 ingredients. Sauté 2 minutes or until liquid almost evaporates; stir in bacon. Yield: 4 servings (serving size: ¾ cup).

CALORIES 74; FAT 0.9g (sat 0.3g, mono 0.3g, poly 0.3g); PROTEIN 3.6g; CARB 14.5g; FIBER 3.3g; CHOL 3mg; IRON 1.2mg; SODIUM 215mg; CALC 52mg

Pork Schnitzel

Grilled Peach Barbecue Pork Chops

Prep: 4 minutes • Cook: 9 minutes

3	large ripe peaches
¼	cup barbecue sauce
1	tablespoon cider vinegar
1	tablespoon honey
4	(6-ounce) bone-in center-cut loin pork chops (about ¾ inch thick), trimmed
¼	teaspoon salt
¼	teaspoon freshly ground black pepper

Cooking spray

1. Preheat grill to medium-high heat.
2. Peel, halve, and remove pits from peaches. Coarsely chop 1 peach. Place chopped peach, barbecue sauce, vinegar, and honey in a blender or food processor; process until smooth. Reserve ½ cup of sauce mixture.
3. Sprinkle pork evenly with salt and pepper. Place pork on grill rack coated with cooking spray. Brush ¼ cup sauce on tops of pork. Grill pork 4 minutes. Turn pork over; brush with ¼ cup sauce. Add peach halves to grill rack, cut sides down; grill 4 minutes or until pork reaches desired degree of doneness and peaches are tender. Remove pork and peach halves from grill; cut each peach half into 3 wedges. Serve pork and peach wedges with reserved sauce. Yield: 4 servings (serving size: 1 pork chop, 3 peach wedges, and 2 tablespoons sauce).

CALORIES 256; FAT 7.5g (sat 3g, mono 3.6g, poly 0.9g); PROTEIN 26.9g; CARB 20.2g; FIBER 1.8g; CHOL 74mg; IRON 1.3mg; SODIUM 320mg; CALC 28mg

serve with:

Grilled Corn with Jalapeño-Herb "Butter"

Prep: 1 minute • Cook: 10 minutes

4	ears shucked corn

Cooking spray

2	tablespoons yogurt-based spread
1½	tablespoons minced seeded jalapeño pepper (about 1 medium pepper)
1	tablespoon chopped fresh cilantro
1	teaspoon grated lime rind
¼	teaspoon freshly ground black pepper

1. Preheat grill to medium-high heat.
2. Place corn on grill rack coated with cooking spray. Grill 10 minutes or until corn is tender, turning occasionally.
3. While corn cooks, combine spread and next 4 ingredients in a small bowl. Spread about 1 tablespoon Jalapeño-Herb "Butter" over each ear of corn. Yield: 4 servings (serving size: 1 ear of corn).

CALORIES 102; FAT 3.6g (sat 0.7g, mono 0.9g, poly 1.9g); PROTEIN 3g; CARB 17.5g; FIBER 2.6g; CHOL 0mg; IRON 0.5mg; SODIUM 59mg; CALC 4mg

make ahead

Make the "Butter" ahead of time and store in your refrigerator. Have any left over? It's yummy on top of any grilled chicken.

Pork Medallions with Spicy Pomegranate-Blueberry Reduction

Prep: 2 minutes • Cook: 11 minutes

The smokiness of chipotle chiles complements the concentrated sweetness of pomegranate and blueberry juices in this tender entrée.

1   (1-pound) pork tenderloin, trimmed and cut crosswise into ¾-inch round slices
¼   teaspoon garlic powder
¼   teaspoon salt
¼   teaspoon freshly ground black pepper
Butter-flavored cooking spray
¼   cup water
⅓   cup frozen pomegranate-blueberry juice concentrate, undiluted
1½   teaspoons minced chipotle chiles, canned in adobo sauce

1. Heat a large nonstick skillet over medium-high heat. While pan heats, pound pork slices slightly with the heel of your hand or a meat mallet; sprinkle with garlic powder, salt, and pepper. Coat pork with cooking spray.
2. Add pork to pan. Cook pork 3 minutes on each side or until desired degree of doneness (do not overcook). Remove pork from pan; place on a serving platter. Add ¼ cup water to pan, scraping pan to loosen browned bits. Stir in juice concentrate and chipotle chiles. Reduce heat to medium; simmer 3 to 4 minutes or until slightly syrupy.
3. Return pork and juices to pan, turning pork to coat. Serve pork with sauce. Yield: 4 servings (serving size: 3 ounces pork and about 1 tablespoon sauce).

CALORIES 147; FAT 4g (sat 1.3g, mono 1.5g, poly 0.3g); PROTEIN 22.5g; CARB 3.3g; FIBER 0.2g; CHOL 63mg; IRON 1.2mg; SODIUM 206mg; CALC 7mg

Pork Medallions with Cranberry Sauce

Prep: 6 minutes • Cook: 9 minutes

Frozen cranberries work well when you cannot find fresh. Complement the sweetness of the cranberry sauce by serving this dish with Swiss chard.

1   (1-pound) pork tenderloin, trimmed
¼   teaspoon salt
½   teaspoon freshly ground black pepper
1   cup fresh or frozen cranberries
½   cup fat-free, lower-sodium chicken broth
¼   cup sugar
1   teaspoon chopped fresh sage
Cooking spray

1. Cut pork crosswise into 8 pieces. Place pork between 2 sheets of heavy-duty plastic wrap; pound to ¼-inch thickness using a meat mallet or small heavy skillet. Sprinkle both sides of pork evenly with salt and pepper.
2. Combine cranberries, broth, and sugar in a small saucepan. Bring to a boil; boil 6 minutes or until berries burst and sauce is reduced to ⅔ cup. Stir in sage.
3. While sauce cooks, heat a large nonstick skillet over medium-high heat. Coat pan with cooking spray. Add pork to pan; cook 4 minutes on each side or until done. Serve pork with sauce. Yield: 4 servings (serving size: 2 pork medallions and about 3 tablespoons sauce).

CALORIES 202; FAT 4g (sat 1.3g, mono 1.5g, poly 0.6g); PROTEIN 23.8g; CARB 16.4g; FIBER 1.1g; CHOL 73.7mg; IRON 1.1mg; SODIUM 278mg; CALC 9mg

Pork Medallions with
Cranberry Sauce

Fiery Grilled Pork Tenderloin

Prep: 4 minutes • Cook: 20 minutes
Other: 5 minutes

A double shot of pepper—black and red—adds kick to this grilled dish. If you want less heat on the pork, use only 1 tablespoon of the ground pepper blend.

1	(1-pound) pork tenderloin, trimmed
2	teaspoons olive oil
1½	tablespoons ground black and red pepper blend
1	tablespoon dark brown sugar
½	teaspoon garlic powder
¼	teaspoon salt

Cooking spray

1. Preheat grill to medium-high heat.
2. Pat pork dry with paper towels. Rub oil over pork.
3. Combine pepper blend and next 3 ingredients; rub over pork. Place pork on grill rack coated with cooking spray. Grill 20 minutes or until a thermometer registers 160° (slightly pink), turning once. Remove pork from grill; let stand 5 minutes. Cut pork diagonally into ½-inch slices. Yield: 4 servings (serving size: 3 ounces).

CALORIES 170; FAT 6.1g (sat 1.7g, mono 3.5g, poly 0.8g); PROTEIN 23.9g; CARB 3.6g; FIBER 0g; CHOL 74mg; IRON 1.5mg; SODIUM 204mg; CALC 9mg

serve with:
Grilled Summer Squash with Garlic and Lime

Prep: 4 minutes • Cook: 10 minutes

2	teaspoons olive oil
4	large garlic cloves, pressed
3	small yellow squash, cut in half lengthwise
3	small zucchini, cut in half lengthwise
¼	teaspoon salt
¼	teaspoon freshly ground black pepper

Cooking spray

4	lime wedges

1. Preheat grill to medium-high heat.
2. Combine oil and garlic in a small bowl; brush over squash. Sprinkle squash and zucchini halves with salt and pepper.
3. Place squash halves on grill rack coated with cooking spray. Grill 5 to 6 minutes on each side or until almost tender.
4. Place squash halves on a serving platter; squeeze lime wedges over squash. Yield: 4 servings (serving size: 3 squash halves).

CALORIES 54; FAT 2.6g (sat 0.4g, mono 1.7g, poly 0.4g); PROTEIN 2.4g; CARB 7.4g; FIBER 2.1g; CHOL 0mg; IRON 0.7mg; SODIUM 157mg; CALC 33mg

quick flip

Instead of squash and zucchini, try grilling red onions and bell peppers.

Teriyaki Pork Medallions

Prep: 5 minutes • Cook: 11 minutes

Mirin, a rice wine with a low alcohol content, is the key ingredient to this teriyaki sauce's authentic flavor. The wine's high sugar content allows it to reduce into a syrup glaze. Look for mirin in the Asian foods section of your local supermarket. Serve with Pineapple Salsa and precooked white rice.

6	tablespoons mirin (sweet rice wine)
2	tablespoons lower-sodium soy sauce
1½	teaspoons brown sugar
1	teaspoon dark sesame oil
1	(1-pound) pork tenderloin, trimmed

Cooking spray
Pineapple Salsa

1. Combine first 4 ingredients, stirring with a whisk.
2. Cut pork crosswise into 8 pieces. Place pork pieces between 2 sheets of heavy-duty plastic wrap; pound each piece to ½-inch thickness using a meat mallet or small heavy skillet.
3. Heat a large nonstick skillet over medium-high heat. Coat pork generously with cooking spray; add to pan. Cook 3 minutes on each side or until done. Remove pork from pan; place on a serving platter. Add mirin mixture to pan. Cook 2 minutes or until mixture thickens slightly.
4. Return pork and accumulated juices to pan. Cook 2 minutes, turning pork to coat. Serve pork with sauce and Pineapple Salsa. Yield: 4 servings (serving size: 3 ounces pork, 1 tablespoon sauce, and ⅓ cup Pineapple Salsa).

CALORIES 284; FAT 8.3g (sat 2.7g, mono 3.4g, poly 1.9g); PROTEIN 35.1g; CARB 9.5g; FIBER 0.1g; CHOL 107mg; IRON 1.9mg; SODIUM 374mg; CALC 11mg

Teriyaki Pork Medallions

Pineapple Salsa

Prep: 8 minutes

1	cup diced fresh pineapple
¼	cup diced red onion
½	medium jalapeño pepper, minced
2	tablespoons chopped fresh cilantro
1	tablespoon fresh lime juice

1. Combine all ingredients in a medium bowl. Yield: 4 servings (serving size: ⅓ cup).

CALORIES 25; FAT 0.1g (sat 0g, mono 0g, poly 0g); PROTEIN 0.4g; CARB 6.5g; FIBER 0.7g; CHOL 0mg; IRON 0.1mg; SODIUM 1mg; CALC 8mg

Hoisin Pork Steaks

Prep: 3 minutes • Cook: 9 minutes
Other: 2 minutes

Butterflying the pork tenderloin and pounding it to a ¼-inch thickness helps these pork steaks cook fast and ensures a fork-tender bite.

1   (1-pound) pork tenderloin, trimmed
¼   teaspoon salt
Cooking spray
¼   cup rice wine vinegar
3   tablespoons honey
1   tablespoon hoisin sauce
¼   teaspoon crushed red pepper

1. Slice pork tenderloin lengthwise, cutting to, but not through, other side. Open halves, laying pork flat. Place plastic wrap over pork; pound to ¼-inch thickness using a meat mallet or small heavy skillet. Cut pork crosswise into 4 steaks; sprinkle with salt.
2. Heat a large nonstick skillet over medium-high heat. Coat pan with cooking spray. Add pork; cook 3 to 4 minutes on each side or until done. Transfer pork to a plate. Reduce heat to low.
3. Combine vinegar and remaining 3 ingredients in a small bowl, stirring with a whisk. Stir vinegar mixture into pan drippings; cook 1 minute. Return pork to skillet; remove from heat. Let stand 2 to 3 minutes or until thoroughly heated, turning often. Yield: 4 servings (serving size: 3 ounces pork and about 1 tablespoon sauce).

CALORIES 214; FAT 4.6g (sat 1.5g, mono 1.8g, poly 1g); PROTEIN 23.9g; CARB 18.8g; FIBER 0.1g; CHOL 74mg; IRON 1.5mg; SODIUM 399mg; CALC 7mg

Hoisin Pork Steaks

serve with:
Sesame Bok Choy

Prep: 2 minutes • Cook: 12 minutes

If you can't find baby bok choy, use a large bok choy, but chop it into large pieces.

6   baby bok choy
Cooking spray
2   teaspoons dark sesame oil
¼   teaspoon salt
⅛   teaspoon freshly ground black pepper
1   teaspoon sesame seeds
1   teaspoon black sesame seeds

1. Cut bok choy in half lengthwise, leaving core intact. Steam bok choy, covered, 4 minutes or until tender; drain well.
2. Heat a large nonstick skillet over medium-high heat. Coat pan with cooking spray. Drizzle cut sides of bok choy with oil; sprinkle with salt and pepper. Place bok choy, cut sides down, in pan; cook 6 minutes or until lightly browned. Turn bok choy over; cook an additional 1 to 2 minutes or until lightly browned. Sprinkle with sesame seeds. Yield: 4 servings (serving size: 3 bok choy halves).

CALORIES 52; FAT 3.1g (sat 0.4g, mono 1.2g, poly 1.3g); PROTEIN 2.6g; CARB 4.9g; FIBER 2.5g; CHOL 0mg; IRON 0.2mg; SODIUM 225mg; CALC 15mg

Seared Pork Tenderloin Medallions with Shallot-Mushroom Pan Gravy

Prep: 4 minutes • Cook: 10 minutes

Combine the cornstarch with the stock and sherry before adding it to the hot pan to keep the gravy smooth.

1	(1-pound) pork tenderloin, trimmed
½	teaspoon salt
½	teaspoon freshly ground black pepper
3	garlic cloves, minced
	Cooking spray
1	teaspoon olive oil
1	(8-ounce) package sliced baby bella mushrooms
⅓	cup chopped shallots (about 4)
2	teaspoons cornstarch
1	cup beef stock
1	tablespoon dry sherry

1. Cut pork diagonally into thin slices. Sprinkle pork with salt and pepper; rub with garlic. Heat a large nonstick skillet over medium-high heat. Coat pan with cooking spray. Add oil; swirl to coat. Add pork; cook 1 to 2 minutes on each side or until done. Transfer pork to a platter; keep warm.
2. Recoat skillet with cooking spray. Add mushrooms and shallots; cook, stirring often, 5 minutes.
3. While mushroom mixture cooks, place cornstarch in a small bowl. Gradually add stock and sherry, stirring with a whisk until smooth. Stir stock mixture into mushroom mixture, scraping to loosen browned bits. Bring to a boil; cook, stirring constantly with a whisk, 1 minute or until thickened. Return pork and accumulated juices to pan; cook 1 to 2 minutes or until thoroughly heated. Yield: 4 servings (serving size: 3 ounces pork and about ¾ cup mushroom gravy).

CALORIES 199; FAT 5.2g (sat 1.5g, mono 2.6g, poly 0.8g); PROTEIN 27.4g; CARB 10.1g; FIBER 1.2g; CHOL 74mg; IRON 2.2mg; SODIUM 490mg; CALC 26mg

Seared Pork Tenderloin Medallions with Shallot-Mushroom Pan Gravy

serve with:
Balsamic-Glazed Green Beans

Prep: 2 minutes • Cook: 6 minutes

1	(12-ounce) package trimmed green beans
1	tablespoon butter
3	tablespoons minced shallots (about 2)
2	garlic cloves, minced
¼	cup balsamic vinegar
½	teaspoon salt
¼	teaspoon freshly ground black pepper

1. Microwave green beans according to package directions.
2. While beans cook, melt butter in a large skillet over medium heat. Add shallots and garlic; cook, stirring constantly, 2 minutes. Stir in vinegar, salt, and pepper; cook 1 minute. Add beans, tossing to coat. Yield: 4 servings (serving size: ¾ cup).

CALORIES 76; FAT 3.1g (sat 1.9g, mono 0.8g, poly 0.2g); PROTEIN 2g; CARB 11.1g; FIBER 2.8g; CHOL 8mg; IRON 0.8mg; SODIUM 515mg; CALC 48mg

Smoked Paprika Pork

Prep: 4 minutes • Cook: 15 minutes
Other: 8 hours and 10 minutes

Infusing the oil with smoked paprika elevates the flavor of the marinade.

¼   cup canola oil
1½ teaspoons smoked paprika
1   tablespoon sherry vinegar
½   teaspoon finely chopped fresh rosemary (optional)
¼   teaspoon salt
2   garlic cloves, minced
2   (1-pound) pork tenderloins, trimmed
Cooking spray

1. Combine oil and paprika in a small saucepan, stirring with a whisk. Cook over low heat 2 minutes or until thoroughly heated. Add vinegar, rosemary, if desired, salt, and garlic, stirring with a whisk. Remove from heat.
2. Place pork in a large zip-top plastic bag. Add oil mixture; seal bag. Marinate in refrigerator 8 hours, turning bag occasionally.
3. Preheat grill to medium-high heat.
4. While grill heats, remove pork from marinade, discarding marinade. Place pork on grill rack coated with cooking spray. Grill 20 minutes or until a thermometer registers 160° (slightly pink), turning every 5 minutes. Remove from grill. Let stand 10 minutes before slicing. Cut pork diagonally into ½-inch slices. Yield: 8 servings (serving size: 3 ounces pork).

CALORIES 170; FAT 7.4g (sat 1.6g, mono 3.8g, poly 1.7g); PROTEIN 23.9g; CARB 0.5g; FIBER 0.2g; CHOL 74mg; IRON 1.5mg; SODIUM 130mg; CALC 8mg

serve with:

Fragrant Saffron Rice

Prep: 5 minutes • Cook: 5 minutes

2   (8.5-ounce) packages microwavable precooked basmati rice
Cooking spray
½   cup chopped red onion
2   garlic cloves, minced
½   cup frozen petite green peas
1   (.035-ounce) envelope flavoring and coloring for yellow rice
¼   teaspoon salt
¼   teaspoon crushed red pepper
¼   cup sliced almonds, toasted

1. Microwave rice according to package directions.
2. While rice cooks, heat a medium nonstick skillet over medium-high heat. Coat pan with cooking spray. Add onion and garlic; sauté 3 minutes. Add green peas; sauté 1 minute or until peas are thoroughly heated.
3. Place rice in a large bowl; stir in sautéed vegetables, rice flavoring and coloring, salt, and crushed red pepper. Toss well. Sprinkle with almonds. Yield: 8 servings (serving size: ½ cup).

CALORIES 120; FAT 1.8g (sat 0.1g, mono 1g, poly 0.4g); PROTEIN 3.2g; CARB 22.7g; FIBER 1.4g; CHOL 0mg; IRON 1.2mg; SODIUM 83mg; CALC 14mg

Smoked Paprika Pork

Spiced Pork Tenderloin

Prep: 2 minutes • Cook: 20 minutes
Other: 13 minutes

A marinade of sugar, bourbon, Worcestershire sauce, and ground cinnamon infuses this succulent grilled pork tenderloin. Arrange the sliced pork over a bed of Sweet Pea and Fresh Mint Couscous for a beautiful restaurant-style presentation.

2	tablespoons sugar
2	tablespoons bourbon
2	tablespoons Worcestershire sauce
½	teaspoon ground cinnamon
1	(1-pound) pork tenderloin, trimmed
¼	teaspoon salt
¼	teaspoon freshly ground black pepper

Cooking spray

1. Preheat grill to medium-high heat.
2. Combine first 4 ingredients in a large zip-top plastic bag. Add pork to bag; seal and shake well. Let stand 10 minutes, turning frequently.
3. Remove pork from bag, reserving marinade. Sprinkle pork evenly with salt and pepper. Place pork on grill rack coated with cooking spray; grill 10 minutes on each side or until a thermometer registers 160° (slightly pink), basting with reserved marinade. Remove from grill; let stand 3 minutes before slicing. Yield: 4 servings (serving size: 3 ounces pork).

CALORIES 178; FAT 4g (sat 1.3g, mono 1.5g, poly 0.3g); PROTEIN 22.5g; CARB 8.2g; FIBER 0.2g; CHOL 63mg; IRON 1.8mg; SODIUM 274mg; CALC 18mg

Spiced Pork Tenderloin

serve with:
Sweet Pea and Fresh Mint Couscous

Prep: 2 minutes • Cook: 2 minutes
Other: 5 minutes

¾	cup water
¼	teaspoon salt
⅛	teaspoon ground turmeric
½	cup uncooked whole-wheat couscous
½	cup frozen petite green peas
2	tablespoons chopped fresh mint

1. Combine first 3 ingredients in a medium saucepan. Bring to a boil. Remove from heat; stir in couscous. Cover and let stand 5 minutes.
2. Place peas in a mesh strainer. Rinse under warm water; drain well. Add peas and mint to couscous. Toss well with a fork. Yield: 4 servings (serving size: about ½ cup).

CALORIES 64; FAT 0g (sat 0g, mono 0g, poly 0g); PROTEIN 2.8g; CARB 13.4g; FIBER 2.4g; CHOL 0mg; IRON 0.7mg; SODIUM 161mg; CALC 10mg

Sherried Pineapple Pork Tenderloin

Prep: 1 minute • Cook: 29 minutes
Other: 3 minutes

Impress your guests with this company-worthy main dish served alongside a colorful slaw.

½	teaspoon freshly ground black pepper
1	(1-pound) pork tenderloin, trimmed
Cooking spray	
1	(6-ounce) can pineapple juice
2	tablespoons sugar
2	tablespoons dry sherry
1	tablespoon lower-sodium soy sauce

1. Sprinkle pepper evenly over pork.
2. Heat a nonstick skillet over medium-high heat. Coat pan with cooking spray; add pork. Cook pork 3 to 4 minutes or until browned, turning occasionally. Reduce heat to medium-low; cover and cook 10 minutes. Turn pork over; cook 10 minutes or until a thermometer registers 160° (slightly pink).
3. Place pork on a cutting board; let stand 3 minutes. Cut into ¼-inch-thick slices.
4. While pork stands, combine pineapple juice and remaining 3 ingredients; add to pan drippings. Bring to a boil; boil 5 minutes or until liquid is reduced to ¼ cup. Spoon sauce over pork slices. Yield: 4 servings (serving size: 3 ounces pork and 1 tablespoon sauce).

CALORIES 190; FAT 4g (sat 1.3g, mono 1.5g, poly 0.3g); PROTEIN 22.8g; CARB 13.5g; FIBER 0.1g; CHOL 63mg; IRON 1.3mg; SODIUM 243mg; CALC 6mg

Sherried Pineapple Pork Tenderloin

serve with:

Red Cabbage and Carrot Slaw

Prep: 6 minutes

2	cups matchstick-cut carrots
¾	cup very thinly sliced red cabbage
½	cup refrigerated prechopped tricolor bell pepper mix
3	tablespoons unsalted, dry-roasted peanuts
2	tablespoons cider vinegar
1	teaspoon grated peeled fresh ginger
⅛	teaspoon salt

1. Combine all ingredients in a medium bowl, tossing gently to coat. Yield: 4 servings (serving size: ¾ cup).

CALORIES 100; FAT 3g (sat 0.5g, mono 1.7g, poly 1.1g); PROTEIN 2.4g; CARB 16.1g; FIBER 1.9g; CHOL 0mg; IRON 0.5mg; SODIUM 78mg; CALC 20mg

Pork Tenderloin with Balsamic Onion–Fig Relish

Prep: 4 minutes • Cook: 19 minutes
Other: 5 minutes

Caramelized onion, balsamic vinegar, and figs combine to create a subtly sweet topping for savory roasted pork. A side of acorn squash, available in peak form throughout the winter, rounds out this hearty meal.

1	(1-pound) pork tenderloin, trimmed
¼	teaspoon salt
¼	teaspoon freshly ground black pepper
Cooking spray	
8	dried Mission figs
2	tablespoons balsamic vinegar
2	tablespoons water
1	tablespoon lower-sodium soy sauce
1	(8-ounce) container refrigerated prechopped onion

1. Preheat oven to 425°.
2. Sprinkle pork evenly with salt and pepper; coat with cooking spray. Heat a medium-sized cast-iron skillet or other ovenproof skillet over medium-high heat. Coat pan with cooking spray. Add pork; cook 4 minutes or until browned on all sides, turning occasionally.
3. While pork browns, coarsely chop figs. Combine vinegar, 2 tablespoons water, and soy sauce in a small bowl. When pork is browned, remove pan from heat. Add figs, onion, and vinegar mixture to pan, stirring to loosen browned bits.
4. Bake, uncovered, at 425° for 15 minutes or until a thermometer registers 160° (slightly pink). Stir onion mixture; cover pan loosely with foil. Let stand 5 minutes before slicing. Yield: 4 servings (serving size: 3 ounces pork and ¼ cup relish).

CALORIES 256; FAT 4g (sat 1.4g, mono 1.6g, poly 0.5g); PROTEIN 24.6g; CARB 30.6g; FIBER 4.6g; CHOL 63mg; IRON 2.1mg; SODIUM 349mg; CALC 81mg

serve with:

Acorn Squash with Butter Sauce

Prep: 2 minutes • Cook: 12 minutes

1	acorn squash (about 1½ pounds)
⅓	cup water
1	tablespoon butter
2	tablespoons maple syrup
¼	teaspoon ground nutmeg
⅛	teaspoon salt

1. Pierce squash several times with a sharp knife; place on paper towels in microwave oven. Microwave at HIGH 1 minute. Cut squash in half lengthwise. Discard seeds and membrane. Cut each squash half lengthwise into 4 wedges. Pour ⅓ cup water into an 11 x 7–inch baking dish. Place squash, cut sides up, in pan. Cover with plastic wrap, turning back 1 corner to vent (do not allow plastic wrap to touch food). Microwave at HIGH 10 minutes or until tender.
2. Place butter in a small microwave-safe bowl. Cover and microwave at HIGH 20 seconds or until butter melts. Stir in syrup, nutmeg, and salt. Spoon sauce over squash wedges. Yield: 4 servings (serving size: 2 squash wedges and about 2 teaspoons sauce).

CALORIES 120; FAT 3g (sat 1.9g, mono 0.8g, poly 0.2g); PROTEIN 1.4g; CARB 24.5g; FIBER 2.6g; CHOL 8mg; IRON 1.3mg; SODIUM 99mg; CALC 64mg

Slow-Cooker Pork Loin Carnita Tacos with Chimichurri Sauce

Prep: 6 minutes • Cook: 8 hours and 13 minutes

These make-ahead tacos are an ideal way to showcase slow-cooked pork. Browning the pork roast before adding it to the slow cooker adds rich flavor.

1	(1½-pound) boneless pork loin roast, trimmed
½	teaspoon salt
½	teaspoon freshly ground black pepper
8	garlic cloves, minced
	Cooking spray
2	cups chicken stock
½	cup water
12	(6-inch) corn tortillas
6	tablespoons light sour cream (optional)
	Chimichurri Sauce

1. Rub pork with salt, pepper, and garlic. Heat a large nonstick skillet over medium-high heat. Coat pan with cooking spray. Add pork; cook 3 minutes on each side or until browned. Transfer pork to a 5-quart round electric slow cooker coated with cooking spray. Add stock to pan, scraping to loosen browned bits; cook 2 minutes. Pour stock mixture over pork; add ½ cup water. Cover and cook on LOW 8 hours or until tender.

2. Remove pork from slow cooker, and place in a medium bowl. Pour broth into a medium skillet. Bring to a boil over high heat; boil 5 minutes or until reduced to ⅔ cup.

3. While broth reduces, shred pork using 2 forks. Stir in broth reduction.

4. Warm tortillas according to package directions. Serve pork with tortillas, sour cream, if desired, and Chimichurri Sauce. Yield: 6 servings (serving size: ½ cup pork mixture, 2 tortillas, and about 2 tablespoons Chimichurri Sauce).

CALORIES 320; FAT 12.6g (sat 3g, mono 6.7g, poly 2.7g); PROTEIN 29.4g; CARB 23.4g; FIBER 2.3g; CHOL 62mg; IRON 1.5mg; SODIUM 506mg; CALC 71mg

Chimichurri Sauce

Prep: 7 minutes

3	garlic cloves
3	small shallots, peeled and quartered
½	cup flat-leaf parsley leaves
¼	cup white wine vinegar
3	tablespoons oregano leaves
2	tablespoons extra-virgin olive oil
½	teaspoon crushed red pepper
¼	teaspoon kosher salt

1. With processor on, drop garlic through food chute; process until minced. Add shallots and remaining ingredients; pulse 8 times or until finely chopped, scraping sides as necessary. Yield: 6 servings (serving size: about 2 tablespoons).

CALORIES 58; FAT 4.8g (sat 0.7g, mono 3.6g, poly 0.4g); PROTEIN 0.8g; CARB 3.6g; FIBER 0.1g; CHOL 0mg; IRON 0.5mg; SODIUM 81mg; CALC 19mg

desserts

Mini Nectarine
Galettes, page 479

Mini Nectarine Galettes

Prep: 12 minutes • Cook: 25 minutes
Other: 10 minutes

Use firm, ripe nectarines instead of soft for the best results. Firm fruit will slice easily and stand up to cooking. You can dress these mini tarts with a bit of crème fraîche, whipped cream, or ice cream, and some chopped or sliced toasted nuts.

½ (14.1-ounce) package refrigerated pie dough
1 large egg white, lightly beaten
2 tablespoons turbinado sugar, divided
3 firm ripe nectarines, pitted and sliced
2 tablespoons apple jelly

1. Preheat oven to 425°.
2. Roll dough into a 13-inch circle; cut into 8 (4¼-inch) circles, rerolling dough as necessary. Place circles on a baking sheet lined with parchment paper. Brush circles with egg white; sprinkle evenly with 1 tablespoon turbinado sugar. Arrange nectarine slices evenly in centers of circles, leaving a ½-inch border. Fold edges over fruit. (Dough will only partially cover fruit.)
3. Brush remaining egg white over dough edges; sprinkle evenly with remaining 1 tablespoon turbinado sugar. Bake at 425° for 25 minutes or until crust browns.
4. Place jelly in a microwave-safe bowl. Microwave at HIGH 1 minute or until melted. Brush jelly evenly over fruit. Let stand at least 10 minutes before serving. Yield: 8 servings (serving size: 1 galette).

CALORIES 147; FAT 6.7g (sat 2.8g, mono 2.5g, poly 0.9g); PROTEIN 1.9g; CARB 22.3g; FIBER 0.9g; CHOL 3mg; IRON 0.2mg; SODIUM 136mg; CALC 4mg

Baklava Bites

Prep: 6 minutes • Cook: 10 minutes

From clarifying butter to managing paper-thin phyllo sheets, making baklava is labor intensive. These bite-sized treats simplify the process while staying true to the traditional flavors.

⅓ cup finely chopped walnuts
⅓ cup finely chopped pistachios
2 tablespoons butter, melted
2 tablespoons honey
1 teaspoon grated orange rind
¼ teaspoon ground cinnamon
⅛ teaspoon ground cloves
1 (1.9-ounce) package mini phyllo shells

1. Preheat oven to 425°.
2. Combine first 7 ingredients in a medium bowl. Place phyllo shells on an ungreased baking sheet. Spoon nut mixture evenly into phyllo shells.
3. Bake at 425° for 10 minutes or until golden. Yield: 15 servings (serving size: 1 filled shell).

CALORIES 71; FAT 5.3g (sat 1.3g, mono 1.9g, poly 1.9g); PROTEIN 1g; CARB 5.3g; FIBER 0.5g; CHOL 4.1mg; IRON 0.4mg; SODIUM 36mg; CALC 7mg

Baklava Bites

Chocolate-Flecked Peanut Butter–Banana Freeze

Prep: 8 minutes

1½   cups diced banana (2 medium bananas), frozen
2   tablespoons creamy peanut butter
1   ounce semisweet chocolate, grated, or 2 tablespoons semisweet chocolate minichips

1. Place frozen diced banana and peanut butter in a food processor; process until smooth, scraping sides of bowl occasionally. Stir in grated chocolate. Serve immediately. Yield: 2 servings (serving size: ½ cup).

CALORIES 247; FAT 11.6g (sat 3.5g, mono 4.4g, poly 2g); PROTEIN 5.7g; CARB 36.1g; FIBER 4.6g; CHOL 0mg; IRON 1mg; SODIUM 77mg; CALC 9mg

fix it faster

To make this refreshing dessert at a moment's notice, have bananas already frozen. Use ripe bananas with lots of brown spots on the skins. When the bananas get to this point, peel them, dice them, toss them in a heavy-duty zip-top plastic bag, and freeze them.

Chocolate-Flecked Peanut Butter–Banana Freeze

Chocolate-Cranberry Refrigerator Cookies

Prep: 10 minutes • Cook: 12 minutes
Other: 1 hour and 10 minutes

Keep the dough wrapped tightly in the refrigerator for up to two weeks. Then it's easy to slice and bake for fresh cookies whenever the craving hits.

4.5	ounces all-purpose flour (about 1 cup)
⅓	cup unsweetened cocoa
½	teaspoon baking soda
¼	teaspoon salt
⅓	cup unsalted butter, softened
⅔	cup sugar
2	tablespoons ice water
½	cup chopped sweetened dried cranberries

1. Weigh or lightly spoon flour into a dry measuring cup; level with a knife. Combine flour, cocoa, baking soda, and salt in a medium bowl; stir with a whisk. Place butter and sugar in a medium bowl; beat with a mixer at medium speed until fluffy. Add flour mixture, beating at low speed until crumbly. Add 2 tablespoons ice water, 1 tablespoon at a time, beating until thoroughly moistened. Beat in cranberries.
2. Shape dough into an 8-inch log. Wrap dough in plastic wrap; chill 1 hour.
3. Preheat oven to 350°.
4. Cut dough into 24 (¼-inch-thick) slices. Place slices 1 inch apart on a baking sheet lined with parchment paper. Bake at 350° for 12 minutes or until set. Cool cookies on pan 10 minutes. Remove from pan; cool completely on a wire rack. Yield: 24 servings (serving size: 1 cookie).

CALORIES 75; FAT 2.6g (sat 1.5g, mono 0.6g, poly 0.1g); PROTEIN 0.8g; CARB 12.3g; FIBER 0.5g; CHOL 7mg; IRON 0.4mg; SODIUM 51mg; CALC 1mg

Chocolate-Raspberry Chews

Prep: 22 minutes • Cook: 10 minutes
Other: 15 minutes

This sandwich cookie highlights the timeless pairing of chocolate and raspberry.

1.9	ounces almond flour (about ½ cup)
1¼	cups powdered sugar, divided
3	tablespoons Dutch process cocoa
⅛	teaspoon salt
2	large egg whites
3	tablespoons low-sugar raspberry preserves

1. Preheat oven to 325°.
2. Weigh or lightly spoon almond flour into a dry measuring cup; level with a knife. Sift together almond flour, ¾ cup powdered sugar, and cocoa.
3. Place salt and egg whites in a medium bowl; beat with a mixer at high speed until foamy. Gradually add remaining ½ cup powdered sugar, 1 tablespoon at a time, beating until stiff peaks form. Sift cocoa mixture over egg mixture; fold cocoa mixture into egg mixture. (Mixture should be smooth and shiny.)
4. Spoon dough into a pastry bag fitted with a ½-inch round tip. Pipe dough into 24 (1½-inch) rounds onto baking sheets lined with parchment paper. Sharply tap pan once on counter to remove air bubbles. Let stand 15 minutes or until surfaces of cookies begin to dry slightly.
5. Bake at 325° for 10 minutes or until cookies are crisp and firm. Cool completely on pans on wire racks.
6. Spoon ¾ teaspoon preserves onto flat side of each of 12 cookies. Top with remaining cookies. Yield: 12 servings (serving size: 1 sandwich cookie).

CALORIES 88; FAT 2.4g (sat 0.2g, mono 1.4g, poly 0.5g); PROTEIN 1.8g; CARB 15.7g; FIBER 0.7g; CHOL 0mg; IRON 0.6mg; SODIUM 36mg; CALC 10mg

Chocolate Granola Yogurt Crunch

Prep: 6 minutes

Crushed crisp granola thins put the crunch on top of this easy sundae.

2	cups vanilla frozen fat-free yogurt
3	(0.6-ounce) dark chocolate granola thins, coarsely crushed
½	cup sliced fresh strawberries
2	tablespoons honey

1. Divide frozen yogurt evenly among 4 bowls. Sprinkle granola thin crumbs over frozen yogurt. Top with strawberries, and drizzle with honey. Serve immediately. Yield: 4 servings (serving size: ½ cup frozen yogurt, 2 tablespoons crumbs, 2 tablespoons strawberries, and 1½ teaspoons honey).

CALORIES 191; FAT 3.1g (sat 1.1g, mono 1.5g, poly 0.4g); PROTEIN 3.9g; CARB 38.3g; FIBER 0.4g; CHOL 0mg; IRON 0.4mg; SODIUM 102mg; CALC 103mg

Chocolate Granola Yogurt Crunch

Peaches-n-Cream Parfaits

Prep: 10 minutes

What's better than eating a juicy, ripe peach? Peaches at their peak in a parfait, for starters. Use tall stemmed glasses to showcase the delicious layering of creamy yogurt and fresh peaches.

½   cup vanilla fat-free yogurt
½   cup light sour cream
4   cups coarsely chopped peeled fresh peaches
¼   cup firmly packed light brown sugar
Chopped fresh mint (optional)

1. Combine yogurt and sour cream.
2. Spoon ½ cup peaches into each of 4 glasses; sprinkle with 1½ teaspoons brown sugar, and top with 2 tablespoons yogurt mixture. Repeat layers with remaining peaches, brown sugar, and yogurt mixture. Sprinkle each with chopped fresh mint, if desired. Yield: 4 servings (serving size: 1 parfait).

CALORIES 181; FAT 2.4g (sat 1.5g, mono 0.5g, poly 0.3g); PROTEIN 4.1g; CARB 38.7g; FIBER 2.5g; CHOL 11mg; IRON 0.7mg; SODIUM 58mg; CALC 78mg

Raspberry-Lemon Parfaits

Raspberry-Lemon Parfaits

Prep: 5 minutes • Other: 5 minutes

2   (6-ounce) packages fresh raspberries (about 2¾ cups)
2   tablespoons sugar
2   (6-ounce) cartons lemon meringue light yogurt
1½   cups (4 ounces) frozen fat-free whipped topping, thawed
3   cups (1-inch) cubed angel food cake
Raspberries (optional)

1. Combine raspberries and sugar in a medium bowl. Let stand 5 minutes, stirring occasionally.
2. Place yogurt in another bowl; gently fold in whipped topping until combined.
3. Layer about ⅓ cup each angel food cake, raspberry mixture, and yogurt mixture in each of 4 glasses. Repeat procedure once. Garnish with additional raspberries, if desired. Serve immediately, or chill until ready to serve. Yield: 4 servings (serving size: 1 parfait).

CALORIES 257; FAT 1g (sat 0.1g, mono 0.1g, poly 0.5g); PROTEIN 5.6g; CARB 56g; FIBER 6g; CHOL 2mg; IRON 0.8mg; SODIUM 327mg; CALC 171mg

Peaches-n-Cream Parfaits

Balsamic Peach Melba Parfaits
with Spiked Mascarpone

Balsamic Peach Melba Parfaits with Spiked Mascarpone

Prep: 9 minutes • Other: 10 minutes

1½	tablespoons sugar
1½	teaspoons white balsamic vinegar
2	small fresh peaches, peeled, pitted, and each cut into 12 wedges (about ¾ pound peaches)
¾	cup fresh raspberries

Spiked Mascarpone

1. Place first 3 ingredients in a medium bowl; toss gently until sugar dissolves. Gently stir in raspberries. Let stand 10 minutes.
2. Spoon half of peach mixture evenly into 4 parfait glasses. Top evenly with half of Spiked Mascarpone. Repeat layers with remaining peach mixture and Spiked Mascarpone. Chill until ready to serve. Yield: 4 servings (serving size: ½ cup fruit and about 1½ tablespoons Spiked Mascarpone).

CALORIES 154; FAT 6.8g (sat 3.5g, mono 1.9g, poly 0.4g); PROTEIN 2.6g; CARB 19.7g; FIBER 2.4g; CHOL 17.8mg; IRON 0.3mg; SODIUM 20mg; CALC 58mg

Spiked Mascarpone

Prep: 4 minutes

2	tablespoons mascarpone cheese
¼	cup plain fat-free yogurt
1½	tablespoons peach brandy
1½	tablespoons sugar

1. Combine all ingredients in a medium bowl, stirring with a whisk until smooth. Cover and chill until ready to use. Yield: 4 servings (serving size: about 1½ tablespoons).

CALORIES 98; FAT 6.5g (sat 3.5g, mono 0g, poly 0g); PROTEIN 1.8g; CARB 5.8g; FIBER 0g; CHOL 17.8mg; IRON 0mg; SODIUM 19mg; CALC 48mg

quick flip

Can't find mascarpone cheese? Substitute crème fraîche for similar rich flavor and creamy texture. You can also substitute amaretto for the peach brandy in the mascarpone for an almond-flavored twist.

Black Forest Trifle

Prep: 15 minutes • Other: 10 minutes

This trifle is a quick take on classic black forest cake. Use thawed frozen cherries when fresh cherries are not in season. You can prepare the trifle in individual dishes or in a 2-quart trifle dish or glass bowl.

2½	cups pitted dark sweet cherries, halved
6	tablespoons sugar, divided
3	tablespoons kirsch (cherry brandy)
½	cup heavy whipping cream
1	(11-ounce) frozen chocolate cake, thawed and cut into 1-inch cubes
1	ounce shaved bittersweet chocolate (optional)

1. Combine cherries, 3 tablespoons sugar, and kirsch in a medium bowl. Let stand 10 minutes.

2. While cherry mixture stands, place whipping cream and remaining 3 tablespoons sugar in a medium bowl. Beat with a mixer at medium-high speed until soft peaks form.

3. Divide half of cake cubes evenly among 8 small bowls or individual serving dishes. Spoon half of cherry mixture over cake, and top with half of whipped cream mixture. Repeat layers. Sprinkle with chocolate shavings, if desired. Cover and chill until ready to serve. Yield: 8 servings.

CALORIES 256; FAT 9.8g (sat 3.5g, mono 3.6g, poly 2.2g); PROTEIN 2.1g; CARB 39.1g; FIBER 1g; CHOL 20.5mg; IRON 0.9mg; SODIUM 98mg; CALC 16mg

Black Forest Trifle

Coconut Rice Pudding

Prep: 5 minutes • Cook: 45 minutes

Prepare the rice ahead so it can chill, or use leftover plain cooked rice for this tropical dessert.

2	cups 1% low-fat milk
1½	cups cooked rice, chilled
⅓	cup sugar
⅛	teaspoon salt
1	(13.5-ounce) can light coconut milk
1	teaspoon vanilla extract
½	cup flaked sweetened coconut, toasted (optional)

1. Bring first 5 ingredients to a boil in a medium saucepan. Reduce heat to medium and simmer, uncovered, 45 minutes or until thickened, stirring frequently. Remove from heat; stir in vanilla. Let cool to warm, stirring occasionally. Spoon evenly into 8 dessert dishes. Sprinkle evenly with toasted coconut, if desired. Yield: 8 servings (serving size: about ½ cup).

CALORIES 128; FAT 3.4g (sat 2.8g, mono 0.3g, poly 0g); PROTEIN 3.5g; CARB 21g; FIBER 0.1g; CHOL 3mg; IRON 0.4mg; SODIUM 73mg; CALC 79mg

Dark Chocolate–Cherry Almond Bark

Dark Chocolate–Cherry Almond Bark

Prep: 10 minutes • Other: 30 minutes

Keep this indulgent treat on hand to satisfy your sweet tooth. A small bite of antioxidant-rich dark chocolate with heart-healthy almonds is an alternative to sugar- and fat-filled candy bars.

8	ounces dark chocolate (70% cocoa), chopped
¼	teaspoon almond extract
½	cup dried cherries, chopped and divided
½	cup whole natural almonds, toasted, coarsely chopped, and divided
¼	teaspoon coarse sea salt

1. Line a baking sheet with parchment paper.
2. Place chocolate in a microwave-safe bowl. Microwave at HIGH 1 minute, stirring after 30 seconds. Stir until smooth. Add almond extract, stirring until blended. Stir in half of cherries and almonds.
3. Spread mixture onto prepared baking sheet. Sprinkle with remaining almonds and cherries, pressing lightly to adhere. Sprinkle with salt. Chill 30 minutes or until firm. Break into 14 pieces. Yield: 14 servings (serving size: 1 piece).

CALORIES 144; FAT 9.5g (sat 4.2g, mono 3.7g, poly 0.8g); PROTEIN 2.6g; CARB 12.2g; FIBER 2.8g; CHOL 0mg; IRON 2.2mg; SODIUM 45mg; CALC 28mg

Coconut Rice Pudding

Dulce de Leche Ice Cream

Prep: 6 minutes • Cook: 5 minutes
Other: 5 hours

Dulce de leche, a milk caramel, combines with low-fat milk to create a rich, silky ice cream.

3	cups 1% low-fat milk
1⅔	cups canned dulce de leche
⅛	teaspoon vanilla extract
⅛	teaspoon salt

1. Bring milk to a boil in a medium saucepan over medium heat. Gradually add dulce de leche, stirring with a whisk. Remove from heat. Stir in vanilla and salt. Place pan in a large ice-filled bowl until mixture cools to room temperature (about 30 minutes), stirring occasionally. Cover and refrigerate 3 hours or until thoroughly chilled.
2. Pour mixture into the freezer can of an ice-cream freezer; freeze according to manufacturer's instructions. Spoon ice cream into a freezer-safe container; cover and freeze 1 hour or until firm. Yield: 12 servings (serving size: ½ cup).

CALORIES 159; FAT 3.4g (sat 2g, mono 1.1g, poly 0.1g); PROTEIN 4.3g; CARB 26.3g; FIBER 0g; CHOL 14.1mg; IRON 0mg; SODIUM 129mg; CALC 165mg

Dulce de Leche
Ice Cream

ingredient spotlight

Pure vanilla has one of the most complex tastes, and there's no mistaking its unique flavor and aroma. Don't be tempted to use imitation vanilla—it is made from chemicals and lacks the depth of flavor of the real thing.

Fudgy Bourbon-
Pecan Brownies

Fudgy Bourbon-Pecan Brownies

Prep: 8 minutes • Cook: 18 minutes

Bourbon adds an extra kick to these fudge brownies.
You can also substitute your favorite liqueur.

Cooking spray
4.5   ounces all-purpose flour (about 1 cup)
⅓   cup unsweetened cocoa
¼   teaspoon salt
1   cup sugar
¼   cup canola oil
¼   cup bourbon
2   large eggs
¼   cup chopped pecans

1. Preheat oven to 350°.
2. Coat bottom of an 8-inch square baking pan with cooking spray.
3. Weigh or lightly spoon flour into a dry measuring cup; level with a knife. Combine flour, cocoa, and salt in a medium bowl; stir with a whisk. Combine sugar and next 3 ingredients in another medium bowl; stir in flour mixture. Stir in pecans. Spread batter into prepared pan.
4. Bake at 350° for 18 minutes or until a wooden pick inserted in center comes out almost clean. Cool completely on a wire rack. Cut into squares. Yield: 16 servings (serving size: 1 brownie).

CALORIES 139; FAT 5.6g (sat 0.6g, mono 3.2g, poly 1.5g); PROTEIN 2.1g; CARB 20g; FIBER 0.7g; CHOL 23mg; IRON 0.8mg; SODIUM 46mg; CALC 6mg

Grilled Fruit Sundaes

Prep: 9 minutes • Cook: 6 minutes

Select peaches that are juicy and ripe yet still firm; they will be easier to peel and chop. If you like, save the juices from the grilled fruit to drizzle over the ice cream.

4   (½-inch-thick) slices fresh pineapple
2   firm ripe peaches, halved and pitted
2   plums, halved and pitted
Cooking spray
1½   cups vanilla light ice cream
12   cinnamon sugar pita chips

1. Preheat grill to medium-high heat.
2. Lightly coat fruit with cooking spray. Place fruit on grill rack coated with cooking spray. Grill 3 minutes on each side. Remove skins from peaches. Finely chop fruit; drain. If desired, cool fruit to room temperature.
3. Spoon ½ cup fruit into each of 6 serving dishes. Scoop ¼ cup ice cream onto each serving. Serve each with 2 pita chips. Yield: 6 servings (serving size: 1 sundae).

CALORIES 135; FAT 2.9g (sat 1.1g, mono 0.9g, poly 0.3g); PROTEIN 3g; CARB 26.4g; FIBER 2.2g; CHOL 10mg; IRON 0.5mg; SODIUM 44mg; CALC 40mg

Grilled Fruit
Sundaes

Grilled Rum Pineapple with Coconut Sorbet

Prep: 4 minutes • Cook: 7 minutes
Other: 5 minutes

1   small pineapple, peeled and cored
¼   cup packed dark brown sugar
2   tablespoons dark rum
Cooking spray
1   cup coconut sorbet
2   tablespoons flaked sweetened coconut, toasted

1. Preheat grill to high heat.
2. Cut pineapple into 8 (½-inch-thick) rings; place in a medium bowl. Combine brown sugar and rum; pour over pineapple. Let stand 5 minutes.
3. Place pineapple on grill rack coated with cooking spray. Grill 3 minutes. Turn pineapple over; grill 4 minutes or until caramelized, basting frequently with remaining brown sugar mixture. Place 2 pineapple slices on each of 4 plates; top each with ¼ cup coconut sorbet and 1½ teaspoons toasted coconut. Serve immediately. Yield: 4 servings.

CALORIES 275; FAT 5.5g (sat 4.2g, mono 0.4g, poly 0.2g); PROTEIN 1.8g; CARB 54.9g; FIBER 0.3g; CHOL 0mg; IRON 0.9mg; SODIUM 21mg; CALC 40mg

Ice Cream Crepes with
Chocolate-Hazelnut Sauce

Ice Cream Crepes with Chocolate-Hazelnut Sauce

Prep: 15 minutes

To keep the ice cream from melting while you prepare all 10 servings, place the filled crepes on a wax paper–lined baking sheet in the freezer. Once you have filled all the crepes, plate the crepes, drizzle with the sauce, and sprinkle with the hazelnuts.

¼	cup chocolate-hazelnut spread
1	tablespoon Frangelico (hazelnut-flavored liqueur)
1½	teaspoons 1% low-fat milk
5	cups chocolate or coffee light ice cream
1	(5-ounce) package refrigerated prepared crepes
5	teaspoons chopped hazelnuts

1. Combine first 3 ingredients in a small bowl; stir with a whisk until smooth.
2. Spread ½ cup ice cream down center of each crepe. Fold sides of crepes over ice cream. Arrange crepes, seam sides down, on each of 10 dessert plates.
3. Drizzle about 1½ teaspoons sauce over each crepe; sprinkle each crepe with ½ teaspoon hazelnuts. Serve immediately. Yield: 10 servings (serving size: 1 crepe).

CALORIES 201; FAT 7g (sat 4.2g, mono 1.6g, poly 0.1g); PROTEIN 4.6g; CARB 28.2g; FIBER 1.5g; CHOL 25mg; IRON 0.4mg; SODIUM 98mg; CALC 70mg

Ladyfingers with Mascarpone Cream and Fresh Orange Sauce

Prep: 15 minutes

Vanilla bean paste is a perfect addition: It has no alcohol to compete with the Grand Marnier, and it adds attractive vanilla seeds to the cheese. Find vanilla bean paste at specialty food stores.

½	cup sugar, divided
2	tablespoons Grand Marnier (orange-flavored liqueur)
2	large navel oranges
1½	cups fat-free cottage cheese
¼	cup (2 ounces) mascarpone cheese
1	teaspoon vanilla bean paste
1	(3-ounce) package ladyfingers (12 ladyfingers), split
2	tablespoons sliced almonds, toasted

1. Combine ⅓ cup sugar and liqueur in a medium bowl, stirring well. Peel oranges; cut each orange in half lengthwise. Cut each half crosswise into thin slices to measure 2 cups. Add oranges to sugar mixture in bowl; toss gently to coat. Let stand at room temperature while preparing cream mixture.
2. Place remaining sugar, cottage cheese, mascarpone, and vanilla bean paste in a food processor; process until smooth.
3. Arrange 4 ladyfinger halves in each of 6 dessert bowls. Spoon cheese mixture evenly into center of ladyfingers (about ¼ cup each). Top each serving with about ⅓ cup orange sauce, allowing syrup to soak into cake. Sprinkle 1 teaspoon almonds over each serving. Yield: 6 servings (serving size: 1 dessert).

CALORIES 247; FAT 6.2g (sat 2.7g, mono 2.3g, poly 0.5g); PROTEIN 9.4g; CARB 38.3g; FIBER 1.4g; CHOL 44.3mg; IRON 0.3mg; SODIUM 321mg; CALC 102mg

Mango-Lime Pudding

Prep: 25 minutes • Cook: 8 minutes
Other: 4 hours

Champagne mangoes are also labeled Ataulfo, Honey, and Manila mangoes. They ripen to a golden yellow and have velvety smooth flesh, a small pit, and almost no fibrous texture, making them ideal for a smooth pudding.

4	cups cubed peeled ripe champagne mango (8 champagne mangoes)
⅓	cup sugar
¼	cup cornstarch
¾	cup evaporated low-fat milk
½	cup water
¼	cup fresh lime juice
½	cup diced champagne mango (optional)
2½	thin lime slices, quartered (optional)

1. Place 4 cups mango in a food processor; process until smooth. Press mango puree through a sieve into a bowl, using the back of a spoon. Discard solids.
2. Combine sugar and cornstarch in a medium saucepan, stirring with a whisk. Stir in mango puree, evaporated milk, water, and lime juice. Bring to a boil; cook, stirring constantly, 1 minute or until thick. Remove from heat. Pour into a bowl; cover surface of pudding with plastic wrap. Chill 4 hours.
3. Spoon pudding evenly into each of 10 dessert dishes. Sprinkle puddings evenly with diced mango, and garnish with quartered lime slices, if desired. Yield: 10 servings (serving size: ½ cup).

CALORIES 94; FAT 0.6g (sat 0.1g, mono 0.2g, poly 0g); PROTEIN 1.8g; CARB 21.8g; FIBER 1.1g; CHOL 3mg; IRON 0.1mg; SODIUM 22mg; CALC 56mg

Mango-Lime
Pudding

Mint-Chocolate Sorbet

Prep: 4 minutes • Cook: 10 minutes
Other: 4 hours

Cool, refreshing, and decadently rich, this sorbet will leave you begging for more on a warm afternoon.

2   cups water
1   cup sugar
⅓   cup Dutch process cocoa
3   ounces semisweet chocolate, finely chopped
½   cup mint leaves

1. Bring 2 cups water to a boil in a medium saucepan. Combine sugar and cocoa. Gradually add sugar mixture to boiling water; reduce heat, and simmer, uncovered, 5 minutes, stirring frequently. Remove from heat; add chocolate, stirring until chocolate melts. Stir in mint leaves. Cover and let steep 30 minutes. Refrigerate 2 hours or until thoroughly chilled.
2. Pour chocolate mixture through a sieve into freezer can of an ice-cream freezer; discard mint leaves. Freeze according to manufacturer's instructions. Spoon sorbet into a freezer-safe container; cover and freeze 1 hour or until firm. Yield: 5 servings (serving size: about ½ cup).

CALORIES 264; FAT 6g (sat 3.3g, mono 2g, poly 0g); PROTEIN 2.4g; CARB 53.6g; FIBER 2.5g; CHOL 0mg; IRON 2.9mg; SODIUM 1mg; CALC 7mg

Orange-Beer Floats

Orange-Beer Floats

Prep: 3 minutes

This adult dessert is a take on the usual orange-slice accompaniment to a Belgian-style wheat ale.

2   (12-ounce) bottles Belgian-style wheat ale
1   cup orange sherbet
2   orange slices

1. Pour 1 beer into each of 2 frozen mugs. Scoop ½ cup sherbet into each mug. Serve with orange slices. Yield: 2 servings (serving size: 1 float).

CALORIES 289; FAT 1.5g (sat 0.9g, mono 0.4g, poly 0.1g); PROTEIN 3.4g; CARB 38.7g; FIBER 1.7g; CHOL 1mg; IRON 0.2mg; SODIUM 38mg; CALC 67mg

Orange-Scented Almond Cookies with Chocolate

Prep: 10 minutes • Cook: 16 minutes

Store the sweet, chewy almond cookies in an airtight container to keep them from drying out.

1	(7-ounce) tube marzipan (almond paste)
¾	cup sugar
2	tablespoons all-purpose flour
1	teaspoon grated orange rind
2	large egg whites
2	ounces bittersweet chocolate, chopped

1. Preheat oven to 350°.
2. Line 2 large baking sheets with parchment paper.
3. Place first 4 ingredients in a food processor; process until mixture is crumbly. Add egg whites; process until smooth.
4. Spoon batter, 1 tablespoon at a time, 2 inches apart onto prepared pans. Bake at 350° for 12 minutes or until puffed and lightly golden. Cool cookies completely on pan on a wire rack.
5. Place chocolate in a microwave-safe bowl. Microwave at HIGH 30 seconds; stir. Microwave 30 additional seconds; stir until smooth. Drizzle melted chocolate over cooled cookies. Yield: 23 servings (serving size: 1 cookie).

CALORIES 80; FAT 2.6g (sat 0.8g, mono 1.4g, poly 0.3g); PROTEIN 1.2g; CARB 13.4g; FIBER 0.7g; CHOL 0mg; IRON 0.5mg; SODIUM 6mg; CALC 12mg

Orange-Scented Almond Cookies with Chocolate

Pistachio
Milkshakes

Pistachio Milkshakes

Prep: 14 minutes

Some supermarkets carry shelled pistachios; if yours does not, buy unshelled nuts and shell them yourself.

⅔   cup unsalted pistachios
¼   cup sugar
3   cups vanilla low-fat ice cream
1½   cups 1% low-fat milk
½   teaspoon vanilla extract
Chopped pistachios (optional)

1. Place pistachios and sugar in a blender; process until nuts are finely ground.
2. Add ice cream, milk, and vanilla; process until smooth. Sprinkle chopped pistachio nuts on top of each shake, if desired. Serve immediately. Yield: 6 servings (serving size: ⅔ cup).

CALORIES 236; FAT 10.2g (sat 3.1g, mono 4.4g, poly 1.9g); PROTEIN 7.9g; CARB 30.5g; FIBER 1.3g; CHOL 23mg; IRON 0.6mg; SODIUM 73mg; CALC 151mg

Roasted Pears with Amaretto and Crème Fraîche

Prep: 8 minutes • Cook: 40 minutes

The butter and sugar caramelize on the bottom of the pan while the pears roast, forming the base of a flavorful sauce for this simple dessert.

1   tablespoon unsalted butter, softened
5   tablespoons sugar, divided
3   Bosc pears, peeled, halved, and cored
3   tablespoons amaretto (almond-flavored liqueur), divided
½   cup water
⅛   teaspoon salt
6   tablespoons crème fraîche
⅓   cup toasted sliced almonds (optional)

1. Preheat oven to 425°.
2. Spread butter over bottom of a 15 x 10–inch pan; sprinkle ¼ cup sugar over butter. Arrange pear halves, cut sides up, in pan. Brush pears with 1 tablespoon amaretto.
3. Bake, uncovered, at 425° for 25 minutes or just until tender. Add ½ cup water, 1 tablespoon amaretto, and salt to baking pan; brush pears with pan juices. Bake, uncovered, an additional 15 minutes or until pears are glazed, basting twice with syrup.
4. Combine crème fraîche, remaining 1 tablespoon sugar, and remaining 1 tablespoon amaretto. Place 1 pear half, cut side up, on each of 6 dessert plates. Drizzle pears evenly with sauce. Spoon about 1 tablespoon crème fraîche mixture onto each pear half. Sprinkle evenly with almonds, if desired. Yield: 6 servings (serving size: 1 pear half, about 1 teaspoon sauce, and 1 tablespoon crème fraîche mixture).

CALORIES 180; FAT 7.4g (sat 4.7g, mono 2g, poly 0.3g); PROTEIN 0.5g; CARB 25.7g; FIBER 3g; CHOL 25.1mg; IRON 0mg; SODIUM 55mg; CALC 21mg

Roasted Pears with Amaretto
and Crème Fraîche

Sour Cream—Peach Tart

Sour Cream–Peach Tart

Prep: 5 minutes • Cook: 20 minutes
Other: 10 minutes

Other summer fruits work well, too. Try cherries, berries, nectarines, apricots, or plums.

1	sheet frozen puff pastry dough, thawed
¼	cup (2 ounces) ⅓-less-fat cream cheese, softened
½	cup light sour cream
3	tablespoons brown sugar
1½	cups sliced peeled ripe fresh peaches

1. Preheat oven to 400°.
2. Line a large baking sheet with parchment paper.
3. Place dough on prepared pan. Roll dough into a 14 x 8–inch rectangle. Lightly score dough along each edge, ¾ inch from edges. Brush scored edges lightly with water, and fold over onto remaining dough, creating a border. Press gently to adhere. Pierce bottom of tart shell with a fork. Freeze 10 minutes.
4. Bake at 400° for 20 minutes or until browned. Cool completely on pan on a wire rack.
5. While tart shell bakes, combine cream cheese, sour cream, and brown sugar in a medium bowl, stirring until smooth. Spread sour cream mixture on bottom of tart shell. Arrange peach slices over sour cream mixture. Cut into 8 rectangles. Serve immediately. Yield: 8 servings (serving size: 1 piece).

CALORIES 90; FAT 4.3g (sat 2g, mono 1.7g, poly 0.2g); PROTEIN 2.3g; CARB 10.8g; FIBER 0.5g; CHOL 10mg; IRON 0.3mg; SODIUM 60mg; CALC 44mg

Watermelon-Mint Sorbet

Prep: 8 minutes • Other: 2 hours

A touch of orange liqueur balances the bright flavor of watermelon and keeps the sorbet from freezing until it's too firm to scoop. Instead, it is slightly soft and light.

4	cups cubed seedless watermelon
½	cup sugar
¼	cup packed mint leaves
¼	cup Cointreau (orange-flavored liqueur)

1. Place all ingredients in a blender; process until smooth.
2. Pour mixture into the freezer can of an ice-cream freezer; freeze according to manufacturer's instructions. Spoon sorbet into a freezer-safe container; cover and freeze 1 hour and 30 minutes or until firm. Yield: 7 servings (serving size: ½ cup).

CALORIES 115; FAT 0g (sat 0g, mono 0g, poly 0g); PROTEIN 0.3g; CARB 26.2g; FIBER 0.6g; CHOL 0mg; IRON 0.3mg; SODIUM 4mg; CALC 8mg

Watermelon-Mint Sorbet

White Grape–Champagne Granita

White Grape–Champagne Granita

Prep: 15 minutes • Other: 3 hours

You don't need an ice-cream maker for this dessert: Freeze it in a square or rectangular baking pan. Scraping the mixture with a fork gives it a flaky, melt-in-your-mouth texture.

2	pounds green seedless grapes
1	cup Champagne or sparkling white wine
2	tablespoons fresh lemon juice
3	tablespoons sugar

1. Place grapes in a food processor; process until pureed. Pour grape puree through a fine sieve into an 8-inch square baking dish, pressing with the back of a spoon to remove as much liquid as possible. Discard solids. Add wine, lemon juice, and sugar, stirring until sugar dissolves.

2. Freeze 3 hours or until firm, stirring every hour. Remove mixture from freezer; scrape entire mixture with a fork until fluffy. Yield: 8 servings (serving size: ½ cup).

CALORIES 122; FAT 0.2g (sat 0.1g, mono 0g, poly 0.1g); PROTEIN 0.9g; CARB 26.3g; FIBER 1g; CHOL 0mg; IRON 0.5mg; SODIUM 4mg; CALC 14mg

Italian Berry Floats

Prep: 5 minutes

2   cups blood orange or lemon sorbet
2   cups mixed berries (such as raspberries, strawberries, blackberries, and blueberries)
2   cups Prosecco or other sparkling wine
Mint sprigs

1. Place ½ cup sorbet in each of 4 glasses. Arrange ½ cup berries evenly around sorbet in each glass. Pour ½ cup Prosecco over berries in each glass; garnish with mint sprigs. Serve immediately. Yield: 4 servings (serving size: 1 float).

CALORIES 203 (1% from fat); FAT 0.3g (sat 0g, mono 0g, poly 0.2g); PROTEIN 0.6g; CARB 30.4g; FIBER 2.7g; CHOL 0mg; IRON 0.4mg; SODIUM 34mg; CALC 13mg

Chocolate-Raisin Bread Pudding

Italian Berry Floats

Chocolate-Raisin Bread Pudding

Prep: 5 minutes • Cook: 55 minutes
Other: 10 minutes

4   large eggs
1   cup sugar
2   cups 1% low-fat milk
5   cups (½-inch) cubed raisin cinnamon swirl bread (such as Pepperidge Farm)
1   cup dark chocolate–covered raisins (such as Raisinets)
Cooking spray

1. Preheat oven to 350°.
2. Combine eggs and sugar in a large bowl, stirring with a whisk. Stir in milk. Add bread, stirring to saturate. Stir in raisins. Spoon mixture into an 8-inch square baking pan coated with cooking spray. Let stand, uncovered, 10 minutes.
3. Bake at 350° for 55 minutes or until set. Serve warm. Yield: 8 servings (serving size: ⅛ of pudding).

CALORIES 349; FAT 8.5g (sat 3.5g, mono 2.1g, poly 2.4g); PROTEIN 8.7g; CARB 63.3g; FIBER 2.3g; CHOL 95mg; IRON 1.7mg; SODIUM 187mg; CALC 88mg

Peach-Pineapple Crumble

Prep: 9 minutes • Cook: 38 minutes

No one will ever guess that the key ingredient to the buttery topping of this fresh, fruit-filled dessert is a pineapple cake mix. Select a cored pineapple with a generous amount of juice in the container to use in the batter.

1	cored fresh pineapple
3	cups sliced peeled peaches (3 large)
Cooking spray	
¼	cup butter, melted
1½	cups pineapple supreme cake mix (such as Duncan Hines Moist Deluxe)
2	cups vanilla low-fat frozen yogurt
¼	cup chopped pecans, toasted (optional)

1. Preheat oven to 350°.
2. Drain pineapple, reserving 3 tablespoons juice. Chop pineapple to measure 3 cups.
3. Combine chopped pineapple, reserved juice, and peach slices in an 11 x 7–inch baking dish coated with cooking spray. Stir butter into cake mix until smooth. Spread batter over fruit; coat with cooking spray.
4. Bake at 350° for 38 minutes or until golden and bubbly. Serve warm with frozen yogurt. Sprinkle each serving with 1 tablespoon pecans, if desired. Yield: 8 servings (serving size: ⅛ of crumble and ¼ cup frozen yogurt).

CALORIES 333; FAT 10.6g (sat 5.5g, mono 2g, poly 0.3g); PROTEIN 5.1g; CARB 58.4g; FIBER 1.8g; CHOL 18mg; IRON 0.4mg; SODIUM 83mg; CALC 90mg

Zabaglione with Fresh Berries

Prep: 3 minutes • Cook: 7 minutes

2	large eggs
2	large egg yolks
½	cup sugar
½	cup sweet Marsala wine
3	cups whole mixed berries
1½	cups light canned refrigerated whipped topping

1. Combine first 4 ingredients in top of a double boiler, stirring with a whisk. Cook over simmering water, whisking constantly, about 7 minutes or until a thermometer registers 160°. Serve over berries. Top each serving with whipped topping. Yield: 6 servings (serving size: about ½ cup zabaglione, ½ cup berries, and ¼ cup whipped topping).

CALORIES 200; FAT 5g (sat 2.8g, mono 1.3g, poly 0.6g); PROTEIN 3.6g; CARB 32g; FIBER 1.8g; CHOL 139mg; IRON 0.9mg; SODIUM 29mg; CALC 32mg

ingredient spotlight

Zabaglione is an Italian dessert custard made with egg yolks, sugar, and sweet wine.

Zabaglione with Fresh Berries

Bananas in Warm Rum Sauce

Prep: 1 minute • Cook: 9 minutes

1	tablespoon butter
⅓	cup dark rum
¼	cup water
¼	cup turbinado sugar or granulated sugar
3	bananas
2½	cups vanilla light ice cream

1. Melt butter in a large nonstick skillet over medium-high heat. While butter melts, stir together rum and water. Add sugar to melted butter in skillet. Stir in rum mixture. Bring to a boil; cook 4 minutes or until bubbly and slightly reduced.

2. While sauce reduces, slice bananas diagonally to create oval-shaped slices; add to sauce. Cook 3 minutes, turning until coated and thoroughly heated. Remove from heat. Serve bananas with ice cream. Yield: 5 servings (serving size: about ⅓ cup bananas with sauce and ½ cup ice cream).

CALORIES 257; FAT 6g (sat 3.4g, mono 1.4g, poly 0.2g); PROTEIN 3.8g; CARB 44.6g; FIBER 2g; CHOL 24mg; IRON 0.3mg; SODIUM 65mg; CALC 107mg

---

quick flip

The caramelized bananas are reminiscent of bananas Foster and would be good served over buttermilk pancakes.

Chocolate-Peppermint Parfaits

Prep: 8 minutes

1	cup coarsely chopped vanilla meringue cookies
2	cups chocolate low-fat ice cream
1	cup refrigerated canned light whipped topping
½	cup finely crushed soft peppermint candies

1. Spoon ¼ cup cookies into each of 4 parfait glasses; top each serving with ¼ cup ice cream, 2 tablespoons whipped topping, and 1 tablespoon peppermint candies. Repeat layers with remaining ice cream, whipped topping, and peppermint candies. Yield: 4 servings (serving size: 1 parfait).

CALORIES 222; FAT 4g (sat 2g, mono 0g, poly 0g); PROTEIN 2.1g; CARB 39.3g; FIBER 0g; CHOL 11mg; IRON 0.4mg; SODIUM 57mg; CALC 80mg

Chocolate-Peppermint
Parfaits

Strawberry-Banana Pudding

Prep: 10 minutes

1   (3.4-ounce) package vanilla instant
     pudding mix
1   cup fat-free milk
1   (8-ounce) container frozen fat-free whipped
     topping, thawed
3   ripe bananas, diced
1½   cups miniature vanilla wafers, divided
2   cups fresh strawberries, sliced

1. Combine pudding mix and milk in
a small bowl; stir with a whisk until
smooth. Fold whipped topping into pudding mixture. Fold in bananas. Layer ¾
cup cookies in bottom of an 8-inch square
baking dish. Spread half of pudding mixture over cookies. Repeat procedure with
remaining cookies and pudding mixture.
Top with strawberries. Serve immediately,
or cover and chill. Yield: 6 servings (serving
size: about 1½ cups).

CALORIES 263; FAT 4g (sat 0.9g, mono 0.6g, poly 1.8g); PROTEIN 3.4g;
CARB 46.4g; FIBER 2.3g; CHOL 4mg; IRON 0.8mg; SODIUM 160mg;
CALC 81mg

Chocolate Pretzel Bark

Chocolate Pretzel Bark

Prep: 6 minutes • Cook: 1 minute
Other: 20 minutes

12   ounces semisweet chocolate chips
2   cups thin salted pretzel sticks
¾   cup chopped dried sweet cherries
½   cup chopped pistachios
¼   cup chopped crystallized ginger

1. Place chocolate in a microwave-safe
bowl. Microwave at HIGH 1 to 2 minutes
or until melted, stirring after 30 seconds.
Stir in pretzel sticks, coarsely chopping
with a wooden spoon. Pour mixture into a
13 x 9–inch baking dish lined with wax
paper, spreading to coat bottom of dish.
Sprinkle remaining ingredients evenly on
top, pressing into chocolate mixture.
Refrigerate until hardened (about 20 minutes). Invert chocolate bark onto a plate;
carefully peel off wax paper. Cut into 16
pieces. Yield: about 1½ pounds (serving
size: 1 piece).

CALORIES 175; FAT 8g (sat 4g, mono 3.1g, poly 0.8g); PROTEIN 2.3g;
CARB 25.8g; FIBER 2.4g; CHOL 0mg; IRON 1.4mg; SODIUM 130mg;
CALC 21mg

Strawberry-Banana Pudding

Peanut Butter Granola Apple Rings

Prep: 7 minutes

Vitamin- and fiber-rich, these crisp apples get extra crunch from a pecan-studded granola topping. We used a Granny Smith apple for crispness and a Braeburn apple for more color, but choose your favorite, depending on your sweet cravings.

1	cup Cinnamon-Pecan Granola
¼	cup natural-style peanut butter
1	tablespoon honey
2	red or green apples, cored and each cut into 6 rings

1. Prepare Cinnamon-Pecan Granola. Place 1 cup granola in a small dish.
2. Combine peanut butter and honey in a small bowl, stirring until smooth. Spread mixture evenly on 1 side of each apple slice. Sprinkle evenly with granola. Yield: 6 servings (serving size: 2 apple rings).

CALORIES 179; FAT 10.1g (sat 1.1g, mono 5.5g, poly 3.4g); PROTEIN 4.3g; CARB 20.4g; FIBER 2.5g; CHOL 0mg; IRON 0.8mg; SODIUM 29mg; CALC 20mg

Cinnamon-Pecan Granola

Prep: 2 minutes • Cook: 31 minutes
Other: 10 minutes

¼	cup brown sugar
1	tablespoon water
2	teaspoons canola oil
½	teaspoon ground cinnamon
1	cup uncooked old-fashioned rolled oats
½	cup chopped pecans
	Cooking spray

Peanut Butter Granola Apple Rings

1. Preheat oven to 300°.
2. Combine brown sugar and 1 tablespoon water in a medium microwave-safe bowl. Microwave at HIGH 30 seconds or until sugar is dissolved. Stir in oil and cinnamon. Add oats and pecans, stirring until coated. Spread oat mixture on a large rimmed baking sheet coated with cooking spray.
3. Bake at 300° for 30 minutes or until browned, stirring twice. Spread mixture in a single layer on wax paper to cool completely. Store in an airtight container. Yield: 12 servings (serving size: about 3 tablespoons).

CALORIES 85; FAT 4.8g (sat 0.4g, mono 2.6g, poly 1.6g); PROTEIN 1.6g; CARB 9.7g; FIBER 1.2g; CHOL 0mg; IRON 0.6mg; SODIUM 2mg; CALC 12mg

Apricot-Pistachio Chocolates

Apricot-Pistachio Chocolates

Prep: 5 minutes • Cook: 1 minute
Other: 10 minutes

Antioxidant-rich apricots and health-boosting bitter-sweet chocolate accented with pistachios and a hit of salt make this a surprise medley of flavors. Apricots and pistachios are popular ingredients in Mediterranean cuisine.

6	ounces bittersweet chocolate, chopped
¼	cup chopped pistachios
¼	cup chopped dried apricots
½	teaspoon coarse sea salt

1. Place chocolate in a small microwave-safe bowl. Microwave at HIGH 1 minute or until melted, stirring after 30 seconds. Spoon chocolate by tablespoonfuls onto wax paper–lined baking sheets. Sprinkle evenly with pistachios, apricots, and sea salt. Refrigerate 10 minutes or until firm. Yield: 10 servings (serving size: 1 piece).

CALORIES 114; FAT 8.7g (sat 3.8g, mono 3.8g, poly 1g); PROTEIN 2g; CARB 11.9g; FIBER 1.8g; CHOL 0mg; IRON 0.7mg; SODIUM 115mg; CALC 6mg

quick flip

Cranberries will also partner deliciously with chocolate and pistachios. Their sweetness plays well against the coarse sea salt finish.

Orange-Sicle Tartlets

Prep: 9 minutes • Other: 3 hours

These citrusy tartlets take you back to that dreamy summertime ice cream pop treat. We just swapped the stick with a tartlet shell to capture the creamy goodness.

1   large navel orange
6   tablespoons fresh lemon juice (about 2 lemons)
1   (14-ounce) can fat-free sweetened condensed milk
2   (1.9-ounce) packages frozen miniature phyllo shells
5   tablespoons frozen fat-free whipped topping, thawed
Orange rind strips (optional)

1. Grate rind and squeeze juice from orange to measure 1 tablespoon rind and ¼ cup juice.
2. Combine orange rind, lemon juice, and condensed milk in a medium bowl, stirring with a whisk. Stir in orange juice. Cover and chill in refrigerator 3 hours.
3. Spoon filling evenly into phyllo shells. Top each with 1 teaspoon whipped topping, and garnish with orange rind strips, if desired. Yield: 15 servings (serving size: 2 tartlets).

CALORIES 55; FAT 1.8g (sat 0g, mono 1g, poly 0.3g); PROTEIN 0.6g; CARB 9.2g; FIBER 0.2g; CHOL 1mg; IRON 0.3mg; SODIUM 29mg; CALC 20mg

Orange-Sicle Tartlets

Mississippi Mud Baby Cakes

Prep: 10 minutes • Cook: 20 minutes
Other: 10 minutes

Mississippi Mud Baby Cakes boast a bonanza of flavor. They may be small, but they live up to the gooey dessert's reputation.

Cooking spray
1   (13.7-ounce) package fat-free brownie mix
1   (6-ounce) carton French vanilla low-fat yogurt
3   tablespoons finely chopped pecans
¾   cup miniature marshmallows (72 marshmallows)
24   chocolate kisses

1. Preheat oven to 350°.
2. Place 24 paper muffin cup liners in miniature muffin cups; coat with cooking spray.
3. Prepare brownie mix according to package directions, using French vanilla yogurt. Spoon batter evenly into prepared muffin cups. Sprinkle evenly with pecans.
4. Bake at 350° for 19 minutes. Remove cakes from oven. Place 3 marshmallows on top of each baby cake; place 1 chocolate kiss in center of marshmallows. Bake an additional 1 minute. Gently swirl melted chocolate kiss to "frost" each cake and hold marshmallows in place. Cool in pans on wire racks 10 minutes; remove from pans. Cool completely on wire racks. Yield: 24 servings (serving size: 1 baby cake).

CALORIES 100; FAT 2.2g (sat 1g, mono 0.9g, poly 0.3g); PROTEIN 2g; CARB 19g; FIBER 0.2g; CHOL 2mg; IRON 0.8mg; SODIUM 69mg; CALC 47mg

Pumpkin-Gingersnap Bars

Prep: 9 minutes • Cook: 26 minutes

The peppery, spicy bite of ginger is tamed by the creamy, fluffy pumpkin layer in these bars. Cinnamon-sugar adds another layer of flavor to the thin cookie-crust base.

1½	cups crushed gingersnap cookies (about 26 cookies)
3	tablespoons light butter, melted
3	tablespoons bottled cinnamon-sugar, divided
	Cooking spray
	Pumpkin Filling
1	cup frozen fat-free whipped topping, thawed

1. Preheat oven to 350°.
2. Combine crushed cookies, butter, and 2 tablespoons cinnamon-sugar in a small bowl. Press mixture evenly into a 13 x 9–inch baking pan coated with cooking spray. Bake at 350° for 6 minutes or until set.
3. While crust bakes, prepare Pumpkin Filling. Spread filling evenly over crust. Bake an additional 20 to 22 minutes or until a wooden pick inserted in center comes out almost clean. Cool completely on a wire rack, and then cut into bars. Serve with a dollop of whipped topping, and sprinkle evenly with remaining 1 tablespoon cinnamon-sugar. Yield: 15 servings (serving size: 1 bar and about 1 tablespoon topping).

CALORIES 202; FAT 4.9g (sat 1.4g, mono 2.3g, poly 1g); PROTEIN 2.8g; CARB 32.9g; FIBER 1.4g; CHOL 3mg; IRON 1.9mg; SODIUM 211mg; CALC 52mg

Pumpkin Filling

Prep: 6 minutes

4.5	ounces all-purpose flour (about 1 cup)
1	cup reduced-calorie sugar for baking blend
1	teaspoon baking powder
½	teaspoon pumpkin pie spice
¼	teaspoon salt
1	cup canned pumpkin
½	cup egg substitute
2	tablespoons canola oil

1. Weigh or lightly spoon flour into a dry measuring cup; level with a knife. Combine flour and next 4 ingredients in a medium bowl. Combine pumpkin, egg substitute, and oil in a small bowl, stirring with a whisk. Add pumpkin mixture to dry ingredients, stirring until blended. Yield: 2¼ cups.

CALORIES 124; FAT 2.3g (sat 0.2g, mono 1.2g, poly 0.7g); PROTEIN 2.1g; CARB 20.7g; FIBER 0.7g; CHOL 0.1mg; IRON 0.8mg; SODIUM 117mg; CALC 33mg

Chocolate-Covered Strawberry Ice Cream Sandwiches

Prep: 6 minutes • Other: 2 hours

Chewy devil's food cookies encase strawberry preserves and ice cream for a double shot of decadence. Keep these guilt-free sandwich treats on hand in your freezer for a quick dessert.

12   devil's food cookie cakes
2   tablespoons sugar-free hot fudge topping
2   tablespoons sugar-free strawberry preserves
¾   cup strawberry light ice cream

1. Place cookies, flat sides up, on a baking sheet. Top each of 6 cookies with 1 teaspoon fudge topping. Top each of remaining 6 cookies with 1 teaspoon preserves and 2 tablespoons ice cream. Place fudge-topped cookies on top of ice cream, topping sides down, pressing gently.
2. Wrap each sandwich in wax paper, and freeze at least 2 hours or until firm. Yield: 6 servings (serving size: 1 ice cream sandwich).

CALORIES 145; FAT 0.8g (sat 0.5g, mono 0.3g, poly 0g); PROTEIN 2.9g; CARB 33.9g; FIBER 0.2g; CHOL 4mg; IRON 1mg; SODIUM 68mg; CALC 38mg

Chocolate-Covered Strawberry
Ice Cream Sandwiches

Chocolate Chip Collision Ice Cream Sandwiches

Prep: 10 minutes • Cook: 9 minutes
Other: 25 minutes

A three-way collision of chocolate defines these confections: A yogurt and chocolate morsels mix sandwiches between chewy, chocolaty, brownielike cookies. Make these bite-sized treats ahead, and freeze them to have on hand when a chocolate craving hits.

1¾   cups chocolate and vanilla low-fat frozen yogurt
¼   cup semisweet chocolate minichips
¼   cup finely chopped toasted pecans
1   (13.7-ounce) package fat-free brownie mix
1   (6-ounce) carton vanilla fat-free yogurt
Cooking spray

1. Preheat oven to 400°.
2. Combine first 3 ingredients in a small bowl. Cover and freeze 20 minutes.
3. Combine brownie mix and vanilla yogurt according to package directions. Drop dough by tablespoonfuls onto parchment paper–lined baking sheets coated with cooking spray to yield 30 cookies.
4. Bake at 400° for 9 minutes. Cool 5 minutes on baking sheets. Remove cookies to wire racks to cool completely.
5. Spread 1 heaping tablespoon frozen yogurt mixture over flat side of each of 15 cookies. Top with remaining cookies, flat sides down, pressing gently. Serve immediately, or wrap each sandwich tightly in plastic wrap, and freeze until firm. Yield: 15 servings (serving size: 1 ice cream sandwich).

CALORIES 173; FAT 3g (sat 1g, mono 1.4g, poly 0.6g); PROTEIN 3.9g; CARB 34g; FIBER 0.6g; CHOL 5mg; IRON 1.4mg; SODIUM 124mg; CALC 106mg

Strawberry-Meringue
Parfaits

White Chocolate Panna Cotta

Prep: 4 minutes • Cook: 3 minutes
Other: 8 hours

Panna cotta is an Italian dessert made from heavy cream that is usually served with fresh berries, caramel topping, or chocolate sauce. Fat-free half-and-half and fat-free sweetened condensed milk for the heavy cream adds a little white chocolate flavor. Since this impressive dessert needs to chill at least 8 hours before serving, plan to make it ahead, and store it in the refrigerator until ready to serve.

1	envelope unflavored gelatin
2	cups fat-free half-and-half, divided
3	ounces white chocolate, chopped
1	cup fat-free sweetened condensed milk
½	teaspoon vanilla extract

Fresh raspberries (optional)
Mint sprigs (optional)

1. Sprinkle gelatin over 1 cup half-and-half in a small saucepan; let stand 1 to 2 minutes. Cook, stirring constantly, over medium heat 3 minutes or until gelatin dissolves; remove from heat. Add chocolate, stirring until chocolate melts.
2. Gradually stir in remaining 1 cup half-and-half, condensed milk, and vanilla. Pour ½ cup custard into each of 6 stemmed glasses or 6-ounce custard cups. Cover and chill 8 hours or until ready to serve. Serve with fresh berries and garnish with mint, if desired. Yield: 6 servings (serving size: 1 panna cotta).

CALORIES 281; FAT 4.6g (sat 2.8g, mono 1g, poly 0.5g); PROTEIN 5.8g; CARB 48.4g; FIBER 0g; CHOL 9mg; IRON 0.1mg; SODIUM 148mg; CALC 216mg

Strawberry-Meringue Parfaits

Prep: 12 minutes

3	(3.75-ounce) cups refrigerated sugar-free vanilla pudding cups
½	cup light sour cream
1	tablespoon grated orange rind
2	cups sliced fresh strawberries
4	chocolate chip meringue cookies, coarsely crumbled
4	teaspoons shaved bittersweet chocolate

1. Combine first 3 ingredients in a small bowl. Layer pudding mixture, strawberries, and meringue cookies evenly in 4 parfait glasses or other dessert dishes. Top each serving with 1 teaspoon bittersweet chocolate shavings. Yield: 4 servings (serving size: 1 parfait).

CALORIES 202; FAT 6g (sat 3.4g, mono 1.7g, poly 0.8g); PROTEIN 2.7g; CARB 36.3g; FIBER 2.1g; CHOL 10mg; IRON 0.4mg; SODIUM 149mg; CALC 45mg

Ginger-Berry
Granita

Ginger-Berry Granita

Prep: 5 minutes • Other: 8 hours

1   (10-ounce) package frozen strawberry
    halves in light syrup, thawed
1   cup fresh blueberries
2   teaspoons grated peeled fresh ginger
2   cups sugar-free ginger ale
Mint leaves (optional)

1. Place first 3 ingredients in a blender; process 30 seconds or until pureed, stopping as necessary to scrape sides. Stir in ginger ale; pour mixture into an 8-inch square pan. Cover and freeze 8 hours or until firm.
2. Remove mixture from freezer; scrape entire mixture with a fork until fluffy. Garnish with mint leaves, if desired. Yield: 16 servings (serving size: about ½ cup).

CALORIES 15; FAT 0g (sat 0g, mono 0g, poly 0g); PROTEIN 0.2g; CARB 3.7g; FIBER 0.4g; CHOL 0mg; IRON 0.1mg; SODIUM 10mg; CALC 1mg

make ahead

Juicy, plump blueberries, convenient frozen strawberries, and fresh ginger make this icy treat satisfying, healthful, and delicious. The make-ahead frozen concoction is a cool ending to a summer meal.

S'mores Shake Shots

S'mores Shake Shots

Prep: 8 minutes • Cook: 2 minutes

S'mores in a glass will capture your guests' attention! This campfire classic reinvents itself to be served in shot glasses as tiny layered parfait treats with big flavor.

4   regular-size marshmallows
1½   cups chocolate light ice cream
½   cup 1% low-fat chocolate milk
2   reduced-fat graham cracker sheets, divided

1. Preheat broiler.
2. Place marshmallows on a small rimmed baking sheet lined with parchment paper. Broil 2 minutes or until toasted.
3. While marshmallows toast, place ice cream, milk, and 1 graham cracker sheet in a blender; process until smooth.
4. Crumble 1 graham cracker (one-fourth of remaining sheet) into each of 4 large shot glasses. Divide ice cream mixture among glasses. Top with toasted marshmallows. Yield: 4 servings (serving size: 6 tablespoons shake mixture and 1 marshmallow).

CALORIES 153; FAT 3.3g (sat 1.7g, mono 1.2g, poly 0.4g); PROTEIN 3.8g; CARB 26.9g; FIBER 1g; CHOL 16mg; IRON 0.3mg; SODIUM 110mg; CALC 117mg

Affogato

Prep: 3 minutes

Affogato is an Italian coffee-flavored beverage or dessert, usually gelato, drowned in espresso. This is a light version of the traditional treat. No espresso? Strong brewed or instant coffee works fine. In Italian, affogato means "drowned."

2	cups vanilla fat-free ice cream
2	cups espresso, chilled
¼	cup frozen fat-free whipped topping, thawed
1	teaspoon unsweetened cocoa

1. Scoop ½ cup ice cream into each of 4 tall glasses. Pour ½ cup espresso into each glass. Top each with 1 tablespoon whipped topping, and sprinkle each with ¼ teaspoon cocoa. Serve immediately. Yield: 4 servings (serving size: 1 dessert).

CALORIES 119; FAT 0.3g (sat 0.1g, mono 0g, poly 0.1g); PROTEIN 3.1g; CARB 26.1g; FIBER 0.2g; CHOL 0mg; IRON 0.2mg; SODIUM 64mg; CALC 83mg

Prickly Pear–Mango Sundaes

Prep: 9 minutes • Cook: 8 minutes

4	Sugary Lime Tortilla Bowls
2	cups prickly pear sorbet
1	cup chopped fresh mango (about 1 mango)

Frozen reduced-calorie whipped topping, thawed (optional)
Mint sprigs (optional)

1. Prepare Sugary Lime Tortilla Bowls.
2. Scoop ½ cup sorbet into each tortilla bowl. Top with ¼ cup mango. Garnish with whipped topping and mint sprigs, if desired. Yield: 4 servings (serving size: 1 sundae).

CALORIES 242; FAT 1.3g (sat 0g, mono 0.9g, poly 0.3g); PROTEIN 3.2g; CARB 54.9g; FIBER 3.7g; CHOL 0mg; IRON 1.7mg; SODIUM 213mg; CALC 74mg

ingredient spotlight

Prickly pear is close in flavor to kiwifruit, strawberries, watermelon, honeydew, figs, banana, and citrus fruits. And, if that's not enough, it boasts a bright crimson color. Substitute raspberry sorbet if prickly pear isn't available.

Affogato

Sugary Lime Tortilla Bowls

Prep: 4 minutes • Cook: 8 minutes
Other: 5 minutes

4   (6½-inch) flour tortillas
Butter-flavored cooking spray
2   tablespoons turbinado sugar
1   teaspoon crystallized lime

1. Preheat oven to 450°.
2. Fit 1 tortilla in each of 4 (10-ounce) custard cups coated with cooking spray. Coat tortillas with cooking spray, and sprinkle with sugar and lime.
3. Bake at 450° for 8 to 10 minutes or until browned and crisp. Let cool in cups 5 minutes or until tortillas retain their shape. Yield: 4 servings (serving size: 1 tortilla bowl).

CALORIES 115; FAT 1.2g (sat 0g, mono 0.9g, poly 0.3g); PROTEIN 2g; CARB 22.9g; FIBER 2g; CHOL 0mg; IRON 1.3mg; SODIUM 212mg; CALC 70mg

Prickly Pear–Mango Sundaes

Strawberries with Fresh
Mango-Mint Sauce

Strawberries with Fresh Mango-Mint Sauce

Prep: 11 minutes • Cook: 5 minutes

Strawberries and mango bring a happy ending to mealtime. Mint freshens and enhances the fruity sauce that tops the ice cream mounds.

Fresh Mango-Mint Sauce
2	cups sliced strawberries
1⅓	cups vanilla low-fat ice cream
8	teaspoons chopped toasted pistachios

1. Prepare Fresh Mango-Mint Sauce.
2. Spoon ½ cup strawberries into each of 4 dessert dishes; top each with ⅓ cup ice cream, ¼ cup Fresh Mango-Mint Sauce, and 2 teaspoons pistachios. Yield: 4 servings. (serving size: 1 dessert).

CALORIES 186; FAT 4.9g (sat 1.7g, mono 2.1g, poly 1g); PROTEIN 4g; CARB 34.3g; FIBER 3.2g; CHOL 12mg; IRON 0.7mg; SODIUM 34mg; CALC 96mg

Fresh Mango-Mint Sauce

Prep: 6 minutes

1	cup chopped peeled mango (1 medium mango)
2	tablespoons agave nectar
2	tablespoons chopped fresh mint leaves

1. Place mango and nectar in a food processor; process until smooth. Stir in mint. Yield: 4 servings (serving size: ¼ cup).

CALORIES 57; FAT 0.1g (sat 0g, mono 0.1g, poly 0g); PROTEIN 0.2g; CARB 15.1g; FIBER 0.8g; CHOL 0mg; IRON 0.1mg; SODIUM 1mg; CALC 6mg

quick flip

Pistachios have a delicate flavor. Substitute macadamia nuts for a buttery-rich flavor. Because macadamia nuts contain more fat than pistachios, use half as much per serving.

Chocolate-Hazelnut Panini Sundaes

Prep: 2 minutes • Cook: 2 minutes

These petite Italian dessert sandwiches make a delicious closing statement. Serve them hot off the press drizzled with chocolate-hazelnut spread. They received the highest rating in our Test Kitchen.

4   (⅝-ounce) slices very thin white bread
¼   cup chocolate-hazelnut spread, divided
1   tablespoon chopped toasted hazelnuts
Butter-flavored cooking spray
1   cup vanilla light ice cream
2   teaspoons chopped toasted hazelnuts
       (optional)

1. Preheat panini grill.

2. Trim crusts from bread slices. Spread 2 tablespoons chocolate-hazelnut spread evenly over 2 bread slices. Sprinkle evenly with nuts. Top with remaining 2 bread slices. Coat both sides of sandwiches with cooking spray. Place sandwiches on panini grill; cook 1½ minutes or until golden. Cut each sandwich diagonally in half.

3. Place 1 panini triangle on each of 4 small dessert plates. Top each triangle with ¼ cup ice cream.

4. Place remaining 2 tablespoons chocolate-hazelnut spread in a microwave-safe bowl. Microwave at HIGH 25 seconds or until warm; drizzle 1½ teaspoons over each scoop of ice cream. Garnish with ½ teaspoon hazelnuts, if desired. Serve immediately. Yield: 4 servings (serving size: 1 sundae).

CALORIES 198; FAT 8.9g (sat 2.8g, mono 4.3g, poly 1.7g); PROTEIN 4.6g; CARB 26.8g; FIBER 1g; CHOL 10mg; IRON 0.8mg; SODIUM 113mg; CALC 65mg

Chocolate-Hazelnut Panini Sundaes

Apple-Granola Crisp

Apple-Granola Crisp

Prep: 8 minutes • Cook: 7 minutes

Sweet-tart Granny Smith apples hold up well when heated and keep their shape in this warm and comforting apple crisp. If you prefer a sweeter apple, try Golden Delicious, Rome Beauty, or York.

4	cups sliced Granny Smith apple (about 3 large apples)
1	tablespoon brown sugar
1	tablespoon cornstarch
1	tablespoon fresh lemon juice
½	teaspoon vanilla extract
	Butter-flavored cooking spray
1¼	cups low-fat granola with raisins
1	cup vanilla light ice cream

1. Combine first 5 ingredients in a large bowl; toss well. Spoon mixture into an 11 x 7–inch baking dish coated with cooking spray. Cover with heavy-duty plastic wrap; microwave at HIGH 5 minutes or until apple is tender; stir after 3 minutes.
2. Stir apple mixture, and top apple mixture with granola. Coat generously with cooking spray. Microwave, uncovered, at HIGH 2 minutes. Serve with ice cream. Yield: 4 servings (serving size: 1 cup apple mixture and ¼ cup ice cream).

CALORIES 247; FAT 3.6g (sat 0.3g, mono 1.1g, poly 0.6g); PROTEIN 4.4g; CARB 51.9g; FIBER 3.4g; CHOL 10mg; IRON 1mg; SODIUM 99mg; CALC 80mg

fix it faster

One (16-ounce) package of presliced apples makes this apple crisp recipe even quicker. You'll find already-sliced apples prepackaged in the produce department of your supermarket.

Fresh Strawberry Tart

Prep: 13 minutes • Cook: 21 minutes
Other: 25 minutes

This elegant tart could be the star in a French pastry shop's dessert case. It combines a creamy, citrusy custard crowned with juicy berries, all atop a flaky crust.

½   (14.1-ounce) package refrigerated pie dough
Lemon Custard
6   cups hulled small fresh strawberries
2   tablespoons red raspberry jelly

1. Preheat oven to 450°.
2. Roll pie dough into a 12-inch circle. Fit dough into a 10-inch round removable-bottom tart pan, and pierce dough with a fork; bake at 450° for 10 minutes or until golden. Cool completely on a wire rack.
3. While crust bakes, prepare Lemon Custard.
4. Spread custard into bottom of prepared crust. Arrange strawberries, hulled sides down, over custard.
5. Place jelly in a small microwave-safe bowl. Microwave at HIGH 30 seconds or until melted. Gently brush jelly over strawberries. Chill tart until ready to serve. Yield: 8 servings (serving size: 1 wedge).

CALORIES 227; FAT 7.9g (sat 2.9g, mono 3.6g, poly 1.3g); PROTEIN 3.1g; CARB 36.6g; FIBER 2.4g; CHOL 30mg; IRON 0.6mg; SODIUM 128mg; CALC 78mg

Lemon Custard

Prep: 2 minutes • Cook: 9 minutes
Other: 5 minutes

1½   cups 1% low-fat milk, divided
⅓   cup sugar
2   tablespoons cornstarch
1   large egg yolk
2   teaspoons grated lemon rind

1. Bring 1¼ cups milk to a boil in a medium saucepan over medium heat, stirring frequently. Remove pan from heat.
2. While milk comes to a boil, combine sugar and cornstarch in a medium bowl. Add remaining ¼ cup milk and egg yolk to cornstarch mixture, stirring with a whisk until smooth.
3. Gradually stir half of hot milk into egg yolk mixture, stirring constantly with a whisk. Stir egg yolk mixture into remaining hot milk in pan; cook, stirring constantly with a whisk, over medium-high heat 3 minutes or until thick. Stir in lemon rind. Spoon custard into another medium bowl. Place bowl in a larger bowl filled with ice water. Cool 5 minutes or until thoroughly chilled, stirring frequently. Yield: 8 servings (serving size: about 3 tablespoons).

CALORIES 66; FAT 1g (sat 0.5g, mono 0.4g, poly 0.1g); PROTEIN 1.9g; CARB 12.5g; FIBER 0.1g; CHOL 27mg; IRON 0.1mg; SODIUM 24mg; CALC 60mg

Fresh Strawberry Tart

Brownie Bites

Prep: 5 minutes • Cook: 8 minutes

When you make this recipe, don't be alarmed that the batter is very wet—the end result will be moist, tender minicakes.

½ cup self-rising flour
⅔ cup sugar
3 tablespoons unsweetened cocoa
4 large egg whites
2 tablespoons canola oil
3 tablespoons chocolate liqueur (optional)
⅓ cup cocoa nibs
Cooking spray
Roasted salted almonds, coarsely
　　　chopped (optional)
Powdered sugar (optional)

1. Preheat oven to 400°.
2. Lightly spoon flour into a dry measuring cup; level with a knife. Combine flour, sugar, and cocoa in a medium bowl, stirring with a whisk.

3. Whisk egg whites until foamy in a separate bowl. Add oil and liqueur, if desired, stirring with a whisk. Add egg white mixture to flour mixture, stirring just until moistened. Fold in cocoa nibs. Spoon batter evenly into 24 miniature muffin cups coated with cooking spray. Sprinkle batter evenly with almonds, if desired.
4. Bake at 400° for 8 minutes. Remove from pans; cool on wire racks. Sprinkle with powdered sugar, if desired. Yield: 24 servings (serving size: 1 brownie bite).

CALORIES 61; FAT 2.4g (sat 0.8g, mono 0.9g, poly 0.4g); PROTEIN 1.2g; CARB 8.8g; FIBER 0.3g; CHOL 0mg; IRON 0.4mg; SODIUM 43mg; CALC 15mg

ingredient spotlight

Cocoa nibs, which are broken bits of husked cocoa beans, add delicate chocolate flavor and delicious nutty crunch to baked goods. You can find cocoa nibs at upscale supermarkets and gourmet cookware stores.

Brownie Bites

Flourless Chocolate Cakes

Prep: 10 minutes • Cook: 10 minutes
Other: 10 minutes

With rich chocolate flavor and a warm gooey filling, these hot-from-the-oven minicakes are the perfect indulgence at the end of a busy day. Many supermarkets stock ground pecans in the nuts section; if you can't find them already ground, chop pecan halves or pieces, and grind them in a food processor, minichopper, or spice grinder.

1	large egg
¼	cup sugar
2	teaspoons unsweetened cocoa
1½	tablespoons chopped pecans, ground
1	tablespoon warm water
1	ounce bittersweet chocolate, melted and cooled slightly

Cooking spray
Powdered sugar (optional)
Fresh strawberries (optional)

1. Preheat oven to 425°.
2. Separate egg, placing egg white and egg yolk in separate medium bowls. Add sugar and cocoa to egg yolk, stirring with a whisk. Add pecans, water, and chocolate, stirring with a whisk.
3. Beat egg white with a mixer at high speed until stiff peaks form. Gently fold half of egg white into egg yolk mixture; fold in remaining egg white. Spoon batter evenly into 4 (4-ounce) ramekins coated with cooking spray.
4. Bake at 425° for 10 minutes or until almost set. Transfer to a wire rack; cool 10 minutes. Garnish with powdered sugar and strawberries, if desired. Yield: 4 servings (serving size: 1 cake).

CALORIES 124; FAT 6.2g (sat 2.1g, mono 1.9g, poly 1.8g); PROTEIN 2.5g; CARB 17.3g; FIBER 1.1g; CHOL 45mg; IRON 0.6mg; SODIUM 18mg; CALC 10mg

Lemon Pudding Cake

Prep: 3 minutes • Cook: 28 minutes
Other: 5 minutes

Prepare this recipe in the summertime when you're craving a dessert that's not too heavy. Lemon rind and juice provide tartness, which is balanced by the sweetness of the fresh berries. This dessert is not quite a pudding and not quite a cake—it's something in between. A puddinglike layer forms under the tender cake topping as it bakes. It tastes best when served warm.

1	(9-ounce) package yellow cake mix
½	cup fat-free milk
¼	cup reduced-fat sour cream
1	lemon

Cooking spray
⅔	cup boiling water
2	cups mixed fresh berries

Frozen fat-free whipped topping, thawed (optional)

1. Preheat oven to 350°.
2. Combine first 3 ingredients in a medium bowl. Grate rind, and squeeze juice from lemon to measure 1 teaspoon and 2 tablespoons, respectively. Stir rind and juice into batter just until blended. Spoon batter into an 8-inch square baking dish coated with cooking spray. Pour ⅔ cup boiling water over batter (do not stir).
3. Bake at 350° for 28 minutes. Remove from oven; let stand 5 minutes. Spoon cake into 8 individual serving bowls; top with berries and whipped topping, if desired. Serve warm. Yield: 8 servings (serving size: ⅛ of cake and ¼ cup berries).

CALORIES 168; FAT 3.4g (sat 1g, mono 0.9g, poly 0.9g); PROTEIN 2.4g; CARB 33.2g; FIBER 0.9g; CHOL 3mg; IRON 0.8mg; SODIUM 229mg; CALC 18mg

Triple-Chocolate Pudding

Prep: 5 minutes • Cook: 10 minutes
Other: 5 minutes

Modest in appearance yet boasting an intense flavor and a made-from-scratch taste, this simple, satisfying chocolate pudding is the quintessential weeknight dessert. Place plastic wrap on the surface of the hot pudding to prevent a skin from forming during chilling.

1   (5-ounce) package chocolate cook-and-serve pudding mix
1   large egg yolk
4   cups 1% low-fat chocolate milk
1   ounce semisweet chocolate, chopped
1   teaspoon vanilla extract
Frozen reduced-calorie whipped topping, thawed (optional)
Semisweet chocolate shavings (optional)

1. Combine first 3 ingredients in a medium saucepan. Bring to a boil over medium heat, stirring constantly with a whisk. Boil 2 minutes, stirring constantly. Remove from heat. Add chopped chocolate and vanilla, stirring with a whisk until chocolate melts. Cool 5 minutes.
2. Spoon ½ cup pudding into each of 8 individual serving bowls. Serve warm, or cover surface of pudding with plastic wrap, and chill thoroughly. Top each serving with whipped topping, if desired; sprinkle with chocolate shavings, if desired. Yield: 8 servings (serving size: 1 pudding).

CALORIES 169; FAT 2.8g (sat 1.6g, mono 0.2g, poly 0.1g); PROTEIN 5.2g; CARB 31.3g; FIBER 0.7g; CHOL 31mg; IRON 0.7mg; SODIUM 187mg; CALC 151mg

White Chocolate–Cherry Rice Pudding

Prep: 4 minutes • Cook: 7 minutes

This shortcut method of using an instant pudding mix delivers the characteristic creamy texture of rice pudding without the long cooking time.

3½   cups 1% low-fat milk, divided
⅓   cup dried cherries
2   tablespoons light brown sugar
¼   teaspoon ground cinnamon
1   tablespoon butter
⅛   teaspoon salt
1   cup instant rice
1   (1-ounce) package sugar-free white chocolate instant pudding mix
Cinnamon sticks (optional)

1. Bring 1½ cups milk, dried cherries, and next 4 ingredients to a boil in a medium saucepan over medium heat, stirring occasionally. Stir in rice; cover, and reduce heat to low. Simmer 5 minutes, stirring occasionally.
2. While rice mixture cooks, prepare pudding mix according to package directions using remaining 2 cups milk. Stir prepared pudding into rice mixture. Serve warm. Garnish with cinnamon sticks, if desired. Yield: 8 servings (serving size: ½ cup).

CALORIES 156; FAT 2.6g (sat 1.6g, mono 0.7g, poly 0.1g); PROTEIN 5g; CARB 27.9g; FIBER 0.7g; CHOL 8mg; IRON 0.9mg; SODIUM 141mg; CALC 142mg

White Chocolate–Cherry
Rice Pudding

Glazed Apples in Caramel Sauce

Prep: 6 minutes • Cook: 45 minutes

This no-fuss treat comes together in minutes. The sauce, made of butter, apple juice, and a homemade caramel sauce, reduces while the apples bake, creating a velvety glaze. Make extra Caramel Sauce, and store it in the refrigerator to serve over pound cake or ice cream later in the week.

4   Granny Smith apples, peeled and cored
⅔   cup no-sugar-added apple juice
2   tablespoons butter, melted
Caramel Sauce

1. Preheat oven to 375°.
2. Cut each apple horizontally into 5 slices. Reassemble each apple, and place in an 11 x 7–inch baking dish. Combine apple juice and melted butter; pour over apples. Bake, uncovered, at 375° for 45 minutes or until apples are tender, basting with juices every 15 minutes.
3. Place an apple stack on each of 4 individual serving plates. Pour ¼ cup Caramel Sauce into center of each stack, allowing sauce to flow over sides. Serve immediately. Yield: 4 servings (serving size: 1 apple and ¼ cup Caramel Sauce).

CALORIES 247; FAT 8.7g (sat 5.4g, mono 2.2g, poly 0.8g); PROTEIN 2.5g; CARB 41.9g; FIBER 1.7g; CHOL 22mg; IRON 0.2mg; SODIUM 102mg; CALC 98mg

Caramel Sauce

Prep: 1 minute • Cook: 18 minutes

1   cup sugar
⅓   cup water
1   tablespoon butter
½   cup fat-free evaporated milk
½   teaspoon vanilla extract

Glazed Apples in Caramel Sauce

1. Combine sugar and water in a large skillet. Cook over medium heat 15 minutes or until golden (do not stir). Brush crystals from sides of pan with a wet pastry brush, if necessary.
2. Remove pan from heat; let stand 1 minute. Carefully add butter, stirring until butter melts. Gradually add milk, stirring constantly. (Caramel will harden and stick to spoon.) Cook, stirring constantly, over medium heat 2 minutes or until caramel melts and mixture is smooth and slightly thickened. Remove from heat; stir in vanilla. Yield: 4 servings (serving size: ¼ cup).

CALORIES 116; FAT 2.8g (sat 1.8g, mono 0.7g, poly 0.1g); PROTEIN 2g; CARB 20.7g; FIBER 0g; CHOL 8mg; IRON 0mg; SODIUM 60mg; CALC 81mg

Marsala-Poached Figs

Prep: 3 minutes • Cook: 10 minutes

This stylish dessert requires little preparation, and you can easily halve or double the recipe to serve fewer or more diners. Give the figs a gentle squeeze to check for their ripeness; they should be quite soft. Serve the figs with toasted pecan halves and small wedges of Gruyère or fontina cheese.

½	cup Marsala wine
1	(3-inch) cinnamon stick
3	black peppercorns
1	tablespoon honey
6	fresh Black Mission figs (about 8.5 ounces), halved

1. Combine first 4 ingredients in a medium saucepan. Bring to a boil; cook 7 minutes or until syrupy. Add figs; cook 1 minute or until thoroughly heated. Remove cinnamon stick and peppercorn. Yield: 6 servings (serving size: 2 fig halves and about 2 teaspoons sauce).

CALORIES 72; FAT 0g (sat 0g, mono 0g, poly 0g); PROTEIN 0.4g; CARB 13.3g; FIBER 1.2g; CHOL 0mg; IRON 0.2mg; SODIUM 2mg; CALC 15mg

ingredient spotlight

Fresh figs need very little adornment and cooking, thanks to their subtle, sweet flavor and dense texture. For a quick, pleasurable ending to a meal, serve figs raw, or gently simmer them in a sauce for just a few minutes. Figs are available twice a year, with the first crop available from June through July, and the second crop coming in early September and lasting through mid-October.

Marsala-Poached Figs

White Chocolate–Hazelnut Tarts

Prep: 11 minutes • Cook: 12 minutes
Other: 30 minutes

These creamy, nutty tarts received our Test Kitchen's highest rating. They're easy and fast for every day, but because this dessert needs time to chill, it's also a terrific make-ahead option.

½   (15-ounce) package refrigerated pie dough
1   (1-ounce) package sugar-free white chocolate instant pudding mix
1½   cups fat-free milk
¼   cup chocolate-hazelnut spread
¼   cup chopped hazelnuts, toasted
Chocolate shavings (optional)

1. Preheat oven to 450°.
2. Roll pie dough into a 14-inch circle. Cut 4 (5-inch) circles from dough; press each circle into a 4-inch tart pan with removable bottom. Pierce bottom and sides of dough; bake at 450° for 12 minutes or until golden.
3. While crusts bake, combine pudding mix and milk, stirring with a whisk 2 minutes.
4. Spread 1 tablespoon hazelnut spread over bottom of each warm crust. Spoon pudding mixture evenly over hazelnut spread in each crust. Chill in refrigerator 30 minutes or until ready to serve.
5. Sprinkle tarts evenly with hazelnuts and chocolate shavings, if desired. Yield: 8 servings (serving size: ½ tart and ½ tablespoon hazelnuts).

CALORIES 200; FAT 10.8g (sat 2.8g, mono 5.1g, poly 2.8g); PROTEIN 3.1g; CARB 22.2g; FIBER 0.8g; CHOL 3.5mg; IRON 1mg; SODIUM 268mg; CALC 70mg

Raspberry–Cream Cheese Tarts

Prep: 8 minutes • Other: 3 hours

Mascarpone, Italy's version of cream cheese, is a sweet, delicate, triple-blended cheese made from cow's milk that is often used in both sweet and savory dishes. Here, we used only a small amount and stretched it with cream cheese to get the richness of the mascarpone with reduced calories and fat. Store the remaining mascarpone in the refrigerator for up to one month.

1   (8-ounce) package fat-free cream cheese, softened
2   tablespoons mascarpone cheese, softened
⅓   cup sugar
1   teaspoon vanilla
6   mini graham cracker pie crusts
⅓   cup seedless raspberry jam
1½   cups fresh raspberries

1. Combine first 4 ingredients in a large bowl. Beat with a mixer at high speed 1 to 2 minutes or until smooth. Spoon cheese mixture evenly into crusts.
2. Place jam in a medium bowl; stir with a whisk until smooth. Add raspberries, stirring until coated; spoon evenly over cheese filling in each tart. Serve immediately, or refrigerate 3 hours or until thoroughly chilled. Yield: 6 servings (serving size: 1 tart).

CALORIES 305; FAT 11.1g (sat 4g, mono 4.3g, poly 2.1g); PROTEIN 7.5g; CARB 44.6g; FIBER 3g; CHOL 15mg; IRON 0.6mg; SODIUM 361mg; CALC 91mg

Dulce de Leche Tartlets

Prep: 5 minutes • Cook: 5 minutes
Other: 2 minutes

Looking for a quick dessert that's ideal for a week-night potluck or party? These petite tarts are the answer. With just the right amount of crunch from the candy bar pieces to complement the rich, smooth dulce de leche filling, they'll disappear fast!

1	(1.9-ounce) package mini phyllo shells
⅓	cup canned dulce de leche
1	cup reduced-calorie frozen whipped topping, thawed
1	(1.4-ounce) English toffee candy bar, finely chopped

1. Preheat oven to 350°.
2. Arrange phyllo shells on a baking sheet. Bake phyllo shells at 350° for 5 minutes or until crisp. Cool slightly.
3. Spoon about 1 teaspoon dulce de leche into each shell, and top each serving with about 1 tablespoon whipped topping. Sprinkle tartlets evenly with chopped candy. Yield: 15 servings (serving size: 1 tartlet).

CALORIES 180; FAT 7.7g (sat 2.8g, mono 2.2g, poly 0.6g); PROTEIN 1.3g; CARB 23.4g; FIBER 0.1g; CHOL 14mg; IRON 0.5mg; SODIUM 83mg; CALC 64mg

ingredient spotlight

Dulce de leche, a sweet Spanish sauce, is made by cooking milk and sugar until it reduces to a thick, amber-colored syrup. Preparing home-made dulce de leche can take up to three hours; for quick weeknight cooking, we recommend purchasing a can at your supermarket or a Latin market. Look for dulce de leche alongside the canned milks.

Hazelnut–Sugar Cookie S'mores

Hazelnut–Sugar Cookie S'mores

Prep: 10 minutes
Cook: 2 minutes 20 seconds

In this takeoff of the campfire classic, we replaced the customary graham crackers with sugar cookies. We slathered them with chocolate-hazelnut spread, sprinkled them with dried apricots and hazelnuts, and, of course, sandwiched them with marshmallows.

2	tablespoons chocolate-hazelnut spread
8	rectangular sugar cookies
2	tablespoons finely chopped dried apricots
16	miniature marshmallows
4	teaspoons chopped hazelnuts, toasted

1. Spread ½ tablespoon chocolate-hazelnut spread on each of 4 cookies; sprinkle each with ½ tablespoon apricots and 4 marsh-mallows. Place on a microwave-safe plate; microwave at HIGH 20 seconds or until marshmallows puff. Sprinkle evenly with hazelnuts, and top with remaining cookies. Yield: 4 servings (serving size: 1 s'more).

CALORIES 150; FAT 6.7g (sat 2.2g, mono 2.1g, poly 2.2g); PROTEIN 2.3g; CARB 20.8g; FIBER 1.3g; CHOL 5mg; IRON 0.7mg; SODIUM 54mg; CALC 15mg

Berry-Lime Angel Food Mini Trifles

Prep: 10 minutes

In a traditional trifle, liqueur moistens cake that's layered with custard and fruit. In our lighter, parfait-like version, we used the sweet juice from mashed blackberries and blueberries to soak into the cake and lime zest to flavor the whipped topping. Fresh strawberries and raspberries will also work well in this recipe.

1	tablespoon grated lime rind
2	cups reduced-calorie frozen whipped topping, thawed
1½	tablespoons fresh lime juice
1¼	cups fresh blackberries, divided
1¼	cups fresh blueberries, divided
2	cups (½-inch) cubed angel food cake

1. Fold lime rind into whipped topping; set aside.

2. Place lime juice and 1 cup each blackberries and blueberries in an 8-inch square glass dish. Mash berry mixture using the back of a spoon.

3. Layer half of cake cubes evenly in each of 4 dessert glasses. Top evenly with half of berry mixture and half of reserved topping mixture. Repeat layers with remaining half of cake cubes, berry mixture, and topping mixture. Top each trifle with 1 tablespoon each remaining blackberries and blueberries. Yield: 4 servings (serving size: 1 mini trifle).

CALORIES 192; FAT 4.6g (sat 4.1g, mono 0g, poly 0.3g); PROTEIN 2.5g; CARB 38.1g; FIBER 4g; CHOL 0mg; IRON 0.6mg; SODIUM 187mg; CALC 53mg

Berry-Lime Angel Food
Mini Trifles

Strawberry-Kiwi Freeze

Prep: 10 minutes • Cook: 1 minute
Other: 9 hours

Use ripe, juicy strawberries and kiwi to achieve the best flavor for this light, refreshing dessert.

1   cup sugar
1   cup water
2   teaspoons fresh lime juice
4   cups fresh strawberries
1½ cups cubed peeled kiwifruit (about 4 kiwifruit)

1. Combine sugar and water in a medium saucepan. Bring to a boil over high heat; cook 1 minute. Remove from heat; cool 1 hour. Stir in lime juice; set syrup aside.
2. Place strawberries in a food processor; process until smooth. Stir in half of syrup. Pour strawberry mixture into an 8-inch square glass dish. Rinse processor bowl; wipe dry. Add kiwifruit; process until smooth. Stir in remaining syrup.
3. Use a measuring cup to drizzle kiwi mixture in a swirl pattern over strawberry mixture. Cover and freeze 8 hours. Yield: 8 servings (serving size: about ½ cup).

CALORIES 148; FAT 0.5g (sat 0g, mono 0.1g, poly 0.2g); PROTEIN 1g; CARB 37.3g; FIBER 2.8g; CHOL 0mg; IRON 0.4mg; SODIUM 2mg; CALC 27mg

Strawberry-Kiwi Freeze

Cherry-Merlot Granita

Prep: 5 minutes • Cook: 3 minutes
Other: 8 hours

This frozen dessert doesn't require an ice cream maker—just freeze the mixture in a pan, and scrape it with a fork. For a nonalcoholic version, use 1 cup black cherry juice in place of the merlot.

1	cup water
¼	cup sugar
1	cup ice cubes
1	large navel orange
1	cup frozen pitted dark sweet cherries
1	cup merlot

1. Combine water and sugar in a small saucepan. Bring to a boil; reduce heat, and simmer 3 minutes. Remove from heat; stir in ice cubes.
2. While sugar mixture comes to a boil, grate rind, and squeeze juice from orange to measure 1 tablespoon and ½ cup, respectively.
3. Place cherries and sugar mixture in a blender; process 1 minute or until pureed, stopping as necessary to scrape sides. Stir in rind, juice, and merlot; pour into an 8-inch square pan. Cover and freeze 8 hours or until firm.
4. Remove mixture from freezer; scrape entire mixture with a fork until fluffy. Yield: 8 servings (serving size: about ½ cup).

CALORIES 70; FAT 0.3g (sat 0.1g, mono 0.1g, poly 0.1g); PROTEIN 0.3g; CARB 11.9g; FIBER 0.5g; CHOL 0mg; IRON 0.2mg; SODIUM 1mg; CALC 8mg

Chocolate-Toffee
Ice Cream Pie

Chocolate-Toffee Ice Cream Pie

Prep: 8 minutes • Other: 8 hours

You'll love the added crunch that toffee bits give this frozen pie. To quickly soften the ice cream, place it in a microwave-safe bowl, and microwave at HIGH 10 to 15 seconds.

4	cups chocolate low-fat ice cream, softened and divided
1	(6-ounce) reduced-fat graham cracker crust
¼	cup fat-free chocolate syrup, divided
¼	cup milk chocolate toffee bits, divided
2	cups fat-free frozen whipped topping, thawed

1. Spread 2 cups ice cream in bottom of crust; drizzle with 2 tablespoons chocolate syrup, and sprinkle with 2 tablespoons toffee bits. Spread remaining ice cream over toffee bits. Freeze 8 hours or until firm.
2. Top pie with whipped topping, and drizzle with remaining 2 tablespoons syrup; sprinkle with remaining 2 tablespoons toffee bits. Yield: 8 servings (serving size: 1 wedge).

CALORIES 268; FAT 7.8g (sat 2.5g, mono 2.5g, poly 2.2g); PROTEIN 3.8g; CARB 46g; FIBER 0.3g; CHOL 8mg; IRON 0.7mg; SODIUM 175mg; CALC 80mg

Nutritional Analysis

How to Use It and Why

Glance at the end of any *Cooking Light* recipe, and you'll see how committed we are to helping you make the best of today's light cooking. With chefs, registered dietitians, home economists, and a computer system that analyzes every ingredient we use, *Cooking Light* gives you authoritative dietary detail like no other magazine. We go to such lengths so you can see how our recipes fit into your healthful eating plan. If you're trying to lose weight, the calorie and fat figures will probably help most. But if you're keeping a close eye on the sodium, cholesterol, and saturated fat in your diet, we provide those numbers, too. And because many women don't get enough iron or calcium, we can help there, as well. Finally, there's a fiber analysis for those of us who don't get enough roughage.

Here's a helpful guide to put our nutritional analysis numbers into perspective. Remember, one size doesn't fit all, so take your lifestyle, age, and circumstances into consideration when determining your nutrition needs. For example, pregnant or breast-feeding women need more protein, calories, and calcium. And women older than 50 need 1,200mg of calcium daily, 200mg more than the amount recommended for younger women.

In Our Nutritional Analysis, We Use These Abbreviations

sat	saturated fat	**CHOL**	cholesterol
mono	monounsaturated fat	**CALC**	calcium
poly	polyunsaturated fat	**g**	gram
CARB	carbohydrates	**mg**	milligram

Daily Nutrition Guide

	Women ages 25 to 50	Women over 50	Men over 24
Calories	2,000	2,000 or less	2,700
Protein	50g	50g or less	63g
Fat	65g or less	65g or less	88g or less
Saturated Fat	20g or less	20g or less	27g or less
Carbohydrates	304g	304g	410g
Fiber	25g to 35g	25g to 35g	25g to 35g
Cholesterol	300mg or less	300mg or less	300mg or less
Iron	18 mg	8mg	8mg
Sodium	2,300mg or less	1,500mg or less	2,300mg or less
Calcium	1,000mg	1,200mg	1,000mg

The nutritional values used in our calculations either come from The Food Processor, Version 8.9 (ESHA Research), or are provided by food manufacturers.

Metric Equivalents

The information in the following charts is provided to help cooks outside the United States successfully use the recipes in this book. All equivalents are approximate.

Cooking/Oven Temperatures

	Fahrenheit	Celsius	Gas Mark
Freeze Water	32° F	0° C	
Room Temperature	68° F	20° C	
Boil Water	212° F	100° C	
Bake	325° F	160° C	3
	350° F	180° C	4
	375° F	190° C	5
	400° F	200° C	6
	425° F	220° C	7
	450° F	230° C	8
Broil			Grill

Liquid Ingredients by Volume

¼ tsp		=	1 ml
½ tsp		=	2 ml
1 tsp		=	5 ml
3 tsp = 1 tbl		= ½ fl oz =	15 ml
	2 tbls = ⅛ cup =	1 fl oz =	30 ml
	4 tbls = ¼ cup =	2 fl oz =	60 ml
	5⅓ tbls = ⅓ cup =	3 fl oz =	80 ml
	8 tbls = ½ cup =	4 fl oz =	120 ml
	10⅔ tbls = ⅔ cup =	5 fl oz =	160 ml
	12 tbls = ¾ cup =	6 fl oz =	180 ml
	16 tbls = 1 cup =	8 fl oz =	240 ml
	1 pt = 2 cups =	16 fl oz =	480 ml
	1 qt = 4 cups =	32 fl oz =	960 ml
		33 fl oz =	1000 ml = 1l

Dry Ingredients by Weight

(To convert ounces to grams, multiply the number of ounces by 30.)

1 oz	=	1/16 lb	=	30 g
4 oz	=	¼ lb	=	120 g
8 oz	=	½ lb	=	240 g
12 oz	=	¾ lb	=	360 g
16 oz	=	1 lb	=	480 g

Length

(To convert inches to centimeters, multiply the number of inches by 2.5.)

1 in =			2.5 cm
6 in =	½ ft	=	15 cm
12 in =	1 ft	=	30 cm
36 in =	3 ft = 1yd	=	90 cm
40 in =			100 cm = 1m

Equivalents for Different Types of Ingredients

Standard Cup	Fine Powder (ex. flour)	Grain (ex. rice)	Granular (ex. sugar)	Liquid Solids (ex. butter)	Liquid (ex. milk)
1	140 g	150 g	190 g	200 g	240 ml
¾	105 g	113 g	143 g	150 g	180 ml
⅔	93 g	100 g	125 g	133 g	160 ml
½	70 g	75 g	95 g	100 g	120 ml
⅓	47 g	50 g	63 g	67 g	80 ml
¼	35 g	38 g	48 g	50 g	60 ml
⅛	18 g	19 g	24 g	25 g	30 ml

index

Chicken (continued)

Sandwiches (continued)